CONVERGING
MEDIA

Converging Media

SECOND EDITION

A New Introduction
to Mass Communication

JOHN V. PAVLIK

SHAWN McINTOSH

New York   Oxford

OXFORD UNIVERSITY PRESS

2011

Oxford University Press, Inc., publishes works that further Oxford University's
objective of excellence in research, scholarship, and education.

Oxford New York
Auckland   Cape Town   Dar es Salaam   Hong Kong   Karachi
Kuala Lumpur   Madrid   Melbourne   Mexico City   Nairobi
New Delhi   Shanghai   Taipei   Toronto

With offices in
Argentina   Austria   Brazil   Chile   Czech Republic   France   Greece
Guatemala   Hungary   Italy   Japan   Poland   Portugal   Singapore
South Korea   Switzerland   Thailand   Turkey   Ukraine   Vietnam

©2011 by Oxford University Press, Inc., ©2004 by Pearson Higher Education

Published by Oxford University Press, Inc.
198 Madison Avenue, New York, New York 10016
http://www.oup.com

Oxford is a registered trademark of Oxford University Press

Library of Congress Cataloging-in-Publication Data

Pavlik, John V. (John Vernon)
  Converging media : a new introduction to mass communication / John V. Pavlik, Shawn McIntosh. -- 2nd ed.
    p. cm.
  ISBN 978-0-19-537910-5 (alk. paper)
1. Mass media.   2. Digital media.   3. Internet.   I. McIntosh, Shawn.   II. Title.
P90.P355 2010
302.23--dc22
                        2009028038

Printing number: 9 8 7 6 5 4 3 2 1

Printed in the United States of America
on acid-free paper

To my wife, Jackie, and my daughters, Tristan and Orianna—J.V.P.

. . .

To my parents, Dennis and Kathie—S.M.

Brief Contents

Contents

Part 2 Mass-Communication Formats

CHAPTER 3 DIGITAL MEDIA: ONLINE AND UBIQUITOUS   64

Part 3 How Digital Media Are Changing Our World

Part 4 Media Perspectives

CHAPTER 10 JOURNALISM   280

Preface

In June 2009 we got a powerful reminder of how convergence has forever changed the nature of communication—and the world in which we live.

After a presidential election in Iran, hundreds of thousands of supporters of the losing candidate took to the streets to protest the results, in the largest protests since the shah was ousted in 1979. Iranian authorities cracked down on the protestors, killing some. Foreign journalists in Iran were banned from reporting on the protests and government responses, but the world received on-the-ground reports and images from Iranian citizens using social media such as Twitter, Facebook, and YouTube. The losing candidate used his website to encourage his supporters and continue the protests. Bloggers helped translate Farsi-language websites and blogs into English. All these activities were reported on by the mainstream media, further keeping the protests and government crackdown on the global stage.

For Iran's leaders, wrestling with this groundswell of protest through social media must have been threatening and confusing, but also hauntingly familiar. Thirty years earlier, *they* were the protestors and revolutionaries in the streets, and their movement succeeded in part because they used similar methods. In 1979, however, the Internet did not exist—there was of course no World Wide Web, there were no video or camera phones, no text messaging, no blogs. Instead, they copied and passed along audiocassettes of sermons from the exiled Ayatollah Ruholla Khomeini to help build popular support to overthrow the shah.

If text messaging to a friend during class about where to eat lunch may not seem like a radical activity, it belies the media revolution we are experiencing today. It is an exciting time to be a communications professional, with a new range of communications tools transforming many aspects of the communications industries and challenging many of our assumptions about their roles and functions. The *digital natives* of today—those young people who have grown up with personal computers, the Internet, and mobile phones—are perfectly poised to be tomorrow's leaders in a converged media world.

However, the digital natives cannot do it without help. In order to understand how convergence is affecting our lives on many levels, we have to also understand traditional mass media forms and industries, which still determine what media content we get. Although it is easy to point to a dramatic example of social-media use and political action like in Iran, the fact is far more of us spend much more time doing things like watching television, listening to music, or playing video games than we do taking part in government protests. In fact, by the time most of us turn seventy-five, we will have spent eleven years of our lives watching television, according to one study. And this study looked only at traditional TV, not the myriad other screens we spend time with today, for movies, computers, PDAs, and cell phones. Today's digital natives likely spend far more time staring at screens in one form or another than older generations, and as we consume even more media in digital form this trend is sure to continue.

Rarely have there been such differences as seen today in media usage between the digital natives and those who grew up in a pre-Internet era of mass communication. One group may enjoy reading a printed newspaper over breakfast; the other group may get their news online—if they read any news at all. One group may have impressive collections of CDs; the other group may have their music collections in computer hard drives. One group may worry at how increased product placement may affect the type of shows that are produced; the other group may wonder what product placement is and why it matters. One group may believe that it is nobody's business what their relationship status is; the other group may publicly post that and much more personal information on social-networking sites.

Today, the divide is usually between college students, as the digital natives, and their professors, who are ostensibly teaching them about a media environment that the professors often do not seem to be a part of. What can that old (or perhaps just "seasoned") person in the front of the lecture hall who doesn't even have a Facebook page and who rarely checks email teach today's youth about mass communication and digital media?

The short answer: A lot. As the Iranian example demonstrates, social media are not simply replacing traditional mass media. Rather, they are influencing and changing each other in unique ways that make it an exciting time to be studying media and mass communication. Social media did not simply spring forth fully formed from the ether, ready for us to use. In order for us to understand how convergence is affecting our media and our lives we have to also look back at the media that have come before and that are still influential and powerful.

Knowing the history of our media and the growth of media industries is one component of understanding today's media world, but no introductory course to mass communication should simply be a media history course. Students must be allowed to experience the excitement and opportunity of media today, a world in which we see long-standing newspapers moving to online-only versions, in which advertising dollars shift inexorably to the Web, where twentieth-century business models that helped build media entertainment empires seem no longer viable even as media conglomerates continue to expand and new models challenge the old.

If these examples seem more threatening than exciting, it is because the glass looks half empty rather than half full. Print newspapers of today may eventually largely disappear, yet that does not mean the need for news and good journalism will stop. The recording industry may have difficulty doing business as usual, but it does not mean that we will stop listening to music. We may not sit down as a family at 8 p.m. on a Thursday night to watch our favorite show, but it does not mean we will stop wanting television entertainment.

One way to look at the state of mass communication today is that convergence is bringing us the kinds of tools that audiences have long wanted with their media—the ability to have some control over what they watch, read, or listen to; and the ability to share their stories and their lives with others. And, as some embattled Iranian revolutionaries could tell us, the ability to connect with others and change the world when needed.

A New Introduction to Mass Communication

Change has been a constant in mass communication the past several years and has sometimes been dramatic, but you would not know it from most introductory textbooks. Students are changing. The field is changing. The world is changing.

Yet these changes go largely ignored in the textbooks. An introductory textbook is supposed to provide a foundation of knowledge for students learning a new field, but when the foundation sits on a bed of sand it is time for a new introduction.

This book embraces the transformations we see today in mass communications and examines the changes even as it prepares students for what comes tomorrow. This book represents the beginning of a third wave in mass-communications textbooks, building on the earlier waves of case studies and critical-cultural approaches. This new approach demands a more balanced and nuanced understanding of the role that technology and digital media have played in our mass-communication environment. Thus, the second edition of *Converging Media* offers the following:

- **A new perspective**—Through the lens of convergence, our book shows how different aspects of media are parts of a whole and how they influence each other. Digital media are not relegated to special features or an isolated chapter; they are integrated throughout every chapter. This better reflects the world as students live in it and prepares them to understand the changes that are taking place. This organization invites students and professors to engage in timely discussions of media within a larger framework of understanding traditional mass-communication topics.

- **Comprehensive coverage of traditional media**—In order to understand the present, we have to study the past. The development and historical influences of print and electronic media, and the issues these media face today, are covered. The communications professions of journalism, advertising, and public relations are viewed from historical, societal, and career perspectives, giving students insights into how they interact and influence each other. Basic information on computers and networks also gives students a new understanding of the media they use every day.

- **Unique coverage of social media**—This is the first introductory mass-communication textbook to devote a chapter to this emerging area, placing social media within a larger media and sociocultural context while explaining basic principles of social networks and why they are important for a basic understanding of today's mass communication. Popular social-media tools used widely by people today are given a historical context and thematically connected to older online communication tools. Social media are such an integral part of the media mix for so many people that they must be covered in an introductory course, not introduced in an upper-division media and technology course.

- **Cutting-edge examples**—We have chosen examples that are fresh, interesting, and up to date. We have written *Converging Media* with students always in mind—understanding the changing world they live in today. Taken from popular media that are familiar and relevant to undergraduates, the examples illustrate how the landscape of media has evolved—and is still evolving.

- **Cultural context**—Mass communication, media technologies, and convergence take place firmly within a sociocultural milieu that simultaneously affects and is affected by these forces. Understanding this cultural context is vital for a complete understanding of convergence and today's media environment. The authors emphasize the cultural influences and implications of media technologies while explaining how they work and how they were developed.

- **Emphasis on ethics**—Early in the book, we provide students with a grounding in ethical principles that can be applied in cases and examples used throughout the course. Students should learn that ethical considerations are tightly linked to a full understanding of mass communication and media. Ethics can also help guide us in the complex and often confusing world of converging media, giving a basis for sound and humane decisions on media use, new technologies, and the ways they affect people.
- **Integration of international perspectives**—In a global media environment, it is hard to package all things international in a stand-alone chapter. Like ethics, global issues affect domestic media and vice versa, and this text highlights international perspectives in features boxes and in the text itself. Through comparisons and contrasts, students obtain an appreciation for different media systems throughout the world and how they work.

How This Book Is Organized

In today's media environment, we have to understand not only digital media and social media but basics of communication theory, ethics, and traditional mass-communication forms while developing media-literacy skills. **Chapter 1** not only explains the multifaceted nature of convergence (and disputes over its definition) but looks at **theories of communication** in general to see how the nature of mass communication is changing. **Chapter 2** discusses **media literacy and ethics**, which may seem like strange bedfellows but actually share a common characteristic—the need for solid critical-thinking skills. Today's students are often sorely lacking in critical-thinking skills and media literacy, despite their apparent technology savvy. Critical thinking and moral reasoning are both crucial when confronting ethical issues, which communications professionals frequently face.

Chapter 3, on **digital media**, starts a section that explores the traditional forms of media: print, radio, photography, movies, and television. Rather than cover these forms and then add a chapter on digital media at the end, we introduce the media world as it is today in Chapter 3 and then give the historical background of the various forms and the industries around those forms. **Chapter 4** examines **print media**, looking at books, newspapers, and magazines and their industries. Although print is far from dead, there is growing concern among some experts about the effects of lower reading rates among young people and whether we read the same way on a screen as we do with print on paper. **Chapter 5** explores sound—namely, the **recording industry and radio**. The recording industry has of course been at the forefront of changes that digital media have brought to their industry through music file sharing, and radio is increasingly facing questions about its role as people come to expect music on demand and there are more options for bands to promote their music, such as video games and television shows. **Chapter 6** looks at visual media—**photography, movies, and television**—and how each of these developed and influenced the ways that we see media. Photography is often ignored in books like this but is an important aspect of the development of our media usage. Technological advances in photography not only led directly to motion pictures, but contributed to the increased importance we place on visual media today.

The part of the book containing Chapters 7, 8, and 9 is unique in an introductory mass-communication textbook. However, we believe these topics are crucial to apprehending the effects of digital media. Without a current perspective on certain aspects of technology, such as storage capacity, user interface, and interactivity, it is impossible to gain a fuller understanding of the social, cultural, and economic effects of digital media. We explain how **storage capacity**, **user interface**, and **interactivity** play fundamental roles in the development of media, especially digital media, the subject of **Chapter 7**. After all, file sharing would not be such an issue if it were not for the MP3 format that allows for compression of digital files. Similarly, the Internet might have become just another form of mass communication if it weren't for all that interactivity brings. Just as knowing the historical development of print media and television helps us put them in a modern context, **Chapter 8** explores the nature of **telecommunications networks** and how networks and government policies have influenced the development and use of the Internet in different countries. **Chapter 9** is unique in that it addresses **social media** and basic concepts around social networks. Even if specific companies that are popular today fail, the principles discussed in this chapter will apply to whatever new social media take their places. Companies have already been adding new positions that are responsible for monitoring and in some cases participating in the discussions taking place online about the companies.

Chapters 10, 11, and 12 examine the history of the communications professions, and the changes now taking place, with in-depth discussions of the ethical issues each profession faces. **Journalism**, the subject of **Chapter 10**, is probably the field most under threat today for a number of reasons. Yet it is also an exciting field to enter precisely because of the nature of social media and journalism's important role for democracy and people wanting more democratic forms of government. Even though journalism is important, we consume far more entertainment than we do journalism. **Entertainment** is sometimes questioned as a form of mass communication, but as we point out in **Chapter 11**, it is hard to ignore as a powerful force when considering the role it plays in terms of culture and economics—and of course when considering the time we spend with it. For example, it is hard to claim that video games are not an important form of media today when video game sales have been higher than U.S. box office sales for several years now. Intertwined with and supporting both journalism and entertainment is **advertising and public relations**, the subject of **Chapter 12**. These two areas are also facing drastic changes in some of their basic professional assumptions, in part because the public can now talk back to media producers and companies and because advertisers face more fragmented audiences with greater media choices than in the past.

For students interested in gaining a deeper understanding of media or who are considering a career in academia, **Chapter 13** provides a good introduction to some of the **media theories** and introduces the communications professional to different types of research and the strengths and weaknesses of each. Budding communications professionals also need to understand the legal and regulatory framework of media and how that affects what media we get. **Chapter 14** explores **legal and regulatory aspects of media**, especially as related to the First Amendment. It includes a brief history on how electronic media have been regulated in the United States, as well as some of the issues that have yet to be decided. **Chapter 15** makes a thorough examination of **politics and communication**, an area that, in introductory books, is often confined to examining U.S. election coverage. We introduce the notions of the public sphere and public opinion and look at the media's role in democratic and nondemocratic countries throughout the world. Of course, with President Obama's 2008 election win and some calling the election "the YouTube election," the media's role in the election cannot be ignored, and we explore how and why the campaign succeeded using the concepts and principles that were discussed throughout the book.

■■■ FEATURES

We have kept features limited and focused on a few key areas that will help bring out interesting and relevant aspects of the content discussed in the book.

- **Convergence Culture** boxes showcase how media impact our social, political, and popular culture in sometimes dramatic ways.
- **Convergence Context** boxes explore hard-to-understand concepts in fresh and engaging ways, making them easier to grasp and more relevant to students' lives.
- **International Perspectives** boxes take a global perspective on chapter topics, showcasing how media and technology use and media industries are similar to or different from the U.S. context and why that is so.

We are also keenly aware of the value of entertaining as a means of educating, so we have provided some features for students that we hope will succeed at doing both:

- **Opening vignettes** with related photos connect the digital-media theme to the chapter content in a student-friendly way.
- **Media Quizzes** provide a lighthearted yet pedagogically sound way to measure students' knowledge of traditional and digital media and to give them a new awareness of their media usage.
- **Discussion questions** and **further reading** assignments round out each chapter.

Changes from the First Edition

This edition has undergone several major changes since the first edition, published in 2003—changes so large that calling this simply a "revision" does not do justice to their depth and breadth.

The most obvious change is organizational. Instead of having the chapter on digital media follow the chapters on traditional media, we decided that digital media should start that section of the book. It brings relevant content to students sooner and gives them a frame of reference as they learn about the traditional media formats and how they have been changed by digital media. The middle three chapters, Chapters 7, 8, and 9, have probably undergone the most drastic changes. When we finished the book in 2002, social media was still in its infancy, the term "Web 2.0" hadn't been thought of yet, and blogs were still something that had to be carefully explained to an audience that likely had never heard of them. Things have changed radically in the past seven years, of course, and these chapters reflect the changes. Much of the overly technical content in Chapters 7 and 8 was removed and the relevant principles and points from those chapters included, along with new material on interactivity, in the new Chapter 7. Chapter 8 contains material on telecommunications networks and the Internet that had been scattered in other chapters, and this was put together in a more reader-friendly way with new material. Chapter 9 is a completely new chapter, with only small portions regarding online communities taken from chapters in the first edition. Finally, from an organizational perspective, we deleted the final chapter on global media and moved much of that material to other chapters, where relevant, including a more robust and expanded chapter on politics and media.

We have also made several big changes from a content perspective. Probably most important is the removal of material that was too technical or that focused too much on how technology works. We include discussions on technology only when knowing something about how the underlying technology works will affect a student's understanding of the influence that technology has on the media or on historical developments with the media. For example, students at this level do not need to know how exactly compression of digital content works, but they do need to know the effect digital-compression technologies have had on our ability to listen to music or watch videos over the Internet and how that in turn has affected media industries. Related to this, and thanks to helpful suggestions from reviewers, we have also included more explanations of how convergence and culture intersect with and influence each other. In fact, a more nuanced approach to the intersection of culture, media, and technology, and a greater appreciation of it, can be seen in this edition compared to the first. Another change in content is that we removed many of the lists, charts, and rankings that we had in the first edition. As reviewers rightly pointed out, much of this information is dated by the time the book is published and is available in more up-to-date forms online. Along similar lines, material that was deemed too detailed was largely removed or was rewritten in a more general way. Exact dates were deleted altogether or changed to years unless it was important to know an exact date; if someone's birthplace or hometown did not seem relevant to his or her fame, it was removed; if an interesting sidebar related to the development of print or television or some other media did not seem needed to the overall story arc, then it was heavily edited or removed.

Supplements

Adopters of the second edition of *Converging Media* will be pleased to know that Oxford University Press offers a comprehensive support package for both students and instructors, for all kinds of introductory mass-communications courses.

■ ■ ■ FOR STUDENTS

- The **Companion Website** at www.oup.com/us/pavlik offers a wealth of study and review resources including activities, flashcards for key terms in the book, interactive self-tests, objectives, summaries, and web links to a variety of media-related websites.

■ ■ ■ FOR INSTRUCTORS

- **Instructor's Manual and Test Bank**, by Tamara Henry of the University of Maryland, College Park, provides teaching tips, exercises, and test questions that will prove useful to both new and veteran instructors. The Instructor's Manual includes chapter objectives, detailed chapter/lecture outlines, discussion topics, and suggested activities for each chapter. The comprehensive Test Bank offers numerous exam questions for each chapter in multiple-choice, true/false, and essay formats.
- **Instructor Resource CD with Computerized Test Bank**, available to adopters, includes the full Instructor's Manual and Test Bank, as well as computerized testing software and new PowerPoint lecture presentations by Michael Evans of Indiana University.

- **Instructor's Companion Website** at www.oup.com/us/pavlik is a password-protected site that features the Instructor's Manual, PowerPoint lecture slides, and links to supplemental materials.
- **Course cartridges** for a variety of e-learning environments allow instructors to create their own course websites with the interactive material from the instructor and student companion websites. Contact your Oxford University Press representative for access or for more information about these supplements or customized options.

Acknowledgments

Creating a book like this is very much a collaborative effort, and the authors have benefited from the advice and wisdom not only of the reviewers, listed below, but of those who adopted the first edition of the book. These early adopters, in all senses of the word, sometimes had to work hard to persuade colleagues and departments that *Converging Media* was the text to use to introduce students to mass communications. We can only hope that the argument is easier to make with the second edition as we witness a growing number of books about media convergence in the market.

We would also like to thank the adopters who wrote to us over the years asking when a revised edition would be published, and who offered encouraging words about the usefulness of the book when there were still plenty of professors who were not convinced that a new approach to teaching mass communication was needed, or who thought that only minor tweaks to curricula would do the trick.

John is especially grateful for the unfailing support and love of his family, including his wife, Jackie, and daughters, Tristan and Orianna. Shawn is similarly grateful for the love and support of his wife, Naren, and son, Altan, who was good at reminding him that there is always time for tickling and "wrestle-fighting."

We want to especially thank the editors at Oxford University Press whom we worked with: Peter Labella, Frederick Speers, and Josh Hawkins. They immediately understood and shared our vision of what this textbook should be and could be to introductory mass-communication courses. Their insights, advice, and willingness to accept sometimes drastic changes to the organization and structure of the text helped this book surpass our expectations. And how many university press book editors over forty would know who Vampire Weekend is—how cool is that? The copyeditors also helped clarify and simplify and made great improvements throughout the book.

And last but certainly not least, we wish to thank the following reviewers for the detailed and insightful feedback on various chapters of this book:

Charles Apple, University of Michigan–Flint

Charlyne Berens, University of Nebraska–Lincoln

William R. Bettler, Hanover College

Joseph S. Clark, Florida State University

David Cundy, Iona College

James Ettema, Northwestern University

Michael Robert Evans, Indiana University

Thom Gencarelli, Manhattan College

Roger George, Bellevue College

Donald G. Godfrey, Arizona State University

David Gore, Eastern Michigan University

Margot Hardenbergh, Fordham University

Chandler Harriss, Alfred University

Karima A. Haynes, Bowie State University

Jeffrey B. Hedrick, Jacksonville State University

Tamara Henry, American University

Patricia Holmes, University of Louisiana–Lafayette

Seok Kang, University of Texas–San Antonio

Greg Lisby, Georgia State University

John Madormo, North Central College

Charles Marsh, University of Kansas

Stephen J. McNeill, Kennesaw State University

Olivia Miller, University of Memphis

James E. Mueller, University of North Texas

Robert M. Ogles, Purdue University

Selene Phillips, University of Louisville

Marshel D. Rossow, Minnesota State University–Mankato

Ted Satterfield, Northwestern Oklahoma State University

Randall K. Scott, University of Montevallo

Brad Schultz, University of Mississippi

Arthur L. Terry, Bethel University

Mina Tsay, University of Kentucky

■ ■ ■ FIRST EDITION REVIEWERS

Robert Bellamy, Duquesne University

Gerald Boyer, Maryville University

Mark Braun, Gustavus Adolphus College

Margaret Cassidy, Adelphi University

Steven Chappell, Truman State University

Joseph Chuk, Kutztown University

Vic Costello, Gardner-Webb University

David Gordon, University of Wisconsin–Eau Claire

Charlotte Kwok Glaser, College of Notre Dame

Colin Gromatzky, New Mexico State University

Steven Keeler, Cayuga College

Yasue Kuwahara, Northern Kentucky University

Dianne Lamb, Georgia Southern University

Mitchell Land, University of North Texas

Jeremy Harris Lipschultz, University of Nebraska–Omaha

Arthur Lizie, Bridgewater State College

John Lule, Lehigh University

Thomas McPhail, University of Missouri

Anthony Olorunnisola, Pennsylvania State University

Kathleen Olson, Lehigh University

Ronald Roat, University of Southern Indiana

Marshel D. Rossow, Minnesota State University–Mankato

Andris Straumanis, University of Wisconsin–Eau Claire

L. Lee Thomas, Doane College

Max Utsler, University of Kansas

About the Authors

John V. Pavlik is professor and chair of the Department of Journalism and Media Studies at the School of Communication and Information, Rutgers, the State University of New Jersey. He is also director of the Journalism Resources Institute at Rutgers and faculty associate at the Columbia Institute for Tele-Information (CITI). He is chair of the editorial board for *Television Quarterly*, the journal of the National Academy of Television Arts and Sciences. Having published widely on the impact of new technology on journalism, media, and society, Pavlik has also authored more than a dozen computer software packages for education in journalism and communication. He received his PhD and MA in mass communication from the University of Minnesota and is a 1978 graduate of the School of Journalism and Mass Communication at the University of Wisconsin at Madison.

Shawn McIntosh is a lecturer in strategic communications at Columbia University's School of Continuing Education, where he teaches graduate courses in critical thinking, ethics, and digital media. He was an adjunct faculty member at Iona College, where he taught online journalism, website publishing, feature writing, and information visualization; he has taught a course on media ethics at Rutgers University. McIntosh was an editor and freelance writer for ten years for various newspapers and magazines in the UK, United States, and Japan. He was also co–site manager and senior producer at Fathom, an online educational website comprising a consortium of leading academic institutions, museums, and research organizations in the United States and England. His research interests include social media; media, power and democracy; and citizen journalism. He received a BS in microbiology from the University of Idaho and an MS in journalism from the Graduate School of Journalism at Columbia University.

CONVERGING MEDIA

Mass Communication and Its Digital Transformation

CHAPTER OBJECTIVES

In this chapter we will:

■ Define convergence.

■ Explore the main types of convergence and their implications for communication.

■ Define mass communication.

■ Review basic theories of mass communication.

■ Identify the basic components and functions of the mass-communication process.

1

Lovesick teenagers in countries such as Pakistan and Iran sit in crowded cybercafes to socialize, flirt, and explore fantasies that could get them arrested if acted upon. But it all takes place online, largely anonymously, and is considered harmless if titillating fun by the teens and young adults.

The Internet may have opened up new communication channels for teens in socially restrictive cultures, but it has also opened the floodgates to mass communication from around the world. China suffered on the stage of global public opinion shortly before the Beijing Olympics when it reneged on a promise to open access to the entire Internet for foreign journalists. China, like some other countries, bans various websites that are deemed harmful to the state or to the morals of the people.

Just as the Internet can be a socially liberating tool for interpersonal communication and simultaneously a politically liberating—or threatening—tool of mass communication, it can also be used to rapidly spread rumors and hate. "At its best, the Internet can educate more people faster than any media tool we've ever had," wrote journalist Thomas Friedman. "At its worst, it can make people dumber faster than any media tool we've ever had."[1] He cited the lie circulated over the Internet and widely believed in the Muslim world that four thousand Jews were warned not to go into the World Trade Center on September 11. The Internet's aura of "technology" gives it unquestioned authority for many people while it provides a forum to meet others who share their views.

Mass media, computer networks, and telecommunications are converging to change the very definition and role of mass communication and the communications professions. This book is about understanding that convergence.

The media of mass communication have long played a fundamental role in people's lives. The media inform, persuade, entertain, and even sell. Media can provide companionship. They can shape perception. They are fundamental to an informed and educated public.

We will examine the nature of mass communication and how it is changing in the so-called digital age, the age of computerization of the media in a world connected by electronic networks. Far more than just a technological change, this change is cultural, social, and economic. Journalists, public relations professionals, advertising practitioners, and content creators, as well as media consumers, are facing a new world of media symbols, processes, and effects.

Few communications technologies better encapsulate the fundamental aspects of convergence than the telephone. The history and evolution of the telephone as a communications device touch on almost every important issue that we are dealing with today in terms of the Internet and digital media. Furthermore, the phone continues to be at the heart of some of the most innovative changes taking place in how we communicate with each other and how we interact with the world and with media.

Telephony: Case Study in Convergence

Consider one aspect of the cell phone today—the fact that it is mobile. This mobility has important repercussions for a wide range of activities. First, we are no longer tied to a specific place when making or answering a phone call. The question "Are you at home now?" when calling someone on a land line does not make sense—of course they are home, otherwise they would not be able to answer the phone.

By being able to communicate anywhere and any time, you are able to coordinate with others in a much more fluid and spur-of-the-moment fashion than in the past. Prior to widespread use of cell phones, if you had a sudden change of plans (or change of heart) regarding a planned meeting with someone, you had very limited ways to let them know you would not show up. Coordinating meeting times and places among several people in a group took much more planning and did not allow for last-minute changes. Also consider how much more we talk on the phone when we have it with us than when we had to be in a certain place to use it. This makes us more likely to call someone and share information on the spot than if we had to wait to get home to make a phone call. However, it also can mean that we are less likely to interact with those around us as we talk to distant others.

Our familiarity with the phone belies its revolutionary character from a communications perspective. Before the phone, people could not talk directly to others whom they could not physically see. If there was an emergency, the only way to inform the proper authorities was to physically go to where they were and let them know. The phone played a major role in changing our patterns of communication with each other and thereby changing social relations. But it was the telegraph, not the telephone, that first revolutionized our speed of communication.

The telegraph was the first means of electronic communication, using a series of dots and dashes on a keypad to spell out words. This was a cumbersome way to communicate that took special training to code and decode messages, but at least information was transmitted much faster than it could be before. Entire industries were created out of this dramatic change in communication; the newswire services such as Reuters and Associated Press are examples.

Telephones adopted the principles discovered with telegraphy but allowed voice to be transmitted. Although Alexander Graham Bell is the inventor of record for the telephone in 1876, others were also working on how to transmit voice electronically through wires, and there is some evidence that Bell's invention may have borrowed liberally from existing patents by inventors trying to build similar devices. Still, after years of lawsuits, it was Bell who won out. This parallels the many suits and countersuits seen today as companies claim patent infringement on Internet or software inventions and technologies.

Regardless of who can claim credit for inventing the telephone, it was easier for the general public to use than the telegraph. Even so, it was not immediately thought of as an interpersonal communication device, largely because it was expensive and difficult to connect every single household to the telephone network. This parallels the "last mile" issue we see today regarding broadband, or high-speed, Internet connections coming directly into homes and touches on the importance of networks in our communication environment. It also highlights how new communications technologies often do not have "obvious" uses that seem apparent much later—how they may be used or adopted is very much an open question that relies not only on the technology itself but on a range of economic, social, and cultural issues at the time.

Despite the dramatic changes to communications the phone would bring, it was initially either ignored or thought of as simply a novelty when it was unveiled by Bell in 1876. Once some technological improvements were made, however, making it easier to hear and increasing the number of voices that could be carried on a single wire, the telephone became more widely accepted. The ring of the telephone was a death knell for most telegraph companies, just as later media technologies rendered earlier technologies from which they were built obsolete, changing entire industries.

As the telephone network spread, telephone lines started to clutter the landscape.

Initially, especially in Europe, the telephone acted as a kind of early radio. Wealthy patrons paid a fee to listen to music performances that were sent along the wires, and some public venues would pipe in sermons or performances for their patrons.[3] For several years in Budapest, Hungary, Telefon Hírmondó delivered news over the telephone, with subscribers dialing in at certain times to listen to someone reading the news of the day. A similar service was also tried in 1911 in Newark, New Jersey, but only lasted for a few months before closing.

Delivering news over telephone wires therefore is not something new with the Internet, and it also shows how long before video recorders or TiVo were used that people recognized a desire for information and entertainment "on demand" by the public. What was still missing at that time was a business model that could support a business like telephone newspapers. This issue is commonly dealt with today by media companies that need to see a return on investments before they are willing to experiment with new ways of doing business.

Although the telegraph really was the first electronic network, the rise in popularity of the telephone made it a much more visible network for the general public, with masses of wires strung along telephone poles, cluttering the landscape. The decision whether to make the telephone a government-run agency or a private enterprise was an important crossroads, and the choices made in Europe (government) differed from those made in the United States (private enterprise). These choices had profound repercussions even into the twenty-first century that have influenced the development and perceptions of the control and use of the Internet. This shows how new technologies often inherit and carry with them the baggage of historical decisions made much earlier.

In the United States, local telephone companies also sold their own phones, which were often incompatible with other telephone systems. We see this issue today with the various IM services, most of which are not compatible with each other, and with problems between different browsers or computer operating systems.

In response, the U.S. government granted one company, AT&T, a monopoly on the telephone system. This too had important repercussions for later developments in telecommunications. Just as the monopoly telegraph company Western Union had done nearly a hundred years earlier when it became apparent the telephone was a threat to its business, AT&T tried to hamper the development of a new kind of network that would potentially hurt its business. The network that was needed for development of the Internet was not compatible with the system that AT&T used. Even though AT&T realized the new network was more efficient, the telephone company feared losing dominance and initially refused to adopt it.

Today's cell phones typically have a variety of functions that have nothing to do with traditional functions of the phone.

Issues of government regulation and private enterprise, monopoly powers, and business interests at the expense of the public interest are still very much with us today. Regulations lobbied for by telecommunications companies and passed by lawmakers can have direct implications for what telephone services we get and what we can do (and pay for) with our cell phones today. How much we pay for services, what companies charge and how they set up payment plans, and a variety of other business decisions are influenced by the laws and regulations that have been created, sometimes as a result of industry lobbying efforts.

Just as payment amounts and methods may influence how we use the telephone, social and cultural factors play an equally important role in determining whether a technology is adopted. With almost any new technology, people do not know how to act or interact with it. There is a story that in the early days of the telephone a farmer came to town to place an order for supplies. The store clerk told him to place his order directly with the company over the phone, so the farmer dutifully wrote out his order, rolled it up carefully, and then jammed the rolled note into one of the holes of the phone handset and waited.

If this seems too silly to be true, consider your own reactions when you are given a friend's phone to use or have to use a remote control that you are not familiar with. The variety of functions seen in phones today stretches the very definition of "phone" compared to even twenty years ago. For young people today, it would seem odd to have a phone that does not take pictures or contain an address book or video games. This can be seen in some of the complaints about the Apple iPhone, which cannot show video.

In short, the phone is continuing to evolve as a multifunctional communications device that connects us to the world of information through the World Wide Web as well as to our friends. It provides an almost seamless interface between interpersonal and mass communication, as we access the Web from it to read reviews on a restaurant we pass by, and as we snap a photo while in the restaurant and upload it to the Web or even post our review on the spot, after which it can be seen potentially by millions of people.

Mass communication often brings the public together, providing people shared topics of conversation, news about the world, and entertainment.

All these aspects of the development and use of the phone, ranging from the technical, legal, and regulatory to the economic, social, and cultural, touch on the notion of media convergence. But as we will see, "convergence" is a debated concept and has multiple layers of meaning. We will start to unpack these layers and will define it to show how it encompasses some of the most dramatic transformations taking place in communications today.

Three Types of Convergence

Although scholars still do not agree on an exact and complete definition of the word, **convergence** is known broadly as the coming together of computing, telecommunications, and media in a digital environment. It is important to study and understand convergence because what would seem like technology or media issues have had profound influences on our economic, social, and cultural lives.

The confusion and disagreements around the definition of the term indicate the far-reaching consequences of the changes taking place in mass communication today. Indeed, they speak to the fact that there are many forces changing in ways that we do not yet have adequate descriptions for, nor do we fully understand yet how these changes will affect us. For now, the term "convergence" seems to come closest to encompassing many of these forces.

We can look at three main categories of convergence as ways to frame our understanding of the changes taking place today in the media industries: technological convergence, economic convergence, and cultural convergence. As you will see, these three categories actually overlap in many respects.

■ ■ ■ TECHNOLOGICAL CONVERGENCE

Perhaps the most easily visible aspect of convergence is the rise of digital media and online communication networks. Technological convergence refers to specific types of media, such as print, audio, and video, all converging into a digital media form. Such types of convergence are becoming increasingly apparent in news organizations, for example, where today's journalists often need to be able to tell stories in text, audio, video, and even interactive media.

Digital media often change the very nature of their traditional counterparts and affect how we use and perceive them. For example, although you can look at reading a book on Kindle as simply "print online," the fact is that a Kindle book alters the reading experience. One obvious way is that because of its storage capacity you can easily carry many books in one device, allowing you to move back and forth between books or to cross-reference passages quickly. Furthermore, you are able to change the text size to make reading more comfortable for you, look up words with a built-in dictionary, annotate and index sections, and even purchase new books on the spot through a wireless Internet connection.

If most of these activities, such as looking up a word you don't know in a dictionary, seem like things that exist already with printed books, that is because they are. The difference is that you can do these activities within a single device rather than carrying a separate dictionary with you, or permanently marking in a book, or having to go to a store or library to get another book by the same author. Activities that used to be separate or cumbersome are now easier and folded into the media experience. It is not simply a matter of convenience—these changes fundamentally alter how we interact with our media. We may be far more likely to look up a word in Kindle than if we had to walk to the shelf to get the dictionary, for example.

The music, television, and film industries, which we will look at in later chapters, provide other examples of how our media use changes thanks in part to changes in technology.

This form of convergence is very relevant today for communications professionals, but it is not the only way to think of convergence. The changes that come from new technologies also affect business models and established industries, which often see the upstarts as threats to their dominance. Sometimes, these upstarts become larger and more powerful than established companies; Google is a case in point. Because of the importance of networks in today's world, it is often advantageous for a company to control not only media content but the means of distributing that content through the networks, which is part of what economic convergence is about.

■ ■ ■ ECONOMIC CONVERGENCE

Economic convergence refers to the merging of Internet or telecommunications companies with traditional media companies, such as AOL with Time Warner. Traditional media companies have grown fewer and much larger in the past fifty years, and this process is also sometimes called convergence. This, however, would be better defined as **consolidation**, or the process of large companies merging with each other or absorbing other companies, forming even bigger companies.

consolidation
The process of large companies merging with each other or absorbing other companies, forming even bigger companies.

An aspect of this process of consolidation does include economic convergence. Entertainment companies may own news stations; large corporations traditionally outside of the media business, such as GE, may purchase media companies like NBC. This can result in conflicts of interest when corporate parents don't want some aspects of their businesses covered in the news or when a news outlet gives prominent coverage to a movie coming out that happens to be from the studio also owned by the corporate parent. The latter occurred in 2000, when *Time* magazine made a cover story out of Stanley Kubrick's last movie, *Eyes Wide Shut*, starring Tom Cruise and Nicole Kidman, which also got prominent play on other Time Warner media news outlets such as CNN's *Larry King Live*. The movie was from Warner Brothers studios.

Economic convergence also has important repercussions for the nature of the media, telecommunications, and computing industries. A telecommunications company that also owns a media company can bolster the user experience for its own content at the expense of content from other companies by doing something as simple as speeding up transmission of its content and slowing that of other content. It could also control the type of content its customers see by blocking material from certain websites.

This is not happening because of the Internet, as there are many historical examples of media owners censoring content that they did not like or did not agree with for one reason or another. But what makes this issue bigger and more prominent is the combination of consolidated media giants and ever bigger audiences. In other words, more people may have fewer real choices than ever before, despite the explosion of channels and media content.

But it is part of the nature of interactive media and the Internet to break down some of these traditional barriers between media producers and the audience, and audiences today potentially have more power than ever before. A kind of cultural shift is taking place, still in fits and starts, in which the relationship between the audience or public and media producers is changing.

CONVERGENCE CONTEXT

User-Generated Content: Creativity or Piracy?

With the ease of copying and altering digital content, almost anyone can take media content and make it into something different. Two or three popular songs from different artists can be combined and made into a new song; an artist's paintings can be manipulated digitally and mixed with one's own work.

Is this kind of content creation original art or is it copyright infringement, since it relies on preexisting art owned by someone else?

Some make arguments that almost any creative work has been influenced by previous works encountered by the artist and that digital content simply makes it easier to make "mash-ups" of content. They argue that notions of copyright—essentially a government-granted monopoly to the content creator (or owner of the copyright, as is often the case with recording labels where the artists don't own the copyright)—is anachronistic in the digital age and increasingly stifles creativity through steep licensing or copyright fees. Copyright reduces the amount of creative material in the public domain, thus reducing the pool of works freely available.

However, copyright is still a cornerstone of media industries and a fundamental way in which media companies gener-

ate revenues. It is hard for most media industries, especially in entertainment, to envision a world with no copyright that would still allow them to create the kind of content they do.

Creative Commons has made a range of "copyleft" contracts for content creators that help ensure creative works remain in the public domain. Under the various contracts, content creators allow their content to be used by anyone for free, but they may make certain stipulations, such as that they must be credited or that the content can only be used if it isn't sold. One common stipulation within the community, however, is that people using the content must allow it to remain free for public use.

Web Link >>>
Creative Commons
www.creativecommons.org

■■■ CULTURAL CONVERGENCE

The term "culture" is often a loaded word, and its definition is even harder to pin down than the term "convergence." The notion of culture can refer to anything from a long-standing tradition or heritage shared by a group of people to a specific professional group's particular way of seeing the world or behaving—as with, for example, "newsroom culture."

Here we will refer to culture as something that characterizes the practices, beliefs, and values that interact with and influence each other in creating a shared worldview, or way of understanding the world, among a group of people.

From this definition, one aspect of cultural convergence comes from the process of globalization of media content. Cultural convergence occurs, for example, when an HBO series like *Sex and the City* becomes wildly popular among female office workers in Thailand, or when a Mexican telenovela, or soap opera, gets high ratings among audiences in Russia. The popularity of such shows across a variety of cultures demonstrates that there is some aspect to them that foreign audiences identify with or aspire to and indicates that there may be more in common between a young professional in Bangkok and one in New York City than would first appear.

But we can also look at cultural convergence from the perspective of how we consume, create, and distribute media content. The shift from a largely passive and silent audience that consumes media produced by large-scale media companies to an audience with nearly equal ability to produce and distribute its own content is one of the major themes of this book and a crucial aspect of cultural convergence.

A central premise of this kind of convergence is that although there will continue to be "mass communication," in the sense that media companies and others will continue to produce messages for large audiences, frequently audiences may receive messages tailored to each individual, and audiences are empowered to become much more active in their engagement with communication than they have been. Furthermore, what was traditionally considered interpersonal communication, such as an email, can be distributed through online networks in the same way that mass communication can, making the dividing line between interpersonal and mass communication increasingly hard to distinguish.

Whether audiences will become more active in media production or not remains open to debate, although there are many examples throughout the book that substantiate this trend.

Convergence and Communications

In this book we will focus on aspects of convergence and how it relates specifically to media or mass communication, only touching on some of the larger issues around culture, media economics, and technological changes, which are beyond the scope of this book.

It is clear that the changes brought about by convergence, however one defines it, have dramatic implications. Within the larger framework of the three types of convergence we see, these implications fall into five areas:

1. The content of communication
2. The audience and communications organizations
3. The structure of communications organizations
4. How communications professionals do their work
5. The global audience

These five implications are recurrent themes throughout this book.

■■■ CONVERGENCE AND CONTENT

Stories told in a digital, online medium can make connections with other types of content much more easily than in any other medium. This is done primarily through the use of **hyperlinks,** or clickable pointers to other online content. For example, advertisements in a digital, online environment permit visitors to click on interactive ads or even images of products that can be purchased directly online. Or, in entertainment programming, hyperlinked content allows a viewer to explore a story in a nonlinear narrative, where the outcome of a story may be unchanged, but the path to get there is determined by the links the user chooses to click.

hyperlink
clickable pointer to other online content.

Moreover, it is increasingly possible to obtain content on demand. In the traditional media world, news, entertainment, and marketing information was broadcast or published on a schedule solely determined by the publisher or broadcaster. Children growing up in an on-demand media world of YouTube, podcasting, and TiVo may quickly become frustrated with traditional radio or television, where they cannot control what they watch or listen to, or how many times.

digitization
....
The process in which media is made into computer-readable form.

Digitization is transforming both how and when media organizations distribute their content. They no longer distribute content solely through traditional channels but instead deliver it via the Internet, satellite, and a host of other digital technologies. They are increasingly making that content available twenty-four hours a day, with news organizations updating the news almost continuously, and to a worldwide audience.

The production cycle and process is similarly being transformed by digital technology. In fact, the transformation may be even deeper in terms of media-content production. Whether in Hollywood motion pictures, television shows or news, books, magazines, newspapers, or online, the process of producing media content is rapidly becoming almost entirely digital. Movies are shot using digital cameras and edited on computers. Reporters working for television, radio, newspapers, or any other news operation capture their raw material with digital devices as well, editing their stories digitally. Even book authors typically write on a computer, with words increasingly remaining digital throughout the entire production process.

Digital technology has allowed more people to create professional-quality videos and other media content.

▪▪▪ CONVERGENCE AND THE AUDIENCE

Mass communication was largely one-way, from the source of a message to the receiver, or audience. The audience was relatively large, heterogeneous, and anonymous. Audience members had relatively few means by which to communicate either with each other on a mass scale or with the creators and publishers. Audiences in the age of convergence can communicate via email, online forums, and other interactive media more easily and quickly with each other and with those who create and publish mass-communication content. In addition, they can create the content themselves and reach far larger audiences for much lower costs than they could have with traditional media. They are generally not anonymous, as they can be tracked through user names or IP addresses.

Mass-communication organizations can keep detailed and automatically updated records on their audiences by tracking their paths within their websites through intelligent software agents and programs known as **cookies**. Cookies allow a website to recognize when a previous user returns and to offer personalized content. Cookies provide invaluable information for media organizations to better understand an audience's media behaviors, preferences, and habits.

cookie
....
Information that a website puts on a user's local hard drive so that it can recognize when that computer accesses the website again. Cookies are what allow for conveniences like password recognition and personalization.

Of course, the same ability that media companies have to track users is shared by any website creator with cheap or free tools. Surveillance is an increasingly powerful tool that is necessary to optimize content and to give advertisers a high

CONVERGENCE **CULTURE**

Mapping Sex Offenders

The role of surveillance in our society becomes especially important when the public has easy access to data that used to be stored only in institutions. It strikes close to home when there are sites that let users type in an address or zip code and see on a map where registered sex offenders live and work. Such sites include not only the addresses of the offenders but their pictures and information such as offense, year released from prison, and personal attributes like height, weight, and identifying marks. Users can sign up to receive email alerts when a sex offender registers or changes address in their neighborhood.

Such sites have been lauded by parents groups

Web Link >>>
Family Watchdog
www.familywatchdog.us

Web Link >>>
Vision 20/20
www.thevision2020.com

and child-safety organizations, yet they also raise some thorny ethical questions regarding rights of privacy and the potential for vigilante justice. One such case occurred in Evansville, Indiana, in early 2008 when would-be vigilantes tried to burn down the house of a registered sex offender—except they set fire to the wrong house.

Cases like this one reveal the power of personalized and localized information in surveillance when combined with easy access.

return on their investment. But of even more importance is how audiences are able to communicate with each other, largely circumventing the traditional media channels and in some cases even challenging them in terms of popularity and ability to reach an audience.

Distribution Alters the Balance of Power

Digital media make it easier than ever for the public to create and distribute media content, whether it is an original drawing done using illustration software, an animation or video, or a song sampled and mixed from current hits by famous recording artists. Writing and music have led the way in media consumers creating content—especially music, where remixes of previously recorded (and copyrighted) material are common.

Audiences are increasingly active in their communication with each other and with the creators of mass-communication content. This gives them much greater

viral marketing
....
Spreading news and information
about media content through
word of mouth, usually via
online discussion groups,
chats, and emails, without
utilizing traditional
advertising and marketing
methods.

peer-to-peer (P2P)
....
A computer communications model
in which all users have equal
abilities to store, send, and
accept communications from
other users.

control over what media they consume and shifts some of the power away from media organizations. Through **viral marketing**, or the online equivalent of word-of-mouth advertising, a popular website, product, or piece of content can potentially reach millions of online users in a very short time, all without corporate promotion or advertising dollars. The success of **peer-to-peer** (or P2P) file-sharing programs shows how an Internet audience shifts the balance of power away from media organizations, even though those organizations created and provided that content in the first place.

Audiences aren't willing to wait for the evening news or the next day's paper for developments in a breaking story. Audiences can get their information and entertainment from literally thousands of sources around the world. Audiences aren't content to sit back and listen in silence to what the media report; they actively seek the most recent information through blogs, instant messaging, and other informal communication channels. There have been cases of employees finding news of their company's planned layoffs through certain websites hours before the company officially announced the layoffs.

Audience Fragmentation and *The Daily Me*

These changes are not without some dangers, however. Actively choosing the media you want to see, hear, or read can narrow the scope of news items or entertainment that you may encounter by accident, that unintentionally inform or entertain. Former MIT Media Lab director, the late Michael Dertouzos, called the specialization of news to one's specific interests "The Daily Me." This phenomenon could fragment audiences into small groups of like-minded individuals who do not interact with other groups or with society as a whole and choose to receive only the news and information that reinforce their beliefs and values. Media fragmentation has already been a trend in analog media, and digital media can easily accelerate that trend. Cass Sunstein, law scholar and author of *Republic.com* and *Infotopia*, voices similar concerns over the social effects in a democratic society when media audiences become increasingly fragmented and stop discussing social and political issues of common public interest. However, personalization and localization of news does have benefits in potentially getting the public to become more engaged in news and in helping people become better informed about current events.

Giving the audience a chance to talk back and interact with journalists, as well as provide news coverage themselves, is another important development in keeping journalists accountable. A mistake in a story can be publicly countered or corrected in the discussion section of the story and, if shown to be correct, can then be incorporated in a revised version. These trends may help slow or even reverse the steady decline in credibility suffered by U.S. news organizations during the past quarter century, though it has yet to be seen. This is just one example of how the nature of the relationship between audiences and media organizations is changing in a world of converged media.

■ ■ ■ CONVERGENCE AND COMMUNICATIONS ORGANIZATIONS

In the preconverged world, centralized media organizations created and published or broadcast content on predetermined schedules. A newspaper was printed and distributed within a certain period of time; a television broadcast appeared within a given time slot. "Centralized" media organizations are ones where content production and distribution, as well as marketing and other functions, are controlled by a central unit or individual. Internet-based media can be less centralized. Many divisions may determine the design or content of individual web pages of a website. Web-based media are certainly not exempt from the economic consolidation of all mass media, but the nature of the Web permits more flexibility and adaptability in publishing or webcasting content.

Although there are many public service media, most media companies throughout the world try to make a profit. Many media companies are among the most profitable private enterprises in the world, with average profit margins often in excess of 20 percent a year—double the average for other industries.

Concentration of media ownership, or consolidation, has been a growing trend, and the same process is taking place in the digital media world. Convergence is in some ways fuelling media consolidation by leading traditional media giants such as Time Warner to join with an online colossus such as America Online, giving rise in 2001 to the short-lived AOL Time Warner, which later jettisoned AOL as a separate unit and reverted once again to Time Warner after plummeting stock prices and executive shake-ups.

However, the trend is clear; analog and digital media are rapidly being consolidated into the hands of a few, very large, very powerful and very rich owners, an economic structure referred to as an **oligopoly**. These media enterprises today are increasingly likely to be part of large, global media organizations publicly owned and accountable to shareholders whose main interest is the financial bottom line. The problem of centralized control of access and content can become especially acute as traditional telecommunications companies, such as Verizon or Comcast, which serve as main Internet service providers, partner with or are part of a media company that has a vested interest in promoting its specific content over that of rival media companies.

oligopoly

An economic structure in which a few, very large, very powerful and very rich owners control an industry or collection of related industries.

This practice has greater implications than simply the kind of media content that audiences may receive; it can fundamentally alter the types of jobs that communications professionals may do and even the standards of those professions.

■ ■ ■ CONVERGENCE AND COMMUNICATIONS PROFESSIONALS

With all the changes brought to mass communication because of convergence, it is obvious that the way communications professionals do their jobs will also change. Just as print, video, and audio become absorbed as types of digital media, so the divisions will disappear between print and electronic journalists and between advertising and public relations professionals. Newsrooms increasingly expect reporters to know how to use video and audio to tell stories as well as to write effectively. Advertising and public relations professionals will have to learn how to best attract the attention of a public that encounters ever more media and in which the public is more active than in the past.

Just what constitutes a television or radio receiver, or TV or radio programming, is in a state of flux. Once it was simple. Radio programming was what a listener heard on a radio. Today, however, there are radio stations that transmit their programming via the Internet and listeners tune in via their computer. Moreover, these radio stations can include images, graphics, text, and video. For example, some Voice of America radio reporters have been trained in digital video shooting and editing and can now be "VJs," or video journalists, webcasting their stories visually as well as through audio. With little more than a small digital video camera

Olympic Mascots of the Apocalypse

INTERNATIONAL PERSPECTIVES

Like other countries that have hosted the Olympics, China created cutesy Olympic mascots amid much fanfare and media hype about what the mascots were supposed to symbolize. It is also no surprise that such mascots lend themselves well to being marketed as stuffed dolls, key chains, and other memorabilia.

However, the five Fuwa, or "good-luck dolls," created for the 2008 Beijing Olympics became seen as harbingers of bad luck after a series of unfortunate accidents. This change in perception by the Chinese public was largely because of the enhanced power of Chinese citizens to communicate directly with each other through blogs, chat rooms, and mobile phones, free of state-run mass media outlets that stick to the party line and are careful about presenting anything that would put the government in a bad light.

An earthquake in Sichuan Province earlier in the summer that killed approximately seventy thousand people was connected to the panda Jing Jing, as Sichuan is where pandas come from. Earlier in the year, extensive flooding was pinned on Bei Bei, the fish. Protests in Tibet that were suppressed harshly were associated with Ying Ying, the Tibetan antelope, and the various protests worldwide during the torch relay were blamed on Huan Huan, the fiery red mascot. A swarm of locusts coming from Inner Mongolia and heading to Beijing was enough to convince many Chinese that Ni Ni, the flying mascot, completed the curse.

The government ordered state-run media to not report on the topic or refer to any "Fuwa" curses, but with so many communication channels open to the people now, it was impossible to suppress such beliefs. The implications of this change in communications dynamics goes far beyond any supposed curse regarding Olympic dolls; it could have repercussions for the Chinese government if dissatisfied citizens used these same communication tools to challenge government authority or to criticize government policies.

and a laptop computer with video-editing software, journalists can now shoot, edit, and produce a professional-quality news-video segment.

But in order to take advantage of digital media, new skills will have to be learned and it will be more important than ever that the fundamental principles and ethics of each profession are not abandoned in the march toward the digital environment. As noted above, this is no easy order given the pressure by corporate parents to blur the lines between news and entertainment, or news and promotion.

■ ■ ■ CONVERGENCE AND GLOBAL MEDIA

Content is much more fluid, dynamic, and rapidly transmitted throughout the globe in an online environment. However, this is not without its dangers, as events in distant places can have far-reaching repercussions to others because of the reach of global media and instantaneous communications. False rumors about companies or company leaders, such as the email in late 2008 that falsely claimed that Steve Jobs had had a heart attack and that sent Apple's shares down for much of the trading day, demonstrate the power and danger of rapid global communication.

The Internet enables audiences around the world to participate in a global dialog about the world's events and issues and can bring individuals into direct contact with each other though they are separated by thousands of miles and political and cultural boundaries. It is not clear what the net effect of this sea change in communication will be, but it is clear the foundation is being laid for a more connected and engaged global public. However, this does not mean that increased connectivity and engagement among people will naturally lead to rational discussions or debates. It is likely the opposite will occur as people from different cultures discover that what they take as cultural "common sense" may be considered heresy by someone else. Consider the amount of vitriol seen in many discussion groups even among people who are from the same culture but who have differing opinions.

Global economic, political, and cultural influences also are reshaping media, just as they have ever since Gutenberg printed his first Bible in 1455. Governments, both domestic and international, regulate most media in an attempt to shape or control them or their content. This is true whether in the analog or digital worlds of media. Broadcast media have traditionally been subject to extensive government regulation, whereas print media in the United States have been relatively free of government regulation, with strong legal independence established in the First Amendment to the Constitution of the United States.

Yet, in the digital, online realm, even "print" media organizations could become subject to greater government regulation, whether in the United States or internationally. As newspapers move from the analog to the digital world and their products reach a global audience, they are finding themselves increasingly subject to international rules, regulations, and restrictions foreign governments place upon the Internet. **Libel** and obscenity laws differ widely between countries, raising the question of whose version of libel should be used when an article published on the Internet libels someone according to that person's local laws. Likewise, should Internet communication be considered under telephone regulations, since many people access it through telephone lines, or regulated according to the cable industry, since it is also available through cable modems? These are just some examples in which digital technology and convergence has sped ahead of our current legal framework.

libel

A type of defamation that is written and published, such as a false attack on a person's character, which damages a person's reputation.

So far we have discussed how convergence has been changing the media industries and their business models, the issues communications professionals have faced that are brought by new technologies, the nature of the relationship between media producers and audiences, and legal matters that have yet to be addressed. You have gotten a glimpse of the powerful transformations taking place today in mass communications and the media and will see even more examples in greater detail in subsequent chapters.

But before we can move forward we have to take a step back and look at what mass communication itself is and even how media scholars theorize how communication works. We will then be able to use these foundations to better understand the changes taking place today.

Mass Communication in the Digital Age

The traditional mass-communication model differs from other forms of communication, such as **interpersonal communication**, which is communication between two or more persons. Interpersonal communication often interacts with and intersects **mass communication**.

Interpersonal communication takes place between two or more people, is interactive, and can happen face-to-face or through a medium.

interpersonal communication
Communication between two or more individuals, usually in a small group, although it can involve communication between a live speaker and an audience.

mass communication
Communication to a large group or groups of people that remain largely unknown to the sender of the message.

medium
A communication channel, such as talking on the telephone, instant messaging, or writing back and forth in a chat room.

■ ■ ■ INTERPERSONAL COMMUNICATION

Interpersonal communication is usually interactive, or flowing at least two ways, is generally one-to-one, and tends not to be anonymous. Think of chatting with a friend or talking with a small group of friends. Responses are generally immediate and the speaker or speakers will often adjust their messages based on the responses they receive.

These same principles apply to live public speaking, even though this is a one-to-many model and opportunities for audience feedback will be more limited than in a casual small-group setting. The speaker and audience can communicate through a variety of nonverbal cues, such as facial expressions, physical contact, or body language. If speakers see looks of boredom or audience members yawning, they can react to that feedback and try to make their presentations more interesting.

Interpersonal communication can also take place through a **medium**, or communication channel, such as talking on the telephone, instant messaging, or writing back and forth in a chat room. Note how the mediation limits some aspects of interpersonal communication compared to face-to-face interactions. There are no visual cues either on the telephone or online (unless using a webcam), and meanings can be misconstrued by text messages. The online medium also blurs the line between interpersonal and mass communication, as a chat room can have hundreds or thousands of participants.

■ ■ ■ MASS COMMUNICATION

Media of mass communication refer to any technologically based means of communicating between large numbers of people distributed widely over space or time.

Since Johannes Gutenberg invented the Western world's first mechanical printing press in Germany in 1455, the media of mass communication have been characterized by a single, overarching model. This model has had the following four main characteristics:

1. Communication flow is largely one-way, from sender or source to receiver or audience.

2. Communication is from one or a few to many (i.e., one or a few sources generate and distribute content to large, heterogeneous audiences).

3. Communication is anonymous (sources generally do not know their audiences and audiences do not know the sources, except at a general level).

4. Audiences are largely passive recipients of the messages distributed by the media, with little opportunity for feedback and practically no opportunity for immediate feedback or interaction with each other.

In other words, media companies create content they believe the audience will want and distribute that content to an audience that has very few ways to provide immediate feedback. This model has characterized all media of mass communication, whether books, magazines, newspapers, broadcast television or radio, cable or satellite TV, recorded music, or motion pictures. Digital media, however, are radically changing that model, as we will see throughout this book.

In the traditional mass-communication model, content creators play a fundamental role in society by representing and defining reality (as done by journalists or other communication professionals), or by authoring fictional narratives to explain, interpret, or entertain (as done by artists, authors, and film auteurs). Authors and artists create stories about issues and events, they write books and articles, they create music or motion pictures, and then they publish, broadcast, or present those stories at set dates or times and in set locations.

Some mass-communications models, such as live television or radio, are **synchronous media**. Synchronous media require the audience to be assembled simultaneously with the broadcast, transmission, or event. Others are asynchronous. **Asynchronous media**, such as newspapers or magazines, do not require the audience to assemble at any given time. Audio and video recording devices let people **time shift** and record a live concert or performance so it can be watched anytime, thereby turning synchronous media into asynchronous media.

■ ■ ■ WHITHER MASS COMMUNICATION?

Digital media and online networks have blurred the line between interpersonal and mass communication, leaving many to wonder how relevant the concept of mass communication remains for media-studies scholars and communications professionals. The media companies built on mass-communication models, despite facing many challenges in the digital era, are not disappearing anytime soon, and neither will certain fundamental aspects of mass communication.

What is changing, however, is the interplay between mediated interpersonal communication and mass communication: interpersonal communication is capable of adopting some characteristics of mass communication, and mass communication is trying to adopt certain characteristics of interpersonal in an attempt to remain relevant to audiences. Let's consider some examples.

Email is considered a form of mediated interpersonal communication, yet as anyone who has had their inbox clogged with forwarded jokes from Aunt Gertrude can attest, it can also be broadcast to many recipients, following the one-to-many model typical of mass communication.

Weblogs, or **blogs**, diary-like entries or comments posted online, often feel interpersonal in tone and scope, yet some blogs have become very influential among the public or among decision makers, with readership greater than many well-established mainstream publications. Blogs may allow immediate feedback or discussion from readers, who often must be registered in order to write feedback and are therefore not anonymous—thereby weakening two of the linchpins in the definition of mass communication. Yet it is hard to claim that the most popular blogs are not a type of mass communication, because of the numbers of audience members reading them.

Similarly, the fragmented nature of audiences on the Web makes defining a "mass" extremely difficult. Some websites have small but dedicated followings, while others have millions of visitors a month, reaching far more people than your typical local newspaper. Yet the local newspaper would be traditionally defined as

synchronous media
Media that take place in real time, such as live television or radio, that require the audience to be present during the broadcast or performance.

asynchronous media
Media that do not require the audience to assemble at a given time. Examples of asynchronous media are printed materials and recorded audio or video.

time shift
Recording an audio or video event for viewing later rather than when the event was originally broadcast. Setting a VCR to record a favorite program while one is out is an example of time shifting.

blog
Short for "weblog," a type of website in which a person posts regular journal or diary entries with the posts arranged chronologically.

a type of mass communication, whereas a YouTube video such as "Charlie bit my finger—again!", with over 95 million views almost two years after being posted and over two thousand various remixes and spoofs, would generally not be.

It is important to remember that much of the interaction and conversation that takes place between members of the public online does so because of the information and entertainment generated from mass communication. There are no "Charlie Bit My Finger" fan clubs, whereas a TV series such as *Star Trek*, which ran for only three seasons in the late 1960s, continues to have a thriving fan subculture that creates—and consumes—content about the series and the actors in it, not to mention the various movies and television-series spin-offs from the original *Star Trek*. The daily mix of news, information, and entertainment that we consume through mass-communication channels gives us the fodder from which to create websites, to blog, to interact with each other—and to talk back to the media producers who are giving us the content.

Web Link >>>
YouTube: "Charlie bit my finger—again!"
www.youtube.com/watch?v=_OBlgSz8sSM

Nature and Function of Mass Communication

Defining mass communication was once a relatively straightforward matter. The media were relatively stable and well known. Print media included books, newspapers, and magazines. Electronic media included television, radio, the recording arts, and cinema, although the latter two were usually created and originally distributed on media such as albums or film.

The functions of mass communication in society were also relatively well understood and thoroughly researched. Studies by Harold D. Lasswell, Charles Wright, and others suggest that these functions have tended to fall largely into four broad categories.[4] These functions can be a useful lens through which to understand how the various forms of mass communication work.

surveillance
. . . .
Primarily the journalism function of mass communication, which provides information about the processes, issues, events, and other developments in society.

■ ■ ■ SURVEILLANCE

Surveillance refers primarily to journalism, which provides information about the processes, issues, events, and other developments in society. This can include news on the latest military developments, weather alerts, and political scandals. Surveillance can also include aspects of advertising and public relations, as well as educational aspects of communication.

One weakness in the surveillance function is that too much news about disasters, murders, or other unusual events can skew the audience's perception of what is normal in society. Another weakness is that too much information can make the audience apathetic. Consider how media coverage of a scandal regarding a sports figure such as Yankees baseball player Alex Rodriguez can take on a life of its own and seem to continue forever, until we are truly sick of seeing any more stories about A-Rod.

The example may seem trivial in the case of celebrity scandals, but it takes on greater importance when one considers coverage of wars or disasters, especially in developing countries.

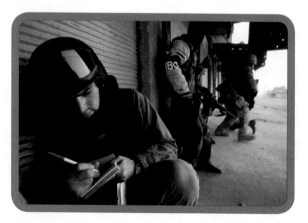

Journalists covering conflicts overseas represent one important aspect of the surveillance function of mass communication.

■ ■ ■ CORRELATION

Correlation refers to the ways in which media interpret events and issues and ascribe meanings that help individuals understand their roles within the larger society and culture. Journalism, advertising, and public relations all shape public opinion through comments, criticism, or even targeted marketing campaigns. Individuals may learn what others think about an issue through polls or surveys and thus get a sense of where their views fit within mainstream opinions. Some people may even subtly shift their views or beliefs to better correlate with a social group they aspire to. By correlating one's views with other groups or perceived notions of general public opinion, the media can help maintain social stability, although this function can be taken too far and the media can thwart social change or block a full range of views from being disseminated to a mass audience.

Interpretation can also tend to favor established business or elite interests over disadvantaged or minority groups, lending a sense of credibility and authority to certain views that may not be fair to all members of society.

■ ■ ■ CULTURAL TRANSMISSION

Cultural transmission refers to the transference of the dominant culture, as well as its subcultures, from one generation to the next or to immigrants. This function includes socialization, which the media perform in helping persons learn society's rules or how to fit into society. This function is especially important for children but also is performed for adults who may have recently immigrated to a new country with a different culture.

The other side of the coin regarding the cultural-transmission function is a criticism that it creates a homogenized culture that promotes mindless consumerism as a means to achieve happiness, rather than imparting more humanistic, and ultimately more rewarding, values to people.

■ ■ ■ ENTERTAINMENT

The entertainment function is performed in part by all three of these activities (surveillance, correlation, and cultural transmission) but also involves the generation of content designed specifically and exclusively to entertain. Although some say that this function helps raise artistic and cultural taste among the general populace, critics argue that mass media encourage lowbrow entertainment at the expense of fine art, encourage escapism, and do not help raise the cultural level of society. It is also important to note that entertainment is often imbued with powerful cultural values and symbols that can easily be taken for granted but that play a role in transmitting specific sets of values.

Entertainment can also perpetuate certain stereotypes about various groups, wittingly or unwittingly. These can be especially hard to notice as they are often part and parcel of a storyline or characters and can often seem "natural" in terms of the show.

Theories of Communication

Underlying the functions of mass communication is a rich history of thinkers who have tried to understand how communication itself works and what exactly "communication" is. They have proposed a variety of theories on communication in

correlation

The ways in which media interpret events and issues and ascribe meanings that help individuals understand their roles within the larger society and culture.

cultural transmission

The transference of the dominant culture, as well as its subcultures, from one generation to the next or to immigrants, which helps people learn how to fit into society.

Wartime propaganda posters provide windows into how public opinion can be shaped.

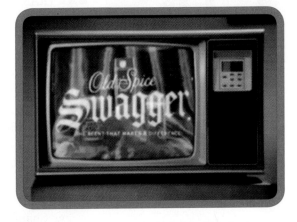

Commercials can be highly influential in shaping public tastes and fashions.

Entertainment is one of the most important functions of mass communication, partly because of the cultural meanings it often transmits.

Aristotle was one of the earliest theorists of communication, and his ideas influenced theorists for generations.

their attempts to explain it. One of the earliest communication theorists was the philosopher Aristotle, who in 300 BCE called the study of communication "rhetoric" and spoke of three elements within the process: the speaker, subject, and person addressed. His basic ideas laid an enduring foundation for communication research, even today.

The need to better understand communication from a theoretical perspective arose with the importance that mass communication began to have in people's lives, especially as electronic communication such as radio and television became so dominant.

■ ■ ■ TRANSMISSION MODELS

In 1949, scientists Claude E. Shannon and Warren Weaver formulated an influential model of communication.[5] It is known as a transmission model of communication and is closely related to communication theorist Harold Lasswell's famous question about media effects, which he posed in 1948. Lasswell asked, "Who says what in which channel to whom with what effect?" This model has allowed for many general applications in mass communication.

The Shannon and Weaver mathematical theory of communication, as they described it, is based on a linear system of electronic communication. The original formulation of the model included five main elements:

- Information source
- Transmitter
- Channel
- Receiver
- Destination

In this model, an information source formulates a message. A transmitter encodes the message into signals. The signals are delivered via a channel. A receiver decodes the signals, "reconstructing" the original message, which reaches its destination. The communication flow in this model is decidedly one-directional, from the sender to the receiver. The system has a limited capacity to provide feedback from the receiver to the information source: to acknowledge receipt of the message, to indicate whether the message has been understood, and to communicate the receiver's reaction. The communication process can be adversely affected by noise, or interference, from the environment, possibly by way of competing, or distracting, messages, or even electrical interference. The original Shannon and Weaver mathematical theory of communication, or model, is depicted in the diagram in Figure 1-1.

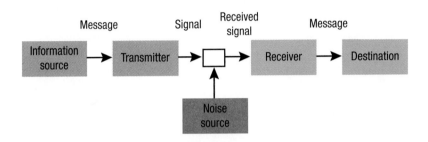

FIGURE 1-1 Shannon and Weaver. Mathematical Theory From *The Mathematical Theory of Mass Communication*. C. Shannon and W. Weaver. Copyright 1949, 1998 by Board of Trustees of the University of Illinois Press. Used with permission of the University of Illinois Press.

The model clearly explains how a telephone works. The information source speaks (encoding a message), the phone (transmitter) transforms the sound waves into electrical impulses (the signal), which are sent over the channel (the tiny box in the center), and those electrical impulses are turned back into sound waves by the phone (receiver) at the other end of the line, where they are heard and (one hopes) understood (decoded) by another person (destination). "Noise" is any interference anywhere along the way.

The Shannon and Weaver model is especially technological in its orientation and therefore limited in its utility for understanding traditional mass communication because it does not fully reflect the role of humans in the process—specifically, how meaning is created. Moreover, the advent of digital, networked communication media is greatly expanding the interactive nature of communication, making the limited feedback capacity of the model more problematic even by its own standards.

Adapting the Shannon and Weaver model and integrating concepts from Aristotle, pioneering communication scholar Wilbur Schramm in 1954 developed a **simplified communications model** in the book *The Process and Effects of Mass Communication*.[6]

In the Schramm model, communication requires three main elements:

1. a source, who encodes
2. a message, or signal, which is transmitted (via the media or directly via interpersonal communication) to
3. a destination, where the receiver decodes it.

Significantly, Schramm envisioned the importance of understanding as part of human communication. Schramm realized that another important aspect of the traditional communication model needed correcting. In human communication, mediated or not, communication is not a one-way process. Schramm wrote,

simplified communications model
....
Developed by Wilbur Schramm in 1954 and based on the mathematical theory of communication. It includes a source, who encodes a message, or signal, which is transmitted (via the media or directly via interpersonal communication) to a destination, where the receiver decodes it.

"In fact, it is misleading to think of the communication process as starting somewhere and ending somewhere. It is really endless. We are little switchboard centers handling and rerouting the great endless current of information." As a result, Schramm and Charles Osgood developed a circular model of communication. The participants exchange roles of source/encoder and receiver/decoder. This model is depicted in Figure 1-2.

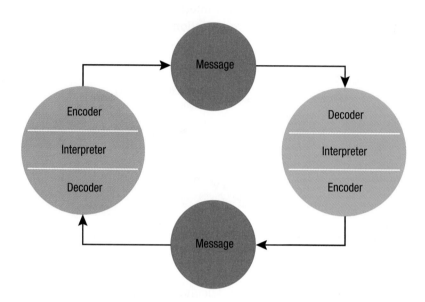

FIGURE 1-2 Schramm-Osgood Model. From *The Process and Effects of Mass Communication.* Wilbur Lang Schramm, ed. Copyright 1954 by Board of Trustees of the University of Illinois Press. Used with permission.

However, even this model, based on certain concepts derived from the transmission model, has its limitations for some scholars. One way to explore the limitations of this and other transmission models is through an example of a simple six-word classified advertisement: "Baby shoes for sale. Never used." Although it is of course possible to put these six words into a transmission-model framework, doing so would destroy the character and evocative nature of those six words. A transmission model–based theory of communication that conceives of people as switchboards of information processing simply does not adequately explain how the ad makes us wonder why the baby shoes were never used and how it sends us on perhaps melancholy flights of imagination regarding what happened to the family that placed the ad. For that we have to look at other theoretical traditions.

■ ■ ■ CRITICAL THEORY AND CULTURAL STUDIES

A typical critique of transmission models of communication (made by others outside the critical-theory tradition as well as within) is that it treats communication as some kind of separate, independent phenomenon outside of the people who are engaging in communication. Its technological orientation may explain an electronic signal well, but it falls far short when trying to explain the deeper meaning behind someone reading a morning paper, or even a classified ad within that paper, as the example above demonstrated. To define humans as a type of "switchboard center" when it comes to communication, as Schramm does, is to leave us unable to explain how media economics may influence what paper we are able to read or if we even have an Internet connection—nor does it help us to better understand the role that power, identity, and a host of other factors can play in how we make and share meaning through communication.

Critical theory is a theoretical approach broadly influenced from Marxist notions of the role of ideology, exploitation, capitalism, and the economy in understanding and eventually transforming society. There are many branches of critical theory, not all of which focus on media and mass communication—and they often disagree with each other on certain fundamental points. We will explore **cultural studies**, which tends to focus more on mass communication than some of the other types of critical theory.

To understand a cultural-studies approach to the subject of communication, it is important to first see its intellectual heritage through the lens of critical theory and to know how it differs from "traditional," or positivist, social science. Critical theorists criticize positivist researchers for inappropriately applying physical science research methods to human behavior. They do not agree that by using various statistical techniques, and with enough research, various "natural laws" of society and behavior can be determined.

Critical theorists not only say that the process of scientific creation of "fact" is a social and variable process like any other (consider how Pluto has gone from being considered a planet to not being one) but they refute that natural laws can be discovered that can explain human behavior. They see the drive to better predict and control society as one more form of oppression. In short, critical theorists would say positivists ask uninspiring questions and get uninteresting—if not misleading—answers that largely describe the societal and cultural status quo as unproblematic.

Cultural-studies researchers join critical theorists in rejecting the positivist scientific approach. They try to examine the symbolic environment created by mass media and to study the role that the mass media play in culture and society by utilizing a host of disciplines ranging from anthropology and sociology to political science and literary theory. For cultural-studies researchers, a television commercial can be a rich source of cultural codes and representations that tell us in subtle and not-so-subtle ways how we should be acting and thinking as members of society.

Communications scholar **James Carey** was a leading cultural-studies theorist and developed what he calls a ritual view of communication. He claims that "communication is a symbolic process whereby reality is produced, maintained, repaired, and transformed."[7] From this view, the act of reading a newspaper has less to do with receiving information than with participating in a shared cultural experience that portrays and confirms the world in a certain way. By reading the paper, we are actually participating in a ritual that produces and reproduces certain sociocultural norms that are played out through our actions and interactions with others.[8] The same dynamic can be said to take place with online media, such as posting photos on MySpace or IMing a friend—you are not simply transmitting information but are sharing ways of doing things and ways of thinking that actually create the society we live in through our repeated actions.

LOOKING BACK AND MOVING FORWARD

This book takes the premise that mass communication as we have known it is fundamentally changing, perhaps to the point where it no longer is a relevant or

James Carey was one of the most influential media and communication scholars of the twentieth century.

even accurate descriptive term for our communication and media landscape. That day, however, is still not here. Convergence is, broadly speaking, the process with which we are seeing these changes taking place on technological, economic, and sociocultural levels. Many of the ramifications of the changes taking place today through convergence will likely not be realized or fully known for years to come, while others seem to have immediate and dramatic effects.

What we have today is a fascinating and confusing mixture of mass-communication industries and business models combining with various emerging digital technologies and communications practices that simultaneously threaten and hold great promise for traditional media companies and the communications professions. Issues of consumer privacy, of copyright, of affordable access to the Internet, and other legal, regulatory, and ethical issues have still to be worked out.

Moreover, the leaders of the industries in the media business have a unique opportunity to transform their media enterprises into institutions that better serve society. Rather than follow the familiar path of the commercially dominated media industry, journalists and other communication professionals can take this opportunity to reinvent media enterprise and help lead troubled industries into a renaissance. But in order to do that it takes money, and media companies for the most part have still not figured out new business models that work with digital media, at least none that would still leave them with the same kind of control they have enjoyed over selling and distributing media content. To date, few media organizations seem willing to relinquish that control.

The public, or audience, may finally have some say in the matter in the new digital media environment. Through communication tools that give the public unprecedented power to share information with each other and to "talk back" to those in power, people are able to connect and organize on any number of issues that are important to them, effecting policy changes through online and offline means. We have already seen the power that online organizing has had for various politicians in terms of getting donations and getting young people more engaged in political campaigns. Will the Internet and other digital media flourish and lead to a rich blend of eclectic voices, or will the emerging global media system be a homogenous blend of commercial banality where news and entertainment are little more than commodities that sit with equally insipid user-generated content? It is still an open question, but dealing with issues like these responsibly is the moral mandate of mass communication in the digital age. This book hopes to give you the tools to do so.

DISCUSSION QUESTIONS

1. Keep a media diary for a day of the media you consume (and create). Include what sources you get your news from, what types of online communication you use with friends and family, and how often you are on the phone. What did you learn from the diary?

2. If you were asked to create a time capsule that would be opened in the year 3000, what would you put in it to help a future society understand the nature of the media of mass communication of the twenty-first century?

3. What are the key functions of mass communication identified by Harold Lasswell, Charles Wright, and others?

4. Based on your own communication experiences, develop your own model of communication. Is it an empirical model or a cultural model?

5. Convergence has many implications for the mass-communication process. What are some of the ways the convergence of media in the digital age affects the relationship between the media and their audiences?

6. What are the key differences between the traditional, analog world of mass communication and mass communication in the digital age?

7. In which direction do you think digital media are more likely to go—toward a more open, diversified, and democratic medium or toward a more corporate, commercialized, and centrally controlled medium? Why?

8. List some changes you have seen in the past few years on the Internet in terms of your own use of digital media, and explain why you think these changes came about and whether you feel they are for better or for worse.

. . . .

FURTHER READING

Convergence Culture: Where Old and New Media Collide; Henry Jenkins (2008) NYU Press.

The Coming Convergence: Surprising Ways Diverse Technologies Interact to Shape Our World and Change the Future; Stanley Schmidt (2008) Prometheus Books.

Understanding Media Convergence: The State of the Field; August Grant, Jeffrey Wilkinson (eds.) (2008) Oxford University Press.

Media Organizations and Convergence: Case Studies of Media Convergence Pioneers (Lea's Communication Series); Gracie Lawson-Borders (2005) Lawrence Erlbaum Associates.

The History of the Telephone; Herbert Casson (2006) Cosimo Classics.

America Calling: A Social History of the Telephone to 1940; Claude Fischer (1994) University of California Press.

The History of Wireless: How Creative Minds Produced Technology for the Masses; Ira Brodsky (2008) Telescope Books.

Speaking into the Air: A History of the Idea of Communication; John Durham Peters (1999) University of Chicago Press.

Understanding Media Theory; Kevin Williams (2003) Oxford University Press.

Understanding Media Cultures: Social Theory and Mass Communication, 2nd ed.; Nick Stevenson (2002) Sage Publications.

Theories of Communication: A Short Introduction; Armand Mattelart, Michele Mattelart (1998) Sage Publications.

Communication Theories: Origins, Methods, and Uses in the Mass Media, 5th ed.; Werner J. Severin, James W. Tankard Jr. (2001) Addison Wesley Longman.

Being Digital; Nicholas Negroponte (1995) Alfred A. Knopf.

What Will Be: How the New World of Information Will Change Our Lives; Michael Dertouzos (1997) HarperEdge.

Media Literacy and Ethics

CHAPTER OBJECTIVES

In this chapter we will:

■ Define media literacy and provide some basic skills to improve critical-thinking ability when consuming mass-communication content.

■ Explain three elements of media literacy: media grammar, fragmentation of media channels, and commercial forces that shape media content.

■ Provide tips on how to recognize reliable online information and evaluate online sources.

■ Define some basic elements in media ethics.

■ Describe the consequences and societal repercussions when ethical principles are not followed in media.

2 The BBC story on December 3, 2004, commemorating the twentieth anniversary of the Bhopal industrial disaster, in which a pesticide plant run by Union Carbide leaked toxic gas, killing at least three thousand people immediately and sickening tens of thousands of others, had some good news for a change. Jude Finisterra, a spokesman for Dow Chemical, which owns Union Carbide, announced in the interview that Dow would finally take full responsibility for the disaster, compensating the victims and their families, and clean up the toxic plant site, as well as push for the extradition of Union Carbide's CEO, Warren Anderson, who fled India after the disaster.

For two hours that day the story was at the top of the rankings on news.google.com. There was only one catch: "Jude Finisterra" did not work for Dow Chemical. Rather, he is a member of a culture-jamming group called "The Yes Men" that practices what they call "attitude adjustment" by conducting media and event hoaxes that attempt to shame corporations and the elite by exposing their hypocrisy and greed.

By the time Dow refuted the story, two hours after it was first broadcast, CNN reported that the company's stock value had dropped $2 billion.[1] Dow sent out a story retraction, which was echoed and amplified by a spoof retraction from The Yes Men that emphatically stated that Dow would not be compensating any victims or cleaning up the site. It remained the top news item the remainder of the day on news.google.com.

This is an excellent example of why media literacy is important. The BBC contacted the fictitious spokesperson through a fake website The Yes Men had created, www.DowEthics.com, not realizing who had actually created the website. Two years earlier, Dow had successfully shut down another Yes Men site, Dow-Chemical.com, through various threats of legal action to the Internet Service Providers (ISPs) hosting the website.

If an esteemed news organization such as the BBC can fall victim to a media hoax like this, what hope is there for the individual to know or trust information found online? This is where media-literacy skills become increasingly important in today's digital-media world.

This incident also highlights the importance of ethical considerations when dealing with media and the public. What responsibility does a group like The Yes Men have in undermining the public's trust in major news organizations like the BBC? What responsibility does the BBC have to check its sources and to make sure it is not duped again? And what ethical obligations does a corporation like Dow Chemical have to be a good global corporate citizen and take responsibility for its past actions?

e live in a media society. Mass media surround us and influence our world in a variety of ways. They entertain us, they inform us, and they sell us everything from household products to political candidates. Although we often tend to study media and mass communications as something separate from our culture, society, and lives, the fact is media are just as real as the "real world."

With the pervasiveness of media in modern life, it is more important than ever to understand how media messages may influence us. We must look critically at all media we receive and understand something about how media organizations work as businesses, how they fit into other aspects of society, and how they influence culture and can manipulate public opinion.

This chapter explains some basic principles behind media literacy while teaching you to critically analyze the media messages you encounter. Finally, we'll explore some important issues in media ethics, laying the foundation for applying critical-thinking skills in moral and ethical reasoning. Communications professionals face a range of ethical challenges that have far-reaching consequences not faced by most other professions, which means media literacy and critical thinking are especially important skills for them.

Education and Media

In school we learn to read, write, and do arithmetic. We learn about history, other cultures, literature, science, and politics. We learn athletic skills and teamwork; we can even learn art, mechanics, computer programming, and how to cook.

But we also learn much from our daily and extensive interactions with media content—some may argue we even learn more of practical value from media than from the typical school day spent in classes. If we think back to the four functions of mass communication mentioned in the previous chapter—surveillance, correlation, cultural transmission, and entertainment—the common component that runs through all of these functions is that they essentially educate and inform us.

This raises the question that if media are so pervasive in our lives, why aren't we studying them in the same way that we study geography, or chemistry, or national politics? Why can we take a class in high school on how to dismantle a car engine, but we do not have a class that teaches us how to deconstruct our modern systems of media and mass communications?

How Media Literate Are You?

Because of widespread media exposure, most young people have a relatively high level of media literacy in some areas. Although you may have seen every movie your favorite actor has been in and can swap MP3 music files with friends over the Internet, it doesn't necessarily mean you have an adequate level of media literacy in today's world.

Get a general idea of how media literate you are by taking the following quiz. Be sure to try this quiz again at the end of the semester and see if your media literacy has improved.

1. Can you name the number one song in the pop chart right now by title and artist?
2. Name other hit songs the group or artist may have had.
3. Name the recording company this artist or group is signed to and who owns the label, if the recording company is a subsidiary of a larger recording label.
4. Name the titles of at least three books by best-selling author Stephen King.
5. Name at least three movies made from Stephen King's books.
6. Describe the last time you saw product placement in a movie.
7. How does a cookie work on a website and why is it important?
8. What information can Web-analytics software determine about visitors to websites?
9. What is a news release, how is it created, and what is the process by which it gets into the news?
10. True or False: Apple can enter your iPhone remotely and "kill" any application you have installed on it without your knowledge.

If you are like most students, some of the questions were much easier for you to answer than others. If you were able to answer up to four questions (such as 1, 2, 4, and 5) correctly, then you have what would be considered a typical, and somewhat limited, level of media literacy. If you got five to seven questions correct, then your media-literacy skills are pretty good but still could be improved. If you got seven to ten correct, then you have a pretty high level of media-literacy skills now—keep up the good work!

The question highlights two interesting issues. First, it shows that "education," like media, is not something that we can easily set aside as a thing separate from our lives. We are learning all the time, even when not in a formal academic setting such as a classroom or doing homework. In some ways, a formal academic environment simply forces us to be aware that we are learning.

Second, if we are learning all the time through our interactions with each other and with media content, then how can we ensure that what we are learning is accurate and useful if we do not have the skills to consider where that learning is coming from and how it may be affecting our thought processes?

Educators have recognized a growing need to teach **media-literacy** skills to school-age children, starting as young as kindergarten or elementary school and

media literacy
....
The process of interacting with media content and critically analyzing it by considering its particular presentation, its underlying political or social messages, and ownership and regulation issues that may affect what is presented and in what form.

Learning media-literacy skills has become even more important for students today.

continuing to high school graduation. Some countries, such as Canada and Australia, have taken the lead in media-literacy education, while the United States generally lags behind in teaching media literacy. However, it is changing, and a growing number of states, such as New Jersey, have implemented statewide media-literacy guidelines for K–12 schools.

What Is Media Literacy?

Being able to read a book, understanding how to navigate a website or send an email attachment, and realizing a scary part of a movie is coming up when the background music changes are all types of literacy that involve media. Some fall under what we would consider the traditional meaning of the term "literacy," and others can be classified as visual literacy or computer literacy. Knowing all the movies a director has ever made, how much money they cost to make, and how much they grossed is also a type of literacy involving media, albeit a limited one. Media literacy encompasses all these skills and much more.

Media literacy can be defined as the process of interacting with media content and critically analyzing it by considering its particular presentation, its underlying political or social messages, and ownership and regulation issues that may affect what stories are presented and in what form. In the age of digital media, additional issues when interacting with media must also be considered, such as erosion of media-consumer privacy and tracking of consumer behavior.

In other words, media consumers should always question what they see, hear, or otherwise experience when receiving or interacting with mediated communication. Is a news story biased? How might the story be slanted through word choices or the people interviewed in ways that do not accurately reflect the situation? Why is it even news? Does a popular television show or video game encourage gender or racial stereotypes? What is an advertiser really trying to sell and to whom? Does the placement of articles and photos in a newspaper fairly represent the relative importance of those items as news? These are just a sample of the kinds of questions critical media consumers should ask.

Developing media literacy is an ongoing process, not a goal. There is no qualification test in media literacy to differentiate the media literate from the media illiterate. You will never receive a certificate in "media literacy." If you do, you should apply your newfound critical-thinking skills and ask whether it is worth the paper it is printed on.

Even though you cannot ever attain "perfect media literacy," it is possible to always improve your level of media literacy and thus be a wiser media user. The importance of media in contemporary society makes it imperative that audience members exercise critical thinking in their consumption of media content so they can better control their actions and not be controlled by media messages.

Media-literacy scholar W. James Potter talks about building "knowledge structures" to improve one's level of media literacy.[2] A knowledge structure is simply a way to visualize building one's level of knowledge on a given topic or topics. For example, if you have a basic understanding of the history of television and someone tells you they remember watching *I Love Lucy* in the 1920s, you can be confident that they are incorrect because television as a mass medium did not yet exist in the 1920s.

It might seem like an impossible task to learn about all the issues surrounding media, especially in the rapidly changing world of digital media that relies so heavily on complex technology. However, four basic categories represent the foundation for critical media consumption. These are

1. Understanding variations in how media are used
2. Knowing media grammar
3. Seeing the effect of fragmentation of media channels
4. Recognizing how commercial forces shape media content

From these foundations, it is possible for us to better navigate the complex interplay of traditional media and digital media that we encounter today. However, understanding media literacy is not enough; we have to use this knowledge and apply it to the myriad ethical issues that arise in mass communication. With media literacy we can understand the "why" of things in our media environment, but with ethics we can make informed decisions on what is right and wrong.

Variations in Media Use

It is important to understand that there is nothing "natural" about how we use media today and how our current media system operates or has evolved. We tend to think of the evolution of media technologies as going from a more primitive state to our current one, which of course we see as the most advanced and best—until a new development comes along.

However, this is a mistaken way to think of media and mass communication. Of course there are improvements in media technologies and changes in media-usage habits that can do things like provide easier and cheaper access to more people, or that provide information or entertainment in new and exciting ways, but it should not be thought of as some kind of inevitable evolution.

There are many factors that can affect the type of technologies we have available to us and the type of media we encounter. It will become obvious even with the brief examples below that there were many other possible outcomes besides what we currently take for granted. This knowledge can be especially liberating, as along with ethics it can help us think more deeply about what is right and wrong about today's media systems and make us aware of forces that could change things for better or worse in the future.

■ ■ ■ REGULATORY FACTORS

Regulations and laws created by politicians or government agencies such as the Federal Communications Commission (FCC) can have profound effects on what type of media are available and what type of content we see. Regulations can directly affect the level of competition in an industry by making it difficult or impossible for companies, or certain types of companies, to enter a market.

An example of regulatory control over media is the restrictions on monopoly ownership of a newspaper, television station, and radio station in a single market. Although these restrictions have gradually been easing, it still generally is not allowed for a single owner to have all three within a specific locale. This regulation was created to ensure that the public could get a diversity of voices through the media.

The debates around **Net neutrality**, which will be discussed in more detail later in the book, are another example of the powerful role that regulations play. Telecommunications companies want to start charging content providers for certain types of content being sent over their networks or charging more for heavy users of bandwidth.

Critics argue that this will lead to telecommunications firms favoring media content that comes from a parent media company, for example, and slowing down content that comes from competing media companies. Despite denials by telecommunications firms that this would happen, there have already been examples of firms favoring some content over others in the past few years. Consider how different your Web browsing experience may be if your Internet Service Provider (ISP) allows content from Universal Music Group to reach you easily while slowing down how fast you can download music or content from Warner, or charges you more to be able to download Warner's content at the same rate as Universal's.

Calls for new regulations or deregulation must be watched very closely, as such calls are often prompted by industry lobbyist groups who want to give their clients a business advantage at the expense of competitors—and often the general public. The issues are often complex and couched in bureaucratic or scientific language, but the effects can be far-reaching.

One example is the case of low-power FM (LPFM), which allows for communities or groups to create nonprofit, hyperlocal FM stations. Despite the potential for such stations to create a range of voices in the media and to offer more choices to the public for radio listening, LPFM advocates faced a long struggle against the broadcast industry—including National Public Radio—which saw a threat to its interests if LPFM was allowed. Regulations or lobbying efforts are not always responsible for hampering new technologies, of course. Sometimes the reasons are more engrained in society or culture.

■ ■ ■ SOCIOCULTURAL FACTORS

Sometimes perfectly good or sensible technologies do not get adopted simply because people do not seem to be ready for them or because using them breaks certain sociocultural practices or codes of acceptable behavior. Consider the devel-

net neutrality
....
A principle that states that broadband networks should be free of restrictions on content, platforms, or equipment and that certain types of content, platforms, or equipment should not get preferential treatment on the network.

opment of video conferences in business settings. Video conferences over broadband Internet offer much in terms of cost and time savings for businesses yet still have not replaced business trips. Despite making it possible to see and hear the people at the other end, a video conference cannot replace the kind of interaction found in face-to-face interpersonal communication.

Regulatory bodies like the FCC often have a great deal of influence over the development of media technologies.

Similarly, sociocultural norms may change over time to accommodate new media technologies and new media uses. Consider the example of the telephone in the previous chapter and how it went from initially being considered a novelty, in Victorian times, to what it is today. Even now we struggle with establishing social norms of polite behavior with mobile phones when talking in public places. Consider our reactions when we hear someone in a restaurant, bus, train, or other public space speaking loudly on the phone. We generally don't show the same annoyance when two people are talking with each other equally loudly, but we do not like it when we hear only one side of the conversation.

There are often unintended consequences of new media and examples of how the media are used that were likely not imagined by their creators. The inventors of video on cell phones no doubt did not think that it would lead to "happy slapping," or groups of youth in England and elsewhere videotaping and posting with their phones their friends attacking total strangers just for the fun of it.

People watching porn on DVD players built into their vehicles has also become a problem, especially in areas where traffic can be at a standstill. Parents have found themselves answering awkward questions from young children about the shows being watched in adjacent vehicles but visible from their own car. This case and the example of happy slapping also show how sociocultural practices may lead to changes in laws regarding media usage or to the application of existing laws (such as not showing porn in public places) in new ways.

In short, it is important to remember not only that technology may affect sociocultural practices and norms but that those norms may have an effect on how that technology is used and perceived, which in turn could have an effect on things like new laws being made.

TECHNOLOGICAL FACTORS

We often want the latest and the best technology, and some people make sure they have the latest, lightest, or fastest high-tech gizmo to show off. Even though we may think we have the best technology, the history of media and technology is littered with the ghosts of better technologies that were never successful.

The classic example of this was the battle in the 1970s between two competing video formats, Betamax, by Sony, and VHS, by JVC. Betamax tapes were smaller and had better picture quality than VHS yet ultimately failed in the marketplace as VHS became the standard, primarily because VHS had a better distribution and marketing network and thus reached a wider audience first. Once people owned a VHS video player, they were unlikely to also purchase a Betamax player and replace their videotapes.

Another example is the competition between Apple computers and PCs. Although Apple computers were in many ways far superior to PCs in terms of usability and capability, they only captured a small part of the market share. Similarly, Microsoft crowded out Netscape in a few short years during the 1990s with its Internet Explorer web browser that came bundled with the Windows operating

Text Messaging and the Thumb Tribe

Text messaging is a prime example of how regulatory, sociocultural, technological, and economic factors all come together to affect whether something gets adopted and how it is used.

In many parts of the world, text messaging has become a predominant way to use a cell phone, and there have been instances of large crowds mobilizing for protests in a very short time through text messages. This happened in Manila in 2001 when Filipinos wanted to oust President Joseph Estrada, who was accused of corruption.

Text messaging is also popular in Japan, where crowded public spaces make speaking on the phone especially bothersome to others and do not allow a private conversation to take place. Young Japanese have become so proficient at texting that they have been dubbed "the thumb tribe" by some social commentators.

Yet text messaging has not caught on in the United States to nearly the same extent that it has in other countries, though that is gradually changing. Why the difference?

The cell phone network in the United States, partly for technological reasons and partly for regulatory reasons, makes phone calls relatively cheap compared to some other countries. The cost of making a phone call, compared to the cost of a text message, is not an issue for most Americans.

Americans generally have more private space than some other countries, as well, making it easier to talk on the phone without worrying about sharing private information with strangers.

Finally, until phones with keyboards came out, texting was cumbersome on most cell phones compared to simply calling, so until the technology caught up Americans tended to disfavor texting.

system. Internet Explorer was not a vastly superior browser to Netscape (both had strengths and weaknesses), yet within six years Internet Explorer captured over 90 percent of the web browser market.

How did Microsoft do it? Although marketing played a role, by and large it was simply a combination of inertia and lack of computer literacy on the part of most computer users. Nothing prevented people from downloading the Netscape browser (after connecting to the Internet through the already-loaded Internet Explorer), but many people learning to use computers simply thought that using Internet Explorer was the only way to see the Web or didn't want to bother trying a new web browser once they became familiar with Internet Explorer.

Why doesn't the best technology always win? Why can't consumers recognize the better product and simply buy or use that one? It can be especially difficult with new media technologies that do not have a track record or long history of use. Most people do not want to spend a lot of time learning how to use new devices, or changing their media consumption, and will stay with what is familiar. Companies that come to market with new technologies that threaten old ones always have to deal to some extent with complacency from the general public. They also have to deal with large-scale economic and business factors ranging from distribution to changes in media formats (such as a new DVD) that could have repercussions far beyond a particular new technology.

■■■ ECONOMIC FACTORS

Economic factors very closely affect how we use media and even what type of media we get. Many towns throughout the United States now only have one newspaper where there used to be two or more competing dailies. This is not because of a cultural tradition of only reading one newspaper or because of government regulations. Economic pressures forced the others to close or to merge with the remaining paper. The high cost of publishing a newspaper or starting a television station prevented most people from even considering such ventures.

Economics can be at the heart of industry lobbying efforts to change regulations so they are more favorable to the industry. It can be an important factor, through licensing or marketing deals, in making an inferior technology more popular than a better one, such as the case with Apple. Unlike Windows and PC makers, Apple did not license its operating system to other companies to make Apple or Mac clones, thus limiting the availability of Macs while keeping the cost relatively high in comparison to PCs. This helped push the PC to the huge majority it has today.

Economic reasons also play a key role in the types of programming we see today and the types of information we receive. It is relatively cheap to produce reality shows, which may account in part for their proliferation in recent years. It is also cheaper to produce news on light, entertainment-oriented topics rather than conduct in-depth investigative pieces on complex social issues. Economics is also driving media consolidation, which further affects the types of content available when media owners or corporations make programming decisions based on their own business interests rather than the public interest.

Media Grammar

Being a critical consumer of media messages begins with understanding the grammar of the media—in other words, how a medium presents itself and is used and understood by the audience. Each medium of mass communication presents its messages uniquely. With mediums that we are familiar with through widespread use or exposure, we often do not think about the role media grammar plays in what we see, how we see it, and what our perceptions are. In many ways, it becomes "background," but it nevertheless can have profound implications for our understanding of media content. We become more aware of media grammar when we encounter a new media type that we do not know the "rules" for yet. Here we will look briefly at the main forms of media and explore some basics about each particular form of media grammar and what it means for our perceptions and expectations of that medium.

■■■ SUBTEXT MESSAGES

Common to the grammar of all media is **subtext**. Subtext is the message beneath the message—the underlying, or implicit, message that is being conveyed by media content. A situation comedy such as Warner Brothers' popular television show

subtext
....
The message beneath the
message—the underlying, or
implicit, message that is being
conveyed by media content.

Friends (aired on NBC) may be explicitly about the humorous lives of a group of friends living in Manhattan, but the subtext may be that friends should be of the same race. In *Friends*, all six friends are white. Viewers, especially children and adolescents, may watch the show to be amused, but they may be subtly learning that they, too, should choose best friends of the same race.

Being aware of subtext messages does not mean becoming a conspiracy theorist and assuming every television producer or book author has a hidden agenda. The creators of content may not be aware that they are propagating subtext messages; they feel they are simply telling an interesting or amusing story or writing about what they are familiar with. But that doesn't mean that the audience should not be on guard for possible implicit messages that reinforce stereotypes or influence one's opinions in the real world.

It is interesting to see how our media literacy has in some important ways become more sophisticated over time. *Gilligan's Island*, a 1960s sitcom about seven shipwrecked characters on a deserted Pacific island, is still often seen in reruns. After the first few episodes aired in 1964, Sherwood Schwartz, the show's producer, said in a 1984 interview he was contacted by the Coast Guard, who told him they had received several dozen serious complaints from people saying that the military should send a ship to find and rescue the people. Schwartz asked, "Who did these viewers think was filming

Many viewers do not realize how highly produced and edited so-called reality shows are.

the castaways on that island? There was even a laugh track on the show. Who was laughing at the survivors of the wreck of the *S.S. Minnow*? It boggled the mind."[3]

Although today we may laugh at the naivete of some members of the public in the 1960s, consider areas in which we may be equally naive if someone looks at our assumptions today in forty years. Consider the willingness of many students to simply cite material they take from Wikipedia, an online collaborative encyclopedia that can be written and edited by anyone. Or consider how fake photos can circulate through the Web, often forwarded with the assumption that the photo is real. Subtext too plays a role in these activities, as faked photos may have more deliberate intended messages and play on popular fears, wisdom, and stereotypes just as easily as mainstream media.

▪▪▪ PRINT MEDIA

Print media, partly due to their long history compared to other types of mass communication, have developed a very sophisticated media grammar. Everything from the physical dimensions of a book to whether it contains pictures or not, the size and style of the typeface, whether it is hardcover or paperback, and the artwork on the book jacket conveys important messages to the potential book buyer beyond the actual content. Within a book itself, there are several aspects of media grammar that have evolved over the years. Spacing between words to aid reading comprehension is an early example, as are page numbering, tables of contents, indexes, and chapter headings. We take many of these conventions for granted, but most took years before they were widely adopted and became standard in books.

Newspapers have their own types of media grammar that have also evolved over time and that continue to change. An obvious example is the amount of color photos and graphics used in newspapers today compared to forty years ago. Since space is limited in a newspaper, more graphics means less room for text. Although many media critics and journalists have complained that this "packaging" of news into relatively short, easy-to-read units accompanied by splashy pictures or graphics does readers a disservice by not providing them with the depth of information they need in today's world, U.S. newspapers have continued to add color and graphics to their pages to make them more visually appealing. Proponents of the trend say that newspapers must compete with television and other visual media for audience attention and so must present news in a way that suits people's busy lifestyles.

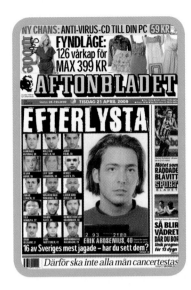

We can often tell what kind of newspaper a foreign paper is, even without knowing the language, simply from the look of the publication.

Most newspapers are organized into sections such as sports, business, and local news. These not only act to help organize information so readers can quickly find stories that interest them, but they create subconscious parameters for readers on what types of stories to expect in those sections. The editorial pages and op-ed pages are where newspaper readers expect to hear opinions on events, either from the newspaper staff or publisher (editorials) or from guest columnists.

In terms of size, newspapers conform largely to the rules of either tabloid (typically more sensational in tone) or broadsheet (more serious). They use headlines to capture attention and "teasers" on the front page or front-section pages to entice readers to see articles inside the paper. They use a variety of graphic techniques to attract and guide the reader's eye. More important stories usually appear "above the fold," or on the upper half of the broadsheet paper, so when it is stacked in a newsstand those stories and graphics are what people first see.

Newspapers typically present hard news using an inverted pyramid organization (most important items first) in the body of the text report, although this structure is slowly starting to change to resemble that of a feature story. Sources, or people interviewed, are quoted to establish the credibility of what is being reported, enliven the report, and show that it's not just the reporter offering his or her views. Photos and illustrations are accompanied by a brief tagline that explains what the artwork is about. Features, such as human-interest stories or profiles, are written in a different style, sometimes starting with a vignette that helps humanize the story and hook the reader.

Magazines similarly use sophisticated graphic and design techniques, even more so than newspapers, and feature more long-form writing, often with just one or two articles per page and multipage articles. Advertising in magazines often takes up a full page, and in some magazines it is hard to immediately tell if something is an ad or graphics at the beginning of a feature. In some ways magazines combine elements of books and newspapers in their media grammar. Because of their length, they usually have a table of contents (many also have an advertiser index), which helps readers find specific articles quickly. Like newspapers, they are often divided into subject-related sections within their topic areas, which usually contain short, newsy items.

With hundreds of years to develop the grammar for print media, it is perhaps surprising to see how quickly we have adapted to the rise of electronic media, especially audio and, later, video.

actualities
. . . .
Edited audio clips from people
interviewed.

voice-over
. . . .
An unseen announcer or narrator
talking while other activity
takes place, either on radio
or during a television scene.

■■■RADIO AND RECORDED MUSIC

Radio and recorded music similarly have their own grammar, one based only on sound. Radio uses a combination of audio techniques to achieve different ends. Among these techniques are volume changes, multiple audio tracks, **actualities** (i.e., edited audio clips from people interviewed), sound effects, and **voice-overs**, all of which can be used to convey information, capture attention, evoke a mood or scene, or achieve some other purpose.

Recorded music typically conforms to particular stylistic conventions, especially with regards to length (less than five minutes a song) and music format. Popular music genres, such as hip-hop, rock, country, or swing, have certain rhythms, lyrical styles, and sounds that make them clearly distinguishable. This underlying media grammar of specific categories or genres makes it easier to market and promote artists.

However, putting music into genres like this has its drawbacks. Radio stations brand themselves by the genres of music they generally play, making it easier for audiences to pick stations that play music they like. Someone with a sound or style that does not easily fit into well-established genres may therefore find it harder to get listened to, as radio stations are hesitant to play something that does not fit nicely into their established formats. An artist may also find it harder to get a recording contract in the first place, as a recording label will not want to sign someone it believes will have difficulty getting promoted on the radio.

Even a format as apparently chaotic as talk radio has a well-defined media grammar. Despite the interactive nature of call-ins from the audience—talk radio is one of the few traditional mass-communication formats to include such a high degree of interactivity—the callers are obviously in a subordinate position in terms of how long they are allowed to speak, what they may say, and the fact that they can be cut off at any time by the host or producers. Many talk radio shows include call-ins from comic imitators of famous people and include a "sidekick" in the studio who supports or provides counterpoints to the main host.

Although radio developed years before television became a mass medium, and some of the earliest television shows were taken directly from popular radio programs, media producers and audiences had already developed a fairly sophisticated visual grammar thanks in large part to the popularity of movies.

■■■FILM AND TELEVISION

Although film and television have much shorter histories as media than print, they have already developed a sophisticated media grammar that is based on editing, camera angles, lighting, movement, and sound.

For example, in the early history of film, most movies were only a few minutes long and either simply recorded daily activities or were essentially uncut filmed short stage plays. Although the short length of movies was more a function of the limited technology at the time, audiences soon tired of the novelty of watching silent filmed plays and wanted something more interesting.

Filmmakers started producing more sophisticated storylines for their short films and introduced a technique that was unique to film at the time—crosscut scenes. By crosscutting different scenes to simulate simultaneous events happening in two different locations (think of the classic scenes of a train heading down the tracks and a woman tied to the tracks by the villain), filmmakers were able to tell much more complex and dramatic stories. Further, increasing the speed between crosscut scenes helped increase dramatic tension in the audience.

Today's filmmakers have many more such tools at their disposal and are able to give audiences a lot of information, all with visual or audio techniques. Think of the combination of low music and strong shadows in many horror movies, or how we understand an on-screen dream sequence or flashback, or how we differentiate "good" from "bad" characters even before they have spoken or revealed their characters through the narrative plot.

The media grammar of television fiction uses many of the same techniques seen in movies, although of course television production budgets are much smaller than movie budgets. Consider the media grammar of your average sitcom—it is usually shot on a set, with perhaps less than half a dozen "locations" generally used, and the actors come and go as if on a stage. The camera is usually stationary, although multiple camera angles are used, and punch lines are reinforced by a **laugh track**, which in some sitcoms can almost be timed with clockwork precision (even if the line isn't particularly funny).

Other types of television shows have their own types of media grammar, such as game shows, soap operas, talk shows, and news. Although we tend to think of the news as objective—or at least the media grammar used in news shows tries to encourage that kind of thinking by the audience—it is important to understand how camera angles, lighting, distance from the subject and interviewer, sound, and intercut scenes all affect our perceptions of the news.

The "objective point of view" used in television news-reporting interviews treats the viewer as an observer. Typically, the camera is kept still, with shots over the shoulder of the journalist interviewing a subject. Prior to the interview, the subject is instructed by the journalist to never look directly into the camera. Rather, only the news anchor or field reporter in his or her stand-up, often used as a means to summarize or conclude the report, is allowed to look directly into the camera and thereby establish eye contact with the audience. This grammar establishes the authoritativeness and objectivity of the journalist and helps the viewer recognize the difference between the subject and the reporter.

It has been interesting to see how television news, especially, has borrowed some elements of media grammar from the online world—which originally had borrowed heavily from television when graphical user interfaces such as windows and digital video started appearing online. Multiple windows on the television screen showing different kinds of information, scrolling news across the bottom of the screen giving updates, and icons such as blinking cursors are just some examples of how television news is borrowing from the interactive online world and thus adding new types of media grammar.

laugh track
A device used in television sitcoms that generates prerecorded laughter, timed to coincide with punch lines of jokes.

Fake news shows use the conventions of journalism and the media grammar of news shows to make ironic or humorous points.

■ ■ ■ ONLINE MEDIA

We may be thoroughly familiar with and comfortable using the Internet and online media, but there are still many people throughout the world who have limited or no contact with the online world. In addition, online media are still new enough that the grammar is still developing. The Web of 2000 bears little resemblance to the Web today and will look even more different in ten years.

Imagine a media world in which we have to teach someone how to turn pages in a book, or where people try to use a remote control on a magazine or are afraid to use their remote control lest they break the television, or where they see a different kind of image on their TV compared to their neighbors because they have a different model. That is roughly the state of online media in the early twenty-first century, and it is unlikely to change anytime in the near future.

However, some media-grammar elements are starting to form. **Hypertext**, for example, is generally either underlined or otherwise set apart typographically or graphically from nonlinked text. More and more web developers are following an unwritten rule to have a website logo in the upper-left corner of the screen linked to return to the website's homepage. Icons are increasingly used to create a visual, interactive "language" that transverses websites in order to allow computer users

hypertext
. . . .
Text online that is linked to another web page, website, or different part of the same web page by HTML coding.

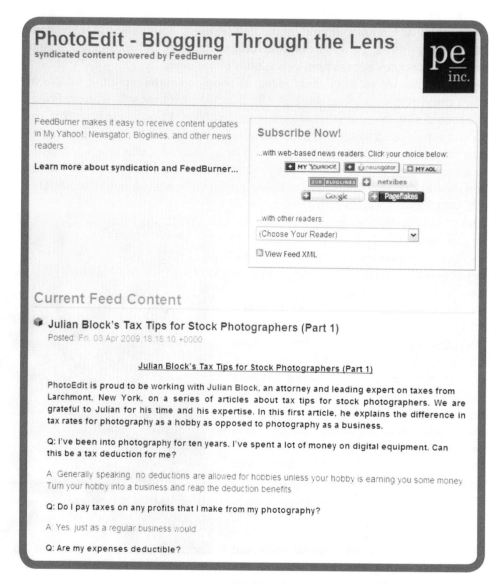

The media grammar of online media is still evolving, sometimes making it hard for users to easily get the information they want.

to quickly learn new types of programs or to utilize interactivity on a website, such as an **RSS feed** or letting someone "**Digg**" a story. Other examples include more or less standardized icons for functions such as printing, opening a document, sending a file, emailing a document, and manipulating images (such as zooming in or out), where applicable.

Mass communication in an online digital environment increasingly exploits a full range of storytelling and communication tools, including text, audio, video, graphics, and animation. This broadened set of tools enables the journalist or other communication professional to tell each story in a manner uniquely suited to that story. Because of the lack of experience of many online-media users and the ever-changing state of technological improvements, it still can be a challenge to guide users to access that information.

RSS feed
....
Short for really simple syndication, it lets users easily subscribe to feeds from a blog or website.

"Digg"
....
A popular website in which users submit material (called "digging") to be voted on by other users, with the most popular material appearing on the homepage.

■ ■ ■ HOW TO RECOGNIZE RELIABLE INFORMATION AND EVALUATE RESOURCES

With the increased availability of media channels, especially online, it has become increasingly difficult for audiences to recognize which channels offer reliable information and how to evaluate the information they encounter. The ability to discern truthful information from false information is essential for us to be autonomous individuals in modern society, which directly relates to deciding right and wrong. Spreading falsehoods, either intentionally or unintentionally through lazy research, can harm others, including people who may find our information at some point in the future and use that.

There are at least three principal ways to evaluate media in the digital age. First is by brand name. Some brands are well established and have proven their reliability over time. Among these are leading news publishers, such as The New York Times Company, which publishes news and information both in print and online, and also on television. News consumers who see this brand, regardless of medium, can count on it to probably be a good source of information. The BBC, despite being tricked by The Yes Men in 2004, is widely respected worldwide as a leading and important source of news.

Second is to examine the new or unfamiliar source's own internal standards, practices, organization, and personnel. Most websites include a section called "About Us," and it usually provides useful information about who operates the site, how it is run, and what procedures are followed in creating content. This information should lay out a compelling case as to why readers should trust the site.

It can also be worth looking at a website called "Who Is?" Who Is? provides a comprehensive and up-to-date database on who leased the domain names for all websites and their contact information. Such information can be useful in establishing the legitimacy of a website and would have saved the BBC reporter for the Bhopal twentieth-anniversary story a lot of subsequent grief. Websites that do not have accurate or complete contact information should not be as trusted in the same way as those that do.

Web Link >>>
Who Is?
www.whois.net

Comparing the new or unfamiliar source of information with other, trusted or independent sources is also useful to determine if a site is trustworthy or not. For example, if one encounters a new website on financial information and is unsure of its veracity, one may find it useful to compare its reports with those of an established or trusted brand, such as the *Wall Street Journal*, which has spent more than a century establishing its reliability. Another option when looking at online news sources is to look at the original source material as well to see if the article accurately portrayed what was important.

Searching online databases such as Factiva or ProQuest Direct, commonly available online through university library services, can show what type of media coverage has been done on a topic and may indicate where your particular source got its news. It also lets you easily compare news stories on a topic. Such databases are tremendously useful sources of information and should be used for research rather than simply citing Wikipedia or taking what is found on the first page of a Google search.

■■■DOS AND DON'TS WHEN EVALUATING ONLINE INFORMATION

The Internet is full of hoaxes, cranks, scams, and cons. The up-to-the-minute, 24/7 nature of news on the Web, and its low-cost distribution, make it an ideal place for misinformation to spread quickly because facts cannot always be quickly verified. How do you know when you are being fed a line when online?

- Do check the About Us section of a website to find out background information on who runs it. Do they clearly state their mission, what they stand for, and who any sponsors are, or do they seem evasive and unclear? If in the latter category, they may not be on the level as to their real purpose.
- Do check what other sites they link to in a Useful Links page and scan what those sites stand for. Most websites link to others who share their views or at least will have more similar-minded links than links to opposing websites.
- Do compare the information in the website with similar stories in other websites, both from branded news names and from smaller sites. If you receive information that a well-known or respected group has made an important announcement, check the organization's website, as they should have that information posted as well.
- Don't trust the name of the organization who owns the website. Lobbying groups and other organizations that are trying to push a specific agenda will often adopt names that mask their true goals or put them in a euphemistic light, or will create front groups to hide their real goals. SourceWatch, a project of the Center for Media and Democracy, is one good website to visit to learn more about the names behind the news.
- Don't immediately trust information that does not have a date somewhere on the page. Information that may have been accurate when it was first posted may well be out of date when you come to the site.
- Don't trust information you read from discussion groups, online chat rooms, blogs, or Usenet, even if the person making the post claims to be an expert or authority on the subject. As the old newsroom saying goes: If your mother says she loves you, check it out.

Web Link >>>
SourceWatch
   www.sourcewatch.org

Web Link >>>
Evaluating Online Information
   http://www.hsl.unc.edu/Services/Tutorials/eval/Index.htm

Fragmentation of Media Channels

Today's media system is increasingly fragmented. The number of media channels has exploded since the mid-1970s, when most people in the United States had access to four national television networks (three commercial, one public), one

Wikipedia in Our Cites: The Trouble with Collaborative Knowledge

Wikipedia has become an amazing cultural phenomenon and source for knowledge in a very short time, surpassing traditional encyclopedias in both scope of topics covered and speed with which information is updated. Furthermore, one study showed that Wikipedia was comparable to the venerable Encyclopaedia Britannica in terms of accuracy.[4]

Wikipedia is a type of **wiki**, or website in which pages can be created and edited by anyone. The scope and depth of knowledge demonstrated by individuals making small contributions to Wikipedia has astounded even skeptics of the idea of just how much the general public actually knows.

Search for a subject on Google, and it is likely that a Wikipedia page on the subject will appear on the first page, if not as one of the first five listings. Complete Wikipedia articles have extensive citations and links to external websites and other Wikipedia entries.

With so much information in one place, and accuracy that is purported to match established and well-respected encyclopedias, the question often arises from dismayed college students why they are not allowed to cite Wikipedia in their papers.

The trouble with Wikipedia is also its strength—the fact that anyone can contribute. Although the overall information of any specific article may be accurate, there could be inaccuracies, either by mistake or put there deliberately by mischievous contributors, that have gone unnoticed. Without knowing where a specific piece of information came from, it is impossible to verify its accuracy.

There have been a number of cases in which misleading information has been added to Wikipedia, either to harm others, simply as a prank, or to put oneself in the best possible light. Even Jimbo Wales, the founder of Wikipedia, has been caught editing his own bio to rewrite history. Similarly, congressional offices are banned from contributing to Wikipedia because aides were frequently caught changing entries on the politicians they worked for.

The best way to use Wikipedia when doing research is as a first stop to get an overview of a subject and to quickly find relevant links to sources that you can trust. Then go to those sources to find more in-depth information and verify the facts presented.

Web Link >>>
Wikipedia
www.en.wikipedia.org

---

or two national news magazines, a local daily newspaper, and a handful of local radio stations. Today, the typical media consumer has hundreds of national channels of television and radio content to choose from, as well as dozens of international channels. Online, media consumers have thousands of media websites from around the United States and the world to explore.

At first glance, having more media channels for the public would seem like a good thing, offering more programming choices and opening our eyes to new worlds of information. But this first impression can be misleading, and it is an important part of media literacy to understand how what seems like more choice may actually give us fewer choices. Similarly, understanding who is left out because of socioeconomic reasons can say a lot about media companies and how well they are fulfilling their ethical obligations in modern society.

wiki
....
Website in which pages can be created and edited by anyone.

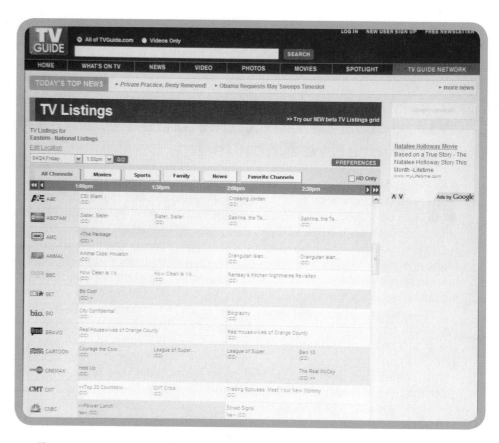

The growing number of channels has made electronic program guides a necessity for most viewers.

electronic program guides
(EPG)
....
Guides available on television
that provide program listings
and some simple interactivity,
such as ordering pay-per-view
programs or buying CDs or DVDs
of listed music or shows.

■ ■ ■ THE MULTICHANNEL UNIVERSE

The explosion in the number of channels has enormous implications for media literacy. In the past, one needed only turn the television dial a few times to see the entire spectrum of television programming. Today, it can take half an hour to navigate through the **electronic program guide** listings of just the current program offerings, not to mention what you may have recorded on your digital video recorder. Making sense of all the media available on the Internet is even more daunting.

The consequences of fragmentation are potentially significant in terms of the impact of media on society. Rarely do national audiences come together for common, simultaneous media experiences. The effects of this fragmentation have been hard to document, but many people have asserted that fragmentation leads to less social cohesion. This fragmentation can be amplified by many of the personalization features on the Web. Internet users can choose what kinds of news and entertainment content they see when they get online, and thus filter differing views and news that they would otherwise be exposed to in traditional media. As mentioned in the previous chapter, a concern is that people will become so focused on some narrow aspect of a particular topic, with other like-minded individuals, that they will ignore larger societal issues that do not directly affect or interest them.

Before television, national magazines were said to help the young American nation define itself and to give people a common platform to look at and discuss issues. A sometimes-heard lament is that when the three networks dominated American television viewing, television played a vital role in establishing or reinforcing a common culture and a common agenda for the nation. Television, for example, provided live coverage of humans' first step on the moon, and this helped foster great national pride.

One also needs to consider other programming commonly seen during the era when three commercial networks dominated. Although there were some great programs, to be sure, such as Edward Murrow's *See It Now* or *Playhouse 90*, among the most widely seen programs were situation comedies such as *The Beverly Hillbillies* and *Gilligan's Island*. Entertaining though these programs may have been, it is hard to argue they provided the glue that held our nation together. Even more, it was during the 1960s, when the networks were at their peak in terms of viewing dominance, that the nation was embroiled in its greatest social upheaval since the Civil War, a century before.

■ ■ ■ DIVERSITY OF VOICES

The flip side of fragmentation is increased diversity of voices. When the three long-standing commercial networks dominated, their programming was almost devoid of cultural diversity. It was an almost entirely white world, frequently suburban in nature. There were occasional programs featuring black, Latino, or other minority-group lead characters, but it was not until the development of Fox, WB, and UPN networks (the latter two merged into The CW Network in 2006) that commercial network television began to show significantly more inclusive programming during primetime—although it is still highly skewed in its portrayal of mainstream white culture over that of many social, cultural, and ethnic groups.

More channels have meant more shows with predominantly minority characters.

Moreover, the growth of cable and direct broadcast satellite (DBS) has ushered in even more cultural diversity and diversity of voices on television. Although it may be hard to get the nation gathered around the television set watching a single program anymore, it is also true that television of the early twenty-first century reveals greater cultural diversity of the nation and the world. Of course, it is still far from a perfect social or cultural mirror.

The proliferation of online media has also led to a huge growth in the diversity or plurality of media voices available to consumers. Although many media consumers may still be most comfortable with a relatively small number of media channels, they now at least have access to a diverse set of voices and perspectives online. Research from the Pew Center indicates that frequent users of the Internet appreciate and value this variety of media voices.

■ ■ ■ MASS AUDIENCES

Despite media fragmentation, certain programs still draw record audiences, especially noted sporting events such as the Super Bowl or World Cup soccer. Another excellent example of a mass audience viewing material on one topic occurred when, after the terrorist attack on the World Trade Center on September 11, 2001, almost all media turned their attention to the attack and its aftermath. For days, weeks, and even months following the attack, it was hard to find any media channel—print, broadcast, cable, or online—that didn't focus in large part on terrorism and the U.S. response to it. In this case, fragmentation of channels likely helped in the depth of coverage, as more media outlets covered various angles of the tragedy and thus gave the public more information than it would have gotten from fewer media outlets.

The notion of "mass audience" also changes with online media, as a specific piece of content such as a YouTube video could have tens of millions of views, but spread over an extended period rather than occurring at one time. This can give some content a kind of extended life cycle that was often absent with traditional media. One reason that this was not the case with traditional media was that it was usually not cost-effective to rebroadcast a specific segment from a show or to reprint a specific article. It was easier to attract new and larger audiences with new material rather than by simply repeating the same material over and over. Television reruns may seem like an exception to this, but audiences for reruns have always been smaller than when the original shows were broadcast (and thus reruns bring in fewer advertising dollars). Even in a multichannel universe in which there is a diversity of voices there is still the need to attract advertising dollars through reaching the largest possible audience, although audience numbers may be smaller for a particular program than they were in the past.

Commercial Forces That Shape Media Content

Even in an open and democratic society with a free press such as in the United States, economic factors and corporate decisions often influence what is and is not covered in the news and what kind of entertainment is created and shown to the general public. Rarely do average media consumers think of how commercial forces are shaping the content they see every day, but these forces affect everything from what types of shows are produced to whether a news report critical of an important advertiser is downplayed or even pulled by a media corporation.

These activities happen at the local, national, and international level. At the local level, a cutback in the number of reporters to help save money can result in a noticeable drop in local coverage, such as coverage of area schools. The newspaper company may save money, but the public is poorer for the lessened coverage of local issues. A company that advertises heavily in a local newspaper may gain undue influence in the decision whether to publish articles critical of it by threatening to withdraw its advertising. A publisher with business interests in other industries, such as local tourism, may influence the types of coverage in the newspaper it owns in order to further these other interests.

But this kind of manipulation of media content is not confined to small-town media outlets. In 1998, Chris Patten, former British governor of Hong Kong, had his book contract cancelled by HarperCollins, which is a subsidiary of Rupert Murdoch's News Corporation. Patten's book, *East and West*, was reportedly going to be highly critical of China's policies, and Murdoch at the time was trying to get China to accept Murdoch's Star TV satellite and cable programs. Similarly, a few years prior to that he removed the BBC from Star TV when Chinese leaders expressed displeasure at the BBC's reports on the killings in Tiananmen Square in June 1989.

These incidents are not meant to show that Rupert Murdoch and News Corporation are particularly greedy or selfish; similar stories of corporate decisions influencing what we see or do not see can be told about all of the major media corporations and will be covered in more detail later in this chapter, in the discussion of media ethics.

Media scholar and political economist Robert McChesney has written several books that show how corporate media have adversely affected the quality of com-

Former Hong Kong governor Chris Patten.

munications content we receive and how media companies have lobbied the government to further their own corporate interests at the expense of the public interest. He claims that today's corporate media giants actually harm our democracy and political processes in a number of ways, ranging from poor news coverage that largely does not challenge the status quo (especially when it comes to media companies' own business interests), to banal entertainment that dulls our senses, to incessant advertising that trains us to be passive consumers rather than active citizens. McChesney's organization, Free Press, is dedicated to trying to reform media in the United States in order to create a better democracy.

Web Link >>>
Free Press
www.freepress.net/

■ ■ ■ PROFIT AND NONPROFIT MEDIA

As McChesney points out, basic to all mass media is the underlying commercial nature of mass communication. As such, there are two main systems for funding media. One system relies on the commercial marketplace, where print and electronic media are run to make money. The other system is not for profit and can rely on a combination of public funding, or support from government or other public institutions, corporate gifts and sponsorships, and audience contributions. This system is used especially for electronic media. There are a variety of other funding models used around the world for nonprofit media, including systems where the public pays a tax on its television or radio receivers, which then is used to fund media programming.

In the for-profit model, ownership plays a key role in determining the nature of the media enterprise. For-profit media companies are either publicly held companies or privately owned operations. For publicly held media companies, shares are bought and sold on the stock market, just like any other company. The people who run these companies are responsible to their shareholders, who, by and large, expect their investments to return a profit.

In recent history, media businesses have been among the most profitable of any industry, with profit margins typically around 20 percent on an annual basis. Sometimes, profit pressures lead media companies, especially publicly traded companies, to focus on the short term—cutting costs, laying off staff, or making decisions that can increase near-term profits but that negatively influence the quality of a product, such as news coverage. The result can be an immediate increase in profitability, but that profitability is not sustainable.

On the other hand, making money can also be an incentive for media companies to produce a better-quality product. The Disney Company, for example, is among the most profitable of major publicly owned media companies in the United States, and it is recognized for its quality products, including award-winning motion pictures, recorded music, and television (it owns the ABC television network and ESPN, the most profitable channel on television).

The influence of this commercial foundation is especially evident in entertainment media, such as in much television programming and many motion pictures. Most of the television schedule is organized with commercial breaks on the hour and throughout each program so advertisers can insert their commercial messages. Broadcast television, although thought of as "free" television, is still essentially paid for by the consumer in the form of higher prices for products as companies have to recoup their expenses for advertising and marketing. But in addition to commercials, advertisers can influence the content of shows and motion pictures directly.

■■■ PRODUCT PLACEMENT AND CORPORATE SPONSORSHIP

product placement

The practice of advertisers paying for actual products to be used and shown prominently in television shows and movies.

Influencing the content of shows and motion pictures can happen in at least two ways. First is **product placement**, where advertisers pay to have their product displayed in a movie or show with the brand name highly visible to the audience. A character driving a name-brand car or drinking from a popular brand of soda is an example of product placement. Second, advertisers or marketers sometimes work directly with media organizations to sponsor specific programs on television or special sections in newspapers. A brand of beer or soft drink sponsoring a concert tour that is televised on MTV is an example of this, as is Ford sponsoring a commercial-free hour of a popular TV show such as *24*.

Even entire channels of content are entirely based on corporate sponsorship. An example is the Hallmark Channel. Launched in August 2001 by Hallmark Cards and Crown Media Holdings, the Hallmark Channel features dozens of series and specials, movies and miniseries, ranging from *Gulliver's Travels* to *Animal Farm*. The Hallmark Channel is widely distributed through 1,700 cable systems and direct-to-home satellite services, across the United States, and worldwide to one hundred international markets, where it is seen by more than 85 million subscribers globally.[5] It's worth noting that simply because a program or channel is advertiser sponsored, it isn't necessarily flawed. In fact, advertising sponsorship has produced some of the best programming on television, including the Hallmark Channel, which features a library of 4,500 hours of programming that has won nearly two hundred Emmy Awards.

■■■ COMMERCIAL FORCES IN PUBLIC SERVICE MEDIA

Although the U.S. media system includes public service broadcasting, even that is increasingly influenced or shaped by commercial forces. In the United States, a large portion of the funding for public service broadcasting comes from corporate sponsors, and those sponsors tend to be most interested in programming that is consistent with the image they want to cultivate among public broadcasting's generally upscale audiences. In 2000, the Public Broadcasting Service (PBS), which produces and distributes public television, received 17 percent of its funding from businesses—its second-highest source. The largest portion, 26 percent, came from member donations, often from large philanthropic foundations. Less than a third of PBS's funding comes from government sources.[6]

As a result of the relatively large portion of corporate sponsorship, and the relaxing of rules that limit corporate advertising on public television, even public service broadcasters sometimes shape their programming in accordance with commercial forces. PBS has also faced especially tough competition from some of the specialized cable channels, which produce targeted or niche educational programming on sciences, nature, or history much like that shown by PBS.

■■■ CONCENTRATION OF MEDIA OWNERSHIP

Regardless of ownership, there are incentives for media companies to seek economies of scale. Strictly speaking, "economy of scale" refers to the decrease in unit manufacturing cost that results from mass production. In the context of media, it means essentially that media enterprises can reduce costs and increase profit by getting larger and reaching a larger market with their content. Of course, just getting bigger doesn't necessarily translate into greater economies of scale, but it is the basic reason behind a fundamental trend in media over the past half century. Successful media enterprises have acquired, either through purchase or merger, other media enterprises and thereby become larger in size and scope. Newspaper companies have bought other newspaper companies, radio-station groups have bought other radio-station groups. Cross-media enterprises have acquired other media enterprises, sometimes extending internationally as well. The result is a media system that is increasingly large, multifaceted, and international in ownership. These companies compete with other large media enterprises and across international borders.

Some critics have argued that despite the possible economies of scale, there is a significant downside to media conglomerates or media monopolies (i.e., when in a community there is just one media organization serving the public). Greater concentration of ownership, or fewer owners owning more media, results in less diversity of media voices, and the public is thus poorly served. Minority voices and non-mainstream views are silenced.

One of the most vocal critics of concentrated media ownership is Ben H. Bagdikian. In his book *New Media Monopoly*, Bagdikian presents evidence that during the 1990s a small number of the country's largest corporations purchased more public communications power than ever before. In 1983, the biggest media merger in history was a $340 million deal involving the Gannett Company, a newspaper chain, which bought Combined Communications Corporation, whose assets included billboards, newspapers, and broadcast stations. In 1996, Disney's acquisition of Capital Cities/ABC was a $19 billion deal—fifty-six times larger. In 2001, AOL's acquisition of Time Warner dwarfed even this deal at $160 billion, or nearly ten times the price of the 1996 Disney deal.

These companies, Bagdikian contends, have built a communications cartel within the United States. A cartel is a group of independent businesses that collaborate to regulate production, pricing, and marketing of goods by the members of the group. In this case, the group is controlling not just industrial products such as gasoline, refrigerators, or clothing. At stake are the words and images that define and shape the culture and political agenda of the country.

"Aided by the digital revolution and the acquisition of subsidiaries that operate at every step in the mass communications process, from the creation of content to its delivery into the home, the communications cartel has exercised stunning influence over national legislation and government agencies, an influence whose scope and power would have been considered scandalous or illegal twenty years ago," writes Bagdikian.

Bagdikian further notes that 99 percent of the daily newspapers in the United States are the only daily in their cities. All but a few of the nation's cable systems are monopolies in their cities. Most of the country's commercial radio stations are part of national ownership groups, and just a half-dozen formats (e.g., all talk, all news, rock, rap, adult contemporary, oldies, easy listening) dominate programming in every city. The major commercial television networks and their local affiliates carry programs of essentially the same type all across the country. By looking at media from this perspective, it seems that perhaps there is not as much diversity in media channels as would first appear.

media oligopoly
....
A marketplace in which media
ownership and diversity are
severely limited and the
actions of any single media
group substantially affect
its competitors, including
determining the content and
price of media products for
both consumers and advertisers.

This system is called a **media oligopoly**. A media oligopoly refers to a marketplace in which media ownership and diversity is severely limited and the actions of any single media group substantially affect its competitors, including determining the content and price of media products for both consumers and advertisers.

Dominating the media worldwide are eight diversified global media giants, as seen in Figure 2-1. These corporations are international conglomerates, many of which are either themselves part of a larger company comprising nonmedia business interests or contain in their financial portfolio significant nonmedia commercial properties and investments. They include a wide range of media or channels of distribution. Of special note is that three of the eight are technology companies and that Google didn't even exist until late 1998.

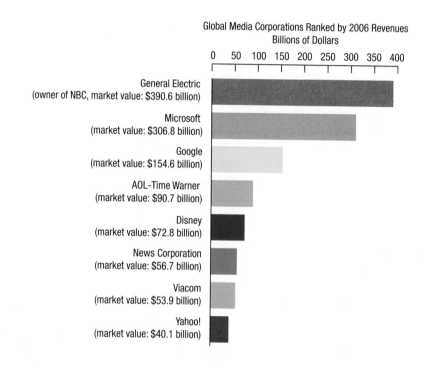

FIGURE 2-1 Global Media Corporations, Ranked by 2006 Revenues, Billions of $ *Mother Jones*, March/April 2007

Much of what we see, hear, or read in traditional media, or interact with on the Web, comes from one of these eight companies. Of course, these are not the only media companies in the world, as there is what McChesney calls a "second tier" of about fifty large media companies operating at the national or international level, each doing more than $1 billion of business a year. Any of these second-tier companies, in and of themselves, can be considered a huge media power with an array of business interests, but their revenues pale in comparison to the big eight.

The trend of media concentration continues, even among the top eight (in 1999 there were nine, and that doesn't include the addition of Yahoo!, Microsoft, and Google since 1999). In 2007 and starting again in late 2008, Microsoft approached Yahoo! with the idea of a friendly takeover. The merger of Yahoo! and Microsoft would make a software and Web-content powerhouse to rival the juggernaut that is Google, but it would further concentrate the channels by which the public receives news, entertainment, and information. Although that deal appears dead at this time, it is likely to arise again either with these two companies or with a similarly large media company. The image in the gatefold insert at the back of this book shows the evolution of the concentration of media ownership over approximately twenty-five years.

The concentration of media ownership and consolidation of media companies into ever larger companies is not simply about learning "the inside scoop" on who owns what. As Bagdikian, McChesney, and other scholars have pointed out, it has serious repercussions for our politics, society, and culture because of the power that media have in our lives. This in turn raises ethical considerations, since media companies have unique and special responsibilities to the public that most other industries do not have to the same degree. The tension that arises from corporate interests in conflict with public interests creates situations in which ethics and moral reasoning must be at their best but often are not.

Media Ethics

It is important to understand the difference between ethics and laws. Although many of our most basic laws are based on ethical precepts, many unethical actions are not actually illegal. Ethics are moral codes that we live by, and philosophers have struggled with understanding principles of ethics for thousands of years. As societal and cultural mores change over time, ideas of what constitutes ethical practices also shift. Ethics can also differ between cultures. For example, lying to someone to save them or someone else from embarrassment may be perfectly acceptable, even expected, in some cultures, whereas people in other cultures would believe lying under any circumstances is unethical.

There is no single, underlying unified ethical principle that all people can follow for complete justice and peace. However, that does not mean that we cannot utilize the thinking and efforts of philosophers, and the guiding principles developed over thousands of years, during which time ethical questions and issues of morality have often been at the heart of our deepest enquiries into what it means to live a good life. At the same time, we cannot simply succumb to relativism, saying that any approach is as good as any other so therefore we do not need to develop good moral reasoning skills or a solid ethical basis for decision making.

A useful approach to applying ethical principles in life and in the practice of mass communication is outlined by prominent ethics scholars in their book *Media Ethics*. Clifford G. Christians, Mark Fackler, Kathy McKee, and Peggy Kreshel outline five theoretical approaches to ethics that can be used as philosophical principles from which to frame ethical issues that arise. We have added a sixth from social theorist and philosopher Jürgen Habermas called "discourse ethics." All of the following are simply snapshots of the principles, not complete explanations, and are meant to provide a general understanding.

■ ■ ■ THE GOLDEN RULE

A basic ethical principle in Judeo-Christian belief, which dominates most Western societies, is often cited as "Do unto others as you would have them do unto you." Another way to phrase the same belief is "Love thy neighbor as thyself."

This principle could be applied by a journalist when she is interviewing a grieving relative, for example. By treating the person with respect and dignity and asking herself if she would want to be treated in the same way in that situation, she can perhaps avoid some of the charges of invasion of privacy or tastelessness in coverage that are often leveled at the media. Some journalists who have been on the receiving end of news stories have often mentioned their shock when they realize how insensitive and intrusive the news media can be during trying times of personal grief.

■ ■ ■ THE GOLDEN MEAN

One of the oldest ethical principles, the Golden Mean was espoused in different forms by Aristotle and Confucius, each of whom said that finding a balance between two extremes is the most ethical way. This "middle way" may well shift as the extremes shift, of course, and even this principle has to be taken in moderation. It would not be ethical to only steal half the money from a cash register rather than all of it, for example, because stealing is wrong in the first place.

Applying the Golden Mean to news stories would involve trying to find balance and fairness among all sides of an issue. It does not mean automatically giving each side the same amount of coverage or space in the newspaper, however, as the relative importance of the groups must be judged.

According to Aristotle, the process of deciding on a mean is how we determine what virtue is, and the mean becomes the standard by which ethical acts are judged. This is part of the reason that acts that are clearly wrong, such as stealing, should not be considered as one extreme.

■ ■ ■ THE CATEGORICAL IMPERATIVE

Immanuel Kant was an influential German philosopher in the eighteenth century who stated that actions should be decided on moral laws that would apply to everyone. In other words, if someone was going to be punished for lying, then everyone should be punished when they lied, even if their lie was told to save a life or protect someone else.

For media organizations, examples of applying Kant's categorical imperative would be in their decisions to publish names of crime victims, or to cover all crimes of a certain seriousness, for example. In this case, if a newspaper published all names of drivers arrested for drunk driving, then even the mayor and newspaper publisher would have their names published if they were arrested for drunk driving. A public relations firm may have a policy about not accepting certain types of clients, such as companies doing business in countries with poor human rights records, and if so would have to apply that policy to any potential client, no matter how big the project promised to be.

Immanuel Kant was an influential eighteenth-century German philosopher who developed the notion of the categorical imperative in ethics.

■ ■ ■ UTILITARIANISM

This philosophical approach states that what is most ethical is what does the most good for the greatest number of people. This means that even if a decision or act severely hurts someone or a small group, if it helps a much greater number of people then it is the right thing to do. But also remember the other side of the premise regarding the greater good: too often it is easiest to quantify the greater number of people who may benefit but forget about the notion of the greatest good, which may help fewer people but help them more than an alternative course of action.

Scientific research on animals operates under a utilitarian principle, with many safeguards to minimize potential suffering and harm of test subjects. It may be harder from a utilitarian ethical perspective to justify testing cosmetics on animals than testing a cure for cancer—a classic case of how both "greatest number" and "greatest good" must be weighed.

Utilitarianism can often be used to justify media coverage of sensitive or painful events for a small number of people, since the coverage can help many others. Examples include investigative reports of government wrongdoing in which a few individuals may go to jail or lose their jobs, but society as a whole is better for exposing the wrongdoers. **Social marketing** operates under utilitarian principles, as it attempts to do the greatest good for the greatest number of people in changing their behaviors, such as to stop smoking or to avoid binge drinking.

social marketing
....
The use of advertising and marketing techniques for social causes, such as anti-smoking or safe sex campaigns.

■ ■ ■ THE VEIL OF IGNORANCE

Twentieth-century philosopher John Rawls argued in his 1971 book *A Theory of Justice* that fairness is the fundamental idea in the concept of justice. However, in complex modern society it is often difficult to establish what is fair, since some groups have greater wealth, power, and advantages than others. In order to better understand fairness, Rawls advocates the parties step behind a "veil of ignorance" in which they are no longer in their usual roles. They must stake out a basic position on the issue not knowing what role they would have after it is decided. From this framework, Rawls says, the parties would be able to better establish fair practices.

Using the technique of applying a veil of ignorance to an issue helps those involved see the issue from a different perspective. An advertising executive may realize that if he were of a different ethnic group or gender he may then find a proposed advertisement offensive. This may lead to a change in behavior.

■ ■ ■ DISCOURSE ETHICS

Noted German social theorist and scholar Jürgen Habermas, most known for his conceptualization of the public sphere, which will be discussed later in the book, has proposed what he calls "discourse ethics" as an ethical framework. Habermas says that communication is at the foundation of how we understand the world and that when we try to communicate with others to truly arrive at a shared meaning of an issue, without the use of coercion or force, that in itself is an ethical act. He proposes several actions for participants in discourse, a kind of formalized discussion that can ensure that all affected parties have a chance to be heard and that everyone's ideas are considered on their own merits—not based on outside factors such as who is dominant in a certain group or who has more power. Like the "veil of ignorance" concept, discourse ethics also comes from a basic assumption that justice and equality are most important for a good society.

Using principles of discourse ethics could work well in an organization in which there are disagreements on the proper course of action. If all affected parties are allowed to participate in the discussion, everyone can better see other perspectives and a decision can ideally be made in which everyone is happy. Note that this process is not about finding a compromise simply for the sake of compromise, but more about directly letting people come to a shared and consensual understanding of what is true, or right based on the merits of the argument, not on the dynamics of who has more power.

■■■ CONFLICTS AND ISSUES WITH ETHICAL DECISION MAKING

It should be obvious that one theoretical approach will not work for all situations and that conflicts between ethical precepts are at the crux of ethical dilemmas in life and in media. The Golden Rule may often conflict with the categorical imperative, as an editor may well imagine he wouldn't want his name to appear in an embarrassing front-page story, but the newspaper's policy is to always print crime victims' names.

Media organizations often do not show the same vigor in reporting about their own business practices and mistakes as they do about those of other businesses. This is a clear violation of the categorical imperative.

The principle of utilitarianism can be used to run roughshod over people's rights of privacy, as editors justify heavy coverage of tragic stories involving famous people as "the public's right to know." But what good does such intrusive coverage actually serve? On the other hand, should a story that could close a polluting factory that employs many people in the town not be published since it would break the principle of utilitarianism by putting the plant's employees out of work? What about the notion of the greatest good, in which stopping the pollution may be a greater benefit for people than the loss of jobs for a large number of townsfolk?

Media professionals must deal with a number of ethical problems in the course of their daily work, some of which are discussed throughout this book and in the chapters dealing with each of the professions. Because of the nature of the work in mass communication, ethical lapses can have repercussions far beyond the unethical media professional, potentially ruining others' careers, affecting the public's perception and trust of media in general, and even in some cases ending lives.

Sometimes corporate decisions made in executive boardrooms far above the typical media professional's level can also have ethical repercussions. Sometimes media professionals may be willing pawns in unethical practices and other times they simply try to do their jobs as best they can within the larger organizational environment.

We will concentrate here on media-ethics issues that arise from commercial forces shaping media content and from the concentration and globalization of media ownership. One such example has already been raised, that of Chris Patten's cancelled HarperCollins book contract as parent-company owner Rupert Murdoch tried to get his Star TV cable and satellite service into the Chinese market.

■■■ PUBLIC INTERESTS VERSUS BUSINESS INTERESTS

Businesses in a capitalist society are expected to make money for their owners, whether they are privately held companies or those traded publicly on the stock market. Members of the public invest in companies that are or that are expected to be successful, which means making profits. Media companies are no different than other types of corporations in that regard.

However, media organizations are in a uniquely powerful position to influence the public compared to other types of companies because of the "product"—media content—they create. Scholars in the Frankfurt School tradition coined the term "culture industry" with media companies to show the power they have in affecting culture. If any other kind of company, such as a shoe manufacturer or cereal maker, wants to influence public opinion, they have to go through the media to do so.

Because of the power of media to shape and influence the public, some aspects of the media industry, such as journalism, are given special protection under the Constitution; the First Amendment is a case in point. Partly as a result of these protections and partly through historical traditions, media—and journalism in particular—have had a strong public service mission. Many questions arise on how seriously the public service mission of news is kept in mind when news organizations become divisions of larger entertainment-media corporations that have little or no tradition in the unique culture of the newsroom and its commitment to public service.

At the heart of many media-ethics dilemmas are the conflicting goals of serving the public with information and maximizing profit for the business. These issues can arise in a number of ways.

Commercial interests can take precedence over what is covered when powerful advertisers cancel or threaten to cancel their advertising in a media outlet. A blatant example may be when an unflattering story on a large local advertiser is going to run in a local newspaper and is either toned down or pulled when the advertiser threatens to withdraw. A far more common case involves advertisers pulling their ads when there is coverage of unpopular issues or when a media organization takes unpopular editorial stands. Examples of this include Southern newspapers that supported the civil rights movement in the 1950s and 1960s losing local advertisers. Although news coverage was not about the advertisers directly, the newspapers became associated with an opinion that the advertisers either did not agree with or were concerned would hurt their businesses if they were seen as advocating it too.

The civil rights movement forced some Southern newspapers to make tough choices when advertisers threatened to pull their ads if the papers appeared to support the movement.

Another way that commercial interests may interfere with the public interest is when media outlets do not adequately cover certain groups or portions of the population because of a lack of audience and advertiser interest. For example, the *Los Angeles Times* had expanded its coverage and spent tens of millions of dollars on creating zoned editions that covered the growing and largely middle-class and affluent surrounding areas of the city even as it largely ignored coverage of the predominantly poor central city. A special section of the paper concentrating on complex urban issues of the south-central area was created in 1992, with the *Times* emphasizing its public service mission, but was closed three years later, despite greater than expected advertising, because of costs associated with the special section.[7]

Related to the case cited above are the costs associated with running a modern newsroom. Cutting staff is one of the surest ways to drastically reduce operating costs, but at what expense in terms of news coverage? Fewer staff means less coverage of certain subject areas and neighborhoods, which can end up giving the public an incomplete picture of what is happening in their town or region as the paper fills the news hole with wire-service copy or light features. Similarly, investigative reports are often time-consuming and expensive and are less likely to be conducted in a media organization intensely aware of maximizing profits.

Professional training and development is another area that often suffers. For many journalists interested in learning how to use computer-assisted reporting tools or digital media in order to help make them better reporters, it is necessary to pay their own way to conferences or workshops and use their personal vacation time in order to attend. This despite a push by some news organizations for journalists to become multimedia reporters, doing their stories in print, TV, and radio formats, which of course is intended to save on production costs when one journalist is doing the work that three had previously done.

■ ■ ■ NEW WORLDS—OR CULTURAL IMPERIALISM?

Media content can open new worlds and new ways of thinking to us as we get exposed to different cultures and lifestyles. The Web has further opened up the possibilities for exploration, especially though video-sharing sites but also as we communicate with each other online.

But when considering the issue of media concentration of ownership and the types of media content typically produced by media companies, questions arise regarding how many diverse voices we actually see. Yes, there are more cable channels than ever, but how many DIY channels such as HGTV are needed for the public, and how fundamentally different are the types of shows on each of the networks?

When we look at the global reach of the media giants and their ability to promote their programming in foreign markets, it raises the issue of what is called cultural imperialism, or the practice of one country dominating a media market through an influx of its media products. The issue is further complicated in that many of these shows imported from the United States, such as *Baywatch* or *The Simpsons*, gain large followings in the foreign countries where they are shown, making it seem like viewers are not forced to watch the programs but are doing so willingly or because the programming is meeting some need that is unmet by domestic television programs.

This may be true to some extent, as many countries cannot afford to produce television shows at the same level of production quality as in the United States, thus giving domestic programs a visually amateurish quality compared to imported programs. However, what can also happen is that domestic television and movie production companies in these countries do not get a chance to fully develop because of the flood of imported movies and shows. The market size in countries with small populations can also be a barrier to the development of robust movie and television industries, because they have no way to recoup the high production costs with such a limited market.

What is of great concern to many in these countries is that their citizens are absorbing alien cultural values that can conflict with their traditional cultural values. Although this exposure to new types of content can lead citizens to question their government about such issues as freedom and democracy, remember that a show such as *Baywatch* does not deal with these issues in any way. The worry is that citizens are losing their appreciation and pride in their traditional culture and replacing it with a prepackaged, homogenized version of what the United States represents—and loving it.

■ ■ ■ MEDIA TYPES INFLUENCING CONTENT

Just as the type of media used to present content influences how that content is created and how it is received and perceived by the public, various business pressures arise with the various media types. The expense of producing feature-length films, for example, is an important factor for large media companies that want to maximize their profits. A film could have a greater likelihood of getting produced if the media company already owns the rights to the character to be used in the film, for example, and if there is good potential for other media content from within the company, such as music and television shows, to be tied in with the movie to help in marketing it.

The individual divisions of a large media company must deal with the demands of the corporate parent to maximize profits. For example, the book-publish-

Video Volunteers: Giving Voice (and Video) to the Voiceless

Founded in 2003 by Jessica Mayberry, Video Volunteers has adopted an innovative program of teaching video production to local communities in India and letting common people tell and share their own stories. It asks, "What if the poorest 1 billion people in the world had their own media industry?"

Using what it calls a Community Video Unit (CVU) model, in partnership with Drishti, an Indian human rights and community organization that uses media in its work, Video Volunteers trains six to ten community members as paid Community Video Producers. Every month, these producers create a new local-language video magazine on a social issue that affects the lives of the local community. They screen the videos in slums and villages on widescreen projectors to up to ten thousand people.

By using video to tell stories, Video Volunteers is not only relying on the power of the visual for storytelling, but also circumventing the low literacy rates that hamper literature-based development projects.

By empowering local communities to become active in critical social issues that directly affect them and teaching them how to tell their stories in a way that can garner attention in the mainstream media, Video Volunteers hopes to effect powerful social changes. Of course, the group is not only relying on the power of the media but also working closely with several Indian nongovernmental organizations (NGOs) to better reach communities and identify important issues that need to be addressed.

Video Volunteers has been recognized for its excellent work and has received several awards by different organizations that are involved in social entrepreneurship and community organizing.

Web Link >>>
Video Volunteers
www.videovolunteers.org/

Web Link >>>
Drishti
www.mydrishtimedia.org/

ing branch may feel pressure to emphasize books from established authors in a popular genre in order to generate sales, but at the expense of finding new authors or types of books that do not fall within established categories.

The need for exciting visual elements has even affected news coverage. *Dateline NBC's* fifteen-minute segment "Waiting to Explode," which ran on November 17, 1992, was meant to demonstrate the danger of the gas tanks exploding with certain models of General Motors' pickups. The only trouble was that the trucks shown exploding on the segment had been rigged by the production team to ensure a fiery explosion and that several elements of the information presented were

Reporters are not supposed to misrepresent the news for dramatic effect, which can often be a temptation in a visual medium such as television.

misleading or inaccurate. Only later, through independent investigations and information from sources who were at the initial filming, did the truth behind the segment come out, forcing NBC to make a public apology and settle the lawsuit that GM had brought against it.[8] In this case, the need to have an exciting visual element likely helped cause the ethical breaches.

On a smaller scale, but no less unethical, was the example of *Today* reporter Michelle Kosinski covering flooding in Wayne, New Jersey, in 2005. She is shown paddling a kayak down a flooded street as she gives her report, only to have two people walk right in front of her, revealing that the water is actually only ankle deep. Despite this incident, she continued with the report as if nothing happened.

Not every dramatic photograph on the front page of a newspaper or in a television news reports is an example of a breach in media ethics, but it is important to have a critical eye and good media literacy when looking at visual media to ask how much of the decision to put that element in the news segment or on the page was driven by the need to capture the public's attention rather than its true news value.

LOOKING BACK AND MOVING FORWARD

Media literacy is not a goal to reach but an ongoing process in which one can always improve in order to become a better mass media consumer and user. Media literacy involves critically thinking about the media and understanding the subtext of messages that mass media may be sending. By developing a better understanding in four key areas—media grammar, commercial forces that shape media content, fragmentation of media audiences, and factors that influence the types of media and technology we have—we can be aware of when mass media are trying to manipulate us and can act accordingly.

It is perhaps hardest for us to recognize how commercial forces shape the type of content we see, largely because we see the end product and not the processes that have taken place behind the scenes to make that media product. But it is arguably the most important aspect of media literacy and of being a critical media user to consider how commercial forces may not always have the best interests of the public at heart, even when media companies claim they are serving the public or simply giving the people what they want.

The conflict of interest between the drive for profits and the public interest is similarly at the heart of many poor ethical decisions made by media companies and communications professionals over the years. It is further complicated by the fact that media companies sit in a unique position among industries, with their ability to greatly influence much of how we view the world and to even influence our ethics and what we see as "right" or "normal."

The changes that we are witnessing with convergence, especially the rise of user-generated content and collaborative media, are perhaps the most direct challenge to some of the traditional media companies who have enjoyed largely unquestioned dominance of the public's attention throughout most of the twentieth century. The way the public is creating media, often on nonmarket principles and simply for the joy of sharing and interacting with others, belies the notion that the public is as happy with its mainstream media content as media conglomerates would have us believe.

Companies' efforts to keep the public satiated with a never-ending stream of media content (that it continues to pay for), and to maintain the largely one-way flow of content from media producer to audience, will continue and even intensify. Scholars such as McChesney are skeptical that the Internet will live up to its promise as a transformational communication technology that can improve democracy and better engage citizens. Whether it does or not will largely depend on how media literate the public becomes and how well we can develop our moral reasoning and ethical thinking to make sure that we do indeed create the kind of society we want to live in, not just have to live in.

DISCUSSION QUESTIONS

1. Go to the library and look at a newspaper from forty years ago (likely only available on microfilm now) and compare the front page with the same paper for the year you were born and that of today. What differences do you notice? What is your first impression of each one? Which one provides more information?

2. Think about your favorite television program and create a list of at least three subtext messages the show may be sending. Explain what effect you think these messages may have on viewers.

3. What do you think the popularity of "reality TV" says about U.S. society and media literacy? Is it a change for the better or for the worse?

4. Would you be willing to pay a mandatory annual television licensing fee if television networks and cable companies promised to show fewer commercials? If so, how much would you be willing to pay? What advantages or disadvantages could there be to a stronger public-supported media presence in the United States?

5. Discuss the moral and ethical implications of using someone else's artistic creation to make something new from it. What steps can be taken to ensure that artists continue to have incentive to create original works even though they can easily be copied, altered, and distributed on the Web?

6. What social or human barriers are there to the public fully utilizing all the capabilities of broadband cable if it were widely accessible? How could these barriers be overcome or minimized?

7. Do you think bloggers should have to follow the same ethical principles as journalists regarding checking the veracity of the information they are reporting on, using authoritative sources, and matters of libel and privacy? Why or why not?

FURTHER READING

Media Literacy, 2nd ed.; W. James Potter (2001) Sage Publications.

The New Media Monopoly; Ben H. Bagdikian (2004) Beacon Press.

Media Ethics: Issues and Cases; Lee Wilkins, Philip Patterson (2001) WCB/McGraw Hill.

The Political Economy of Media: Enduring Issues, Emerging Dilemmas; Robert W. McChesney (2008) Monthly Review Press.

Rich Media, Poor Democracy: Communication Politics in Dubious Times; Robert McChesney (1999) The New Press.

The Problem of the Media: U.S. Communication Politics in the Twenty-First Century; Robert McChesney (2004) Monthly Review Press.

Jamming the Media: A Citizen's Guide to Reclaiming the Tools of Communication; Gareth Branwyn (1997) Chronicle Books.

Citizen Muckraking: How to Investigate and Right Wrongs in Your Community; The Center for Public Integrity (2000) Common Courage Media.

The Conquest of Cool: Business Culture, Counterculture, and the Rise of Hip Consumerism; Thomas Frank (1997) The University of Chicago Press.

Living Ethics: Across Media Platforms; Michael Bugeja (2007) Oxford University Press.

Ethics for the Real World: Creating a Personal Code to Guide Decisions in Work and Life; Ronald Howard, Clinton Korver (2008) Harvard Business Press.

Habermas: A Very Short Introduction; Gordon Finlayson (2005) Oxford University Press.

. . . .

MEDIA QUIZ ANSWERS

Of course the answers to some of the questions will depend on when students take the quiz, but as far as the timeless answers go, here they are:

4. *Lisey's Story* (2006), *Hearts in Atlantis* (1999), *Bag of Bones* (1988), *The Tommyknockers* (1988), *It* (1986), *The Shining* (1977), *Salem's Lot* (1975), just to name a few.

5. *The Green Mile, The Shining, It, Salem's Lot, Hearts in Atlantis, Cujo, Carrie,* just to name some.

7. A cookie is a small snippet of code that is inserted by a website into your machine that allows the website to better track and recognize you. Cookies help make websites more usable, as they allow for personalization of content and are why you do not need to log in every time you visit a website. However, cookies can also invade privacy and track user actions in ways that have nothing to do with making a better Web experience.

8. Web-analytics software can determine, among other information, what type of computer you have (Mac or PC), what type of web browser you are using, what page you came from to get to the website, what page you went to, how long you spent on each page, whether you are a first-time visitor to the website or not (and if not, when the last time you visited was), and even roughly where you are connecting from even if you have not registered to the site and provided that information.

9. A news release, or press release, is written by a public relations agency or by the company itself and is written like a news story. It is then sent to newswire services and individual journalists, after which editors determine if the news outlet will do a story on the topic or not. In theory, news organizations would simply take the news release as a rough source of information and do their own reporting on the story. In practice, however, especially among smaller news organizations, news releases may get printed as a news story largely as written by the company or PR firm, without any identification of its source.

10. True. Apple received negative publicity when it was learned that it could—and had—remotely killed harmful applications for the iPhone and did not have an easy way for customers to get refunds from the applications that were killed. T-Mobile's G1 phone also has a kill switch for harmful applications, but T-Mobile announced the fact even before the phone was available to the public.

Digital Media:
Online and
Ubiquitous

⊙ CHAPTER OBJECTIVES

In this chapter we will:

- Describe what makes digital media ubiquitous and different from other types of media.

- Provide a new and deeper understanding of how and why digital media and the online environment work the way they do.

- Explain the historical development of the Internet and World Wide Web and its relevance to digital media.

- Examine how traditional types of media content are changing, and will likely change further, in a world of digital media.

- Look at the role that digital TV plays in the convergence of the PC and TV.

- Explore business models currently being tried with online media.

The still frames from the film *Workers Leaving the Lumière Factory* may seem an unlikely example to use when talking about digital media. However, when one considers the size and resolution of the images, there is a striking parallel to early video on the Internet. With tiny video screens on computer monitors, poor resolution, and the jerky motions of streaming video that too often froze completely, many initially asked why anyone would want to watch television over the Internet. They concluded that online video had no future.

However, despite continued limitations in picture quality because of Internet connection speed and other technological issues, and content of often questionable quality or value, video-sharing sites like YouTube have become wildly popular in recent years.

Consider further parallels between early film and online video. Lumière asked himself the same question about films such as *Workers Leaving the Lumière Factory* that video skeptics asked: How long would people be willing to watch something they could see every day? His question was valid only as long as that was the only thing filmmakers were producing and only if film technology never improved—both of which of course turned out to be false assumptions. He did not see that technology would improve the picture quality and that filmmakers would use human imagination to portray fantastic and engaging stories.

The same considerations can be applied to online digital media today. The Web is not even twenty years old and has undergone dramatic technological and visual changes in its short life. Companies that did not even exist fifteen years ago are now global media and technology powerhouses that rival established media companies.

An important point to consider, and perhaps the most important lesson to be learned from this chapter and even from this book, is that digital media are not only the same old media delivered digitally, though they can be that. With creativity and imagination, they can be much, much more, leading us to futures we can hardly imagine today.

Digital media are not simply an improvement on or enhancement of other forms of media, in the same way that radio could be thought of as "wireless telegraphy," or broadcast television could be thought of as "radio with moving images," for example. Changes in media brought about by digitization and the Internet are much more fundamental and transformative.

Yet, ironically, many of these fundamental changes will not be immediately apparent to the average media consumer. People will still watch movies and television, still read books, magazines, and newspapers, and will still want to listen to music. Some people even avoid the Internet or are not able to access it easily and still rely heavily on traditional media products for their information and entertainment.

For many people it will not matter that a song was created, produced, and even distributed digitally. But digitization of media alters and threatens existing media

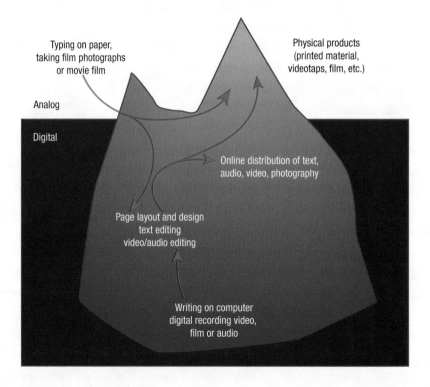

FIGURE 3-1 "Media Iceberg"

How Tech-Savvy Are You Really?

1. (T/F) The World Wide Web and the Internet are the same thing.
2. Is a hyperlink a form of free speech that is protected by the First Amendment? Why or why not?
3. Can an Internet Service Provider (ISP) such as Verizon be sued if one of its customers conducts illegal activities by using the network?
4. (T/F) The United States leads the world in broadband penetration and Internet affordability.
5. If a person sues a media company in another country for libel, whose libel laws are used for the suit?
6. (T/F) Instant messaging is the most used application on the Internet.
7. What does "http" stand for, at the beginning of most website addresses?
8. (T/F) It is legal for employers to read employees' emails sent from work computers.
9. Can you name an example of a new technology causing people to act a certain way?
10. Is Wi-Fi more or less secure than a wired broadband connection?

business models, creates new opportunities for media-content creators, and causes shifts in how media consumers access, use, and interact with media.

A useful way to visualize the states of digital and analog media today is to picture an iceberg floating in the ocean. Just as only a small percentage of the whole iceberg is visible above the water, today the primarily analog end media products we see, such as books or DVDs, are only a small part of the overall media-creation process. Most mass media today already utilize digitization in some way, even if the final product that generates revenues is still predominantly analog. But this will change over time as consumers get more of their media content digitally. In other words, the iceberg will continue to be submerged into an entirely digital sea of content production and distribution, though it will never entirely disappear, of course.

Key Concepts in Digital Media

Digital media are those that have been created in or transformed into machine language, or computer-readable form. Computers can only understand "on" or "off" states, or the presence or absence of information, represented by either a 1 or 0, called a "bit." Each bit of information (the term "bit" is a shortening of "**b**inary dig**it**") in a computer is stored in what is called "binary code." Eight bits make a byte (pronounced BITE). A series of bits, a byte, or a series of bytes can represent any information. For example, the number five in binary code is "000101," or "101" for short. Each letter of the alphabet is one byte, so capital A is represented in computer-readable code as "01000001," for example. Every digital word, image, song, or movie is represented by nothing but a string of 0's and 1's, or electronic on-off states. This may seem like an inefficient system to process information—

and it is—but computers process all these 0's and 1's extremely quickly. A computer makes no distinction between a digital video clip and a digital text document, except for the differing amount of memory each takes up in the computer. The process in which media is made into computer-readable form is called **digitization**.

Although it may be extremely useful to have a computer that can solve complex calculations or make it easier to write and edit a novel, its use is greatly diminished if the computer user cannot share information with other computer users. If other computer users are nearby, then using some kind of physical medium such as tape or a diskette to transfer information between computers can work, but that does not solve the problem of distant computer users wanting to share information or what to do when multiple users are working on the same information and need to share with each other. The solution to this problem is to put the computers on a network.

The term **analog media** derives from the world of audio recording, in which the modulation of the sound carrier wave is analogous to the fluctuations of the sound itself. Because of the on-off nature of digitization, it can never exactly capture a sound in the way analog media can; the best it can do is sample the original data and get as close to the original as possible. Figure 3-2 shows the difference between an analog sound wave and a digital sample of the same wave.

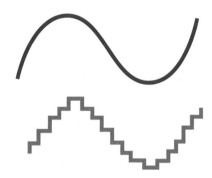

FIGURE 3-2 Digital Sampling. A digital sample can never exactly match its analog counterpart because digital media only have two states, "on" and "off," which are represented in the steplike pattern. The reason a digital recording can sound as good as an analog recording is that the digital sampling can be done at small enough intervals that the human ear cannot detect the gaps between the steps.

Analog media work differently. Consider, for example, how Thomas Edison's original phonograph, created in 1877, worked. Edison's phonograph, an analog-media device, required the user to speak into a sound horn while rotating an attached tin cylinder. A needle, attached to a diaphragm that vibrated in corresponding fashion to the sounds of the speaker's voice, "recorded" or scratched onto the tin cylinder a pattern analogous to the sounds emitted by the speaker. Playing back the sound required the needle to move over the groove etched during the recording. The needle would vibrate as it moved over the groove, which caused the diaphragm to vibrate and emit via the sound horn a replica of the original voice. Modern phonographs use essentially the same principles, although helped greatly by improvements in materials, design, and the use of electronic rather than mechanical amplifiers.

There are four main concepts that underlie the digital media world—multimedia, interactivity, automation, and ethereality. Some of these are not unique to digital media, as there are examples in the analog media world as well, but digitization

digitization
The process in which media is made into computer-readable form.

analog media
Term originally used in audio recording for media analogous to the sound being re-created. It now refers to all nondigitized media, such as print media, audio and video recordings, photography, and film.

Web Link >>>
How Stuff Works: Analog-to-Digital Conversion
www.howstuffworks.com/analog-digital.htm

makes them easier than ever before. Each plays an important role in giving digital media the power that they have.

■ ■ ■ MULTIMEDIA

When all information consists of bits, it becomes easy to juxtapose various media types that could not coexist in the analog media world. There will never be an option to watch a video clip in a print newspaper or listen to the interview of the story; the nature of print as a medium and physical laws of nature simply will not allow it. The best that can be done to read and perhaps look at a photograph or use other media such as a radio or television to supplement the reading. Likewise, it is impossible to retrieve the written lyrics of a song directly from the radio.

The idea of **multimedia**, or combining various media types into one package, is not new. Putting photographs with text is a type of multimedia, but a better example is the combination of moving pictures and sound, as in film and video. In the digital world, however, there are more opportunities for multimedia. Video can sit side-by-side with a text transcript, and audio can play while the media consumer reads the lyrics of a song or reads information about the artist or even watches a concert by the artist.

multimedia

A combination of different types of media in one package; thus, film or video with sound is a type of multimedia, because it combines visual and audio elements. Web pages that combine text, video, animation, audio, or graphics are another type of multimedia.

■ ■ ■ INTERACTIVITY

Interactivity is a crucial aspect of digital media but is, ironically, extremely hard to define to everyone's satisfaction. There is no doubt that the term is misunderstood, misused, and abused. According to WhatIs? online encyclopedia, it is defined this way:

> In computers, interactivity is the dialog that occurs between a human being (or possibly another live creature) and a computer program. . . . In addition to hypertext, the Web (and many non-Web applications in any computer system) offers other possibilities for interactivity. Any kind of user input, including typing commands or clicking the mouse, is a form of input. Displayed images and text, printouts, motion video sequences, and sounds are output forms of interactivity.[1]

Media and Internet scholar Sheizaf Rafaeli states that interactivity is "the condition of communication in which simultaneous and continuous exchanges occur."[2] In other words, interaction involves two or more parties to a communication engaging in an ongoing give-and-take of messages.

For our purposes, we will define interactivity as having the following elements:

1. A dialog that occurs between a human and a computer program (this includes emails, online chats, and discussion groups, as at either end of the communication flow it is a human interacting with a computer program—the Internet is simply the channel).

2. The dialog affects the nature or type of feedback or content that is received, changing as the dialog continues.

3. The audience has some measure of control over what media content it sees and in what order (getting personalized information, magnifying an image, clicking on a hyperlink, etc.).

These three components of interactivity include almost all of the activities that we typically engage in with digital media and make interaction with digital media fundamentally different than that with traditional media. Turning the pages of a

interactivity

Although an exact definition is still being debated, for digital-media purposes interactivity can be defined as having three main elements: (1) a dialog that occurs between a human and a computer program, (2) a dialog that occurs simultaneously or nearly so, and (3) the audience has some measure of control over what media content it sees and in what order.

A visualization map of the connections in the Internet shows how some parts are more highly connected than others.

magazine may be considered "interactive" by some, but the reader is unable to engage in dialog with the article, cannot change the size of text or personalize the information in the article, and the article itself will remain unchanged no matter what the reader writes in the margins.

■ ■ ■ AUTOMATION

Computers can be programmed to automate many complex and time-consuming tasks, which are made easier since all data exists in essentially the same format. Search engines and other elements that make computers and the Web relatively easy to use are all possible through automation. Automation enables computers to draw 3-D objects, it makes computer games engaging, and it is changing the way journalists and other media professionals do their work. But automation also makes it much easier for companies to find and track individuals and makes media use no longer anonymous.

Automation plays a crucial role in the ability of online media to be **personalized** and **localized** or to provide user-specific or geographic-specific information. Users can specify what kinds of news or information they want to receive based on any number of factors, such as geography, interests, or specific topics. With automation, computer programs can even select media content that is more likely to be of interest to a specific user simply based on tracking of websites or type of content the user has visited.

personalization
....
The ability of media-content producers to provide content that is of interest to a specific user based either on criteria the user has selected, such as a zip code, or on automated tracking of their Web-viewing habits.

localization
....
The ability of media-content producers to provide content based on a user's locale, either done automatically based on an ISP or after the user has provided information such as a city name or zip code.

■ ■ ■ ETHEREALITY

We've just taken a look at digital media and how it's made up of representations of 1's and 0's. In some ways digital information is better without a physical presence, as often the need to put it in some sort of physical form makes it lose its natural digital characteristics.

The "immaterial" quality of digital information has far-reaching consequences for distribution of content, media companies, the law, and society. Digital libraries will not need time limits for books that are checked out, as online visitors simply download a perfect copy to their own computer and leave the original for others. In fact, the concept of "checking out" a book becomes meaningless. The concept of watching a show broadcast at 8 p.m. on a certain night of the week is similar. The shows are available, all the time, and can be accessed and watched on demand. Endless copies of media content can be made and easily distributed, as file-sharing services have shown.

Discussing Digital Media: Networks Are Key

But even as far-reaching as these elements are in changing the media landscape, they are still incomplete without one important element: a network that connects computers or media devices to each other so they can communicate. There are many kinds of networks, but we will concentrate primarily on the Internet and the World Wide Web here. All data that pass through the various networks—telephone, cable, or satellite—are at one or more stages digital, but we will use the term "digital media" to refer to networked, or online, digital media.

The broader topic of online communications, of which the Internet is a vital part, must be clarified. Although many may consider the term "online" synonymous with the Internet, "online" is in fact a term with a larger meaning. "Online" refers to the interconnected, networked media that permit the direct, electronic exchange of information, data, and other communications. Everything from local area networks (LANs) to wide area networks (WANs), such as the Internet, is part of the online world. In other words, the Internet and the World Wide Web are part of the online communications world; they are not the entire online world. However, the Internet and the Web are among the most important parts of the online world for mass communication because they are where much media content resides and where most of the public gets its digital content.

Out of all modern media, the Internet/World Wide Web reached 50 percent of U.S. households faster than any other media technology. It is important to note here, however, that the Internet is more complex in its requirements for adoption than other media. One can't simply go out and "buy an Internet" as one could with a radio or TV. Instead, one must first have a computer and a means of connecting it to the Internet, plus a higher level of technical media literacy to use the computer than is required for a television or VCR, so direct comparisons with older media types can be problematic. Nevertheless, even with these technological hurdles, Table 3-1 shows the relatively rapid adoption rate of the Internet.

TABLE 3-1

Number of Years to Reach a 50 Percent Penetration of U.S. Households

TECHNOLOGY/MEDIUM	YEARS
Newspapers	100+
Telephone	70
Phonograph	55
Cable Television	39
Personal Computer	19
Color Television	15
VCR	10
Radio	9
Black & White Television	8
Internet/World Wide Web	7

John Carey ("The First 100 Feet for Households: Consumer Adoption Patterns," paper presented to "The First 100 Feet: Options for Internet and Broadband Access" conference by the Freedom Forum in Arlington, VA [October 29–30, 1996]. Retrieved June 20, 2002, from http://www.ksg.harvard.edu/iip/doeconf/carey.html); Electronic Industry Association; U.S. Dept. of Commerce

Social and Cultural Implications of Digital Media

Digital media of course play a role in every communication function that analog media play, ranging from surveillance to entertainment. Whether society ultimately will be better served by an Internet-connected world is impossible to say. However, there is no doubt digital media are changing and will continue to change the relationship between mass-communication industries and the public. Media organizations face many challenges, but so do media consumers as the nature of our media environment changes. Some general trends can be discerned that will provide a better perspective on how our digital-media use is changing our media world and, by extension, our social and cultural worlds.

■ ■ ■ PERVASIVE MEDIA

The pervasiveness of the media system means that wherever one goes there will likely be unprecedented access to mass communication. With today's global satellite communications, it is not possible to truly "escape" anywhere on the planet. In May 1996, climber and guide Rob Hall was trapped high on Mt. Everest for more than a day after a sudden storm hit. Unable to descend, unable to be rescued, and knowing he would die there, he was able to talk to his pregnant wife in New Zealand by satellite phone.[3]

A 24/7 media environment had begun to emerge even before the arrival of the Internet, and now it is fully here. This media environment has had several implications for how we use and what we expect from media, as well as for media industries. The public has become used to getting increasingly large chunks of its news and entertainment on demand, thanks largely to interactivity. This trend toward on-demand viewing has moved beyond the online environment, getting impetus with digital video recorders (DVRs) and cable providers that allow their viewers to watch a range of programming whenever they want.

Media companies face many challenges in the digital age.

Portable media devices and flat-screen technologies mean that we can take our media with us and access it in places where we previously did not encounter media. Video displays in elevators or at checkout registers are two examples of how advertisers are using technology to reach captive audiences.

Pervasive mass communication means better access to entertainment, information, and news—in theory. It can also mean that media organizations can turn us into super-consumers of media of questionable social or civic value. The ability to watch a lowbrow sitcom or reality show on your mobile phone while riding the bus can be challenged as a worthwhile goal to strive for in the digital media world, just as tuning out the world around you when listening to songs on an iPod can be questioned.

■■■ FLUID MEDIA

Our understanding of most types of media content as static or unchangeable, such as a book, is being challenged by digital media. In 1999 a company, Third Voice, created an application that allowed website visitors to annotate any web page with their own comments. The idea was to generate a more democratic forum for discussions among users, but the service quickly drew the wrath of website creators, who likened the annotated comments to graffiti. Two years later, Third Voice quietly closed down.

However, the spiritual inheritor of the principle that Third Voice espoused can be seen in a **wiki**, a type of website that can be edited by anyone, and the growing popularity of wikis, thanks in part to the success and attention of Wikipedia, shows that there was a pent-up demand among Web users for such a function. Now, that most staid form of print media, the authoritative encyclopedia article, begins to blur the line between news and encyclopedia as breaking developments are added to Wikipedia articles.

Of course content was never actually unchangeable; it just seemed that way. A book could be reprinted as a new edition, yet for most readers the changes made between editions were almost impossible to discern. A book can now be seen as a much more fluid and changeable document online, with discussion forums on book material incorporated into the contents, ongoing interactions between the author and readers, and interactions between readers.

Similarly, the idea of mash-ups of existing media has become common, thanks to digital editing tools for music and video. Any popular item produced from mass media has the potential of being transformed very quickly into a number of user-generated mash-ups, most done simply for the fun of creating something rather than for commercial gain. Online discussions and mash-ups both share an important change taking place in digital media: that of audience participation being more visible and having a greater influence on media content.

■■■ ACTIVE AUDIENCES

Digital media do not cause people to become active media producers, or "**produsers,**" as they are sometimes called in an attempt to capture how we use (not just consume) and produce media content now. However, they do give people ready tools to produce media if they wish and to do so far more cheaply and easily than analog media. Active audiences have two important implications for media companies: they compete for limited time among the potential audience, and they become more critical media consumers of the mass media they do receive.

Furthermore, the ability to widely distribute **user-generated content** (UGC) on a par with major media companies gives audiences unprecedented power in relation to traditional media producers. This is not to say that the average person now has the same ability to produce and create a hit song as a major recording label, as an individual does not have the marketing and promotion capabilities that a recording label has at its disposal, but the basic capability of producing and distributing at least exists.

As produsers, audiences also learn to become more critical media consumers and to raise questions on the quality of news, information, and entertainment they get. The channels available through interactive media let the public speak directly to traditional media producers in a public way, thereby giving a sense of shared experience, even perhaps community, as people see that others may feel as they do

wiki
A type of website that can be edited by anyone.

Cell phones or other portable devices may be the primary way people access the Internet rather than desktop PCs.

produsers
The notion that audiences cannot simply be considered consumers anymore but also often take an active role in producing content or information.

user-generated content
Content that has been created by users of a website or that has been uploaded to a website.

that an advertisement was offensive or that a news story was inaccurate in some important respects.

Active audiences are more likely to organize and work together on common problems, especially if they have developed trusted relationships through interacting with each other, than if they perceive themselves as isolated individuals or anonymous faces in a crowd who have no choices in determining what media they get.

■ ■ ■ TRUST, TRANSPARENCY, AND REPUTATION

Members of the public are coming to expect a certain amount of transparency in their communications with each other and with leading organizations, including media organizations. There have been a growing number of cases in which organizations have been caught deceiving the public and have suffered damage to their reputations. One such example was Edelman, a global PR firm that financed the "Wal-Marting Across America" blog in 2006. The blog was ostensibly done by a couple traveling around the country in an RV, "who just happened" to like to stay at Wal-Mart parking lots because of the free services offered for RVs. Of course, the couple had nothing but good things to say about Wal-Mart. When the truth was revealed that the couple was actually being paid by Edelman, whose client was Wal-Mart, debates raged on how ethical it was to have such a blog.

User rankings are an important means for the public to determine whether to trust information received on the Internet.

Because most people on the Web do not physically make contact with each other and know one another only through their online interactions and communication, establishing a sense of trust has become crucial. There are a growing number of reputation systems on the Web that attempt to help Web users do this, ranging from rankings such as on Amazon or eBay to the "karma points" on Slashdot, a popular news and discussion website.

This idea of managing one's reputation online, and how that may affect the offline world (imagine the consequences of getting some bad reviews on eBay if you are trying to make a living selling items on the site), becomes important not only for companies but for individuals as well. Companies can fall prey to disinformation campaigns, as the example of Dow Chemical showed in Chapter 2, and monitoring blogs and online discussions of a company becomes important.

At the heart of reputation and transparency is the idea of building relationships based on trust and essentially respect. Media companies that do not realize this will suffer in the digital media world in the long run. For many, it means a shift in corporate policies or philosophies and a loss of the control they have enjoyed through much of the mass-communications era. There is a conventional wisdom among some executives that employees are more willing to spend company time doing personal things, like shopping online, than they were in the past. But on the other hand companies are also expecting employees to stay longer at work and must realize that the blurring of company time and private time is a large-scale trend.

■ ■ ■ CHANGING CONCEPTIONS OF PRIVACY

The convergence of digital media has led to confusion over our traditional notions of privacy, both for individuals and for companies. Although there have been a number of clear violations of privacy laws, even by traditional standards, there is also a lot of confusion over what is acceptable or even legal and what is not.

For example, a person writing a blog may consider it a private journal, or something intended for only a select audience of friends, and thus feel like her privacy was invaded and get angry when a potential employer mentions inappropriate postings during a job interview. Similarly, information that always has been public, such as property deeds or arrests by the police, but that has generally been cumbersome to retrieve, can now be easy to find online.

One component of privacy is the ability to be left alone, and this has become increasingly difficult in an age of pervasive media. It can be easy to turn off a mobile phone, but maintaining a sense of privacy can be more problematic when instant messaging and getting unwanted messages from others who see you are online.

Wireless communication between devices, without the need for specific human direction—such as swiping a debit card at a supermarket checkout—makes it increasingly easy to paint a picture of a person simply through his or her electronic transactions over a short period of time. The ability to track consumers with such accuracy, especially on the Web, means that we can get more relevant or personal media content, but it also means we have provided a great deal about our personal habits and interests, not all of which we may wish to share with companies or advertisers.

■ ■ ■ DIGITAL DIVIDE

All of the implications mentioned here make a large assumption—that individuals have ready access to computers, a broadband Internet (wired and Wi-Fi) connection, and the knowledge and skills to know how to use them. It is a world that many in advanced, industrialized countries may take for granted, but it is still far from a universal condition, even within developed countries.

Better Internet access has not come evenly to all, nor allowed everyone to benefit equally from that access. People in lower socioeconomic groups in the United States and other industrialized countries have lagged in almost every category of Internet access. The high cost of telecommunication services, including broadband Internet, keeps many from being able to develop the skills and knowledge that can help them fully participate in society.

The United States has been slipping in both high-speed Internet penetration and affordability for the services that are available. The United States ranks twenty-second in terms of affordability and has slipped from fourth place in 2001 to fifteenth place for Internet penetration in 2008.[4]

Exploring the Foundations of Digital Media

The convergence of digital technology has blurred the lines in many legal matters that were never an issue in the analog media world. This means that if we are to understand the ripple effects that technology changes have brought to media and the ways we use media, then we have to understand at least some basic aspects about digital and online technology. This is because digital technologies create functionalities that no other media has previously been able to do. Hyperlinks are a fairly simple, yet illustrative, example.

CONVERGENCE CONTEXT

The Trouble with "The Technology Made Me Do It"

It is easy to get carried away with the power of technology when looking at the changes occurring with digital media. However, it is important to maintain a critical distance, especially when dealing with new and emerging technologies and social and cultural behaviors.

Technological determinism is a perspective that states that technology essentially "causes" certain behaviors and the creation of social systems. It is easy to look at developments in new technologies and see subsequent changes in society that are sometimes quite revolutionary.

An example of an argument that uses technological determinism would be looking at how the invention of the mechanical printing press changed European history and helped usher in the Renaissance. The printing press could be seen as causing the Catholic Church to lose power, as it could no longer control the distribution of texts. Because of the ease of distribution of written materials, the printing press could also be seen as increasing literacy rates and helping to excite greater interest in a range of literature.

The argument seems logical enough, but consider it from a different perspective. The printing press was not invented by Gutenberg in 1455. In fact, the Chinese invented printing a few hundred years earlier, and the Koreans had the first metal printing press a couple hundred years after that. If the printing press "caused" all these developments in Renaissance Europe, then why didn't it have the same effect in China or Korea hundreds of years earlier?

You can see technological determinist thinking today when people claim that any new technology has more or less caused a certain behavior. Think of cell phone use and social attitudes, or the amount of time people spend on the Internet and deteriorating social skills, or any number of new technologies that are credited or blamed for causing certain behaviors. It is important to remember that the relationship among technology, society, and culture is a complex one in which a simple cause-and-effect explanation often masks underlying factors.

---

technological determinism

A perspective that states that technology essentially "causes" certain behaviors and the creation of social systems.

hyper text transfer protocol (HTTP)

A protocol that enables the standardized transfer of text, audio, and video files, as well as email, from one address to another.

deep linking

Creating a hypertext link to another website's inside page or pages rather than to its homepage.

Until the creation of **hyper text transfer protocol (HTTP)** in 1991 by Tim Berners-Lee, hyperlinks only existed as hypertext within certain types of Mac files, not between computers. But after hyperlinks were created and started being used by larger numbers of people, new issues began to arise.

Although in theory hyperlinks can take the user anywhere else on the Web, in practice many organizations protested the practice of **deep linking**, or linking to one of the website's inside pages, such as a particular story. This is because commercial media sites charged advertising rates based on how many visitors came to their home pages, and deep linking skirted that business model. Some websites compiled links of other websites and put them under their own Web address, making it look like the content was theirs. On the other hand, it is of little use to provide a link to a specific story, only to send users to a website's home page and make them find the story themselves.

Company attitudes against deep linking began to change a few years ago as blogs became popular and media companies realized that the gains in website traffic, and the potential for garnering new readers from links on a popular blog, outweighed the fact that the visitors were not coming to the home page. Getting mentioned on popular sites could leave some websites unprepared; the term "Slashdot effect" was coined to refer to a huge spike in website traffic that sometimes crashed website servers when a company's link was posted on the popular website Slashdot.

Another issue has arisen regarding whether a hyperlink is a form of free speech or simply a device that takes a user elsewhere. The answer, according to a federal court in *Universal City Studios v. Reimerdes* (2000), is that links are both expressive and functional and could be subject to regulation. The object of contention in this case was a computer program known as DeCSS, which enabled users to effectively copy DVDs. The judge ruled that it was illegal not only to publish the program on the Web, but also, more extraordinarily, to link to any website containing the illegal computer code. However, simply writing the website address without actually linking to it would be protected as free speech, as the judge ruled that it is equivalent to the printed word whereas the link acted as a mechanism to take the user to the illegal site.

Hyperlinks are a fundamental aspect of the Web.

In the case of hyperlinks, without an understanding of how they work and what characteristics make them different than traditional media, it is impossible to fully understand how digital media are changing the overall media framework economically, legally, and in terms of media use. The same reasoning can be applied to many aspects of digital media. Hyperlinks may give users the mechanisms by which to connect to other places on the Internet, but without a network in place that allows for such connections, hyperlinks would do little good. The Internet, like some other revolutionary media before it, was not created with the intent of becoming a hugely popular mass medium.

Historical Development of the Internet and World Wide Web

Prior to the creation of the Internet, institutions or organizations that had computers had no simple way for the computers to communicate with each other, even if they were connected by a wire, as computers ran machine-specific languages and programs that could not be understood by other computers.

In 1969, the foundations for the Internet were laid when the Defense Advanced Research Projects Agency (DARPA) launched the Advanced Research Projects Agency network, or ARPAnet. ARPAnet was the first national computer network, connecting many universities around the country for advanced, high-speed computing applications and research. It was not yet the Internet, but it was the beginning of online communications. There was still no "common language," or protocol, that computers could use to easily transmit information via the network. A protocol, just like a diplomatic protocol, is essentially a set of rules that allows for easier communication between two parties who normally speak different languages.

Email is often called the "killer app" (killer application) of the Internet, yet in some ways it has been taken for granted in recent years in the barrage of other ways to communicate online, such as through instant messaging or chat rooms. Email is usually one of the first things people learn to do when getting on the Internet, and it doesn't take long even for computer novices to get hooked enough to check their email inboxes several times a day. More messages are sent via email now than through the U.S. Postal Service. Email combines aspects of casual conversation with the permanence of text, as well as speedy transmission of messages.

"E-mail kind of announced itself," said Ray Tomlinson, the computer engineer who invented email in 1971. After debugging his program and giving it several trials to make sure it worked properly, he sent a message to his coworkers saying they could now communicate with people on other computers. The first email message? According to the *Guinness Book of World Records*, it was QWERTYUIOP—the keys on the third row of the keyboard. Tomlinson said that testing and debugging his original program was a process of trial and error, and he actually doesn't remember what the first message was.

Once messages could be moved from one machine to another, Tomlinson had to decide on a symbol that would separate the name of the individual from the machine he or she was working on. He said that the symbol @ ("at") was the obvious choice, as any single letter or number could cause confusion. "As it turns out, @ is the only preposition on the keyboard. I just looked at it and it was there. I didn't even try any others," Tomlinson said.[5]

It was clear to computer engineers that some type of simplified, common language was needed, a language that computers could speak with each other and by which they could send and receive information was needed—something more robust than what email could offer.

■ ■ ■ CREATING AN INTERNET PROTOCOL

transmission control protocol
....
A part of the main protocol for
the Internet that allows for
computers to easily communicate
with each other over a network.

In 1974, Vinton Cerf and Robert Kahn published their classic article, "A Protocol for Packet Network Intercommunication." In the article, they specified the design of a **transmission control protocol** (TCP) as a part of the main protocol for the Internet and introduced the term "Internet." Also important to the creation of the Internet was the work of Jonathan Postel, who, when a graduate student at UCLA, outlined along with Cerf some of the key principles that underlie today's Internet protocols (IP). Together, these two protocols, TCP/IP, became the foundation for how computers would communicate with each other.

Although it is difficult to pin down an exact date when the Internet officially started, it was in 1982 that the Defense Department adopted TCP/IP as the basis for the ARPAnet. Essentially, this meant that if universities wanted to remain in the network, they had to adopt the TCP/IP protocol. Moreover, at this time researchers began defining an "internet" (lowercase *i*) as a connected set of networks using TCP/IP, and the "Internet" (uppercase *I*) as a set of connected TCP/IP internets.[6]

■ ■ ■ CREATING THE WORLD WIDE WEB

For the first decade of the Internet's existence, its usage was limited largely to academic and government researchers. Use of the Internet required knowledge of a variety of arcane commands and terminology. The limited, specialized nature of

Milestones in the Development of the Internet

1958 In response to the 1957 Soviet launch of Sputnik, the U.S. Department of Defense establishes the Defense Advanced Research Projects Agency (DARPA), whose mission is to develop advanced communications capabilities.

1969 Laying the foundations for the Internet, DARPA launches the Advanced Research Projects Agency network, or ARPAnet, the first national computer network.

1971 Email invented.

1973 Vinton Cerf and Robert Kahn develop the basic concept and architecture for the Internet.

1974 Cerf and Kahn specify the design of a transmission control protocol (TCP), the basic protocol for the Internet, and coin the term "Internet."

1975 Researchers successfully conduct the first TCP communication tests via satellites linking locations across the Atlantic and Pacific oceans.

1982 DARPA adopts the TCP/IP protocol as the standard for communication among computers in ARPANet.

1991 Tim Berners-Lee creates the World Wide Web, a global publishing platform, on the Internet.

1993 Mark Andreeson and others create Mosaic, a Web browser, or graphical user interface for the Web, that permits anyone to easily navigate and view pages on the Web using a computer mouse and keyboard. This helps bring the Web out of the specialized domain of scientists and into the mainstream of media and the public.

1994 Mosaic Communications Corp. (later Netscape) is formed by Marc Andreeson and colleagues who left the National Center for Supercomputing Applications (NCSA).

1994–1995 First blogs created, although they are not yet called blogs and many of the automated tools that help make blogs a popular form of online communication will not be developed until the late 1990s and early 2000s.

1995 WikiWikiWeb, the first wiki, is created and named by Ward Cunningham.

1998 Microsoft antitrust trial begins, with the Department of Justice and twenty states claiming that Microsoft illegally blocked web browser competition from Netscape by bundling Microsoft's Internet Explorer browser with the Windows operating system.

1998 Google founded by Larry Paige and Sergey Brin, two Stanford graduate students.

2000 The dot-com economic bubble bursts in March, ending a run since the late 1990s that saw huge increases in valuations of Internet companies and a kind of frenzy that dot-com companies would sweep aside traditional media companies.

2008 The Firefox Web browser, a free, open-source browser, gets almost 20 percent of the worldwide browser market, second only to Internet Explorer.

Tim Berners-Lee, creator of the World Wide Web.

hypertext mark up language (HTML)
....
A coding format that describes how information should look on the Web.

extensible mark up language (XML)
....
A coding format similar to HTML but that allows for easy sharing of information and data about the information on the Web, not only how it looks.

the Internet underwent a fundamental change in 1991 when Tim Berners-Lee, a British researcher at a physics laboratory in Switzerland, invented the World Wide Web, which began to open the Internet to a much wider set of users.

The advent of the Web as a global publishing platform made possible the most fundamental shift in human communication since the advent of the printing press five centuries earlier. The Web enabled easy many-to-many communication over distance and time. In addition, in contrast to traditional media of mass communication, anyone can create and publish on the Web for very little cost and with little technical expertise.

The World Wide Web (WWW) is a subset of the Internet and is perhaps best described as a global electronic-publishing medium accessed through the Internet. Technically speaking, the Web is made up of an interconnected set of computer servers on the Internet that subscribe to a set of TCP/IP network-interface protocols. These technical protocols include assigning to a website a Uniform Resource Locator (URL) based on its TCP/IP Internet address, which is the website address that web users are familiar with. URLs include the instructions that are read by a web browser, a navigational tool to travel the Web.

A web page is any document, or collection of content, that resides on a website. The content can take any form, including text, graphics, photographs, audio, video, or interactive features, such as surveys or discussion forums. A website can consist of one page of content or many such pages and can include hyperlinks to other websites.

Content on a web page is marked up using what is known as **hypertext markup language**, or **HTML**, or variations of HTML such as **extensible markup language** (XML), to format the content so it displays correctly on a screen. In addition, each document uses hyper text transfer protocol (HTTP), which enables the standardized transfer of text, audio, and video files from one address to another.

■ ■ ■ CREATING GRAPHICAL WEB BROWSERS

Another huge gain in making the Internet accessible to even more people was the creation in 1993 of Mosaic by Marc Andreeson, then at the National Center for Supercomputing Applications (NCSA) at the University of Illinois at Champaign-Urbana. Mosaic, which eventually became Netscape, provided a graphical user interface (GUI) for the Web that computer users who had Macs or Windows PCs could quickly understand and use. Although GUI browsers Viola and Erwise were also created in 1992, by the end of the year Mosaic was being written about in mainstream media and became the most well-known web browser at the time before becoming Netscape.

Microsoft created its own graphical browser, Internet Explorer (IE), in 1996 to compete with Netscape's browser, then called Netscape Navigator. By offering Internet Explorer free and eventually bundling it with the Windows operating system, IE was able to become the dominant web browser in only four years, with 75 percent usage compared to Netscape's 25 percent. By 1999, at its peak, IE had 99 percent of the browser market. The same year, Netscape was bought by AOL, a year before AOL acquired Time Warner.

Although other browsers were created, such as Opera or Apple's Safari, the first serious competition to IE came from open-source browser Firefox, created by the Mozilla Foundation. Launched in late 2004 under the Firefox name but built on versions of the browser that had been launched under other names since 2002, by

2008 Firefox had captured nearly 20 percent of the browser market, most of it from IE, all without advertising or marketing.

As any regular web user can attest, websites and text size often look different not only on different browsers but on different versions of browsers. More advanced functions or codes on websites may not show up on earlier browser versions, thus making it difficult for web designers and content companies to create websites that are consistent across the online audience.

For most users, the web browser is their window into the world of online communication. Yet this window is constantly changing in ways that can be exciting and confusing, and we are still in the early stages of development with the Internet as a medium of mass communication.

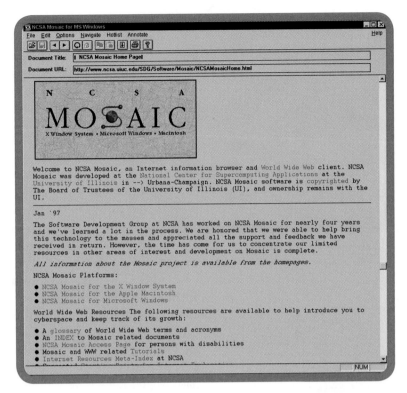

The Internet Today

The Mosaic browser, the first widely used graphical user interface for the Web.

In its broadest sense, the Internet encompasses virtually all other media, as well as a broad cross-section of human culture, commerce, and creation. Virtually anything one can think of almost certainly is accessible in some form on the Internet, from information in the Library of Congress to deliberately misleading information created by hate groups or individuals. As distinguished communications scholar Fred Williams once observed, "Going on the Internet is like going through someone else's trash."

Web Link >>>
Last Page of the Internet
www.1112.net/lastpage.html

There are two contrasting trends taking place on the Internet regarding revenues and accessibility. One trend is a decrease in the costs of software and hardware that makes computers and computer equipment (such as storage devices) cheaper and more powerful than ever before. This is making computers more affordable for people and allowing those in a lower socioeconomic status to buy at least a basic computer and to connect to the Internet.

On the other hand, there is an increasing trend for rising costs of telecommunications services and for web services that have previously been free to move toward partial subscription-based models. This trend of partially free services or content, with payment for what is considered "premium," more valuable content, can also be seen among media companies online, and it is still too early to tell whether these strategies will be successful in generating revenues.

Online media companies are also experimenting with increasingly obtrusive online advertising, such as larger pop-up ad windows or automatic pop-under ads that are changing the look and experience of the Web for users. In the early 1990s there were many debates among users of online discussion groups about whether *any* advertising should even be allowed on the Internet, considering it was created using taxpayers' money. These discussions have been abandoned as advertising has come to be expected on most websites; the discussions have shifted to what

Advertising on the Web has become more obtrusive as companies try to figure out how to earn revenue online.

kinds of ads are most effective, how they can collect data on users, and what Web users are willing to accept. One important issue in this discussion is how fast content can arrive at users' computers, as anything that slows this down affects the user experience with online media.

■ ■ ■ BANDWIDTH

Although former Alaska Senator Ted Stevens famously described the Internet as "a series of tubes," during a debate on **Net neutrality** in 2006, a description that was gleefully mocked for its simplistic description of the Internet, he did at least have a hazy—if misguided—notion of the importance of bandwidth.

Bandwidth is a crucial element for online communication to reach its full potential as a mass medium. Without what is called high-speed, or **broadband**, connections to the Internet, most people online are unable to receive audio or video in real time or at the same quality as they are used to from television or radio. **Narrowband** is the term used for low-bandwidth communications, such as dial-up phone modems. Bandwidth available for Internet service has traditionally been narrowband via dial-up modems, typically delivering anywhere from 28 kilobits to 56 kilobits per second. Video at these narrowband rates is very limited, usually a small window of jerky motion, low-resolution imagery, and only marginally better sound.

In a technical sense, bandwidth refers to the electromagnetic frequency or spectrum available for delivering content. Bell Labs scientist Claude E. Shannon in 1948 provided a precise mathematical definition of bandwidth, defining the capacity of a communications channel in terms of bits per second. A voice phone call, for example, uses about 3,000 hertz (Hz) bandwidth, whereas a telephone modem operating at about 33.6 kilobits per second requires a little more bandwidth, or about 3,200 Hz.[7]

Think of bandwidth not so much as electromagnetic frequency, however, as in terms of how large "the pipe" is that comes to your home delivering data (rather than a physical thing like water). It is not an actual pipe, of course, but a coaxial or fiber-optic cable that has greater or lesser capacity to carry data. If people are able to tap the large "data pipe" directly, then they can access the flow of data at equally high speeds. Sometimes this is called a "fat pipe." However, if their pipe accessing the main pipes is very thin, data will come to them at only a trickle, no matter how fast their personal computer is.

■ ■ ■ TELEPHONE AND CABLE COMPANY BROADBAND SERVICES

One of the great challenges that cable and telecommunication providers have begun to solve in the past decade is the so-called last-mile obstacle (not always literally the last mile, but somewhere from a few hundred yards to more than a mile or so). For more than a decade, many cable and telephone companies have had considerable bandwidth available in their backbone or trunk lines, which are generally fiber-optic lines, but it has not been profitable for them to run the same broadband connectivity over the "last mile" to the end consumer. Verizon FiOS service is one of the first to connect homes directly to a fiber-optic network, giving consumers faster Internet connections than they can get with cable modems or DSL, which is a broadband connection carried over traditional phone lines.

TABLE 3-2
Connection Speeds to the Internet by Carrier Type

CARRIER TECHNOLOGY	SPEED*	PHYSICAL MEDIUM
Dial-up Access	2400 bps to 56 Kbps	Twisted pair (regular phone lines)
ISDN	64 Kbps to 128 Kbps	Twisted pair
Cable	52 Kbps to 512 Kbps	Coaxial cable
ADSL	512 Kbps to 8 Mbps	Twisted pair (used as a digital, broadband medium)
Wireless (LMCS)	2 Mbps or more	Airwaves
Satellite	400 Kbps	Airwaves
T1	1.544 Mbps	Twisted pair, coaxial cable, or optical fiber
T3	44.736 Mbps	Optical fiber

Source: Internet Connection Speed Comparison Chart
*bps = bits per second; Kbps = kilobits per second; Mbps = megabits per second

Cable companies have started to fight back with sometimes inaccurate advertising campaigns touting their Internet connection speeds or the fact that they, too, use fiber-optic networks. That is technically true, though what they fail to mention is that they do not have fiber-optic lines directly to the end user's home, meaning that the "fat pipe" of fiber optic narrows dramatically just before getting to an end user.

There has been increasing competition between telecommunications companies and cable companies in providing broadband services to customers. Today, most consumers can get some type of broadband service, through DSL lines that come through existing telephone wires at higher speeds than typical phone lines, through existing coaxial cable lines that are used to receive cable television signals, or, in the case of Verizon, in some limited markets, through fiber-optic lines directly to the home. Most telecommunication and cable companies in the United States have structured the data flow so that it is faster to download content from the Internet than to upload it, which tends to favor media consumption by Web users rather than media production and distribution by users.

Despite the growth of broadband services in recent years, consumers still have many complaints about both telephone and cable companies regarding service, late or bungled installations, actual connection speeds that are slower than what is promised, and a lack of choice for their broadband provider, as well as high monthly charges. The lack of choice is not a surprise, as cable companies have monopolies in most markets where they operate, and if the local telecommunications company, the only potential competitor for broadband service, does not provide DSL or fiber-optic connections, then the consumer essentially has no choice at all.

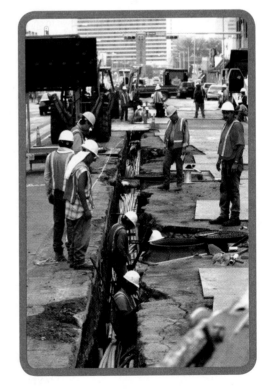

Laying broadband cable the "last mile" to homes will help increase Internet connection speeds.

Broadband connections have been shown to change patterns of Internet use, including making it easier to play video games with others online.

The importance of broadband capability to usage patterns on the Internet may be profound.[8] Research shows that Internet users with broadband access already have substantially different behaviors than when they used dial-up connections. One trend that has been noted is that they are more likely to create and distribute media content than dial-up users, even though upload speeds are still slower than download speeds. Online expenditures more than double for users of broadband services. In 1999, David Clark predicted that broadband Internet would bring "Real-time high-fidelity music, telephone, videoconferencing, television and radio programs... There will be new entertainment options, such as movies-on-demand, and new features, such as the ability to call up information about a movie's director or its actors as they appear on screen. Users will be able to play online games—live— against many contestants scattered around the globe."[9] Although not all of what Clark predicted in 1999 is actually available, most of it is, on broadband connections.

The World of Digital Media

Digital media did not simply spring from the ether, untouched by the existing media environment. Rather, the development of digital media has been influenced by traditional media businesses and the types of media content available, just as it has influenced that content.

Discussing online mass communication means essentially talking about all of mass communication. Today, countless offline mass-communication products, whether print or electronic, also exist in some form online, or the physical product can be bought online. It is unusual today if a newspaper, magazine, recording artist, television network or station, or even individual movie does not have its own website.

Even companies not traditionally involved with mass communication have found that maintaining their own websites is an excellent way to communicate directly to a large audience. For many young people, especially, who are comfortable online, if an organization does not have a website, then for all intents and purposes it does not exist.

The following discussion describes the current state of digital media as well as emerging trends among the major forms of mass communication. In subsequent chapters the history and development of these forms will be explored to show how they have influenced digital media today.

■ ■ ■ DIGITAL PRINT

The printed word was the forerunner, just as it was in the traditional media world, to mass communication online. Technological limitations related to computing power and Internet connection speeds have favored, for much of the history of the Internet, the use of text over audio or video. Although this is changing in recent years as audio and video begin to play more prominent roles on the Internet, text will always continue to be important for web users.

Mobile Telephony in the Developing World

Despite the prevalence of the Internet and personal computers in the United States and other industrialized countries in Europe, South America, and the Asia-Pacific region, an even stronger competitor to the Internet and PC has emerged in the developing world—the mobile phone.

Mobile telephony holds several advantages over the Internet in many developing countries. First, the telecommunications infrastructure in these countries is often in poor condition, making land-line phone calls expensive and sporadic at best for those who have phones.

Without adequate phone lines, let alone consistent electric power, it is nearly impossible to depend on a PC or have regular Internet service, even a dial-up service. Needless to say, many of these countries do not have cable television industry wires, relying instead on satellite transmission of cable content, when allowed by the governments. (In countries like Malaysia, owning a satellite dish is a crime.)

Mobile telephones provide an easy and relatively cheap way for people to communicate with each other, and text messaging allows further mass coordination so that the phone becomes part of a larger, ad hoc mass-communication system.

There are even cases of mobile telephones helping foster a sense of community among phone users. In Nigeria, for example, women generally ran the various market stalls throughout urban areas. By using mobile phones, they were able to easily coordinate prices with each other in different parts of the city. What's more, they recognized that they shared common interests and had common grievances, joining together to try to alleviate some of the problems they faced as sellers in markets.

Digital Books

Digital books offer a variety of advantages over printed books, including permitting the reader to not only read the text but to make electronic annotations and bookmarks, access the content of the book via an interactive table of contents, and search the entire text by keyword. Digital books and their sale online also point to a fundamental issue in the future of how mass-communication industries will derive much if not most of their revenue: from online transactions, or what is called ecommerce.

In the late 1990s, major publishers prepared for a surge in consumer demand for electronic books, and many experimented with the online sale and distribution of digital books. However, after the economic slowdown in 2000 that hit technology and Internet companies particularly hard, and a subsequent slowdown in sales of digital books, publishers started to adopt a slower, more cautious approach.

The launch in 2007 of Amazon's Kindle ebook reader, which stores up to two hundred titles, was heralded as the latest technology breakthrough that may finally be the tipping point toward digital books. Major publishers such as Random

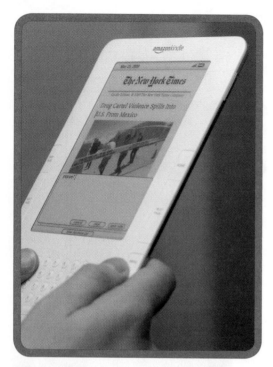

Ebook readers such as Amazon's Kindle promise to change the reading experience.

citizen journalism

Journalism done by amateurs or volunteers, either with citizen journalism websites, blogs, or as part of a mainstream news organization's website.

House, Simon & Schuster, and HarperCollins have embraced ebook readers like Kindle and the Sony Reader, making many more titles available for downloading.

Free sample chapters and other marketing techniques will also likely help aid the growth of digital books, as will improvements in technology such as screen clarity. The growth in digital books, though still minute when compared to traditional publishing sales, has been remarkable, going from $7.3 million in sales in 2003 to $31.8 million in 2007.

Digital Newspapers and Magazines

One notable difference between online and offline newspapers is that the online "newspaper" sites are in direct competition with the leading national "broadcast" and "cable" television news sites. In fact, with growing calls for converged newsrooms and wider broadband access among the general public, newspaper websites increasingly contain audio, multimedia features, and video clips.

Online newspaper sites also face direct competition on a number of other fronts in the online arena, such as blogs, growing numbers of **citizen journalism** websites, and news aggregators like Yahoo! News or Google News that combine news stories from a number of sources.

Advertising, especially classified ads, is another big area in which newspaper companies are threatened by the Internet. Classified ads make up a large portion of advertising revenues for most newspapers, but online classified-ads aggregators can allow people to search far more ads than are usually covered in a newspaper's circulation area. Similarly, users can visit an online auction site like eBay and reach a nationwide group of potential sellers or buyers, communicating with them directly.

There are very few online magazines that were created to be solely online: Slate.com and Salon.com are two of the most prominent ones. However, a growing number of print-based magazines have ceased publishing and moved to online-only versions in response to rising production costs and slowing readership growth.

There are several likely reasons online magazines have fared poorly in the digital world. One of the main reasons is technological: computer screens, especially mobile devices with small screens, still cannot match the clarity of the printed page.

Changing behavior among members of the public in how they consume media is another factor weighing against long-form, text-based narratives like those found in the *New Yorker* or the *Atlantic Monthly*. With greater competition for their attention during the day, people seem less willing to spend the time necessary to read long articles. In an online environment, readers are also more likely to click on hyperlinks to get more information rather than wait for the author to fully explain a point. Likewise, an article may be a starting point for a much more robust discussion among Web users in the form of online discussion groups, further detracting from the controlled narrative of a single author.

However, there could be an important niche for magazines to provide a measure of distance and perspective on issues and to thereby be a voice of authority in their specialized area. If a magazine is perceived as having suitable authority and is respected highly enough by its readers, it seems the public is willing to pay for an online subscription. Consumer Reports Online is one of the few success stories in the online-magazine world, when it comes to subscriptions, with over six hundred thousand subscribers who can access archived articles and reviews on various products.

■ ■ ■ DIGITAL AUDIO

The MP3 file format represents an interesting example of how the new networked digital marketplace could work. It's indicative of how the recording industry will likely sell much of its music in the future, as the recording industry has been at the forefront of dealing with issues of piracy and other threats to traditional media business models. There are few case studies that better highlight the changes digital media are bringing to traditional mass-communication companies.

Some online magazines, such as Slate.com, have proven to be popular despite general declines in reading online.

The MP3 file format is used to compress near-CD-quality audio, which then lets the files, which generally range between 2 and 4 MB in size, be distributed easily over the Internet. There is nothing inherently illegal in the MP3 file format itself; it is simply the technology used to compress audio files.

The problems with the recording industry arise because consumers can copy, download, and distribute music largely for free through file-sharing services. The recording industry has long held that it is acceptable for an individual who purchases a CD to make a copy for personal use, and it is of course not uncommon for friends to exchange copies of music among themselves.

File sharing of online music takes these exchanges to completely new levels, however. At any given time during the day, it is not unusual for millions of users to be on a file-sharing service, exchanging hundreds of millions of files. These are not simply audio, of course, and can include video, text, and images as well, but it would be safe to say most of the files being shared are music files.

The iPod and iPhone have changed the music-listening experience for many consumers.

Peer-to-peer file-sharing systems have been at the core of this phenomenon and have faced the brunt of the recording industry's wrath, though the industry has not been afraid to periodically threaten and even sue its own customers or push institutions like universities to take action in trying to stem the tide of file sharing. The issues surrounding peer-to-peer networking and the public sharing of music online are discussed in more detail in later chapters.

For now, suffice it to say that the major labels and everyone else in the recording-industry value chain are enormously threatened by this development. They lose significant control, and, they say, their profits and investments are being reduced through the piracy of their intellectual property. It was not until 2001 that the major record labels finally began getting into the online music business themselves, even as they maintained their lawsuits against file-swapping services.

Finding new songs and artists you like may become more difficult than ever in the digital age as production and distribution costs decrease, allowing more people to create their own professional-sounding (although not necessarily good) recordings and distribute them digitally. One emerging solution is the use of intelligent agent-based collaborative filtering, a sort of music club for the digital age. Amazon.com and other ecommerce organizations already are making use of collaborative filtering to alert their customers to new books and music that they would likely find appealing, based on previous purchases and the purchasing patterns of people with similar buying tastes.

Radio has traditionally been the main avenue by which songs and artists are promoted. Yet in the digital world, the concept of radio is starting to change as consumers become used to being able to listen to music on demand through **podcasts** or downloaded music. In that way, online "radio" is technically audio programming, not true over-the-air broadcasting, and in some ways will seem much closer to the current state of on-demand online music downloads, even though the term "radio" may stay with us.

podcast
A program that is usually audio or video that lets users easily subscribe, much like subscribing to a blog.

Web radio would seem to offer the best of both worlds—a radio format that provides access to any number of songs whenever a user wants to listen to them— yet a ruling in 2002 by the U.S. Copyright Office declared that webcasters must pay royalties for songs based on the number of their listeners. The ruling forced many webcasters from the Internet, as they could not afford to pay the backdated royalty payments from 1998.

Online radio stations must abide by the **Digital Millennium Copyright Act**, however, which prohibits the advance posting of playlists, which would permit users to plan when to copy songs. Even before the 2002 rulings on royalty payments for webcasts, some online radio stations paid royalties to one of the two music licensers in the United States, the American Society of Composers, Authors and Publishers (ASCAP), or Broadcast Music Inc. (BMI).

digital millennium copyright act
A copyright law in the United States that makes it a criminal act to circumvent or alter digital rights management technologies that protect copyrighted works.

Live transmissions of sports events have emerged as an important part of online radio. In the case of Major League Baseball, Internet users must pay a fee to listen to live audio webcasts of professional baseball games.

Satellite radio, though not technically online, is also competing with traditional radio programming. Largely free of advertising and based on a subscription model, satellite radio offers many specific programs of sports, entertainment, talk radio, and music.

■ ■ ■ DIGITAL VISUAL MEDIA

The Internet has proven a valuable means of distribution for film, especially independent and short films, which have traditionally found distribution to be the most vexing bottleneck in becoming successful. Because independent and short films vary widely in quality and style and are produced outside the mainstream of Hollywood, few theaters, or theater chains, have been interested in showing them. Because of the low cost of online distribution and the potential to build audiences over time and space, a growing number of websites provide an extensive selection of independent and short films online, typically for free viewing.

Digital video has also been a godsend for low-budget directors, who can shoot professional-quality footage at a fraction of what it would cost for actual rolls of film. Editing and other postproduction work can also be done on computers or dedicated editing workstations.

There is a growing variety of sources of video content online, ranging from the popular YouTube to many video-sharing sites cloning the YouTube model. Most television stations and all major networks maintain websites with some or most of their television coverage available for viewing, something not generally seen even ten years ago.

Bandwidth considerations have been the main issue that has hampered wide distribution of video content. However, as more people get broadband access, it is clear that video content will be shared in the same way music has been shared, and the film and video industries have tried to learn the hard lessons from the recording industry in dealing with the potential threat to their business models.

Television stations seem to be taking a more conciliatory approach toward video-sharing sites than the recording industry did with music, though not after some initially negative reactions and demands to remove content. Realizing that YouTube was actually serving a useful function in promoting a network's shows, more networks began allowing clips from shows to be uploaded. In 2008, CBS agreed to have entire shows available on YouTube, no doubt hoping that the YouTube traffic would generate interest among the public to watch the shows on television as well.

Online video has been transformed through video-based sites such as YouTube.

TV/PC Convergence

It is still too early to predict whether the television will absorb the functions of the PC or the PC will adopt more TV-like functions, but either way, what we know today as two separate items (essentially two separate monitors) will merge into one, and in the end it largely will not matter.

That is not to say most households will only have one monitor; it can almost be guaranteed that American households will maintain their multimonitor way of life, just as most have more than one TV today, plus one or more computers. If anything, it is likely that households will have more screens than they do today, as flat-panel monitors become prevalent and are placed on or embedded in walls, refrigerator doors, or other areas in the house that currently do not have screens.

Several factors will play a role in determining which way the convergence goes—toward the PC or toward the TV. Economic decisions can be a major factor, depending on whether computer and television manufacturers, along with media companies, see more profit potential in either device. The type of content and the way the audience interacts with that content will affect how the PC and TV converge. Currently, the PC is far more interactive and requires the user to be far more active than the television, as shown in how we generally refer to people as "computer users" or "television viewers." With computers, users are actively involved in

CONVERGENCE **CULTURE**

A Brief History of Interactive TV

Almost as soon as the TV became a mass medium, people were looking for ways to improve interactivity with the television set. The technology itself does not allow for true interactivity between viewers and media producers. Nevertheless, there have been some notable attempts at interactive TV (ITV), and earlier than you may assume.

The first regularly scheduled television show that encouraged interactivity was called *Winky Dink and You* and was produced for CBS in 1953.[10] It was interactive by inviting children to help the animated character Winky Dink escape from situations (such as being chased by wild animals) by drawing things (like a bridge over a yawning chasm) on a piece of wax paper placed on the screen. The show was short-lived, partly because children frequently failed to put the wax paper up before drawing the bridges, rope, ladder, or whatever else Winky Dink needed, and drew directly on the screen.

Warner Amex's QUBE experiment, the first two-way cable TV system, launched in 1978 in Columbus, Ohio. The interactive video system permitted viewers in their homes to participate in public opinion polls by punching buttons on a device. Warner concluded the experiment in 1984 after winning the local cable franchise and deeming it no longer necessary to continue an expensive showcase experiment to demonstrate their superiority over competing cable companies.

A trial of ITV in the early 1990s by Time Warner in Orlando, Florida, called the Full Service Network, collapsed under its own weight because of high costs and the creation of the World Wide Web, which had interactivity built into it.

After initial enthusiasm for ITV and glowing promises of how it would transform the audience experience, the cable and ITV industries have toned down their rhetoric markedly in recent years, though talk of the promise of ITV is once again on the rise.

Video games such as Wii have added physical activity to the playing experience.

getting information or communicating with other individuals, whereas with traditional television, viewers are largely passive and in fact do not have any way to communicate directly either with other audience members or with media producers.

From a content perspective, already most programs actively promote either their own show or other shows on the network through an increasingly intrusive range of techniques, such as roll-over graphics at the bottom of the screen during programming and a logo in one corner of the screen. Programs also encourage viewers to visit their websites to participate in games, contests, or discussions with other viewers, and sports programs often have trivia questions for viewers to answer via text messaging.

Video games could be the interactive barbarian at the gate to reconceptualizing the television as an interactive media device. Video games, which will be discussed in a mass-communication context in more detail in Chapter 11, are one of the few activities that have transformed the passive television box into an interactive (some say addictive) entertainment center. Computers also allow for games, but television video games such as Nintendo's Wii, Microsoft's Xbox, and Sony's PlayStation are far more popular than computer games. Because the public is now comfortable with using the television as a dual-purpose device (active gaming and passive television viewing), an Internet-connected and interactive television may well be easier for the public to accept than an antenna-ready PC.

If television content is to become more interactive, then devices to interact with on-screen content will have to be revised or wireless keyboards made available. The relatively simple multibutton devices for gaming, or remote controls, do not offer the same level of control and manipulation over content that a mouse offers with a computer, with its ability to select parts of a screen by dragging and clicking, for example. Keyboards will likely remain the primary input device for text for some time, which means they would be necessary for activities like online chat or emails while watching a show. How exactly someone will balance a keyboard in their lap while holding a drink and eating chips while watching a sports game is a matter for engineers and entrepreneurs to ponder.

The type of content that is made available for interactivity will affect how the converged PC/TV of the future is used and thought of. If media companies only

More people today watch TV while using a computer, often having the two nearby each other.

create or encourage interactive content for such programs as game shows or popular programs, then it is likely that interactivity with the "television" will be less than what is done with the "computer."

Screen resolution is important so that text and other detailed graphics that may be interactive can be displayed clearly on a large TV screen. At any rate, the Internet will become more TV-like in how it is presented as broadband becomes more common and video and other multimedia can be shown over the Internet more easily.

The eventual convergence of the PC and TV is not some futuristic fantasy; it is happening today in ways that we often do not realize because it is taking place in small, gradual steps. One simple example is where people place their computers in relation to their televisions. In the early days of desktop computers, the computer was often confined to a little-used room. Today, however, you often see computers near or within easy viewing distance of TVs, and with home Wi-Fi connections TV viewers on the couch can get online with their laptops and be on the Internet while they watch shows. Handheld wireless devices that connect to the Internet are also making the living room couch less relevant as a place to consume media, as people can view or listen to content and play video games with others on a portable device.

Another good example is the role that digital television is playing in merging the TV and PC.

Digital Television: Preparing the Way for Convergence

Although electronic television has always utilized a video display terminal, it has gone through various stages in terms of picture and sound quality. In the first stage (the 1950s), the video display was relatively small, black and white, and with monophonic, low-fidelity sound (i.e., no directionality and not high quality). In the second stage (the 1960s and 1970s), color television and stereophonic sound were developed, greatly increasing the realism of the viewing experience. All the while, the level of resolution of the display was relatively unchanged.

The third stage arrived in 1981, when NHK (Japan Broadcasting Corporation) engineers demonstrated analog **high definition television** (HDTV), calling it Hi-Vision. HDTV was a significant advance because it presents a much higher resolution image, sharper color, a wider aspect ratio, and superior audio. NHK had begun its research on HDTV in 1973, long before the digital revolution was on the global radar screen.

In 1990, General Instrument Corporation proposed an all-digital television system, something initially deemed technically impossible, especially for over-the-air broadcasting. But this proved not to be the case. **Digital television** (DTV) became the accepted global standard for next-generation TV. It is important to note that DTV and HDTV are not the same thing. HDTV as invented by the Japanese was analog in format. DTV was invented in the United States as a response to the Japanese invention of HDTV. HDTV can be digital, and digital TV can be HDTV, but the two were not always synonymous.

Since June 2009, all television broadcast signals in the United States are mandated to be digital. TVs that were not created to receive digital signals must be fitted with digital encoders. TV sets today that are promoted as HDTV are invariably digital as well.

high definition television (HDTV)
....
Television with a much higher resolution image and sharper image than a standard television signal.

digital television
....
Television signals that are transmitted digitally rather than over-the-air, as in analog television broadcasting. Digital TV provides better picture and sound quality and has greater capabilities to include interactive functions than analog television.

■ ■ ■ WHY DTV MATTERS IN MASS COMMUNICATION

In comparison to analog TV, digital TV provides higher-resolution video images, better color, and digital sound. HDTV offers even higher resolution and a wider aspect ratio (more cinematic wide screen). These advantages make it possible to use DTV or HDTV effectively in the presentation of text. Prior television displays were too low in resolution to effectively permit text for reading.

DTV is more important than HDTV from the point of view of media programming. Digital TV enables the convergence of computing, television, and telecommunications and brings the possibility of interactivity. This means that with DTV new storytelling techniques are possible, as well as the ability to link to **multicast** (also known as multiplex), which means simultaneously transmitting multiple channels of compressed content, or in some cases the same content but at different times. DTV brings possible functions to the television set that have been used in recent years on computers and the Web, taking yet another step toward converging the TV and PC.

multicast
....
Simultaneously transmitting multiple channels of compressed digital content over the television airwaves.

■ ■ ■ CAPABILITIES OF DTV

DTV has many capabilities simply not possible with analog television. They make possible a wide variety of creative options for novel program formats. They also enable more user control and navigation through the video, including video delivered on demand. Among the opportunities are the following:

- Enhanced TV, seamless linking of video to the Internet and Web.
- Viewer control of camera angles, allowing the viewer to use a remote control or voice command to pan, tilt, or zoom through 360-degree still or full-motion video to look around a scene.
- Object-oriented multimedia, or layering interactive objects into a motion video the way objects are incorporated into today's static websites. This is an important capability that will permit digital TV programs to include embedded information graphics in the news, commercial product placements in entertainment programming, and pointers to related websites.
- Meta–data manipulation, which allows producers to process any of the digital objects in the video and use the data for purposes of analysis, for example.
- Three-dimensional video, graphics, and animations that allow the viewer to explore an entire scene or virtual location using a remote control, mouse, or even voice command.

New technologies allow for interesting effects in news stories, such as 3D perspectives.

Technology of course is not the only factor that will affect the development of DTV; media economics have already played an important role and will continue to do so, just as with other types of media.

Digital Media Economics

Traditionally, media enterprises, like other industrial-age businesses, required heavy capital investment. Capital was required to build the transmission towers for television and radio stations. It was required to buy printing presses and to build cable systems. Not only was the infrastructure expensive, but it created enormous barriers to entry for prospective competition.

In the digital age, these rules are changing. Some of the most significant barriers to entry are shrinking. Capital costs are reduced, as almost anyone who is online can create a website and potentially compete with established media companies. It is part of why relative newcomers such as Google, Yahoo!, and Craigslist have been so successful. Moreover, few media enterprises have found a formula for making profits in the online world, as most people seem unwilling to pay for content and traditional advertising has not been very effective.

Most large online media outlets have the backing of traditional media companies, such as MSNBC.com, a joint venture between NBC and Microsoft, or CNBC.com. With advertising and other revenues generated from the parent companies, these online endeavors can afford to take losses for a while as online revenue models are tried and tested. Many smaller, independent dot-com media companies were not so fortunate, especially after the economy and stock market spiralled downward from spring 2000. Some severely scaled back their business plans, and others, such as award-winning crime-news website APBnews.com, went out of business.

■ ■ ■ THE OPEN-SOURCE MOVEMENT

One of the biggest challenges to the usual business models has come from the open-source movement. The open-source, or free-software, movement began with creating software and programs that were freely available for anyone to use. Further, the source code, or code that created the programs, was purposely left accessible so others could tinker with it and improve the program, sharing it with yet more people to do the same. This was the spirit of community and sharing on nonmarket principles that embodied the early development of computers and the Internet.

Today, the public benefits from a range of high-quality open-source software, most available for free or at a fraction of the cost of similar software. The operating system Linux is one example, as is OpenOffice, the software suite that includes word-processing, spreadsheet, database, presentation, and drawing software. With capabilities that rival if not surpass what Microsoft Office offers, it has the added advantage of being free to download and without the requirement for subsequent purchases of updates or new releases, as they are free as well.

The notions of the open-source movement have moved to content production as well, with Wikipedia being a prime example of how many volunteers can come together on their own and create something far grander than any individual or smaller group could create, all for no monetary compensation. The logic seems to defy explanation in an economic system that has been based on producing commodities (including media) that are bought and sold, yet it has become a powerful competitive force for mainstream computer makers and for media companies.

For example, some countries have adopted OpenOffice as the standard office-suite software for all government agencies, which can easily lead large-scale organizations such as educational institutions to also adopt OpenOffice in order to have compatible file types when communicating with the government agencies that oversee them. This of course is a threat to Microsoft's business model of selling its proprietary software Microsoft Office and then charging customers for periodic updates. In order to counter OpenOffice, Microsoft has provided computers (loaded with Microsoft Office, of course) free to libraries in some developing countries. The hope is that once people become familiar with a certain type of software, they will be reluctant to switch. Microsoft, with its billions of dollars in revenues, can take a small loss initially in giving away computers with the goal of attracting long-term customers.

For media companies such as Encyclopaedia Britannica or Microsoft's now-defunct Encarta, an open-source encyclopedia free for anyone to use was a direct threat to their subscription business model. Of course, the open-source challenger would have to be as accurate and have the same high quality as the products that a person would normally pay for. As mentioned in the previous chapter, this has not been an issue by and large with Wikipedia, where the self-correcting mechanisms of many volunteers working together have helped make it a dynamic and relevant source of information.

■ ■ ■ REVENUE MODELS FOR DIGITAL MEDIA

One of the most significant challenges all online media properties face is building a revenue stream to not only cover costs but to return a profit. There are several ways online media companies can generate revenues—at least in theory. These include traditional methods such as advertising, subscriptions, and syndication, as well as methods that are either unique or feasible in an online environment, such as ecommerce or joint offline and online activities. However, none so far have proven to be inherently better than other methods, and dot-com companies as well as online media companies are still experimenting with ways to earn profits. It is likely that more advanced technology will open the door to creative revenue-generating models that are unavailable today.

For the time being, the revenue streams that appear most viable for content sites involve a combination of advertising, subscription, ecommerce, and leveraging content in partnerships online and offline.

Advertising

Traditional banner advertising has proved disappointing in generating revenues for all but the largest sites that attract millions of visitors. Media companies both offline and online charge advertisers for the cost per thousand (**CPM**) of audience members. This means a magazine with a circulation of one hundred thousand can receive more for carrying ads than a magazine with a circulation of ten thousand.

Banner ads still exist but have largely been superseded by other types of ads. A **banner ad** is one that sits at the top or along the side of a web page. They have had a history of very low **click-through rates**, or the rate in which people click on the ad.

In the online media environment, technology allows website owners to not only see exactly how many people have visited a given page on the site, but to track whether people clicked on the advertisement on that page or not. When advertisers are able to see how low the click-through rates are, they question the effectiveness of the ads in attracting customers.

Online companies have tried a number of things to improve click-through rates on ads and thereby increase revenues. Larger ads, animated ads, and pop-up and pop-under ads have all been tried. Some show slightly higher click-through rates than static banner ads, but they also run the risk of annoying Web users who

CPM
Cost per thousand. The standard unit for measuring advertising rates for publications, based on circulation.

banner ad
An advertisement across the top or along the side of a website, and the original form of advertising on the Web.

click-through rate
Rate in which people click on the ad.

do not want to have to click "close" on a number of ads just to get to the content they initially wanted.

Search engine advertising has become the most important form of advertising on the Web, and the most successful. Based on the fact that people increasingly go to search engines such as Google as the first place to start looking for content, the placement on a search-results page can be the difference between success and failure for a company. **Search engine marketing** (SEM) involves paying a search engine to have a listing in a specific part of a search-results page, while **search engine optimization** (SEO) uses careful keyword choices, site design, and linking strategies to get a site listed higher in a search engine's ranking.

Subscriptions

The most successful revenue-producing media sites have been those that have carved out an important content niche, produced original, quality content, and designed an effective, efficient online presence—and charged a subscription for their site. The two best examples are The Wall Street Journal Interactive and Consumer Reports Online. Consumer Reports Online provides all the content from its well-known magazine, plus additional customizable information and reports on product testing and ratings. With a fee of less than fifty dollars a year, Consumer Reports Online has captured over six hundred thousand paid subscribers. This is only a fraction of its 3 million paid subscribers to the printed magazine, but it is nevertheless a significant number and revenue stream (nearly $30 million a year).

Most other sites that have tried subscription models, however, have not been as successful. Even the esteemed *New York Times* failed in its experiment with a partial subscription model, its Times Select product, in which op-ed columnists could not be accessed unless a subscription fee was paid. This essentially quarantined some of the most popular content of its online newspaper, and after two years the *Times* announced it was abandoning Times Select. The *Times* still does charge for archived content, however, something many other magazine and newspaper sites do as well. This partial subscription model is being tried by a number of online media companies as they look for what types of content the public is willing to pay for in a medium that started out with, and still has, most of its information available for free.

Ecommerce

Ecommerce refers to the electronic commercial environment that emerged in the 1990s, primarily on the Internet. Although the potential of ecommerce was likely overhyped in the late 1990s, it could be argued that it has likewise been looked at overly skeptically in the post-dot-com-boom era.

Yet, ecommerce presents an interesting opportunity in the long run for media businesses operating in the digital age. The online arena is an environment in which consumers can not only get information about products on demand, but, conversely, media and other organizations can deliver promotional messages specifically targeted to individuals based on their online profiles. In many cases consumers can also purchase those products or services and even have them delivered digitally via the Internet, as is the case for music, computer software, digital books, video games, and some other products. Those that can't be delivered electronically are mostly shipped via commercial delivery services anywhere in the world.

A major issue for online media organizations is how to provide a secure environment for payments in online transactions. Something else online media orga-

search engine marketing (SEM)
....
Paying a search engine such as Google to have a listing appear prominently when searched.

search engine optimization (SEO)
....
A strategy that utilizes website design, careful choice of keywords, links, and other techniques to show prominently in online searches.

Web Link >>>
The Wall Street Journal Interactive
www.wsj.com

Web Link >>>
Consumer Reports Online
www.consumerreports.org/

nizations must consider when venturing into ecommerce is maintaining viewer trust in their content by disclosing potential conflicts of interest or even the appearance of conflicts of interest.

For example, an online magazine may have a book review on its site, along with a link to online bookseller Amazon.com. It would seem to be a convenient way for a reader who likes the review to buy the book, and it is. However, if the website is an "affiliate member" of Amazon, a common program in which a member receives a commission on each book sold if consumers come to Amazon through a link on the member's site, then the website's or reviewer's journalistic objectivity could be called into question. It is in their best financial interest to get people to buy that book, making it appear less likely that a reviewer would give a negative review or write reviews on books that might not sell very well. This kind of behavior, for which several large media organizations have been called to task in the past several years, further erodes public trust in content produced by media companies.

Related to making ecommerce successful is that media companies must show a willingness to surrender some of the control they have had over packaging media content. Allowing customers to buy individual songs rather than an entire CD is one simple example of something recording labels showed remarkable resistance to until recently. Allowing a good deal more "try before you buy" free trial samples, such as Kindle's free book chapters, is another business practice that will have to be encouraged for online customers. Eventually, some publishers may even be willing to allow customers to create their own books by combining the essays of a favorite author, for example, or putting book themes together. By encouraging promotion of such user-created books (yet while still providing royalties to authors), publishers may find that some of their readers have a better sense of how to tap into popular tastes than the companies themselves.

· ·

LOOKING BACK AND MOVING FORWARD

Broadband digital media present both an opportunity and a threat for those in the media and communication industries. On the one hand, long-standing corporations, institutions, and entire industries are being turned upside down by the digital revolution. Businesses built on analog technologies of production and distribution are trying to figure out how to adapt in the digital age. New efficiencies of creating and delivering content in a digital, networked environment are emerging throughout the world. Long-held, highly profitable business models based on the analog world are less viable in a digital marketplace.

Yet, uncertainty prevails in the largely digital world. Converting to digital production and distribution costs a lot of money, and the returns are not guaranteed. No wonder so many executives in the media business are nervous about digitization choice and change.

Nevertheless, the new digital world means new business opportunities. It means opening new markets that formerly were restricted by political, economic, and geographic boundaries. It means new storytelling formats that bring true interactivity to television and radio. It means creating immersive audio and video on demand for consumers who want their media, in all its forms, customized not only according to their preferences but to their current geographic location and many other factors.

Overall, the digitization of television and radio means an expansion of the business pie. In other words, the size of the marketplace is growing, which means extraordinary business opportunities for those brave enough, talented enough, and persistent enough to enter the fray in a creative manner. Established businesses face the additional hurdle of their own entrenched corporate culture that insists on placing a priority on protecting existing business interests. This shortsighted thinking opens new opportunities for entrepreneurial start-ups nimble enough to adapt to an uncertain and rapidly changing marketplace.

As some open-source advocates are discovering, profits do not necessarily have to come from the sale of packaged media products such as books. Seth Godin, a noted author on Internet advertising and marketing, makes his books freely available for download on the Internet. This would appear to be the fast track to the poorhouse, but Godin's success stems from the fact that his strategy helps get his book in the hands of many influential people, including business leaders and conference organizers for business leaders, who then invite him (and pay him) to speak at events and conferences.

Other potential business models exist besides actually selling a media product. The media product becomes the focal point or thing that generates interest among an audience, and through partnership or licensing deals, syndication, or ancillary product sales based on the media product, one is able to generate revenues.

The conflict between open-source philosophies in the realm of cultural production and proprietary business models based on traditional, industrial-era models of media production is one of the main ideological struggles on the Internet today. At stake are notions of intellectual property protection, the availability of cultural material in the public domain, and the future of the audience as either passive media consumers with limited choices or active produsers in a vibrant, interactive community.

The issue is complex, as even open-source proponents acknowledge that people and organizations must generate income in order to survive. At the heart of the debate, however, is how exactly these revenues will be generated. Will media companies try to force traditional ways of making money on consumers in the digital and online realms, or will they adapt to the various possibilities that could be explored and that may better suit the unique nature of digital media?

. . . .

DISCUSSION QUESTIONS

1. If electrical power were to go out, shutting down all computers, which mass media type would be most likely to be able to keep operating, if any? Why?

2. If online news websites merged into combined newspaper/radio/television news stations or channels, which group do you think would be better prepared to learn new skills—print journalists learning broadcast skills or broadcast journalists learning print skills? Why do you think so?

3. What are the primary reasons the recording industry is so threatened by file-sharing services? Are their reasons justified?

4. What open-source software do you use? Where did you first hear about it? Why did you decide to try it? Why do you still use it?

5. Which revenue models have the most potential to be successful for digital media? Why?

6. Try to create the perfect media/technology company by taking units from various existing companies. What would the strengths and weaknesses of your company be? How could you enhance the strengths and reduce the weaknesses?

7. Describe your vision of how the media world will be for most consumers five years from now. Discuss audience behavior, expectations, media industries, and the ways people will access media content.

FURTHER READING

Convergence Culture: Where Old and New Media Collide; Henry Jenkins (2008) NYU Press.

New Media Old Media: A History and Theory Reader, Wendy Hui Kyong Chun and Thomas Keenan (2007) Taylor & Francis.

Wikinomics: How Mass Collaboration Changes Everything; Don Tapscott and Anthony Williams (2008) Portfolio Hardcover.

The Wealth of Networks: How Social Production Transforms Markets and Freedom; Yochai Benkler (2007) Yale University Press.

Bodies in Code: Interfaces with Digital Media; Mark Hansen (2007) Routledge.

Infotopia: How Many Minds Produce Knowledge; Cass Sunstein (2007) Oxford University Press.

Unspun: Key Concepts for Understanding the World Wide Web; Thomas Swiss (ed.) (2001) New York University Press.

The Digital Dialectic: New Essays on New Media; Peter Lunenfeld (2000) MIT Press.

MEDIA QUIZ ANSWERS

1. False.

2. No, because it is considered a mechanism and not just speech.

3. Yes.

4. False.

5. It is still an open question that is being debated in the courts.

6. False.

7. Hyper text transfer protocol.

8. True.

9. Any number of possibilities—Tivo, cell phones, the Internet, MP3 downloads, etc.

10. Less secure than broadband.

Print Media: Books, Newspapers, and Magazines

CHAPTER OBJECTIVES

In this chapter we will:

- Identify print media: books, newspapers, magazines.

- Describe functions of print media.

- Review the historical foundation and evolution of print media.

- Outline readership and distribution patterns of print media, including book sales and newspaper and magazine circulation.

- Identify forces—including political, cultural, economic, technological—that have shaped development of print media.

- Describe content characteristics of print media.

4 *GOOD* magazine, with the tagline "for people who give a damn," puts its money where its mouth is. Founded in 2006 by Ben Goldhirsh when he was twenty-six years old, staffed entirely by friends and former classmates of Goldhirsh rather than by established magazine editors and journalists, the magazine was meant to speak to an audience of young people who cared about the world but who did not feel like thought-leader magazines like the *Economist* or the *New Yorker* really spoke to them.

GOOD magazine targets the so-called millennial generation with snappy writing on a range of social, political, and pop-culture issues and eye-catching graphics and illustrations. In one issue it compared the largest corporate donors to the Obama and McCain presidential campaigns by decking out line drawings of the candidates in suits covered with racing-driver logos.

GOOD magazine's unique subscription model got it noticed by the media, even as others in the magazine industry tended to dismiss its chances of success. All subscription revenues are donated to one of several charities from which the subscriber can choose, and after two years of publishing, *GOOD* had raised over $850,000 for various charities.

Goldhirsh's idealism that a company can both be profitable and have a social conscience, and his willingness to sink money into the venture, was helped by the fact that as son of Bernie Goldhirsh, founder of *Inc.* magazine, he had inherited a fortune after Bernie's death from cancer in 2003—only four years after his mother also died of cancer.

Ben also inherited his father's desire to make the world a better place. When Bernie sold *Inc.* magazine, he gave $20 million to his employees and used $50 million to establish the Goldhirsh Foundation.

Although it is still too early to tell whether *GOOD* magazine will be one of the small minority of magazines that survive past their first five years, Goldhirsh has made the magazine only one part of the larger *GOOD* business that organizes events (entry cost for some events is a subscription to *GOOD* magazine) and produces videos in partnership with community organizations and individuals who also "give a damn" and want to see the world become a better place—while still being able to make a living.

the High Tech / Low Tech issue   it's all true

GOOD

THE OLDEST PROFESSIO
GET A SECOND LIFE 76
L.A.'S URBAN
CATASTROPHE 102
ALSO
POSTAL MULES / STEPHEN COLBERT / MA
MIRANDA JULY / EGYPTIAN HEAVY METAL
STUDENT DEBT / AL-QAEDA'S PR / and MO

This man predicts the future (correctly)

How game theory can tell us who the next president will be, if we'll bomb Iran, and the outcome of other world events

COOL
007 GADGETS
INSIDE!

GOOD is for people who give a damn. It's an entertaining magazine about things that matter. Find out more: GOODMAGAZINE.COM

Issue
Nov/Dec
$4.95 U.

Shelves full of books, racks brimming with magazines, and newsstands overflowing with newspapers are familiar to generations of people the world over. Yet print media are undergoing momentous changes as they move from analog to digital form, emerging transformed in the online world of the Internet and World Wide Web. This chapter examines the history, traditions, and business of print media and touches on some of the changes brought by the digital age.

Print media represent the foundation, the beginning of the system of mass communication. Their origins lie in the "typographical era" of the Middle Ages. The rise of mass forms of mechanical printing and typography played a role in sweeping social change in Europe, including mass literacy and the Renaissance. The advent of print media challenged society in its ability to adapt to technological change, just as modern society is struggling to adapt to the change brought about by digital media today.

Some scholars, such as noted communication scholar **Marshall McLuhan**, even claim that reading printed words has changed the way we think. Reading, as opposed to viewing or listening, lets us ponder what the author is saying; we can go back and reread and think about passages of text and develop arguments for or against points that are made, in ways that we simply cannot do when watching someone speak or listening to them. The format of the printed word, some scholars claim, helps us develop solid critical-thinking skills and teaches us how to build arguments using logic. It is interesting to consider how electronic media and, especially today, the Internet could be affecting our thinking just as much. What McLuhan wrote about electronic media in 1962 in *The Gutenberg Galaxy* could equally be applied to the effect of digital media: "We are today as far into the electric age as the Elizabethans had advanced into the typographical and mechanical age. And we are experiencing the same confusions and indecisions which they had felt when living simultaneously in two contrasted forms of society and experience."

Marshall McLuhan
....
A communication scholar who
wrote Understanding Media and
The Gutenberg Galaxy, among
other books. He is perhaps
most famous for creating the
"global village" metaphor
regarding electronic media and
his often-misunderstood phrase
"the medium is the message."

Print Media and Their Functions

Although young people may spend more time watching television, listening to recorded music, or playing video games than reading, print media still hold a special place in the lives of many people. Reading is the basic building block for literacy, whether analog or digital. By age five or six, most children can already read begin-

Print Media

1. What was the last book you read for pleasure? What made you decide to read it?
2. Where did you buy your latest book that was not a textbook?
3. What is the oldest book you own?
4. Did you read a print newspaper today? If so, describe at least one story from the front page.
5. Compare the print version of your local newspaper with its online version. Are there stories found in one format but not the other?
6. Did you read any news today from a website? If so, describe at least one story.
7. Do you subscribe to any magazines? Which ones?
8. If you subscribe to a magazine, describe how you typically read it. For example, do you read some sections first and jump around, or cover-to-cover? Do you read it over a month, or soon after getting it?
9. What do these reading patterns say about your relationship with the magazine?
10. What makes you decide to print out an article you read online rather than read it on the screen?

ner books. Print media continue to play a central role in the lives of vast numbers of Americans, whether for entertainment, education, or escape.

However, there have been some studies in recent years that show a marked drop in reading among the American public, with fewer than half of American adults saying they read literature. The steepest decline in reading literature is among young people, although reading has declined across all age groups.[1]

Print media, in the form of books, newspapers, and magazines, serve many functions in society. Among the most important are the transmission of culture from generation to generation, the diffusion of ideas and knowledge, and entertainment.

■■■ TRANSMISSION OF CULTURE

From childhood on, people learn the language, values, and traditions of a culture from all types of media. Although not the sole means of transmitting culture, books, newspapers, and magazines teach what is considered right or wrong in a society, what is socially acceptable and what is unacceptable. Immigrants often learn about the rules and norms of a society from reading. In learning how to read, children absorb the basic principles and practices of a culture. On a grander scale, consider the lasting impact of ancient religious texts such as the *Bible, Koran*, or *Torah* in imparting cultural mores and values.

■■■ DIFFUSION OF IDEAS AND KNOWLEDGE

An important part of the transmission of culture is education. Books lay the foundation for formal education and are central to many people's lifelong continuing

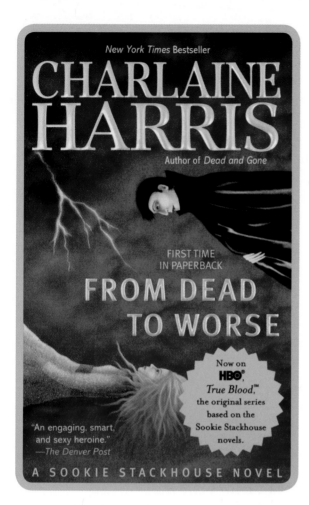

Books have long been a main source of entertainment for the reading public.

education, formal and informal. Textbooks and other works of nonfiction impart everything from scientific knowledge to psychological self-help. Books teach not only how to do things, but explain what is known about the arts, literature, history, contemporary society, and social and natural sciences.

Newspapers and magazines keep us informed of the latest events and offer interpretations of those events in order to help us make sense of the world. We read about new discoveries, fashions, trends, and other parts of the world through newspapers and magazines. Special-interest magazines give us knowledge of specific fields or hobbies and help us connect with others who share our interests.

Print media can teach both knowledge and values, and often the two are intertwined. Even textbooks, which are supposed to primarily impart knowledge, can also transfer values, as much by what they omit as by what they contain. Consider the debates in some states in the United States about whether to include both evolution and creationism in high-school science textbooks. Or examine the vocal criticisms Japan faces from China and Korea when Japanese history textbooks either ignore or euphemize Japan's military atrocities during World War II.

■ ■ ■ ENTERTAINMENT

Whether you find reading this book a pleasure or not, reading is often done purely for the joy it provides. Reading can offer escape or diversion, and millions of readers travel to exotic places or faraway planets, or experience fantastic creatures and memorable characters, all through the printed page.

Just because something is read primarily for entertainment does not mean that it also cannot impart knowledge to the reader at the same time. We can gain access to what the ancients thought through their books, often making connections across centuries as we find commonalities in the human condition. Great literature can elevate our senses and make us feel new emotions as memorable characters come to life. Readers who may not otherwise know or care how our legal system works, or what it is like to be in military intelligence, nevertheless can learn a lot when they read legal thrillers such as *The Firm* by John Grisham or military action stories such as *The Hunt for Red October* by Tom Clancy.

Even books written for entertainment can cause controversy because of cultural values they supposedly do or do not impart. Some have criticized the Harry Potter children's book series, written by J. K. Rowling, for not featuring stronger female characters in central roles, and others have said the books promote witchcraft.

Historical Development of Books

Since the Sumerians of 3500 BCE pressed marks into wet clay tablets to create what some scholars consider the first form of books, authors have been writing long-form text narratives to record and convey their ideas in packages more portable than clay tablets. By 2500 BCE writers in western Asia were using animal skins to publish books in scroll form. The ancient Egyptians wrote the *Book of the Dead* in 1800 BCE on papyrus. Between the first century BCE and the sixth century CE the **codex**, or manuscript made of bound individual pages, began replacing the scroll-form book and established the modern book form. Book publishing continued to evolve, with block printing invented in China by 600 CE; movable copper-alloy type invented in Korea in 1234; and the Western world's first mechanical printing press in Germany in 1455. The portability of books and their wider distribution after the development of printing gave rise to the earliest form of mass media. Books have had profound effects on culture and society in disseminating new ideas and building a common body of knowledge that can be shared across generations.

codex

A manuscript book of individually bound pages.

Korean copper-alloy type was the first printing to use metal plates, hundreds of years before Gutenberg's European press.

■■■ MONASTIC SCRIBES

Until the invention of printing, books had to be laboriously copied by hand. In the Middle Ages, this work was done by specially trained monks called scribes, who worked in monastic scriptoria, or writing rooms. Scribes copied religious and classical works, and work in a scriptorium was considered an important task dedicated to promoting the ideas of the Catholic Church. Many of the books published in the Middle Ages were written in beautiful calligraphy and are richly illustrated.

Early books were published in scroll format, but eventually the codex, or bound manuscript, replaced scrolls. Until paper arrived from China via the Middle East in the later Middle Ages, scribes wrote on parchment or vellum, which were specially treated hides of goats, sheep, or calves. Copying and illustrating books by hand was extremely time-consuming and creating parchment was expensive, so books were generally not widespread before the end of the Middle Ages.

■■■ JOHANNES GUTENBERG

As the Christian Church grew in Europe, the need for religious texts grew as well. It was out of this need that **Johannes Gutenberg** found his inspiration for the invention of printing with lead, using movable type, in 1455 CE in Mainz, Germany. Gutenberg's invention employed oil-based ink on paper using a converted wine press.

Johannes Gutenberg was born to one of the region's patrician families about 1400 and died about 1468 in Mainz, Germany. Gutenberg met the silversmith Waldvogel in Avignon in 1444, who taught the craft of "artificial writing," as early printmaking was called. In 1450, Gutenberg formed a partnership with the wealthy Mainz burgher Johann Fust, in order to complete his own printing invention and to print the famous Gutenberg "forty-two-line Bible." The publication of the **Gutenberg Bible** in 1455 is considered the beginning of mechanical printing.[2]

In the early years of printing, illustrators embellished printed pages with drawings and artistic flourishes in order to more accurately represent handwritten manuscripts. By combining a printing press with existing technology such as book binding, it was possible to begin the mass production of books at a fraction of the time and cost it took to produce an equal number of hand-copied books. The printing press spread rapidly and was initially met with enthusiastic reception by the church and in the centers of culture throughout Europe.

Johannes Gutenberg

German printer credited with creating the first mechanical printing press in Europe in 1455.

Gutenberg Bible

One of a handful of surviving Bibles printed by Johannes Gutenberg; considered the first mechanically printed works in Europe.

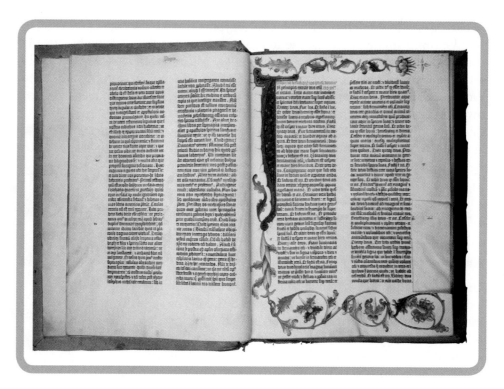

The Gutenberg Bible, like most books of the period, had lavish hand-colored illustrations alongside the printed text.

■ ■ ■ BEGINNINGS OF MASS COMMUNICATION AND MASS LITERACY

The printing press had an important role in the growth of Renaissance culture, the sharing of scientific discoveries, and the spread of religious beliefs—some of which challenged the authority of the Catholic Church. The availability of greater numbers of books and other printed materials helped increase literacy among the populace and laid the foundation for the rise of mass communication in the Western world. Many books, especially scientific works, were printed in Latin, which effectively reduced readership to elites who were educated in the classics. Books and other material such as broadsheets printed in the local vernacular usually found a much wider audience. Books had left the quiet monastic scriptoria and entered the bustling commercial world of printmakers and the average person.

Despite a greater number of books and printed materials from the Renaissance onwards, large numbers of Europeans and Americans remained illiterate until the nineteenth century. In the American colonial era and early years of the United States, education was available largely to the wealthy, who could afford to hire and house private tutors for their children. Increased public education in the early 1800s helped reduce illiteracy among the general populace, and textbooks played a crucial role in the public education system.

One of the first textbooks published in America was the *New England Primer*, published initially in about 1690 by Benjamin Harris. The textbook introduced children to the English alphabet, the rudiments of reading, and basic Christian religious values.

Noah Webster, known today for his *Webster's Dictionary*, wrote his 1783 textbook, *A Grammatical Institute of the English Language*, as a reaction to the textbooks imported from England that were commonly used and that taught English cultural

Noah Webster is most famous for his dictionary, but he also published a grammatical textbook widely used throughout much of the nineteenth century.

values. Known popularly as the "Blue Back Speller," Webster's textbook provided tutorials on language, religion, morals, and domestic economy. McGuffey Readers, first published in 1836, became standard reading books for schoolchildren throughout the nineteenth century.

Textbooks of the 1800s often reflected the power structure of contemporary society, just as modern textbooks do. In order to appeal to the widest cross-section of society, textbooks generally avoid controversial subjects and embrace perspectives and bodies of knowledge in which there is general agreement among members of the dominant group.

■ ■ ■ CHEAPER AND SMALLER BOOKS

Changes in technology since Gutenberg's time have radically altered the production and printing of books. However, the very same forces that helped drive the invention of the printing press—wider distribution of printed materials and lower cost to produce books—have continued to play major roles in successful publishing ever since 1455. To some extent, books entering the digital realm can be seen as a continuation of these same historical forces on publishing.

One way to make money publishing is to publish a book that many people want to buy and read, which usually means publishing books that entertain people. Another way is to make the book affordable enough for many people to buy (with the assumption that it is also something that people will want to read). The invention of the dime novel and later the creation of mass-market paperbacks satisfied both these criteria.

dime novel
....
The first paperback book form, which cost ten cents. This made it accessible even to the poor.

Dime Novels

The **dime novel** was the first paperback book form and, as its name suggests, sold for ten cents. This made it accessible even to the poor. Introduced in 1860 by Irwin P. Beadle & Company, the dime novel initially featured stories of Indians and pioneer tales that were often nationalistic in tone. Ann S. Stephens wrote the first dime novel, *Malaeska: The Indian Wife of the White Hunter*. Within a year of publication, *Malaeska* sold more than three hundred thousand copies. The 1870s saw an expansion of dime novels to include melodramatic fiction, adventures, detective stories, romances, and rags-to-riches tales.

Mass-Market Paperbacks

Mass-market paperbacks were introduced in the United States in 1939 by Robert de Graff's company Pocket Books. Pocket Books, with its familiar kangaroo mascot, Gertrude, published a line of plastic-laminated books priced at twenty-five cents each that were small enough to be carried in a back pocket. It ushered in the paperback revolution by offering books to the public in places like drugstores and supermarkets, an alternative mass-distribution network to established bookstores.

The post–World War II baby boomers who became the students of the 1950s and '60s were dubbed "the

Dime novels were the nineteenth-century equivalent of the paperback novel, making stories more accessible to the public.

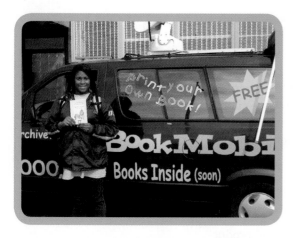

The Internet Archive's Bookmobile is an example of how print on demand can bring a huge variety of books to communities that do not have easy access to them.

paperback generation." They were raised on Dr. Benjamin Spock's popular best-selling paperback, *Dr. Spock's Baby and Child Care,* and influenced by paperback copies of J. D. Salinger's *Catcher in the Rye* and Kurt Vonnegut's *Slaughterhouse Five.*

Print-on-Demand

One interesting development in printing that began in the late 1990s is print-on-demand (POD). POD employs low-cost technology to enable writers to publish using printers who specialize in the technology and to have their paperback books available online or even in some bookstores. High-quality color laser printing and binding machines can print a book in a few minutes at a fraction of the cost it would take for a traditional print run.

The combination of low-cost, digital, online technologies may release a flood of POD authors publishing their own books in the twenty-first century. A growing number of POD publishers, such as Xlibris, Virtual Bookworm, and Lulu Publishing, let authors publish their books for as little as four hundred dollars. Even more importantly, POD can bring to readers a range of books cheaply that otherwise may be out of print or hard to obtain.

In 2002 the Internet Archive, a group dedicated to digitizing and archiving all kinds of media, started the Internet Bookmobile, consisting of a Ford minivan with a computer and POD printer in the back. It tours various cities, giving people access to over twenty thousand public domain books in its digital archive, all available on the spot and in a matter of minutes for a fraction of the cost of similar books sold in bookstores.

Three Major Trends in Today's Book Industry

Books are part of a global publishing industry. In 2007, the book-publishing industry's annual U.S. sales volume was $37 billion, about a 4.4 percent increase from the previous year.[3] As a result of the enormity of this market, there has been tremendous consolidation of ownership in the book-publishing industry worldwide, which has significant repercussions for the diversity of book titles and perspectives that are published.

There are at least three significant trends affecting the business of book publishing. First, mergers and consolidation in the industry enable publishers to reduce operating costs, including the costs associated with warehousing titles, marketing, and sales, and thus increase profit margins. Size also gives the book-publishing giants more leverage in negotiations on terms with retail giants such as Barnes & Noble and Amazon.com, who dominate the industry. Such negotiations include obtaining good display locations in bookstores and on the Web.

Second, the book-publishing industry is intertwined with the global media and the entertainment industry. All of the biggest publishers have an increasingly large part of their profits in selling technology products and services, such as electronic databases or educational-testing services, rather than only selling printed books. Likewise, some books are published and subsequently produced as motion pictures or made-for-television movies or miniseries, from Mary Wollstonecraft Shelley's *Frankenstein* (written in 1818 and made into movies many times) to

Education for All 2015

INTERNATIONAL PERSPECTIVES

In countries with literacy rates that approach 100 percent, it is hard for people to understand the devastating effect that illiteracy can have on a country's development. Without even basic literacy skills, large swaths of the population remain trapped in cycles of poverty, unable to participate in larger public discussions that take place in the pages of newspapers or magazines, or to better their lives through reading books and educating themselves. Furthermore, the public becomes easy to manipulate by cynical leaders who use easy-to-understand catchphrases or slogans to garner support from the uneducated masses.

UNESCO estimates that there are 774 million adults worldwide who lack basic literacy skills, and 64 percent of them are women. In 2000, UNESCO launched the Education for All 2015 project, with 164 governments making a pledge at a conference in Senegal to vastly expand educational opportunities for people worldwide.

Through an annual commissioned Global Monitoring Report, UNESCO has been able to track the progress of various efforts toward providing education to children, youth, and adults. There have been tremendous strides in many countries, creating mandatory child-education laws and abolishing tuition for elementary schools, thereby removing one of the major barriers that kept many children from attending schools.

One part of this effort is getting affordable computers into the hands of school children. One Laptop Per Child (OLPC) encourages people to donate rugged, specially made cheap computers to children in the developing world to help with education, literacy, and simple computer skills.

However, there is still a long way to go in many countries. A lack of schools, teachers, and supplies remains a top concern, and efforts to educate adults have generally lagged behind the education of children. It is important for adults to recognize the value of literacy so they can encourage learning among their children as well.

Out of 177 countries, 17 have adult literacy rates below 50 percent. These range from Pakistan, at 49.9 percent, to last-place Burkina Faso, at 23.6 percent. Fourteen of the 17 countries are in Africa, with Nepal and Bhutan completing the list.

Web Link >>>
One Laptop Per Child
http://laptop.org/en/

Steven Gould's debut novel *Jumper*, written in 1992 and made into a movie starring Hayden Christensen in 2008.

Third, book sales and distribution are being transformed by the emergence of online booksellers, electronic books, and on-demand printing. Online booksellers such as Amazon.com, bn.com, and others are capturing an increasing portion of total book sales. Moreover, these and other online booksellers are distributing electronic books. As electronic books and online book sales grow, the future of traditional brick-and-mortar bookstores is uncertain. Another big shift has been toward megabookstores and the sale of discounted books at warehouse shopping outlets. These venues offer brick-and-mortar booksellers the needed economies of scale to compete with online enterprises. Independent bookstores are on the decline.

Thomson Reuters became the world's largest publisher in 2007, even before acquiring news giant Reuters earlier in the year and after selling its Thomson Learning division. Thomson Reuters is a prime example of how mergers and digital media are affecting the publishing industry, as the majority of their revenues are made through electronic products and services rather than through printed book or journal sales.

Only seven of the top fifty book publishers are headquartered in the United States; publishers whose names you may recognize, such as Random House and HarperCollins, are owned by overseas companies (Bertelsmann, based in Germany, and News Corporation, based in Australia, respectively). McGraw-Hill Education is the top-ranked U.S. company, ranking seventh in the world in 2007, followed by Reader's Digest in eighth place. Like the other large publishers, these two companies have extensive international operations. The smallest American publisher on the list, Marvel Entertainment, ranked thirty-ninth and generates revenues from books, comics, and licensing deals.

Book Sales and Readership

Book sales have been in a mixed pattern for over twenty years, with revenues increasing a percent or two some years and then dropping a few percent in other years, though there has been growth overall. Growth in some categories may be balanced by decreases in sales or books sold in other categories, with some patterns going back and forth from year to year.

Books are divided into various categories, all with different markets and different strategies for reaching their audiences. As Figures 4-1 and 4-2 show, only looking at sales or the number of units sold can give a misleading picture of the industry. If looking at net dollar sales, one may presume that the professional category is on par with the adult trade category, but when looking at units sold it is clear that far fewer professional books are sold than adult trade books. The rough parity in dollar sales between the two is obviously because professional books are much more expensive than most adult trade books, meaning fewer books can be sold to equal the same dollar amount of much cheaper books.

Trade books, or books intended for general readership, produce the greatest revenues and are second only to juvenile books in terms of units sold. Paperbacks used to dominate the trade book industry, but in recent years hardcover books have made a comeback. There has been a seesawing in yearly sales between hardcover and paperback books.

Mass-market book sales have declined sharply in the past few years, and the industry does not expect an uptick in sales or units sold until 2010. Religious books in general performed well and are expected to continue showing strong growth, though unit sales in the subcategory of "Bibles, testaments, hymnals, and prayer books" were slightly down in 2007, with flat to lower sales projected through to 2012.

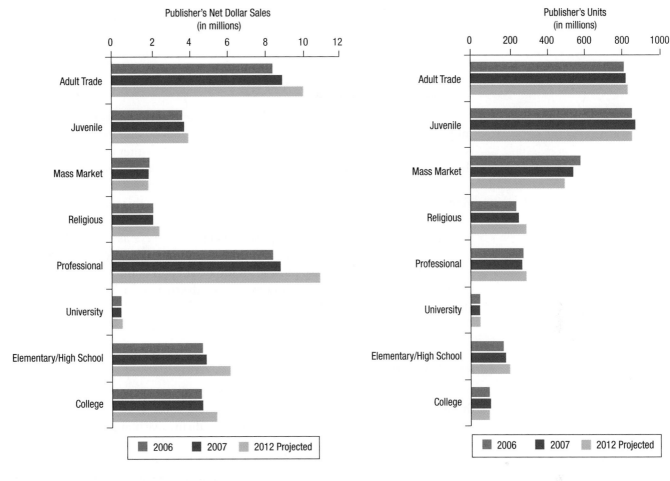

FIGURE 4-1 Book Publishers' Net Dollar Sales: 2006, 2007, 2012 Projected. *Book Trends*, 2008.

FIGURE 4-2 Book Publishers' Units: 2006, 2007, 2012 Projected. *Book Trends*, 2008

Newspapers and Their Functions

Newspapers, as most everyone knows, consist largely of words, pictures, and graphics printed on lightweight, inexpensive paper stock. They are very portable and inexpensive. They are typically printed either daily or weekly. Although they are called "news" papers, most newspapers consist mostly of advertising. The typical daily newspaper in the United States, for example, is roughly 60 percent advertising and about 40 percent editorial content. Similarly, about two-thirds (65 percent) of the cost of producing a newspaper goes into printing and distribution, and only about a third (35 percent) goes into the actual creation of the "news" (reporters' salaries, etc.).

The most important function served by newspapers in modern society is **surveillance**, or to inform the public of important events taking place. However, they also play a role in the **correlation** and **entertainment** functions. Typically, the front page of a newspaper is all "news," with section front pages similarly constructed, and most news placed "above the fold," or on the top half of the page, on other pages.

Newspapers have tended to serve communities bounded by geographic, political, cultural, and economic borders. Correspondingly, newspapers are generally organized into sections often defined by geography, including local, national, and

surveillance
....
Primarily the journalism function of mass communication, which provides information about the processes, issues, events, and other developments in society.

correlation
....
The ways in which media interprets events and issues and ascribes meanings that help individuals understand their roles within the larger society and culture.

entertainment
....
A function of mass communication that is performed in part by all three of the other four main functions (surveillance, correlation, cultural transmission) but also involves the generation of content designed exclusively to entertain.

international news; and topic, including business, culture, health, science, sports, and technology.

■■■ LOCAL NEWSPAPERS

The vast majority of newspapers in the United States serve local geographic communities (usually city based, but with suburban, zoned editions). Local newspapers tend to provide coverage of the local communities they serve, monitoring the activities of local government, law enforcement, business, religion, education, the arts, and other area institutions. In addition to local news, they carry some regional, national, and international news, although most of this tends to come from other news-gathering organizations better equipped to cover these broader areas, including the news services. Local papers also tend to serve as the legal record of public communications in their communities, running obituaries and various legal announcements. They also provide an important part of the local community's economic infrastructure by carrying extensive advertising for local products, services, and businesses with local interests and markets.

■■■ NATIONAL NEWSPAPERS

A few newspapers have emerged as truly national newspapers, with readership throughout the country. These include the *New York Times*, *USA Today*, and the *Wall Street Journal*. Each of these papers offers its own distinctive brand of news. The *New York Times*, known as the paper of record in the United States, as well as the "Old Gray Lady," offers especially strong coverage of international events and issues.

Japan's *Yomiuri Shimbun* is the largest circulation newspaper in the world.

USA Today offers a strong mix of general-interest news packaged in well-designed, colorful, easy-to-read sections. Launched in 1982, *USA Today* was the brainchild of newspaper mogul Al Neuharth and ushered in a new age of newspaper design. The paper took ten years to become profitable, but in the meantime transformed the look and feel of most newspapers in the United States and many around the world.

Prior to *USA Today's* launch, many twentieth-century newspapers were dull in appearance and filled with long columns of text. *USA Today* introduced colorful graphics and an overall design that was inspired by television and easy to read. *USA Today* also succeeded in becoming a national newspaper because the new age of satellite communications made it technically and economically feasible to distribute the content of the paper electronically via satellite to printing and distribution centers around the country and the world for local distribution in a timely, cost-effective, and inexpensive manner.

The *Wall Street Journal* is the nation's leading newspaper covering business and finance. Many in the world of business or finance consider the *Journal* a must-read for their work. Despite the relatively large circulation of the *Wall Street Journal* and *USA Today* compared to most U.S. newspapers, they are dwarfed by the circulation numbers of the world's largest dailies in Japan, the *Yomiuri Shimbun* (over 10 million), the *Asahi Shimbun* (over 8 million), and the *Nikkei* (over 3 million), the latter of which is similar in coverage to the *Wall Street Journal*.

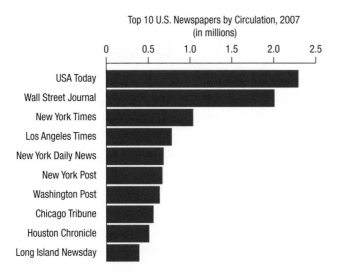

Top 10 U.S. Newspapers by Circulation, 2007
(in millions)

	0	0.5	1.0	1.5	2.0	2.5

USA Today
Wall Street Journal
New York Times
Los Angeles Times
New York Daily News
New York Post
Washington Post
Chicago Tribune
Houston Chronicle
Long Island Newsday

FIGURE 4-3 Top 10 U.S. Newspapers by Circulation, 2007. *Newspaper Trends*, 2008

Historical Development of Newspapers

The first English-language newspaper published in what is today the United States was *Publick Occurrences, Both Foreign and Domestick*. It was first published on September 25, 1690, in Boston.

The American colonial press took two forms: political papers and commercial papers. This duality was reflected in the names of the papers of the day, such as the *Boston Daily Advertiser*, the *Daily Mercantile Advertiser*, *Federal Gazette*, and *Federal Republican and Daily Gazette*. They were physically quite small, usually no more than four pages and ten by fifteen inches in size.

The broadsheet format common to most daily newspapers today is partly a result of British tax law—which the colonies were subject to—that in the eighteenth century placed a tax on the number of pages contained in a newspaper. As a result, newspaper publishers created papers with larger sheets and smaller text in order to reduce the amount of tax they paid.

Publick Occurrences, although only published once, is considered the first newspaper in colonial America.

■ ■ ■ THE COMMERCIAL PRESS

The commercial papers were published by merchants who printed reports on the arrivals and departures of ships, contents of their cargo, weather, and other information useful to commercial enterprises. Both commercial and political papers were sold by subscription at a cost of eight to ten dollars per year, or about six cents an issue. Since the average worker made just eighty-five cents a day, the subscription price of most newspapers put them out of reach of the masses. By 1750 most colonialists who could read had access to a newspaper, although literacy was generally limited to the elite.

■ ■ ■ THE PARTISAN PRESS

After United States independence and prior to the 1830s in North America most newspapers were affiliated with a political party or platform. Political papers were

History (and Pre-History) of Newspapers

200 BCE *Tipao* gazettes distributed among Chinese officials.

59 BCE Julius Caesar orders publication of first daily news sheet, Acta Diurna (*Daily Events*)—Rome.

748 CE First printed newspaper—Beijing, China.

1502 *Zeitung* ("newspaper") published in Germany.

1513 Earliest known English-language news sheet and first illustration in a news sheet—*Trewe Encountre*.

1609 First regularly published newspaper in Europe (Germany)—*Avisa Relation oder Zeitung*.

1620 First English-language newspaper—*The new tydings out of Italie,* published in Amsterdam.

1621 First English-language newspaper printed in England—*Corante, or, Newes from Italy, Germany, Hungarie, Spaine and France*.

1638 First printing press arrives in what later became the United States—Cambridge, Massachusetts.

1665 First issue of the *Oxford Gazette* published at Oxford, England, offering first use of double columns in a news publication. Considered the first true newspaper.

1666 The *Oxford Gazette* becomes the *London Gazette* and is published continuously for more than 300 years.

1690 First newspaper published in what is now the U.S., in Boston—*Publick Occurrences Both Foreign and Domestick*.

1702 First daily newspaper—the *Daily Courant*, published in London.

1704 North America's first regular newspaper—the *Boston News-Letter*.

1721 First independent newspaper in North America, the *New England Courant*, published by James Franklin, Benjamin Franklin's brother.

1764 The *Hartford Courant* established, the oldest continuously published newspaper in the United States.

1784 First daily newspaper in the United States—the *Pennsylvania Packet*.

1800 First iron hand press—Stanhope, England.

1830s First steam-powered rotary press makes mass distribution possible; prints on both sides of paper, 4,000 sheets per hour. Prior hand presses printed just 200 sheets per hour.

1880s–1900s "Yellow journalism" is coined as competition between Pulitzer's and Hearst's New York papers leads to flashy and often inaccurate stories to gain readership; the precursor to today's tabloid journalism.

1932–1944 Despite most newspaper editorials being against President Franklin Roosevelt and his New Deal policies, he wins election a record four times, using the power of radio to talk to Americans directly through his "fireside chats."

1971 Newspapers switch from hot metal letterpress to offset printing.

1977 *Toronto Globe and Mail* offers public access to newspaper text database.

1982 *USA Today* founded; typeset in regional plants by satellite commands.

1995 *Metro*, distributed free to subway commuters in Stockholm, Sweden, launches what becomes a worldwide newspaper chain that focuses on younger, urban readers.

2005 The *New York Times* acquires About.com, a leading online site of consumer information, for $410 million.

2008 The New York Times Company, Tribune Company, Gannett, and Hearst Corporation announce creation of quadrantONE, an online sales organization for national advertisers.

Web Link >>>
Media History Project
www.mediahistory.umn.edu/

sponsored by political parties and the articles were often written by political figures, usually anonymously. The partisan press, as it was called, did not subscribe
to the modern notions of good journalism, free of bias and impartial in its coverage
of the day's events and processes. The newspapers of the late eighteenth and early
nineteenth centuries were decidedly opinionated and took a position not only on
their editorial pages but throughout the entire papers. Readership was also limited
in at least two ways. First, readership was largely limited to those who supported
or agreed with the political position of the paper. Second, readership was largely
limited to society's elite, well-educated, land-owning and economically advantaged
groups.

■■■ THE GOLDEN AGE OF NEWSPAPERS

Technology has always shaped the newspaper. A series of changes beginning in the
1830s, led by technological developments, led to a transformation of newspapers
and the emergence of a "golden age" for newspapers in America. This golden age
lasted until about 1930 and the arrival of electronic mass communication, first in
the form of radio, and later, television and other media. For one hundred years,
however, newspapers exerted perhaps their greatest influence on American society.
In many ways, the rise of newspapers came in response to an appetite for news in
large eastern cities such as New York, Boston, and Philadelphia. Between 1870 and
1900, the U.S. population doubled, the city population tripled, and the number of
daily newspapers quadrupled. In fact, the 1880 U.S. Census counted 11,314 newspapers, compared to 2,344 newspapers in 2006. Papers serving growing metropolitan areas sprouted throughout the nation, led by press innovators such as James
Gordon Bennett, Horace Greeley, Joseph Pulitzer, William Randolph Hearst, and
E. W. Scripps.

Prior to the 1830s, printing technology was largely powered by hand, and briefly
by horses, and could print from two hundred to six hundred sheets per hour. This severely limited the circulation of the papers of the day. But in the 1830s steam-powered

printing presses were developed. These could print up to four thousand sheets per hour printed on both sides. This made mass-scale printing possible. Seizing the opportunity, publisher **Benjamin Day** ushered in this new era, offering on September 3, 1833, a mass-medium daily newspaper, the *New York Sun*, for one cent. The paper was sold by newsboys in the streets each day rather than by subscription. Unlike the partisan press or commercial papers, this **penny press** offered news for the masses. News was written to appeal to the lowest common denominator, and sensationalized news frequently appeared in the paper. Day's paper quickly reached a circulation of eight thousand, and within three years its circulation had reached thirty thousand, astounding other contemporary publishers.

The penny press denoted newspapers for the mass public and exerted important social effects. These metropolitan dailies developed large circulations aimed

The *New York Sun* was the first of the penny papers.

Freesheets: Riding the Rails of Newspapers' Future?

It looked like a crazy idea, even back in 1995. At a time when newspapers were already struggling with rising costs and budget crises, and just starting to understand the threat that the World Wide Web would have on their readership, Pelle Tornberg launched a free daily newspaper in Stockholm targeted to subway commuters.

The paper, called *Metro*, was created to be read in fifteen minutes. Tabloid-sized and colorful, with short articles covering a variety of topics, *Metro* aimed squarely at an elusive yet lucrative readership for advertisers—young, affluent, and urban. This was also precisely the demographic that had largely stopped reading newspapers.

Now there are 210 free newspapers in 50 countries, with a total worldwide circulation of 40 million. The *Metro* chain of freesheets has expanded throughout Europe, Latin America, and Asia and into New York, Boston, and Philadelphia in the United States. They now are in 81 cities in 19 countries and publish in 18 languages.

Free newspapers remain the fastest-growing segment of newspapers worldwide, although growth has slowed in some key markets. The *New York Metro* and its competitor, *amNewYork*, have been struggling to gain the kind of popularity of the freesheets in Europe. Even in Europe, however, freesheets have had to close down in some cities.

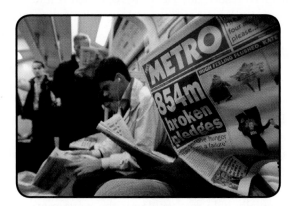

Are freesheets just a fad, or can they get young people back into the habit of reading a newspaper, even if it is only for fifteen minutes while riding the subway? There does seem to be an increase in young urban readership, but it remains an open question whether this increased readership will transfer to paid circulation newspapers as the readers get older and whether it will instill a lifetime habit of reading newspapers.

at expanding audiences that included, even focused on, the middle class. In many ways, it was analogous to the social shift that accompanied Gutenberg's printing press some four centuries earlier. News was no longer for the political or commercial elite; it was for everyone.

The penny press changed the nature of news by employing reporters to seek out the news, not just publish items that came into the office. The penny press also brought a new marketing function to newspapers. The price for a newspaper did not cover printing and distribution costs, but because the penny press brought large audiences, businesses seeking to sell their products to mass markets saw potential in advertising. The penny press began advertising medicines, entertainment, and jobs, as well as items the commercial and partisan press frowned upon, such as ads for theaters, lotteries, or abortionists. Advertising emerged as the primary revenue source in the modern newspaper business model. Today, about 70 percent of newspaper revenue typically comes from advertising.

Newspapers Today

Just as improvements in technology helped in driving the rise of newspapers as a mass medium, technology has also played a role in the decline and transformation of newspapers in the last half of the twentieth century. A combination of sociological forces in post–World War II America, including a change to a largely suburban society and increased use of automobiles, along with electronic media such as radio, television, and later the Internet, helped draw audiences away from newspapers as their primary sources of news.

Television's ease of use and entertainment value contributed to the continuing decrease of American newspapers, especially afternoon papers, in the second half of the twentieth century. Previously, cities usually had two or more competing daily newspapers, but now many cities have only one newspaper or a morning and evening paper. These are ostensibly competitors but are sometimes owned by the same company or work under a **joint operating arrangement** that leaves virtually monopolistic control over the circulation area. A joint operating arrangement, or JOA, is a legal agreement that permits newspapers in the same market to merge their business operations yet maintain separate editorial operations. Today, ten cities in the United States are served by two or more major daily newspapers operating under a JOA, with eleven cities served by different newspapers under common ownership. JOAs are permitted under the **Newspaper Preservation Act of 1970**, which is intended to preserve a diversity of editorial opinion in communities where only two competing, or independently owned, daily newspapers exist. Critics argue, however, that JOAs essentially allow virtual monopoly control of a market.

Modern newspapers are still undergoing significant changes, including marked change in their news and advertising content. As newspaper circulation numbers become more important in an increasingly competitive market, even leading newspapers are more likely to pander to popular taste. Departing from the established editorial tradition of selecting newsworthy topics regardless of general appeal, many newspapers are deferring to marketing polls and focus groups when setting standards for content, tone, and layout.

Brightly colored photos and graphics like those pioneered in *USA Today* can, when they are done properly, actually help readers digest the news more easily. However, when done poorly they can trivialize the news and at worst be confusing or misleading.

How newspapers reach the reader is changing dramatically, especially with the rise of the Internet. Newspapers have been in the forefront of experimenting with the electronic delivery of news to news consumers since the late 1970s, when newspapers like the *Toronto Globe and Mail* allowed public access to their news databases. Most of these early efforts were not very successful, however, as many people at the time did not have computers or Internet access and the state of technology with screens made reading text on the computer tiring.

As the Internet has grown as a medium of public communication, most daily newspapers have launched online news operations. They have increasingly used this new medium as a vehicle for serving an audience no longer limited to or defined by geographical, political, or even cultural or linguistic boundaries. Still, most newspapers have seen the Internet as a bigger threat to their business model than a boon in terms of gaining paid subscribers or advertisers. As a sign of trends to come, two major newspapers, the *Christian Science Monitor* and the *Seattle Post-Intelligencer*, announced in late 2008 and early 2009 that they would no longer publish papers and

joint operating arrangements (JOAs)

Legal agreements that permit newspapers in the same market or city to merge their business operations for reasons of economics yet maintain independent editorial operations.

Newspaper Preservation Act

Created in 1970, it is intended to preserve a diversity of editorial opinion in communities where only two competing, or independently owned, daily newspapers exist.

would exist only online. Other newspapers will likely follow suit, either scaling back their print publishing operations or closing them down altogether.

Newspaper Readership, Circulation, and Advertising

Newspaper readership, circulation, and advertising have continued to decline for more than five decades, along with the number of daily newspapers. Newspaper readership refers to the number or percentage of people who read a newspaper, which is larger than the circulation number (number of copies sold or distributed) because some copies are read by more than one person. This is called "pass-along readership." Because of the growth of the U.S. population, the actual number of persons reading newspapers does not show a large decline. However, the percentage of the U.S. population that reads a daily paper has been declining, and the amount of time people spend reading newspapers has been slipping as well.

Readership among the young is lower than for people between thirty-five and sixty-five and has been showing sharp declines in recent years, though some statistics by the newspaper industry have shown that the young are reading news online in higher numbers than they were. Of course, many of these online sources are published by daily-newspaper parent organizations.

■ ■ ■ DECLINING NUMBER OF DAILY NEWSPAPERS

Since 1940, the total number of daily newspapers has dropped more than 21 percent, with 1,422 daily papers in the United States in 2007. Most of the decline has been in evening papers, which decreased 51 percent since 1940. In 2000, for the first time the number of morning dailies exceeded the number of evening papers, and it has remained that way since then. Since 1940, the number of morning papers has increased over 100 percent, doubling since 1980 to 867 morning daily papers, with 565 afternoon daily papers in 2007. The number of Sunday papers increased 65 percent since 1940, reaching a high of 917 papers in 2005, but falling to 907 by 2007.[4]

FIGURE 4-4   Circulation Numbers of Morning, Evening, and Sunday Papers, 2007.
NAA.org

■ ■ ■ DECLINING ADVERTISING

Of equally great concern to newspaper publishers is the decrease in advertising in newspapers, as advertisers mostly move their ad dollars to the Internet—though generally not to online newspaper websites. In 2007, advertising expenditures for newspapers were down 9.4 percent from the year before, the largest drop since 2001, with classifieds seeing the biggest drop, 16.5 percent. Since 2001, advertising expenditures have either been in low single digits or dropping.

Advertising expenditures on the Internet, however, have shown double-digit increases since recording began in 2003, with increases of between 26 percent and 31 percent up to 2006. The rate of expenditures slowed markedly in 2007, to 18.8 percent. It would seem to be a good thing for newspapers if advertisers are simply shifting their ads from the print product to online, but that is not what is happening. Internet advertising expenditures were $3.2 billion in 2007, compared to $42 billion for print. So even though Internet advertising has been increasing dramatically, the amounts still fall far short of making up for the decreases in print-advertising expenditures.

The Newspaper Industry Today

The newspaper business continues to evolve in significant and sometimes unpredictable ways. Trends suggest that newspapers' presence on the media landscape will continue to decline, at least from an economic perspective. Newspaper publishers and editors have been trying to find ways to make printed newspapers more valuable to their audiences and more viable as successful business enterprises. However, most proposals to do so involve some combination of an expanded online presence for the newspaper and greater interactivity with the audience, including user-generated content, that begins to blur the line between the traditional conceptions of professional journalist and audience.

Increasing concentration of ownership, which was discussed in earlier chapters, has also taken place in the newspaper industry and continues to play an important role in how newspapers are meeting the challenges of the twenty-first century and the digital age.

■ ■ ■ NEWSPAPER CHAINS; NEWSPAPERS CHANGE

Throughout much of the history of newspapers in the United States, newspapers were family owned, or owned by individuals, and in some cases by political parties. These owners generally lived in the communities their newspapers served. The twentieth century brought new patterns of ownership to newspapers, both in the United States and around the world. The most fundamental shift has been toward increasing concentration of ownership. In other words, most newspapers today are part of newspaper groups or chains, some of which are privately held and some of which are publicly traded companies. The increasing concentration of newspaper ownership is the result of many forces, primarily economic. The newspaper business has traditionally been highly profitable, with profit margins often in the range of 20 percent of gross revenues. This placed the newspaper industry among the most profitable in any sector of the economy and represented double the average profit margin for all industry sectors.

The high profit margin of many newspapers has made them a desirable target for investors, and there are certain economies of scale that newspapers can enjoy through chain ownership. Consequently, facing declining audiences and declining advertising revenue, as well as rising costs for newsprint and other necessary resources, larger newspapers and newspaper groups have acquired smaller newspapers and newspaper groups. Newspaper chains bring both benefits and problems to formerly independent local or regional papers.

Benefits of Chains

One of the benefits is that smaller, struggling newspapers can gain access to the resources of the entire chain. This can be especially important in communities where a single advertiser or industry controls an especially large share of the advertising revenues. A single advertiser can pose a strong economic threat to the commercial viability of the local newspaper by threatening to reduce or remove advertising. Subject to this influence, the newspaper can find itself in the compromising position of not reporting as rigorously on an advertiser as may be warranted.

Chains also offer newspapers the advantage of shared resources for news gathering, especially when covering regional, national, or international stories—much as newspapers have benefited from the shared news-gathering resources made possible through the Associated Press news service.

Problems with Chains

Chain-owned newspapers also bring certain problems to the communities they serve. Among these problems are an increasing disconnection between the local media and the local communities. As local reporting gets squeezed out by wire service or chain-produced content, communities are being forced to look elsewhere for local news and information.

Among the most significant considerations is the potential for chains, especially those that are publicly owned and traded on the stock market, to place increasing pressure on local newspapers to bring greater levels of profitability. This pressure can mean many things, including cutting editorial costs. One common strategy is to cut costs by reducing the size of the reporting staff and filling the news hole with wire service copy or material from the chain's other papers. Thus, the amount of local news is reduced, but the overall newspaper does not shrink in size—just expenses.

■ ■ ■ LEADING NEWSPAPER CHAINS

In general, the trend is toward more concentration of ownership and control of circulation. Most chains are publicly traded, with some still under family control, but increasing pressure is being felt to provide greater attention to the bottom line.

An example of this increased pressure among all newspapers, but especially the chains, can be seen with some of the buying and selling between chains recently that has changed the newspaper landscape. In 2006, it was announced that Knight Ridder, the second-largest newspaper chain in the United States, known for its innovative use of new technologies, would be sold to The McClatchy Company, the eighth-largest chain, for $4.5 billion.

Knight Ridder was a merger of two companies that had both gone public in 1969, having started as family-run newspaper businesses. One of the founders' descendants, Tony Ridder, was CEO and chairman of the company, which published thirty-one daily papers in twenty-eight markets, including many respected papers such as the *Miami Herald*, the *Philadelphia Inquirer*, and the *San Jose Mercury News*. The company had been under increasing pressure from shareholders to cut costs and raise profits in recent years, and some press critics charged that the papers had been sacrificing quality.

The sale took place in June 2006 and, for various reasons, McClatchy immediately started to sell a dozen of Knight Ridder's newspapers. Because McClatchy already owned the *Minneapolis Star Tribune*, it had to sell the *St. Paul Pioneer Press*, and it sold other papers, mostly in Rust Belt cities, to various chains such as MediaNews Group, which also bought the *Mercury News*. The *Philadelphia Inquirer* was also sold, to a group of private investors in the Philadelphia area. Despite the fact that some papers were reverting to private ownership independent of a newspaper chain, it is important to remember that investors buying these papers were doing so largely because of the potential they saw for profits, not out of a desire to return a paper to its roots as an important local voice for news.

Another widely heralded sale in 2007 shook the news world when the Bancroft family, owners of Dow-Jones and the *Wall Street Journal*, agreed to sell the paper to Rupert Murdoch's News Corporation (News Corp.). Many journalists fretted that Murdoch would meddle with the content, as he has done with other papers he has bought, and quit in protest. Murdoch promised he would not, and it remains to be seen if he will keep his promise and allow the venerable *Wall Street Journal* to maintain its standards of high journalistic quality. One big change did take place soon after the sale, however. Murdoch moved the paper's offices from the financial district in downtown Manhattan to the News Corp. offices in midtown.

■ ■ ■ NEWSPAPER ECONOMICS

The cost of the printing press, the newsprint or paper, the ink, the press operators (or "pressmen," as they are known in their union), the delivery trucks and drivers, and the maintenance of subscriber databases, as well as various other non-news-related production and distribution costs, make up roughly two-thirds of the overall cost of publishing a newspaper.

It is ironic that most of the cost of a newspaper goes to functions other than producing news—which represents an interesting opportunity for newspapers in the digital age. Today, only a handful of newspapers, most in small markets, have stopped print versions of the paper and gone entirely to the Web. Although printing and delivery costs are of course greatly reduced, there are other economic and customer issues to consider for online newspapers. One is the cost of maintaining Web servers and other computer equipment, especially for sites that receive lots of traffic. Although still less than printing a physical product, the costs can be substantial for large sites, especially as online news shifts to video and audio formats in addition to text and images. With a plethora of news and information available online, most newspapers without an established and respected brand are simply not important destinations for online readers, making it unlikely that people will subscribe to an online-only version of their local paper. And as other sites siphon advertising revenues, especially those of the classifieds, online-only papers lose valuable potential ad revenues.

The Future of Newspapers

"The rumors of my death have been greatly exaggerated," once quipped American novelist and humorist Mark Twain, a former journalist himself, after reading his own obituary in a local newspaper. This may have been true for Twain, but can the same be said for newspapers?

With only three exceptions (Cox Enterprises, Bertelsmann, News Corp.), the world's largest media companies do not own newspapers. It is likely that the unique newspaper culture that places a premium on public service is not well understood by the owners and leaders of media firms, which are largely entertainment companies. But some of the readership and circulation factors discussed earlier, as well as the economic pressures associated with the printing and publishing business, declining circulation, and reduced advertising, make publishing on dead trees look like a dead end. Most of the world's media giants don't want to be part of this disaster waiting to happen.

As newspapers, at least in their current printed form, become less important as primary sources of news and continue to suffer staff reductions—which further erode their relevance, readership, and advertising revenues—serious questions for society must be asked. Foremost, what will fill our need for news in today's world, when most media companies find it cheaper and more profitable to simply provide entertainment? Weeklies and nationals may survive, but many local dailies face a very questionable future unless they adapt to the digital, online world. Where might the public interest fit into the bottom line?

At the heart of these questions are considerations about how the public wants to get its information and how often. In our media-saturated world with 24/7 news cycles and constant news updates, newspapers will have to adjust their content to better fit audiences' needs, as they no longer are the first to inform. This may speak to newspapers changing to be more interpretative, or to analyze news events, to a greater extent than they do now, which could make them seem more like today's weekly news magazines than traditional daily newspapers. However, this change will bring them into competition with news magazines. As we will see in the next section, magazines are facing their own demons in the digital, multimedia world in which audiences read less and seem to prefer shorter articles when they do read.

Magazines and Their Functions

There are three factors that most clearly distinguish magazines and newspapers. First, magazines tend to feature more long-form writing, whether in the form of news and analysis or features and human-interest articles. Historically, many journalists and other writers who are today most famous for their books or novels often introduced their works in serial form in contemporary magazines. The great English writer Charles Dickens, author of *A Tale of Two Cities*, *A Christmas Carol*, and *Oliver Twist*, had many of his classics first published in this fashion, typically one chapter at a time. American writer and sometimes journalist Edgar Allan Poe, whose dark tales are still popular today, also had many of his stories first published in magazines. His *Murders in the Rue Morgue*, said to be the first modern detective story, was published in the April 1841 issue of George Rex Graham's *Lady's and Gentleman's Magazine*, whose circulation jumped from five thousand to twenty-five thousand the year Poe started writing for it. Many contemporary writers also use magazines, both in print and online, to introduce their books, either by featuring chapters and other excerpts for new readers or by creating books out of a series of magazine articles they have written.

Second, magazines are published at regular intervals but tend to be published less frequently than newspapers, most typically on a monthly basis, although weeklies and quarterlies are also common. This contributed to the alternative writing

FIGURE 4-5
Major Newspaper Chains in the U.S.

THE MCCLATCHY COMPANY

The McClatchy Company became the third-largest newspaper publisher in the United States after its purchase of Knight Ridder in 2006 and after selling its largest newspaper property, the Minneapolis Star Tribune. It owns thirty newspapers in twenty-nine markets and has focused on owning newspapers in fast-growing markets. Its purchase of Knight Ridder also gave the company some nondaily newspapers and added ten foreign news bureaus as well as expanding the Washington, D.C., news bureau.

Newspapers include: *Anchorage Daily News, Sacramento Bee, Fresno Bee, Modesto Bee, Miami Herald, El Nuevo Herald, Idaho Statesman* (Boise, ID), *Wichita Eagle, Kansas City Star, News & Observer* (Raleigh, NC)

Website: www.mcclatchy.com

TRIBUNE COMPANY

Tribune Company is the second-largest newspaper publisher in the United States, though it has been struggling with a large debt load after going private in 2007. A merger with the Times Mirror newspaper group in 2000 added the Los Angeles Times, the Baltimore Sun, New York–based Newsday, and several other Times Mirror newspapers. The company also owns twenty-three television stations, a radio station, and the Chicago Cubs baseball team.

Newspapers include: *Chicago Tribune, Baltimore Sun, Los Angeles Times, Newsday, Orlando Sentinel, Newport News* (VA)

Website: www.tribune.com

E. W. SCRIPPS

The E. W. Scripps Company is a publicly traded company under family control. Family trusts own 60 percent of the company and control 90 percent of the votes. The Cincinnati, Ohio–based chain owns seventeen newspapers in fifteen markets, as well as the Scripps Howard News Service and Scripps Media Center in Washington, D.C. Its television group has six ABC-affiliated stations and three NBC-affiliated stations.

Newspapers include: *Rocky Mountain News* (Denver), *Commercial Appeal* (Memphis), *News Sentinel* (Knoxville, TN)

Website: www.scripps.com

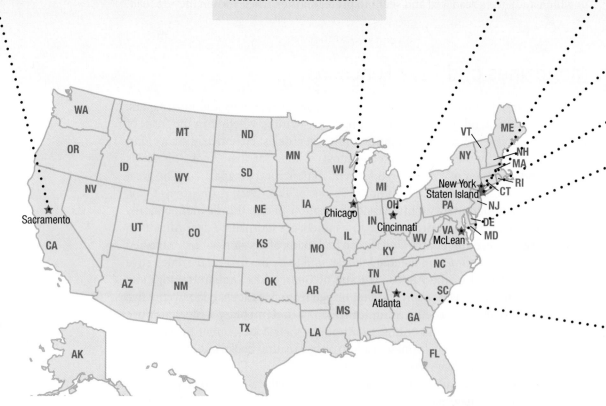

THE NEW YORK TIMES COMPANY

The New York Times Company also is publicly traded, but it is controlled by the Sulzberger family. It owns twenty daily newspapers, including the New York Times, the Boston Globe, half of the International Herald Tribune, and eighteen other regional daily newspapers through two regional media groups, as well as eight network-affiliated television stations, two New York radio stations, and more than forty websites, including About.com.

Newspapers include: New York Times, Boston Globe

Website: www.nytco.com

ADVANCE PUBLICATIONS

Advance Publications Inc. is a private, family-controlled company, led by chairman and CEO Samuel I. "Si" Newhouse Jr. Advance owns newspapers in twenty-two cities, Conde Nast Publications, Parade Publications, the Golf Digest companies, and has interests in cable television and the Internet.

Newspapers include: Newark Star-Ledger, Times (Trenton), Birmingham News, Huntsville Times, New Orleans Times-Picayune, Plain Dealer (Cleveland), Oregonian (Portland)

Website: www.advance.net

THE HEARST CORPORATION

The Hearst Corporation's diverse media properties include television, radio, cable network programming, online services, and twelve daily newspapers, eighteen weeklies, and sixteen consumer magazines.

Newspapers include: Houston Chronicle, Seattle Post-Intelligencer, Seattle Times

Website: www.hearst.com

GANNETT

Gannett, a publicly controlled chain, publishes ninety-five daily newspapers, including USA Today, in forty-one states and the United Kingdom, and owns more than three hundred nondaily newspapers and shoppers. It also owns several magazines and twenty-two television stations nationwide.

Newspapers include: Greenwich Time (CT), Florida Today (Melbourne), Honolulu Advertiser, Indianapolis Star, Des Moines Register, Courier-Journal (Louisville, KY), Detroit Free Press, Clarion-Ledger (Jackson, MS), Reno Gazette-Journal, Home News Tribune (East Brunswick, NJ), Statesman Journal (Salem, OR), Argus Leader (Sioux Falls, SD), Tennessean (Nashville, TN), Burlington Free Press (VT)

Website: www.gannett.com

COX ENTERPRISES ATLANTA

Cox Enterprises is a global media giant whose interests include fifteen daily newspapers and almost a dozen nondailies through ownership of newspaper groups in Austin, Texas; North Carolina; and Ohio. Cox's flagship newspaper is the Atlanta Journal-Constitution.

Newspapers include: Atlanta Journal-Constitution, Palm Beach Daily News, Palm Beach Post, Daily Sentinel (Grand Junction, CO)

Website: www.coxenterprises.com

In the latter nineteenth century, national magazines helped the growing U.S. establish a common sense of identity and culture.

format of the content of magazines, typically less time sensitive, often more analytical or interpretative, creative, or fictional.

Finally, magazines often have been published on higher-quality paper stock than newspapers and are often designed to be kept considerably longer than dailies. Magazines have tended to be printed in a certain size, namely eight and a half by eleven inches. However, certain clever magazine publishers have sometimes reduced the size of their magazines—what is known as the "trim size"—by a quarter inch or half inch in order to save money on printing costs, yet maintained the same cost to advertisers and subscribers. On the other hand, some magazines, such as *Rolling Stone* and *ESPN Magazine*, print on larger stock, which helps make their magazines stand out on shelves crowded with other magazines.

Charles P. Daly, Patrick Henry, and Ellen Ryder outline in their definitive book on magazine publishing, *The Magazine Publishing Industry*, several additional qualities magazines possess. Perhaps the most important of these is that magazines have a defined audience. Although this is true today in a generally descriptive sense, it is not necessarily true conceptually and has not always been true historically. General-interest magazines of the mid-twentieth century such as *Look* and *Life* are two notable exceptions.

Magazines serve several important functions in society. Among the most important functions are surveillance, correlation, entertainment, and marketing of goods and services. Surveillance is the most basic function magazines perform. However, unlike most newspapers, magazines tend not to specialize by reporting on local geographic communities, although some do. Rather, most magazines specialize by subject matter. They cover relatively narrow topics, such as science, health, or sports. Some concentrate on extremely specialized topics, such as doll collecting, harness racing, or scuba diving.

Many magazines have national, regional, or even international readership and distribution. A few major news magazines, such as *Time*, *Newsweek*, and *U.S. News & World Report*, take a broader approach to their reporting on the goings-on of society. Magazines can provide information in relatively great detail compared to newspapers, because they tend to feature longer stories. Since magazines are typically printed on higher-quality paper, they can provide exceptionally effective photography and illustration, making them well suited to covering fashion, nature, and science.

Many magazines are either exclusively or largely designed to provide entertainment and are mostly read as a leisure activity. Magazines such as *People* or *Entertainment Weekly*, with their coverage of celebrities and Hollywood, are illustrative of magazines that emphasize the entertainment function.

Almost all magazines serve a vital marketing function for a broad cross-section of goods and services. It often happens that readers spend more time looking at ads than reading editorial content as they browse a magazine. This is especially true of fashion magazines, such as *Vogue*, *Glamour*, or *GQ*, which often feature not just the latest news on designer clothes but the hottest advertising.

Historical Development of Magazines

In some ways, the early histories of magazines and newspapers are interwoven, with technological, business (i.e., advertising), and journalistic/entertainment functions overlapping between the two. It was not until 1731 that the first English-language periodical used the word "magazine" in its title: *The Gentleman's Maga-*

zine, published in London. Benjamin Franklin published *Poor Richard's Almanack* in 1732, a predecessor of the modern-day magazine. The first magazine published in North America was the *American Magazine, or A Monthly View of the Political State of the British Colonies*, published in 1741 in Philadelphia. The first newsweekly magazine was *Niles' Weekly Register*, first published in 1811.

In the nineteenth century, magazines helped a young United States define itself, as they reached a nationwide audience. This was in contrast to newspapers, which were primarily metropolitan or local in scope.

Also important in this period were Frank Leslie and Miriam Florence Folline Leslie. Frank founded a variety of periodicals, including one of the first influential newsweeklies, *Frank Leslie's Illustrated Newspaper*, launched in 1855. In 1871 Leslie hired Miriam as editor of *Frank Leslie's Lady's Journal*; the two married in 1874. Frank's business went bankrupt in 1877, but Miriam took over upon his death in 1880 and skillfully restored the enterprise to financial health. She became one of the wealthiest and most powerful women in journalism and bequeathed some $2 million to the cause of suffrage.

Important magazine developments in the late 1800s and early 1900s include the 1888 debut of *National Geographic*, founded by the National Geographic Society. *National Geographic* introduced color plates in 1906. Time Inc., founded by Henry Luce, launched *Life* magazine in 1936, a large-format, general-interest magazine with excellent photography.

Specialization of Magazines

A series of major sociological and media shifts in the 1940s and 1950s brought major change to the magazine industry. These complex changes included not only a dramatic decline in public appetites for general-interest magazines and afternoon newspapers but a marked shift in advertising dollars from these media to television. Television quickly became the dominant medium of mass communication and drew national advertisers seeking large audience reach. As a result, general-interest magazines such as *Life* and *Look* saw their business base dissolve.

Magazine publishers had to adapt in order to survive. Overall, they stopped publishing general-interest magazines in favor of specialized magazines on almost every conceivable topic, with highly targeted audiences. Advertising returned, too, as advertisers found appeal in the target marketing possible in specialized publications. This is a trend that has continued in the online arena. There are nearly eighteen thousand largely specialized magazines available in print and online.

One entrepreneur who decided to do something to serve the media needs of African Americans in the mid-1900s was John H. Johnson, then a young African American whose hometown high school in Arkansas City, Arkansas, was "whites only." As a result, Johnson's family moved to Chicago, where Johnson got his formal high-school education. His mother funded his business undertaking by pawning her household furniture and giving her son five hundred dollars to start *Ebony* magazine. *Ebony* has become one of the leading magazines targeting the interests of African Americans, with a circulation of more than 1.5 million. Johnson became one of the leading

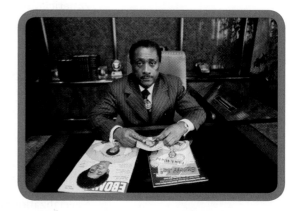

John H. Johnson, founder of *Ebony* magazine, started his media empire by borrowing $500 from his mother.

cross-media owners in the United States, with a book-publishing company, a nationally syndicated television program, and two radio stations.[5] Johnson was the first African American to appear on the Forbes 400 Rich List, and when he died in 2005 he was estimated to have a fortune of $500 million.

Circulation Patterns and Titles

Contemporary magazines, like all media, are increasingly subject to ownership consolidation and media concentration, although in contrast to newspapers, many magazines are seeing their circulations increase, and the number of magazines is also gradually increasing. The number of magazine titles has increased from 13,541 in 1988 to 19,532 in 2007, according to the National Directory of Magazines, with only seven years during that time when there were decreases in the number of titles.

Despite overall increases in the number of magazine titles, many magazines go out of business every year or suspend publication, including some well-established titles. Sometimes they announce that they will go to online-only editions, as Hearst Publications did in 2008 with *CosmoGirl*. In general, the teen-girl magazine market has seen a narrowing of titles in the past few years, reflecting the changes in reading habits of the target audience from print to online. In 2007, Hachette Filipacchi, the publisher of entertainment magazine *Premiere*, announced it would stop print publication of the magazine and have it only online. In August 2008 *Playgirl* made a similar announcement.

The leading circulation magazines are reflective of the general trends in magazine publishing. The top magazines target specific audiences. They cover specialized subjects in depth, and they do so with quality. However, not even these titles can buck the trend of larger societal changes in readership or the unwillingness to purchase or subscribe to print magazines. Those with the largest circulation appeal to the audience segments that are relatively large and, in many cases, growing, such as older adults, who are less likely be online as much as younger people.

Table 4-1 shows the top-ten paid-circulation magazines in the United States in 2000. Both *Modern Maturity* and *NRTA/AARP Bulletin* are publications of the American Association of Retired Persons (AARP). Moreover, among these top circulation magazines, most are either targeted toward senior citizens and retired persons (the fastest-growing demographic segment of the U.S. population) or women, with five of the seven major women's magazines—dubbed the "seven sisters"—among the top ten. The other major women's magazines are also in the top fifty. All these magazines also have robust and increasingly important websites that include material not available in the magazines.

Content Specialization

Specialization in the magazine industry breaks out into several major topical areas. In fact, Bacon's, the publisher of an annual directory of magazines, lists 225 "market classifications." Ten of the most important, at least in terms of circulation, are news, fashion, women (with at least three major subgroups, middle-aged and older women, women under thirty-five, and teenage girls), families (especially aimed at parents of children under age twelve), sports (with some general interest, but

TABLE 4-6

Top-Ten Paid Circulation Magazines in the U.S. in 1972 and 2000

	1972		2000	
	TITLE	**CIRCULATION**	**TITLE**	**CIRCULATION**
1	Reader's Digest	17,828,000	NRTA/AARP	20,826,000
2	TV Guide	16,411,000	Modern Maturity	20,824,000
3	Woman's Day	8,192,000	Reader's Digest	12,590,000
4	Better Homes and Gardens	7,996,000	TV Guide	10,388,000
5	Family Circle	7,890,000	National Geographic	7,892,000
6	McCall's	7,517,000	McCall's (ceased publishing)	n/a
7	National Geographic	7,260,000	Family Circle	5,002,000
8	Ladies' Home Journal	7,014,000	Good Housekeeping	4,532,000
9	Playboy	6,401,000	Woman's Day	4,195,000
10	Good Housekeeping	5,801,000	Ladies' Home Journal	4,137,000

many specialized by type of sport), ethnic, medical/health, political, farm (*Farm Journal* alone has a circulation of 815,000), and lifestyles (many by type of home, region, or cooking).

Notably, most of the new titles introduced each year tend to be in relatively new or smaller, less established niche specialties where growth potential may be greater. For instance, of the almost 250 titles introduced in 2007 (half the number introduced in 1998), the largest number were in the interest category of "metropolitan/regional/state," with 38 new titles, followed by "crafts/games/hobbies/models" with 27 titles. By contrast, in 1998 the largest category was "media personalities," followed by "sex" and "crafts/games/hobbies." In 2007, only three titles were introduced in the category of "sex" and one in "media personalities." This dramatic change in trends perhaps speaks to the changes in how people choose to access these topics, primarily going online and not relying on a single publication for most of their entertainment and information about entertainment.

The Future of Magazines

In some ways, magazines are at the eye of the storm when it comes to how the Internet is changing reading habits and how readers are interacting with content. Magazines have several trends going against them but continue to maintain some

CONVERGENCE CONTEXT

Will Printing on Dead Trees Ever Die?

It is easy to think in the digital age that printed materials will soon be seen only behind glass cases or in musty libraries. However, there is strong evidence that this will not happen. The "paperless office" was widely touted as offices became computerized and connected by networks, yet paper use increased dramatically thanks in part to the availability of photocopiers and cheap printers.

Printed materials also maintain several advantages over their electronic brethren, the main ones being portability, disposability, and durability. Although electronic readers match the portability of

books and actually exceed books in terms of the amount of material they can hold, printed matter still holds the advantage in the other two areas. Forget your newspaper at a coffee shop and you shrug it off; leave your laptop or Kindle there and it can ruin your week. Similarly, printed materials never need recharging and hold up much better to being dropped than most electronic devices. But this too may change as electronic readers become more rugged or disposable.

The relative importance of printed materials may change, however, with printed newspapers, especially, becoming less common than they were in the past, but it is unlikely that they will completely disappear anytime in the near future.

Before you lament the decline of print too loudly, however, remember how environmentally unfriendly the publishing industry is. Paper is of course made from trees, and it is estimated that one tree can make 2,700 thirty-five-page newspapers. Today, printers use more recycled paper and tree pulp for paper, but pulp mills are some of the worst polluters among modern industries. Combine the papermaking process with the many harmful chemicals used in inks, and the environmental damage caused by fleets of delivery trucks, and it adds up to a large environmental footprint, although some publishers have been trying to reduce the amount of pollution printing creates.

Publishing is a resource-intensive enterprise, requiring not only pulp and paper mills but printing plants, inks and dyes, and a large distribution network.

important advantages over newspapers, for example, in terms of staying relevant as print-based products.

Going against magazines are the trends in online reading toward relatively short pieces as opposed to long, in-depth features. This could mean that directly transferring print content to their online counterparts may not be as successful as creating new, shorter content better geared to the online environment. There are exceptions to this, most notably online-only magazines such as *Slate*, but these are not the rule.

As readers expect to be able to interact with authors and with each other through discussion forums, blogs, and chat rooms, the long-form, authoritative or idiosyncratic authorial voice of many magazine features may seem antiquated or limiting. Readers may feel that they are being forced to listen to a long lecture rather than take part in a conversation.

Web Link >>>
Salon
www.salon.com

On the economic side, with full-color pages and generally high-quality, glossy paper, magazines are both expensive to produce and environmentally unfriendly, even when special steps are taken to reduce the environmental impact by using recycled paper, for example.

However, the pages of magazines may also be their saving grace, as they remain more visually enticing and more readable than any mobile electronic screen can yet be. Advertisements can be works of graphic art in and of themselves, and the portability and relatively low cost of magazines make them almost as disposable as newspapers.

The generally interpretative nature of many magazines may also help them survive, as they may provide a perspective and distance to issues of the day that could be hard to find or digest in an online environment. Though the same content could be found online in the magazine's website, of course, strong forces may be at work to create the desire for a portable, nonelectronic version of a magazine that interprets rather than just reports the news of the day.

Some magazines can also serve an important social function that is likely to keep people subscribing for a long while. Although reading a newspaper may not be an accurate indicator of one's social aspirations or intelligence (especially in one-newspaper towns), publicly reading the *New Yorker* or the *Atlantic Monthly* imparts a very different impression of the reader than *Popular Hot Rodding*. In fact, prestige magazines, either through content or through excellent graphics, can often be used as subtle social markers by being left on the coffee table in the home or apartment (even if the magazine is never actually read).

Over the long term, however, it is likely that magazines, like their fellow print-based media books and newspapers, will lose their relative importance as a form of delivering content as more and more readers make the online environment their primary source for information and entertainment. The type of magazine content we see today may not change much, but the way in which we see it will, though this change will likely be slower than that occurring with newspapers.

LOOKING BACK AND MOVING FORWARD

In a world of eye-catching multimedia, flashy graphics, and media saturation, it would seem that gray, boring, and quiet print media will take a backseat. Indeed, some studies have shown a worrisome decline in reading among adults and especially young people. If print has affected our ability to think logically and rationally, as some scholars believe, that raises questions about how today's digital media may be affecting our thinking, adversely or otherwise.

However, even with so many other media options, reading remains an important component of our media consumption—some may say it even could become more important, especially if media literacy and critical-thinking skills decline.

From an economic perspective, media industries that have relied on words being printed on paper are facing grave challenges. This is not because what is written has become irrelevant, but because the packaging that the content comes in is changing. Just as scrolls gave way eventually to books, and in the change the form of writing also changed, printed books are beginning to give way to online or digital formats, and the changes in appearance and content could be equally revolutionary.

Similarly, newspapers and magazines are facing drastic changes brought on by digital media. There is nothing sacred or magical about the form of the modern newspaper (although for people who grew up reading newspapers it may seem so), and if newspapers are to survive, they very well may need to move from paper to digital-only formats—which we are already starting to see with some major newspapers. This change is not simply one of form: it will alter the nature of the newspaper and likely even the nature of news itself and will allow print to sit alongside audio, video, and multimedia. Whether this reduces the importance of the written word, or how it alters it in our minds, remains to be seen.

Print published on paper will never disappear entirely, of course, just as sailboats did not disappear with the rise of steamships and horseback riding did not disappear with the invention of railroads and cars. But the changes that will inevitably occur will be a window on convergence and its effect on our society and culture, and the records that will be kept—most likely in written form—will give historians of the future a rearview mirror that will tell far more about us than we realize today.

DISCUSSION QUESTIONS

1. Do you think that, with the Internet and digital media, we are in the midst of a media revolution as far-reaching as that brought on by the printing press? Why or why not? What are some societal and technological similarities or differences between now and the mid-1400s that will support your argument?

2. If you were to travel into the future to a postapocalyptic world to build a new civilization, what three books might you bring and why?

3. If you had to make a choice today for the rest of your life to receive your textual news and knowledge about the world only from printed materials or only from online sources, which would you choose? What are your reasons?

4. How did the development of the penny press change the nature of mediated communication in the nineteenth century?

5. Why have magazines seemed to adjust better than newspapers to societal and technological changes brought on primarily since World War II? Create a brief outline of a business plan that a twenty-first-century newspaper could follow in order to survive, including its target audience and type of content.

6. What forces led to the specialization of magazines in the years following World War II? What factors will shape the future of magazines in the twenty-first century?

7. Magazines survived by moving from general-interest to niche markets, a trend followed by cable television today. Given that fact, what would a good marketing strategy for magazines be?

8. Local advertisers can exert undue control over small, independently owned papers by threatening to reduce or stop advertising. What factors could hurt public-service journalism in an age of media concentration by companies whose primary business interests are not journalism?

FURTHER READING

A History of Reading; Alberto Manguel (1997) Penguin.

An Introduction to Book History; David Finkelstein and Alastair McCreely (2005) Routledge.

The Smithsonian Book of Books; Michael Olmert (1992) Smithsonian Press.

The Evolution of the Book; Frederick G. Kilgour (1998) Oxford University Press.

Preserving the Press: How Daily Newspapers Mobilized to Keep Their Readers; Leo Bogart (1991) Columbia University Press.

-30-: The Collapse of the Great American Newspaper; Charles M. Madigan (ed.) (2007) Ivan R. Dee.

The Vanishing Newspaper: Saving Journalism in the Information Age; Philip Meyer (2004) University of Missouri Press.

The Magazine from Cover to Cover; Sammye Johnson and Patricia Prijatel (2006) Oxford University Press.

Magazines: A Complete Guide to the Industry; David Sumner and Sherril Rhoades (2006) Peter Lang.

Pulp Culture: The Art of Fiction Magazines; Frank Robinson and Lawrence Davidson (2007) Collectors Press.

Audio Media: Music Recordings, Radio

CHAPTER OBJECTIVES

In this chapter we will:

■ Define the nature and functions of the recording arts (i.e., music).

■ Review the history of the recording arts.

■ Identify the changes digitization, the Internet, and file-sharing services have brought to the recording-industry business model.

■ Examine the basic functions served by radio.

■ Review the history of radio.

■ Outline the basic structure of the radio industry.

5 The woman waiting for the subway, fiddling quietly with her iPod to get the song she wants to listen to, may seem quiet and removed from the world around her, but in fact she is at the center of a transformation taking place today in the music industry.

Whether she downloaded the songs for free from a file-sharing service or paid for them a la carte from iTunes, her actions challenge the major record labels to come up with new ways of marketing and distributing their product.

The newfound freedom among music lovers to discover new music or artists that may only be heard on college radio stations or in a rare indie music shop seems like a boon to the recording industry. Yet it is exactly this kind of freedom that the industry fears.

The recording industry has been built on a model of mass-producing albums by a select number of artists and using its marketing might to convince consumers to buy the product. This still works to some extent, but it is not nearly as powerful as it was before digital media and the Internet. Furthermore, the record labels have been unable to stop the flood of free versions of songs found on file-sharing services, giving little incentive to many consumers to buy the physical CD.

Independent artists would seem to be the main beneficiaries of this new system, but in taking advantage of a more level playing field to distribute music, they have created a din that is nearly impossible to break through. Furthermore, their songs are just as likely to be shared for free as those from an international pop star.

The recording industry has been at the vanguard of where established media business interests and digital media clash, and the recording industry has not been shy about voicing its concerns or protecting its interests. It has been watched closely by other media companies, who have so far been able to avoid many of its mistakes. From enabling through inaction the rampant use of file-sharing services to suing its customers for copyright infringement, the recording industry has made its share of poor decisions from a business perspective and in the spotlight of public opinion.

Radio is the most familiar and far-reaching medium of mass communication in the world. Just about everyone listens to radio. Unlike computers, radio doesn't require any particular technical skill from the listener—and doesn't even need an electrical connection, with hand-cranked or battery-powered radios. Unlike print media, radio doesn't even require literacy; all you have to do is listen (although the listener does need to know the language spoken).

One principle in particular has guided the development of radio and other wireless communication media in the twentieth century: that the airwaves belong to the public, that they are a public good, and that those who use them have a responsibility to serve in the public interest. This concept, in tandem with the notion that the airwaves are a limited resource, laid the foundation for the regulation of radio and other electronic wireless media. Important changes to this principle are happening in the twenty-first century, however, as digitization transforms the potential use of the broadcasting spectrum and commercial interests increasingly dominate the character of radio and other wireless communications.

The Recording Industry

The recording industry has shown the best and the worst of what mass communication and entertainment can offer. On the one hand, the public has been exposed to a much greater variety of music than before. We are all familiar with stories of recording artists from humble origins being discovered and becoming wildly successful entertainers. On the other hand, careers and lives have been ruined because of the excesses that the recording industry is partly responsible for encouraging. Despite the variety of music we have available to us, the industry itself has made it especially hard for artists who do not fit established genres or styles of music to get contracts and be heard by a mass audience.

MEDIA QUIZ

The Revolution Will Not Be Televised (It Will Be Listened To)

1. Have you ever bought a vinyl LP?
2. Have you ever bought an audiocassette by an artist?
3. Do you own an MP3 player? When did you get your first one?
4. (T/F) Revenue from downloads of music surpassed CD revenue for the first time in 2008.
5. Where is the dividing line between radio stations that have call letters starting with K and those starting with W?
6. What is the most popular music format for radio stations?
7. Why is radio called "the wireless" in other English-speaking countries?
8. (T/F) Satellite radio does not have the same restrictions regarding content as do broadcast radio stations.
9. Who owns the radio station that you normally listen to?
10. How much would you be willing to pay per month to listen to commercial-free radio?

The recorded-music industry has similarities to other large media entertainment companies. It is a business controlled mostly by a few very large firms (which are often subsidiaries of even larger media corporations), and it has been primarily promoted through radio, television, and movies. Because of this strong mass-market emphasis, recording labels do not have any benefit in promoting music that will not have large numbers of sales. This leads to a certain homogenization of music styles that are often formulaic and sound much the same. This situation is beginning to change with the emergence of online music distribution, in which fans can find music styles and artists that would not be available in the traditional marketing and distribution structure because they would not make enough money for the labels.

Functions of the Recorded-Music Industry

Recorded music serves a variety of functions, primarily entertainment, art, and education. The principal service to the audience is to provide musical entertainment. From children to senior citizens, just about everyone in contemporary society finds at least some recorded music to their liking. Although largely a commercial enterprise driven by profit motive, the recording industry has helped produce media art, as well. Whether recordings of jazz, opera, or even hip-hop, many recorded musical performances and studio productions have achieved a cultural impact or enduring quality that critics have praised or acknowledged. Recorded music provides another important function: to educate. Children, especially, listen to recorded music, sometimes the same songs over and over, learning vocabulary and much more.

phonograph

First patented by Thomas Edison in 1877 as a "talking machine," it used a tinfoil cylinder to record voices from telephone conversations. Successive technological improvements in electronics and the type of material the sounds were recorded on made sound quality better.

graphophone

An improvement on Thomas Edison's phonograph in recording audio, it used beeswax to record sound rather than tinfoil. Developed by Alexander Graham Bell and inventor Charles Tainter.

gramophone

Developed by inventor Emile Berliner, it used a flat disc to record sound rather than the cylinder that was used up to that time.

Historical Development: From Edison to CDs

It was a technological challenge to record sound on devices that would be easy for the public to use.

The dog Nipper "listening to his master's voice" is a widely recognized symbol of what started as the Victor Talking Machine Company.

The recorded-music industry, or the recording arts, is the oldest of the electronic media of mass communication. Having begun to develop as a mass medium in the 1870s, the recording arts predate even the development of cinema, which did not develop as a mass medium until the turn of the century. Radio, which was invented in the 1890s, did not develop as a mass medium until the 1920s.

Audio recording began when Thomas Edison patented his first "talking machine" in 1877, the **phonograph**, using a tinfoil cylinder as a way to record telephone messages. Edison held a monopoly in the recording industry for nine years until telephone pioneer Alexander Graham Bell and inventor Charles Tainter developed an improved audio-recording device called the **graphophone** that used beeswax rather than tinfoil cylinders. Based on their invention, the American Graphophone Company was launched in 1887.

The Columbia Phonograph Company soon entered the scene, launching its own technology to sell recordings on wax cylinders that could be played on coin-operated machines. The Victor Talking Machine Company was also launched, employing technology developed by inventor Emile Berliner called the **gramophone**, which used a flat disc to record sound rather than a cylinder, as proposed by Edison.

Certain technological hurdles hampered the development of audio recording. In order to record sound, it first has to be accurately captured. A microphone gathers sound energy and converts it to electrical energy with similar wave characteristics.

History has obscured the exact origins of the microphone. Some suggest that D. E. Hughes of England invented it in 1878, although some evidence indicates that Scottish inventor Alexander Graham Bell may have been the one. Bell had been interested in the education of the deaf, which led him to invent in 1876 his "electrical speech machine," now known as a telephone.

There were very few dramatic changes in recording-arts technology over the first one hundred years of its existence. Even the creation of vinyl long-play (LP) albums at 33 1/3 rpm, or revolutions per minute, in the mid 1950s, which allowed playing times of forty to forty-five minutes rather than the two-and-a-half minutes of the shellac 78 rpm albums, were simply improvements in existing production processes and sound quality rather than radical new technologies.

Electromagnetic tapes such as eight-track tapes, and later cassettes, created in 1965, actually provided poorer sound quality than LPs, but consumers were willing to trade audio quality for portability.

Compact discs, developed in 1980, were the first conveyor of digitally recorded songs and the first real technological breakthrough in the recording arts since Edison's time. Digital technology not only can improve the sound quality on older recordings by removing the unwanted noise such as pops and hisses, but it has also allowed for easy creation of "duets" by live and dead singers, such as the song "Unforgettable" by Nat King Cole and his daughter Natalie.

The Recorded-Music Industry Today

By 1909 a handful of companies controlled the recording-arts industry. Recording-arts scholar Geoffrey P. Hull notes that although the companies went through major changes, a three-way corporate oligarchy dominated the music industry until the 1950s, when a variety of industry-wide changes set in. The growth of rock and roll music introduced much greater competition into the recording industry, with the emergence of various new recording labels such as Detroit's Motown, although it was relatively short-lived diversity.

Through extensive merger and acquisition activity, the 1990s saw the reemergence of tight oligarchy control in the recording arts. The Internet and online music distribution has triggered a titanic struggle to redefine this structure, however. Today, the recording-arts industry is perhaps best thought of as the world of musical recording and distribution for profit. It is a more than $25 billion business worldwide. The industry is dominated globally by four companies, the **major labels**. They are Universal Music Group, Sony Music, EMI, and the Warner Music Group. Similar to other media companies, the record labels have been consolidating. In 1998 there were six major labels, and in 2004 there were five, which included Bertelsmann Music Group (BMG). In 2008, BMG was absorbed into Sony Music, leaving the four remaining major labels.

Each of the big-four recording-industry giants is either a subsidiary of a larger media empire or has other media and entertainment interests that stretch beyond music. Combined, these companies control much of the recording and entertainment industries. Universal Music Group alone controls 25 percent of the worldwide market for recorded music.

Independent labels—ranging from small local companies producing and distributing music from even a single artist or two to large labels such as Disney—produce the majority of music titles, estimated at about 66 percent by SoundScan and the Recording Industry Association of America (RIAA), yet only about 20 percent of the sales.

Similar to book publishing, the vast majority of recorded-music releases sell less than 5,000 copies per year, with only a handful of recordings, numbering in the hundreds, selling more than 250,000 a year. Yet these few account for over half the total sales volume, and most are released by the major labels.

How do the major labels manage to produce so many of the big hits? There are at least two answers, and no one knows for sure which is correct. One answer is that they produce the best music from the best artists, market it the best, and reap the rewards. Although there is no doubt at least some truth to this, answer number two also rings at least partly true. The major labels so dominate the entire production and distribution process that even if they produce collectively only marginal-quality recorded music, they will also dominate music sales because of their ability to market what they do produce.

Independent releases have risen dramatically, especially with the rise of the Internet, but sales continue to be small compared to most major-label releases. Some websites have dedicated themselves to promoting and selling independent artists, although their marketing might pales in comparison to the resources of the major labels. Marketing is not the only reason that independent labels are at a disadvantage compared to the major labels. Despite changes in the industry, the basic business model remains largely the same.

Alexander Graham Bell is credited with inventing the telephone, although historians disagree on how much his invention relied on several other inventors' patents.

major labels
....
The four biggest recording-arts companies that control much of the music industry partly through their powerful distribution channels and ability to market music to mass audiences. They are Universal Music Group, Sony Music, EMI, and the Warner Music Group.

independent labels
....
Any small record-production and distribution companies that are not part of the four major-label companies. They include companies producing only one or two albums a year, as well as larger independents such as Disney. The independent labels produce 66 percent of the albums each year but only 20 percent of the sales.

TABLE 5-1
The Major Record Labels and Their Main Subsidiary Labels

MAJOR LABELS	Universal Music Group	Sony Music	EMI	Warner Music Group
Subsidiary labels (and select artists)	**Interscope Geffen A&M** (Beck, Black-Eyed Peas, Marilyn Manson, New Kids on the Block, Weezer) **The Island Def Jam Music Group** (Rihanna, The Killers, Kanye West) **Universal Motown Republic Group** (Amy Winehouse, 3 Doors Down, Nelly) **Universal Music Group Nashville** (Shania Twain, Trisha Yearwood, Ryan Adams, Willie Nelson) **Decca Label Group** (Andrea Bocelli, Boyz II Men, Elvis Costello) **The Verve Music Group** (Billie Holiday, Ella Fitzgerald, John Coltrane) **Universal Records South** (Allison Moorer, Dean Miller, Bering Strait) **Universal Music Latino** (Juanes, Café Tacuba, Luis Fonsi) **A&M/Octone** (Flyleaf, Hollywood Undead, Dropping Daylight)	**Arista/ J Records** (Alicia Keys, Boxie, Santana) **Arista Nashville** (Brooks and Dunn, Brad Paisley, Alan Jackson) **RCA Records** (Kelly Clarkson, Foo Fighters, Kings of Leon) **RCA Records Nashville** (Martina McBride, Jake Owen, Chris Young) **BNA Records Label** (Kenny Chesney, Pat Green, Craig Morgan) **Burgundy Records** (America, Chaka Khan, Julio Iglesias) **Columbia** (AC/DC, Bruce Springsteen, System of a Down) **Columbia Nashville** (Keith Anderson, Montgomery Gentry, Gretchen Wilson) **Epic** (Brandy, Ben Folds Five, Michael Jackson) **Zomba-Jive Label Group** (Britney Spears, Chris Brown, Justin Timberlake) **Legacy Recordings** (Johnny Cash, The Clash, Miles Davis)	(Bebe, Trouble Andrew, The Decemberists, Coldplay, REM, Trace Adkins)	**Atlantic Records Group** (Kid Rock, Matchbox Twenty, Staind) **Rhino Entertainment** (Aretha Franklin, Chicago, Black Sabbath) **Rykodisc** (Frank Zappa, Joe Jackson, Freezepop) **Warner Bros. Records** (Red Hot Chili Peppers, Linkin Park, Seal)

TABLE 5-1
The Major Record Labels and Their Main Subsidiary Labels

MAJOR LABELS	Universal Music Group	Sony Music	EMI	Warner Music Group
Subsidiary labels (and select artists) (cont'd)		**Sony BMG Latin** (Alicasto, Calle 13, Marc Anthony)		
		Masterworks (Leo Bernstein, Yo-Yo Ma, Beverly Sills)		
		Provident Label Group (Annie Moses Band, Jars of Clay, Pillar)		
		Verity (gospel) Windham Hill (New Age)		
Other interests or parent companies	Parent company is Vivendi, involved in publishing, TV and film production, and video games	Parent company is Sony		Parent company is Time Warner, involved in publishing, TV and film production

Recording-Industry Business Model

Web Link >>>
CD Baby
www.cdbaby.com

Throughout much of the twentieth century, the basic business model in the recorded-music industry could be divided into three main parts: creation, promotion, and distribution. Even in the digital world these main parts have not changed, though components of the parts have of course changed with digital technology and the Internet.

Web Link >>>
cdpulse
www.cdpulse.com/

■ ■ ■ CREATION

Web Link >>>
Independent Distribution Collective
www.independentdistro.com/

The major record labels sign artists and financially back those artists in the creation and recording of the music. Because of their financial investment in the process, the recording labels have historically received the majority of the financial rewards, with most artists receiving royalty payments of approximately 10 percent of gross, or overall, sales for their endeavors. Since recording labels obviously want to sign artists whose music will sell well, they can be seen as a gatekeeper or filter of talent, although not necessarily a perfect one, much like book publishers can be filters of writing talent.

Being signed to a major label may seem like a struggling band has finally "made it," but remember that most music sells fewer than 5,000 copies annually, with only a handful selling more than 250,000 copies. When seen this way, 10 percent of sales suddenly does not seem like much income for a band.

■ ■ ■ PROMOTION

Promoting artists and their music is crucial to an album's success. There are several venues for promoting music to fans and the public. Artists perform in concerts, for which additional royalties are received, but radio is a primary promotional vehicle for music. In the past two decades, music videos have also become an important promotional vehicle, and the use of music from new bands on TV shows and in video games in recent years have become important ways to help bands reach wider audiences.

The record labels traditionally provide the radio stations and television programmers with free copies of the recorded music and music videos in exchange for playing them on their stations and channels. Sometimes certain unscrupulous programmers or disk jockeys in major markets have demanded illegal cash, gifts, or other payments under the table—known as **payola**—from the labels in exchange for promoting a song by playing it more frequently than other songs. The labels have sometimes paid this fee because of the importance of radio, especially certain major stations, as a promotional vehicle. Payola was very big in the 1950s, until the FTC ruled it was unfairly stifling competition. Payola favors the major labels over small labels, because small labels lack the financial resources to make these payments. Moreover, payola reduces the potential for diversity on the air.

Perhaps the most famous case of radio payola involved rock-radio DJ Alan Freed. Freed is credited with naming the emerging rhythm and blues–type music "rock and roll" while working for WJW-AM in Cleveland in the early 1950s. His career in radio was ruined in 1964 when he was convicted in New York on commercial bribery charges for accepting payoffs, or payola, to play certain records. After a series of radio jobs in various cities and a worsening drinking problem, Freed died in Palm Springs, California, in 1965. In 1986, Freed was inducted into the Rock and Roll Hall of Fame.[1] Today, payola, or what is now called "pay for play" (and some suspect still done extensively), is punishable with a fine or even imprisonment and is enforced by the FCC. Record labels have devised ways to get around a clear "pay for play" format by doing things like having artists visit radio stations for interviews in exchange for promoting their music, special events in certain markets, and other ideas for promotions in which the labels and radio stations work together.

payola
....
Cash or gifts given to radio disc jockeys by record labels in exchange for greater airplay given to the label's artists or most recent songs. The practice is now illegal after several scandals involving payola in the 1950s.

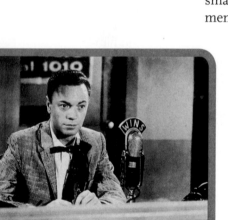
DJ Alan Freed, who was at the heart of the payola scandals between the record labels and radio stations.

■ ■ ■ DISTRIBUTION

Although recorded music has appeared in different ways over the years—first as tin or beeswax cylinders, then on grooved plastic as albums, then on magnetic tape as eight-tracks and audio cassettes, then in optical form on compact discs—the method of distribution has essentially remained unchanged. The record labels make copies of the music from a master copy and send the albums, tapes, or CDs to local retail outlets that sell them to consumers. Online stores, such as Amazon, act much like their real-world counterparts, except consumers receive the CDs at their homes and Amazon does not have to be concerned about display space in stores.

Because online stores such as Amazon do not have to worry about display space, they are able to carry a larger number of CDs than retail stores, which lets them carry CDs that are far less popular. This is an example of what is called the **long tail**, where businesses are able to succeed by selling a greater variety of items but fewer of each item.

Another aspect of digital media and the Internet has been changing distribution much more radically. Consumers do not even have to buy a physical product and are able to download songs in compact file formats such as MP3. Not only can songs be copied and distributed easily by the general public, but flawless copies can be created with no loss in sound quality. This is having profound effects on the control the recording industry has on distributing music, which will be examined later.

long tail
....
The notion that selling a few of many types of items can be as profitable or even more profitable than selling many copies of a few items. The concept works especially well for online sellers such as Amazon or Netflix.

■ ■ ■ PRICING STRUCTURE

A major source of debate in the industry is the pricing structure for recorded music. Price, of course, is a major determining factor in both sales and profitability for the label and royalties for the artist, as well as income for all others in the distribution chain. In the 1970s, when vinyl LPs were the standard means of distributing recorded music, list prices (what the consumer paid) were about $6 (about $19.50 in 2009 dollars). In the 1980s, the compact disc was introduced as the new means of distributing music, and CDs as a percentage of album sales gradually increased from just 22 percent in 1988 to 91 percent in 2001. List prices for CDs were about $19 in the early 1980s (about $34 in 2009 dollars), with wholesale prices about $12.

Over time, with increases in production volume, the cost of producing CDs has fallen, and as a result, wholesale prices have fallen to about $10, with list prices at about $17. Inside the labels, manufacturing costs are today about $1 per CD, with artist and producer royalties about $2 per album (roughly 10–20 percent of the list price) and distributor charges about $1.50. Marketing costs (roughly 50¢) tend to be quite low, because most of the promotion is provided free by radio stations and music television. Thus, a label typically has a gross profit of $5 per CD sold. This is a simplified model, but it illustrates the immense profitability in the recorded-music industry.

Recording-Industry Reality Today: A Complex Landscape

From a high of $14.6 billion in revenues in 1999, the recording industry has seen sales of recorded music steadily decline to $8.5 billion in 2008, according to the RIAA. The RIAA claims that file-sharing services that encourage song piracy are to blame for the decline in sales, though other industry observers say the picture is more complex than that.

First, although the vast majority of music sales in 2008 were still CDs, making up 84 percent of sales, CD sales declined 20 percent compared to 2007. Music download sales have increased markedly, up 27 percent from the year before and going over 1 billion units for the first time in 2008, but are still not high enough to compensate for the decline in CD sales.

The music industry is getting caught in a downward distribution cycle with major retail chains like Best Buy and Wal-Mart, where 65 percent of all CD sales occur. As CD sales drop, retailers devote less floor display space to CDs, making it

Web Link >>>
RIAA
www.riaa.com

even harder for the record labels to distribute all the new CDs they produce. However, even this picture is muddied by the fact that the fifth-highest-selling album of 2008, AC/DC's *Black Ice*, was sold through an exclusive distribution deal with Wal-Mart.

The music industry has started to encourage online sales in recent years, although critics of the recording industry argue it is several years too late, while some major artists like Kid Rock and AC/DC refuse to allow their songs on download services like iTunes. AC/DC and other recording artists argue that selling songs a la carte outside of a produced album destroys the artistic continuity of the album. A la carte sales also are much less profitable for the record labels than album sales.

To further complicate matters, whole new categories of revenue generation have been created in the past few years, such as ring tone sales, that had nothing comparable in the predigital age. Although still a small part of the overall recording industry's revenue generation, these different avenues hint at new ways the record labels can make money outside of their old models.

Security of copyrighted material remains a prime concern to the record labels, and many of their past initiatives in **digital rights management** (DRM) have been heavy-handed and raised the ire of customers, such as limiting the number of digital copies a customer can make of purchased music. Most DRM efforts have also proved short-lived, as hacks have quickly emerged to break the security codes.

Critics of the music industry and major record labels say they only have themselves to blame as they scramble to stop the decline in music sales. Rather than embracing the potential of digital technologies and the Internet early on, they fought it in a number of ways that proved to be valuable lessons for television networks and movie studios.

The recording industry sued various file-sharing services and Internet Service Providers (ISPs), successfully shutting down and eventually bankrupting music file-sharing pioneer Napster. The RIAA even sued several thousand individuals who were sharing files, creating a huge amount of bad publicity. At the end of 2008 it announced it would stop suing individual file sharers and would instead put pressure on the ISPs to cut off those people from the Internet.

Many ISPs have blocked access to file-sharing services because of both threatened lawsuits and the heavy load that such sharing can place on networks, thus slowing the networks down even for users not sharing files. Universities, with their fast Internet connections and large groups of music-loving young people, have been prime targets of the RIAA, which has pushed for special ethics education for incoming students to discourage music-file sharing and to remind them that sharing copyrighted works is illegal.

Lobbying efforts by the recording industry have resulted in some politicians proposing legislation that would further strengthen the legal positions of the recording industry, with suggestions such as requirements for electronic-equipment manufacturers to install digital security devices in their products. Manufacturers are resisting such directives, and groups like the Electronic Frontier Foundation and others also fight these efforts from a citizen or consumer rights perspective.

In short, the music industry finds itself caught between old models of doing business and new ways for customers to get what they want—without paying for it or at least not getting it in the prepackaged ways the industry has traditionally used. Although its problem is not unique, the music industry has been at the forefront of this revolution and made numerous strategic mistakes that have hurt the industry's public image, as well as revenue opportunities. Other media industries,

Some popular artists have refused to let their recordings be sold by the song through digital downloads, saying it destroys the artistic integrity of the album.

digital rights
management (DRM)
....
Various technologies or
security codes used to protect
copyrighted works from being
illegally copied.

Giving consumers more choice in how they get their music has been a difficult adjustment for the major record labels.

especially the film and television industries, have been watching and learning from the recording industry's mistakes.

What Is Broadcasting?

The term **broadcast** was used much earlier than the development of radio or television broadcasting as we know them today, as far back as 1883. Even the term "broadcasting" was borrowed from agriculture, where it referred to a form of planting seeds by casting them widely in a field rather than depositing them one at a time.

In its early days, wireless communications, which was initially only radio, provided point-to-point communication where telegraph lines were impractical or unreliable. The main purpose early wireless inventors saw was ship-to-ship communications or ship-to-shore communications, which would allow ships to communicate emergencies quickly to others. Subsequently, radio technology was developed to permit the broadcasting of messages through wireless means to multiple locations to distribute information widely. The subsequent development of television broadcasting several years later offered the opportunity to transmit moving pictures as well as audio via wireless technology.

Whether it is radio or television, however, broadcasting works essentially the same way. A transmitter sends messages over a part of the electromagnetic spectrum to a receiver, or antenna, which translates the message to a device such as a radio or television. The electromagnetic waves, whether they are audio or images, are then decoded by the receiving device so they can be heard or seen.

broadcast

The original usage was agricultural, referring to casting seeds widely in a field rather than depositing them one at a time. The notion was transferred to the fledgling electronic medium of radio and later television.

The Alphabet Soup of Spectrum Allocation

Since the electromagnetic spectrum used for wireless communications is a limited resource, the FCC allocates various portions of it to different uses so these applications do not interfere with each other. Electromagnetic waves are divided into cycles per second, or hertz. If a radio station is at 99.5 on the radio tuner, this means its transmitter is oscillating at 99,500,000 cycles per second, or 99.5 megahertz (MHz).

"AM" stands for **amplitude modulation** and refers to how the audio signal is encoded on the carrier frequency. AM radio broadcasts between 535 kilohertz (KHz) and 1,700 KHz (1.7 MHz), and was the only radio signal to reach the public for a number of years.

"FM" stands for **frequency modulation**; this refers to the modulation of the length of the wave. FM radio broadcasts in the 88–108 megahertz (MHz) portion of the radio spectrum. This band is used exclusively for FM radio.

Other portions of the wireless bandwidth spectrum are used for other applications, such as **Global Positioning System** (GPS), a system of satellites that provide location information anywhere in the world, between 1,227 and 1,575 MHz. Citizens band, or CB, radio (26.96 to 27.41 MHz) enjoyed short-lived popularity among the public in the 1970s and is still commonly used by long-haul truckers today.

Web Link >>>
How Stuff Works
   electronics.howstuffworks.com/radio3.htm

Web Link >>>
U.S. Frequency Allocation Chart
   www.ntia.doc.gov/osmhome/allochrt.html

Radio

Radio is the most widely available medium of mass communication around the world. It is also the most heavily used medium in the United States, where people listen to radio on average over 2.5 hours per day, although there are sometimes great disparities in reported radio listening depending on how the information is obtained. For example, when filling out a diary of radio usage compared to observational studies, people tend to greatly underreport their radio listening. This is likely because radio is often playing "in the background" while they do other things, even while they consume other media such as reading a book or going online, and they tend not to think about it.

At least 99 percent of all U.S. households have at least one radio receiver and there are similar levels of penetration in most industrialized countries. Even developing nations have a relatively high radio penetration. Radio is less expensive to produce, transmit, and receive than television; radio receivers are highly portable—even wearable—and radio doesn't require literacy to understand. There are basically three types of radio broadcasting, AM, FM, and satellite radio. However, satellite radio, like so-called Internet radio, is an entirely different method of delivering audio

Early radios were often built to fit in with other living room furniture.

programming and is not the same form of broadcasting as traditional AM and FM, even though some in the industry call it "radio." Its method of delivery makes it more akin to audio programming like that in an airplane than true broadcasting, although both are "broadcast" in the sense that they reach mass audiences.

Functions of Radio

Around the world, radio is a medium of entertainment as well as of news and information, or surveillance, and marketing. The U.S. radio industry generated $16.7 billion in annual revenues, according to BIA Advisory Services, the lowest in more than five years, with further declines expected in 2009 and 2010.

Even in remote rural areas, radio is used to disseminate important news and information, as it can distribute instructions for farming and agriculture easily, cheaply, and rapidly. Radio is also used as an emergency broadcast medium in all parts of the world, for such events as severe storms, natural disasters, or military conflict, largely because of its portability and flexible power source. Radio is especially well suited for emergencies, when electrical power may be lost, since radio receivers can easily operate for extended periods on battery power alone.

In American society, radio offers a diverse array of functions, perhaps more diverse than any other of the traditional analog media. Talk radio provides information, debate, and even limited audience interactivity with call-in shows. News programming offers breaking news reports as well as traffic and weather reports, school closings, and more. The mainstay of commercial radio has been the broadcasting of recorded music for entertainment. This latter function also serves artists and the recording industry, who want their music promoted.

Radio's Historical Development

Radio is a medium with a remarkable history. Technically, economically, and programmatically, radio has evolved considerably since its early development, and it continues to evolve as we enter the digital age. The following discussion reviews the development of radio, from its early days in the late nineteenth century to the early twenty-first century.

■ ■ ■ WIRELESS TELEGRAPHY

Many inventors and scientists around the world were experimenting with radio technology at almost the same time. In 1884, German **Heinrich Hertz** began experimenting with electromagnetic waves, and in 1885 he demonstrated the existence of radio waves. His discovery was based on earlier theoretical notions proposed by Carl Friedrich Gauss and James Clerk Maxwell. Hertz's work set the stage for the development of modern wireless communications, both fixed and mobile, a portion of which Americans have come to know as radio. In much of the rest of the English-speaking world, radio has been known as "the wireless." The measurement unit of electromagnetic frequencies was named for Hertz.

Another scientist experimenting with radio technology was African American **Granville T. Woods**, who in 1887 invented what is known as "railway telegraphy." His invention allowed messages to be sent between moving trains, and between

Granville T. Woods
....
Inventor of railway telegraphy in 1887, a type of wireless communication that allowed moving trains to communicate with each other and with stations, greatly reducing the number of railway collisions.

Guglielmo Marconi invented radio telegraphy, or the wireless telegraph, in 1899.

moving trains and a railroad station, reducing the frequency of railway collisions and informing engineers of obstructions ahead on tracks.[2]

At the twilight of the nineteenth century, in 1899, Italian **Guglielmo Marconi** invented radio telegraphy, what he called "the wireless." Marconi's invention made possible real-time transmission of audio, although in the form of dots and dashes of Morse code, over distance without a wired connection; it was what might be called the first real radio transmission.

As is typical for notable inventions, there is some debate regarding whether Marconi can be credited as the inventor of radio. Marconi was not the only inventor at the time working on wireless communications technology. Called by some the *real* inventor of radio, Kentucky farmer Nathan B. Stubblefield created and demonstrated in 1892 a wireless communications device that could even transmit voice and music over a short distance, about five hundred feet. Stubblefield was a mysterious figure who made his invention available to the Wireless Telephone Company, which proved to be a fraud, and Stubblefield never patented his device. He ultimately failed to reap the commercial rewards of his invention and in 1928 died of starvation, alone and penniless on the dirt floor of a shack.[3]

■ ■ ■ EXPLORING RADIO'S EARLY POTENTIAL

In the United States, the Department of Agriculture saw radio's potential and in 1900 financed Canadian Reginald A. Fessenden's early research for gathering reports and then for distributing them over a broad area. The USDA started using radio broadcasting to transmit weather reports in 1912, although its initial transmissions were in telegraphic code, not in human voice. Fessenden in 1901 obtained a U.S. patent for his new radio transmitter engineered to use a high-speed electrical alternator to produce "continuous waves." His design is the basis for today's AM radio.

■ ■ ■ VOICE TRANSMISSION

In 1906, Swedish-born inventor Ernst Alexanderson was among the first to build a working high-frequency, continuous-wave machine capable of transmitting a radio broadcast of the human voice and other sounds. His invention permitted the station to transmit a radio broadcast featuring a human voice and a violin solo.

Although much of the early work on radio was done by Italian Marconi and Canadian Fessenden, a U.S. pioneer in radio was **Lee de Forest**, who developed a unique transmission technology for radio broadcasting of human voice. His arc transmitter for voice transmissions proved reliable for both point-to-point communication and for broadcasting entertainment and news, and by 1907 de Forest's company supplied the U.S. Navy's Great White Fleet with arc radiotelephones for its pioneering around-the-world voyage. This helped establish de Forest as the "father" of radio, although in reality, radio had at least three "fathers."

Lee de Forest, one of the three "fathers" of radio.

Milestones in Early Radio Technology Development

1839 Carl Friedrich Gauss proposes the Earth's atmosphere contains a conducting layer.

1864 James Clerk Maxwell predicts the existence of electromagnetic or radio waves that use the conducting layer in Earth's atmosphere (i.e., that electric waves can travel through the air).

1885 Heinrich Rudolf Hertz demonstrates the existence of radio waves, based on Maxwell's prediction.

1887 Granville T. Woods invents railway telegraphy, which allows messages to be sent between moving trains.

1892 Nathan B. Stubblefield creates and demonstrates a wireless communications device that can transmit voice and music.

1893 Nicola Tesla demonstrates a wireless communications device.

1899 Marchese Guglielmo Marconi invents radio telegraphy, which he calls "the wireless."

1901 Reginald A. Fessenden obtains a U.S. patent for his new radio transmitter engineered to use a high-speed electrical alternator to produce "continuous waves." It will be the basis for Amplitude Modulation, or AM (medium-wave), radio.

1906 Ernst Alexanderson builds a working high-frequency, continuous-wave machine capable of transmitting a radio broadcast of the human voice and other sounds.

1907 Lee de Forest develops a reliable transmission technology for radio broadcasting of human voice, for both point-to-point communication and for broadcasts of entertainment and news.

■ ■ ■ RADIO BEFORE, DURING, AND AFTER WW I

Despite evident practical uses for radio, radio technology still needed to improve before it could become a mass medium. With considerable financial support from and direction by the U.S. military, research on the vacuum tube helped produce a reliable radio transmitter and receiver by about 1915. Using the perfected vacuum-tube radio transmitter, de Forest's Highbridge Station 2XG introduced nightly broadcasts, which offered listeners a so-called wireless newspaper for amateur radio operators.

All this activity ended with the entrance of the United States into World War I in April 1917. At this point, all radio stations were either taken over by the U.S. government or shut down completely. For the duration of the war it was illegal for private citizens to own or operate a radio transmitter or receiver without special permission. The military continued to conduct research on radio technology, and with the end of the war in late 1918 radio restrictions were lifted.

Commercial broadcasting in the United States began in 1920, as well as the first election-night coverage. Regular commercial radio broadcasts began when

Guglielmo Marconi
Italian inventor and creator of radio telegraphy, or wireless transmission, in 1899.

Lee de Forest
Considered the "father" of radio broadcasting technology because of his invention that permitted reliable voice transmissions for both point-to-point communication and broadcasting.

AM station KDKA of Pittsburgh, Pennsylvania, reported results of the Harding-Cox presidential election.

■■■ WIDESPREAD PUBLIC ADOPTION OF RADIO

In the early 1920s in the United States there were roughly 6,000 licenses for amateur radio stations and 4,600 commercial stations, or stations run for profit. Up to this point, general public interest in radio had been slow to develop. There were amateur enthusiasts, who could be likened to the computer geeks in the early days of the Internet, but to most members of the public, radio was a bit of a novelty whose application to their lives was limited.

However, a sporting event on July 2, 1921, would help establish radio as a major medium of mass communication. People across the country were keenly interested in the heavyweight boxing title fight between champion Jack Dempsey and challenger Georges Carpentier.[4] Radio networks did not yet exist, however, so only one station, a temporary long-wave station, WJY, broadcast the bout live, with technical help from the Radio Corporation of America (RCA). RCA, of course, had a financial incentive to see the success of the event. As a manufacturer of radio receivers, it wanted to see a radio set (or two) in every American household.

Organizers of the broadcast telegraphed a transcript of the commentary to pioneering station KDKA in Pittsburgh, which then broadcast the fight to its listeners on a slightly delayed basis. Because most people did not have their own radio receivers at this time, most listeners were in halls where local organizers, including volunteer amateur radio operators, set up receivers and charged admission to offset costs. Because of the sensational nature of the event, much subsequent media commentary was given to the technical breakthrough and promise of the new medium of radio, helping propel radio as a medium of mass communication.

A broadcasting boom began after the Dempsey-Carpentier fight, with hundreds of radio stations springing up across the country, similar to how web servers became widespread in the mid- to late 1990s. Radio receivers were selling as fast as RCA and others could manufacture them. American Telephone and Telegraph Company (AT&T) drafted a plan to create a national radio network. AT&T began implementing the programming for its national network in 1922 with flagship station WEAF in New York City and quickly set the standard for the entire industry.

■■■ FM RADIO, EDWIN HOWARD ARMSTRONG, AND DAVID SARNOFF

Edwin Howard Armstrong
....
Inventor of FM radio
transmission; Columbia
University engineering
professor.

David Sarnoff
....
Head of RCA. He helped push
the development of television
as a mass medium yet blocked
the development of FM radio
for years because its adoption
would hurt AM listenership and
reduce demand for AM radio
receivers, which RCA produced
and sold.

In 1934, an important breakthrough in radio transmission technology occurred when Columbia University engineering professor **Edwin Howard Armstrong** (1890–1954) invented FM (frequency modulation) radio, and later stereo FM radio, with his colleague, John Bose.

Armstrong completed his first field test on June 9, 1934, sending an organ recital, via both AM and FM, from an RCA tower on top of the Empire State Building to the home of a trusted old friend on Long Island. The FM organ came through loud and clear. The AM version had much more static.

Armstrong and **David Sarnoff**, head of RCA, had started out as friends, both seeing the great potential of radio broadcasting. But RCA had made much of its fortune from the mass sales of AM radio sets, called "radio music boxes." FM radio threatened to destroy the RCA empire.

Once Sarnoff realized the magnitude of the invention, he blocked Armstrong by ordering RCA engineers to ask for more tests, lobbying federal regulators to deny Armstrong a license to test his invention, and even trying to obtain Armstrong's patent. Armstrong responded as best he could, filing suit against RCA and many other radio companies who were infringing on the Armstrong FM radio patent.

Tragically, Armstrong never reaped the commercial rewards of his invention and ultimately committed suicide virtually penniless in 1954 over his long-running legal battles with Sarnoff and other companies, as well as the end of his marriage. Ironically, his many lawsuits were settled shortly after his death, leaving a fortune to his widow and the Armstrong Foundation.

The story of Armstrong's invention and Sarnoff's machinations to protect the RCA business model mirrors some of the developments that have taken place with the Internet, in which sometimes legal wrangling or threatened business interests have prevented the better technologies from winning out.

Edwin Howard Armstrong, inventor of FM radio, spent much of the latter part of his life battling companies that tried to quash FM radio because it threatened their business models that were based on AM radio.

Development of a Radio Business Model

Just as with the Internet, the question of how to make a viable business out of radio broadcasting would prove a complex and controversial subject. Many stations in the United States experimented with commercial sponsorship, but through the mid-1920s there were many outspoken critics of advertising on the public airwaves. The May 1924 issue of *Radio Broadcast* magazine sponsored a five-hundred-dollar contest for the best essay on "Who is to Pay for Broadcasting—and How?" The fact that the magazine ran this contest suggested it wasn't convinced on-air advertising was a viable solution.

However, a confluence of commercial interests, government decisions (sometimes influenced by commercial interests), and lack of coordination among advocates of publicly supported broadcasting made privately owned stations with on-air advertising the standard radio-broadcasting business model that continues to this day. As a result, the engine that drives profits is audience size, especially among key demographic groups that are attractive to the advertisers who provide sponsorship.

The Networks

During the 1920s the first commercial broadcasting networks were formed, initially as radio networks—affiliated radio stations in multiple cities all broadcasting a common core set of programming—and later as national television networks. Prior to the passage of the **Radio Act of 1927** and the creation of the **Federal Radio Commission** (FRC), the predecessor to the **Federal Communications Commission** (FCC), broadcasting was lively but haphazard and not well organized. There were numerous stations competing with each other on the same or nearby frequencies, which often caused reception interference. There were also few regulations regarding the power of transmitters, so powerful transmitters could drown out with a stronger signal the lower-powered, local transmitters. The FRC revoked thousands of radio broadcast licenses and instituted a system that favored fewer, high-power stations over smaller but more numerous local low-power stations. This policy benefited large commercial broadcasting companies over educational and small, private broadcasters.

Radio Act of 1927

An act of Congress that created the Federal Radio Commission and that was intended to help establish some sort of regulation and order over the chaos of the largely unregulated airwaves. It helped establish the principle that the airwaves were a limited public good and that companies using those airwaves had a duty to act responsibly toward the public in terms of the type of material they broadcast.

Federal Radio Commission (FRC)

Formed by the Radio Act of 1927, the commission was the precursor to the FCC and created a policy that favored fewer, high-power radio broadcasting stations rather than more numerous, low-power stations.

Federal Communication Commission (FCC)

The principal communications regulatory body at the federal level in the United States, established in 1934.

The National Broadcasting Network, or NBC, was the first network to form, having been created in 1926 when RCA, under the leadership of Sarnoff, purchased New York station WEAF (now WNBC) from AT&T for $1 million. That same year, NBC bought WJZ (licensed to Newark, New Jersey, but transmitting in New York) from Westinghouse and thus created the first network.

CBS was the second network to be formed, first as the United Independent Broadcasters in 1927 and then, after going on the air with a partner, the Columbia Phonograph and Records Company, becoming the Columbia Broadcasting System. In 1928, cigar maker Sam Paley bought CBS for four hundred thousand dollars and installed his son, William, as its head, moving the network's headquarters from Philadelphia to New York. Under William's longtime leadership, and later under that of his corporate heir Frank Stanton, CBS held to the number-one position among the networks and described itself as the Tiffany Network—although

Trusting in the Power of the Airwaves

Radio has proven to be very important as an information source in developing countries, where spotty electricity service, government regulations, low education, and scant incomes have kept most people from owning a television, let alone a computer and Internet connection.

Radios, however, are nearly ubiquitous thanks in part to their portability, low cost, and ability to run on batteries, solar power, or by hand cranks.

INTERNATIONAL PERSPECTIVES

A survey conducted overseas in 2009 by the International Center for Media Studies found that people in the developing world tended to trust radio more than any other source of information. Muslim respondents even said they trusted radio more than their religious leaders and that they were five times more likely to trust radio to tell them "how to live life" than other forms of media.

The implications of these findings are important for NGOs and others working in the developing world, as they highlight how important it is for those from developed nations to not take for granted certain cultural assumptions about media and how they are used. For example, an award-winning print-advertising campaign about disease prevention in the United States or Europe may not be understood or even seen by wide swaths of the population in a developing country, whereas a radio ad could reach many more people and have a greater effect.

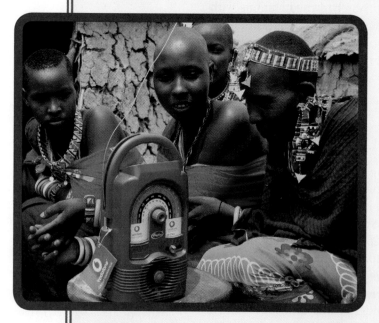
Maasai women listening to a hand-cranked radio provided by Feeplay Foundation.

others sometimes called it Black Rock, in partial reference to the black marble façade of its midtown Manhattan headquarters.

By 1935, fifty-eight of sixty-two stations nationwide were part of either the NBC or the CBS network. It was not until the 1940s that a third competing commercial network emerged, in television: ABC.

Radio Station Programming

Perhaps the most fundamental development in commercial radio in the twentieth century was its eventual specialization. Radio grew in its early years to become a dominant medium of mass communication. Large audiences assembled to listen to individual programs during much of the first half of the twentieth century. But with the rise of television as a medium of mass communication in the years following World War II, radio fell from a position of media dominance and, like magazines, adapted to the new media landscape by specializing.

This specialization takes a number of forms, including program formats, time of day for certain formats, and especially audience demographics. In radio, a day is broken up into different time segments called "dayparts." The 6 a.m. to 10 a.m. **daypart**, for example, is a time when most people listen to the radio as they get ready for work or school or are commuting. Therefore, the programming emphasizes frequent news, traffic, and weather reports as well as some of the more outspoken talk radio shows such as *Imus in the Morning.*

Radio stations are organized according to the type of programming they air. There are dozens of radio-programming formats.[5] Formats vary widely in terms

Radio plays an integral role in promoting music and making some recording artists top stars.

daypart
....
A segment of time used by radio and television program planners to decide who the primary audience is during that time of day or night.

TABLE 5-2
Most Popular Radio Programming Genres

FORMAT	% LISTENING AUDIENCE	# OF STATIONS (U.S.)
Country	12.7	1,683
News/Talk/Information	10.7	1,553
Adult Contemporary	7.5	798
Pop Contemporary Hit Radio	5.6	381
Classic Rock	4.5	514
Rhythmic Contemporary Hit Radio	4.0	156
Urban Adult Contemporary	3.7	170
Urban Contemporary	3.7	154
Mexican Regional	3.4	302
Hot Adult Contemporary	3.2	451

Source: Maximi$er Plus National Regional Database, Spring 2007

NPR and PRI: America's Public Radio Networks

National Public Radio (NPR) is a not-for-profit membership organization with 490 member public radio stations nationwide and a weekly audience of 17 million.[6] It produces and distributes news, cultural, and informational programs for public radio in the United States, linking the nation's noncommercial radio stations into a national network.

Public Radio International (PRI) produces and distributes additional public radio programming, such as *Marketplace* and Garrison Keillor's *A Prairie Home Companion*, to nearly 600 affiliate stations in the United States, Puerto Rico, and Guam, as well as international programs including the BBC World Service.[7]

NPR debuted on April 19, 1971, with live coverage of the Senate Vietnam hearings, and a month later broadcast *All Things Considered*, establishing NPR as an important provider of news and information programming. Today, NPR broadcasts each week one hundred hours of original programming.

Public radio distinguishes itself from commercial radio in a number of ways, including more extensive, impartial, and original audio news, especially long-form audio reporting, as heard on *Morning Edition* and *All Things Considered*. NPR also offers extensive music programming in classical and folk music, jazz, and opera, featuring a variety of live transmissions of the performing arts from theaters and concert halls. Evening programs include ones that introduce listeners to classical music as well as international musicians and unique musical formats beyond the standard genres.

Web Link >>>
NPR
www.npr.org

Web Link >>>
PRI
www.pri.org

---

of the audience they draw. Contemporary hit radio, for example, draws a much different audience than the country format, which is by far the most popular radio format in the United States. Over 1,600 stations are devoted to country music.

Radio Stations: The United States Today

There are approximately 10,000 commercial radio stations and 2,500 noncommercial stations in the United States. Noncommercial stations include NPR-affiliated stations, college radio stations, and community and religious stations.

All stations in the United States are assigned call letters, which designate the station and its geographic location east and west of the Mississippi River. For stations east of the Mississippi, W is the first call letter, and for stations west of it K is the call letter, although there are some exceptions that used call letters before the boundaries were determined, such as KDKA in Pittsburgh. Under an international agreement issued at the London International Radiotelegraphic Conference in 1912, different countries were awarded different letters. The United States received "KDA" to "KZZ."

For most of the first half of the twentieth century, AM radio listenership far exceeded FM listenership. But in the late 1970s this turned around, and today FM listenership is far greater than AM listenership, just as the number of FM stations exceeds AM stations. The ascendancy of FM radio in the 1970s was due to a number of factors, among them the inclusion of an FM dial in most automobile radio

Web Link >>>
FCC website
www.fcc.gov

receivers, changes in programming, and regulatory changes, combined with the fact that FM has less static.

Radio Station Ownership

In its early days, radio in the United States was a largely uncontrolled medium of public communications, not unlike the Internet in its early days. But the free-for-all quickly gave way to largely commercial interests and government regulation of the airwaves. Throughout most of the twentieth century, ownership of radio was relatively diverse. This was partly a result of federal laws that prohibited any one person or organization from owning more than twenty FM stations and twenty AM stations nationwide.

Regulatory changes in 1992 and the passage of the Telecommunications Act of 1996 resulted in new FCC radio-ownership rules. These new rules put no limit on the number of radio stations that can be owned or controlled by a single entity nationwide, although it is still required that the owner be a U.S. citizen. Since the passage of the act, more than 4,400 radio stations have changed ownership, and the radio industry has become more of an oligopoly, in which fewer companies own a greater number of radio stations.

Regulatory changes altered the FCC's "duopoly rules" on local station ownership. Duopoly rules refer to a prohibition on any one person or group owning, operating, or controlling more than two AM stations and two FM stations in the largest markets. The rules had also restricted the combined audience share of the co-owned stations to 25 percent, with smaller markets having even more restrictive limits. The act ended these duopoly restrictions and the FCC now permits a single entity to own substantially more in the same service market than it could in the past.

This shift in regulatory policy led to a trend in the 1990s and early twenty-first century toward increasing consolidation of radio ownership. For most of the first fifty years of radio broadcasting, radio was a small business, with owners longtime residents of the towns in which the stations operated. Although many stations in smaller towns are still locally owned and operated, most radio stations in big cities have become corporate enterprises.

In order to reduce operating costs, more and more stations are relying on computerized automated systems with prerecorded DJs and set music programming. Although the DJs' chatter may sound like they are in the local studio at the time and choosing songs as they go along, in fact it is more likely that it was all prerecorded and the playlist has been generated by computer program.

Increasingly, with the end of the duopoly rules, some groups now control eight or more stations in a single market, and most of the big, highly profitable stations are owned by the most powerful media groups. Those who support the changes in station ownership say consolidation is a good thing for many reasons, including increased efficiency; more economical, centralized production; larger budgets that permit greater programming experimentation and development; and more effective management. Critics argue that group ownership typically means less sensitivity to local concerns because owners are often remotely located.

There has been an interesting trend in the past few years toward radio groups deconsolidating and selling some of their vast holdings; Clear Channel is the most obvious case, as it has sold more than half of its 1,200 radio stations and all of its 51 television stations since 2007, partly because of its announcement to become a

TABLE 5-3

Top Radio Groups in U.S. by Number of Stations Owned, 2007

OWNER	# OF STATIONS
Clear Channel	636
Cumulus Broadcasting	286 (2005)
Citadel Communications Corporation	204
CBS Radio	140
Entercom	114
Salem Communications Corporation	97
Saga Communications Inc.	91
Cox Broadcasting	79
Univision	74
Radio One Inc.	53

Source: BIAfn Media Access Pro, PEJ Research, December 2007

privately held company and partly because of FCC regulations. Cumulus Broadcasting, the second-largest radio group, also went private in 2008.

Table 5-3 provides a breakdown of the top radio groups in the United States by number of stations owned. Although the move away from consolidation may seem like a good thing for the radio industry, the shift from publicly traded companies to privately held firms may also mean that the new owners make decisions based purely on the bottom line rather than considering the role that radio stations play for the public.

Satellite Radio

Satellite radio is touted by its supporters and many loyal listeners as the future of radio, while its skeptics say that it is an unsustainable business model that will ultimately disappear.

More akin to audio programming than to traditional broadcast radio, satellite radio uses digital radio signals broadcast from a satellite, beaming the same programming across a much wider swath of territory than what terrestrial broadcast stations can do. With up to fifty channels of CD-quality music in a variety of formats and a variety of third-party news, sports, and talk radio programs (most of them commercial free because it is a subscription-based service), satellite radio has won a loyal following of over 18 million listeners in the United States. Because it is subscription based, like cable television, it does not have the same restrictions regarding content that terrestrial broadcasters face.

Some of the popularity can be attributed to the fact that a growing number of new cars come with the service, and an increasing number of electronic gadgets that allow access to satellite radio in the home have also hit the market, though in-home adoption has been slow.

Sirius Satellite Radio, which started out as CD Radio in the early 1990s, launched its satellites for its radio service in 2000 and began broadcasting in 2002. XM Satellite Radio launched soon after, and the two companies competed vigorously in offering exclusive access to various sports channels, hosted music channels, and noted talk radio hosts.

In 2004, shock jock Howard Stern signed an exclusive five-year, $500 million contract with Sirius, to begin in 2006. The signing was widely debated by media watchers, some saying it signaled a sea change in the importance of satellite radio in comparison to terrestrial radio and others saying it was reminiscent of the wasteful spending seen during the dot-com boom of the late 1990s and that Stern would essentially disappear from the public's eye (or ear) because he would not be reaching nearly the same number of people on satellite radio.

In mid-2008 Sirius completed its acquisition of former competitor XM Satellite Radio and became Sirius XM Satellite Radio. The company almost filed for bankruptcy in early 2009 as large debts came due, but was rescued at the last minute.

Radio shock jock Howard Stern's move to satellite radio was hailed by some and criticized by others.

Web Link >>>
Sirius XM Satellite Radio
www.sirius.com

LOOKING BACK AND MOVING FORWARD

It is still unclear whether Sirius XM Satellite Radio will survive, and, if it does not, whether another satellite radio service will take its place and try to pick up where it left off. However, even if the future is not in the heavens, it will be grounded in certain behaviors and consumer desires that have become readily apparent across all media but especially regarding music.

First, although the way radio is transmitted and the devices the public uses to listen to it will change, radio itself—or, more accurately, the transmission of audio content to a mass audience—will remain an important form of mass communication. A primary reason for this is that radio, almost alone among mass media, allows people to easily engage in other activities while listening. No matter how advanced or portable media technology becomes, there is no way that we can watch TV or read a book or newspaper while driving safely, as we can do when listening to audio content.

However, as with other digital media, the shift to an on-demand media environment will become more important. This is one shift that satellite radio has signaled already, along with even further specialization and fragmentation of music types. A service like Pandora Internet Radio may well be where the future of radio lies: a highly personalized system that not only responds to your musical tastes but uses special algorithms and collaborative filtering to suggest new artists who play similar styles of music. These kinds of changes may so drastically alter how radio stations think of their programming that the term "radio" may technically become obsolete or come to mean something very different.

Of course, tied closely to the future of radio is the recording industry, which has relied largely on radio as a promotional vehicle for new music. Until the advent of digital media, the recording industry had little incentive to change its business model or ways of creating, promoting, and distributing music. Although advances in technology helped both the sound quality and portability of recorded music, little changed regarding basic business policies.

PANDORA®
internet radio

account | sign out | subscribe

Your Profile | About the Music ▼ | Share ▼ | Mobile | Help

Create a New Station...

Your Stations

Led Zeppelin Radio
add variety | edit

Kalmah Radio
Gabriel & Dresden ...
Zero 7 Radio
Strung Out Radio

QuickMix

Come Together
by: The Beatles
on: 1967-1970

Purple Haze
by: Jimi Hendrix
on: Voodoo Child

Touch Me (Take 3 Previously Unliss...
by: The Doors
on: Perception O...

About This Music | Artist | Album | Song | Lyrics | Fans

The Doors

The Doors, one of the most influential and controversial rock bands of the 1960s, were formed in Los Angeles in 1965 by UCLA film students Ray Manzarek, keyboards, and Jim Morrison, vocals; with drummer John Densmore and guitarist Robby Krieger. The group never added a bass player, and their sound was dominated by Manzarek's electric organ work and

Similar Artists:
The Rolling Stones
Jimi Hendrix
The Animals
Led Zeppelin
The Beatles

more...

Buy | Bookmark | Share

Pandora Internet radio is an example of what online audio has to offer listeners, providing recommendations of other artists and styles of music based on listening preferences.

Web Link >>>
Pandora Internet Radio
www.pandora.com/

This radically changed with the MP3 format, which made music files small enough to easily be sent via the Internet and stored on computers. The recording industry has become a poster child for other entertainment companies worried about a similar fate for their products, as file-sharing services make illegally copying and sharing of copyrighted material easy.

There are two main camps, or schools of thought, regarding the state of the music industry today. One camp claims that the music industry has only itself to blame in not realizing earlier that digital media would alter established business models and that it would need to adapt rather than try to bully consumers and the government with lawsuits and legislation benefiting the industry at the expense of the public. They point to growing sales of digital downloads of a la carte songs and ring tones as areas in which record labels can find new revenue streams.

However, these new revenue streams are still far from making up for the decline in music sales seen over recent years, which the recording industry blames on illegal file sharing of music. The interest in music remains as strong as ever, but music sales have declined. Supporters of the recording industry say that illegal file sharing hurts not only corporations but more importantly the artists who rely on royalties to survive and that file sharing is theft, pure and simple.

These two schools of thought are not confined only to the world of recording artists; there are echoes of this found especially in other entertainment, such as television and film. Even in the world of journalism we can see repercussions of these debates as media companies struggle to find new business models and adjust to differences in ways that audiences get and use their content.

· ·

DISCUSSION QUESTIONS

1. The public appetite for recorded music is great, but especially so among teenagers. Why do you think music is generally more important for teenagers than for people in their forties, for example?

2. In what ways have MTV and the music video influenced the recording-arts industry and popular music?

3. What suggestions would you make to a record-label executive regarding creating a successful business model in the digital age?

4. If you were an emerging artist starting to build a following of fans online and were approached by a major recording label, would you sign a contract with the major label or would you prefer to be with a small, independent label that let you keep a higher percentage of your royalties? Why?

5. Which do you think was more important in the development of radio: the shift in its early days to favor large-scale, powerful commercial stations over small, independent stations or the shift from terrestrial to satellite radio?

6. Listen to your favorite radio station with a critical ear and list the techniques it uses to give a certain character to the music format and the station itself. Listen for things like use of sound effects, how promos are done, and tone of the DJs. Now find a station of similar genre elsewhere in the country (via the Internet), listen to it, and find similarities.

7. Look at your music library and count how many songs you have that you have downloaded for free. Now put a value on each song of ninety-nine cents and calculate how much you would have spent if you'd purchased the songs legally.

8. Look at your music library and determine how many songs downloaded from new artists persuaded you to purchase that artist's CD or to purchase other songs by the artist.

. . . .

FURTHER READING

All You Need to Know About the Music Business, 6th ed.; Donald Passman (2008) Hal Leonard Corp.

The Business of Music, 10th ed.; William Krasilovsky, Sidney Shemel, John Gross, Jonathan Feinstein (2007) Billboard Books.

The Future of Music: Manifesto for the Digital Music Revolution; David Kusek (2008) Berklee Press.

Appetite for Self-Destruction: The Spectacular Crash of the Record Industry in the Digital Age; Steve Knopper (2009) Free Press.

Empire of the Air: The Men Who Made Radio; Tom Lewis (1993) Harper Perennial Library.

Hello, Everybody! The Dawn of American Radio; Anthony Rudel (2008) Houghton Mifflin Harcourt.

Censorship: The Threat to Silence Talk Radio; Brian Jennings and Sean Hannity (2009) Threshold Editions.

Something in the Air: Radio, Rock, and the Revolution That Shaped a Generation; Marc Fisher (2007) Random House.

Right of the Dial: The Rise of Clear Channel and the Fall of Commercial Radio; Alex Foege (2009) Faber and Faber.

. . . .

MEDIA QUIZ ANSWERS

4. False.

5. Mississippi River.

6. Country music.

7. Because it was originally called wireless telegraphy.

8. True.

Visual Media: Movies and Television

CHAPTER OBJECTIVES

In this chapter we will:

- Appreciate the role photography has played in our visual culture and its continued importance within mass communication.

- Understand the impact technological changes have had on the film and television industries and their content.

- Recognize the ways business models and structures have influenced the film industry.

- Understand the development of television from its origins to digital TV.

- Know the differences between terrestrial, cable, and satellite broadcasting and what they mean for viewers.

- Appreciate the implications of the convergence of telecommunications and content companies.

6 The screen pops on and you see various channel and show logos mixed with CD covers of your favorite bands. You click on the icon for a new show and choose to read some online reviews of the show before deciding to watch it. The reviews, from users you trust, are generally positive and you decide to give it a try.

As you watch the show, you see that one of your friends has also started watching it, so with your remote control you contact him and start a casual IM chat about the show you are both watching.

A song plays in the show from a band you haven't heard of, so you click on the link for the band name and see a list, with reviews, of their albums. You pause the show, click on the song you heard, and see the lyrics next to the snippet of the song that is playing. You put the song in your online shopping cart and put the album on your Wish List and get back to watching the show, making sure to program your on-demand service to automatically notify you when a new show airs.

Welcome to your television-viewing experience, coming soon to a living room near you.

This scenario, which would have largely been science fiction even five years ago, is now much closer to re-ality thanks to online services such as Boxee. Although Boxee may not be the company everyone uses, its services or something very much like them will be

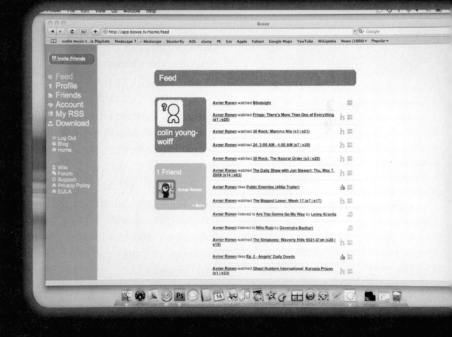

used by television viewers, drastically altering how they consume media and giving them much more control over what they watch, how they watch it, and when they watch.

hotographs and film have played a fundamental role in framing our world through journalism, entertainment, and art and giving us a sense of the importance of the visual in our lives. Even as digitization dramatically alters aspects of visual media, in other ways these media continue to shape our perceptions of what we create in a digital environment. Photojournalists, cinematographers, and videographers have used the frame of the photographic lens to place a defining structure on the linear narrative of visual storytelling.

The visual media grammar that filmmakers have created in the past hundred years of filmmaking provides the foundation for digital videographers as they explore the limits of the new medium with more portable equipment and more sophisticated editing tools.

The Internet and online consumption of video, film, and television are only starting to have serious ramifications on our understanding of the role of television in the future, but the changes are happening rapidly. Already for many younger people the Internet is a more important medium than television, which is still the dominant medium for the majority of people.

Although technological advances in visual media have been linked to genres and media content, in this chapter we will focus primarily on the role that technology has played with photography, film, and television and touch only briefly on the impact that has had on content. This and the role that business models have played with content will be looked at more carefully in Chapter 11, when we discuss entertainment.

Photography

Still images, or photographs, have long been important to mass communications. Still images have performed—and continue to perform—at least three significant functions in mediated communication.

First, photographs can tell a story or convey information quickly. At a glance, a reader can scan the photos or images in a newspaper or magazine. These photos might tell the story of a daring rescue in a fire, provide a glimpse of a reclusive celebrity, or show the latest fashions on the runways of Paris or Milan.

Second, photos and other images can provide verification of factual claims. While words might provide the narrative, photos confirm the truth of what those

Eye-Q Test

1. (T/F) The principles used in photography were known for hundreds of years before the first photograph was ever made.

2. What did the invention of roll film do for photography?

3. If someone stands on the street in front of your house and takes a picture of your house without your permission and then posts it on the Internet, is that an invasion of privacy?

4. Why did some of the earliest film pioneers, such as the Lumière brothers, believe that film was mostly a novelty and would simply be a short-lived fad?

5. What movies have paid tribute to the famous Odessa Steps sequence in *Battleship Potemkin*?

6. Why have independent or art house movies inherently been at a disadvantage in the Hollywood studio production system?

7. If you live to be 75, how many years out of your life will you have spent watching television?

8. What is the most common way Americans get television signals—over-the-air broadcasts, cable, or satellite?

9. (T/F) Government regulations and the FCC forbid television networks from posting their shows online as Internet TV stations.

10. When did all television signals in the United States convert to digital format?

words say, whether it is a plane crash, an alleged extramarital affair, or a mass grave in a war-torn part of the world.

Finally, photos can engage, entertain, or elicit emotion in a way that words alone might not. Seeing photos of the devastation left from the September 11, 2001, terrorist attacks on the World Trade Center and Pentagon can stir feelings that mere verbal descriptions might never produce.

■ ■ ■ HISTORICAL DEVELOPMENT OF PHOTOGRAPHY

The principles involved in creating photographs had been known and used for hundreds of years before photography was invented, so in one respect it was perhaps surprising that photography had not been developed earlier. The earliest recorded use of a **camera obscura**, a dark box or room with a small hole in it that allowed an inverted image of an outside scene to be shown on the opposite inner wall, is in the writings of Leonardo da Vinci. He explained how a camera obscura can be an aid to drawing scenery, as one simply moves a sheet of paper around until the scene comes into sharp focus and then traces the scene.

The other important element is understanding how light can affect certain chemicals, which was also known for hundreds of years before the first photograph was developed. Although some scientists could produce photographs by using various light-sensitive chemicals, they had no way to make the images permanent. In June 1827, Joseph Niépce created a picture using

Photography can often capture powerful emotional moments in ways few other mediums can.

The Photojournalist's Dilemma: Sudan, Starvation, and Suicide

INTERNATIONAL PERSPECTIVES

On March 23, 1993, the *New York Times* ran a photo taken by South African photojournalist Kevin Carter that seemed to epitomize the human suffering and anguish in Africa.

A small, starving Sudanese girl tried to crawl to a feeding station in a remote area while a vulture stood nearby, waiting for her to die. Carter said he waited for about twenty minutes, positioning himself for the best shot and careful not to disturb the bird, hoping it would spread its wings. When it did not, he snapped some pictures, chased the bird away, and watched as the little girl resumed her struggle. A friend and colleague of Carter's said that afterward Carter was depressed and kept saying he wanted to hug his own young daughter. The photo touched many who saw it, and hundreds of people asked the *Times* if the girl had survived, but there was no way the *Times* could find out the girl's fate.

On April 12, 1994, Carter learned that he won the Pulitzer Prize for photography, even as some colleagues and media outlets strongly criticized him. The *St. Petersburg* (Florida) *Times* said, "The man adjusting his lens to take just the right frame of her suffering might just as well be a predator, another vulture on the scene."

Carter was painfully aware of the photojournalist's dilemma but said, in describing photographing a gunfight, that one simply had to think visually first and think about the other issues later. American photojournalist James Nachtwey, who often worked with Carter and his photo-

journalist friends, says, "Every photographer who has been involved in these stories has been affected. You become changed forever. Nobody does this kind of work to make themselves feel good. It is very hard to continue."

This was apparently the case for Carter, who committed suicide by carbon monoxide poisoning in his truck on July 27, 1994, near a park where he used to play as a child. He was 33.[3]

What responsibility, if any, does a photojournalist have to help the subjects he or she photographs? What implications could there be if photojournalists regularly helped people during conflicts or in times of tragedy?

documentation. Muybridge took a famous photo series through which he was able to document, for the first time, how a horse runs. Such applications of photography are of great importance in mass communications, especially where they can help us see things that human eyes, unassisted, would be unable to see. This is an opportunity taken to new heights in the digital age. Today, not only photographs of the microscopic can captivate us but images of the heavens as well. Some scientific images have even been considered visual art.

Photography remains an especially important component of modern magazines, even reaching high art in some cases, and has had powerful effects on what we perceive as ideals of beauty or fashion (which few of us can ever reach). The power of the image can persuade just as effectively as it can educate.

There were many reasons for the move to Hollywood, not the least of which was better weather. Actors, producers, and directors found their way to the growing movie-making center, creating a split between the theater (and later television) in New York and film in Hollywood that largely continues to this day. Most television shows are now filmed in Hollywood studios as well, even the comedies and police dramas ostensibly set in New York.

The warm, dry weather in Hollywood allowed filmmakers to produce films year-round to feed the hungry distribution chains a nonstop flow. Success bred more success, and today the U.S. movie industry is securely based in Hollywood, although there are a number of regional centers for movie production across North America, including Toronto and Vancouver, Canada.

Since its birth, the industry has grown to a multi-billion-dollar giant that, with a distinctly American influence, not only provides global entertainment but also shapes global culture, commerce, and imagination. The development of the Hollywood movie industry very much reflects the social, business, and political climate of the times and continues to be heavily influenced by technological changes that bring about different business models. One example of how intertwined commerce and pop culture are in the movie industry can be found in the development of the Hollywood studio star system and its dismantling.

Hollywood Star System

Today we often feel that the term "movie star" is synonymous with a glamorous lifestyle and even with Hollywood itself. But for the first several years of movies, actors' and actresses' names did not even appear in the movie credits. However, it was not long before audiences showed an interest in learning not only the names but also the personalities and histories of the people they were watching on-screen. Fan magazines helped stoke interest in stars. Shrewd studio heads created and cultivated personas for their popular stars, even giving them false histories in order to better market them. Although not as blatant as in early years, the embellishment of stars' backgrounds for marketing purposes continues today.

In the early 1930s a new era began in American film and lasted until 1949. This was the era of the Hollywood studio star system. Paramount Pictures (1912), Columbia Pictures (1920), Metro-Goldwyn-Mayer (1924), Warner Brothers (1923), and 20th Century Fox (1935) all held long-term contracts on star directors and actors and built their success on those stars. Many are still familiar today, more than a half century after the era ended.

During this era, stars were unable to seek their own contracts for individual films, but they could be loaned from one studio to another, often in exchange for other stars. Stars were also expected to be highly productive, often starring in five or six films a year. Warner Brothers' Humphrey Bogart starred in forty films between 1934 and 1943, and perhaps his most famous, *Casablanca*, was just one of four films he made in 1943.

Many of the films of this era, including *Casablanca*, were not made as great works of cinematic art. Rather, they were made as popular entertainment to make profits for the studios. These films made a great deal of money for the studios, which also typically owned large theater chains where the films were shown. People often went to see these films for the stars they had come to know and for the characters they often represented. Gary Cooper, star of *Mr. Deeds Goes to Town* (1936) and *Meet John Doe* (1941), was known as a tall, clumsy, and humble man who may have been naive but was also a man of integrity. He was the quintessential American, the strong, silent type. Jimmy Stewart was in many ways the same

Recent years have seen the growth of imagery and video from satellites. Remote-sensing satellite imagery has since the end of the Cold War grown dramatically to become an almost daily part of media content.[4] On the Web, through applications like Google Earth, members of the public can see satellite images of their homes and even in many cases street-level photographs.

Just as early photography raised new ethical issues for photojournalism regarding capturing actual scenes and creating more visually compelling scenes, digital photography combined with social media like MySpace or Facebook have created new ethical debates among the general public around privacy issues. It is a testament to the continued power of the visual image that these debates arise when there are new ways to see things or when more people have access to photographs.

However, the ethical debates and concerns over the power of the image pale in comparison to what evolved from some of the earliest developments in capturing still images—capturing the moving image.

Satellite imagery like Google Earth's has helped the public see the world in new ways but sometimes raises privacy concerns.

Movies

Even before the invention of daguerreotype photography, inventors had tried to re-create the perception of motion through a variety of devices that were often as awkwardly named as they were difficult to use. Most were never more than novelties. If still images proved important to mass media of the mid-nineteenth century, then the development of motion pictures at the end of the nineteenth century dramatically transformed the nature of mass communications and entertainment in the twentieth century. The introduction of motion pictures meant that for the first time activity could be recorded. More importantly for the movie industry, the technology could re-create reality and *create* visual "realities" that never could exist in the real world.

■ ■ ■ THE FUNCTIONS OF THE MOVIE INDUSTRY

The motion picture, or movie, industry dates back to the 1890s, when Thomas Edison and the Lumière brothers developed motion picture cameras and projection devices. The primary function of motion pictures is to entertain, with many millions of movie watchers enjoying the sweeping epics, slapstick comedies, romance, and adventure they see in feature-length films.

Yet, many fans and critics alike consider the cinema to be more than simple entertainment and appraise its value and function as a serious visual art form comparable to painting, sculpture, or architecture, with a history of important social

CONVERGENCE CONTEXT

3-D Movies: Perennial Fad, or Wave of the

Movie studios are once again promoting 3-D movies as The Next Big Thing, but this time several noted directors are also cheerleaders, including Steven Spielberg, Peter Jackson, and James Cameron, all of whom are working on 3-D movies. Some proponents even claim that 3-D will revolutionize cinema in the same way that sound revolutionized the early film era.

Others remain skeptical, however. The need to wear special glasses—no matter how cool the glasses look—is a barrier to watching a movie in 3-D. Price is another issue, as 3-D movies tend to

cost about 25 percent mo[re tha] at the box office, in part to make equipment needed to show them.

There is also the issue of the m lend themselves to 3-D—generally films that can allow for the full arr. fects that come with 3-D.

Genre has also been a sticking movies, as in the past they have ten ror movies or other cheesy types, ar image of 3-D as a gimmick to attrac otherwise poor films may be hard.

As with many other developm ies, the desire to make the m even more lifelike goes way b movie audiences saw a series tary shorts in 3-D by Edwin Porte *The Great Train Robbery*.

In just about every decade le now, the movie industry and the hyped 3-D as something new in n ing. In the early 1950s, it was large get audiences back from their tele where they were watching old m new programs for free.

Today, with increasingly lavis entertainment systems and wid television sets, filmmakers are once a ing to give the viewing public som cannot get at home. Whether 3-D wil tionize the movie industry—this time one more example of a cyclical cinem remains to be seen.

■ ■ ■ INTRODUCTION TO THE MOVIE INDUSTRY

The United States motion picture industry began on the eastern seaboa cially New York, but soon moved to Los Angeles, where the powerful movic of the early 1900s created Hollywood. The main reason the industry si New York was because at the time it was the center of entertainment in the States, with its Broadway and vaudeville theaters. Thomas Edison's labo were also located nearby in New Jersey.

months, depending on schedules and other issues that may arise. After shooting is done, the filmmaker is still looking at several more months of postproduction work and editing the hours and hours of footage into a typical movie length. This too can often lead to serious creative differences, as studio executives may demand a more upbeat or otherwise different ending based on early audience feedback, which often means editing out other scenes or even in some cases reshooting scenes or shooting new ones. The Ridley Scott classic *Blade Runner* (1982) is perhaps one of the most famous cases in which the director's ending did not meet with the studio's approval after early audience testing and had to be redone to be more upbeat. Of course, several versions of the movie were later released, including a "director's cut" that more closely adhered to Scott's vision of the movie. Postproduction is also the phase during which musical scores are added and dubbing and voice-overs put in.

Marketing and distribution are quite expensive and are often the keys to a movie's success. A well-attended movie that debuts in one thousand theaters nationwide simply will not earn as much as a movie that fills half the seats but that is distributed to over three thousand theaters. This is where the power of the major studios still comes into play, as they can more easily get a movie distributed widely than an independent film can.

Exhibition Windows for Movies

Movies have a regular pattern of exhibition "windows," or places where they are shown, that help increase revenues. When studios were at their strongest, they could control theatrical releases to what were deemed "first-run" theaters; then, after the movies lost their appeal at those, they were placed in second-run theaters. Movie studios determined which theaters were first-run and which were second-run and had agreements with theater owners that ensured theaters would have exclusive showing privileges within a certain geographic area for a certain amount of time. However, studios also often forced theaters to buy package deals of movies that included a few hits but also many lower-quality films that would not be as popular. This is one of the practices that became forbidden in the 1948 *Paramount* antitrust case.

The movie industry boycotted television when it first arrived, refusing to provide movies that could be shown on television and even blacklisting actors who acted on television. Studios felt that television would draw audiences away from theaters and thus ruin the movie industry. This resistance to technological change has become a common pattern among entrenched media-entertainment industries.

However, it was not long before the movie industry realized that television could be used to give new life to movies that had run through their life cycle in theatrical release, and they started selling their previously released movies to the television networks. A similar pattern of resistance, and then acceptance, by the studios occurred as they saw more revenue opportunities with VCRs and cable television. Currently movie studios are insisting that digital media include guaranteed security measures to avoid illegal copying of their movies. Until recent years, studios had been hampering development of digitally delivered video-on-demand or movies-on-demand for fear of piracy like that seen with music.

The usual windows for a movie start with domestic theatrical release then proceed to international release, video, pay-per-view on cable, pay cable, network TV, and then syndicated TV. Each of these windows has a specified time for its showing, and windows generally do not overlap. However, depending on the success of the movie, it may get released to video earlier than usual in order to take advantage of residual popularity of the theatrical release. In fact, video rentals and sales are usually the biggest money-generator for movies, long since surpassing box office revenues. As video-on-demand becomes more widespread, it will likely become the first window after theatrical release.[7]

Going Digital

Digitization has had profound effects on the movie industry, some of which are already being seen both in the industry itself and in the theater. Amazing special effects can be created, using digital technology, that far surpass previous special-effects efforts. Computer-created characters have become increasingly lifelike, and, as computer power increases, computer artists and programmers continue to improve their skills to render surfaces like snow and fur more realistically.

Digital distribution of films also promises huge cost savings for movie studios. It costs up to two thousand dollars to produce, duplicate, and ship one forty-pound celluloid film print to a movie theater, and most studios ship prints to three thousand theaters nationwide if they hope the movie can be a blockbuster. That means $6 million just in distribution costs for a major film.[8] A digital film, on the other hand, would simply be sent over satellite or through broadband to a movie theater, thereby avoiding all the costs associated with shipping a bulky physical product. In addition, endless perfect copies could be made, just as with other digital media, eliminating the need to receive even more prints when film breaks or loses its quality after repeated showings.

Digital technology has allowed filmmakers to combine live actors with computer-generated animation to produce interesting new effects.

The movie industry has been relatively slow to wholly embrace digital technology on the distribution end, however, for a number of reasons. One reason is the high cost of outfitting theaters with digital projector systems, computer servers, and satellite dishes or high-speed wiring. Theater owners argue that since it is the movie studios that will get the greatest savings through digital distribution, they should pay at least part of the cost of upgrading theaters to digital systems. As of May 2002, there were only twenty-three all-digital theaters throughout the United States, and the conversion process was going slowly. But in 2008, five of the major studios struck a deal with movie-theater chains to rapidly convert thousands of theaters to digital projection systems.

Another reason the movie industry has been slow in moving to digital technology, despite potential cost savings, is its concern over piracy and subsequent loss of revenues. The studios have watched the music industry's battles with file-swapping services such as Napster and realize that they are prime targets for similar practices because of the popularity of movies.

Assuming that the movie industry does eventually adopt digital technology at all levels of production, it is likely that the moviegoer will see great changes not only in digital effects, such as improved picture quality (including 3-D) and better sound, but in the availability of types of movies as well. Independent movies may more likely be shown in major theaters, as the theaters or studios will not be

Television Learns Music's Lessons

As YouTube rapidly gained popularity, television networks were seeing more and more of their shows being uploaded to the site. Snippets of *Saturday Night Live* skits, clips or scenes from shows, and even whole episodes were being made available to YouTube's millions of users.

Learning from the mistakes made by the music industry, most networks took a more subdued approach to the content that was being uploaded. Although YouTube did get "cease-and-desist" letters regarding copyrighted material, which it would then remove from the site, some television companies got together and decided that they would take control of their content online.

However, rather than create some kind of subscription model, they decided to provide the content for free, just as YouTube was doing. In March 2007 Hulu.com was founded, co-owned by NBC Universal, News Corp., and Providence Equity Partners.

Because of the number of subsidiary media companies both NBC Universal and News Corp. have, they were easily able to add content from Fox, NBC, Sony Pictures Television, Warner Brothers Televi-

Web Link >>>
Hulu
www.hulu.com

sion, and others. Furthermore, they have made a notable effort to have high-quality streaming video online, which is quite different than the varying and generally poorer-quality videos found on YouTube.

Supported by an advertising model, Hulu is still too new to know whether it will be successful or not. However, it is yet one more example of how media companies are realizing that the old models of business simply will not work and that if they do not do something online, other upstart companies simply will.

these issues have arisen in the form of the debates about Net neutrality, covered in a later chapter.

. . . .

DISCUSSION QUESTIONS

1. With the existence of film and television, do you think still photography is as relevant as it used to be? Why or why not?

2. The ability of the earliest filmmakers to tell stories was hampered by technological limitations that kept film reels short, so only a few minutes of filmed footage could be shown at a time. In what ways could current technological limitations hamper our ability to tell stories through the Internet?

3. Recent movies seem to consistently break box office records. Why do you think this is so?

4. Could a group of young digital filmmakers revolutionize the industry and dominate movie production and distribution like the Hollywood movie moguls did in the earliest days of Hollywood? Why or why not?

5. Discuss new ways movie theaters might be able to use their large screens and space to show digital film not only from big-name moviemakers but from local artists as well. What effects might this have for the local movie theater and for its role in the community?

6. Keep a diary for a week of the television shows you watch, how long you watch them, and how (TV, computer, video-on-demand, etc.). What patterns do you see and what implications do they have, if any, for your media consumption?

7. Research one of the top ten cable MSOs (or top twenty-five) and find out what people are saying about it in online discussions such as forums and blogs. Compare your findings with classmates.

. . . .

FURTHER READING

American Photography: A Century of Images; Vicki Goldberg, Robert Silberman (1999) Chronicle Books.

Film Art: An Introduction, 8th ed.; David Bordwell, Kristin Thompson (2008) McGraw-Hill Higher Education.

Hollywood! A Celebration; David Thomson (2001) DK Publishing.

The Film Snob's Dictionary: An Essential Lexicon of Filmological Knowledge; David Kamp, Lawrence Levi (2006) Broadway.

Film: A Critical Introduction, 2nd edition; Maria Pramaggiore, Tom Wallis (2007) Allyn & Bacon.

The Film Encyclopedia: The Complete Guide to Film and the Film Industry, 6th ed.; Ephraim Katz (2008) Collins.

The Business of Television; Howard Blumenthal, Oliver Goodenough (2006) Billboard Books.

The Columbia History of American Television; Gary Edgerton (2009) Columbia University Press.

Career Opportunities in the Film Industry; Fred Yager, Jan Yager (2009) Checkmark Books.

. . . .

MEDIA QUIZ ANSWERS

1. True.

2. Make photography accessible to the general public.

3. No.

4. Because they took film of people doing everyday activities and they felt the novelty of watching such things on screen would soon wear off.

5. The Untouchables, among others.

6. Because they generally do not get large audiences and are not profitable.

7. 11 years.

8. Cable.

9. False.

10. June 2009.

Information Overload, Usability, and Interactive Media

CHAPTER OBJECTIVES

In this chapter we will:

■ List the five fundamental principles that make something a storage technology and how they relate to mass-communication issues.

■ Compare and contrast various historical and current storage technologies in terms of how well they meet the five fundamental principles.

■ Describe the consequences of storage technologies for mass communication and society.

■ Describe why user interface is important to mass communication.

■ Explain how emerging trends will affect user interface and the way we use media.

■ Define the elements of interactivity.

■ Describe the importance of interactivity in terms of modern media.

7

Imagine a world without paper. No books, magazines, or newspapers as we know them. There are still libraries to store knowledge, of course, but they are likely vastly bigger to store the material in whatever form is most common—probably something similarly portable to paper but perhaps harder to use, perhaps more fragile, or more expensive to make.

Now imagine a world much like ours today except digital audio files use a device the size of a brick to store a single song. Rather than downloading dozens of songs effortlessly, you have to agonize over your choice of song to take with you, something that you will be willing to listen to repeatedly to and from class. Likely as not, you won't even bother.

Consider a world in which you look at a TV-like screen but with no buttons or switches of any kind—no way to understand how to turn it on, how to change channels, or perhaps even understand what it does, exactly.

These three examples show how important the type of storage technology and the interface we get accustomed to using are to our media environment. They affect how we access and think about information and how we use media devices.

A common thread with the examples is the idea of interactivity—the notion of how we engage with the media and the devices we use. This, too, greatly affects our position in relation to media: interactive media change us from passive media consumers to potentially active users—and creators—of media content.

his chapter focuses on three major aspects of digital media that make them different than traditional media: storage technology, user interface, and interactivity.

The term "**storage technology**" simply refers to any type of device or medium in which information can be kept for later retrieval. An ideal storage technology will be strong in five components common to all storage technologies: longevity, capacity, portability, accessibility, and reproducibility.

However, throughout history various technologies have been strong in some aspects but not others, and attempts to find a perfect balance continue today. In addition, digital technology and the importance of information in the modern age bring their own unique issues to storing and retrieving content in a mass-communication context.

Even if storage is dealt with, there still remains the important question of how to easily access the information we want when we want it. Related to this is the problem of the relative newness of digital media and our lack of understanding of how to use it in even basic ways sometimes. This is why user interface is so important in today's media. Poor user-interface design can keep people away from websites or content and can affect how subsequent technologies are developed. Similarly, good interface design can enhance the user experience and open up new realms of information and entertainment.

Interactivity is a key aspect differentiating today's digital media from traditional media or from putting traditional media simply in a digital, noninteractive format. The power that interactivity has to engage and involve users changes our relationship with media and raises new ethical issues, which will be explored in this chapter.

storage technology
....
Any type of device or medium in which information can be maintained for later retrieval.

Characteristics of Storage, Representation, and Retrieval

How information is stored is critical to communication, whether analog or digital. Since only a portion of media content is distributed live, or without storage, an overwhelming amount of the media content we read, see, or hear has first been stored for subsequent editing, distribution, and access. Whether through letters on a page, a magnetic tracing on a computer disk, or etchings on an optical drive, information must be represented in a fashion that allows for people to access it. The following discussion identifies the five concepts of longevity, capacity,

Searching for Knowledge

MEDIA QUIZ

1. (T/F) Kilobytes are named after Anastasios H. Kilobyte, the nineteenth-century Greek mathematician who discovered them.
2. (T/F) Until humans invented written language, there was no way to store information or knowledge.
3. What does GUI stand for?
4. (T/F) Out of all the fundamental characteristics of storage media, longevity has actually decreased compared to older storage media.
5. (T/F) MP3 stands for MPEG-3, a type of audio compression format.
6. What is the estimate of how much money is lost a year by companies because of information overload?
7. Which was the last network to switch from film to videotape for its news coverage? What year did it switch and why?
8. Name the top three languages used on the Internet.
9. (T/F) Even the best search engines only cover about 30 percent of the Web.
10. What is a Google bomb?

portability, accessibility, and reproducibility that help to define the nature and quality of stored information.

■■■ LONGEVITY

In one sense, longevity, or how long information can be retained in a medium, is most critical. The oldest known media, petroglyphs, or cave paintings, have lasted for many millennia, as have hieroglyphics, also painted on rock. It is their longevity that has given us a window into the past and a glimpse into the world of early humans.

Information-storage technologies have generally sacrificed longevity for increases in the four other characteristics, such as capacity or portability. In other words, storage technologies such as paper, film, or magnetic tape do not last nearly as long as some of the earliest storage technologies, such as petroglyphs, for example. Compare the life span of four-thousand-year-old hieroglyphics in Egyptian tombs with that of cinema film stock from the early 1900s, which is already disintegrating only one hundred years after it was created.

Hieroglyphs written on stone have great longevity but are not very portable.

Longevity, though undoubtedly useful from a historical perspective, has turned out to not be as important as how much information can be stored.

■■■ CAPACITY

Newer storage technologies have greatly increased the capacity to store information but at the expense of longevity. Books and other print media, such as newspapers and magazines, can retain greater amounts of information than petroglyphs, but they begin to decay almost immediately and are unlikely to survive more than a few hundred years.

Consider the size of a floppy diskette and how much more information it can store in a smaller space than a book. Expand that to CD-ROMs (700 MB versus 1.2 MB for diskette) and then to DVDs, which store up to 4.7 GB (9.4 GB double-sided) in the same amount of physical space as a CD, and you can begin to see how much more information we can access in a very small space than ever before. And that doesn't include using compression algorithms that can cram even more material into the same amount of disk space.

However, being able to store large amounts of data is not very helpful if the medium used to store it also increases in size, thus making it hard to move around.

Books and scrolls help make information very portable, but at the expense of longevity, as paper or parchment disintegrates.

■■■ PORTABILITY

Tied closely with increasing capacity has been increasing portability. Although cave paintings endure, they are essentially immovable. Stone or clay tablets improved portability of information, although not by much. Papyrus and parchment, first developed in Egypt and widely used in the Greek and Roman worlds of the late fourth century BCE until the middle of the seventh century CE, created a dramatic improvement in portability of information.

The development of paper and printing made distributing information easier as well. Portability can also be tied to the notion of capacity. Carrying a Kindle or other type of ebook, which can store two hundred titles, is much easier than actually having to move all two hundred printed versions of the same books. However, greater portability through electronic storage devices comes at a cost—unlike a book, you cannot access the content if the battery is dead.

■■■ ACCESSIBILITY

Better accessibility of stored information can be looked at from two perspectives. On one hand, the need to use electronics to access television, radio, or computer is a limitation. With no power, there is no information. But books or clay tablets can be accessed directly, simply through looking at them.

International standards and devices to retrieve the information on digital storage media continue to change so rapidly that in just a few years it can become virtually impossible to access the content stored on a particular device. For example, try to find a $5\frac{1}{4}$-inch computer floppy disk drive—a storage medium that was common in the 1980s. VHS videocassettes are also increasingly hard to find in stores, having been replaced by DVDs. Will DVD players manufactured in the early twenty-first century have a longer life span? Will a member of a human civilization living three thousand years from now—or even three hundred—be able to find a machine to play a DVD?

On the other hand, modern electronic-storage technology, especially in digital form, provides much greater access to information to a larger number of people than ever before, if they have the right equipment. A person does not have to be present at the cave to see the cave drawings, or have an actual photograph to see the drawings, or wait months for a book or magazine to arrive by post. Today, people can use the Internet to instantly access information of any type, almost anywhere they are.

Accessibility of information can be a problem in the electronic age, as old media formats get replaced by newer ones and manufacturers stop making equipment that used the older formats.

■ ■ ■ REPRODUCIBILITY

In many ways digital media can be seen as improving on trends in storage technology that have continued for thousands of years, but in terms of reproducibility digital media represent a radical departure from anything that has come before, for a number of reasons. The ease and accuracy of reproduction in digital media far surpasses analog media. Prior to the printing press, the only way to copy written text was by hand—a laborious, time-consuming, and error-prone process. Visual media had to be hand copied until the nineteenth century, when photography "automated" the copying process to some extent.

Digital media can be easily reproduced because they exist only as bits and bytes and not anything physical. In other words, the very fact that digital media are not a physical object of any sort makes them easier to copy and allows for an infinite number of copies without reducing the number of copies available.

This same characteristic also makes it possible to produce not only perfect copies of the original but *better* versions than the original, such as when imperfections of sound recordings are removed digitally. In analog media, copies of the original are inevitably changed and lose some quality compared to the original version—again, think of audio recordings, in which a third- or fourth-generation audiocassette copy of a recording from a CD is noticeably poorer in sound quality. In digital media it is much easier to retain the same quality as the original, although for storage-space reasons reduced-quality versions are often saved.

Nonelectronic Media Versus Electronic Media

In terms of storage technology, there is a fundamental difference between nonelectronic media, such as print, painting, or photography (including film), and electronic media, such as radio, television, and digital media. In the former types of **mediated communication**, their storage capacity is inherent in the medium itself. In other words, in painting a picture or writing words down the information is being stored.

Books have medium- to long-term longevity (in modern terms), are very portable, and are fairly easy to reproduce. They are accessible, assuming one can read, but their accessibility drops markedly if one is searching for a specific piece of information. Think of searching for a favorite quote or passage in a novel read long ago.

In storage-technology terms they can be described as "**sequential-access memory**" devices; i.e., a reader must go through each page to find some specific piece of information in the book. Developments such as page numbers, a table of contents, and an index (the latter two being of no use without page numbers) all help make

mediated communication

Communication that takes place through a medium, such as writing or recording, as opposed to unmediated communication, such as face-to-face discussions.

sequential-access memory

A type of medium in which a reader, viewer, or user must go through the medium in the order received in order to find specific information.

the book more of a "**random-access memory**" device—meaning, the accessibility of random content in it is increased. Dictionaries, encyclopedias, and telephone books, where information is listed either alphabetically or by some other logical category, are examples of books created specifically *as* random-access memory devices.

Electronic media, on the other hand, can be broadcast live and unrecorded. In fact, one way of looking at electronic media such as radio and television is that in their purest forms they are not storage technologies at all—once they are broadcast they have absolutely zero longevity and cannot be "stored" in any physical sense except through the memories of listeners or viewers. Imagine living in a world in which every television show, every news broadcast, and every song on the radio was done live over the air, with no way to go back and listen or watch again unless it was performed again.

TIMELINE

Development of Electronic Recording Devices

1875 Thomas Edison successfully records and plays back the song "Mary's Little Lamb" from a strip of tinfoil wrapped around a spinning cylinder.

1888 American inventor Oberlin Smith introduces the concept of recording sound on magnetic tape.

1898 The Telegraphone, the first operating magnetic recording device, is developed by Danish engineer Valdemar Poulsen.

1900 Austrian emperor Franz Josef records his voice with the Telegraphone at the Paris Exposition, causing a sensation among the public as people begin to realize the implications of being able to record the human voice.

1928 Austrian chemist Fritz Pfleumer invents a recorder using lightweight tape coated with magnetic particles.

1930 Stereo recording is invented at Bell Labs in the U.S. using the concepts created by Alan Blumlein, an employee of Electrical and Musical Industries (EMI), in London.

1936 The Magnetophon, a cheaper and easier-to-use device than previous magnetic recorders, is used to record a performance of the London Philharmonic Orchestra in concert in Germany.

1947 *The Bing Crosby Show* is recorded using the Magnetophon. Crosby switches from NBC to ABC radio network in order to use the recording device. Bing Crosby Enterprises sells hundreds of the devices to radio stations and recording studios throughout the country.

1956 Ampex Corp. manufactures the first practical magnetic videotape recorder, the VR-1000, for use by television stations. Cost: $50,000.

1961 The Society of Motion Picture and Television Engineers (SMPTE) establishes the standard for time-code format on recorded audio and video (first on tape, but now on any storage medium). Time coding is the basis for modern postproduction or editing.

1963 Philips introduces the compact audiocassette recorder, followed by the eight-track recorder and microcassette.

1968 First portable video-recording equipment is developed in Europe, allowing journalists to shoot video in the field instead of film.

1975 NBC is the last of the major television networks to switch to videotape in news footage after its filmed report on the assassination attempt of Gerald Ford is aired several hours after the reports from ABC and CBS.

1977 Philips (Netherlands) introduces the videocassette recorder.

1986 Digital audio tape (DAT) is created in Japan. Consumers now use digital videotapes almost exclusively, such as in digital video cameras.

1988 MPEG standard established (acronym for "Moving Pictures Experts Group") for compressing digital data.

1992 MPEG-2 becomes the new compression standard, which allows the coding of studio-quality video for digital TV, high-density CD-ROMs, and TV broadcasting.

1998 MP3 is a new file-storage format for digital audio recordings.

2006 Sony introduces a digital, high-definition, tapeless camcorder for consumer market.

Social and Political Impact of Storing Information

Canadian media scholar Harold Innis and his famous protégé Marshall McLuhan formulated well-known hypotheses about the longevity and portability of media and their resulting cultural meanings. It is worth reading McLuhan's book *Understanding Media: The Extensions of Man* (with Lewis H. Lapham) or Innis's *The Bias of Communication* for a detailed understanding of how the life span and portability of a medium might affect its nature and role in a society.

The storage capacities of nonelectronic media brought their own challenges and influences over millennia, as did the storage of electronic media once recording became available. Digital media, and their capacity for easy random-access memory, have also brought many changes. The ability to easily store and find digital information has become one of the most important aspects of turning the Internet into a fully developed mass medium, and companies such as Google, which were created to help people search for information, are now global media behemoths.

■ ■ ■ STONE TABLETS TO PAPYRUS

Innis argued that from papyrus to printing, the social and political development of the Western world has been profoundly shaped by the qualities of media-storage technology. Civilizations that used stone or clay tablets, such as Babylon, tended to favor centralized administrative systems where knowledge was concentrated in the hands of a few powerful elites—either religious or political leaders, or both. The formulation of written laws, such as Hammurabi's Code in Babylon, is an example of how the advent of writing and recording in clay tablets affected the development of civilization.

Papyrus lent itself to political organization of a different kind that allowed more decentralization, as written laws and other information could be easily distributed, thus facilitating the development of early civilizations such as that of ancient Egypt. It also assisted commerce, as records of business transactions could easily go from one place to another, enhancing the development of ancient trading civilizations such as Phoenicia.

■ ■ ■ VELLUM TO PAPER

In the Middle Ages, the adaptability of the alphabet to printing became the foundation for literacy, advertising, and trade. Equally important as the development of printing, however, was the creation of paper. Prior to the invention of paper, documents were written on vellum or parchment, which were time-consuming and expensive to create. Paper was initially made in China in the second century CE and gradually arrived in Europe via the Middle East hundreds of years later.

Paper was also relatively expensive to produce, being made of a combination of wood pulp and cloth rags, and had to have a good balance of absorbency for the ink, smoothness to make sure images and text could be printed, and sturdiness to make sure it wouldn't disintegrate in the publishing process. It wasn't until the nineteenth century, when steam-powered paper mills could make paper solely out of wood pulp, that the cost of paper dropped dramatically. This of course led to cheaper printed products and more widespread distribution of books, magazines, and newspapers.

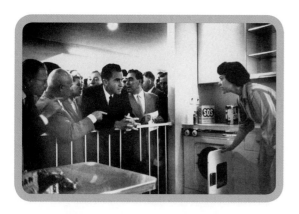

The impromptu "kitchen debate" between then vice president Richard Nixon and Soviet premier Nikita Khrushchev is an example of how recorded television could give prominence to a single event.

■ ■ ■ THE KITCHEN DEBATE TO WATERGATE

Although electronic media have a much shorter history than non-electronic media, the ability to record and store them has already had significant impacts in the twentieth century. It has played a role in making or breaking political careers, spurring urban riots, and winning (or losing) court cases.

A dramatic example is the so-called kitchen debate in 1960, the height of the cold war. U.S. vice president Richard M. Nixon, who himself would later become president, was visiting the Soviet Union. While there, Nixon met with Soviet premier Nikita Khrushchev. An impromptu debate occurred between Khrushchev and Nixon while the two were touring an exhibit of home appliances in Moscow. Thanks to the "miracle" of recently invented portable magnetic-videotape recorders, the "kitchen debate" was caught on videotape and subsequently replayed to 72 million TV viewers in the United States.

Fourteen years later, Nixon was again at the nexus of recording technology. In 1974, Nixon resigned after audiotapes (despite missing portions of recordings) documented his role in the 1972 cover-up of the break-in of the office of the Democratic National Committee, located in the Watergate building. Because of the publicity of the scandal, which sent several of Nixon's aides to prison, any incident today that has the whiff of scandal gets the "-gate" suffix attached to it.

Web Link >>>
watergate.info
watergate.info/

■ ■ ■ RODNEY KING TO THE OVAL OFFICE

In 1991 an amateur videotape of Rodney King being beaten by the L.A. police led to riots in that city. This tape provided a record of the controversial use of force by police in arresting an African American suspect. It also offered the entire U.S. population a window into the simmering racial tensions of the second-largest city in the country—in addition to showing how portable video-recording technology made recording events much more ubiquitous.

In 1998, Linda Tripp's secret audio tapings of her telephone conversations with White House intern Monica Lewinsky led to a sex scandal involving President Bill Clinton. After a major investigation by the Office of the Independent Counsel, on December 19, 1998, President Clinton was impeached by the U.S. House of Representatives, but he was acquitted of impeachment charges by the Senate two months later.

■ ■ ■ EMAIL TO FACEBOOK

Email has played an increasingly important role in recent years in court cases and political scandals. Although emails can be deleted from inboxes, they actually can be recovered in many cases. Partly to get around this, some high-ranking members in George Bush's White House, such as Karl Rove, used alternative email accounts to conduct White House business, which is forbidden.

Republican vice-presidential candidate Sarah Palin and members of her staff were also accused of using Yahoo accounts to conduct government business, knowing that these accounts could not be accessed in the way that government email accounts could be. A minor scandal erupted several weeks before the 2008 presidential election when a University of Tennessee student correctly answered Governor Palin's security questions on her Yahoo account and accessed her emails.

The ramifications of the public's ability to store and publish information on social networking sites such as Facebook are still to be fully understood.

Social networking sites such as Facebook have also shown the potential ramifications of information storage, with many stories of recent college graduates being embarrassed during job interviews when potential employers asked about photos or posts found on their sites. In October 2008, the British tabloid press published pictures taken from a U.S. teenager's Facebook page in which she and a friend were posing provocatively with U2 singer Bono and a musician friend while they were on vacation—without their wives.

Managing Information

We have become used to rapid changes in technology, and particularly to changes in storage capacity, so that we take developments largely for granted. But the gains in storage technology, especially storage capacity, are happening with a speed previously unseen in the development of media.

byte
....
The most common base unit
used to measure computer
storage and information, it
consists of eight bits, in a
combination of 0's and 1's, to
form letters, numbers, and all
modes of computer information
that are displayed.

A **byte** is eight bits of data, such as 0110011, and is the common unit used to denote memory storage. The standard sizes most people are familiar with are kilobyte (KB, or 1,024 bytes), megabyte (MB, or 1,024 KB), and gigabyte (GB, or 1,024 MB). Note that the increases in storage capacity are exponential. That is, a gigabyte doesn't store two thousand times more than a kilobyte, but a *million* times more (i.e., a thousand thousands). Terabyte-level (TB, or 1,024 GB) storage capacity is already available in some computers and will soon become standard in desktop PCs. Petabyte (PB) and exabyte (EB) are the next two higher levels, with 1 exabyte storing a billion times that of a gigabyte.

With such rapid and dramatic changes in storage capacity come new problems in figuring out how to manage the information we have available. Two main trends can be seen in the development of digital storage: miniaturization and increased capacity. With miniaturization comes increased portability, especially when considering the amount of information that is transported. Increased capacity has led to many changes in how we interact with media, ranging from listening to music to watching television on a digital video recorder (DVR).

■ ■ ■ DEVELOPMENT OF DIGITAL STORAGE DEVICES

A first step toward automated computation and digital storage of various types of data was the introduction of punched cards, which were first successfully used in connection with computing in 1890 by Herman Hollerith when he worked for the U.S. Census Bureau. Hollerith developed a device that could automatically read census information that had been punched onto a card, an idea developed from watching a train conductor punch tickets. Hollerith, who also developed the first electromechanical tabulator, later went on to establish his own firm to market his electromechanical tabulator—a company that later became International Business Machines (IBM).

Punched cards continued to play an important role in computing well into the 1980s, but the development of magnetic recording technologies in the 1950s would gradually play a more dominant role in computing. However, the low storage capacity of magnetic tape initially limited its usefulness. The first hard-disk computer shipped by IBM in 1957 had a combined storage capacity on fifty disks of 56 MB, not even enough for computers today to run Windows Vista operating system.

Early computers used tape to store information and required their own rooms, making them seem like impractical media devices for the general public.

The trend toward increased portability and capacity is evident in the development of the floppy disk, which first appeared in 8-inch format, then 5.25-inch and finally in 3.5-inch format, each time increasing its storage capacity even as it got smaller. Today, most computers do not even come with floppy disk drives, as other portable memory devices such as flash cards, SD cards, memory sticks, or USB drives have more capacity and are even smaller. A 2 GB USB drive, for example, holds the equivalent of nearly two thousand 3.5-inch floppy disks.

optical storage
....
Uses light in the form of
lasers to store and read data
of all types, whether text,
audio, or video. Using light is
highly efficient: it permits
storage devices to record
vastly greater amounts of data
in small spaces and enables
faster retrieval of the stored
data than from magnetic storage
devices.

Optical storage devices such as CDs or DVDs also show remarkable increases in storage capacity, even though they have generally stayed the same dimensions. DVDs became the first optical storage medium to be able to store an entire full-length movie and within ten years of being introduced had largely replaced the standard storage device for movies to that time, the videocassette, which itself had been in households only since the mid-1970s.

Developments continue in storage technology, including research into **nanotechnology** and quantum computing. "Nanotechnology" refers to ultrasmall technology, involving devices built or operating at nanometer sizes, or one billionth of a meter. Nanotechnology promises to transform a variety of fields, including elec-

Development of Digital Storage Media

1957 IBM ships first hard-disk computer with total capacity of 256 MB on fifty disks.

1971 Floppy disk introduced, initially in 8-inch format (later in 5.25- and then 3.5-inch).

1982 Sony and Philips introduce the CD-ROM, the first optical, digital storage medium.

1997 DVD introduced.

1999 Portable MP3 players introduced.

1999 First consumer DVRs, ReplayTV and TiVo, debut at the 1999 Consumer Electronics Show in Las Vegas.

2000 IBM sells first USB flash storage drive.

2001 Sony introduces the USB memory stick.

2008 Blu-ray high-definition DVR adopted as standard.

tronics, manufacturing, and information storage and retrieval. Nanotechnology may one day produce the only viable information-storage media capable of storing massive quantities of data on incredibly miniature devices. This means that the contents of the entire Library of Congress of the United States, the largest library in the world, could be stored on a single device no larger than the tip of a finger.

Because of its enormous potential, researchers expect nanotechnology to be an increasingly significant part of information storage and other fields in the twenty-first century. In 2001, the National Science Foundation awarded funding for the establishment of national nanoscale research centers at six major research universities.

nanotechnology

A cutting-edge field of technology research that involves items that are nanometers (10^{-9} meters) in length and that promises to revolutionize many fields, ranging from electronics, information storage, and even medicine.

■ ■ ■ COMPRESSION OF DIGITAL AUDIO AND VIDEO

The technological development of digital storage and distribution has not proceeded at an even pace. As our ability to store information digitally increases, our desire to store more memory-hungry content such as audio and video seems to increase as well.

What has not kept pace with increases in storage capacity is the storage capacity of the lines, or "pipes," to people's homes that transmit that data between users in a network. This is one reason why it is necessary to compress digital data. A useful analogy might be the need to roll up and stuff a sleeping bag into its original carrying case in order to easily haul it from one campsite to another. Once it is finally in a compact form, it can be carried relatively easily. And, like the contortions and struggles that go into cramming a down sleeping bag into a space the size of two loaves of bread, engineers have had similar troubles trying to compress audio and video so they too can be easily transported.

DVRs: Changing Television Viewing Habits—and the Industry

Probably the most prominent example of how a storage technology has played a role in altering established media-consumption habits is the digital video recorder (DVR) or personal video recorder (PVR). A DVR is essentially a set-top box with a large storage capacity that can keep several hours of programming and automatically search for shows.

First marketed to the public in 1999, DVRs such as ReplayTV and TiVo gave television viewers capabilities for viewing that they had never had before.

It is no accident that the panelists on *American Idol* have Coke so prominently displayed, as it is an example of product placement.

Some of these included being able to pause live TV, rewind or fast-forward television programs, and set the DVR to automatically record shows by search terms (such as a favorite actor or favorite show) rather than simply by preset showing times.

DVRs have given viewers the ability to personalize their viewing experiences, making TV schedules and, to some extent, the notion of specific channels much less important than they used to be. With the set-top box automatically searching for shows across channels and time slots, the viewer no longer has to remember that a certain show is on a certain channel at a certain time on a certain day.

Of even more importance—and concern to advertisers—is the ability of DVRs to skip commercials. This has led to increased use of **product placement** in TV shows, in which advertisers have their products used by characters or displayed in scenes as natural props. Most viewers are not aware of product placement or the deals made behind the scenes to get products placed in shows and movies, raising important questions about the nature of advertising.

Cable and satellite companies have started to compete with the original DVR companies. ReplayTV is now owned by satellite provider DirecTV, and most cable providers offer their customers some degree of DVR-like service with special set-top boxes and video-on-demand.

MP3 players utilize the digital format of the same name to put music files into a manageable size with decent sound quality.

MPEG, or the Moving Picture Experts Group, was established in 1988 and is also the name for the encoding process used to compactly represent digital video and audio for general distribution. MPEG compresses, or squeezes, the video or audio by removing any redundant information from one frame of video or segment of audio to the next. In other words, it removes the part that doesn't change and only transmits the part that changes from frame to frame or segment to segment.

The audio component of MPEG (Moving Picture Experts Group-1, Audio Layer III) emerged in the mid-1990s as an ad hoc standard for pirated digital audio and is today known simply by its nickname, **MP3**. There are other MPEG formats being developed and used that have different capabilities. MPEG-21 represents the convergence of all the existing MPEG standards, integrated into an international digital standard for the twenty-first century. At this writing, the final specifications of MPEG-21 are still being crafted but will likely contain important specifications to ban illegal copying of digital information.

Web Link >>>
MPEG Industry Forum
www.mpegif.org/resources.php#section42

■ ■ ■ THE ROLE OF SEARCH ENGINES

With vast amounts of information available to us at the touch of a few keys, finding and retrieving the information that we want becomes a crucial issue. It serves little purpose if a library is stored in the space of a desktop computer if the books are essentially randomly scattered on the library floor.

Google is a prime example of how search engines have become immensely powerful in today's media landscape. Starting as a search engine company in 1998, it has quickly grown into an Internet and media powerhouse that rivals or exceeds older and more established media companies and software giants. As Google's services have expanded from simple Web page searches to searches for images, blogs, academic texts, people, automatic translation, and many other areas, it has become more central to users' experience of the Web.

As search engines become the primary portals for many users when they begin to look for information on the Web, search engine advertising has developed. For many companies, showing up on the first page of Google, or showing up as the first listing on Google, has become an important means of driving traffic to the website.

Paid search listings or sponsored links have been one way search engines like Google make money. These can include **keyword auctions**, in which companies bid for relevant keywords and then pay the search engine company a certain amount every time that link is clicked. **Search engine optimization** (SEO) and **search engine marketing** (SEM) have joined the toolbox of skills needed for modern marketers alongside traditional advertising techniques.

Search engines often use "spiders," or intelligent agent programs (sometimes called "bots," which is short for "robots"), to search the Web for content, thus compiling databases or snapshots of Web pages. Despite the apparent vast stores of websites found on the likes of Google, Yahoo, and Ask, none of the search engines actually captures more than a fifth of what is on the Web—some argue even much less, with the rapid expansion of content every day. Microsoft entered the search engine field with its launch of Bing in mid 2009.

Metasearch engines such as Dogpile have become more popular, as they save users the trouble of having to go through various search engines and deal with overlapping or irrelevant entries. On the other end of the scale are **vertical search engines**, which focus on a specialized topic rather than trying to cover all areas. Vertical search engines are especially useful for professions in which similar terms may be used by other fields. For example, a dentist searching for information on ceramic fillings would have to wade through many irrelevant entries on pottery, if using Google, whereas a vertical search engine that focused on dentistry would quickly produce relevant entries.

In 2008, Google was able to show through compiled results of its search engine queries that it could predict flu trends in given areas up to two weeks earlier than traditional flu predictors.[1] This shows the power of data aggregated simply

product placement
....
The practice of advertisers paying to have their products displayed prominently and used in television shows and movies.

MPEG
....
Moving Picture Experts Group, established in 1988 and responsible for creating the standards for digital and audio compression. The abbreviation is also used to denote the types of compression, such as MPEG-1, MPEG-4, and so on.

keyword auction
....
One method in search engine marketing in which companies bid for words and pay the search engine a certain amount every time the word is searched and their listing is clicked on.

search engine optimization
....
A strategy that utilizes website design, careful choice of keywords, links, and other techniques to show prominently in online searches.

search engine marketing (SEM)
....
Paying a search engine such as Google to have a listing appear prominently when searched.

Web Link >>>
Google
www.google.com

Web Link >>>
Yahoo!
www.yahoo.com

Web Link >>>
Ask
  www.ask.com

Web Link >>>
Dogpile
  www.dogpile.com

Web Link >>>
Bing
  www.bing.com

metasearch engines
....
A search engine that searches
search engines for information,
compiling the results for
users.

vertical search engines
....
A specialized search engine
that searches within a highly
specific field, thus giving
users more relevant results
within that field than more
general search engines.

information overload
....
The difficulties associated
with dealing with the vast
amounts of information
available to us and making
sense of it.

from search terms, and the knowledge that can be gained from it, as well as the increasing importance of search engines in how we try to make sense of the complex media and information environment today.

■ ■ ■ SOCIAL AND POLITICAL IMPACT OF INFORMATION OVERLOAD

The social and political impact of our increasing ability to create and store information is vast, though it rarely surfaces as a public topic. We have already discussed the issues around being able to store information in formats that will be accessible to future generations, but there are also important issues around how we make sense of the information we currently have available to us and who has access to it.

The problem of dealing with the enormous amounts of information available to us is known as **information overload**. It affects everything from the ability of government agencies to act rapidly on intelligence they have gathered, or to combine intelligence from different sources to discern a pattern, to workers being able to share relevant knowledge within companies. It has become commonplace in meetings for participants to text or email while someone is presenting or speaking, and this lessened attention to the speaker has resulted in missed important information and misunderstandings.

Some people claim that the constant interruptions typically seen in the workplace have hampered productivity and creativity, with tasks taking longer to complete than in the past and workers showing a reduced ability to concentrate for any length of time to tackle complex problems. Email has been considered a main culprit in information overload. One company claimed in 2007 that firms waste approximately $650 billion a year because of information overload, just from the interruptions caused by email.[2]

The Importance of User Interface

The term **user interface** is a technological way of referring to the junction between a medium and the people who use it. We are usually familiar with our everyday media and so don't give user interface a second thought. Nobody has to remind us how to turn a page in a book, for example, or how to find the sports section in the newspaper, or tune a radio dial.

However, it is easy to forget that the knowledge of using everyday media was learned. Watch a baby with a children's book to see how he explores the book. He chews the corners of the book, holds it upside down, shakes it, tears pages, and randomly goes through the book. It does not take long for babies to figure out that they should turn the pages in sequence, even long before they can actually read.

Comparing a baby exploring the world with rational, thinking adults might not seem completely fair. But consider a case in which many adults are left as helpless as a baby: programming a DVD player. Or think about the last time you were able to immediately turn on someone else's television and stereo system with their remote control. Chances are you needed to ask for help in doing so, even though it was likely just a matter of pushing a couple buttons. But knowing which buttons to push in what order made all the difference.

Computers, because of their relative complexity and their newness for most people, make us even more aware of user-interface issues. Even something as simple as using a mouse is a completely new and nonintuitive experience for a computer novice, let alone the functions that right-clicking a mouse or double-clicking can accomplish. Even after the mechanics of mouse clicking have been mastered, there is still an entirely new world of user control with the interface that must be learned, including the concepts of adjusting window sizes and moving or hiding windows within the screen.

Audiences have long been accustomed to using traditional media to receive content. But they are not "users" of traditional media in the same sense that they are users of a computer to run applications such as word processing, a web browser, or email. With the rise of digital media, the audience consists of more active users, and the interface has become a key element in shaping that use.

The interface transformation is in many ways about empowering the user, or audience. The user is critical to the future of mass communication. The user interface, or how the user interacts with a medium or its content, is a cornerstone for media success. If a user cannot find her way to a website or cannot get the information she wants when she needs it, then even great media content will essentially be unusable. To be practical, the user interface should be intuitive and natural yet appropriate to the medium and its content and customizable to each user's preferences. This is why the user interface is critical to mass communication in the digital age.

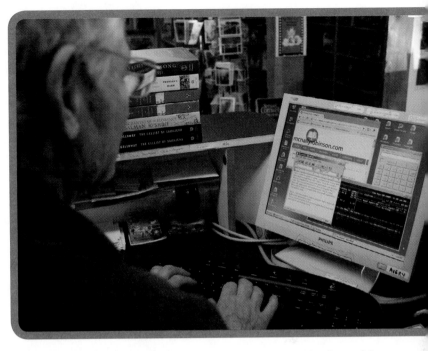

Learning how to cope with the vast amounts of information available online and the different ways the information is presented is a major hurdle for some people.

Current Problems with User Interface

There are advantages to a simple, unchanging user interface. The user always knows what to expect, always knows where to find things, and doesn't need a user's guide each time she tunes in a new channel, reads a different newspaper, or opens a new book. As long as the user interface is well designed, a static design offers efficiency to the user. Traditional media have had decades, even centuries, to create the most efficient user interface. They have evolved slowly, carefully, and thoughtfully into highly effective systems.

This is unfortunately not the case with digital media and the Internet. User interface has become a critical issue for a number of reasons. First, digital media are very new and have not had time to evolve. Second, rapid advances in technology radically alter any user-interface assumptions that are made. Think of how different content may appear in a world in which tiny screens on cell phones with keypads are the primary method of accessing media, as opposed to one in which there are large, flexible screens that can be put up almost anywhere. Third, varying computer standards mean not all technology is accepted, so what may appear in one web browser may not appear correctly—or at all—in a different, or older, web browser. Finally, audience members too often remain media illiterate from a technological standpoint, making them unable to access media simply because they do not understand how to do the online equivalent of turning a page in a book. To be fair, it is not always the public's fault; poor or confusing design choices by website designers frequently create confusion.

However, most of these problems will eventually sort themselves out as people become more familiar with digital media and as technology becomes easier to use. It will likely take some time, however, and will happen only after many stops and starts. These kinds of problems are to be expected with digital media, which fundamentally challenge the centuries-old model of a relatively noninteractive system and a static user interface that has gone unquestioned.

Development of the User Interface

From a historical perspective, the evolution of the electronic user interface, or how people access electronic mass-communication content, began with the development of radio and television, two important electronic media whose "user" interfaces were critical to their success.

Before the development of the computer, we did not generally employ the term "user interface" in discussions of the media. This is because the traditional, analog media were not designed to be interactive, and what we call the user interface was generally unchanging. It was easy to understand how to turn a dial or push a button to receive content, which appeared in the same way everywhere it was broadcast.

There are two main elements in the development of the electronic user interface. One is the technological innovations that have led to how we use computers and other devices in the modern era. The other element is social, or getting people accustomed to using new technologies in a mass-communication context. We will look at an example that combines both elements in order to better understand the evolution of user interface and how it influences our media usage today.

■ ■ ■ THE TELEVISION SCREEN

cathode-ray tube (CRT)
....
A device that is still used in most television screens and computer monitors, in which electrons are transmitted to a screen for viewing.

aspect ratio
....
The ratio of a screen's height to its width. Incompatible aspect ratios of films and television mean that either films have to be cropped to fit within a television screen, or, in order to keep the original aspect ratio, black borders must appear on the top and bottom of the screen.

Until recent years, with the rise of flat-panel displays, desktop computer monitors used **cathode-ray tube** (CRT) technology identical to that in a TV. Technology improvements in computer monitors, once they became the standard interface with computers, have largely been driven by the desire for more of the televisual qualities that we have come to expect from screens, such as color, a certain dimension, and crisp images.

Because computer monitors largely adopt the screen **aspect ratio** of television screens, that has affected a great many subsequent design and user-interface choices. The fact that a "page" of text cannot be seen and read in its entirety on a screen sometimes bothers new computer users, for example, who would like to see at a glance where items are spaced on a page *and* read text at the same time. For word processing, it would seem more natural to have a vertically oriented screen, as if the standard monitor were turned on its side.

When people watch movies on their computer monitors or flat-panel screens, the aspect ratio also has an effect on how these appear, since the aspect ratios of films and television are different (thus forcing movies on television to either cut off part of a scene or keep the original aspect ratio but have black spaces above and below the scenes).

It is interesting to note that although computer makers originally borrowed from television in creating monitors, television has returned the favor in borrowing from the online world of screen windows, scrolling text or tickers, and multiple items on various topics on a single screen. This can especially be seen in newscasts.

■■■ TELEVISION AND REMOTE CONTROL

The TV remote control is not only one of the most important transformational technologies in television but has also often been the source of friction between the sexes and among family members. In many households, the person who wields the remote control wields the power.

The first TV remote control was introduced in 1950.[3] Zenith introduced the Lazy Bones, a remote control connected by a wire to your TV set. In 1955, Zenith introduced the Flash-matic, the first wireless TV remote, which used a flashlight to change channels. Then in 1956, Zenith's Space Command (remember, it was the dawn of the space age) used ultrasound to change channels but also produced unfortunate reactions among household pets. Most modern TV remote controls use infrared technology.

The remote control, besides being one of the earliest examples of consumers using wireless technology in the home (along with the radio), had important effects on TV viewers. Perhaps most importantly and obviously, it enabled easy channel changing. Before the remote control, viewers had to get up and walk to the set to change the channel, which significantly inhibited channel changing. The remote control altered viewing habits, as viewers could now easily move back and forth between channels, or "channel surf," and avoid commercials or uninteresting segments in programs or simply watch multiple sports events. In other words, they were almost effortlessly interacting with their televisions, albeit in a very limited way because of course they could not actually change the nature of the content they were receiving.[4]

In addition, frequently changing channels could be considered a simple form of **multitasking**, a common phenomenon in the computer environment in which people do several simultaneous activities. Less patience in watching content can also be seen in the way computer users access a number of different media outlets in pursuing their objectives without spending a long time on any specific item.

However much remote controls are taken for granted today, they did play an important role in subtly altering and expanding the parameters of media usage. The computer of course has played a much more prominent role in bringing user-interface issues to the forefront of mass communication.

■■■ THE COMPUTER INTERFACE

Since computers and humans use different languages, some kind of interface, or "translator," is needed to allow communication between the two. In the earliest days of computing, the user interface was anything but simple. Usually, only the inventor or a highly trained specialist could operate a computer, interact with it, or access information contained within it.

Data were entered on punch cards, often requiring hundreds of cards to represent even a simple piece of information, such as a series of numbers or names. The output of a computer analysis was typically printed on paper, which might take many minutes or even hours with a slow, dot-matrix printer. If computers were to

Remote controls have grown increasingly complex as we have gained more functions and channels on our television sets.

multitasking
....
In a computer environment, doing several activities at once with a variety of programs, such as simultaneously doing word-processing, spreadsheet, and database work while conducting real-time chat through an instant-messenger service.

be more useful for people, they needed not only to become more powerful but also to develop a better interface both for inputting information and for output.

From the 1970s, personal computers started having electronic monitors, which were generally monochrome, either a black screen and white text or a black screen with luminous green text. The display let users input information or see output without having to wait for a printout.

The development of speakers for use with a computer was critical to creating a full, multisensory experience for the user. This laid the foundation for a multimedia computer. Today, it is standard for every computer to have an electronic display with audio capability, and most come with a microphone or microphone port so users can input audio information. Increasingly, laptops come with built-in cameras as well. All this makes a computer a potentially complete digital media-production facility, with the proper software.

■ ■ ■ THE CREATION OF INTUITIVE INTERFACES

In the 1960s, an important series of advances were made in the computer user interface. Most of these developments helped make the computer simpler and more natural, or intuitive, to use, more efficient to work with (i.e., to enter information and access information contained in the computer), and more capable of dealing with multimedia content such as audio, video, photos, and graphics. The process is still evolving even today as improvements and refinements are made in the interface methods discussed below.

Keyboards

Typewriters were developed in the 1870s as a way to make writing faster. At first, the typewriter keyboard was arranged alphabetically, but it turned out this was a poor design since some keys were used more often than others and, if typed too quickly, would jam together. Instead, Christopher Latham Sholes developed what is known as the QWERTY keyboard (after the first row of letters in the upper-left-hand corner of the keyboard), which has the most frequently typed keys spread far apart (such as "a" and "t"). The QWERTY keyboard slows down the user and prevents the keys from jamming in a typewriter.

Jamming keys became a nonissue with the invention of electric typewriters, but the QWERTY keyboard was by then standard and is what most people are trained on today. Since there are no keys to jam on a computer keyboard, it would make far more sense to have a keyboard that is designed for maximum typing efficiency. Unfortunately, the QWERTY keyboard is a standard part of the computer user interface, and such legacies are very hard to change, even when changing them would greatly improve things.

The Dvorak keyboard is designed for maximum typing efficiency. Created by August Dvorak in the 1930s, the keyboard allows the user to type more than three thousand words without reaching with the fingers. The standard QWERTY keyboard can be reprogrammed to the Dvorak layout quite easily. The software to automatically reprogram a QWERTY keyboard is available for free downloading. Once the keyboard has been reprogrammed, the user simply installs new key caps with the letters corresponding to the new layout as needed.

Web Link >>>
Switch Your Computer to Dvorak
www.mwbrooks.com/dvorak/support.html

Beyond the specific inherited inefficiencies in the QWERTY design, the keyboard in general suffers from other drawbacks as an intuitive interface. First is the need for literacy to understand its use and second is the need for typing training

The Dvorak keyboard is much more efficient for typing than the standard QWERTY keyboard, greatly increasing typing speed and accuracy.

in order to use it more efficiently. An intuitive interface does not require hours of training. A keyboard is also slower as an input device than simply speaking to a computer, for example.

As computers and other media devices have become smaller, the keyboard has also proved to be a limited input device, as keys can become no smaller than what can be comfortably pressed with fingers or thumbs. Small keyboards often leave users with cramped hands or cause them to hit the wrong keys. One benefit the keyboard does have over some other types of interfaces is the ability to input information privately. Typing, unlike a voice interface, can be done without disturbing others in the vicinity.

Computer Mouse

A major development in the evolution of the intuitive computer user interface occurred in 1968 when Douglas C. Engelbart invented the computer mouse. His invention was made of wood and was used with a companion keyboard. The germ of the idea came in 1945, during WWII. Engelbart worked as a radar technician in the South Pacific, and he realized the potential for people to interact with a monitor. His inspiration came while reading a now-classic article in the July 1945 edition of the *Atlantic Monthly* by Vannevar Bush, then science adviser to President Harry S. Truman, titled "As We May Think." The article discussed how the computer could be a desktop tool to help people in their work.

Engelbart initially proposed his idea for a better computer user interface in an article in 1963 when he wrote that through a better-designed computer interface, "people could cope better with complex, urgent things." His vision involved creating better intuitive tools for people to interact with and control the information they input, access, and process in a computer. The computer mouse was one of the most important tools he developed for implementing his vision. The mouse allowed the computer user to easily manipulate data in the computer, pointing and clicking as desired.

The mouse is important for mass communication because it makes it easier, not only for

A Better Mouse, the first mouse that changed the computer interface to one of pointing and clicking rather than simply typing.

Web Link >>>
"As We May Think"
www.theatlantic.com/unbound/flashbks/computer/bushf.htm

The Internet of Babel

It is easy for Americans, especially, to forget that not everyone speaks English, even as a second language. To date, language has generally not been a major issue on the Internet largely because Internet users have tended to be well educated and able to communicate in English even if it is not their native language.

As Internet use spreads among people throughout the world, it is important to remember that English will soon lose its dominance. Although in 2008 the largest share (29.4 percent) of people online used English as a native or main second language, Chinese speakers are rising fast and are now in second place, with 19 percent—a growth rate of 755 percent from 2007.[5]

Arabic, though only at 4.1 percent of Internet users, showed remarkable 2,000 percent growth in 2007. Together, the top ten Internet languages (English, Chinese, Spanish, Japanese, French, German, Arabic, Portuguese, Korean, and Italian) make up almost 85 percent of Internet users worldwide.

As foreign-language users increase, it means that monolingual users could be missing out on huge opportunities to get important information and communicate with others. It also means there could be more conflicts between different groups, as occurred in the popular social-networking site Orkut as Brazilians started to join in higher numbers, speaking among themselves in Portuguese and making English speakers feel left out.

Translation programs are still relatively primitive, doing poor translations at best and incomprehensible, sometimes funny translations at worst. It will likely be a while before automatic translation approaches the level of sophistication of human translators.

Even as the Internet gains more non-English speakers, there is hope for the monolingual English speaker—a growing number of foreign-language tutorials are available online for free or low cost, making it easier than ever to learn a foreign language. Even better for some, a growing number of volunteer translators are willing to fill in the gaps that computer translations miss.

content producers to work more effectively and quickly, but for the audience to access and obtain information. Despite the huge leap in creating a more intuitive interface that the computer mouse represents, it still has its limitations. First, the functions of buttons or wheels on a mouse are not immediately clear and have to be learned.

Second, there is still a disjunct between moving a mouse across the desktop and where the cursor actually goes. This is why computer novices often have trouble at first using a mouse—a small hand movement on the horizontal plane of the desk toward the computer actually corresponds to a relatively large upward vertical movement on the computer screen, which isn't initially intuitive. It takes practice to become accustomed to how hand movements translate to cursor movements.

Touch-Sensitive Screens

Another important development in the evolution of a more intuitive computer user interface occurred in 1974. In that year, the Control Data Corporation (CDC) introduced PLATO (Programmed Logic for Automated Teaching Operations), the first computer system to have a touch-sensitive video display terminal.[6]

The importance of a touch-sensitive screen is that it greatly simplifies the **human-computer interaction**. With a touch-sensitive screen, children and adults alike, without any prior training, or even the ability to read, can interact with images or applications by simply touching the screen with their fingers. ATMs are probably the most common example of touch-sensitive screens, as are automated supermarket registers, but the iPhone and other PDA interfaces are also examples of a touch-sensitive screen.

Despite being perhaps one of the most intuitive interfaces, there are several drawbacks to touch-sensitive screens as a standard interface. First is the need to be within reach of the screen to touch it, which means large screen sizes would be uncomfortable on our eyes. Second, extremely small screen sizes limit interaction, just as with keyboards, since items that can be manipulated can be only as small as a fingertip can comfortably select. A stylus or other thin device can help overcome this latter drawback, however.

Natural Input Methods

Handwriting, voice recognition, and speech systems are all steps toward providing more intuitive, natural methods of interacting with computers and media content. The first computer that could accept natural handwriting with an electronic stylus was sold in 1979, although it could not translate the text into computer-readable text. This did not occur for almost twenty years.

Although there have been vast improvements from the 1990s, handwriting recognition still has a ways to go before it can easily translate a person's natural scrawl into machine-readable text. It will also always have limitations for portable computing devices, as the writing surface must be big enough to write comfortably and so must be at least the size of a small notepad.

One of the most natural, or intuitive, user interfaces has also been one of the most elusive. Computer voice recognition and speech synthesis have been a hallmark of science fiction for generations and are slowly becoming a central part of the real-world computing environment. Most of the current voice-recognition systems are really nothing more than voice typewriters, translating spoken words into printed ones. Some can respond to simple, preset commands, such as "open file," but have no understanding of semantics.

Speech recognition could greatly simplify many interactions with computers, although it is not without its weaknesses as well. One issue, especially for people in urban areas or in public spaces, is noise. Imagine the noise level in a classroom if everyone had to speak to their computer to input their lecture notes, or the noise on a city bus as everyone spoke not into cell phones but to their portable computers. But on the other hand, imagine the ease if your computer could automatically

human-computer interaction
The general term for any interaction between humans and computers, either through devices such as keyboards, mice, touch screens, or voice recognition.

Communication between computers and humans using natural language remains in the realm of science fiction, although researchers continue to get closer to that goal.

transcribe a professor's lecture, leaving you free to listen and annotate the notes being transcribed.

Graphical User Interface

graphical user interface (GUI)
....
A computer interface that shows graphical representations of file structures, files, and applications, in the form of folders, icons, and windows.

The foundation for the modern graphical user interface, or **GUI** (pronounced GOO-ey), was created, like so many other computer innovations, at Xerox Palo Alto Research Center (PARC). In 1974 Xerox created the Alto, a computer that used a graphical user interface that allowed users to simply point and click various objects on the screen to access applications or files.

The Alto, apparently ahead of its time, never caught on. It took a visit to Xerox PARC by Apple cofounder Steve Jobs to see Xerox's graphical user interface and to decide to use that with Apple computers. Several years later Microsoft's Windows followed Apple's lead in using a graphical user interface for its operating system.

Prior to the GUI, computer users had to memorize or have at hand a series of arcane commands to open, save, and move files as well as to use applications. When the GUI was introduced, there was a widespread feeling among established computer users that it "dumbed down" computer use and was not a good development, despite (or perhaps because of) its ease of use and the way it opened up computer use to the nontechnical public.

The Desktop Metaphor

Most computer users, whether using Macs or PCs, are familiar with the graphical user interface of the computer desktop. Software applications are represented as icons and placed in resizable "windows" within the screen space, which can be layered on top of one another or moved around. Computer files are "placed" in folders that sit on the screen or can be put within other folders.

Some of the earliest graphical user interfaces for the PC even tried to carry the desktop metaphor further, by having images of an actual desk as if the user was sitting at it and with images of items like a Rolodex (for contacts and addresses), file cabinet, and other office equipment to represent various computing functions. These kinds of attempts at realistic user interfaces failed primarily for a couple reasons. One reason was the computing power needed to show detailed 3-D images, which was beyond the capacity of most PCs until fairly recently, and another reason was that the realistic interface imposed real-world constraints on obtaining and manipulating information that computers would otherwise not have.

Some computer-interface designers have said that the desktop user interface has outlived its usefulness. It was fine in the early stages of GUIs, when computers were less powerful and computer users mostly had text files rather than a range of multimedia types and far less storage for files. But nowadays, the desktop can actually hinder the most efficient way of getting or manipulating information for the user. The office iconography of the standard desktop can also be confusing at first to people who are not

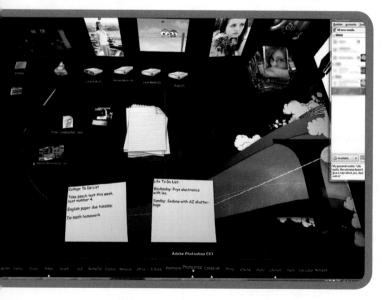

Some say the desktop metaphor for computer screens actually hampers our ability to fully utilize the range of information and media types we have today, and these people have created alternative ways to visualize and manage information.

familiar with such real-world office standards as file folders, printers, or floppy diskettes—the latter of which are rarely used anymore but still often remain as icons for "save." Consider the time spent searching for lost files, either in directories filled with hundreds of various files or in sub- sub- sub-folders of different categories.

There are some interesting attempts to create a better PC user interface that can more fully accommodate the complex media needs of today's computer user. Whether any of these new types of user interfaces will catch on and replace today's desktop interface is impossible to predict. On one hand, users may feel comfortable enough with the desktop icons that they choose not to switch, much as users have grown accustomed to the inefficient QWERTY keyboard layout. On the other hand, user-interface design is still in an early enough stage that a radically new system that makes using a computer much easier could catch on rapidly, just as the GUI garnered widespread use over the command-line interface in a very short time.

Implications of User Interface for Mass Communication

The GUI for personal computers and later for the World Wide Web probably had the single greatest impact in changing the public's behavior and attitude toward computers and helped usher in digital media as a competitor to traditional mass-media formats. Once basic knowledge such as what mouse buttons to click or where to search for files was learned, much could be done on a computer even without any technical knowledge. The graphical browser took the Web out of the labs of engineers and computer scientists and into the living rooms of the public.

The modern user interface not only changes how the audience can access and utilize information, transforming people from passive media consumers to active media users, it also changes how media organizations must create, produce, and present stories. The GUI holds the potential to bring news, information, and entertainment to audiences in ways that engage, educate, and entertain that were unimaginable with analog media.

Graphical browsers also helped lead to the commercialization of the Web (and some would say its destruction) as businesses sought to reach the growing number of consumers online. Examples of a windowed environment that most computer users are unfortunately all too familiar with are pop-up ads or animated ads that must be closed before one can access content.

For those who are not convinced that user interface has become an important issue, consider the lawsuit filed by the U.S. Department of Justice and eighteen states in May 1998 against Microsoft, accusing the company of violating antitrust laws. One of the key issues was whether Microsoft used its near monopoly of the operating system market (90

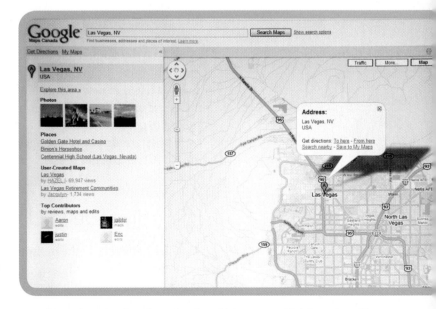

Interactive maps show the power of combining geographic information with multiple layers of other kinds of information for a richer user experience.

Croquet is an example of
a 3-D user interface.

percent of PCs run Windows) to unfairly promote its Internet Explorer browser by making it part of the Windows operating system. The case hinged in part on evidence of Microsoft's unfair tactics because its Internet Explorer web browser came bundled with new operating systems while the browser Netscape did not. In the mid- to late-1990s, Internet Explorer rapidly rose in popularity as Netscape declined.

Although Microsoft eventually emerged largely unscathed from the suit, making only minor concessions regarding allowing third-party software with its Windows operating system, for a while during the trial there seemed to be the very real possibility of Microsoft being broken up into three separate companies. What was one of the main factors in an event that could have seen the breakup of one of the world's richest and most powerful computer corporations? An icon in the graphical user interface for the Web.

Interactive Media

The examples of new types of user interfaces exemplify how computers have brought a new dynamic to mass communication—the ability of audience members to interact with content and with each other. This applies not only to changing the desktop background or screen resolution but also to how they get their news and entertainment and even perhaps how they make sense of the world.

In the past, the audience has been limited largely to the role of passive recipient of news and entertainment by the media. Newspapers, magazines, and books could be limited by locale and could only contain a certain amount of news or information. Likewise, radio and television stations covered only specific geographic areas. The advent of cable and satellite television largely eliminated the issue of limited televised content, but the audience was still by and large passive. Media content was sent by a publisher or broadcaster to a large audience that could do little about changing its experience of what was sent, short of not watching or reading at all.

Today, the audience can choose not only the type of content and the media source it comes from but, in many cases, how to experience it. People can choose audio to listen to news while they work on other things, or watch a video clip of an interview, or get the full text transcript of that interview to read later. They can also choose to get the content in a format that they can listen to, watch, or read later.

These are dramatic changes in how the public receives—and perceives—its media. At the heart of these dramatic changes is the notion of interactivity.

Interactivity Defined

We will briefly review the definition of interactivity that was introduced in Chapter 3 and explore aspects of each component of the definition in greater depth. Interactivity has the following elements:

1. A dialog occurs between a human and a computer program (this includes emails, online chats, and discussion groups, as at either end of the commu-

nication flow a human is interacting with a computer program; the Internet is simply the channel).

2. The dialog affects the nature or type of feedback or content that is received, changing as the dialog continues.

3. The audience has some measure of control over what media content it sees and in what order (getting personalized information, magnifying an image, clicking on a hyperlink, etc.).

The notion of a dialog occurring, either between two or more people or between people and computer programs, is crucially important. Although some have made an argument that traditional media also encourage a kind of dialog as readers or viewers consume content and consider what is being seen or read, it must be said that this level of interactivity simply does not match that of interactive media.

One reason these two kinds of interactivity cannot really be compared is because with traditional media a true dialog does not really occur. The media consumer can "talk to" the media (as people often do to their TVs), but the media cannot actually react. The importance of a sense of dialog is that both parties alter and adjust their messages in response to feedback, thus changing the nature of subsequent messages and modes of communication.

Consider a simple example. You may have a funny story to tell a friend but, upon calling and hearing that he sounds depressed, decide to ask what is wrong rather than launching into your story. The feedback you received altered your message. If you had sent the story as a letter, the receiver would have gotten the message regardless of his state of mind.

The same thing happens in an interactive media environment, not only between users but between computer programs and users. Someone reading a news story may decide to click on a hyperlink of a name within the story because he is not familiar with that person, taking him to another website that describes the person, which in turn may lead to other links to other pieces of interesting information. All of this is essentially "changing the story" for that particular user, who will have a very different sense of it than someone who read the same story but did not click on those links.

Similarly, regarding the third element in our definition of interactivity, two people may have very different impressions of the same story after typing in their zip codes to get personalized or localized information relating to it or viewing a multimedia slideshow of the story as opposed to simply reading text or listening to a podcast. In traditional media, the consumer of course cannot switch between one type of medium and another within the same medium, such as listening to a story she is reading in the printed newspaper.

The Importance of Interactive Media

Interactive media can present information in a way that encourages users to learn and explore. Online quizzes, surveys, and games are currently being used in many places on the Web, ranging from news to interactive advertising. Many of these examples could be classified as gimmicks, and many are, but that is not the only role that interactivity plays. A far more important component to interactive media is how it changes the media experience for users. As mentioned above, the dialogic nature of interactive media can make our relationship with the media we encounter far more personalized. By making media content more relevant to our lives and individual needs, we become more engaged with it.

Not only do we become engaged with media content, but with interactive media we can become engaged with others through discussion forums, online chat, instant messaging, emails, and other ways. This increased interactivity with each other does not make media content irrelevant in our lives. On the contrary, it could be argued that such content becomes more integrated and relevant to us as it provides much of the fodder for our discussions with each other.

Our concept of what makes a story and our expectations with narrative also change with interactive media. The control in storytelling enjoyed by authors or producers in traditional media could well be a thing of the past in an interactive media environment. Users may have less patience with long, complex stories and be more inclined to take hyperlinked detours as their interests and desires arise. Although with entertainment the story ending may be the same, users may arrive at that destination through a variety of routes that could include experiencing the story through the eyes of different characters or using different media. An example of this could be downloading a novel to an electronic reading device such as a Kindle but then listening to the audio version when unable to read, such as when driving. Interaction is important for media companies in other ways. Companies can see who has commented on a particular story, how many visitors have come to a story, how long they have stayed there, and what they went to next. This kind of knowledge can be extremely powerful in that it could influence editorial content as publishers seek to attract the most viewers to their websites. A story that gets many more page views than others may tempt publishers to encourage the editorial team to publish more such stories.

On a related note, the ability to interact with the media and share one's opinions or knowledge has embarrassed some news organizations as readers have pointed out errors or bias in news stories. Although newspapers have long had the ability to publish corrections, the lag time, space limitations, and amount of editorial control over what gets an official correction and what doesn't has limited the corrections' usefulness. In an online, interactive environment, readers can see comments and corrections from users along with the story.

The ability to get a sense of what others may be thinking and saying about a particular news story or type of media content greatly democratizes our information environment. It helps us understand others as a kind of community, albeit perhaps a specialized or temporary one. However, it also threatens the traditional power relationship between media organizations and the audience, which has led to some difficult decisions for many media companies in dealing with the newly empowered public in an interactive media environment.

Ethics of Interactive Media

The power of interactive media to engage users and get them involved with media content raises a host of interesting ethical issues. Some of these are similar to ethical issues faced in the traditional media world, but amplified, and some are largely new. Some touch on age-old concerns regarding free speech, the role that advertising plays in our society, and basic notions of trust.

Trust is an important concept for interactivity to work well, as users have to learn to trust those they are dealing with on the Web. In face-to-face communication, we pick up on certain cues and mannerisms that help us establish trust with others, but without this social context on the Web we have to rely on what we say to each other and what happens between us through our interactions.

Consider what would happen if you were in a chat room discussion with a number of members over the course of several days, greatly enjoying the discussions and the feeling that you have met some interesting, like-minded individuals. Then imagine your sense of betrayal if you learned that one or more of the participants were actually computer programs that gave context-specific responses to posts by real humans. Your trust in that chat room—and perhaps all chat rooms in which you did not personally know the individual participants—would likely be broken.

Trust between people is similarly relevant, as we expect (or hope) that others will respect our views even if they disagree with us and that they will debate in noninflammatory ways. Most people know how disruptive an obnoxious poster can be to a discussion group, making others respond angrily to views perhaps simply spouted to draw a reaction, a practice called **trolling**. Not only do such practices degrade the quality of the discussions taking place but they waste others' time in reading and responding.

trolling
The practice of posting deliberately obnoxious or disruptive messages to discussion groups or other online forums simply to get a reaction from the participants.

■ ■ ■ FREE SPEECH FOR EVERYONE?

We also expect to trust our news organizations to give us accurate and timely information. As news organizations have had to adapt to the world of blogs and an empowered audience, they have also had to deal with issues of free speech, which can sometimes come in the form of hateful speech from the public.

The *Los Angeles Times* was forced to shut down a "wikitorial" site it had created for readers in 2005 because of foul language and inflammatory comments from readers on it, and in 2006 the *Washington Post* was criticized for removing negative comments from readers about a column that had some factual errors in it.

Although critics did not question the need to remove offensive language or posts that were clearly written just to be inflammatory, they did question why the paper also removed many thoughtful, critical comments by readers who pointed out errors in the original column. In a forum on the matter, Jeff Jarvis, a journalist and creator of the media blog Buzzmachine, said, "The age of controlled conversation is over. The age of open conversation is here. But that is damned hard for the controllers to get used to."[7]

The ability for users to post to blogs or news articles and point out errors, spout political opinions, or argue with the journalists or other users has become expected, and media organizations who do not allow this functionality make it seem as if they are still trying to control the conversation by not letting the audience speak. On the other hand, when audiences react in ways that are not deemed suitable for public, civic discourse, it raises questions on who can (or should) control or moderate the conversations.

Interactivity brings the issue of free speech into sharper focus as questions are raised regarding what is protected and what is not. Can a "sucks site" that is dedicated to complaining about a specific company and that has been designed to look like the company's site be an infringement of trademark or an example of free speech?

■ ■ ■ INTERACTIVE ADVERTISING

The complaints against advertising and the control it is claimed to have in directing our tastes and desires for goods is intensified in an interactive environment. At the forefront of this are video games for children that are created by companies,

Web Link >>>
Buzzmachine
www.buzzmachine.com

such as breakfast-cereal manufacturers, that prominently feature their products in the games.

Because of the high level of engagement in video games, which are of course interactive, some groups have been concerned that the hidden commercial messages are being absorbed by children who are not even aware that they are being exposed to advertising.

The level of violence in video games, discussed more in the chapter on entertainment, is also a major concern to some groups who claim that the interactivity in the games influences children more than simply passively watching violence on television.

■■■SEARCH ENGINE KEYWORDS

A practice largely hidden from the public's perception of how it receives information on the Internet is how keywords are used in search engines. As more and more people go to search engines first to find information, keywords also become increasingly important as pointers to websites.

metatag
....
A word or words used by websites to help search engines index and describe a site, typically unseen by humans unless looking at the website's code.

There have already been several court cases in which companies have claimed that competitors are unfairly using their name or brand in their search engine keywords, or **metatags**. For example, if I own a video-rental shop and add "Netflix" as one of my metatag keywords, meaning search engines could use that term to identify my site, then in theory if someone does a search for "Netflix" they could come to my site. It is important to note that my site doesn't have to look like or claim to be Netflix's site (which would be a clear case of fraud); I am still acting illegally because I am tricking users to come to my site through keywords that actually do not accurately reflect the content of my site because I am not Netflix.

Being able to trust keyword searches is fundamental to a good user experience on the Web and to interactivity. Without sound ethical principles regarding interactivity, the door is open to abuse, by individuals and companies, that detracts from the overall Web experience for many.

LOOKING BACK AND MOVING FORWARD

Storage of media content, user interface, and interactivity may not seem like typical issues that would affect mass communication, but the fact that they are is yet another signal of the changes that convergence is bringing.

Computing technology changes rapidly, sometimes radically altering the industry and the way people use computers. With the convergence of computing, telecommunications, and media, this means that technological changes can have a strong ripple effect on media and mass communication. One example is how the increase in computer processing power created better opportunities for a graphical user interface and how the GUI then made computers much more accessible to the average person, which helped create large audiences online. It is likely that advances in technology will further alter the way we interact with computers in ways that we cannot foresee.

However, some general patterns can be examined, giving us a sense of what to expect in the future. These patterns fall into the following broad categories: easier accessibility, more immersive media environments, and seamless or fluid interfaces.

Wireless and handheld devices have become more commonplace in recent years and raise important user-interface questions for content on small screens.

CONVERGENCE CULTURE

How I Learned to Stop Worrying and Love the (Google) Bomb

Although Google's method and algorithms for ranking search listings is a closely guarded secret, some programmers and Web developers have been able to manipulate search results based on certain known facts about how listings are generally ranked.

In 2003 and 2004, computer users could type in "weapons of mass destruction" and hit the "I'm Feeling Lucky" button on Google, which takes users to the top-ranked page for that search term, and they would see what looked like the standard "Page Not Found" error. However, on closer reading, it was actually a parody page that discussed how weapons of mass destruction were not found in Iraq.

Similarly, typing in "miserable failure" would take users to the White House official biography page of former president George Bush. It did not take long for conservatives to use similar techniques so that "miserable failure" could bring users to home pages of filmmaker Michael Moore or former president Jimmy Carter.

This practice, known as Google bombing, was an innovative example of how people will find ways to bend technology to make others laugh or to make a political point.

However, it was also deeply threatening to the perceived relevance of Google search listings and to audience trust that search results would be helpful and accurate. In 2007, Google changed the way it ranked pages and thus made it harder to create Google bombs.

At first glance this looks like a standard "error" page, but when reading the text one sees it is actually an example of a Google bomb.

Flexible, portable **OLED** screens will greatly increase accessibility and may mean that users are not confined to small screens on mobile phones. However, even with OLED screens that can be placed on a wall or window, for example, issues of bandwidth may still need to be considered in terms of providing content. If OLED screens do enter the market, they could provide a similar user-interface experience to what we are accustomed to on desktop PCs or laptops.

Geography and location will become more important as more devices are equipped with GPS receivers. From a user-interface perspective, this means that maps will become increasingly important as on-screen graphics that contain layered information. Map-based GUIs can provide everything from information on the nearest restaurant, including reviews, to local points of cultural or historical interest.

Accessing media content will be increasingly easy, but accessing the content one *wants* when and where one wants it may be harder than ever unless sound principles in user-interface design are applied to search-and-find functions.

OLED
....
Organic light-emitting diode screen, a type of thin, flexible screen that will change how and where we are able to view content on screens.

A variety of forms of immersive media are emerging in the online environment and seeing increased use in a number of ways. These include three-dimensional (3-D) visualizations, virtual reality, 360-degree photography and video, and augmented reality. Immersive media environments can provide media experiences unlike those encountered in traditional media or even in the typical digital media environment and can provide new opportunities—and new challenges—for user interfaces.

Our conceptions today of largely static web pages will gradually be replaced by interfaces that are more fluid and that change to suit our informational and entertainment needs. We will not have to necessarily "go to" a website to get the information we want; rather, we will develop our own personalized home page or site that collects the information we want from various sources. We see the precursors to this with RSS feeds and other tools that "push" content to subscribers.

It is important to remember that the online environment of the future will not simply be one of receiving a variety of media content in different forms, though that will continue to be a large part of it. It will also include various ways to communicate directly with media producers, other audience members, and one's social network. We will expect our user interface to help us receive the kind of information and entertainment we want, but we will also demand that we can easily communicate and interact with others. In fact, interactivity is one of the key characteristics of digital media that not only create new kinds of user-interface issues but that set digital media apart fundamentally from traditional media forms.

DISCUSSION QUESTIONS

1. Which characteristic of storage technology do you think is most important for a society to run day-to-day business? What about to preserve its cultural heritage? Do you think the characteristics of storage technology have changed in relative importance with the advent of digital media? Why or why not?

2. Imagine a world in which audio and video could not be recorded. Discuss how media would be different in terms of content creation, performance or distribution, media organizations, and economics.

3. Some contend that secretly recording conversations or activities in audio or video format, even when the acts recorded occur in a public space, is a violation of privacy. State and defend your position on the matter.

4. Discuss ways in which you would like to see search engines improved.

5. Compare the benefits and drawbacks for media professionals of having large amounts of information readily at hand. How might the balance of information versus ease of retrieval affect how journalists do their jobs?

6. If almost all information were available to anyone at any time on a compact, easy-to-use device, how do you think this would affect the level of people's general knowledge or education? Would people become more knowledgeable and more active in society? Would they become more apathetic, or would they be more or less the same? How might this device affect different people within society, such as rich versus poor, or various ethnic or language groups?

7. Compare the user interface of a newspaper with that of the newspaper's website. What elements are similar and what elements differ? Explain why they may be so.

8. Visit three different websites within a specific industry (i.e., car rental agencies, airlines, or newspapers) and note user-interface differences between them. What elements did you like and dislike about each site? Why? What ways could they be improved?

9. Consider the differences between immediate interactivity, such as pushing a button or discussing on IM, and delayed interactivity, such as email or a discussion board. How does the change in time affect the conversations and relations between people?

. . . .

FURTHER READING

Understanding Media: The Extensions of Man, reprint ed; Marshall McLuhan, Lewis Lapham (1994) MIT Press.

Bias of Communication, reprint ed.; Harold Innis (1991) University of Toronto Press.

A History of Modern Computing; Paul E. Ceruzzi (1999) MIT Press.

Dark Ages II: When the Digital Data Die; Bryan P. Bergeron (2001) Prentice Hall.

Interface Culture: How New Technology Transforms the Ways We Create and Communicate; Steven Johnson (1999) Basic Books.

The Rise of the Image and the Fall of the Word; Mitchell Stephens (1998) Oxford University Press.

About Face 3: The Essentials of Interaction Design; Alan Cooper, Robert Reimann, David Cronin (2007) Wiley.

The Google Story: Inside the Hottest Business, Media, and Technology Success of Our Time; David Vise, Mark Malseed (2006) Delta.

Planet Google: One Company's Audacious Plan to Organize Everything We Know; Randall Stross (2008) Free Press.

Click: What Millions of People Are Doing Online and Why it Matters; Bill Tancer (2008) Hyperion.

. . . .

MEDIA QUIZ ANSWERS

1. False, it is 1,000 (kilo) bytes.

2. False, cave paintings and petroglyphs are forms of information storage that predate writing systems.

3. Graphic user interface.

4. True, current media like videotape and DVDs are expected to last only about fifty to seventy-five years.

5. False, it stands for MPEG-1, Audio Layer-III.

6. $650 billion.

7. NBC, after the assassination attempt on President Ford in 1975.

8. English, Chinese, Spanish.

9. True.

10. A technique that manipulates search engine results to get high rankings for a certain site, usually for humorous or political purposes.

Networks and Distributing Digital Content

CHAPTER OBJECTIVES

In this chapter we will:

■ Outline the characteristics that distinguish digital distribution from traditional forms of distribution of media content.

■ Examine the implications new forms of digital distribution have on mass-communication organizations.

■ Describe the historical development of telecommunications and of networks that have created the current status of digital distribution.

■ Highlight the future development and potential problems of digital distribution.

8

The example may seem like ancient history according to Internet time, but it foreshadows several important elements that have stayed with us as the Internet has developed and more people use it.

Mahir Cagri was just another Turkish journalist until November 1999. Then his cell phone and home phone began ringing constantly, with people from all over the world who wanted to talk to him about his home page.

Even in the earliest days of the Web in the early 1990s, his home page was considered technically crude and poorly designed. Visitors were greeted by

This is my page ....

WELCOME TO MY HOME PAGE !!!!!!!!!

I KISS YOU !!!!!

This was followed by a picture of a smiling Cagri in a brown suit, then

I like music , I have many many musicenstrumans my home I can play

I like sport , swiming , basketball ,tenis , volayball , walk ....

I like sex

I like travel I go 3-4 country every year

Web Link >>>
I Kiss You home page
www.ikissyou.org/famous_site/
famous_site.html

Several pictures of Cagri followed—him playing table tennis, him lying on a beach in a red Speedo—interspersed by similar English statements, and at the bottom he invited anyone to visit him in Turkey and gave his phone numbers. Even though Cagri's grasp of written English was as tenuous as his grasp of basic website design, it didn't stop him from becoming a Web sensation. Within days a million people had visited his page.

Cagri said that apparently someone in Turkey copied his home page and republished it to another site, sending it to some friends as a joke. From there it quickly spread. The interest in his site peaked at the end of 1999, but numerous parody sites sprang up and some advertising firms tried to copy the style to pitch products. Cagri recorded a pop single, "I Kiss You," and an ad for a British Internet company. He also wrote a book. His website gave him the chance to meet many women, some who specifically came to Izmir to see him, and he became a local celebrity.

Internet commentator and author David Weinberger said it would be a mistake to dismiss Cagri and his home page. "The absurdity is the point," says Weinberger. "Hollywood has been cynically handing us stars, and we reveled in showing that now we are the ones who will decide who to notice. I think the general Web reaction was: 'We made this relentlessly ordinary guy a star! Cool!'"[1]

The ability to cheaply and easily distribute content to a mass audience, along with the chance for people to interact with each other, is probably the most crucial and visible aspect of how the Internet is transforming mass communication. Computerized production and editing technologies, storage media, and interface design have important implications in a range of areas involving mass communication, but none of these implications would be so great if media distribution had remained only in the hands of a select few media companies.

Digital distribution has gone from a unidirectional model, in the analog world, in which large media companies send out messages to a mass and largely silent audience, to one in which the public can distribute content as widely as an established media company, all without spending money on advertising or marketing.

The continuing battles the recording industry is having over file-sharing services, although framed in terms of intellectual property and copyright infringement, are an issue primarily because of changes brought about in distribution.

The public is behaving no differently than it did prior to the Internet, when a music fan would make an audiocassette copy of an album for a friend or compile songs from a favorite band onto a cassette to be listened to in the car. A primary difference is that, rather than making a couple of tapes and giving them to friends, millions of people can now get free copies of music and send those copies to others throughout the Internet, all with very little effort and almost no cost.

A. J. Liebling once said, "Freedom of the press is guaranteed only to those who own one." With digital media and the Internet, now practically anyone has a "printing press" that can distribute not only printed text but audio or video as well.

In order to understand how these changes have come about, it is important to know how today's telecommunications networks originated and how what we experience with these networks today has many past influences, not all of them beneficial.

Historical Influences on Modern Networks

The telecommunications networks we rely on today for everything from talking with friends to banking have been influenced and shaped by a wide range of social, political, and historical factors. Because these networks generally operate hidden from us, or seemingly invisibly, it is easy to overlook how crucial they are to our media system. But no understanding of media today is complete without under-

Network Knowledge

1. If you were allowed to use only one telecommunications device, what would it be?
2. (True or False) The fax machine was invented before the telephone.
3. Which is older, the electric telegraph or the optical telegraph?
4. If you had the choice between taking $1 million right now and getting a penny doubled every day for a month, which would you choose?
5. What does "P2P" stand for?
6. How does P2P work?
7. What is the debate over Net neutrality about?
8. What are three characteristics of digital distribution that give it advantages over physical products?
9. (True or False) File-sharing networks such as BitTorrent are technically illegal.
10. (True or False) Members of the public who post content online are not bound by the same restrictions regarding privacy and libel as professional journalists.

standing how modern networks work and the historical influences that made them what they are today.

One of the fundamental changes that telecommunications networks have brought to our social and political life is what is called **time-space compression**. This futuristic-sounding term means that networks have "sped up" time and have "shrunk" space. Prior to the invention of the first electronic communication, the telegraph, communication could be distributed no faster than the fastest means of transportation, whether it was a horse, train, or ship.

The slow pace of long-distance communication meant that it was almost impossible for governments such as the British Empire to easily control far-flung colonies. A message from India would normally take several weeks to reach London and of course the same amount of time to get back to India. In the meantime, circumstances might have changed drastically, making the response largely irrelevant depending on what had developed during the interim period.

However, in the early days of the telegraph, it only took a matter of hours for a message to reach London from India through various overland telegraph routes, and that time shrank as telegraph connections and technology improved. This "shrinking of space" helped rulers control things much more closely than they had in the past—essentially bringing faraway lands "closer" than they had been before.

Another way to think of how time-space compression works is to consider the effect the cell phone has on us. You may be in a college far from home, but your parents are still able to "be present" through a simple call or text message. Your physical distance may be great, but activities or decisions in one place can instantly affect people in a different place. Your decision to stay on campus over Thanksgiving Break, phoned to your parents, may have an immediate impact on their Thanksgiving plans.

time-space compression
The idea that electronic communication has essentially reduced distances between people because of nearly instantaneous communication, which has also "sped up" our notions of time.

This shrinking of space and speeding up of time had several important repercussions for the media. Timely information became increasingly important in order to make good business decisions. Firms were created to provide timely news and business information, such as the national wire services Reuters and Havas. Companies or countries that were cut out of this informational loop were often at a disadvantage.

In our always-on, almost instantaneous information environment it is hard to imagine the drastic transformations that the earliest telecommunications networks had on society, but by looking at some of the ways their development was influenced we will better understand our networks today and how certain echoes of the past continue to affect us.

■ ■ ■ GOVERNMENT AND PRIVATE INDUSTRY

An important communications network that existed long before the invention of the telegraph in 1837 was the postal system. Although not typically thought of as a communications network, it nevertheless played a vital role in the colonial era and early years of the United States in disseminating information.

The importance of the postal system as a means to distribute news was understood by the Republic's early leaders, who subsidized newspapers by allowing them to be sent at reduced postal rates. A common practice among newspaper publishers at the time was to directly copy news from other papers (usually without attribution), so when access was provided to greater numbers of papers, news was able to spread much further and much faster than it otherwise would have.

The postal system was a government-run service, supported by taxes and charges for deliveries, rather than a for-profit company. The desire on the part of leaders to keep even this rudimentary communications network within government control highlights the importance they gave it. This thinking would have significant implications for how modern telecommunications networks evolved in various countries.

For example, in almost all European countries the telegraph was considered something that should be state-owned—an extension of the mail system—and thus was put within the country's postal service. However, in the United States, the government at first refused to provide funding when Samuel Morse requested it for further work on his nascent telegraph and several years later also declined to offer public money to fund what was called an "information railroad" that would string telegraph lines from coast to coast. Instead, private companies, each trying to establish its own network, strung telegraph wires, and the telegraph was perceived as primarily a network that would operate within a competitive environment of private industry.

There are benefits and detriments in both systems. The private-industry model for the telegraph (and later the telephone) led to chaos in the early years, as competing companies vied for market share and required customers to purchase equipment that was incompatible with other companies' equipment. This led to great waste and hampered the rapid development of the network, at least until some companies either went out of business or merged with other companies.

In the case of the United States, Western Union ended up with a monopoly on the telegraph network. Access to telegraphs could vary greatly; areas that had high market potential had competing services, while large swaths of the country, especially rural areas, did not have any access at all, as the decision to connect an area was based on making a profit.

On the other hand, competition also helped lead to rapid technological and service improvements, although (as we have seen) it is not always the case that the best technology wins out in the end. A highly competitive environment does encourage more risk taking and greater innovation as companies try to gain market share through better products or services. Once a monopoly exists, however, the sole company in the market then has little incentive to innovate or remain competitive through service or price.

The government-run model had the benefit of building the network on principles of public service and universal access rather than where the most profitable market is located. Once the government decided on a system, customers could be assured that equipment would work everywhere on the network, ensuring rapid use of the network. Certain costs could also be absorbed within the government system, making the network cheaper to use than it might have been if a company sought a profit.

However, government bureaucracy can often inhibit further development and growth of new technologies that challenge the established system, making change or improvements difficult. The centralized process of decision making can also hamper innovation and the adoption of new technologies.

In the United States, balancing government interests with those of private industry has been especially difficult with communication networks. Government policies have shifted over time, from letting the market decide who wins, to allowing government-granted monopolies to certain companies in a regulated industry—much like how the utilities companies are run. The amount and degree of regulation has been another arena of conflict over the years.

The tension between the public interest in easy and affordable access to communication networks and the drive for profit and business success continues today. We see it in the many government regulations that dictate what telecommunications companies can and cannot do, in the different laws that govern the industry, and in the frequent lawsuits that challenge the status quo. We will see that these are not new, either, and have often gone hand in hand with new communication-network technologies.

■ ■ ■ EVOLVING TECHNOLOGY: FROM THE TELEGRAPH TO FIBER OPTICS

Technology is of course always changing and evolving. In only a handful of other areas can we see the same dramatic effects that new communication technologies can have on industries, people, and society. The path of evolving communication technologies is not a smooth one and is littered with bitter lawsuits among inventors, technologies that were developed ahead of their time and not adopted, short-sighted government officials, and unintended consequences. It is worth briefly exploring some of these interesting developments.

Telegraphy

The idea of sending information faster than what could be physically transported is as old as smoke signals or lighting fires on mountaintops. However, these earlier systems were extremely limited in terms of the amount of information they could carry and of course depended on the weather.

In 1837, American Samuel Morse created and patented the electromagnetic telegraph, which marked the beginning of today's information age. Morse's invention, building on earlier attempts at electric telegraphy by British inventors, was

Samuel Morse and his telegraph.

the first technology that could put information into electric form and transmit it reliably over great distances.

By tapping dots and dashes representing letters on a keypad, in what is now called Morse code, telegraph operators could rapidly spell out messages. Because the cost was higher for longer messages and there was always a chance the wrong people could see a message, businesses quickly adopted a number of abbreviations for commonly used words and phrases, with elaborate codebooks that allowed the recipients to decipher the messages.

Despite what we see today as obvious benefits of getting information quickly, there was not much enthusiasm for the telegraph initially. It was not until 1844 that an experimental telegraph line of forty miles was actually built, between Baltimore and Washington, D.C. The nomination of the Whig Party presidential candidate, Henry Clay, was sent to the capital, and the information age was born.

Many in the newspaper business and businesses in general then realized the important role the telegraph could play in the rapid delivery of news and information. Within the next two decades, telegraph lines quickly spread throughout the country and throughout Europe. Submarine cable lines across the Atlantic were attempted in the latter 1850s, but it was not until 1866 that the first successful transatlantic cable began operation.

Some scholars have claimed that the telegraph played a direct role in shaping news stories. Because of the unreliability of the early telegraph lines, it was important to write concisely and include the most important facts of a story first, with facts of lesser importance coming later. This led to the style of news writing still practiced today, the inverted pyramid style.

Others have questioned this, however, saying that an analysis of papers from the mid-nineteenth century reveals that stories received over wire and stories received through traditional means had no substantial differences. Both were often written in flowery language using chronological narrative, with little regard to what was most important. These scholars credit Lincoln's second secretary of war, Edwin Stanton, with creating the inverse pyramid style. Stanton's terse missives about Civil War battles were often used directly by U.S. newspapers.

The fax machine, invented by Alexander Bain, is an example of a technology that was developed long before it could be widely used.

Sometimes it's easy to think that "new media" technologies are truly new and revolutionary. Frequently, the truth is far different. The facsimile, or fax, is a very old technology whose invention coincides with the telegraph. Although it became widely used in the 1980s, the fax was actually invented in 1842 by Scottish psychologist Alexander Bain as a way to send images over telegraph wires. It was sometimes used during the U.S. Civil War to send images of maps, but the limited carrying capacity of telegraph wires hampered the facsimile's usefulness.

Telephony

Even as telegraph lines continued to expand, and technological advances allowed for more carrying capacity on the lines, the telegraph quickly faced a serious competitor that would eventually take its place as the most important form of telecommunication.

Bell's 1876 invention of the telephone launched the national system of telephony, which operated much the same as the telegraph except that sounds could be transmitted over the wires. The introduction of the telephone provides an interesting look at how the development of technology has unintended consequences, how advances in technology change and threaten established business models, and how the careful dance between government regulation and corporate interests often contains stumbles.

Bell was not the first person to think of trying to transmit sounds over electrical wires; many people had been working on it ever since the telegraph was unveiled. However, his experience in working with the hearing impaired gave him an advantage over others in understanding how sound, especially the voice, works. His research for the hearing impaired on using technology to amplify sound also played a key role in being able to transmit and receive audible voice messages. Bell did not start out to create a national telecommunications network that would quickly supersede the telegraph network, but that is what happened.

Similar to Henry Ford's famous line about choosing a car color, AT&T let customers choose a color for their phones—as long as it was black.

The American Telephone and Telegraph Company (AT&T) and the American Bell Telephone Company existed as regulated legal monopolies for most of their history, based on the principles outlined by former AT&T president Theodore Vail in 1907. He said that the telephone, by the nature of the underlying technology, could operate most efficiently as a monopoly providing universal service. The notion of universal service was present in the age of the telegraph as well, as noted in the suggestion by Ephraim Farley in 1853 that all homes "would be in immediate communication with each other."

Vail and others realized that competing telephone systems, in which users of one telephone system could not communicate with users of other telephone systems, would hurt the growth of telecommunication. This principle guided U.S. telecommunications policy for most of the twentieth century. Although it may well have helped ease the early adoption of telephones (and helped AT&T, whose system was eventually adopted), the monopoly control AT&T had over telecommunications systems also slowed innovation.

In the early 1960s, researchers were attempting to create what would eventually become the Internet and decided that, rather than build an entirely new network, they could simply use the extensive telephone network, controlled by AT&T. However, the structure of the telephone network relied on analog **circuit switching**, which was a centralized system in five-level hierarchies. Messages transmitted through switching centers would degrade in quality, just as third- or fourth-generation videotape dubs degrade the quality of the original recorded video. If a central switching center was destroyed, the entire telephone system could be incapacitated.

circuit switching

The original system used for telephony, in which circuits connected two people communicating. Once the circuit was connected, or "on," the people on either end of the circuit used the whole circuit exclusively, even if they didn't speak. When they hung up, the circuit was disconnected by an operator and available for others to use.

The researchers asked AT&T if they could test a digital, **packet-switched** network via telephone lines, but AT&T refused. Paul Baran, who conceived of the Internet's architecture in the early 1960s, said that even when the air force offered to give AT&T money to develop a digital, packet-switched network, AT&T said, "It's not going to work. And furthermore, we're not going into competition with ourselves."

AT&T was eventually forced to change to digital packet-switching modes and similarly lost its monopoly control over the telephone network in 1984 when the company was split into several regional "Baby Bells" throughout the country. Today, the basic architecture of the telephone system is digital and packet-switched, just like the Internet.

packet switching

A type of switching within a network, in which information is divided up into pieces, or packets, and transported as separate packets using the least congested routes. At the end of the route the packets are reassembled in their proper order and delivered over the telephone line or Internet.

■ ■ ■ WIRELESS TELECOMMUNICATIONS

Just as the idea of transmitting voices over wires was explored almost as soon as the telegraph was invented, the idea of transmitting sounds over the air, or wirelessly, also was tried by many people before it became a success. The development of radio

Sputnik I, the first satellite sent into orbit, started the space race between the Soviet Union and the U.S.

and television was covered in earlier chapters, so we will not rehash here how they evolved. What is important to keep in mind in terms of their role as telecommunication networks is how they also were initially created with other purposes in mind.

Radio, for example, was not conceived as a popular mode of mass entertainment but as a way for ships to communicate with each other or with people on the coast in order to improve safety. Wireless communication also would help solve the problems that came with severed undersea cables or downed telegraph or telephone lines that halted the normal flow of communication until they were repaired.

And just as the development of the telegraph and telephone spawned whole new industries and government regulations, so too did the development of wireless telecommunications. Two examples that will be explored in later chapters are the far-heavier regulation of television and radio than print media because of spectrum scarcity (the electromagnetic spectrum that can carry audio or radio waves is a limited resource) and the wireless-spectrum auction that took place in the United States in 2008.

■ ■ ■ SATELLITES

Television was still not a mass medium when the concept of wireless telecommunication was considered for space. Communication satellites were first proposed in 1945 by science fiction writer Arthur C. Clarke. Clarke was trained in communications and helped invent radar during World War II.

On October 4, 1957, the Soviet Union launched Sputnik I ("traveling companion"), the first communications satellite. Sputnik I was a 23-inch, 184-pound ball of metal that contained a radio receiver and transmitter, using what is today the Citizens Band, or CB, radio frequency, and signaled not only the beginning of instantaneous global communications but an important milestone in the cold war. It was the Soviets' launch of Sputnik that led U.S. president John F. Kennedy to declare, four years later, that the United States would be the first country to put a man on the moon, by the end of the 1960s.

Although some scholars have questioned the importance of the invention of the communications satellite as a transformative technology, Arthur C. Clarke disagrees, saying that claiming it is simply an extension of existing communication technologies is like claiming the atomic bomb was simply an extension of conventional warfare.

Communications satellites have substantially upgraded communication networks in at least two ways. First, they have substantial bandwidth, or communications capacity. This means more information, communications, or media content can be distributed. Second, because they are positioned high above the earth (typically twenty-two thousand miles), satellites permit ground-based media to communicate with parties in remote corners of the globe. A signal can be sent from one location on earth, bounced off the satellite, and relayed to a distant location that also has a line of sight with the satellite. The two terrestrial locations might be thousands of miles apart and, because of the earth's curvature, unable to reach each other with regular wireless terrestrial communications.

■ ■ ■ FIBER OPTICS

It is ironic that one of the newest, most powerful telecommunication technologies, fiber optics, is derived from one of the oldest attempts at telegraphy. In 1794, French clergyman Claude Chappe and Swedish nobleman Abraham Niclas

Al Jazeera: CNN of the Middle East?

INTERNATIONAL PERSPECTIVES

Since the terrorist attacks on the World Trade Center and Pentagon on September 11, 2001, a largely unknown satellite news channel—unknown outside the Middle East, at least—based in Qatar (pronounced like "cutter" rather than "guitar"), has beaten CNN at its own game with several scoops.

Al Jazeera, which means "the peninsula" in Arabic, was the only news organization broadcasting live in Afghanistan when the United States started bombing the country. It was the first to obtain copies of videotapes of Osama bin Laden, broadcasting them when some Western networks refused to do so out of fear they might contain hidden messages to Al Qaeda operatives.

Government officials in the United States have complained that Al Jazeera is little more than a mouthpiece for Osama bin Laden and that its unbalanced coverage fans anti-Semitism and anti-American feelings. Whether that is true or not, Al Jazeera is accustomed to criticism from government authorities: the news organization has outraged almost every Arab government as it has tried to follow its motto, "We get both sides of the story."

Founded in 1996 by Qatar's ruler Sheik Hamad bin Khalifa Al Thani, who was dismayed by the lack of press freedom in much of the Middle East, the station prides itself on its independence. Al Jazeera's coverage of sensitive topics has often led to strained relations between Qatar and other Arab nations, as well to Al Jazeera's expulsion from some Arab countries.

Al Jazeera claims at least 35 million viewers in the Arab world and 175,000 cable subscribers in North America. Its website gets 17 million hits a day, it alleges.

"Al-Jazeera is undoubtedly a new trend in Arab media," said Roger Hardy, a Mideast specialist for the BBC World Service in London. "And as far as I can tell, it's the station of choice for Arabs, whether you're a Palestinian in Gaza . . . or you're part of the Arab diaspora in Canada or America."[2]

The website includes a program that translates Arabic articles into English and, in addition to its own stories, a number of links to various stories about Al Jazeera itself. Because of the unequalled access that Al Jazeera reporters often have in the Middle East, they can be one of the primary sources for news when Western reporters are barred from entering hotspots, such as Gaza in early 2009.

Web Link >>>
Al Jazeera
english.aljazeera.net/

Optical telegraphs were created in the late 1700s but were limited by weather conditions.

Fiber-optic lines transmit information by using highly concentrated light waves.

Edelcrantz built the optical telegraph so that news could be brought from Finland to Stockholm, Sweden, and also from Denmark to the Swedish coast and from there to the Swedish capital. The optical telegraph worked by means of a series of signaling stations, each within sight of the next, usually less than a kilometer apart. A person standing in a lookout platform on the station would watch the next tower for a visual signal, which would represent a letter, word, or number. A series of signals could represent a message, which would then be relayed to the next tower, and so on. Experienced signalers could transmit even a fairly complex message quickly.

England used an optical telegraph system to communicate between London and its south coast, and Napoleon also used one in Europe in the early 1800s during his military campaigns. But for the most part, European governments failed to see the practicality of optical telegraphs and did not encourage their growth. Likewise, the few that were built in the United States, such as between Cape Cod and Boston, were never commercially viable.

In many respects, the story of fiber optics goes all the way back to the optical telegraph created by Chappe and Edelcrantz, since it uses light to transmit information. Even though telegraphy eventually developed around using electromagnetism, rather than light, the concept of transmitting information with light was not abandoned. Alexander Graham Bell patented an optical telephone system—the photophone—only four years after his invention of the telephone, but his earlier telephone was more practical.

Transmitting light through the air had many problems, the main one being that the light became diffused. Numerous inventors and scientists worked on concentrating and focusing the light, usually through glass tubing of some type. In the 1950s and 1960s, two developments helped make the transmission of information by light a reality. One was the reduction of light leakage from the glass or plastic fibers by covering them, and the other was the invention of the laser in 1960. Sending light long distances without degrading the signal still proved to be problematic, making fiber optics not practical as a communication medium until further technological improvements in 1970.

Today's fiber optics can send information through hair-thin glass or plastic fiber by laser almost one hundred miles without using a repeater, or device that boosts the signal. Fiber not only has much more capacity to carry information than traditional copper wires, it moves information much faster—at the speed of light, in fact.

Almost all of the major communication lines within the United States now use fiber optics to send information. However, laying fiber-optic lines directly to homes is still not cost-effective for telecommunications companies, so most information travels by fiber optics to switching stations near the destinations. The switching stations send it further by copper wires or coaxial cable, which are slower than fiber-optic lines. Verizon's FiOS service, being rolled out gradually in various regions within the United States, provides fiber-optic connections directly to homes. Some countries, such as Japan, have encouraged the building of fiber-optic lines to homes and thus have far more homes connected that way.

The Nature of Networks: Key Concepts

Some characteristics of networks have been discussed in earlier chapters, and here we will more thoroughly examine some of the networks that have been mentioned. We will also cover key concepts that must be understood to better comprehend mass communication and the Internet.

There are many types of networks, but in this chapter we will focus on telecommunications networks as they relate to mass communication and the Internet. In the next chapter we will look at social networks on the Internet and what is called Web 2.0 and how they relate to media.

One useful way to consider networks is by looking at three network "laws." These are not scientific laws, in the same way that there is a law of gravity, but actually ways to describe and analyze different kinds of networks.

■ ■ ■ SARNOFF'S LAW

RCA executive and radio and television pioneer David Sarnoff is the creator of **Sarnoff's Law**, which states that the value of a network increases linearly with the number of people on it, as Figure 8-1 shows. This description applies to mass-communication networks such as radio or television networks.

Defining "value" can of course be tricky, but in the case of radio or television, consider how much more a network can charge an advertiser if it has ten million audience members than if it has ten thousand.

Sarnoff's Law
....
Created by RCA executive David
Sarnoff, it states that the
value of a network increases
linearly with the number of
people on it.

FIGURE 8-1 Sarnoff's Law shows how the value of a network increases linearly with the number of people on the network, which applies to traditional broadcasting.

It is important to also think of the communication flow in such a network; it is the very definition of mass communication. A single person or group broadcasts a message to a large audience whose members have no means to communicate with each other or the sender through that network. The audience is essentially silent and passive; viewers or listeners have no way of knowing how many others are also receiving the same message or content, let alone whether others like or do not like it.

Sarnoff's Law may be useful for understanding radio and television networks, but it fails miserably when used to consider a network in which the members can communicate with each other in some form, such as the Internet.

■ ■ ■ METCALFE'S LAW

Metcalfe's Law
....
The value of a network rises
in proportion to the square of
the number of people on that
network. In other words, the
more people who are connected
to a network in which they can
communicate with each other,
such as the Internet, the more
valuable that network becomes.

Robert Metcalfe, creator of the Ethernet protocol and founder of networking company 3Com, came up with the law bearing his name in 1993. **Metcalfe's Law** states that in a communication network with n members, each member can make $n-1$ connections (because a member cannot connect with him- or herself), which means that the value of a communications network increases roughly to its square, or n^2.

It is easy to underestimate the growth rate when considering the square of numbers. A simple example will help illustrate. If a communication network has 10 members, each of whom can communicate with the others, then there are 90 possible communication connections that can be made (see Figure 8-2). If the number of members in the network doubles to 20, then the number of possible connections doesn't simply double to 180 (as Sarnoff's Law would predict) but quadruples to 360.

This is similar to the old trick question "Would you rather take $1 million right now or have a penny doubled every day for thirty days?" It does not look very promising for the lowly penny for most of the month, until it surpasses the $1 million mark on day twenty-eight and you end up with $5,368,709.12 by day thirty.

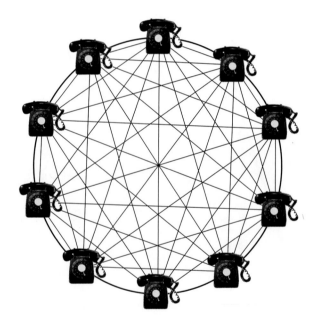

FIGURE 8-2 Metcalfe's Law shows how the value of an interactive network increases approximately to its square because of all the possible combinations of communication between members.

Metcalfe's Law was used to rationalize the fervor of the dot-com boom in the late 1990s, with many experts claiming it was the reason the New Economy would replace the old ways of doing business. That, of course, did not happen.

Critics of Metcalfe's Law point to a number of problems with it. One criticism echoes the problem with Sarnoff's Law in that the term "value" is not defined and can mean different things to different people.

Another major criticism is that the law assumes that connections in the network are all equal, which is rarely the case. Consider your own communications network, perhaps listed in the address book on your cell phone. You do not regu-

Web Link >>>
Penny Doubled
http://pennydoubled.com/

larly communicate with every member on the network every single time you want to send a message, and neither do they. Therefore, the simple number of members in a network will not produce the growth in value that Metcalfe's Law predicts.

Even with the criticisms of Metcalfe's Law, it nevertheless does a better job than Sarnoff's Law of explaining the power more members add to an interactive communications network. Some people, in fact, have claimed that Metcalfe's Law does not go far enough in explaining the power of network effects.

■ ■ ■ REED'S LAW

Though not negating Metcalfe's Law, David Reed claimed in 1999 to have discovered another effect of network scaling that is especially relevant in the Web 2.0 world. **Reed's Law** claims that the utility of a network with n members increases exponentially, or 2^n (2 to the nth power). The rapid growth curve with Reed's Law is shown in **Figure 8-3**, and it is clear how much faster utility, or value, grows when such a network gets more members.

Reed's Law

The utility or value of an interactive communication network with n members increases exponentially, or 2 to the nth power.

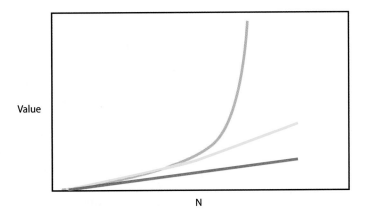

Value

N

FIGURE 8-3 The difference in growth of value between Sarnoff's Law (red), Metcalfe's Law (yellow), and Reed's Law(green) is clearly shown in this graph.

We will discuss Reed's Law in more detail in Chapter 9, but for now it is enough to know that it helps to explain the power of social networks and the various groups that form because of network affiliations. Reed does not claim that they will inevitably form, just that there is greater potential for them to form when there are more members in a network. This is because of the nature of peer-to-peer networks such as the Internet, which we will look at now.

Computer Networks: Key Concepts

Computer-based networks operate differently than traditional broadcast networks. They permit the distribution of content to be more flexible, so if one route of the network is unavailable, the network can automatically and efficiently reassemble the message through a different route. Digital networks permit compression of data, which enables a mass communicator to send more information in the same amount of space on the network. Finally, a computer network easily permits downstream and upstream communications cheaply (from the source to the receiver, and vice versa), whereas traditional networks were largely one-way and relatively expensive.

A **modem** (a foreshortening of **MO**dulate-**DEM**odulate) is used to convert the digital information in a computer to signals for transmission over a phone or cable TV line and to convert signals from the network to the computer. Modems can also operate wirelessly by converting data into radio signals. Modems were invented in the 1960s, before the days of the personal computer, as a means of letting "dumb terminals" (electronic machines with keyboards but no storage capacity) dial in to a remote computer.

■ ■ ■ PEER-TO-PEER MODEL

The **peer-to-peer (P2P)** network model is what the Internet was initially supposed to be: an interconnected group of computers, all essentially "equal" in their ability to send, store, and receive information, i.e., a network of peers. P2P networking is by its architecture decentralized and nonhierarchical.

Usenet is an early example of a P2P network and one that highlights some of P2P's flaws in the current Internet environment. Because of the nonhierarchical nature of Usenet, it was relatively easy for some people to abuse the system by doing things like sending **spam**. Spammers not only take away bandwidth from legitimate Internet users, slowing the system down, they also clog inboxes with advertising messages not related to the topics being discussed. The result? People avoid visiting discussions on Usenet, reducing the number of members and thereby diminishing its usefulness.

Another hurdle for P2P applications in reaching their full potential on today's Internet is the amount of bandwidth available to upload content. Since in a P2P network anyone can be a content distributor, users need as much bandwidth to upload content as they do when they download content. However, broadband providers such as cable companies, in order to conserve the amount of total bandwidth on the network, limit the upload speeds.

Many of the best applications being developed on the Internet combine aspects of client/server networks and P2P. Napster, for example, was not a true P2P application since it stored information on a central server, from which files were available for downloading. This classic client/server network characteristic, although helping searches, also helped make Napster an easy target when it was sued by the Recording Industry Association of America.

■ ■ ■ CLIENT/SERVER MODEL

The **client/server** model is what the Internet—for reasons such as limited bandwidth, Internet Protocol (IP) addresses, and its rapid rise in popularity via the Web—largely developed into. This model of a network simply means there is a centralized computer, or server, that stores content that the audience (clients) can access on the network. It is a hierarchical system in which most computer users do not contribute content to the Internet; they simply receive content.

A client/server network model has strong points and weak points. Among its strong points is that the centralized storage location makes information easy to find (it always has the same virtual address—in the case of the Web, a URL). Among its weak points is that a single server can easily become overloaded if many clients request content from it at the same time. The single location also makes

modem

Derived from the terms modulate-demodulate; a device that converts digital signals from a computer to analog signals for transmission over a phone line, as well as converting transmitted analog signals to digital signals.

peer-to-peer network (P2P)

A network in which all computers on the network are considered equal (peers) and can send and receive information equally well. This is the basis of file-sharing services.

spam

Unwanted email sent out by advertisers as a mass mailing.

client/server

A network model, predominant in the Internet today, that relies on a centralized computer, or server, that stores content that the audience, or clients, access.

it vulnerable to attack or destruction. If the server or servers with the hard drives containing the information are destroyed, such as in a fire, the information is lost unless backup copies were made and stored somewhere else.

Servers are an important part of how mass-communication content is moved about in a digital, networked environment. Audience members access a growing portion of the content produced by media organizations via web servers.

FIGURE 8-4 A client/server network relies on a server to provide content to people on the network, while content on a P2P network exists on various individual computers and is shared among them.

■ ■ ■ WIRELESS NETWORKS

Wireless computer networks operate much like radio or TV signals but use a different part of the electromagnetic spectrum to send and receive data. Some wireless networks have extremely short ranges—only several feet—and allow mobile devices to communicate with each other. Bluetooth is one such technology that allows for wireless communication between a headset and a laptop, for example.

The most familiar wireless network for most people is the mobile-phone network. Voice and data can be transmitted, allowing people to connect with the Internet as well. In many developing countries, this is the primary way people access the Internet, not through desktop computers.

The benefits of wireless networks are many, with a main one being that people can access the network from virtually any location (assuming they have a connection). This gives emergency services an easy way to contact large numbers of people at once, and it also means that people can easily get geographic-specific information from where they are. Want to know if the restaurant you are standing in front of is any good or not? Access the Web through your phone and read reviews on it.

However, there are also some drawbacks with wireless networks that the wired computer networks do not face to the same degree. One is the poor level of security wireless networks offer. It is relatively easy to hack into a wireless network and "eavesdrop" on it, stealing data (such as credit card information) as it is being sent, for example. And even though there has been no medi-

Bluetooth devices and other wireless technologies let us communicate easily on the go.

cal evidence of harm from wireless networks, some people still believe that the electromagnetic waves can hurt us in ways that will show up years from now.

Whether a telecommunications network such as the Internet is wired or wireless, it has two important characteristics that must be considered: connectivity and quality of service.

■ ■ ■ CONNECTIVITY

Connectivity can be defined in terms of the ability of people and their computers, digital television sets, or other digital devices to link to the Internet and other online communications media. Connectivity is critical for at least two reasons.

First, without a connection, the citizen, or media consumer, has no access to the online communications network. This means he or she can neither communicate electronically with others nor access content published online.

Second, as Metcalfe's Law and Reed's Law state, the value of a communications network rises rapidly, the more members are on that network. In other words, the more people connected to a communications network who can communicate with each other, the more potential there is not just for sharing information but for content creation, forming new groups, and even creating new economic models.

Although some in the industry would argue that universal service, or connectivity, is too expensive, the reality is that in network economics, complete connectivity only increases the value of the system to the entire society and is ultimately of economic benefit to the whole.

Without complete connectivity, not only will new economic models fail to be realized, but the function of mass communication in democratic society also fails to reach its potential. It is necessary for all citizens to have access to basic information, even if that access is unequal. Access will always be and has always been unequal, even in the days of analog media. But remember that in an online environment connectivity means that people are able to receive and send messages within the network, not merely be passive recipients of information from a central source.

■ ■ ■ QUALITY OF SERVICE

Quality of service, or the reliability, efficiency, and effectiveness of one's connection, is an important element in the world of online communications and networks. If one cannot trust one's online connection, then it is impossible to make it a cornerstone of civil society, much less of commerce and culture. Today's Internet cannot guarantee a high quality of service. Its strength lies in the ability of anyone to access it, any time, from anywhere to send or receive content.

Some critics contend that the Internet, by its very nature, will never be able to provide a high quality of service. Instead, because anyone can use it at virtually no marginal cost, at any specific moment a user may not get the bandwidth needed for high-quality video or audio or may not be able to access the server needed for a critical journalistic or ecommerce transaction.

This argument may have some truth to it, especially as more people upload videos and other high-bandwidth content. As a result, some point to alternative proprietary high-bandwidth telecommunications-transmission systems where quality of service is guaranteed—but at a cost. Broadcasters pay for the use of satellites or private fiber-optics networks to reliably transmit their video to affiliate stations.

Another solution is to use a combination of the Internet and private networks. However, using private networks could create a new kind of digital divide in which the majority of Internet users have a cheap or free network with severe limitations

The Great Network Neutrality Debate

The concept of Network neutrality, or Net neutrality, is that the Internet should not discriminate among the types of content that pass through it. This equality and openness is what the Internet pioneers believed the Net should be about, and these qualities have been espoused by other, equally influential Net researchers and innovators.

However, after the FCC passed some regulations in 2005, the leading cable and phone companies began lobbying Congress to make changes in the laws governing how the Internet operates. Essentially, these companies sought a tiered system in which content providers would pay according to how much content they sent over the Internet.

Critics of the lobbying efforts claimed that this would destroy the democratic nature of the Internet and make the telephone and cable companies Internet gatekeepers, with the power to decide what type of content would be sent fast and what type sent slow, and from whom, and even whether some sites or content would be completely blocked. The companies claimed that it was not fair that cer-

tain content providers who were using most of the bandwidth were not required to pay more.

The companies also claimed that they had no desire to censor the Internet or to control content in the way the critics charged, but during 2007 and 2008 there were several examples in which companies were doing exactly that. One case involved a company slowing the speed of content delivery from a rival media company, and another involved AT&T when it censored part of a comment from Eddie Vedder during a Pearl Jam concert when he criticized President George Bush.

The debate is a complex one that will not soon go away and is well worth staying abreast of. Changes in the basic architecture of the Internet could have dramatic effects, changing how we use the Internet and limiting its capabilities as an open, interactive communications network to one that favors a broadcast model in which passive recipients of content have little ability to communicate on equal terms. Two main camps are trying to sway public opinion on the matter and thus shape legislation. The website SavetheInternet.com is a coalition of citizen groups, media reform groups, and content providers who want to keep Net neutrality. The website Handsoff.org was created by cable and telephone companies to look like it is a grassroots campaign (known as an **Astroturf** site), and it says that Net neutrality has actually hurt innovation.

Web Link >>>
SavetheInternet
www.savetheinternet.com/

Web Link >>>
Hands Off the Internet
www.handsoff.org

on transmitting or uploading multimedia content, while large media corporations or wealthy individuals have high-quality, high-speed private networks that transmit content to a paying audience.

The quality-of-service issue came to a head in 2007 and 2008 in a debate between telecommunications providers and the public over what was termed **Network neutrality**.

Astroturf
....
The practice of creating a movement or campaign so that it looks like it was created by concerned citizens as a grassroots movement, but was actually created or controlled by a large organization or group.

Characteristics of Digital Distribution

Digitization of media, as we have seen, has radically altered many aspects of mass communication. Distribution is no different. Some of these characteristics have been mentioned before, but they will be touched on again here in order to give a complete picture of what makes digital distribution so different from analog distribution and to highlight why it is a key component in changing our media landscape.

■ ■ ■ DISTRIBUTING BITS

A fundamental characteristic of digital media, that they consist of electrons rather than anything physical, is the cornerstone of the characteristics that follow. Although data still must be stored in some physical location, such as a hard drive, the space required is virtually nonexistent in comparison to that required by analog media. The number of books that can be stored on a computer the size of a small suitcase would fill a town library if they were in physical form. As we have seen, digital data can of course be converted into physical form, such as a printed book, DVD, or CD, but it does not *need* to be put into such a form as long as someone has access to a computer network and the data are stored there.

■ ■ ■ LOW DISTRIBUTION COSTS

With nothing to physically create and send, distribution costs are greatly reduced. There is no need for trucks, trains, or planes to move products from manufacturing or printing plant to warehouses and then to retail stores—and no need to send back unsold copies. Media content can travel at the speed of light over hair-thin wires directly to computers.

This does not mean that distribution over the Internet is free, however. Internet users must still pay for access to the Internet, and distributors of content often have to pay the web-hosting companies for the amount of bandwidth they use as the public requests streaming audio or video.

Sometimes these costs can be quite substantial—several thousand dollars a month—for popular websites that contain video clips. Although the costs are technically not distribution costs, they act much the same way, because companies or individuals unable to pay the extra costs for Internet traffic essentially have their website "closed" to further visitors after their monthly limit has been reached.

Distribution costs can still be quite high, especially when websites are large or when companies like Amazon must hold and ship large inventories of products.

■ ■ ■ PERFECT INFINITE COPIES

A factor in reducing distribution costs is that creating copies of digital content is largely free. Unlike with analog media, in which there are fixed costs associated with creating physical copies such as books or albums, digital media have no such restrictions. This is because, unlike analog media, a digital piece of content never runs out. If a member of the public downloads a book from a publisher's website, it does not mean that there is one less book for somebody else to download or that the publisher will have to order more copies of the book in order to meet demand. The person simply has downloaded a perfect copy to his or her computer, taken from a digital version of the book on the publisher's website that is still there and available to anyone else.

The ability of anyone to create an infinite number of copies of digital media and make them available to anyone else on the Internet is the crux of what has media companies concerned about their current business models. It is also the primary motivation behind the various initiatives to create secure digital content that cannot be copied without the copyright holder's permission.

■ ■ ■ INSTANTANEOUS DISTRIBUTION

Although not truly instantaneous, by analog-media standards the ability to distribute media content over the Internet is instantaneous. A click of a mouse can send content to tens of thousands or hundreds of thousands of people, nearly at the speed of light. Although network congestion can slow down how quickly something is actually received, it can reach a wide audience in an extremely short period of time and much faster than what it takes to create a physical product to send.

Rapid distribution can make official release dates of popular CDs, books, or videos largely superfluous, as digital copies can be sent and shared in advance to encourage interest when the final product is released. However, it can also hurt sales if consumers end up not liking the sample they receive early or believe they got what they wanted from it and do not need to buy the whole thing—as in wanting a particular song but not an entire CD.

■ ■ ■ NEW DISTRIBUTION DYNAMICS

The fact that once a piece of digital content is available on the Internet there is currently essentially no way to completely control how it is distributed is another cause for serious concern amongst media companies.

Let's look at an example such as a photograph from a local online newspaper. It is a simple matter for a user to copy the picture to his local drive, separate from the article it accompanies (it is also easy for the user to manipulate the photo, but for our purposes here that is not important). He could then send the digital photo as an attachment by email to twenty of the people in his email address book.

Assume that only half of those twenty people like the photo enough to send it to twenty other people in each of their address books and half of those people do the same, a kind of reduced Metcalfe's Law effect. Within three "generations" after the original sender, the photo could be seen by over 2,200 people, all within a matter of minutes and at virtually no cost to the senders. Add one more generation of senders and the number jumps to over 20,000—again for no cost. This example does not even take into account somebody putting the photograph on her own website, which could have tens of thousands more visitors, or posting it to a photo-sharing website or a blog.

This example shows that distribution is no longer dependent on a central location sending out content to a passive audience. Distribution has essentially become decentralized and takes places "at the edges" of the computer network. In other words, rather than central servers containing media content that the public accesses, the audience can now store media content on their own computers and make it available to others on the Internet. A few, centralized distribution points are replaced with many, localized distribution points. This is the basis for peer-to-peer (P2P) applications, such as the popular music-sharing services available.

Decentralization of distribution means a loss of distribution control for media companies, since a single company cannot dictate what every single PC among the public may or may not distribute. This translates into potential lost revenues as copies are made and shared among millions of Internet users without paying the copyright holders. This is precisely what is happening with music online, although some studies have countered the music industry's claims that it is losing revenues from CD sales by showing that increased exposure to different music and artists actually helps increase sales. The music industry's concern stems from the fact that each member of the public who uses file-sharing applications becomes a potential distributor of content merely by having certain files others would like to download. No one has to send anything.

A benefit of widely distributed content among the public is that it is far less likely, should a central company server go down, that the content becomes unavailable. In a P2P system, as long as someone with that content is online, it can be downloaded.

File-Sharing Services

File-sharing services using P2P networks started making the news in late 1999 primarily because of the rapid rise in popularity of Napster, a program created by eighteen-year-old Northeastern University student Shawn Fanning. However, Napster was not the first file-sharing service, Usenet actually was. Usenet members posted files to a newsgroup to share with anyone subscribed to that group, and group members could then download and save the files on their computers.

Shawn Fanning created Napster while still a student at Northeastern University.

Napster let Internet users easily share MP3 files, a compression format for digital music. College campus networks slowed as millions of students downloaded and shared music files, and the music industry got a rude awakening to the power of digital distribution of media content.

Although music files and their widespread free distribution among users led the Recording Industry Association of America (RIAA) and the major record labels to take legal action against Napster and other file-sharing services, P2P networks are being used for a variety of other purposes as well. These range from looking for signs of extraterrestrial intelligence to solving complex model simulation problems to creating an information network that is impossible to shut down or censor.

File-sharing services have evolved over time and can work in different ways. Let's examine some of the most common ones.

■ ■ ■ CENTRALIZED FILE SHARING: THE CASE OF NAPSTER

It is ironic that the program and company largely responsible for starting the rapid popularity of P2P file-sharing services did not even follow a true P2P model. Napster used central servers to store information detailing what music files were available on what users' computers. Napster users searched the Napster database, saw the music they wished to download, and then connected directly with that user to download the song. Napster simply facilitated searches and was not involved in actually transferring files between users.

But the ability to easily search and share files for free is exactly what the record labels saw as a threat, and in December 1999 they filed suit against Napster saying that it facilitated massive piracy among its tens of millions of users. Napster claimed that its service exposed emerging and unknown musicians to the general public and said that any copying of music files should be considered **fair use**. Napster also argued that it should be protected under the 1992 Audio Home Recording Act, which allows consumers to make digital recordings for their personal use. Since it was simply facilitating this process, Napster said, albeit on a much larger scale, it should be protected under the act.

The courts did not agree. Initially, Napster was told to shut down completely but received a stay of that injunction for six months. Under a court-brokered agreement, Napster blocked access to any copyrighted songs it did not have license agreements for, even as it started negotiations with one of the record labels in the original lawsuit, Bertelsmann AG's BMG label, to develop a fee-based service that would give it access to all songs in the BMG music archive. The other major labels maintained their lawsuit while they developed two music subscription services of their own, MusicNet and Pressplay.

Bertelsmann invested about $85 million in Napster as it tried to establish a subscription service and kept the struggling company on life support. Napster was finally shut down in July 2001. In May 2002 Bertelsmann bought Napster's assets for $8 million, and in June 2002 Napster declared Chapter 11 bankruptcy and its brand and logo were bought at auction by music company Roxio to rebrand its Pressplay subscription music service. Napster currently operates as a paid music subscription service and, in September 2008, was bought by Best Buy for $121 million.

The centralized database that Napster used was what led to its legal troubles and downfall. However, the numerous file-sharing services that arose to fill the void created by the demise of Napster have learned that lesson.

fair use

An exception to copyright law that allows someone to use an excerpt of a work without paying for its use. Reviews of works or their use in commentary or criticism are examples of fair use.

■ ■ ■ DECENTRALIZED FILE SHARING

Napster's centralized servers made it an easy target to shut down through legal action. During Napster's struggles, several other music file-sharing services sprang up. Some were small and threatened with legal action by the record labels and subsequently shut down before they could catch on.

Austin-based Audiogalaxy, which included in-house music reviews and tried to promote obscure bands, was sued quickly after the record labels' success against Napster. Before shutting down, it paid the labels a "substantial sum" that neither party disclosed. But other file-sharing services that do not rely on centralized servers have been nearly impossible to bring to court.

Sharing music files is not the only thing that P2P networks can be used for. Other applications have been developed that take advantage of P2P's inherent strengths—specifically, the amount of unused computing power on individual PCs at the edges of the network and the inability to track the numerous computers.

Gnutella

Gnutella's existence owes much to the mass-communication power among Internet users. Gnutella gets its name from GNU ("GNU's Not Unix!") and Nutella (a hazelnut and chocolate spread). Gnutella was created over two weeks in March 2000 by two developers, Justin Frankel and Tom Pepper, who a few years earlier had created the program Winamp, which allowed digital music files to be played. AOL, who had bought their company in 1999, deemed Gnutella an unauthorized research project and quashed it. However, **open-source** developers were able to post Gnutella's code to other developers as well as give them access to a type of chat room in which they could communicate with each other in real time as they worked on developing Gnutella. Through this loose-knit collaborative network of volunteer developers, Gnutella was improved and distributed on the Internet as an open-source program that nobody could claim ownership of.

Although Gnutella started out as an application, it has transformed into a P2P protocol. Gnutella lets users exchange not only music files but other kinds of files as well. Late Gnutella developer Gene Kan said Gnutella's strength is in how it mimics natural communication. He compared a file request made over the Gnutella network to someone arriving at a crowded cocktail party and asking where the sushi is. The query goes from one person to another through the crowd until it reaches people with sushi and they say, "It's here!" The news is passed back to the person wanting sushi, and the person goes through the crowd and gets it. The truly decentralized nature of Gnutella makes it extremely difficult, if not impossible, for any one company or person to control. A drawback to Gnutella is that it sometimes takes longer for queries to "ripple through" the network than if there were a central server with a database of everything available. Two popular Gnutella-based software programs are BearShare and LimeWire.[3]

Freenet

Freenet was created as a system utilizing a P2P network structure that would allow people to freely publish or view all types of information from all over the world. Like Gnutella, it is an open-source system in which volunteers work on developing and improving the application. According to Freenet's founders, its main goals include the following:

- Uncensorable dissemination of controversial information
- Efficient distribution of high-bandwidth content
- Universal personal publishing[4]

Although the second goal is what has attracted the most media attention and the wrath of media companies because of the potential to distribute audio and video files, Freenet's first and third goals could have much more of an effect on online mass communication.

Freenet protects freedom of speech by enabling anonymous and uncensorable publication of material ranging from grassroots alternative journalism to banned exposés. This could have important implications for distributing news that otherwise would not be seen in the mainstream press. By letting anyone have a website, even if the person doesn't own a computer, Freenet essentially gives every member of the public a printing press.

Jabber

Jabber, as its name suggests, concentrates on real-time messaging, much like other instant-messaging (IM) systems such as AOL's Instant Messenger (AIM), ICQ, or Yahoo! Messenger. One problem with proprietary IM systems currently is that users of one system cannot communicate with users of another system, although other programs have been created in recent years to largely overcome that problem.

It is the equivalent of a person on an AT&T telephone system not being able to communicate with someone on a Verizon system. This obviously reduces the effectiveness of IM systems. Jabber uses a set of XML-based communication protocols that do allow users from a variety of platforms to communicate with each other, although some companies have blocked or frequently change their protocols so Jabber no longer works with them.

BitTorrent has become a widely used file-sharing service.

■ ■ ■ STREAMING FILE SHARING: THE NEXT WAVE

There are various ways for Internet users on a P2P network to share streaming files without using a centralized server. One of the most popular methods is called **swarming** and uses a protocol such as BitTorrent, perhaps the most popular file-sharing protocol on the Internet today.

BitTorrent works very efficiently and allows users, who would otherwise have to pay high server and bandwidth costs, to easily distribute large video and music files over the Internet. It generally operates on a principle that encourages sharing among peers, so that the more content a user shares the more content that user can likewise access. Internet TV services such as Joost and PeerCast use similar swarming techniques to encourage efficient use and sharing of video files streamed over the Internet.

swarming
....
The process used by some P2P systems in which multiple downloaders of the same file are temporarily coordinated in order to speed up the downloading process.

New Distribution Technologies, New Legal, Ethical, and Social Issues

Along with the amazing empowerment that digital distribution brings to the general audience, there is also the potential for abuse from companies and from the public.

Record labels and other large media companies are relatively unsympathetic targets of the changes wrought by the Internet and digital media. Considering rising prices for entertainment, the homogenous nature of much of the content, and how disappointing it often is, it is hard to feel sorry for large media corporations as old distribution models are disrupted by new technologies.

The differences look especially stark when the volunteer open-source movement of software programmers and developers—in which information is freely shared and all efforts go toward a "virtual commons" from which all can benefit—is contrasted with the proprietary and copyrighted material from companies trying to maximize their profits, giving consumers very little say.

However, it is important to remember that the public can also abuse the system. Consider a new artist who self-produces her song and uploads it to her MySpace page. It becomes popular and is freely shared on the Internet. She receives some revenue from users who purchase the song, but likely misses out on far more revenue because of the number of people who get the song for free.

Similarly, although a service like Freenet, by protecting whistleblowers, would seem to reinforce the ability of people to keep governments honest, it could also facilitate false claims by a disgruntled employee against a company or government organization, with no fear of being discovered.

CONVERGENCE CULTURE

SETI@home: Is There Anybody Out There?

Mass communication does not stop at the communication satellites circling the earth. Ever since the first radio stations started transmitting their signals, the earth has inadvertently been broadcasting into space. It occurred to some astronomers that, if there are extraterrestrial intelligent beings in the universe, they would also be sending out electromagnetic waves as byproducts of their technological development in communication. The search for extraterrestrial intelligence (SETI) began.

SETI is a massive project that involves radio telescopes pointing at small slivers of the sky and recording radio waves, which emanate from many types of celestial bodies, and then trying to determine if there are patterns among the waves that would demonstrate signs of intelligent life. Processing the massive amounts of data being returned is beyond even the most powerful supercomputer.

SETI@home was developed to harness the unused computing power among millions of home PCs to analyze the radio data that have been transmitted. Volunteers in the project download the software and data at certain intervals and their computers work through the information even as the computer owners use their computers normally. When each segment is complete, it is transmitted back to a central computer and a new packet of data is sent. There are safeguards in the system to make sure users cannot tamper with the data and make a false claim that they have found proof of extraterrestrial life.

Although not purely peer-to-peer computing, since a central server and database keeps track and stores the information, it is a good example of how digital distribution can be used. In what is called **distributed computing**, any number of volunteers can assist a project without inconveniencing themselves, since the program works in the background, and the free computing power amassed through the various users is many times more than what any research project could afford. The website also informs people of progress being made, thereby engaging the public in a field it otherwise might not get involved in.

Several other projects have also begun that use the power of distributed-computing networks, including searching for cures for diseases such as cancer, working on models of global warming, and solving mathematical problems.

Web Link >>>
SETI@home
  setiathome.ssl.berkeley.edu/

Web Link >>>
Distributed computing projects
  http://distributedcomputing.info/

distributed computing
....
Individual, autonomous
computers that work together
toward a common goal, typically
a large, complex project that
requires more computing power
than any individual computer
could have.

Along with new technologies must come new thinking on not only social but legal issues and ethical responsibilities.

■■■ LEGAL ISSUES

Media organizations and writers, artists, musicians—anyone creating copyrighted media content for a living—want to be fairly compensated for their work. There would be no incentive, the reasoning goes, for an artist to create something only to have it rapidly copied and distributed without the artist reaping the financial rewards of its popularity. With digital media, the very notion of copyright has been called into question, and several lawsuits are working their way through the court system that in some ways could increase control for copyright holders—which, in most cases, are media organizations and not individuals.

Digital **watermarks**, which allow content to be visibly or invisibly marked so it either cannot be altered, can be traced as it is distributed, or shows a history of how it has been altered, will be needed to make digital distribution more secure. However, many experts say this is a losing battle, as media companies spend millions trying to make digital content conform to real-world constraints. Whenever a new secure system is proposed, it is guaranteed that a crack, or way to break the system, is not far behind. Rather than deal with this fundamental issue, media organizations have tried to have laws changed to favor the nondigital systems over the digital and have taken people to court for merely publicizing the fact that there are security weaknesses in encrypted or watermark systems.

Other legal issues involve the status of messages sent by private citizens. Is a posting to a discussion board considered "publishing," and could a poster be sued for libel? What if a person writes something libelous in a private email to a friend and that friend includes the email in a discussion-board topic? Who could be sued for libel? These and many other similar legal issues have yet to be resolved.

In other words, the public will have to start considering issues of privacy, libel, defamation, and possibly lawsuits—all issues traditional media companies must consider every day—as it gains access to a worldwide distribution network.

watermark

A symbol or mark embedded in a photograph that identifies who owns the copyright for that photograph. With digital media, any piece of content can be watermarked, and the watermark, itself digital, can be completely invisible.

■ ■ ■ ETHICAL ISSUES

We have mostly concentrated on media organizations and how digital distribution affects them. However, now that anybody can essentially be a publisher with their own website, sometimes private individuals can unwillingly be thrust into the public eye.

Let's return to Mahir Cagri's experience mentioned at the beginning of this chapter, in which his unintentionally humorous home page was sent by others as a joke and seen by millions of people within days. What if the subject isn't able to make light of the situation but instead suffers public humiliation or loss of employment because of something he puts on the Web? Is it his fault for putting it on the Web in the first place, or do the people who distribute it share some of the responsibility?

Some websites advertise nude photographs of ex-girlfriends or ex-wives, presumably taken by boyfriends or husbands in happier, more carefree and trusting times. Sent to websites out of spite or greed, these photos can now be seen by millions worldwide. Personal reputations, careers, and even relationships could be ruined.

Or consider a case involving Bill Owens, whose online persona was Buck Hunter. He claimed he was pressured to leave his job at Home Depot and suffered sexual harassment from female coworkers after they learned of a pay-per-view pornographic website he and his wife ran from home that contained streaming video and pictures of them in various sexual acts. Cases like this are becoming more common as employers realize how widely a website can be seen and worry how it may reflect on a company's image. Several similar cases are currently working their way through the courts. The defendants argue that what they do in their private lives away from the company is none of the company's business.

Beyond the issue of legality is the question of ethics. What ethical principles should be followed by media companies and the general public in deciding whether to post or publish material? Companies often have codes of conduct or codes of ethics, but no such general code yet exists for the public.

The public's "right to know" is often cited by journalists as a guiding principle when weighing ethical issues regarding publishing a story that is damaging to someone. Yet it is hard to say that the "right to know" outweighs someone's right to privacy when publishing a nude picture of an ex-girlfriend or when making defamatory claims about someone on a blog.

■ ■ ■ SOCIAL ISSUES

It is useful to revisit some of media guru Marshall McLuhan's observations, even though he died in 1980 and his comments on electronic media were made before the Internet revolution. McLuhan argued that print media disconnected people from their basic tribal emotions and behavior, which were generally visual, oral, and interactive. McLuhan suggested that satellite-based electronic media were re-tribalizing society. By reconstituting a worldwide oral tradition and bringing all senses into full play, the electronic media were leading to the creation of a "global village." McLuhan argued that electronic media help put people back in touch with basic tribal emotions and reconnect with each other around the world.

Though it is perhaps an overly simplistic view, consider how McLuhan's notion of a global village might today be applied to the Internet and other online media. With its global reach and interactivity, the Internet takes us even further toward a notion of simultaneous worldwide communications. Email may have the potential to reconnect people to their tribal emotions, even though it is still primarily text based. Imagine the transformations that can take place when email or other communication technologies are video based.

There are still many unresolved issues regarding how people socialize with each other online. Almost everyone who has been on discussion groups or in chat rooms has seen someone making verbal attacks, often far more abusive than the attacker ever would make in person. Others may find the comments offensive, but there is little they can currently do except chastise the attacker either by email or on the discussion board—and perhaps get attacked as well.

With greater ability to mass distribute messages also comes greater responsibility in thinking how that distribution will affect others. This even applies to the level of forwarding a humorous photograph received by email. Will the busy colleague really appreciate receiving this? Could this be considered offensive to others who may receive it, because it perpetuates gender or ethnic stereotypes?

Some of the socialization issues regarding the Internet will gradually work themselves out as

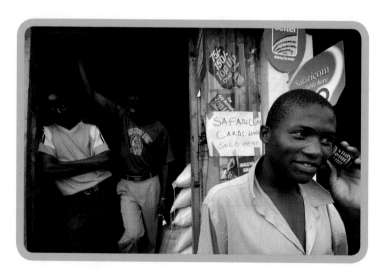

Cell phones and portable computers can be especially important for communication, especially in remote or developing regions.

9

The Egyptian street protests of Israel's attack on Hamas in Gaza in late 2008 had become a standard sight for Egypt's government, but discussions and anger spilled from the street to another type of social venue—Facebook.

Facebook has become wildly popular in much of the Arab world, typically ranking in the top ten of most-visited Internet sites in the region and ranking third in Egypt, behind Google and Yahoo.

Partly because Egypt's restrictive laws hinder the ability of journalists and citizens to criticize the government publicly, Facebook has become an important space for dissenters to gather and discuss. As with most social-networking sites, groups can wax and wane according to the whims of its users, but one group has attracted seventy thousand members in only about a year.

The April 6 Youth Movement is a group created in spring 2008 to help organize a nationwide strike. The group's members, mostly young and educated Egyptians, now use the group to discuss ways to improve Egypt, ranging from freeing jailed journalists to making the economy stronger.

Another aspect of social media has become evident. Members are not content simply talking about the issues online but have organized events and protests. (This use of social media and the interactions they encourage has also become evident in the United States and elsewhere, particularly in political campaigns.) Furthermore, all the interaction occurs without the need for any traditional media channels, making Egypt's government controls on the press and broadcast stations largely ineffectual for those with access to Facebook.

The tools and capabilities of social media have been around in some form ever since the earliest days of the Internet, but not until the past few years has their true potential been realized in business and media companies. Many of the changes have been driven from the ground up, rather than by traditional media companies, a fact that simultaneously gives power to social media and often greatly threatens traditional business models. In some cases, the nature of certain professions is being called into question, due in part to a combination of economic forces and new ways of producing and sharing content.

The term "Web 2.0" has become popular in describing various aspects of social media. Coined at a 2004 conference by technology publisher O'Reilly, the term, despite its popularity, has had questionable descriptive value. Although catchy in that it mirrors the terminology used for new versions of software, it also to some extent misleads.

There was no major technological shift or improvement in the Web that would differentiate "Web 1.0" from "Web 2.0." Rather, the term was meant to symbolize a few changing aspects of the Web. One was the sense of the Web being revived after the dot-com collapse of 2000, when much of the hype surrounding the Web economy during the late 1990s turned out to be so much hot air. Another was the changing uses of the Web, involving more people working with and talking to each other than had been seen before. Wikipedia is a notable example of this kind of sea change in cooperation and content creation, but there are many other examples, some of which will be discussed in this chapter.

Although Web 2.0 (along with the many variations it has spawned since then—Me 2.0, etc.) will likely remain as a general term to describe the fundamental changes taking place in online media today, we will try to avoid the term and use the more descriptive "social media." As we will see, this term also needs to be carefully defined.

Defining Social Media

"Social media" is still a new enough idea that it continues to be defined by scholars, professionals, and the press. It is hard to find a definition everyone agrees on, partly because the tools for social media change with advances in technologies, and

How Connected Are You?

1. How do you define "social media"?
2. How many social-networking sites do you have profiles on?
3. Which social-networking site do you use primarily? Why?
4. How often do you add content to your page on your main social-networking site?
5. (T/F) "Web 2.0" refers to a radical technological updating of the Web in 2003 that allowed for the creation of social-networking sites like Facebook.
6. Have you ever contributed content to a wiki, such as Wikipedia?
7. Have you ever tagged content?
8. Do you share your bookmarks on sites like Delicious?
9. How would you feel if a total stranger approached you and started talking to you as if he knew you because he saw your profile page on a social-networking site?
10. What is your Kevin Bacon number?

popular sites or trends seem to lose popularity almost as quickly as they came into the limelight and were touted as The Next Big Thing.

We can look at some commonly used definitions and from these definitions start to parse underlying elements common to all of them, then apply these to the realm of mass communication.

According to John Jantsch, author of the Duct Tape Marketing blog, "social media" can be defined as "the use of technology combined with social interaction to create or co-create value."[1] He keeps the definition concise because his readers are busy marketing professionals.

PR professional and social-media expert Brian Solis defines social media as "a shift in how people discover, read, and share news and information and content. It's a fusion of sociology and technology, transforming monologue (one to many) into dialog (many to many.)"[2]

Anvil Media, a search engine marketing firm, provides a definition derived from sociology:

> An umbrella term that defines the various activities that integrate technology, social interaction, and the construction of words and pictures. This interaction, and the manner in which information is presented, depends on the varied perspectives and "building" of shared meaning, as people share their stories, and understandings.[3]

There are certain common aspects of these definitions. All mention the intersection of technology, social interaction, and information sharing. These may seem like simple elements, but they have transformed many aspects of mass communication and promise to disrupt them even more.

Before looking at the elements in more detail and exploring how they are disrupting mass communication and media industries, it is necessary to see how social media differ from traditional media.

Web Link >>>
Duct Tape Marketing
www.ducttapemarketing.com/

■ ■ ■ DIFFERENCES WITH TRADITIONAL MEDIA

One clear difference between social media and traditional media is the change from a broadcast or monolog model of one-to-many to a more dialogic model of many-to-many communication. Of course this does not mean that mass media audiences prior to the Internet never spoke with each other—there were fan clubs, letters to the editor, and a variety of ways people did interact. However, the flow of communication favored the broadcaster sending a message to many people simultaneously, with audience members having limited means to share their thoughts with each other.

Consider how someone in the 1970s might be able to share his thoughts on the previous night's episode of a popular yet controversial situation comedy like *All in the Family*. If he watched with friends or family he could of course share his thoughts with them during or after the show. Similarly, he might discuss the show at the office the next day.

However, if the viewer felt particularly strongly about a racist remark made by the character Archie Bunker and felt that others should be aware of the harm such a remark could have, his options to communicate his feelings to a broad audience were limited, expensive, and generally did not generate dialog. He could write a letter of complaint to the network or the FCC, with no guarantee that he would hear from either. He could write a letter to the editor of the local newspaper, but even if it was published, it would reach a limited audience of only the paper's readers (and only those who read the letters to the editor that day). He could purchase an advertisement in the newspaper, which might get more attention than a letter to the editor, but that would be expensive or the paper might choose not to accept such an ad. Or he could create a flyer, make photocopies, and hand them out or mail them to people, which would be both expensive and time-consuming.

If the viewer was persistent (or flamboyant) enough, or if he got enough people to join his cause and perhaps hold a demonstration or march, his crusade might get picked up as a news story in the local press, perhaps even local television, thus perhaps attracting more people to his cause. Although at first glance this would seem to be a kind of many-to-many form of communication, consider the mechanisms by which it occurred—his message was communicated primarily through mass media channels. Furthermore, it is unlikely that he would have had the resources—either time, money, or media attention—to carry out a campaign like this in the first place.

Now let's look at what this viewer would do circa 2009. Let us say that a regular viewer of 24 gets offended at a stereotypical depiction of an Arab as a terrorist.

His first public complaint is likely not a letter to the FCC or the Fox network but to the discussion-board area of the show's website, where fans of the show talk about a range of issues. Or maybe he goes to any number of other discussion groups or fan sites devoted to the popular show and com-

Today viewers of popular programs have many ways to communicate with each other through social media, creating discussions on all aspects of a show.

ments there. He may find that many others share his opinion and have already suggested ways to show their displeasure to the show's creators.

Perhaps one of the members in the group has created a mash-up video of such stereotypes found on various prime-time shows or in the news. The video is uploaded to YouTube, where it gets viewed hundreds of thousands of times within a couple weeks, generating further discussions among YouTube viewers in the comments section of the video. If the video is viewed enough times or talked about enough, mainstream news organizations may cover the story, amplifying the interest among the public and getting more people to the discussions.

What is notable in this latter example is that, except with the original source material, traditional mass media organizations are not involved (until perhaps later in the process), yet far more members of the public may be affected in a very short time than would be the case in the 1970s—or even the 1990s. More importantly, our viewer may never even think to write a letter to the editor of the local newspaper or try to get news-media attention for his campaign. A complete media ecosystem can be created and sustained through social interaction using tools that social media provide. Mainstream media may still play a role, of course, but they do not have to be involved like in the past.

This follows what new-media scholar and NYU professor Clay Shirky calls a "publish, then filter" model. Traditional media industries such as news are based on a "filter, then publish" model of information. From a vast universe of possible information, specialists or professionals (editors, music producers, etc.) select which information will be used as their content. They act as a bottleneck to the flow of information available to the public by the decisions they make (and the limitations of their medium, such as time limits in TV news or space limits in print media).

This material—the news in a newspaper or the bands promoted by a major record label or MTV—is then distributed to the general public. The public is likely completely unaware of all the other possible types of information it could have received. Media business models have been built around this way of controlling and disseminating information, and even entire professions have made this model an essential part of their professional identities. An example is journalism, which many journalists recite is necessary for a healthy democracy because of the role they play in informing the public and being watchdogs of government. This puts journalists squarely in the role of gatekeepers of information, as professionals with special access to the halls of power and unique skills and training that presumably give them the ability to decide what information should be disseminated to the public.

However, as seen in the "publish, then filter" model, which is prevalent in social media, many of these professional assumptions are being challenged, as are the business models. If the public can connect directly with the vast universe of information out there and find what is relevant through a combination of social networks, ratings systems, and online discussions, then what role do organizations that restrict the flow of information serve?

Another big difference between social media and traditional media is cost. Most people cannot afford to start a newspaper, or to create a radio or television station, as the costs are simply too high. However, as has been noted earlier in this book, with digital media and the Internet the costs for creating media content and widely distributing it have been greatly reduced, to the point that they are well within the reach of many.

This is not to say that traditional mass media are no longer important or powerful, as they clearly are for a couple different reasons. First, they provide much of the source material that the public then discusses. In this way, the media can be said to serve an important **agenda-setting** function, in that they give us much of the material that we talk about, even if they do not necessarily tell us what to think. Second, they tend to amplify events through media coverage and because they generally have larger audiences than the majority of social-media sites. Audiences may be fragmenting with traditional media channels such as cable television, but for the most part the audiences with traditional media are still larger than the majority of social-media sites.

agenda setting
....
A role the media play in deciding which topics to cover and thus, by virtue of the fact that the media has covered them, which topics the public deems important and discussion-worthy.

What Is "Social" About Social Media?

There has always been a social component with media, of course. From the earliest days of print, reading was usually done aloud and in groups. Families gathered around the radio in the 1930s and 1940s to listen to their favorite radio shows, and people came together to listen to music, dance, and of course socialize. Even television, that maligned most passive and isolating of mediums, often has important social aspects, as families and friends gather to watch shows or sporting events and of course talk about the programs afterwards. Some of HBO's most popular original series generated what became known as "water-cooler buzz," or discussions among workers about a show the day after it aired, which in turn created more interest among people who hadn't seen the show.

When looking at social interaction compared to traditional media, perhaps a more accurate question is actually this: How are social media more "social" than traditional media?

It is a fundamental and important question. If it can be shown that traditional media are no less social than what is being touted as a revolutionary, transformative new kind of media, then it would follow that Web 2.0 and all the talk around it is just the latest hype about new technology.

The Center for Social Media in the School of Communication at American University says that there are five fundamental ways in which people's media habits are changing: choice, conversation, curation, creation, and collaboration.[4] Although others may use different terms, or scholars may place more emphasis on one activity or another, these five components provide an excellent framework within which to better understand social media.

■ ■ ■ CHOICE

The public of course has far more media choices than it did in the past and far more options of styles and genres within media types than it ever did. Even so, thinking of the public or audience primarily as passive consumers of media ignores the variety of ways people can interact and find the media content they want. Through search engines, recommendations from friends (often known only from online interactions), RSS feeds, and of course traditional media channels people today are generally more proactive in getting the type of content they want than in the past.

Note that "choice" does not necessarily mean "quality." Simply that there are many more options does not mean that the quality of content people may seek is going to be better. However, greater choice does mean that more media types and channels are competing with each other to attract the attention of the audience.

This alters how some media are produced, how they are promoted and marketed, and even what types of content may be created in the first place.

■ ■ ■ CONVERSATION

From the earliest days of the Internet conversation was important, and it continues to be a defining characteristic of social media. Discussion groups, Usenet, email, IM, and Twitter have been or continue to be important tools that give people the ability to communicate easily with each other on a scale and in ways not possible with traditional media.

Companies have had their reputations tarnished or made because of online conversations, unknown artists have become famous through them, and funny or embarrassing moments caught on videotape have made some people instant (if short-lived) celebrities.

Comcast has learned the hard way about the power of social media. In 2006, a customer posted a video on YouTube of a Comcast technician sleeping in the customer's home while waiting on hold—with Comcast—for over an hour. In 2008, Comcast was ranked at the bottom of the American Customer Satisfaction Index, and hundreds of customers contributed their complaints to the website Comcast-MustDie.com. As part of its efforts to improve customer service, Comcast started monitoring blogs and online conversations. Many companies follow online discussions about themselves, but Comcast took an extra step in often responding to bloggers and engaging in conversation with them.

Many companies have discovered that their brands and corporate images are not what they claim, in traditional advertising or public relations efforts, but what the customers say they are. The focus on conversation is one other example of the shift from a lecture to a dialog between companies (including media companies) and the public.

■ ■ ■ CURATION

With so many options available today, how do people begin to make sense of it all? The traditional gatekeepers of information and knowledge, such as media professionals and librarians, are finding their roles changing in the social-media environment. One major change is a shift from a "gatekeeping" model to what Australian media scholar Axel Bruns calls a "gatewatching" model, in which people act as their own filters, classifiers, and reviewers.

Classifying content happens through an activity such as **tagging** or creating **folksonomies** of definitions. This helps bring some order to the vast array of content that is out there and helps in searches. An important difference in tagging is that people are not waiting to hear from an authority on how to classify terms, such as a librarian would do—they are doing it themselves. Sites such as Delicious, photo-sharing site Flickr, and YouTube have all encouraged tagging among users, which makes the content more searchable and helps users see relations they may never have seen before between terms.

Digg is an example of how curatorial activities among users can enhance a site's relevance for everyone. Users vote on stories that have been submitted, and stories with the most votes get pushed to the front page. This creates a kind of natural hierarchy of content, where typically material that is deemed most relevant or interesting to the Digg community becomes more visible to other users of the site, even if they do not vote on stories themselves.

tagging
....
Defining a piece of information, file, image, or other type of digital media in a non-hierarchical system that helps describe what the information is.

folksonomies
....
A collection of tags created by users that provide meta-data, or data about data, regarding information.

The online environment lends itself to a curatorial mode of contributing to the social-media space. It is much easier to tag something with terms, or to write a one-paragraph review of a book, or to write a few lines on a product recently purchased. Similarly, it is much easier to find fault with something. Online reviews have become increasingly important in consumers' decisions ranging from household goods to media products.

■ ■ ■ CREATION

The digital media tools that make it easy for people to create content have played a major role in the rise of user-generated media content. The other important factor, as discussed in the previous chapter, is the low cost of distributing that content through online networks. Without the ability to easily and cheaply disseminate content, the media landscape today would look vastly different. It could even be said that social media as we know them now would not exist.

Simply because the tools are readily available to create media does not of course mean that everyone will start churning out great works of art. Most people in fact will be satisfied consuming media and not creating anything, and there will be far more amateurish or poor-quality types of content online than there will be high art. Even with something like Twitter, in which messages are 140 characters or less, 90 percent of the content is generated by only 10 percent of the users.[5] However, even if a small percentage of the people online create and share content, there will still be a larger pool of media content than existed in the traditional media world because of the sheer numbers of people online.

Creating content is not without its challenges. As noted elsewhere in this book, intellectual property laws are being challenged by a digital culture that sees nothing wrong with borrowing freely from existing media to create something new. Furthermore, many people online have come to expect a variety of media content for free. Rather than encourage creativity, as intellectual property laws were meant to do, more restrictive laws may have the opposite effect in that they will remove creative material from the public domain. But by the same token, content creators should be compensated for their work.

■ ■ ■ COLLABORATION

Although it may not seem like collaboration is an important element of social media, when reading some of the vitriol, name-calling, and inane comments often found on discussion groups, in fact collaboration underpins much of social media.

The willingness of people to collaborate on a common good for no personal monetary gain is perhaps one of the biggest surprises one encounters when first examining social media. It is one thing to spend hours creating a **widget** with the hopes of selling it or copyrighting it for licensing, but quite another to do so and provide it to the Web community for free use, or to provide open access to your project and invite others to work on it and improve on it, as Linus Torvalds did with what became the Linux operating system.

There have been a number of cases of collaboration extending from the online realm to offline, especially in organizing people around politics or social movements. In fact, the most successful uses of online tools in political campaigns have included ample opportunities for people to socialize in real-world settings as well. This was the lesson learned by the Howard Dean campaign in 2004, from looking at Al Gore's failed presidential campaign in 2000. Dean used online tools to

Widgets are useful applications created and shared by members of the public, often for free but sometimes for a small fee.

encourage supporters to get together in person and act, generating millions of dollars for his campaign in the process. Although Dean eventually dropped out of the presidential race, the lessons learned from that campaign were applied to Obama's presidential campaign in 2008.

In some ways, the realization that people need real-world socializing to complement their online socializing harkens back to the earliest days of social media, long before that term was applied. In fact, the need to meet, interact, and discuss was an impetus for the earliest online communities, many of which are precursors to today's social-media tools and still widely used today.

widget
....
A portable chunk of code that can be embedded in HTML pages and that often gives users extra functionality to their pages.

Lily Allen: MySpace Star Reaches the Stars

A single by an up-and-coming artist is nothing new, but what makes Lily Allen's rise to pop stardom in the music charts unique is her use of MySpace and the role it played in getting her noticed by mainstream music media and launching her to fame.

Allen was not a complete newbie to the music and arts scene in the UK. She already had some experience singing and performing in some films, and had a record contract with Regal Records, but they were unable to support her album much due to their commitments with other recording artists.

So Allen used her MySpace page to release and promote demos of her songs, and her site started attracting thousands of listeners. When a music publication noted her growing popularity on MySpace that attracted even more people to her site to download her music. By early 2009, her songs had been downloaded from the site more than 32 million times, and she had nearly five hundred thousand MySpace friends.

As a sign of the different dynamics of social media and the complexities that come with stardom in the mainstream, Allen often used her MySpace page to discuss personal issues or criticize her press coverage and even her own behavior. Similarly, when she had a miscarriage in 2008, the page became the hub for countless condolences from fans. But by 2009 she stopped making personal posts, as she felt her words were often getting twisted in the mainstream media.

In 2007 her second album, *It's Not Me, It's You*, debuted at number one on the charts in Australia and the UK. Her first album, *Alright, Still*, has won her numerous awards and sold over 2.6 million copies worldwide.

Web Link >>>
Lily Allen MySpace page
www.myspace.com/lilymusic

Types of Social Media

In 1980 France launched its videotext service, or text delivery over the air or by cable for presentation on television screens or other electronic displays, known then as Teletel and today as Minitel. Ahead of its time, Minitel survives to this day, and in the 1980s was pointed to as an example of an early successful interactive online information service. Minitel worked because the government subsidized it and provided access devices to every home. Its biggest problem turned out to be the emergence of the World Wide Web, which has made the stand-alone Minitel model, with its slow modem speeds and clunky graphics, obsolete. One part of Minitel that really did point the way toward how popular social media would become was the "blue rooms," or adult-oriented chat rooms, which were the only part of the service that generated a significant revenue stream.

Wireless connections with PDAs have made it easy for people to keep up with emails or online news at all times.

Many of the tools we now commonly associate with social media actually were used before social media or Web 2.0 were defined as such in 2004. Some, like Minitel, were used even before the Web was created. In that respect, there is nothing particularly new about today's social media. However, one main difference has been the development of tools that make creating and sharing content easier than ever. Another big difference has been the rise in people going online and the increase in broadband Internet connections, which change the user experience of the Web. Wireless Internet capabilities in mobile devices such as cell phones, PDAs, and laptops have also played a role in increasing our ability to share content.

Here we will look specifically at some of the social-media tools and how they have developed and changed over time. Just as it is important to understand how print media developed in order to understand how the industry works today and why it works the way it does, it is useful to know how some of what we use online came about and how that has affected our social-media experiences.

■■■ EMAIL

Email, or electronic mail, was one of the first uses of the Internet and is still the most popular use, accounting for most of the traffic on the Internet. It is easy to overlook email as an element of social media, but its ease of use, prevalence, and capabilities to send messages to more than one person make it a powerful communication tool.

Although email is an exchange of messages via telecommunication between two people, it is quite easy for an individual to create a mailing list and send out a single message to multiple people, in a sense "broadcasting" the message. This capability has caused more than a few red faces, as anyone can attest who has been on a mailing list in which one member made disparaging remarks about another, thinking the response was only going to an individual and not to the entire list.

listservs

Also known as listserves, they are automated mailing-list administrators that allow for easy subscription, subscription cancellation, and sending of emails to subscribers on the list.

Mailing lists differ from discussion boards in that messages posted get sent directly to subscribers' email inboxes rather than remaining in a location that a member must visit in order to read the messages. **Listservs** are automated mailing-list administrators that allow for easy subscription, subscription cancellation, and sending of emails to subscribers on the list.

Mailing lists offer some of the same benefits as discussion boards. Longer discussions can take place, with comments written when it is convenient for participants to write, and often complex arguments can take place. Messages have the added benefit of arriving directly to a member's email inbox, making it more likely a participant will read or at least scan them. Drawbacks of mailing lists include information overload as the inbox gets full of messages and potential monopolization of the list by one or a few members sending multiple posts each day or sending irrelevant or inflammatory messages. It does not take too many of these types of posts for the value of a listserv to diminish for most participants.

Media organizations have taken advantage of mailing lists to help attract Internet users to their sites or to send them information they have specifically said they want. When registering for a website, a person is often asked to check boxes indicating content preferences for emails or whether any should be sent at all. This is called an **opt-in** list and can be especially valuable to marketers, as the customers have given permission in requesting certain types of content. Email newsletters may be used to keep an audience informed about the organization or for marketing purposes. Sending email newsletters and email marketing messages helps reduce mailing and printing costs for companies using direct mail marketing.

The principles that allow for easy creation of mailing lists are also responsible for what many consider the scourge of email: **spam**, or unsolicited email advertising. Spam, once rare and considered extremely bad form in the early days of the Internet, is now unfortunately all too common. Companies buy lists of email addresses much like print publishers buy mailing addresses from other magazines or organizations. They create a bulk mailing list and send mass mailings advertising their products or services.

Computer programs troll the Internet and find email addresses, "harvesting" them to a central location that a spammer can then use to send messages or sell the list of emails to other companies.

opt-in
....
A mailing list in which the
user has chosen to receive
emails and marketing materials.

spam
....
Unwanted email sent out by
advertisers as a mass mailing.

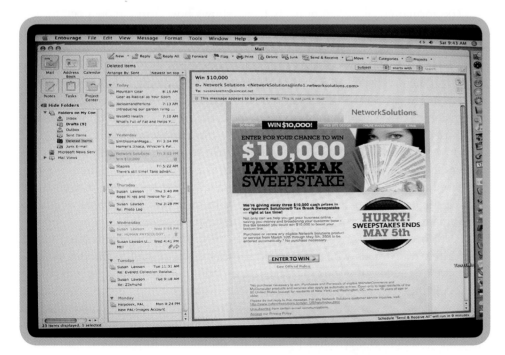

Spam has become a huge problem, clogging inboxes and costing companies millions of dollars.

A battle continues between spammers and companies creating software to block spam. Automated filtering software often removes much of the spam but may also inadvertently remove desired messages.

The problem with spam clogging the Internet and inboxes reflects the downside of easily being able to share content. Just as lowered costs of distribution on the Internet have helped create online communities and give the public a chance to distribute media content on a par with established media companies, it has also made it easier for individuals and companies to abuse that distribution system, making it less valuable for all. Legislators are fighting back in several states, however, with increasingly stringent antispam laws that penalize spammers. Still, antispam laws are generally not effective if the spammers are based overseas, as many are.

■ ■ ■ DISCUSSION BOARDS AND WEB FORUMS

A discussion board is a type of online "bulletin board" where Internet users can post messages that can be seen by others coming to the discussion board and in which they can post responses to previous messages, or posts, or create their own discussions on a new topic. Series of messages that reply to a certain post are organized by threads according to their subject headers, making it easier for users coming to a discussion topic to follow the thread of the discussion back to earlier replies and the original posting.

Today, most discussions are on Web-based forums, which provide a variety of user-friendly tools to create and post discussions. The precursor to the web forums was Usenet, created in 1979, which even today provides thousands of discussion boards, each separated by categories called **newsgroups**. Separating newsgroups by general categories, as well as letting anyone create their own newsgroup on any topic, helps make finding discussions of interest to users easier and facilitates users starting their own communities.

newsgroups
....
Categories for discussion
groups within Usenet.

The formation of newsgroups by users shows how firmly rooted certain aspects of social media are in the Internet. Within general categories already created, users can create very specific subcategories, thus defining communities of interest. Until recently, most news organizations did not permit or encourage discussion boards on their websites, in part because of their fear of being held liable for what readers might say on the boards and in part because they were worried that such discussion boards would detract from the focus the news organization wanted the audience to have—consuming the news content created by the organization.

However, now most news organizations have seen that providing a forum for readers to discuss news stories or other topics of interest related to the news has increased readers' engagement with the organization. At times, the conversation about a single news article may take on a life of its own, even perhaps outweighing the original article in terms of the value of information provided.

Partly because of the ease of sending messages, discussion boards often suffer from a few individuals who either send messages not related to the discussion-board topic or send numerous messages on variations of the same topic, effectively monopolizing the conversation space. Some discussion boards are moderated, which means a moderator either approves all messages before they are posted or has the ability to kick anyone off the discussion board or to block his or her posts. Another weakness of discussion boards is the difficulty in fully exploring an issue, especially when many people are commenting on various aspects of a complex topic, and the ease in which members can go off-topic.

Discussion boards are a vital form of mass communication on the Internet. Their format and asynchronous nature (i.e., not requiring users to be online at the same time) allow for relatively lengthy expositions on topics written whenever is convenient for the person sending the message. They also provide value even to members who do not post messages but simply read what others are writing, a practice called **lurking**. Some discussion-board creators encourage newcomers to lurk for a while so they can become familiar with the tone and type of topics being discussed on the board before posting messages of their own.

One of the earliest online communities, created through discussion groups, is still thriving today. The WELL (Whole Earth 'Lectronic Link) began in 1985 and continues to do well as a place of high-quality and interesting discussions among its members, many of whom are noted intellectuals, artists, authors, and creative thinkers.

The WELL has been likened to "the Park Place of email addresses" in a *Wired* story, and its unusual policy of demanding that users provide their real names rather than user names is supposed to have both helped the quality of discussion and fostered the strong sense of community that has built up among its members. Now owned by the Salon Media Group, publisher of *Salon* magazine, it charges its members fifteen dollars a month to belong (which, in Internet terms, may also help distinguish it as a Park Place address). It is one of the few online communities that have been successful in charging members to get in simply for discussions.

lurker
A person on an online discussion board who does not contribute to discussions by posting messages but who simply reads what others write.

Web Link >>>
The WELL
www.well.com

■ ■ ■ CHAT ROOMS

A chat room is a "virtual room" in which a community of users can visit and talk with each other through text messages, in real time. Like discussion groups, chat rooms are usually divided by topic, ranging from highly technical computer issues to pop stars to sex. Chat rooms differ from **instant messaging**, which also takes place in real time, in that instant messaging usually involves an online conversation between two or at most a few people.

Since chat rooms are synchronous, or take place in real time, they can be effectively used by media organizations to promote special guests online and let the audience "speak" to them, much like a radio station would have a musician visit the station and talk to callers.

Even without a star attraction, a chat room can often be chaotic and much like trying to talk to someone across the room at a crowded, noisy party. It can be difficult to tell who is being addressed, although some chat rooms have general rules and guidelines posted for proper behavior. Although messages may be sent in real time, the fact that they must be typed inevitably slows down the give-and-take that occurs during natural conversations—which can lead to confusion, as one chat room member may be responding to something asked two or more comments ago. Some chatters can monopolize the conversation as well or repeatedly post the same message, a practice called **scrolling**, which quickly draws the ire of other chatters in the room.

Chat rooms are perhaps best used when the topic of conversation is focused and relatively narrow. Viewers of a television show, for example, could be in a chat room during the show and discuss aspects of the stars, plot, or series with each other. This type of interactivity, although not directly part of the show, greatly empowers audience members as they establish connections between like-minded individuals in online communities and inform, educate, and entertain each other.

instant messaging
Often abbreviated to IM, it is a form of real-time communication through typed text over a computer network.

scrolling
The practice of simply repeating the same message in a chat room, which quickly draws the ire of other participants.

■ ■ ■ BLOGS

Weblogs, or **blogs**, are web pages of short, frequently updated postings by an individual that are arranged chronologically, much like a series of diary entries or journal pages. Blogs can contain thoughts, links to sites of interest, rants, or whatever the blogger wants to write about. The earliest blogs go back to 1994, although it was more cumbersome to update posts then because of the technology.

The role that technology plays in social media is clearly evident with the rise in popularity of blogs. It was not until 1999 that blogs started increasing in popularity, largely due to new software tools that made blogging easier and did not require knowing HTML code or programming. Blogger.com, created in 1999 and bought by Google in 2003, is one such tool that makes creating, posting, and sharing a blog easy even for nontechnical people.

Some blogs, such as BoingBoing or the Huffington Post, have readerships in the millions and are quite influential, having an agenda-setting function much like mainstream media. Agenda-setting is when a topic is covered by the media and therefore becomes a subject of discussion among the public.

When a blog becomes popular and attracts a lot of readers, it becomes impossible for the blogger to respond to most of the comments or discussions. In this way, blogs tend to develop the characteristics of traditional media, acting as a kind of "broadcast" or "publishing" model of information or news. A key difference between blogs and mainstream media remains the ease in which blogs have traditionally allowed users to subscribe and forward posts to others, as well as allowing for comments, although this difference is becoming less prominent as more mainstream media companies adopt the same techniques to encourage sharing of their content.

News organizations were even slower to adopt blogs as part of their media environment than they were to adopt discussion groups. In 2002, Steve Olafson, a longtime journalist for the *Houston Chronicle,* was fired for having a pseudonymous blog in which he criticized local politicians. Today, many big news organizations encourage their journalists to have blogs. However, news organizations must be careful about blogs from their journalists so as not to undermine the image of objectivity that journalists are supposed to present and not to undermine the organization's own credibility as a source for important news. A concern is that readers may not distinguish between an opinion shared in a journalist's blog and the news stories he or she files as part of the news organization.

Another element of blogs that often makes their use in the business world problematic is that they tend to have a raw, honest, and unfiltered quality. If a blog is too highly polished, or if it simply repeats public relations platitudes, it is unlikely to be respected or followed. This has been difficult for companies that are used to carefully controlling their messages to the public. The raw, honest element of blogs is a vital part of conversation, or true dialog.

Blogs have also moved from their text roots to easily include video, audio, and multimedia. This is an example of how users are creating content by mixing and matching different media types to make something new. Blogs also play an important curatorial role, as some popular blogs are followed because the blogger finds the best and most interesting ideas and makes relevant comments about that content, which helps the blog's readers find information of interest to them and see it within a larger context.

■ ■ ■ WIKIS

Wikis have become more widely known thanks to the phenomenal success of Wikipedia, the collaborative encyclopedia that has been created entirely by volunteers

Arianna Huffington, founder of the
influential blog The Huffington Post

and has quickly come to rival the established encyclopedias in terms of scope and accuracy. However, like most other social-media tools used today, the roots of wikis go back much further.

A **wiki**, which means "quick" or "speedy" in Hawaiian, is essentially a web page that allows anyone to edit it. Vannevar Bush, in his remarkably prescient *Atlantic Monthly* article "As We May Think" in July 1945, envisioned an editable, hypertext microfilm system, which he called a "memex." The actual creation of something along these lines did not happen until the 1970s, and it wasn't until the advent of the Web that the idea became more practical.

The first wiki was created by Ward Cunningham in 1994. He called it Wiki-WikiWeb, and it was designed to easily allow computer programmers to share information with each other. He took his wiki public in 1995 and asked developers to improve on it.

In 2001, Wikipedia used a version of a wiki system for its new encyclopedia that encouraged anyone to contribute and edit. This was a drastic change from traditional encyclopedias, which are the epitome of the gatekeeper media model of authoritative, unidirectional communication to a silent and passive audience.

Today a number of varieties of wikis are used for different purposes, especially in education. Corporations have also been using wikis to encourage knowledge sharing between groups, especially when offices are far apart. One important aspect of wikis is the ability to see the editing history of any particular page and revert to an earlier version if needed. This function keeps a kind of automatic journal of editing changes, identifiable by user. In combination with discussion or talk pages,

wiki
A website that lets anyone add, edit, or delete pages and content.

Wikipedia is an excellent example of what can be created online by many people working together on nonmarket principles.

which are associated with each article, it provides a ready way for participants to discuss and debate points related to the content they are working on.

What would seem like a major weakness of wikis—the ability of anyone to change any content on a page at any time—has actually turned out to be a strength. The barriers to creating content or adding some special expertise a user may have are so low that it makes it easy to participate. Although not without its share of **trolls**, or people who purposely vandalize Wikipedia entries by inserting false or nonsensical information, the Wikipedia community has shown a remarkable ability to police the vast and growing amount of content on the site.

Wikipedia has been able to avoid major disruptions at the hands of vandals, thanks partly to technology but mostly to the norms and rules that have been created over time by the Wikipedia community. It is an example par excellence of how social media have the power to transform media audiences and how they work on principles different from traditional media economic models. However, Wikipedia is not without its growth pains. In August 2009 it announced that they would institute more restrictive editing rules for content to ensure accuracy, a move away from its earliest, free-wheeling days.

■ ■ ■ SOCIAL-NETWORKING SITES

The various social-networking sites today are perhaps the most visible face to social media, and their popularity cannot be discounted, but as is clear from the brief look at the other types of social media available they are by no means the only ones, or even the most important.

What distinguishes social-networking sites from other types of social media is that in some manner they allow users to show the connections they have, or they allow others to see their social networks.[6] The ability to share the map of one's social network, and allow others to tap into that map by contacting other people in the network, has become an incredibly powerful tool.

Classmates.com, founded in 1995, and SixDegrees, started in 1997, were two early examples of social-networking sites. Classmates.com, as its name suggests, primarily focused on getting people back in touch with former classmates from college, high school, and even grade school. However, Classmates did not provide the same level of network sharing as is commonly seen today. SixDegrees focused on helping people find social-network connections that they may not have otherwise realized existed. Other social-networking sites that appeared in 1999, such as AsianVenue or BlackPlanet (both of which relaunched in 2005), were focused on relatively narrow audiences, such as certain ethnic groups. **Figure 9-1** shows a timeline of social-networking-site launches.

Launched in 2003, Friendster was created as a site to help people connect with old friends and make new ones. It was the first social-networking site that had features similar to what we see today with Facebook, LinkedIn, and MySpace. Although the popularity of Friendster rapidly waned in the United States and Europe, it has remained very popular in Asia, with over 90 percent of its traffic coming from the region. With over 90 million registered users and 61 million unique visitors a month, it ranks as one of the top twenty most visited websites.

MySpace also launched in 2003, and in 2006 became the most popular social-networking site, only to lose that position in 2008 to Facebook. MySpace and its parent company, Intermix Media, were purchased by News Corp. in 2005 for $580 million, and MySpace is now run as part of a division of Fox Interactive. At the time of the purchase, there was concern among many Internet users that News

troll
....
A person who purposely vandalizes Wikipedia entries by inserting false or nonsensical information.

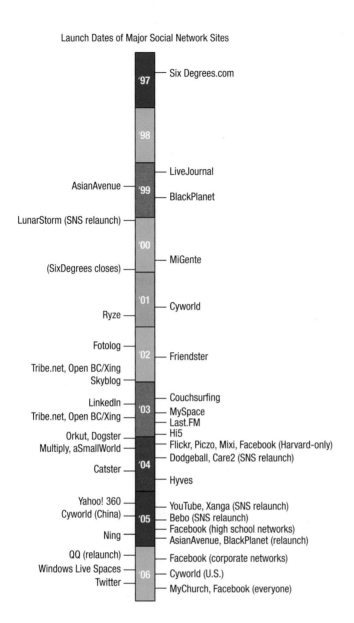

Launch Dates of Major Social Network Sites

'97 — Six Degrees.com

'98

LiveJournal
AsianAvenue — '99
BlackPlanet

LunarStorm (SNS relaunch) —

'00
(SixDegrees closes) — MiGente

'01 — Cyworld
Ryze —

Fotolog —
'02 — Friendster
Tribe.net, Open BC/Xing
Skyblog —

LinkedIn — Couchsurfing
'03 — MySpace
Tribe.net, Open BC/Xing — Last.FM
Orkut, Dogster — Hi5
Multiply, aSmallWorld — Flickr, Piczo, Mixi, Facebook (Harvard-only)
Dodgeball, Care2 (SNS relaunch)
Catster — '04
Hyves

Yahoo! 360 — YouTube, Xanga (SNS relaunch)
Cyworld (China) — '05 Bebo (SNS relaunch)
Facebook (high school networks)
Ning — AsianAvenue, BlackPlanet (relaunch)

QQ (relaunch) — Facebook (corporate networks)
Windows Live Spaces — '06 Cyworld (U.S.)
Twitter — MyChurch, Facebook (everyone)

FIGURE 9-1 Timeline of Social-Networking-Site Launches. Taken from http://jcmc.indiana.edu/vol13/issue1/boyd.ellison.html

Corp. would mine the vast amount of data that MySpace had collected and use it for marketing purposes. There were also concerns that News Corp. owner Rupert Murdoch would try to make MySpace a platform for promoting Fox media content, but he has remained largely hands-off as MySpace has evolved.

Facebook began as a project within Harvard University in late 2003 called Face-mash, a version of the website Hot or Not, and launched as a social-networking site under its current name, but available only for Harvard students, in early 2004. A couple months later it opened to other Ivy League schools and then expanded to include all college students. The next year it expanded to allow high-school students and then companies, and in 2006 it opened to anyone thirteen or older. It rapidly overtook MySpace as the most popular social-networking site thanks to these expansions.

Facebook's rapid rise in popularity led to frequent media reports of potential buyouts from larger media companies, such as Microsoft. Microsoft has invested hundreds of millions of dollars in Facebook and is the sole supplier of advertising on the site, and today's estimated value of Facebook is up to $5 billion. Some see the shadows of the exuberance of the dot-com boom in valuing a company so high that still has not made any revenue.

There are many other social-networking sites that have sprung up since 2003, with some focusing on professional interests, such as LinkedIn; topic interests, such as Dogster or Twine; media or photo sharing (Flickr); and microblogging and IM (Twitter, launched in 2006). Some sites, such as Orkut, have undergone changes as they have gained popularity overseas. For example, as mentioned in Chapter 7, in the early days of Orkut, the English-speaking users started to feel left out as the site became wildly popular in Brazil and more Portuguese-speaking participants joined. Today Orkut remains a primary social-networking site in Brazil and Latin America.

All of the social-networking sites developed within the past few years provide a variety of communication and sharing tools, and many encourage users to develop applications that make the sites even more useful to participants. There are two main influences at work in these developments: the importance of social networks in and of themselves and the culture of the open-source movement, in which people collaborate for reasons other than monetary rewards. Understanding these two driving forces helps us gain a better picture of why social media are transforming not just our media habits but our world today.

Why Social Networks Matter

Understanding how social networks work and the role such networks play in our lives, the way we communicate, and even how we make sense of the world has been an area of social scientific research long before social-networking sites became prominent, going back all the way to the earliest days of sociology itself, in the late 1800s.

A social network consists of nodes, which can be people or even organizations, and links, which are the connections between nodes. The links can represent any number of things, depending on what the researcher is studying, but generally have some communicative function.

The power of mapping social networks can be seen by comparing Figures 9-2, 9-3, and 9-4. In the first figure, we are simply looking at a collection of people

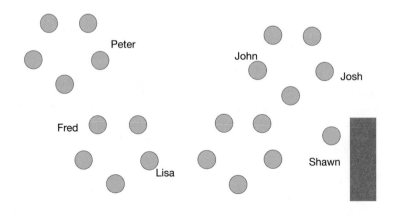

FIGURE 9-2 Without any sense of the social-network connections, we have no idea what relationships there are between members at a party.

mingling at a party; we may gather some information by watching the party long enough and noting certain interactions, but we are missing some important information regarding the underlying relationships, or social structure, of the party.

If we do not already know anyone, we could make a social blunder by talking to the "wrong crowd," which could affect our perceptions of the party or the people at the party—and affect their perceptions of us. This may seem a mundane reason to understand social networks, but consider if you want to meet someone specifically for a potential job or if you are an artist wanting to promote your new song. You could ask every single person there if they knew of any job openings or if they wanted to hear your song, but this is an inefficient (and annoying) way to go about it. Who at the party is most likely to help make the contact you need with that potential employer? Who at the party is an **influencer** others tend to follow? There is no way to tell in Figure 9-2.

However, let us overlay a network diagram over the same members of the party and see how that changes things, as in Figure 9-3. The black lines represent what

influencer
....
A person who can influence others in their social network to perform an action or change an attitude.

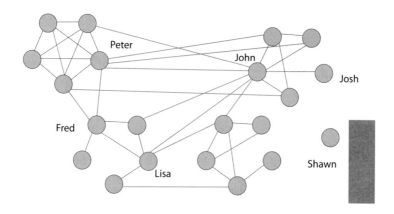

FIGURE 9-3 After connections are shown, indicating both strong and weak links, we see that John is an important person at the party, in part because of the number of weak-link connections he has to others.

are called **strong ties**, or strong links, and represent close bonds between nodes. The red lines represent **weak ties**, or weak links, which means there are connections but they are not as frequent or as close as strong ties. In this example, we will assume the connections represent friendship, or who someone claims as a close friend (strong tie) or friend (weak tie).

Several things become clear when looking at the map of relationships with this party. Shawn, the only node not connected to any other node, is standing by the snack table (likely in the desperate hope of connecting with someone). In social-network terms, he is called an isolate. The group of individuals in the upper left appears to be a very tight-knit group of friends, all connected to each other, but with few connections to other groups at the party. Other groups are less connected with each other, and a few individuals have a connection to only one other member.

Note the number of connections John has, especially the weak ties to multiple members in all the other groups. John is what is called a **hub**, or a node with many connections to other nodes, and hubs are generally influencers in social networks, partly *because* of the number of connections they have. If you are new at the party and want to be introduced to someone else (for whatever reason),

strong ties
....
In social network analysis, the tight bonds between people in a "small world" of close connections.

weak ties
....
In social network analysis, the connections between people in different "small worlds," which tend not to be as tight or as close as strong ties but that are nevertheless extremely important in social networks.

hub
....
A node that has many connections to other nodes in a social network.

Today that has changed. Although the traditional brands still (for the most part) retain their meanings for us, it is more difficult than ever for us to determine how to trust information if it comes from unknown sources. How do we know that the Amazon review of a book we are considering was not written by someone paid to write a glowing review or by the author's mother? How do we know that a Wikipedia entry about a politician was not written by the politician's aides, highlighting only positive information and ignoring past scandals? How do we know that the blog about the problem of obesity in children is not created by a pharmaceutical company trying to promote their dieting drug?

These and other issues are all extremely important in today's media world, thus the importance of critical thinking and media literacy. Similarly, issues of trust and reputation become vital in figuring out what information we can trust. Ratings systems, in which participants can rank how useful a review or comment is, help us in making that decision. But the question also arises whether the raters are trustworthy or not.

This is where social networks enter once again, as we generally trust friends or people we have let into our social networks and are more likely to listen to what they say or recommend. This is one reason **word-of-mouth** or buzz marketing has become so important for advertisers. Ratings systems as a measure of gauging trust will develop and become more important in our social-media landscape, but there will be some thorny ethical and legal questions that arise as well.

Ethical and Legal Issues with Social Media

The legal world has not nearly begun to catch up with the many issues that online media have raised, let alone social media. Issues of trademark infringement or other intellectual property issues have generally been dealt with using existing case laws, but other issues will need new legal thinking to be dealt with properly.

One big issue arising in the legal arena is figuring out who owns user-generated content on social-media sites. If someone decides to write a book based on discussions taken from a site like The WELL, using extended passages of actual discussions, is this a breach of copyright? How should the poster be compensated, if at all? Is permission needed to use the post or an excerpt of it? If so, how much is fair use and how much is an infringement of intellectual property? These are just some of the issues that social-media sites will have to wrestle with in the future.

The ethical and legal boundaries between privacy and transparency blur online, and it is especially true with social media. The norms of acceptable limits of privacy have never been fixed, and the ease of social interaction online combined with the lack of face-to-face interaction often makes a volatile mix for individuals as well as for companies.

■ ■ ■ PRIVACY

The norms for privacy are also changing. For those older than Gen Y, the notion of making so much of one's life public through posting photos, discussing one's thoughts or desires on a blog, or sharing other highly personal information feels strange. There is a sense that much of that is nobody else's business or that that information should only be shared with a select group of people one knows and trusts.

This "living publicly" generally does not seem to bother Gen-Yers in the same way, yet many are rudely awakened to a sense of having their privacy invaded when they learn that an employer is raising questions about material found on a blog or information gleaned from a social-networking site. Most employers today do Google searches on job applicants and examine social-networking profiles if they can. Many also make decisions about who will be called for an interview in part based on these searches. The goofy profile picture of you half-naked at a college party may be hilarious to your friends on Facebook but not so amusing to a potential employer trying to gauge your value as an employee.

Along similar lines, Facebook has gotten into trouble at least three times from its users for unannounced policy changes perceived to invade users' privacy. One notable case was Facebook's Beacon, which tracked users' activities even after they had left Facebook—without informing them. To make matters worse, these off-site activities—such as purchasing a product or registering for a website—were broadcast to a user's network of friends.

There are many temptations for companies such as Facebook to invade users' privacy by tracking their online behavior. The data collected could be immensely valuable to marketers trying to figure out how to best tap certain markets—especially the lucrative eighteen-to-thirty-four demographic. It is especially problematic when companies still have not found sustainable business models to support their activities and are looking for ways to earn revenue.

Companies that are bought by other companies or that go out of business have databases of registered users and online activity that could provide very valuable information. However, when users registered to a site, they likely did not consider that their personal data and search history might at some point end up in the hands of a different company.

■ ■ ■ TRANSPARENCY

Even supposedly tech-savvy companies leading the social-media revolution seem to regularly make blunders similar to traditional media companies when it comes to understanding some of the new dynamics with their audience, as the Beacon example shows.

Companies trying to create faux-viral videos or making fake grassroots blogs, a practice called **astroturfing**, are often punished severely in the court of public opinion once their machinations are learned. Sudden shifts in things like privacy policies, either unannounced or not adequately announced, have produced similar audience backlashes.

Facebook once again learned this the hard way in early 2009 when a change in their privacy policy, which had been made a few weeks earlier but went unnoticed by the general public, stated that Facebook would own the rights to user-generated content on the site, including posted photos. Found and publicized by a consumer interest group, the change elicited immense and immediate outrage, including a threat by the Electronic Privacy Information Center (EPIC) to file a complaint with the Federal Trade Commission.

Facebook quickly did an about-face on the policy and created a group of users to discuss future privacy-policy changes. The actions and reactions are emblematic of the shifting power dynamic between companies and the public and something that other companies should note carefully. It would have been far better if Facebook had created such a group in the first place, rather than only after receiving complaints. Further, Facebook's own customers were able to use the very tools that helped make Facebook so popular to organize against the company.

astroturfing
....
The practice of creating a movement or campaign so that it looks like it was created by concerned citizens as a grassroots movement, but was actually created or controlled by a large organization or group.

Web Link >>>
Electronic Privacy Information Center
epic.org

Web 3.0: The Semantic Web

If you thought that social media and Web 2.0 have transformed media, wait until the semantic Web is fully developed.

The semantic Web is the next big project that Tim Berners-Lee, the creator of the World Wide Web protocol, is working on. The idea behind the semantic Web is that it builds on and extends the existing Web to make it even easier for people to share information across platforms and for the Web itself to essentially be able to satisfy requests regarding web content.

The project is not simply about creating a better search engine that responds to natural queries. It contains a variety of suggestions on protocols and some operating principles that are meant to help reduce incompatibility between software formats, as well as a component that attempts to classify all information on the Web according to a formal system that can be read and understood by all computers.

We see some of the classifying and categorizing taking place among users now with tagging, but this promises to be all-encompassing. It also raises interesting questions about who gets to define what terms will be used. This is bound to raise conflicts with various groups who may define themselves one way but that are defined another way by society.

Regardless of the difficulties ahead, and the time it will take for the semantic Web to be inte-grated into the online space, it promises to revolutionize our online experiences in a way that will make our current Web look like a hand-cranked telephone from the early twentieth century.

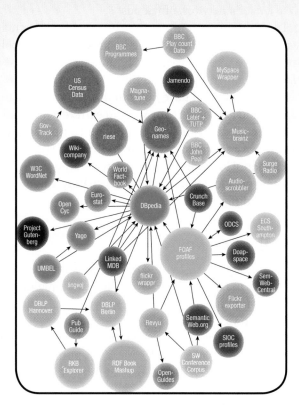

The need for transparency is becoming increasingly important with social media—a fact that individuals and organizations forget at their peril. However, transparency often works against strategy making and planning by companies, as they do not want to give away secrets to competitors.

Transparency is starting to be built into some ratings and review systems, so reviewers can state how long they have had a product, for example, which helps give readers a chance to gauge if the glowing review is about a product that is just out of the box or if it has been used for a while.

The balancing act between privacy, transparency, and tapping into the rich databases of compiled data from user interactions will continue to be a struggle for social-networking sites.

. . . .

LOOKING BACK AND MOVING FORWARD

Like much of "new" media, social media actually have firm roots and influences in many aspects of "old" media, although in this case the term "old" refers more to the earliest days of PCs and the Internet than it does to radio, TV, or print media. Even so, the changes that social media have brought in a relatively short time have long-lasting implications for culture, business, and society that researchers are only beginning to explore.

One of the biggest changes, discussed throughout this book, is the difference in relationship between media producers and the audience. Even without the large marketing and promotion budgets that some major media companies have, average people have been able to create content that has been seen, heard, or read by millions or even tens of millions of people worldwide.

The networks that have formed through online communication, and that have become ever more visible thanks to social-networking sites, have given people even more power. Through collaboration, people have shown in numerous projects what can be accomplished when many work willingly together and how their efforts can benefit even greater numbers of people. Wikipedia is one such project.

What may be of even more significance over the long term, however, is how social media have encouraged people to create and share knowledge structures, not just knowledge. Through the sometimes heated discussions in forums or on the talk pages of wikis, participants are exposed to different viewpoints and ways of looking at the world. In collaborative projects they have to come to some sort of understanding or agreement, thus modifying what is written to satisfy everyone. Although this does not guarantee a change in anyone's views, simply being exposed to other viewpoints has an effect on our thinking.

Sharing knowledge structures, or ways of looking at the world, is also done through curation, such as tagging information. Providing information about information is just as valuable as creating information and in some ways can reflect worldviews just as accurately as direct comments on a discussion board. A user who tags a photo of fighting in Somalia as "genocide" may suddenly see connections to other photos with the same tag and learn of past incidents elsewhere.

Following the actions of many users who are collaborating without even knowing it by using automated systems can yield amazing results. One example is Google flu trends, which uses aggregated data of search terms in the popular search engine to predict flu outbreaks. Google has found that, simply based on search terms, it has been able to predict flu outbreaks up to two weeks earlier than traditional methods.

Of course, the social-media tools available are only as good as the way they are used. It could be argued that a community of sorts exists around a site like Goth or Not, but its value to all but a few may be questionable. Simply because we have the tools now does not mean we will always use them in a productive or efficient way.

Media companies are struggling to adapt to the world of social media, with mixed success. Companies not willing to give up control of their messages are having more difficulty than those that are more open about stepping into the controlled chaos that is social media. Of bigger concern to companies, however, is how to earn revenues from all the conversations sprouting up, conversations often based on content the companies have spent money to create.

There are no easy answers to this question, as we will learn in the next section. Some industries may find it easier to adapt, or to shape the social-media landscape in ways that benefit them, while others may be looking at a bleak future in which the profession or industry as we know it today may be nearly unrecognizable in ten or twenty years.

DISCUSSION QUESTIONS

1. Today many television shows and advertisements try to look amateurish or "homegrown" to emulate what is often seen on the Web. Do you think professional production values will continue to drop, or do you think amateur user-generated content will get better over time? Why?

2. Find a news article and write down tags you would use to define what the article is about. Now go to Digg or another tagging site to see how others have tagged it. What did you learn from the differences or similarities in tagging?

3. Write a review of a local bar, restaurant, or store on a site like Citysearch or Yelp. What did this process make you think about, and did it change what you thought you would write initially?

4. Post a comment on a local news story and follow any discussions that come from it, reporting on what happened.

5. What's your Obama number? Using a rather loose definition of "friend" to show a weak link (i.e., meeting or seeing the person face-to-face), try to figure out if you are separated from President Obama by six degrees or less. (*Hint: including your professors as part of your social network may help.*) Share your story on how you arrived at your number. Now try the same thing to learn your Saddam Hussein number.

6. Why is transparency such an important concept in the social-media world? Is it more or less important than in the offline world? Why?

FURTHER READING

Wikinomics: How Mass Collaboration Changes Everything. Don Tapscott, Anthony Williams (2008) Portfolio.

The Wealth of Networks: How Social Production Transforms Markets and Freedom. Yochai Benkler (2007) Yale University Press.

Here Comes Everybody: The Power of Organizing Without Organizations. Clay Shirky (2008) Penguin Press.

The Wisdom of Crowds. James Surowiecki (2005) Anchor Press.

Going to Extremes: How Like Minds Unite and Divide. Cass Sunstein (2009) Oxford University Press.

The Wikipedia Revolution: How a Bunch of Nobodies Created the World's Greatest Encyclopedia. Andrew Lih (2009) Hyperion.

Blogs, Wikipedia, Second Life, and Beyond: From Production to Produsage. Axel Bruns (2008) Peter Lang.

Groundswell: Winning in a World Transformed by Social Technologies. Charlene Li, Josh Bernoff (2008) Harvard Business School Press.

Social Media Is a Cocktail Party: Why You Already Know the Rules of Social Media Marketing. Jim Tobin, Lisa Braziel (2008) Createspace.

Tribes: We Need You to Lead Us. Seth Godin (2008) Portfolio.

Six Degrees: The Science of a Connected Age. Duncan Watts (2004) W. W. Norton.

. . . .

MEDIA QUIZ ANSWER

5. False.

Journalism

CHAPTER OBJECTIVES

In this chapter we will:

■ Explain what journalism is and its role in mass communication and society.

■ Outline important historical developments in journalism that affect how it is practiced today.

■ Discuss journalism today, including types of journalism, and what the future may hold for journalism in a convergent journalism environment.

■ Outline legal and ethical issues in the practice of journalism, with special emphasis on ethical issues in the digital world.

■ Highlight some aspects of the business of journalism and how they affect the practice of journalism.

■ Examine how convergence is affecting business models and careers in journalism.

10 For the millions of CNN viewers on election night 2008 the moment was strikingly similar to the familiar scene in Star Wars in which a hologram of Princess Leia is beamed from the robot R2-D2.

Except, rather than calling for help against the evil forces of the Empire, CNN correspondent Jessica Yellin was reporting live from Chicago outside of Barack Obama's headquarters in a 3-D image inside CNN's New York studio.

Later on, hip-hop artist and activist will.i.am similarly appeared in holographic form to be interviewed by Wolf Blitzer. The moments were hyped as the first use of holograms in news coverage, although it turned out they were technically not holograms.

Holograms have been used by some technology companies, such as Cisco, but the technology is still generally too expensive to be commonly used by media companies. It is also unclear what value a holographic projection of a correspondent adds as opposed to a video feed.

Although the "holograms" got most of the media hype, CNN actually used other innovative technologies in its election coverage that could be more far-reaching for news organizations in the future. Touch-based screens and easy user interfaces allowed CNN analysts to easily manipulate information in front of the viewer's eyes, making valuable comparisons to past elections and voting records. It is a

reminder that in the convergent journalism newsroom of the future, the tools that help journalists better utilize and interpret information will have the biggest impact, not the gee-whiz tech toys.

ournalism's purpose, according to some journalists, is to "comfort the afflicted and afflict the comfortable." The societal roles and responsibilities of journalism have often been discussed—as government watchdog, as advocate of the common citizen, as panderer to baser tastes among the public, as big business, as influencer of public opinion. Heated discussions on how well journalism is fulfilling its roles continue to this day in letters-to-the-editor pages, call-in talk shows, on the Internet, and in newsrooms. These discussions should not be seen as some inherent failure of journalism; rather, they should be understood as signs of how important journalism continues to be in the modern world.

Journalism plays an important part in three of the four main functions of mass communication: **surveillance**, **correlation**, and **cultural transmission**. It can also play a major role in mobilizing the public. These functions are carried out by the coverage of news. The public learns of events and happenings locally and around the world, and good coverage puts the events in a context that helps people form a picture of what the world is like. Through articles and shows on cultural and artistic figures, culture is transmitted and the public learns the mores of society. To a lesser extent, journalism also serves the entertainment function of mass communication through coverage of entertainment events and news on popular stars.

In order to get a good understanding of journalism, however, it is important to first understand what news is.

surveillance
....
Primarily the journalism function of mass communication, which provides information about the processes, issues, events, and other developments in society.

correlation
....
The ways in which media interprets events and issues and ascribes meanings that help individuals understand their roles within the larger society and culture.

cultural transmission
....
The transference of the dominant culture, as well as its subcultures, from one generation to the next or to immigrants, which helps people learn how to fit into society.

What Is News?

The journalist's old adage that news is "when man bites dog" rings true in the sense that news is something that occurs that is out of the ordinary. News usually is about an event that affects the public in some way, or that at least has some element of public interest. It includes coverage of recent events, such as breaking news of a fire or accident, and recent discoveries of events that have already taken place, such as financial wrongdoing by corporate executives or politicians.

Several issues arise on examination of this basic assumption about the definition of news. First is the often-heard complaint by the public that news concentrates too much on negative events—crime, accidents, wrongdoing, etc. Critics say that this overwhelmingly negative coverage gives the public a misleading impression that things are worse than they actually are, such as making it seem

A Nose for News

1. (T/F) Broadcast journalists, unlike their print counterparts, must be licensed by the FCC.
2. How would you define "news" in one sentence?
3. What publisher was the model for Orson Welles's classic movie *Citizen Kane*?
4. What has replaced the goal of objectivity in journalism today?
5. What is a "pseudo event," and how does it relate to news?
6. Which is older, public journalism or alternative journalism?
7. (T/F) Some of the most popular news websites now are citizen-journalism sites.
8. How does a 24/7 news cycle affect news organizations?
9. (T/F) The percentages of minorities in newsrooms still do not reflect the percentages in the general population.
10. On average and all things being equal regarding years of experience and size of the media market, who makes more money—a journalist or a PR professional?

that local crime is rising by intense coverage on a spate of robberies when in fact the crime rate has dropped. News organizations do include positive news, such as heartwarming human-interest stories or new store openings, but then they can be accused of acting as a public relations mouthpiece for organizations or individuals and not adequately informing the public of important issues.

Conventional wisdom suggests that news means reporting the unexpected. But the truth is that a large portion of news is largely predictable a day, a week, a month, or sometimes years in advance. Consider the types of news stories about any annual holiday or event, such as advice on shopping for Christmas gifts—a look at the news organization's archives will likely uncover a very similar story the previous year or the year before that.

It is vital that media consumers realize this because news doesn't just happen. It is in many ways manufactured and influenced by a wide variety of people, organizations, and forces—often including advertising and public relations. Historian and Pulitzer Prize–winning author Daniel Boorstin describes what he calls **pseudo events**, such as press conferences or other staged events, like marches and rallies, as an example of how groups can influence what is covered in the news. These events are often known about days or weeks in advance and in the case of press conferences are held specifically to attract media coverage. What kind of news shows up on television or in a newspaper depends on a number of factors, including what other events are happening that day, the type of publication or broadcast organization, and even the political views of the owner, in some cases.

A **soft news day** is when editors feel not much has happened that is newsworthy and therefore will air programming or include articles such as human-interest stories. A flood in India that kills five hundred people may be included as a "World News Brief" on an inside page of a local paper on a slow news day and may not be included at all on a day that has important local news. How do editors

pseudo events
An event that is created specifically to attract the attention of the media, particularly the news.

soft news day
A day in which not much of importance happens, so that editors are more likely to add features with less real news value, such as human-interest stories.

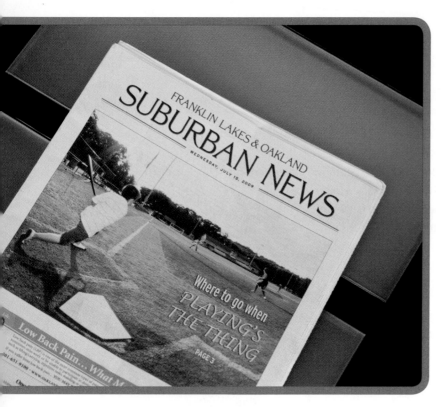
On slow news days editors are more likely to include features or photos that have little true news value.

decide that a story on a popular local high-school athlete killed in a traffic accident is more important than five hundred killed in India? They try to determine what is of most interest to their readership. In this way, journalists have an important agenda-setting function, which means they can influence by their coverage what is deemed as important by their audience and what is therefore more likely to be discussed by the public.

Although journalism has a strong public service mission, it is nevertheless subject to the realities of the commercial media system. Without significant audiences and typically substantial advertising revenues, most newspapers, news magazines, and news programs on television and radio would cease to exist. Most newspapers and magazines are actually more advertising than news, in terms of the amount of space devoted to each type of content. The Internet has challenged many of journalism's traditional business models, and declines in advertising revenues for traditional media outlets have still not been outweighed by the gain in Internet advertising.

Let's look at two sides of the historical development of journalism—as a profession and as a business—to see how each has influenced the practice of modern journalism.

The Historical Development of Journalism

penny press

Newspapers that sold for a penny, making them accessible to everyone. They differed from older newspaper forms in that they tried to attract as large an audience as possible and were supported by advertising rather than subscriptions.

The advent of the **penny press** and mass distribution of newspapers in the early nineteenth century, discussed in Chapter 4, brought about a sea change in the concept and definition of journalism. Prior to that, editors of newspapers mostly relied on "news" brought to their offices by citizens or gathered by a small staff, as well as liberally copying from other newspapers, often without crediting the sources. Editors' or publishers' (they were often the same person) opinions were often freely mixed with other editorial content, and no thought was given to presenting all sides of an issue fairly. There was also no established practice of putting the most important news first. Articles were usually written chronologically, regardless of the relative importance of the information.

With the penny press and the need to appeal to as wide a readership as possible, however, newspaper publishers often toned down opinions in articles and concentrated more on covering sensational crimes or events. In order to fill their pages, they also had to hire reporters who looked for news to cover rather than passively waiting for news to come to them.

Further fueling the transformation of newspapers were competitors such as **James Gordon Bennett**, who founded the *New York Herald* in 1835. He added a

James Gordon Bennett

Founder of the New York Herald in 1835. He started many features found in modern newspapers, including a financial page, editorial commentary, and public-affairs reporting.

number of features that are now staples in modern journalism, including a financial page, editorial commentary, and public-affairs reporting.

In order to maintain their objective stance throughout the rest of the paper, or at least the public appearance of impartiality, newspaper editors began publishing their points of view exclusively on a special page dubbed the "editorial" page, which is a tradition maintained today by the Western press. Editorials provide a valuable service to the public, helping to guide opinion on matters of public importance, as with endorsements for candidates for public office.

Newsboys helped mass distribute penny papers by selling them throughout cities.

■ ■ ■ OBJECTIVITY AND THE ASSOCIATED PRESS

The notion of what is news continued to evolve and was shaped by the democratization of politics, the expansion of the market economy, and the growing impact of an entrepreneurial middle class. One reason news became more impartial—what is known in journalism as **objectivity**—was the emergence of the newswire service in the 1840s. In 1848, publishers of six New York newspapers organized the **Associated Press** (AP), in large part to take advantage of the capabilities of the telegraph as a high-speed communications medium. Telegraphy was too expensive for any single newspaper to afford, so a consortium, or association of leading press organizations, made economic sense.

Because the AP gathered news for half a dozen newspapers with varying political viewpoints, it needed to publish news reports that were politically neutral and thus acceptable to all its member papers. By the dawn of the twentieth century, AP dispatches had become virtually free of editorial comment.

The Associated Press is still based in New York and is the world's largest news-gathering organization, providing textual, audio, and video news, photos, and graphics to its members. The AP is a not-for-profit members' cooperative including 1,700 newspapers and 5,000 radio and television news operations. That means that the members provide much of the content distributed by the AP, and in turn any member can use the content distributed by the AP. The AP employs 4,100 people (3,000 of whom work as journalists) in 243 news bureaus in 97 countries.

■ ■ ■ MINORITY NEWSPAPERS

Also important during the 1800s was the rise of various minority or ethnic newspapers. These newspapers served the needs of niche audiences, including Native American, African American, Jewish, and other ethnic groups. Among the earliest minority newspapers was *El Misisipí*, the first Spanish-language newspaper in the United States, which began publication in 1808 in New Orleans.[1] The first Native American newspaper, the *Cherokee Phoenix*, began publication in 1828. The first African American daily, the *New Orleans Daily Creole*, began publication in 1856.

American abolitionist and former slave Frederick Douglass was not only a great statesman but also a journalist, publishing an antislavery paper called the *North Star*. Among the most notable minority newspapers of the day was the *Provincial Freeman*, a newspaper founded and edited by **Mary Shadd Cary**, the first African American woman in North America to edit a weekly newspaper.

Born a free black in 1823 in Wilmington, Delaware, Mary fled with her family to Windsor, Canada, after the Fugitive Slave Act was passed in the United States in 1850. Under this act, free northern blacks and escaped slaves were threatened with a return to slavery. In response to a vigorous campaign to deter runaway slaves from escaping to Canada, Mary wrote a forty-four-page pamphlet, "Notes of

objectivity
....
A journalistic principle that says journalists should be impartial and free of bias in their reporting. This principle has come under attack in recent years, because of the impossibility of people being completely objective, and has largely been replaced by the concepts of fairness and balance.

Associated Press
....
Founded as a not-for-profit members' cooperative in 1848 by a group of six New York newspaper publishers in order to share the costs of gathering news by telegraph. Today 1,700 newspapers and 5,000 television and radio stations are members of this news-gathering organization.

Web Link >>>
The Associated Press
www.ap.org

Ida B. Wells was a noted African American journalist of the nineteenth century who spent her life fighting racism.

Canada West," outlining the opportunities for blacks in Canada. Building on the success of this widely read publication, Mary established her weekly newspaper, the *Provincial Freeman*, targeting blacks, and especially fugitive slaves. Her newspaper reported on a variety of important topics, among them the lies being spread in the United States that African Americans in Canada were starving.

Another important African American woman journalist in the nineteenth century was **Ida B. Wells**. Born a slave in 1862 six months before the signing of the Emancipation Proclamation, Wells spent her adult life fighting racism and especially the lynching of African Americans. Wells wrote for the religious weekly *The Living Way* and for various African American newspapers, including the *Free Speech* and *Headlight*. She was elected secretary of the Afro-American Press Association in 1889.

■ ■ ■ PULITZER AND HEARST: THE CIRCULATION WARS, SENSATIONALISM, AND STANDARDS

Although the practice of objective reporting became the norm for the AP, it was well into the twentieth century before most newspapers had adopted this model of reporting for their own staff. Throughout the latter half of the nineteenth and early in the twentieth century another form of reporting became prevalent in many U.S. newspapers. **Sensational journalism**, or news that exaggerated or featured lurid details and depictions, came to dominate much newspaper content of this period. Two of the greatest newspaper publishing titans of this era were **William Randolph Hearst**, publisher of the *San Francisco Examiner* and the *New York Journal*, and **Joseph Pulitzer**, publisher of the *New York World*, the *St. Louis Post-Dispatch*, and other papers.

Joseph Pulitzer

Joseph Pulitzer was born in 1847 in Budapest, Hungary. He emigrated to the United States in 1864, serving in the Union army during the Civil War. In 1868 he moved to St. Louis and went to work as a reporter for a German-language paper. Pulitzer purchased the bankrupt *St. Louis Dispatch* in 1878, later merging it with the *Evening Post*, thus creating the *St. Louis Post-Dispatch*. In 1883 he bought the *New York Post* and later the *New York World*.

He was elected to the Forty-ninth Congress of the United States but resigned after three months because of failing health. His health continued to deteriorate, however, and by 1890 he was almost completely blind and became extremely sensitive to sounds. Despite officially resigning as editor of the *World*, he continued his involvement by communicating through secretaries and assistants while he sought various treatments.

He became embroiled with Hearst in the newspaper circulation wars during the 1890s, using frequent illustrations, a racy style, and colorful headlines to build the circulation of the *World*. Pulitzer wanted his papers to focus on city news and encouraged his reporters to seek out original, dramatic, and compelling stories, especially humorous, odd, romantic, or thrilling ones, and to write accurately and with attention to detail. Pulitzer built the circulation of the *New York World* to three hundred thousand by the early 1890s by mixing good, solid reporting with sensational photographs, comic strips, and "crusades" against corrupt politicians, support for increased taxes, and civil service reform.

After the four-month Spanish-American War in 1898, Pulitzer withdrew from the sensational tools and techniques that had helped build his newspapers' circulations and replaced them with a vision of journalistic excellence, which he outlined in a 1904 article for the *North American Review*.[2] During this time, Pulitzer was instrumental in the passage of antitrust legislation and regulation of the insurance industry because of investigative stories his papers ran. This emphasis on public service journalism and accurate reporting is still a cornerstone of the annual Pulitzer Prizes, which he bequeathed along with an endowment for the Columbia University Graduate School of Journalism after his death in 1911.

One of Pulitzer's most successful undertakings was the introduction of color printing of comics in his Sunday papers. The most notable example was *The Yellow Kid*, a comic strip drawn as busy, single-panel illustrations. Although *The Yellow Kid* was not the first newspaper cartoon, its innovative style contributed much of the comic strip format many today take for granted.[3]

The Yellow Kid was a creation of cartoonist Richard Felton Outcault during the Pulitzer-Hearst newspaper circulation war in the 1890s and was characterized by rude, vulgar, and brash behavior on the backstreets of the fictional Hogan's Alley. In some ways, *The Yellow Kid* was a late nineteenth-century precursor to the crude kids of *South Park* created during the cable and broadcast television ratings battles of the late twentieth century.

The Yellow Kid quickly became a central figure in the circulation battles between newspaper giants Pulitzer and Hearst when Hearst hired Outcault away from the *World*. The brashness of *The Yellow Kid* reflected well the *Journal*'s overall dramatic style. In reference to the Kid's well-known yellow shirt, critics coined the term **yellow journalism** to describe the sensational style of the newspapers of Pulitzer and his competitor, Hearst.

Joseph Pulitzer was a Hungarian immigrant who founded a newspaper empire in St. Louis and New York.

William Randolph Hearst

William Randolph Hearst was the son of a self-made multimillionaire miner and rancher in northern California. Hearst studied at Harvard and became "proprietor" of his first newspaper, the *San Francisco Examiner*, in 1887 at the age of twenty-three. His father had acquired the paper as payment for a gambling debt. The younger Hearst then acquired in 1895 the *New York Morning Journal* and debuted the *Evening Journal* a year later, hiring away many of Joseph Pulitzer's best reporters and editors by offering them higher pay. He increased his newspaper and periodical chain nationwide to include the *Boston American* and *Chicago Examiner*, as well as magazines *Cosmopolitan* and *Harper's Bazaar*.

Later immortalized in Orson Welles's cinematic triumph, *Citizen Kane*, William Randolph Hearst sensationalized the news by printing colorful, banner headlines, adding splashy photography, and some say even inventing the news. Hearst's stories did not always capture the truth, and his readers probably knew it, but they enjoyed reading the accounts and his newspapers' circulation increased tremendously.

Often criticized for his sensational tactics, Hearst nevertheless articulated news standards that resonate even today. Hearst's editorial guidelines from 1933 stated: "Make the news thorough. Print all the news. Condense it if necessary. Frequently it is better when intelligently condensed. But get it in."

One historian has summarized Hearst's actions as inflammatory. Ernest L. Meyer wrote: "Mr. Hearst in his long and not laudable career has inflamed

yellow journalism

A style of journalism practiced especially by publishers Joseph Pulitzer and William Randolph Hearst during the late 1890s in which stories were sensationalized and often partly or wholly made up in order to be more dramatic.

William Randolph Hearst's newspapers often had sensational coverage that helped give rise to the term "yellow journalism."

muckrakers
....
A group of journalists in the latter nineteenth and early twentieth centuries who investigated business and political corruption. Their activities were likened to raking up mud, or muck, by Theodore Roosevelt, who meant it as a term of derision.

Americans against Spaniards, Americans against Japanese, Americans against Filipinos, Americans against Russians, and in the pursuit of his incendiary campaign he has printed downright lies, forged documents, faked atrocity stories, inflammatory editorials, sensational cartoons and photographs and other devices by which he abetted his jingoistic ends."[4]

Hearst's ornate, 130-room mansion, San Simeon, built in the 1920s and nicknamed the Hearst Castle, today stands as a California landmark. In 1945 Hearst established the Hearst Foundation (now the William Randolph Hearst Foundation), which today provides important support for journalism education and other concerns including health and culture. Hearst died at age eighty-eight in 1951 in Beverly Hills, California.

■ ■ ■ THE MUCKRAKERS

Just as the efforts of renowned newspaper publishers Hearst and Pulitzer laid a foundation for many of the practices of contemporary journalism, so did the efforts of a number of very important magazine journalists from the late nineteenth and early twentieth centuries. Among the most important were the **muckrakers**. Journalists such as Ida Minerva Tarbell, Joseph Lincoln Steffens, and Upton Sinclair (author of *The Jungle*) were dubbed "muckrakers" by a disapproving President Theodore Roosevelt because they pioneered investigative reporting of corrupt practices and problems in government or business. The process was analogous to raking muck, the polite term for the manure, mud, and straw mixture found in stables. Many of the most important muckrakers reported for magazines of the day, in large part because their investigations required considerable time to complete, which fit better with magazine publishing deadlines than with newspapers.

■ ■ ■ THE RISE OF ELECTRONIC JOURNALISM

The golden age of newspapers started its decline when radio became a medium of mass communication in the 1920s. The public did not have to wait a day or more for news of events like it did with newspapers, and furthermore radio was "free," as it was entirely advertising supported. But television news started the steep decline and eventual eclipse of newspapers as the public's main source of news.

The late 1940s and early 1950s marked the beginning of television news. News was and still is an important part of how broadcast television fulfills its federal mandate to serve in the public interest.

Many of the early news programs were produced by the television network news divisions in New York. In 1947, NBC debuted *Meet the Press*, a made-for-TV news conference, with journalists asking questions of various news makers, often government officials. The program continues today and is the oldest series on network TV. In the 1950s, NBC introduced the *Today* show, the first and still-running early-morning network news show. *Today* had a decidedly entertainment quality back then, with host Dave Garroway joined by chimpanzee sidekick J. Fred Muggs.

Murrow and News in TV's Golden Age

Setting the standard for television news during television's golden age in the late 1940s and the 1950s was the distinguished journalist **Edward R. Murrow**, who first achieved fame by broadcasting dramatic radio news reports from London during World War II. Murrow produced the popular television programs *See It Now* and *Person to Person* at CBS News.

Murrow's comments on television at the Radio-Television News Directors Association (RTNDA) meeting in 1958 ring equally true today for the Internet: "This instrument can teach, it can illuminate, and yes, it can inspire. But it can do so only to the extent that humans are determined to use it to those ends. Otherwise it is nothing but wires and lights in a box." The same year he also wrote in *TV Guide* that viewers must realize "television in the main is being used to distract, delude, amuse and insulate us."

Changes in Television News Coverage

The introduction of video cameras into the television newsroom brought important changes to television news. **Electronic news-gathering** (ENG) equipment allowed journalists in the field to capture and send videotaped news by satellite to the network, where it could be edited and broadcast much more quickly than film. This has influenced the nature of video storytelling. The late CBS news veteran Bud Benjamin likened it to "NTV," or the video-journalism equivalent of "MTV," or music television, with rapid-paced cuts and entertainment values becoming increasingly paramount in journalism. The growth of cable television has also led to an increasing number of local twenty-four-hour cable news operations.

Edward R. Murrow was a noted radio and television journalist in the earliest days of television.

Foundations of Journalism

Digital technology and the Internet will continue to transform journalism, but professional, mainstream journalism today is still largely practiced as it has been.

Edward R. Murrow

A radio and, later, television journalist and announcer who set the standard for journalistic excellence on television during television's golden age.

electronic news-gathering (ENG) equipment

Tools such as video cameras and satellite dishes that allow journalists to gather and broadcast news much more quickly than in the past.

CAMPBELL BROWN   CNN

Although when CNN came out with the first 24-hour cable news channel it was predicted to fail, in fact there are a growing number of such channels today.

Reporters cover events and write stories, editors select what stories get published or aired and where they appear, and how many pages they have for news depends on how many advertisements were sold. Digital technology will not change the fact that reporters need to visit places and interview people. Nor will digital technology replace an experienced editor's judgment on what makes a good story and how to edit that story.

In order to understand what aspects of journalism have changed already and what will likely change some more with convergence, we will first look at basic issues of journalistic responsibility and how journalism is practiced, at least in its ideal form.

■■■ THE HUTCHINS COMMISSION AND A FREE AND RESPONSIBLE PRESS

In 1947 what became known as the Hutchins Commission published a landmark report titled *A Free and Responsible Press*, offering a critique of the state of the press in the United States. The 133-page report of the Commission on Freedom of the Press was written by Robert Maynard Hutchins and a dozen other leading intellectuals. The report argued that the public has a right to information that affects it and that the press has a responsibility to present that information. Because the press enjoys constitutionally guaranteed freedom, the press carries an additional moral duty to fulfill this responsibility. The commission recommended that the government, the public, and the press could all take steps to improve the functioning of a healthy press. Among these steps, the commission recommended the government recognize that all media have the same constitutional guarantees traditionally enjoyed only by print media.

The commission recommended that the agencies of mass communication assume the responsibility of financing new, experimental activities in their fields. Moreover, the members of the press should engage in vigorous mutual criticism. The commission called on the public to create academic-professional centers of advanced study, research, and publication in the field of communications. Among the first such centers was the Media Studies Center, founded by the Freedom Forum in 1984, nearly forty years after the report. The commission also recommended that existing schools of journalism exploit the total resources of their universities to the end that their students obtain the broadest and most liberal training. Finally, the commission recommended the establishment of a new and independent agency to appraise and report annually on the performance of the press. This has been tried at a national level in the form of a National Press Council but has failed, although a similar idea has had marginal success in some states.

■■■ THE SEPARATION OF EDITORIAL AND BUSINESS OPERATIONS

In newsroom parlance commonly called the "separation of church and state," this is a basic principle in ensuring that news coverage is not influenced by business decisions or advertisers who threaten to stop advertising because they do not like coverage of an issue. This separation is supposed to carry over to the page layout of a newspaper or magazine as well by showing clear differences between advertising and editorial content.

However, many media critics complain that this separation has been breaking down in recent years as publishers or large media corporations that own news organizations increasingly let business decisions influence editorial content. This can

Let's talk CORK

For centuries now, people in the wine trade the world over have trusted cork. The best wines from the top French chateaux, from Domaine de la Romanée Conti to Château Lafite Rothschild, along with virtually every top winery in the USA, continue to trust their wines to cork closures. That's because wine drinkers trust cork. We know it has a beneficial effect on aging wines. What other closure can guarantee that?

The love affair between wine consumers and cork began back in 1670, when French monk Dom Perignon first used it for the sparkling wine of his Hautvillers' monastery. Since the 1700s natural cork has been the leading closure for fine wines from every part of the world. Nine out of ten U.S. consumers feel that non-cork closures cheapen wine, a 2006 survey of the wine trade here found. In survey after survey, wine lovers show cork is still the preferred closure for fine wines by a wide margin.

Over the past ten years the cork industry has invested literally millions of dollars to improve cork quality and consistency. Those efforts have now produced significant results for wineries and the consumer. Production techniques and rigorous quality control procedures have developed this past decade to deliver the most widely accepted stopper for wine, despite competition from other wine closures. The corks produced today are the best corks in history—a suitable partner for today's exceptional wines.

It's not just about romance, but quality. Time after time.

Real Cork. Real Wine.

Advertorials are designed and written to look like news content but are in fact paid advertisements.

happen blatantly, as when the owner of the *Los Angeles Times* used staff reporters and editors to create a special "news" section on the Staples Center that was entirely sponsored (and had content approved by) Staples without explicitly saying so; or it could be more insidious, as when management lays off editorial staff, which has the effect of hampering original local reporting and forces the paper to rely on cheaper but perhaps less relevant wire service news.

fairness

In news coverage, the concept of covering all relevant sides of an issue and allowing spokespeople representing those various sides a chance to be covered in the same way.

balance

In news coverage, the concept of presenting sides equally or of reporting on a broad range of news events.

frame

The notion that every story is told in a particular way that influences how readers think of the story.

■ ■ ■ FAIRNESS AND BALANCE IN NEWS COVERAGE

Fairness and **balance** in news coverage have replaced the goal of objectivity in journalism. Objectivity, or the principle that news is reported on and presented in a completely unbiased manner, has come under attack in recent years. Critics say that people cannot be completely unbiased and to claim objectivity in a given situation is simply masking the bias of the reporter. In addition, everything from the subsequent editing or placement of a story in a newspaper to the time slot for a news segment can reflect biased coverage, even if the reporter has no strong bias when writing the story. Unintended biases can also show up in the people a journalist decides to interview and the choice of story assignments an editor makes.

The terms "fairness" and "balance" mean that journalists try to present all sides of a topic equally and in a way that does not favor one side. Fairness and balance do not mean that all participants in an issue get equal space for their views, however. A small group of fifty vocal people supporting a minor-party candidate would not get the same amount of coverage as a popular candidate from a major political party simply because they are fielding a candidate in an election or hold nightly protests. Factors such as the relative importance within the context of the story and validity or authority of the news source must be considered when a journalist decides how much coverage to give a person or group.

■ ■ ■ FRAMING THE NEWS

Traditional news media often decide how they will **frame** a story before the reporting is completed and sometimes before it has even begun. This is one of the biggest problems in journalism today, because frequently the facts of a story are forced to fit into the frame, or angle, regardless of reality. Yet framing cannot be avoided, simply because it makes writing a news story easier and faster. Balance, or fairness, is often not achieved, and often journalists are not even aware that they are framing stories. They see their work as simply reflecting reality.

Perhaps even more problematic, however, is the fact that frequently events in the real world are forced into an existing frame, when reality is in fact more complex and defies framing. The need for journalism often to demonize one side over another can have serious repercussions for reporting on each side and even for what words are used to describe certain actions. Depending on one's loyalties, a "terrorist attack" could also be described as "armed resistance."

■ ■ ■ EXPERT SOURCES

A related issue to framing, also problematic in the media—especially on television—has to do with the use of "expert" sources to give the news more credibility. At the three main television networks, ABC, CBS, and NBC, most speakers selected to give their views during the news or other public-affairs programs are white and male. The Tenth Annual Women, Men and Media Study, conducted by ADT Research in conjunction with the Freedom Forum, shows that during the first six months of 1998, "Nearly nine of ten 'expert' sound bites (87 percent) on the network newscasts were provided by men, and *more* than nine in ten (92 percent) were provided by whites." Women were featured in just 13 percent of expert sound bites and people of color just 6 percent. In contrast, nonexperts on network news programs are much more likely to be of diverse backgrounds.

"Individuals of either sex, any age and all races can be heard from on the network news, as long as they are not wielding power or offering expertise. The networks'

Covering Islim

INTERNATIONAL PERSPECTIVES

Framing in the news occurs everywhere, but it is arguably most prevalent in coverage of international news. In the 1980s, when Japanese companies were buying American companies, the American media often depicted the trend in almost warlike terms. This was echoed in recent years as China gained economic might, yet similar language is not seen when a Canadian or British company buys an American company.

Due partly to the terrorist attacks on September 11, Islam has largely been framed in the U.S. media as a monolithic religion advocating violence and repression of human rights, argues scholar Edward Said in his book *Covering Islam*.

Said says that the inaccurate depictions of Islam are created by a complex web of media that rely on self-proclaimed "Islamic experts" who pontificate on the Middle East and who often equate fundamentalism with Islam, even though Judaism and Christianity face similar fundamentalist movements.

The depictions feed into a nationalistic "us-versus-them" mentality that is similar to the anti-Communist fervor during the cold war. Not only do these inaccurate portrayals of Muslims hurt our ability to see them on equal terms or humanistic terms, they provide a cover for repressive regimes that use Islam as an excuse for their policies.

Framing, in other words, paints over a complex reality and, more importantly, shapes our reactions and beliefs to the new reality that it creates.

'golden rolodexes' of expert consultants are badly in need of updating," said Andrew Tyndall, director of the study, titled *Who Speaks for America? Sex, Age and Race on the Network News*. Research about other mainstream media, including important print media such as news magazines *Time, Newsweek,* and *U.S. News & World Report,* show similar results.

■ ■ ■ THE NEWS AGENDA OF NEWSPAPERS

An important change in newspaper content has to do with the basic news agenda of newspapers. Research by the Pew Research Center for the People & the Press, an independent opinion research center sponsored by the Pew Charitable Trusts, indicates that in 1980 the front page of the average daily newspaper was quite different in its news agenda than it is today.

One of the most important differences is that, in 1980, one of every three front-page news stories dealt with government or public affairs, compared to just one in every five today. Government and public-affairs matters are traditionally considered

Studies have shown that news shows predominantly use white males as subject experts and guests.

the cornerstone of journalism in a democracy. A second important difference is that in 1980, only one in every fifty front-page daily newspaper stories dealt with celebrities, popular entertainment, and other related subjects. Today, one in every fourteen front-page daily newspaper stories deals with celebrities and the like.

There are a number of reasons for this dramatic shift away from public affairs and toward popular entertainment. An increasingly competitive media environment, in which newspapers must compete against electronic entertainment media, is one. Also important is the changing ownership structure and economics of newspapers. Further, technological change is contributing to this transformation, as newspapers struggle to reinvent themselves in an online, digital age.

Web Link >>>
Pew Research Center for the People & the Press
www.pewcenter.org

■ ■ ■ THE NEWS AGENDA OF TELEVISION NEWS

Television news counts on interesting visuals to help tell its stories, and this can often dictate the ordering of stories in a newscast or even whether a story is aired or not. Stories with dramatic video footage, such as fires or accidents, are more likely to air than stories in which stock footage is needed or ones with poor-quality video.

Time constraints of less than thirty minutes or an hour to cover local, national, and international news, business news, sports, and weather also place limitations on how long particular stories can be within a newscast. In-depth looks at news-worthy issues must be sacrificed in order to cover a wider range of news stories. The need for scheduled commercial breaks often means that guest experts are asked to explain complex subjects in less than a minute.

Perhaps because of the visual nature of television, television news has always had an eye on the entertainment aspect of media, as demonstrated as far back as the early days of the *Today* show mentioned earlier. The rise of twenty-four-hour news channels also means that there is much more of a **news hole** to fill, which encourages stations to be less discriminating about what they consider newsworthy. Sometimes this is a good thing, as events that would otherwise not reach a televised audience are covered, but other times the material serves mainly a public relations or entertainment purpose. Worse still is that some print publications take their lead from news channels regarding what should be covered.

news hole
....
A term typically used with newspapers, it refers to the amount of total space available after advertisement space has been blocked out.

From Event to Public Eye: How News Is Created

There must always be news to fill the regularly scheduled evening broadcast on television, the morning's paper, or the weekly news magazine. Like an accordion, news can expand or contract as required by the day's events, but only to a limited degree. The fact is, whether anything important happens today or not, the networks will still have at least a thirty-minute newscast (actually, twenty-two minutes, after subtracting the time for commercials). Sometimes, during a major breaking news event such as the September 11 World Trade Center and Pentagon attacks, they will extend the news to an hour or even have continuous coverage.

Techniques of gathering, reporting, and presenting the news to the public have been refined over the years and have changed surprisingly little. There are variations between techniques that print journalists and television journalists must use, of course, but the basic principles are largely the same. We will look at some of the basic steps in the news-gathering process for print and television.

■■■ GATHERING THE NEWS

The Associated Press news service publishes for its members a daily listing of upcoming news events such as important court cases, demonstrations, and press conferences. It's called the AP daybook, and most journalists or their assignment editors refer to it at night to get ideas for stories to cover the next day. The daybook is a pretty good predictor of the next day's news. Some media critics claim that much news is actually manufactured by media organizations, with the help of public relations professionals sending press releases and creating pseudo events such as press conferences, marches, or awards ceremonies with the sole purpose of getting the attention of the press or public.

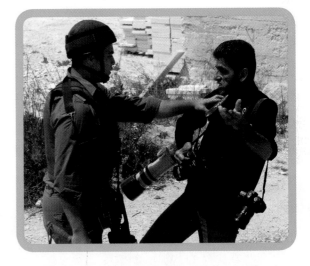

Sometimes during protests or demonstrations people act up when they see TV news cameras covering the event.

Although news covering pseudo events or based on press releases may well be "manufactured," the fact is journalists must largely rely on these sources in order to be informed of what is happening. But journalists also use sources they have developed through experience covering a **beat**, or subject area they specialize in. Initially beats covered geographic areas, much like a police officer's beat. Geographically based beats still exist, but increasingly beats cover specific subject areas, such as education, city hall, the state capital, or science. Through their reporting, journalists become aware of interesting developments that may be newsworthy and can cultivate sources that inform them further. Small newspapers cannot afford to have highly specialized reporters and often simply have general-assignment reporters who cover a range of topics.

Moreover, the media tend to spotlight selected issues and stories. These stories often resonate through the entire media system, whether about the release

beat
....
A reporter's specialized area of coverage based on geography or subject. Common beats in large or medium-sized newspapers include education, crime, and state politics.

of a highly anticipated movie, a natural disaster, or a U.S. presidential campaign. An unusual advertising campaign for a movie, for example, may trigger news stories about the campaign and its effect on the success of the movie, which in turn generate more publicity for the movie—which adds to its popularity. Some news filters up through the media network, starting as a story in a local paper that is then covered by a regional television station, where it is seen by a reporter for a national newsweekly, who covers the story and thus brings it to a national audience.

■ ■ ■ PRODUCING THE NEWS

Once a story has been assigned or chosen and the raw material—interviews, background facts, or video footage—has been gathered, the reporter then has to make sense out of it all and shape it into a compelling piece that accurately reflects the facts. Depending on whether the story involves breaking news or not, the reporter sometimes has very little time to write or produce it before a deadline. Few journalists have the luxury of putting a story aside for a week to ponder word choices or polish their prose.

Newspaper editors decide which stories are most important and where they will be placed in the newspaper in meetings several hours before story deadlines, and these spaces are blocked out (advertising space has been blocked out first). Sometimes breaking news or an unexpected event may push planned stories from their slots or from the newspaper entirely.

Editors look for logical weaknesses or errors in stories, often asking reporters to get more information or make more calls to make the story complete. Fact checkers research all facts stated in the story for accuracy and, depending on the media organization and the laziness of the reporter, sometimes have to replace many TKs (used in journalism to mean "to come") in a "finished" story with hard facts based on their research. Copyeditors correct writing errors and make sure everything is written according to the proper style. In larger newspapers, headline and caption writers read the stories and come up with headlines and photo captions that fit within the space allotted. In smaller newspapers, journalists may have more than one role or may be responsible for fact checking or suggesting headlines as well.

Design and page-layout artists put the copyedited articles and graphics in a digital version of the paper using a page-layout program such as QuarkXpress. Proofreaders check for editorial errors, and after the issue is approved by an editor, it is sent to the printer. This used to be done by taking negative photographs of hard copies of the pages, but now it is mostly done entirely electronically, and the printer receives the pages digitally through a high-speed Internet connection.

In television news, camera crews and reporters usually return to the station to

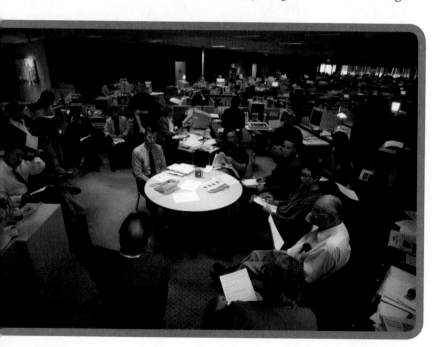
Formal and informal editorial meetings take place throughout the day in newsrooms.

Platypus Journalism: Journalism's Future, or Evolutionary Dead End?

News organizations have been slow to realize how drastically digital media are changing their business and the nature of the profession itself, but with losses in advertising revenues, lower readership, and job cuts they cannot ignore it any longer.

As news organizations scramble to figure out their way in the digital news environment, one model of the future of journalism has seemed particularly appealing: that of the one-man or one-woman correspondent in sole possession of all the tools to report, produce, and file stories from the field.

The idea is that with the new, cheaper digital tools, wireless Internet connections, and more powerful computers, journalists on the road could shoot video, record audio, write a story, and possibly create an interactive multimedia graphic.

The notion has appeal to management, as one reporter would now be doing the work of at least three. Some early experiments in one-person news operations seemed promising, such as Kevin Sites's reporting for Yahoo News from a number of global hotspots.

However, the model has also been ridiculed as "platypus journalism" or "Inspector Gadget journalism," with critics saying that journalists cannot do the same in-depth coverage when juggling all the tech gadgets as they could if they focused on one medium, such as writing or video. The critics say that the future of reporting more likely lies in some form of **crowd sourcing**—utilizing raw data gathered from the public, as well as reports from citizen journalists—than a one-man band of technology gadgetry.

edit footage shot on location and to add voice-overs and graphics to the video. Since time is so critical, news segments are edited and rehearsed down to the second to fit into their selected time slots. With breaking or international news, reporters will report live from location, often broadcasting via satellite.

Television news, because of the amount of equipment needed to shoot video, requires more people to gather and produce a story. A crew of two people, a camera person and a reporter, is usually needed. Digital video technology has helped reduce the number needed to shoot broadcast-quality video to a single camera person and reporter, but there are still many more technical steps involved in assembling a television news package than in writing a print story.

At the station, the producer and reporter decide on what to edit and how the story will be put together, usually working with video editors or other technicians to carry out their instructions. At some stations, news anchors also have a role in editorial decisions, while at other stations they simply present the news.

crowd sourcing
....
Utilizing raw data that
the public has gathered,
in addition to reports from
citizen journalists, to help
create a news report.

The goal of both print and electronic media in distributing the news is the same: to attract as large an audience as possible. The reasoning is simple: a larger audience means a higher advertising rate and more income for the media organization.

Newspapers and magazines use colorful or dramatic photos on their front pages or covers, often with what the editors have decided is the most enticing story. Some magazines may send press releases about what they feel are particularly noteworthy stories coming out in the next issue, with the hope that other media outlets will report on these and generate more sales. Individual stories can be syndicated and appear in other print-media outlets.

Print media are distributed through subscriptions and newsstand sales. Subscribers are more valuable to media organizations because they represent a stable revenue base and provide mailing lists that can be sold or rented to other organizations. Material costs for print media, ranging from paper to ink to delivery trucks, can be quite high.

Television stations have short teasers during commercial breaks throughout the evening, usually asking a provocative question such as, "Could the food you are eating be dangerous? Find out at eleven." Often the stories that have acted as the bait to get viewers to watch the news are not the lead story but appear later in the program, in order to keep people watching. This is also the reason weather forecasts usually come toward the middle or end of a news broadcast. National news shows are transmitted by the network to affiliate stations, sometimes with time slots available for additional local news content. Networks also send video feeds of international and national news coverage to local affiliates so they can use the footage in their news reports.

Types of Journalism

The basic outline of the way news is produced in professional journalism does not show how its tenets have been challenged over the years by other types of journalism that have developed. These other types are a testament to the importance many people put on journalism, making claims of varying severity that mainstream or professional journalism is not living up to its ideals in informing citizens or acting as a watchdog of government.

Much serious questioning of journalism took place during the 1960s, even among established journalists, when social upheavals led many to question norms in established society. Leading reporters such as James "Scottie" Reston of the *New York Times* and Paul Anderson of the *St. Louis Post-Dispatch* perceived the limits of "objective" news reportage that simply stated the facts in a story and developed the beginnings of **interpretive reporting**, which tried to explain the story by placing the facts into broader context.

interpretive reporting
....
A type of reporting that tries to put the facts of a story into a broader context by relying on knowledge and experience the reporter has about the subject.

Critics of interpretive reporting argue that it does no better at adequately representing the complexity of reality than objective reporting. Still, interpretive reporting opened the door to a variety of journalistic styles during the 1960s, including New Journalism, literary journalism, and advocacy journalism.

New Journalism developed in the 1960s and 1970s during a time of great social, political, and economic upheaval in the United States, ranging from the Vietnam War to Watergate. Many journalists sought to present a true account of the complexity or spirit of the times. What emerged was a form of reporting that often used literary techniques such as point of view, exploration of characters' emotions, and first-person narrative. Topics included popular social issues and the drug culture. Truman Capote, Tom Wolfe, and Norman Mailer were three prominent writers using New Journalism techniques in their books. Critics charged that the literary style often blurred the line between fact and fiction.

Literary journalism in some ways has roots that go back to the muckrakers, although its modern form does not always tackle social problems with the same fervor as the muckrakers. Literary journalism stays closer to true, observable narrative in its storytelling, and its pace may be slow, with frequent lengthy side trips on other topics. Because of the length of articles and variety of topics covered, literary journalism does not generally deal with breaking news events, though news events may be the basis for some literary-journalism stories. One of the finest literary journalists is John McPhee, who combines immersive reporting, solid research, and excellent writing to create engaging stories. Other practitioners of literary journalism include Joan Didion, James Fallows, and Robert Kaplan, all of whom write on a range of issues, including foreign affairs and politics.

Another descendent of muckraking, one that keeps the muckraker's critique of society firmly in focus, is advocacy journalism. It maintains a strong commitment to political and social reform. Leading examples of advocacy journalism are Gloria Steinem (founder of *Ms.* magazine and a leader of the women's movement), Pete Hamill (one-time editor of the *Daily News* in New York), and Nicholas von Hoffman. Much of early environmental journalism was a type of advocacy journalism.

■ ■ ■ ALTERNATIVE JOURNALISM

Alternative journalism, often called radical journalism in the past, departed considerably from the traditions of objective reporting and has a much older lineage than some of the types of journalism just mentioned. Its roots go back to some of the radical and socialist newspapers published in the nineteenth century in the UK that were meant to give workers a united voice and sense of injustice. Some radical papers had large circulations in their heyday, comparable to some of the most popular traditional papers of the day, but the advertising-supported model put these newspapers at a disadvantage because advertisers did not want to be associated with radical political movements. In addition, most readers of these papers were working class, so were not considered desirable customers. As a result, such papers tended to struggle to stay afloat or toned down their political rants to be more attractive to advertisers.

Alternative journalism often purposely defied the conventions of professional journalism, both in tone and choice of topics, much as the New Journalists did decades later. Despite existing on the fringes throughout most of the twentieth century and never seriously challenging mainstream journalism, it did provide an outlet for stories not seen elsewhere, some of which would then make their way into the mainstream.

Magazines such as *Mother Jones*, *The Progressive*, and *The Nation* can be seen as inheritors of the radical-journalism tradition and examples of alternative journalism that straddle the gap between radical journalism and mainstream standards of

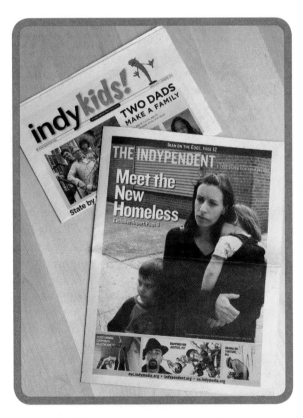

The *Indypendent* is a print newspaper published by the Indymedia group in New York.

professional quality. And of course the alternative weeklies available in most urban areas, such as the *Boston Phoenix* and the *Houston Press,* are examples of the genre, with their edgy, contrarian coverage of topics that is often geared to a younger audience.

Alternative journalism was given new life in 1999 during the WTO protests in Seattle, when an ad hoc group of protesters created their own media to cover the event because they felt the mainstream press was misreporting or underreporting the events. The independent media movement, called Indymedia for short, was founded and has quickly spread worldwide thanks to the growth of the Internet. Although most Indymedia groups remain small, their decentralized structure and open publishing systems allow people to easily contribute stories, providing outlets for many who would not otherwise get involved in journalism. Some local groups, such as Indymedia NYC, publish professional-quality newspapers along with a robust website.

■ ■ ■ PUBLIC JOURNALISM

Public journalism, sometimes called civic journalism, developed in the early 1990s out of dissatisfaction among some editors and journalists over how poorly mainstream journalism seemed to be covering important social and political issues. They saw the growing cynicism and apathy among the general public in civic affairs, and the increased distrust of journalists, and wondered if perhaps mainstream journalism coverage had an influence on those attitudes.

Public journalism takes a much less radical approach to engaging the public than alternative journalism, mostly because it originated from longtime and respected professional journalists. It expands on the watchdog role of journalism but tries to engage the citizenry more closely with creating and discussing the news. Public journalism also tries to avoid framing the news in terms of conflict and extremes and examines the news in a more nuanced fashion.

Newspapers experimenting with public or civic journalism around the country have reported a higher level of trust toward the press by their readership and some signs of increased civic participation and awareness of social and political issues. Critics of civic journalism charge that it is little more than boosterism or advocacy journalism and weakens the role of the press as a sometimes unpopular but critical voice of a community's conscience. Others criticize it for not going far enough in breaking the barrier between professional journalists and audiences, seeing it as a way for journalists to try to maintain their privileged position as professionals who for some reason can report better on the news than citizens can.

Partly because of the two forces of criticism—that of professional peers and that of citizens—public journalism has waned in recent years. Later studies in communities with papers that followed public-journalism principles noted no significant increase in political awareness or participation among the public, so the results of its success seem to be mixed.

What the debates on public journalism did do was provide a precursor to the challenges professional journalists would face in the early twenty-first century with the rise of citizen journalism.

■ ■ ■ CITIZEN JOURNALISM

The Internet and especially social-media tools have allowed the rapid growth of what is called citizen journalism. Although it takes many forms, and is still being

Web Link >>>
Public Journalism Network
pjnet.org

defined, it broadly encompasses everything from blogging to Slashdot to more formal ventures such as OhMyNews that emulate professional journalism in important aspects. Some scholars even include product-review sites by consumers as a form of citizen journalism.

Citizen journalism differs from the other types of journalism already mentioned in that it is usually not created with an explicitly political or radical agenda, like advocacy or alternative journalism, and its driving force has been citizens rather than professional journalists, as in public journalism.

It is partly for these reasons that mainstream journalism has been more willing to embrace some citizen-journalism efforts, even if cautiously in many cases. Some news organizations have tried to cultivate its viewers and readers as sources of raw news footage, such as CNN's iReporter. Other news organizations, especially some newspapers, have adopted a more integrated and thorough approach in which citizen journalists post news and stories on a stand-alone website, perhaps partially cobranded with the newspaper, and the best of the stories get published in a weekly edition. Still other organizations have conducted training sessions for citizen journalists, teaching them interviewing, reporting, and writing skills.

Original citizen-journalism sites have had a rougher time of it, some proving wildly successful and others failing miserably. One success is OhMyNews, the South Korea–based citizen-journalism site that operates much like a traditional news organization, with paid editors and a hierarchy in the editing process before stories are posted. Another is Vancouver-based NowPublic, which launched in 2005 and now has reporters in 140 countries. Citizen-journalism advocate Dan Gillmor launched Bayosphere in 2005, a citizen-journalism site that was intended to cover the San Francisco Bay area. However, after seven difficult months, the

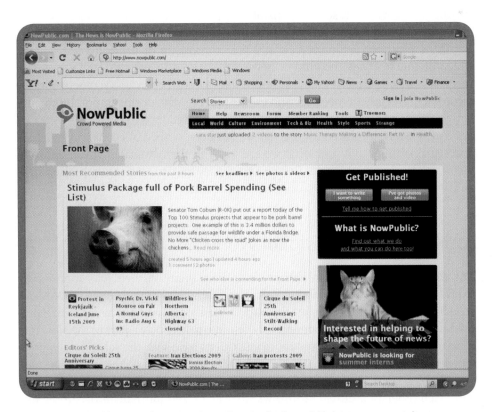

NowPublic is an online citizen-journalism site that has quickly become very popular.

Web Link >>>
OhMyNews
www.ohmynews.com

Web Link >>>
NowPublic
www.nowpublic.com

Web Link >>>
Wikinews
wikinews.org

project was largely abandoned. Gillmor continues to believe in the potential of citizen journalism, but he learned some hard lessons about the practicality and economics of making it a reality.

One common thread in citizen-journalism sites is the emphasis on conversation and interaction between participants and a blurring of the lines between journalist and audience. Many professional journalists find this development very threatening, as it challenges their privileged position as the arbiters of what is important enough to be considered news. In this way, journalists are losing their gatekeeping function and journalism is evolving into what Australian media scholar Axel Bruns calls a gatewatching function, as discussed in the previous chapter.

Despite the great potential in increasing participation and interaction between citizens who practice citizen journalism, there still is no clear business model to ensure the success of the movement. For most citizen-journalism sites, even ones founded by news organizations, citizen reporters are unpaid volunteers. This can be a barrier to attracting top-quality reporters and editors, and it hampers news gathering, which can be time-consuming and costly.

■ ■ ■ AN INTERNATIONAL PERSPECTIVE

There is nothing sacred about the inverted-pyramid style for news stories or the emphasis on fairness and balance in news that is taken for granted in the United States. Most Americans do not realize that there are a number of ways journalism can be practiced because they generally do not see news from other countries—or if they do, it is likely the English-language BBC, which follows the same tenets of fairness and balance in its coverage.

However, a look at news styles, even in other European countries, will often show a surprising variety in how news is written. Reporters' opinions may be more prevalent or obvious in some ostensibly factual news accounts, or reporters may insert their own thoughts or feelings about the news they are covering.

In many countries journalists still face censorship or licensing restrictions, which of course shape the kind of news that appears in print or on TV or radio. In these cases, journalists may act more like government stenographers, simply recording government meetings and events that the state deems important to publicize, with the only editorial voice being that approved by the state.

These examples show how journalism has been shaped by economic, political, and social realities and how what we see today in the newspaper, given different historical developments in the United States, may have turned out very different—and will continue to change.

Journalism in the Digital World

The digital tools available to journalists to help them do their jobs more effectively have been slow to be adopted by mainstream news organizations. Busy work schedules and unwillingness on the part of media corporations to subsidize professional training and development for their journalists play a part in the slow rate of adoption. However, more and more journalists have seen the value in using one tool—the Internet—in making their jobs easier.

The increased power of the audience to communicate with journalists and with each other in a public forum, whether as citizen journalism or simply discussions on blogs or forums, also can be threatening to some journalists who are accustomed to being the gatekeepers of information. Now readers and viewers online can point out, quite publicly, when a journalist errs. News sites have found that if they do not provide a discussion forum for their readers, the readers will simply go elsewhere to discuss stories and point out errors.

As Table 10-1 shows, out of the top ten news sites in 2008 three were based on print publications, four were based on television news networks, and three were essentially news aggregators, such as Yahoo News and Google News, which use stories from the wire services and other news sources. All of the sites showed substantial growth of online viewers between 2007 and 2008, a trend that was even greater among the top twenty online newspapers.

The growth in online viewers of news sites may seem like a good thing, as it shows people are still engaged with the news, but it has put the news industry under even greater pressure. Not only must news organizations compete with their traditional media counterparts, but they also have to compete with the online versions of their competitors. Furthermore, ad revenues have not counterbalanced the drop in ads from the traditional media product, especially in print.

Advances in technology not only threaten business models, but they can bring about changes in how people use the Internet,

The Web changes how people get and read their news.

TABLE 10-1

Top Global News Sites, by Unique Visitors: March 2009

RANK	SITE	UNIQUE AUDIENCE	YOY CHANGE
1	MSNBC Digital Network	39,900,000	9%
2	CNN Digital Network	38,724,000	4%
3	Yahoo News	37,902,000	16%
4	AOL News	23,604,000	1%
5	NYTimes.com	20,118,000	7%
6	Fox News Digital Network	16,791,000	48%
7	Tribune Newspapers	16,513,000	16%
8	Google News	13,668,000	18%
9	McClatchy Newspaper Network	12,508,000	20%
10	ABC News Digital Network	12,189,000	4%
11	Gannett Newspapers and Newspaper Division	11,609,000	(−11%)
12	USAToday.com	9,961,000	(−7%)
13	CBS News Digital Network	9,599,000	(−7%)
14	Washingtonpost.com	9,367,000	5%
15	BBC	9,022,000	61%

Source: Nielsen Online

thereby changing the role online news may play in the public's overall picture of media use. Even so, there are some trends that perhaps show the way to what role online journalism fills in providing news and information to the public.

■ ■ ■ THE 24/7 NEWS CYCLE

Online news is not tied to a printer's schedule or specific broadcast slot, which means that it can be presented twenty-four hours, seven days a week. This can cause the increasingly common situation in which a media organization's website scoops its print newspaper or television news show. Many media companies used to avoid this by putting an **embargo**, or temporary hold, on publishing the news on the Web until the traditional media product had published or aired the story. However, as the chance for getting scooped by the competition rose, the practice became less common, and news organizations have grown accustomed to their websites being the place where news breaks. A non-deadline-driven news cycle wreaks havoc on the way news is usually processed and could add to production costs as more reporting and editing staff are needed to process news around the clock.

■ ■ ■ NONTRADITIONAL NEWS SOURCES

The public's ability to access nontraditional news sources has two components: getting news from traditional news outlets that are not usually viewed or read by the public and getting news from a wider variety of nonjournalism sites, such as blogs or discussion groups. An example in the former category is viewing an online newspaper from the Middle East to see how a story is covered there or watching an Al Jazeera newscast. Even looking at UK media coverage of international issues can often be a valuable and educational experience for U.S. audiences who receive a fairly narrow range of international news. With nonjournalistic, nontraditional outlets, users should have a high degree of media literacy so they can weigh sources of news and any biases the website creator may have.

News sources increasingly view themselves as content providers who can publish without relying on a traditional journalistic publisher or gateway. NBA.com, for example, publishes extensive news about its basketball games and includes video clips. Why would a viewer go to CNN or ESPN when he or she can get sports news straight from the source? Subscribing to follow an influential person's Twitter account or blog can often point people to news that they would not otherwise see, which could come from mainstream media or from other blogs.

The danger in nontraditional news sources like these is that they may not have the same commitment to fairness and balance of coverage that a professional news organization would have. It is unlikely a user would find an exposé on NBA.com about financial wrongdoing by the league, for example. On the other hand, many members of the public may not care about such news and simply want to get basketball scores and news on the latest trades. In that case, going to a site like NBA.com may be fine.

■ ■ ■ ONLINE USERS' MEDIA HABITS

Online users' media habits differ from traditional media use in a number of ways. First, online users are generally more active in their media use and will easily visit different websites to find the information they are seeking. This shorter attention span for viewing media content means that news stories have to compete harder

---

embargo
....
The practice of sending news releases to news organizations with the stipulation that the information cannot be broadcast or print until after a specific day or time.

Web Link >>>
OnlineNewspapers.com
www.onlinenewspapers.com/

for the audience's attention. Most people do not like to read large amounts of material online and tend to skim written material. This also encourages producing shorter printed stories or stories with interactive graphics or multimedia.

Users want to quickly understand not only the essential facts in a story but its context as well and will readily use hyperlinks to click to related stories or other websites. However, from a business standpoint, media organizations do not want visitors to leave their website, so there is a natural tension regarding what hyperlinks to provide and how to provide them in a way that allows users to explore further yet encourages them to remain.

On the other hand, with the rise in popularity of blogs, news sites want their stories to be mentioned and linked to in order to drive traffic to their site. Some blogs are so heavily read that a mention in an entry can crash a smaller news site's web server because of the high volume of people visiting the site, something called the **Slashdot effect**. This refers to what has frequently happened when a site is mentioned on the very popular news site Slashdot.

Slashdot effect
. . . .
The occurrence of a website's servers crashing because of a large increase in visits to the site after its being mentioned on the popular website Slashdot.org.

■ ■ ■ PERSONALIZATION

The Internet allows users to personalize the content they receive, ranging from localized weather forecasts to choosing news on favorite sports teams or companies in a stock portfolio. Personalization is one of the unique features of online media that traditional media simply cannot compete with, and its development will play a key role in making the Internet an increasingly important source for news. Personalization could lead to changes in the way journalists write or produce stories. For example, a standard version of a story could also include various hyperlinked informational modules, or types of sidebars that can be called up on demand, that would be of interest to users in specific demographics.

Journalists will obviously not be able to write individual stories for each user, but it is likely that elements of stories could be broken up by computer and reconstituted in a personalized format based on demographic data or user characteristics.

Personalizing web pages gives users the ability to get exactly the kind of news they wish.

■■■ CONTEXTUALIZATION OF NEWS

Despite often being able to access the raw material that a journalist has used to write a story, users will still want some kind of context for the data and some kind of interpretation of it. If anything, the interpreting function will become more important for journalists, as most people will not have the time, ability, or desire to sift through raw data to determine the important points in a story.

For example, a user may click on an interactive crime map when reading an online news story about a certain crime in a different part of town and then select her own zip code to call up an interactive map of her neighborhood. She can see on the map what types of crimes have been committed in the neighborhood within the past year. Ideally, she will also be able to click to get more information on a specific crime, when it occurred, what the rate of occurrence is for that crime, and whether it's increasing or decreasing—with possible explanations from expert sources on why. Hyperlinks to archived news stories of the crime, if there are any, would also help put the interactive map in context. Such **mash-ups** that combine geographic data overlaid with editorial content are becoming increasingly popular and easy to create.

mash-up
....
Combining textual information over geographic, map-based information so users can access multiple layers of data.

■■■ CONVERGENT JOURNALISM

Online video, audio, and interactive graphics are increasingly used with text stories to enhance and supplement them. Likewise, text can be added to primarily video stories to offer different ways of accessing the information and to provide more depth and context than video or audio alone can do. Journalists will have to become versed in the various tools of online journalism, including video, audio, and writing.

A truly interactive multimedia experience that allows the user to stop or replay segments at will, skip familiar information, and learn background information as needed will help differentiate online journalism from its nondigital counterparts.

Technology can change not only the production and presentation of the news but how it is gathered. Digital cameras and video cameras have made photography and videography much easier for journalists, so much so that a single reporter can videotape interviews or footage that can be used in a multimedia news story. Voice of America radio journalists have received digital-video shooting and editing training and have been able to add video elements to their stories online, and other news organizations such as the BBC are training many of their journalists in video techniques.

Unmanned air vehicles (UAVs) can be useful news-gathering tools and much cheaper than leasing helicopters for such activities as traffic coverage.

Journalists will have to be conversant, if not necessarily expert, in a range of digital media tools. Unmanned air vehicles (UAVs), smaller and cheaper versions of what the U.S. military uses, can also be useful news-gathering tools. Already, some local law enforcement uses UAVs for surveillance, and there is no reason news organizations couldn't use them for certain kinds of stories or for covering traffic conditions, for example.

Journalism Ethics

Because of journalism's unique role in society, its protection by the First Amendment, and its public service mission, many ethical dilemmas arise in the course of practicing it. Ethical questions play a role in the entire news-gathering and production process, and many questions do not have easy answers. Ethical issues become even more important as more citizens practice journalism or some form of it.

Editors must consider whether headlines and captions accurately reflect the important points of a story or simply titillate. Privacy issues play a role when private citizens are thrust by circumstance into the media spotlight. Reporters must consider fairness and balance in their choice of interview subjects. Photo editors and designers must avoid the temptation to alter elements of photos to make them more dramatic. Societal mores and cultural values of the audience must be considered when determining what qualifies as news and how it is reported, although newspapers must also sometimes take highly unpopular stands on issues when acting as the public's conscience.

■ ■ ■ PRIVACY RIGHTS VERSUS THE PUBLIC'S RIGHT TO KNOW

Although there is no actual law stating the public has a "right to know," it is often cited as a commonly understood principle when journalists are trying to obtain information that can help the public make better-informed decisions regarding anything from political candidates to corporate wrongdoing to potentially dangerous foods, drugs, or buildings.

Gathering proof of wrongdoing is one of the biggest challenges journalists face. Admissions of guilt are unlikely to come out during an interview—if the subject even agrees to an interview, which is often not the case. Journalists are often barred from the very locations they need to visit in order to gather information. Employees are forbidden by management to speak to journalists or threatened with losing their jobs if they do; police or public officials refuse to see or talk to journalists or are slow in providing requested documentation, even if the documents are public.

New technology such as miniature microphones and cameras, or the old technique of going undercover, may seem easy answers to the journalists' dilemma. But the ethics and legality of these tools and actions must be considered. Sometimes these techniques are the only ones that will give access to people engaged in illegal or unethical behavior, such as selling drugs or arms.

Federal law prohibits the media or anyone else from intentionally intercepting, or attempting to intercept, anyone's communication by wire, oral, or electronic means. Citizens have a reasonable expectation of privacy for oral, or spoken, communications, including via a telephone or over the Internet. However, it is complicated in that states have varying laws on whether only one person or both people in a conversation must give consent to have a conversation recorded.

Regardless of the legality of intercepting communications, is it ethical? There is no easy answer, as it depends on the circumstances. It also depends on whether it is print or broadcast media. The FCC generally prohibits the use of wireless microphones to overhear private conversations unless all parties to the communication have given prior consent. Conversations that occur in a public place, such as a bar, however, would not be subject to the same prohibition, since people in public places cannot expect the same right to privacy. Broadcast television or radio stations may not record telephone conversations without the consent of all parties, and they must notify the parties prior to broadcasting any of the recorded content. Long-distance calls can only be recorded under limited circumstances, including an announcement made at the beginning of the call indicating it will be recorded or possibly broadcast. Violation of these rules can result in the forfeiture of the station's license, fines, or other penalties.

One area of confusion regarding privacy is whether posting material in a blog or on a social-media site like Facebook is public or not. Some claim that it is the same as a public space, but it gets more complex when one considers the shelf life of material online. An offhand comment in a bar disappears once it is said, but an inflammatory blog post written years ago and later deleted may still exist somewhere on the Web.

■ ■ ■ GOING UNDERCOVER

The legality and ethics of journalists going undercover are also not settled. It in many ways depends on how ethical or responsible the media professional was in using these techniques. Questions that may be asked in a court of law include the following: Were the media being fair? Does going undercover or using hidden cameras somehow manipulate or distort the situation? Do the undercover techniques help build meaningful information or simply sensationalize the story? If a media professional (or anyone else, for that matter) is convicted of violating the law in going undercover, there are a variety of potential penalties, including substantial prison terms and fines.

The Internet raises new questions about a journalist not announcing her identity. If she engages in a discussion in a child-pornography online discussion group without revealing her identity as a journalist pursuing a story, is it ethical to use others' posts without their permission? Is it ethical to pose as someone other than a journalist in order to get people to talk as they naturally would in an online forum?

■ ■ ■ VICTIMIZING THE VICTIMS

Crime victims can feel doubly victimized when their names are made public by the media, especially with crimes such as rape that still carry a social stigma. Most newspapers and television stations do not make rape victims' names public, although critics of this practice argue that it further stigmatizes rape rather than educating the public about the crime of violence that it is.

Publicizing details of crimes can also contribute to copycat crimes, and journalists must always consider what kinds of information in a story are important and what are simply lurid or titillating details. Needlessly mentioning race, gender, or sexual orientation can often be unethical in framing a subject in a way that may reinforce social stereotypes.

Photographs and video have a power to sometimes tell a story in a way that words alone cannot. Yet, publicly presented dramatic photos or footage are not always justified for their news value alone. In fact, in cases of human tragedy, sadness, or crime, personal grief has been violated by the repeated presentation of pictures or video in newspapers, magazines, or on television.

Do the Ends Justify the Means?

On November 5, 1992, ABC's *Primetime Live*, a weekly newsmagazine show, broadcast a report claiming labor and food-handling problems at Food Lion, a nonunion supermarket chain and at the time the fastest-growing supermarket chain in the United States, with more than one thousand stores. The program's producers had been contacted by the United Food and Commercial Workers International Union (UFCW) in early 1992 about doing a story on alleged unsanitary conditions at the supermarket chain.

The show's producers designed a scheme to obtain hidden-camera footage from inside Food Lion stores. The scheme required *Primetime Live* produc-

ABC's story about food-handling practices at Food Lion in the early 1990s raised serious legal and ethical questions regarding investigative techniques.

ers to obtain jobs at Food Lion under false identities and fraudulent employment applications. Once they started working at Food Lion, the producers brought in hidden cameras and recorded what they saw inside the stores, including harried employees, unsanitary conditions, and wasted food. The problem was, many of the bad conditions observed were due to the fact that the ABC producers neglected their own cleaning duties as Food Lion employees.

Food Lion objected to the airing of this report and sued ABC, which in the meantime had been purchased by the Walt Disney Company in 1995. The case went to trial in late 1996 and concluded in January 1997. The jury found for Food Lion on all counts and against Disney/ABC, awarding $5.5 million in damages to Food Lion. The jury concluded that *Primetime Live* based its report on unlawfully obtained videotape and that the program's producers had committed fraud and illegal trespass.

However, later rulings by judges overturned the jury award, first reducing the damages to $315,000 and then in 1999 overturning the ruling altogether and only awarding $2 in punitive damages to Food Lion.

Do you think the decision against ABC was justified? In what other ways could the journalists have obtained the kind of information they did on unsanitary practices at the supermarket chain?

On Sunday, June 11, 2000, the annual Puerto Rican Day Parade in New York City was marred by a group of fifteen to twenty-five men who assaulted women attending the parade. Amateur video documented many of the assaults, and the footage was used by the police to apprehend suspects. Television also aired much of the video and newspapers published print photos extracted from the video, sometimes revealing the identities of the women who were being assaulted.

This is a typical situation a news director or editor faces when deciding what to print or air as news. There is no doubt that footage and pictures of seminude women would attract a larger audience (along with vociferous complaints from various groups), but the ethics of showing such material must be considered in the effects it would have on the victims and their families.

■ ■ ■ SOCIETY OF PROFESSIONAL JOURNALISTS CODE OF ETHICS

The Society of Professional Journalists (SPJ) is a large organization of working journalists and student chapters that tries to ensure that journalism is being practiced professionally and ethically and that it is fulfilling its role in society. The SPJ's code of ethics states that journalists should "seek truth and report it" and that "journalists should be honest, fair and courageous in gathering, reporting and interpreting information." These are some of the other principles in the code:

Web Link >>>
SPJ Code of Ethics
www.spj.org/ethicscode.asp

- Test the accuracy of information from all sources and exercise care to avoid inadvertent error. Deliberate distortion is never permissible.
- Diligently seek out subjects of news stories to give them the opportunity to respond to allegations of wrongdoing.
- Identify sources whenever feasible. The public is entitled to as much information as possible on sources' reliability.
- Make certain that headlines, news teasers, and promotional material, photos, video, audio, graphics, sound bites, and quotations do not misrepresent. They should not oversimplify or highlight incidents out of context.
- Never distort the content of news photos or video. Image enhancement for technical clarity is always permissible. Label montages and photo illustrations.
- Avoid misleading reenactments or staged news events. If reenactment is necessary to tell a story, label it.
- Support the open exchange of views, even views journalists find repugnant.
- Avoid undercover or other surreptitious methods of gathering information except when traditional open methods will not yield information vital to the public. Use of such methods should be explained as part of the story.

The Business of Journalism

The early years of the twenty-first century have been especially challenging for the media business, especially for news organizations. Advertising revenues have been in steady decline for the past several years, especially in print media. Although online advertising is growing, it still makes up a small portion of overall revenues and does not compensate for the reduced revenues in traditional media.

Some media companies that predicted new business opportunities in media convergence, such as the former AOL Time Warner or Bertelsmann, spent large amounts to provide services or media that never made a profit. Other media companies that adopted a more cautious approach with digital media see even fewer reasons to invest in new technologies. However, even the executives who have been burned say the changes will come and that they simply moved too quickly.

The loss in advertising revenues, combined with a recession that began in December 2007, has severely strained news organizations. In 2008, the American Society of News Editors (ASNE) found that the newspaper industry had suffered its largest drop loss in thirty years, with a 4.4 percent workforce decrease compared to 2007.

Not only have layoffs become common, but entire news bureaus are closing down. In 2000, Cox newspapers had thirty correspondents in Washington, D.C., to cover the inauguration of President George Bush. In 2008, Cox announced that it would be closing its Washington bureau early in spring 2009. Some news organizations have taken what are considered even more drastic steps. In 2009, the respected newspaper *Christian Science Monitor* announced that it would stop publishing a print newspaper and only exist online. In March 2009, the 146-year-old *Seattle Post-Intelligencer*, a Hearst paper, ceased publishing its print edition and went to online-only.

In order to cut costs, news organizations may use other methods that affect the quality of the final news product even though staff may not be laid off. It has already been mentioned that using a greater percentage of wire service copy rather than original local reporting saves money, but at the cost of making the news less relevant to a local audience. Investigative journalism is usually scaled back substantially when a news organization is trying to cut costs. Publishers may increase the advertising percentage in a newspaper or raise advertising rates in order to increase revenues, although there is debate whether these practices hurt a newspaper in the long run.

There will always be a tension between the business side and the editorial side in a news organization. The editorial side is looking for stories in line with the adage that journalism should "comfort the afflicted and afflict the comfortable," and often publishers or their corporate parent are "the comfortable." Journalists can sometimes face severe pressures or even get fired if they do not go along with a publisher's wishes in either killing a story on a subject that a powerful advertiser does not want to see or downplaying news that is embarrassing to the publisher's associates or friends. Rare is the media owner who is willing to turn the investigative spotlight on himself as readily and thoroughly as he is on others.

■ ■ ■ SALARIES

Salaries for journalism professionals vary according to several factors, including the type of medium one works in (television is the highest paid, print media the lowest), the location or market (i.e., the larger the market, the higher the pay), the type of position one occupies (farther up in management, ownership, or celebrity status correlates positively with pay), experience, and a variety of other less definite factors, including gender, with men generally being paid more than women, as unfair as that may be. Salaries and overall compensation vary so widely—from fifteen thousand dollars a year to many millions of dollars—that crude averages are relatively meaningless.

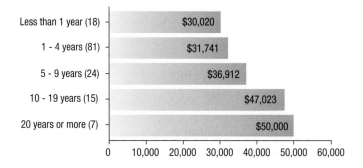

FIGURE 10-1 Average Salaries for Journalists, by Years Worked. Source: payscale.com

In general, network television offers the highest salaries for midlevel jobs as producers. National magazines and newspapers offer fairly good pay, while papers in mid- and small-sized markets offer relatively poor salaries in comparison to jobs of a similar level in public relations, for example. Internet media offer fairly good salaries, and until the dot-com bust their stock option plans made a lucky few journalists instant millionaires when the companies went public. Many more people missed that train than rode it, however, as Internet media companies started going bankrupt.

Radio journalist Condace Pressley, former president of the National Association of Black Journalists (NABJ).

■ ■ ■ DIVERSITY IN THE NEWSROOM

Circumstances in American newsrooms have been slow to change. In 1950, African American journalist Marvel Cooke (1903–2000) was hired as a reporter and feature writer for the *New York Daily Compass*. She was the only woman and the only black person on the staff of the paper and was among the first blacks to work for any white-owned daily newspaper.

The American Society of News Editors (ASNE) regularly conducts a survey on employment of women and minorities by U.S. daily newspapers. The numbers of minority and women hires have fallen short of mirroring the percentages found in the general population and fall far short when it comes to management. Because of the layoffs and hiring freezes throughout the newspaper industry in recent years, the percentage of minority employees has actually risen slightly, to just over 13 percent.

Industry watchers worry that the persistent dominance of white males in newsrooms skews news coverage toward the type of material that appeals to them, as opposed to stories relevant to underrepresented minority groups.

Careers in Journalism

The employment outlook for journalists in the digital age is generally not good, as it largely reflects how well the overall economy is doing combined with the trends already mentioned among news organizations. After a decade of strong growth in employment and business, the twenty-first century got off to a troubled start, and media and technology companies have been especially hard hit with the downturn in the economy.

However, it is an exciting time to be a journalist. Online journalism is still in its infancy and plays an increasingly important role in the overall journalism picture, and there are still possibilities for journalists in traditional print, radio, and television. And within specialty areas such as financial journalism or science journalism, there is an almost endless number of niches that can be pursued.

■ ■ ■ SPECIALIZED JOURNALISM TYPES

With an increasingly complex world, not only do reporters often specialize in a subject area in order to better cover that topic, but there are whole branches of specialized journalism, complete with their own support organizations. Working in a small or medium-sized newspaper or broadcast station means journalists are less likely to be able to focus on one field, but working in bigger publications lets

Entertainment journalism plays an important role in helping promote upcoming movies, albums, and shows.

journalists specialize. Following is by no means a complete list, as it does not cover beats like education or local or national politics, but it should give a general idea of the range of specialties.

Business and Financial Journalism

Business news is often read by a highly educated, knowledgeable audience seeking specific information. It can be difficult for journalists to penetrate an organization's public relations office to get access to executives, and when they do it can be hard to get candid information. Understanding business practices (such as accounting procedures) and being able to read and understand various complex forms are important, as is being able to write about complicated issues, such as changes in tax laws, that the general public may find boring. On the other hand, investors are usually very interested in learning the truth about companies, and financial journalists must be able to separate the hype from the reality.

Arts and Entertainment Journalism

As mentioned earlier, entertainment-related stories have become more prominent in the news in recent years. Much of entertainment journalism, especially on television, on programs like *Entertainment Tonight*, is little more than orchestrated interviews and video shoots with artists or stars that essentially help them promote their latest films. "Behind-the-scenes" segments serve this purpose as well and help viewers feel like they are seeing the "real" person behind the star, even though there is little of true informational value in such features.

On the other hand, cultural and art criticism play an important role in helping define public tastes and form cultural trends in everything from fashion to film. Reviews in prestigious magazines like the *New York Times Review of Books* can be the deciding factor for a book's success. Coverage of the entertainment industry as a business can yield important information on corporate changes occurring with media companies.

Sports Journalism

Sports journalism shares many of the characteristics of both arts and entertainment journalism and business journalism. Like popular singers or movie stars, popular athletes can be almost impossible to approach for in-depth interviews, and journalists may mostly get the usual mumbled platitudes in the locker room after the game.

A sports franchise is a business and the owners treat it as such, jealously guarding company secrets just like businesses everywhere, yet sometimes asking for public funds to build facilities like stadiums. In addition, media access is strictly controlled by the various leagues, making it easy for journalists who pry too closely into touchy issues to be barred from further access to the team or players. This can have a dampening effect on thorough coverage of important issues, such as drug use by players.

Health or Medical Journalism

Health or medical news is almost always of high interest to the public, and journalists in this area have an especially important responsibility to report information accurately and fairly. Claiming that a drug company will have a cure for cancer within three years only gives cancer sufferers and their families false hope, despite what the company may say. Journalists specializing in health and medicine must not only have a good grasp of medical terms and drugs, but they must also be able to read and understand the medical literature and critically analyze statistics and complex studies. They must also know the business side of the health care and pharmaceutical industries, which have tremendous public relations machines to promote their interests, and report this complex information in a way that engages the audience.

Science and Technology Journalism

Science journalists have a double challenge in covering their areas, as the U.S. public generally does not understand basic scientific principles or care about science-related topics compared to other types of news, such as sports or entertainment. The science journalist must interpret and explain complex concepts or findings in an easy-to-understand way and show why the public should care about the topic. Hot-button issues such as cloning or genetically modified foods have many facets that defy quick explanations and are often misreported. Scientists are notoriously hesitant to announce findings with the kind of certainty or sound bites that journalists seek in order to make a good story.

Technology coverage has many of the same issues, in addition to difficulties in accessing executives of technology companies and getting beyond corporate PR hype. Much of the technology press failed miserably in predicting the dot-com collapse in 2000 or pointing out weak companies. Sometimes technology companies were out of business by the time a glowing profile of them appeared in a magazine, such as *Business 2.0*'s positive feature in its June 2000 issue on APBNews.com, which went bankrupt earlier that month.

Environmental Journalism

Like science journalists, environmental journalists often have to explain complex concepts in interesting and clear ways that the general public can understand. As many environmental processes take place slowly and there is often disagreement over what a finding may mean, it is often hard to find a solid angle within the traditional media framework for environmental stories. Environmental catastrophes such as oil spills often become major news events but suffer from the **media spotlight effect**, in which there is intense coverage for a short time and then the media flock moves on to another news item. Environmental journalism started out as a form of advocacy journalism but has shifted in recent years to be more impartial in environmental coverage.

media spotlight effect
The phenomenon that occurs when the media has intense coverage of a certain event or person for a short time, but then moves on to other issues soon after.

LOOKING BACK AND MOVING FORWARD

Journalism plays a crucial role in informing the public of important events taking place domestically and internationally and providing a context that helps people understand the world better. News is the bedrock of journalism, although news is often manufactured by public relations professionals, individuals, or organizations, and the amount of news coverage on any specific topic can change from day to day depending on the perceived importance of other news events.

The challenges that the Internet and digital media have brought to journalism are great, and the industry and profession has for the most part resisted change rather than embracing it. This resistance has had negative effects in that many news organizations, especially newspapers, are only recently trying to figure out ways to exist in the media system today. For many, it is already too late, as advertisers go elsewhere and they cut back staff, making themselves seem even less relevant to the public.

Despite the bleak employment picture for journalism graduates in the past several years, the rapid changes in the industry mean that there are jobs available for the candidates with the right skills to work in the convergent journalism newsroom of the future. Knowing how to use technology is of course important, but it is not considered the most important factor in being marketable.

Time and time again news organizations lament the poor writing skills of recent hires, and this does not change in an online news environment. If anything, even for Web-based video, writing well becomes even more important than in the nondigital forms of journalism. Practice your writing skills and master the forms of journalism and get some published clips in order to make yourself more marketable.

However, the days of journalists being able to say "I am a print journalist" or "I am a radio journalist" are soon coming to an end. Increasingly, print reporters are given a digital video camera or audio recorder and asked to shoot or record footage. Similarly, television journalists are being asked to write text stories to accompany video. The convergent journalist of tomorrow cannot be expected to be an expert in every type of media but should be comfortable using all of them.

Appreciating the power of storytelling is also important, and being able to tell a story using multimedia, hyperlinks, and other forms of interaction in an appropriate way will be what separates good journalists from hacks. Knowing some multimedia tools, such as basic image editing, will be required. But knowing how and why to use various digital tools will be even better.

In some ways, journalism has always been about knowledge creation and knowledge management. Good reporters have extensive files of sources and contacts they can reach out to when they need to get information quickly, and they have developed a sense for differentiating good information from bad. These are exactly the kinds of skills that any citizen will need in the future.

This does not change in the world of convergent journalism and in fact becomes more important as there are more potential sources for information. This is one reason it is good, in college, to focus on a subject area other than journalism. Learning economics, history, sociology, political science, biology—or any number of fields—can provide valuable critical-thinking skills and a base of knowledge to draw from while working as a journalist. Minoring in journalism or, better yet, getting experience as a student journalist at your school's newspaper, radio, or TV station can be an invaluable education in and of itself, even if you do not think you want to be a journalist. The critical-thinking skills you will learn, the practice in writing under deadlines, and the experiences you will gain will be useful in any career.

DISCUSSION QUESTIONS

1. Look at the front page of your local paper and analyze the placement of stories and photographs. What reasons could there have been for placing the stories where they are? Think about placing the stories in other places on the front page or moving a story from the inside to the front page. How would this change your impression of the importance of the story?

2. Choose an article from your local paper and see if you can find a likely source for the article from a public relations department. Compare the original press release, if available, with the final article.

3. Discuss a current event being covered in the news and how it is being framed. Examine how this framing may affect the way the topic is being covered, and suggest frames that may allow for more balanced, complete coverage.

4. Choose one of the alternative journalism types, and explain potential pitfalls of that type and how these pitfalls may be overcome—if they can be.

5. Keep track of your online news reading habits for a day or two, including every website you visit to get news, any hyperlinks you click on, and why. Discuss what you learned.

6. Should there be penalties for breaches of ethics by journalists? If so, what kinds? Who should enforce the penalties? What effects could these have on the practice of journalism?

FURTHER READING

The Elements of Journalism: What Newspeople Should Know and the Public Should Expect. Bill Kovach, Tom Rosenstiel (2001) Three Rivers Press.

News About News: American Journalism in Peril. Leonard Downie Jr., Robert G. Kaiser (2002) Knopf.

Custodians of Conscience. Theodore Lewis Glasser (1998) Columbia University Press.

The Vanishing Newspaper: Saving Journalism in the Information Age. Philip Meyer (2004) University of Missouri Press.

Digitizing the News: Innovation in Online Newspapers. Pablo Boczkowski (2005) MIT Press.

Convergent Journalism: The Fundamentals of Multimedia Reporting. Stephen Quinn (2005) Peter Lang Publishers.

Convergent Journalism: An Introduction. Stephen Quinn, Vincent F. Filak (2005) Focal Press.

The Elements of Online Journalism. Rey Rosales (2006) iUniverse.

We the Media: Grassroots Journalism by the People, for the People. Dan Gillmor (2006) O'Reilly Media.

Literary Journalism. Norm Sims, Mark Kramer (1995) Ballantine Books.

. . . .

MEDIA QUIZ ANSWERS

1. False.

3. William Randolph Hearst.

4. Fairness and balance.

5. An event created to attract media attention, such as a press conference.

6. Alternative journalism.

7. False.

8. A bigger news hole to fill, shorter deadlines, and some traditional news products such as newspapers may get dated more quickly.

9. False.

10. PR professionals make more.

Entertainment

CHAPTER OBJECTIVES

In this chapter we will:

- Understand the functions of entertainment.

- Appreciate how pervasive entertainment is in our lives and the social role it fulfills.

- Describe how major entertainment industries have developed and how they influence the entertainment we see today.

- See how entertainment industries are connected both to journalism and to advertising and public relations.

- Understand how ethics in entertainment can often have great influence on the public and society.

- Understand some of the main types of careers in the entertainment industry.

11

Air guitar has moved from in front of a mirror and behind closed doors to in front of friends or even total strangers at a local bar. And it has done so with all the fanfare that rock music can muster.

Thanks to video games like *Guitar Hero* and a number of spin-offs, the line between the geeky computer nerd playing video games and the hip rocker is also being blurred. Video games, it seems, can be cool—and, more importantly, are also social, even educational.

This trend toward more active, social video games has been helped by game consoles like Nintendo's Wii, in which players can participate against each other in a range of sports.

But what *Guitar Hero* also represents is an important shift in entertainment in which convergence starts to come into its own. Because of the popularity of *Guitar Hero*, downloads of songs for the game have risen, creating new revenue opportunities for the sagging music industry.

Furthermore, there has been some evidence of greater interest, among *Guitar Hero* players, in learning an actual musical instrument. As some bars replace their karaoke nights with *Guitar Hero* nights, it also brings the video game out of the living room and into the street, as it were, acting as a spur for further social interaction—which goes against the stereotype of video games as adding to social isolation.

such as swing, enjoy a short resurgence. Mainstream country music has come to sound much more like country rock, for example, and some hit songs appear on both pop and country charts. One element that has changed the music industry in the past twenty years is the development of MTV, or music television.

■ ■ ■ MUSIC AND MTV

The launch of MTV in 1981 provided a new venue for promoting music. The twenty-four-hour format required many music videos to fill the airtime, and music videos changed the nature of music promotion and, to a large extent, what artists or bands were promoted. Suddenly, it became just as important how a band looked on television as how they sounded.

Music videos have often been criticized by various groups as encouraging sexual or violent imagery, sexism, antisocial behavior, and even Satanism. Studies have shown that viewers like watching music videos more than just listening to music, and when controversial lyrics are combined with controversial video, it is feared that young people may be internalizing socially unacceptable messages.

Researchers have reported that between 40 percent and 75 percent of music videos contain sexual imagery, although it is generally mild and nongraphic. Sexism remains strong, however, with over half the women dressed provocatively but only 10 percent of the men dressed so and women much more likely to be treated as sex objects or dominated by men than the other way around.[5]

Dave Matthews has established a reputation as a popular artist whose songs are hard to classify by a specific genre.

New music channels began on cable in the 1990s, including channels devoted to specific genres, such as country music or heavy metal. Because any music video must have interesting visual elements throughout the entire song, it is interesting to ponder what effect music videos may have on slower-paced songs that do not lend themselves to the typical quick cuts.

Books and Magazines

Despite the perception among many adults that young people do not read anymore, "reading for fun" is still a surprisingly popular activity among young people (although one suspects "reading for school" may fall far lower on the list).

The portability and inexpensiveness of magazines and to some extent books, when compared to other entertainment media, will likely make them a part of the entertainment landscape for quite some time. Novels can engage media consumers in their stories like few other media can, since characters, scenes, and situations are pictured in readers' minds. Every genre is available, appealing to a variety of literary (and not so literary) tastes.

Magazines help guide people in their social behavior and to better understand what the culture deems standard or normal. Not only are they more visually appealing than newspapers, their length allows more depth in stories.

Of course, reading is not confined to print media; much reading takes place online now as well, and there are even novels for cell phones. Although the articles may be shorter and there may be different reading patterns than with print media, reading is still an important element of media consumption online.

Entertainment Ethics and Law

With the important role that entertainment plays in our lives, an especially sensitive issue that media-entertainment companies must constantly deal with is how to mitigate and eliminate messages of negative social values or harmful stereotypes their content may contain. Even apparently minor decisions, such as how some characters dress compared to others, may promote gender or ethnic stereotyping, for example. Repeated viewings of certain ethnic groups or minorities in a bad light or in stereotypical "bad guy" roles may cause an unconscious shift in attitudes among some viewers that all such people are bad.

Portrayals of sex and violence have often been issues by which groups criticize media companies. Although the old adage "sex sells" is usually true, entertainment companies have an ethical responsibility not to pander to baser instincts among the public simply to increase their revenues.

Despite some progress in more balanced, fully developed portrayals of women and ethnic groups, there are still many instances in which media companies fall short. For at least three reasons, the media industries in the United States have often sought to regulate themselves. First, self-regulation can be a responsible form of self-discipline, which can improve the media's actions. Second, and as a consequence, in the court of public opinion self-regulation can improve the media's reputation by signaling a willingness to act responsibly. Third, self-regulation can solve or reduce problems before they lead to unwanted government regulation.

Comic books showing graphic horror and violence in the 1950s were said to cause juvenile delinquency. As a result, ratings systems were developed, similar to what we see today in other entertainment media.

■ ■ ■ THE CENSORSHIP OF COMICS

A fascinating historical and continuing case of censorship is the comic book. Popular among children and adults, comics have long been under the scrutiny of critics in both government and the public. Criticism and censorship reached a peak in the

McCarthy-era 1950s when psychologist Fredric Wertham, MD, published his book, *Seduction of the Innocent*, which contended that the reading of violent and sexually graphic comic books caused juvenile delinquency and worse. Wertham's book captured public and media attention and quickly led to intense pressure from the government and other groups to curtail the graphic sexual and gruesome violent content of comic books, especially the horror comics such as *Tales from the Crypt*, *Haunt of Fear*, and *Vault of Horror*.

Wertham based his argument on his own observations of juvenile delinquents. He found that many delinquents read a lot of comic books, especially horror comics. He also found that many of these kids were poor readers. Wertham concluded that reading comics, especially horror comics, caused both juvenile delinquency and illiteracy. Although his reasoning and methodology were flawed, in response to Wertham's claims the U.S. Senate conducted a full-scale investigation in 1954 into the nature and effects of comics on children.

The Senate did not take any formal legal action against the comics industry. Instead, a consortium called the Association of Comics Magazine Publishers formed the Comics Code Authority (CCA), a sort of industry censorship review board. The CCA began reading every comic book published and effectively put a ban on sexual content and the most graphic material popular in many horror comics of the day, including torture, sadism, and detailed discussion of criminal acts. A CCA seal of approval then was emblazoned on the cover of acceptable comics. As a result of the CCA action, many of the most graphic horror comics were put out of business.

■ ■ ■ THE HAYS CODE

Hays Code
....
A code established in 1930 by the movie industry to censor itself regarding showing nudity or glorifying antisocial acts in movies. Officials for the Hays Office had to approve each film that was distributed to a mass audience.

Some early films, especially some of the black-and-white films prior to 1920, contained considerable nudity or near nudity, particularly some of the biblical films, such as those created by D. W. Griffith (e.g., the 1919 *Fall of Babylon*). Hollywood's original vamp, actress Theda Bara, was often shown in revealing costumes.[6] Although the nudity and sexuality were popular with many early filmgoers, some conservative groups were outspoken in their criticism, especially of bare-breasted women or women dressed in revealing clothing, and the movie moguls feared the possibility of government censorship. As a result, they joined forces to create their own industry self-censorship in the form of the Hays Office.

The office produced what was called the **Hays Code** in 1930, outlining many dos and don'ts for the film industry. The Hays Code articulated three general moral principles. First was the intention to prevent production of any motion picture that would "lower the moral standards of those who see it. Hence the sympathy of the audience should never be thrown to the side of crime, wrongdoing, evil or sin." Second, every picture was to present "correct standards of life, subject only to the requirements of drama and entertainment." Third, no picture was to ridicule "natural or human" law.

The code went on to prescribe the proper depiction of content in twelve specific areas, including criminal activity, sex, and religion. By today's standards, many of these prescriptions seem quaint—though well intentioned—and some are offensive, racist, or at least politically incorrect. In some ways, the Hays Code was little more than a public relations stunt to

The Hays Code was created to censor movies that depicted violence and sex.

deflect criticism, and some moviemakers treated the code as little more than a joke, initially.

However, if a movie did not have the stamp of approval from the Hays Office, it might not receive mass distribution by a major studio—a chance most producers were not willing to take. In the mid-1960s, after a series of Supreme Court cases involving obscenity, and a general change in public mores regarding depictions of sexuality, the Hays Code underwent a major revision and was not enforced as stringently as it had been. By 1968 the movie rating system of G, M, R, and X, today modified as G, PG, PG-13, R, NC-17, and X, had essentially replaced the Hays Code. The movie ratings code has served as a model for industry self-censorship "ratings" for music, television, and video games.

■ ■ ■ STEREOTYPES IN ENTERTAINMENT

Because entertainment plays such an important part in our lives and is a powerful force for transmitting cultural values, the depiction of stereotypes in the media can be especially hurtful or damaging to groups. At the turn of the twentieth century, minstrel shows were popular in vaudeville, with white actors made up in "blackface" to depict African Americans, often in demeaning or clownish roles. Jewish minstrel shows were also popular and similarly played on popular stereotypes of the time.

Asians and Asian Americans have faced both positive and negative stereotypes over the years. As many Asians immigrated to the United States in the nineteenth and early twentieth centuries, they were often depicted in the mass media in negative ways. Today they are often touted as a "model minority" because of the achievements of many Asian American young people in school and professions. However, hidden racist stereotypes still appear far too often in the media, such as an April 2004 full-page feature in *Details* magazine entitled "Gay or Asian?" that used dozens of stereotypes of both gays and Asians.

Some may wonder what harm some good-natured joking about stereotypes can do, especially when it is meant to be humorous or simply to entertain, such as the *Details* feature. However, that is exactly the danger with stereotypes in entertainment—precisely because the underlying stereotypes are taken for granted, they are influential in molding norms and beliefs about certain groups, especially when the primary exposure to those groups comes through the media.

Stereotypes related to Italian Americans are a good case in point. According to a Zogby poll in 2003, 78 percent of teenagers associated Italian Americans with either criminal activity or blue-collar work. Another poll showed that 74 percent of adult Americans believed that Italian Americans had some connection to organized crime.

These kinds of misperceptions influence in subtle and sometimes not-so-subtle ways how we interact with the groups that are stereotyped, and the misperceptions no doubt come from the number of media depictions and popular movies and shows in which Italian Americans are shown as gangsters or part of organized crime.

Some Indian tribes have protested the use of depictions of Indians as sports-team mascots.

Web Link >>>
Stereotype This
www.stereotypethis.com

Because of the popularity of entertainment, there is a strong inclination in other fields, such as advertising and journalism, to emulate certain entertainment values. However, this can undermine the role that a profession like journalism plays, in terms of informing the public.

Entertainment may have a more insidious effect in the digital realm, making it easier than ever for people to get the kind of entertainment they want when they want it. This could come at the expense of personal interaction or discussion of important social topics, as the public settles into a more passive mode of media consumption rather than produsage. Similarly, produsage efforts by some people online may be more focused on copying what is seen among mainstream entertainment rather than trying to create something truly new and original.

The rapid media feedback loop seen online is especially prominent with entertainment. **User-generated content** (UGC) or a viral video can quickly be copied by a mainstream entertainment company for its own purposes, making the public quickly tire of the latest "new thing." Something that may have been creative and original can quickly look old or uncool if adopted and widely copied by mainstream entertainment companies.

The prevalence of entertainment can also affect the nature of our interactions online. Whether we spend our time interacting with others in heated discussions about political policies or in arguments about whether a popular TV-show character should have changed her hairstyle has repercussions for the quality of knowledge we have about our world and our ability to change it. If our worldview is largely defined by the types of entertainment we consume, then our discussions with others will be similarly limited, no matter how active we are online.

Entertainment of course does not exist in a vacuum. It has a complex relationship with both journalism and, especially, the worlds of advertising and public relations, which we will see in the next chapter.

user-generated content (UGC)
Media content that has been created by consumers or audience members, including videos, music, or other forms of content.

DISCUSSION QUESTIONS

1. Count the maximum number of TVs, VCRs, stereos, CD players, and other media devices your family had at a certain time. How do your numbers compare with the national average? If you had a higher-than-average number of media devices, discuss what factors led to getting these and the effect they had on you and family life after getting them. If you had fewer-than-average numbers of media devices, discuss what effect that had on family life.

2. Keep a daily log for one week of how many conversations you have with friends, classmates, and family that have to do with media entertainment. This can include talking about an episode of a previous night's TV show, an upcoming movie, or any entertainment-related area. Write down when the conversations took place and how long they lasted and compare your log with classmates.

3. Keep a daily log of how much time you actually spend with media entertainment, either watching TV, listening to the radio, playing video or computer games, or going to concerts, sporting events, or movies. Compare this amount of time with the time spent discussing the entertainment event and share the information with classmates.

4. Make a short list of some of your favorite TV series or movies and see if you can research where the ideas for these shows or movies came from. Are they remakes of much older shows? If they are original, what influences did the producer or filmmaker have?

5. Most people do not like to watch a movie or read a book more than once or twice. However, people can often play the same video game for hours on end, repeating levels and characters. Why do you think this is so?

6. How might negative ethnic or gender stereotypes have a greater impact on players of video games than on viewers of TV shows?

7. Discuss whether you think the movie rating system, and the music and video game rating systems that is based on it, is a good thing and useful.

. . . .

FURTHER READING

Television Disrupted: The Transition from Network to Networked TV, 2nd ed. Shelly Palmer (2008) York House Press.

Stay Tuned: Television's Unforgettable Moments. Joe Garner (2002) Andrews McMeel Publishing.

Cinema Year by Year 1894–2002. David Thomson (2002) DK Publishing.

Noise/Music: A History. Paul Hegarty (2007) Continuum.

Genre in Popular Music. Fabian Holt (2007) University of Chicago Press.

Changing the Game: How Video Games Are Changing the Nature of Business. David Edery, Ethan Mollick (2008) FT Press.

Paid to Play: An Insider's Guide to Video Game Careers. Alice Rush, David Hodgson, Bryan Stratton (2006) Prima Games.

Trigger Happy: Videogames and the Entertainment Revolution. Steven Poole (2000) Arcade Publishing.

Advertising and Public Relations

CHAPTER OBJECTIVES

In this chapter we will:

- Provide an overview of strategic communications.

- Explore the theoretical foundations of advertising and public relations.

- Examine the purpose and form of advertising and public relations.

- Outline the history and structure of the advertising and public relations industries.

- Identify the impact of digital technologies on advertising and public relations.

- Review the ethical challenges of persuasive communications.

- Discuss the role of evaluation research in advertising and public relations.

12

The two men dressed as scientists stand amidst a spray of fountains created to imitate the water-fountain display at the elegant Bellagio Hotel in Las Vegas. The fountains in the video, however, are created entirely by dropping rolls of Mentos into two-liter bottles of Diet Coke.

Fritz Grobe and Stephen Voltz videotaped what is now known as the Extreme Diet Coke and Mentos Experiments (Experiment #137 to them) on Saturday, June 3, 2006. They uploaded the video to their site, EepyBird.com, and sent the link to one person to watch. By Monday, *The Late Show with David Letterman* called and wanted them on the show to perform the experiment there.

From those beginnings, Grobe and Voltz performed variations of their Mentos and Diet Coke experiments for audiences around the world throughout 2006. The video spawned countless imitations, also posted online, as well as websites and comments suggesting which sodas and which types of Mentos work best (apparently fruit-flavored Mentos do not work as well because of their coating).

None of this was done as part of a sponsorship deal with either Mentos or Diet Coke, yet the publicity around their experiments was worth countless advertising dollars. Mentos responded more enthusiastically to this unique use of their candies than did Diet Coke, even bringing the two to the company headquarters for a factory tour.

This is but one example of how viral videos online have helped change the equation involving advertising, public relations, and the public.

Many diverse forces shape the media of mass communication. Among the most important are advertising and public relations, which can be categorized broadly as types of strategic communications. This chapter examines the nature and history of these two essential media industries and how they are adapting to the shifting nature of mass communication in the age of digitization and convergence.

Advertising has traditionally been the method by which companies or stores reach a mass audience, utilizing the distribution system that newspapers or electronic media outlets have created. Public relations has typically involved managing the public "persona" of a company, also using media outlets and their mass-distribution networks.

In a digital, networked world, however, the power for almost anyone to distribute information cheaply has been greatly enhanced. This would seem to indicate that a company, especially a large, well-known company such as Coca-Cola,

News conferences or other scheduled announcements by companies or government officials are examples of "pseudo events," or events designed to attract media attention.

The Powers of Persuasion

Test how savvy you are about advertising, branding, and public relations.

1. (T/F) Branding is important for corporations but not for nonprofit organizations or educational institutions.
2. (T/F) Advertising has become less important as a revenue source with online media compared to traditional media.
3. What is product placement? Can you name an example and the product?
4. What is the main source of advertising revenue for newspapers, display ads or classifieds?
5. What does CPM stand for, and why is it important?
6. What are SEM and SEO? Why are they important?
7. (T/F) Before the twentieth century, there was often little difference in newspapers between public relations and news content.
8. What is an astroturf campaign?
9. What war was "sold" to the American public partly through unethical public relations techniques?
10. How does a viral video work?

for example, could reach audiences directly. Although this is happening in some cases, it is not as common as one would think.

Just as everyone can be an online journalist, filmmaker, or musician with the digital tools available today, but does not necessarily want to be one or have the skills for it, advertising and PR professionals are experts in their fields but do not fully understand strategic communications and how the media works. This is where the expertise of strategic-communications professionals is used. The modes of communication and distribution structure may change, but the ability to reach audiences with powerful messages will not, nor will the knowledge of how to craft persuasive and memorable messages or how to create an enduring brand or company image.

Advertising is the most prevalent form of media content. This can easily be seen in print media, where the typical **news hole**, or portion of the product devoted to editorial or news content, is just about one-third of the total space. In other words, two-thirds of most newspapers and magazines are filled with advertisements (not including advertising inserts). And even though most television programming time is devoted to content rather than commercials, consider the number of times the audience sees the same commercial during the course of a program.

Advertisements, whether in print, in the form of commercials on broadcast radio and television, as classifieds, on billboards, or online, provide the basic financial revenue that pays for the creation of media content. As advertising decreases, newspaper publishers have had to make serious cuts elsewhere in their company, including laying off journalists and reducing the number of pages in the paper.

news hole
Typically used with newspapers, it is the amount of total space available after advertisement space has been blocked out.

Public relations also plays a vital role today. Although public relations is really about managing relations between organizations or people and their relevant publics, much of the public relations function involves media relations in the form of publicity and other influences on media. Many organizations have historically sought to influence media content and thereby public opinion. They have done everything from generating publicity to staging events to get the attention of the press. Further, most news organizations are dependent on the public relations function of organizations—whether corporate, government, or not-for-profit groups—for information. This includes everything from scheduled announcements and research studies or reports, such as government reports on the economy, to corporate financial statements and information during crises.

Strategic Communications

Advertising and public relations represent two types of strategic communications. Strategic communications is a broad field that is being redefined today, thanks in part to the changes that digital technology is bringing to the communications industry.

Strategic communications can refer to advertising, PR, branding, and even aspects of organizational communications such as internal communications or corporate communications. At the heart of strategic communications is the goal of delivering a persuasive message to an intended audience with some desired effect. Let us break down this definition into its parts and examine each more closely.

Delivering a message can take place through any number of media channels. We will be looking primarily at mass communications and online communications in this chapter, but it can be done at a companywide meeting, face-to-face, or any number of other ways. Part of what makes strategic communications challenging is knowing which channel will be most effective for a particular message to a particular audience. Some companies have been heavily criticized in the media for delivering notices of layoffs via emails rather than telling employees face-to-face.

Making a message persuasive is another challenging task. Persuasion has been studied by many notable researchers over the years, and there are still no clear answers on why some people find a particular message persuasive and others do not. Some may be persuaded by appeals to logic or lists of facts, and others may be persuaded because their favorite movie star endorses a product.

Perhaps the most important factor is the audience, or, more accurately, the need to know and understand the audience. Without knowledge of who audience members are, what they think and feel, their likes and dislikes, and a host of other factors, it is virtually impossible to know what will be persuasive and what the best channel will be to reach them. A large direct mail campaign via email does little good if your audience communicates primarily through IM or text messaging or only checks email once a week.

Finally, the whole purpose of using strategic communications is that you want audience members to act in a certain way. Perhaps you want them to change their behavior, such as to stop smoking or to eat healthier, or maybe you want them to donate to a cause or buy your product—or even buy more of your product—or maybe to just register on a website or pick up the phone and call their congressperson.

The desired action connects to the other components very clearly. What kind of message will be most persuasive to the audience—what is most likely to change people's attitude so they take the desired action? Will a personalized message be the most effective channel, or will an advertising campaign on TV or in print be the best way to reach and convince them? How should the message be crafted and what tone should it use?

Note that these elements apply equally to an executive deciding how to propose company expansion to the board of directors as they do to a company launching a new product or to a nonprofit trying to get more volunteers or donors. Here we will focus on advertising and PR and leave corporate communications aside, but remember that the principles are largely the same.

■ ■ ■ PERSUASIVE COMMUNICATIONS

As noted, a crucial aspect of strategic communications is the need to persuade an audience. The most effective campaigns use persuasive techniques that encourage audiences to agree with the persuader's point in an apparently "natural" or commonsense way. In other words, members of the audience may have started out thinking one thing before being exposed to the message, but afterward think differently, often feeling like they came to the conclusion themselves. However, they have been persuaded.

We may think of persuasive communications as a modern phenomenon that developed along with the rise of mass communications, but in fact it has roots that go much further back in history, at least to the time of the Greek philosophers.

At that time called **rhetoric**, it was one of the three classical areas of learning that any educated person should know, along with logic and grammar. The Sophists, a group of Greek philosophers focused entirely on rhetoric, taught their knowledge to whoever could pay them. For Sophists, the truth of a matter was largely unimportant—they might even claim that truth is in the eye of the beholder—and the most important aspect of an argument was whether one could persuade others by whatever means possible.

rhetoric
....
One of the ancient arts of discourse, it involves using language to persuade others.

Despite strong objections by the likes of Plato, Socrates, and Aristotle that truth should prevail over rhetoric, its importance in politics, business, and life continues to this day. Some may even argue that in an age when more people can speak publicly than ever, the ability to be persuasive and to make your voice heard above the others is now even more important than it was.

There are at least two dozen major modern scientific theories of persuasive communication and audience decision-making. These theories help explain or provide models of how persuasive communications work, as well as guide the strategic communication campaigns that advertising and public relations professionals create and carry out via the media.

At the core of most theories of persuasion are certain assumptions about how we think and feel and how those thoughts and emotions affect the way we act. The assumptions can be broadly categorized as follows:

1. People's behavior and actions are somehow linked to their cognitions about the world, which generally include attitudes, beliefs, and values, as well as their general knowledge and social influences.

2. How people process information about the world (thinking deeply about issues or simply taking someone's word about issues) can play an important part in what types of messages they find most persuasive.

3. A persuader's credibility, authority, and attractiveness all play important roles in successful persuasion.

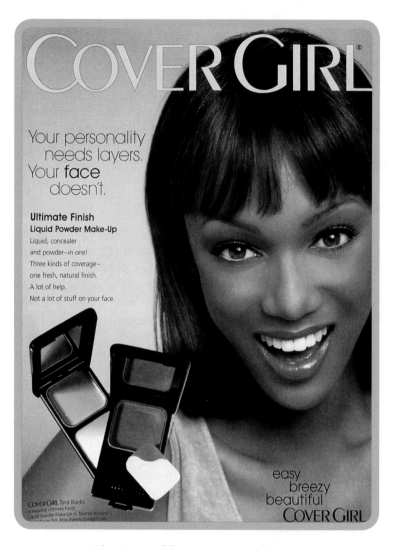

Advertisers carefully consider a range of factors
in making ads as persuasive as possible.

One theory of note that takes a different viewpoint from most theories of persuasion is called the **theory of cognitive dissonance**. This theory says that we act first and then rationalize or create reasons for our behavior afterward in order to fit our actions into our self-perceived notions of who we are. The theory of cognitive dissonance helps explain a range of otherwise puzzling behaviors, such as why freshmen will subject themselves to humiliating circumstances in the form of hazing rituals to join a fraternity or sorority.

■ ■ ■ THE ROLE OF MEDIA IN PERSUASION

Media of course play an important role in persuasion. One obvious way is that media channels are the means by which the public becomes aware of a product or issue. Getting an advertisement on national television that is seen by millions of people at once may be an effective way to raise awareness of a product. However, simple awareness is not enough. Too often, marketers assume that once people know about their product (or cause, or whatever), then they will want to buy it or participate. This is not the case.

The media often have their own kind of credibility. An appearance on national television may lend someone a new air of authority. Receiving a link to a YouTube video from a trusted friend is more likely to persuade you to watch the video than if you received it from someone you did not know. The media play such a role in creating and establishing reputations of famous people that now there are many celebrities who are known simply for being celebrities, not for notable singing or acting careers.

Underlying all this is the notion that mediated communication has some effect on our thoughts that can lead to changes in behavior. Although the **direct effects model** of media influence has been largely disproved, there is still a lurking sense that media can influence the public in some way. From this assumption, it is further assumed that media-based communications campaigns can be strategically designed to produce the kind of attitude and behavior shifts that are desired by persuaders.

Advertising

Advertising is an ancient form of human communication generally designed to inform or persuade members of the public with regard to some product or service. In the modern age, advertising has taken its basic shape as sponsored, or paid-for, communication designed to inform and persuade the receiver of a message to buy a good or service, to accept a point of view, or to act in some fashion desired by the sender of the commercial message.

Print and electronic media have developed around this advertising model and in effect are in the business of selling mass audiences to advertisers who wish to reach them. From a business perspective, the media exist primarily as the means to gather an audience. However, many communications professionals, although recognizing an element of truth in this view, would counter that audiences will not gather if media content is not interesting, useful, or entertaining to them in some way.

Media organizations determine how much they can charge advertisers for space in their publication or airtime on their station based on the audience reached or delivered to the advertiser. In broadcasting, this number is called the **rating**. In print and online media, it is called the **CPM**, or **cost per thousand** audience members. The online model is still evolving, however, and CPM may include the cost per thousand page views or unique visitors to a site or web pages. In **performance-based advertising**, also used online, advertisers only pay for results of an advertisement, such as actual click-throughs to the advertiser's site, rather than the total page views a site has. One of the largest areas of online advertising has become **search engine marketing**, discussed in more detail later.

Advertising rates within media or specific media vehicles vary as well according to the size and quality of the target audience. In radio, for example, the most expensive time to purchase advertising is "a.m. and p.m. drive time." These are the morning and afternoon prime radio time slots for advertising and programming, when audiences are at their peak. An advertiser for a youth-oriented product may choose to show its commercial on prime-time MTV rather than a late-night slot on a network because, although the viewing audience is smaller than on a broadcast network, it is a more targeted audience that is more likely to want the product.

Jade Goody used her fame as a reality TV star in the UK to publicize the need for women to test for cervical cancer, which she eventually died from.

search engine marketing

Paying for certain key words in order to show up high in rankings in search engines such as Google or Bing.

In its earliest form, advertising was conducted as face-to-face, word-of-mouth communication in which buyers and sellers negotiated for the best bartered arrangement for a good or service. In ancient Egypt advertisements for products and services were written on papyrus and posted in common, public areas for passersby to see. The advent of the printing press in the fifteenth century gave rise to advertising in mass-communication settings, usually in the form of posters, flyers, or broadsheets. Broadsheet advertisements were a popular technique to attract people to emigrate to the New World. Colonists in the eighteenth and nineteenth centuries could obtain information from advertising about everything from where to buy groceries and patent medicines to when a ship was sailing.

Advertising was used heavily, early in American history, to attract settlers to new lands.

Greater Prominence of Advertising

By the mid-1800s, advertising had become a mainstay for U.S. firms marketing their products and services. With the advent of the penny press, newspaper publishers relied more heavily on advertising revenue to make up for the lost revenues in subscription income. Advertisements became more prominent and were designed to stand out better from surrounding editorial content. Individuals also used advertising to promote their unique services. In 1856, publisher Robert Bonner ran the first full-page advertisement in a newspaper to promote his own literary paper, the *New York Ledger*.[1] At this time there were no standards in advertising, and medicinal advertisers often made extravagant and untrue claims as to the curative powers of the products they were selling.

The early twentieth century brought the rise of mass-produced, packaged goods and the automobile industry. Today, the automobile industry is the largest advertiser, followed by retail, business, and consumer services. Advertising for cigarettes and other tobacco products grew during the twentieth century, but not without criticism. In 1919, the magazine *Printer's Ink* warned against "an insidious campaign to create women smokers," in reaction to the portrayal of women smoking in cigarette ads.

Development of the Advertising Agency

Early advertisers bought newspaper space and primarily targeted local audiences. It was not until the 1860s that advertising went national via nationally distributed monthly magazines.

Among the most successful early sellers of newspaper advertising space was Volney B. Palmer, who created both the first advertising agency in 1841 and the long-standing business model for the ad-agency industry. Palmer provided his advertising clients with circulation data, gave them copies of the ads, and deducted an **ad-agency commission** from the advertising fee to the publication as compensation for his effort.

ad-agency commission

A percentage amount of the cost of an advertisement that is taken by the advertising agency that helped create and sell the ad.

Advertising in the early twentieth century helped make it acceptable for women to smoke cigarettes.

The advertising business grew quickly as the penny press grew into a mass-circulation medium. By the 1860s, there were more than twenty advertising agencies in New York City. N. W. Ayer & Partners, an advertising agency founded in 1869 by Francis Wayland Ayer, bought Palmer's firm, and the trend toward consolidation of the advertising business had begun. Ayer built on Palmer's basic media billing model, which charged clients a fee for placing ads in newspapers and magazines, and he established a standardized ad-agency commission: 15 percent of the total media billings.

N. W. Ayer also set the standard for creative services, with some of the most well-known ad slogans of the twentieth century, including the De Beers tagline, "A diamond is forever," AT&T's "Reach out and touch someone," and Camel cigarettes' "I'd walk a mile for a Camel." N. W. Ayer & Partners is now part of Bcom3 Group, Inc., one of the world's largest advertising firms.

The new electronic media in the twentieth century drew heavily on the resources of the advertising industry, which effectively used radio and television to promote a wide variety of products and services to audiences throughout the United States and internationally. Television quickly surpassed print media as the main vehicle for reaching a national advertising market.

Growth of Commercial Television

There was never any widespread debate on whether television should be publicly funded or run on a commercial basis, as there had been in the early days of radio. Three of the four early TV networks were affiliated with the radio networks, and it was assumed that television would be supported by advertising just as radio was. The questions raised were not about whether to support television through advertising but about the best way to do it.

Web Link >>>
Television Bureau of Advertising
www.tvb.org/

Commercials quickly became a mainstay on television. The year 1948 established an early high watermark for advertising, with 933 sponsors buying TV time—an increase of 515 percent over 1947. *Variety* reported in 1957 that during a typical week, viewers saw 420 commercials totaling five hours, eight minutes. In the early days of television, advertisers often sponsored whole shows and had their names included as part of show titles, such as *Texaco Star Theater*.

The Television Bureau of Advertising was also launched in the mid-1950s, responding to the emergence of television as the leading medium for advertising. The bureau is a not-for-profit trade association of America's broadcast-television industry and provides a variety of tools and resources to support the use of television as an advertising medium.

Tony Schwartz was a master of audiovisual techniques in advertising.

One of the most talented advertising professionals of the audiovisual realm was Tony Schwartz (1923–2008). Schwartz had a career in advertising spanning most of the twentieth century. He was the master of using implied messages to their greatest effect. He achieved perhaps his greatest fame in the realm of political advertising for a spot that ran in 1964 known harmlessly as "the Daisy Spot," which cleverly implied that Republican presidential candidate Barry Goldwater, known as a war hawk, would likely get the United States embroiled in a nuclear war. Political communication scholar Kathleen Hall Jamieson considers the Daisy Spot to be among the most powerful political ads ever aired.[2]

Commercial developments have continued to reshape the TV landscape. In the 1960s, ABC extended the station break between programs from thirty to forty seconds in order to increase its profits, and other networks soon followed suit. Within a few years the breaks had become even longer, and standard commercial lengths had reached one minute.

By 1971, the networks had further increased profits by cutting the standard commercial length from sixty seconds to thirty seconds without reducing rates a corresponding 50 percent. Networks began the practice of advertising "piggybacking," or running messages for two related products from one company in the same one-minute commercial.

In 1969, New York's WOR-TV became the first station to air a program made up of exclusively commercial messages. This is called paid programming, or an **infomercial**. With the growth in cable channels and need to fill programming time, along with the smaller audiences cable attracts, there has been a rise in infomercials.

Also in 1969, the U.S. Supreme Court applied the **Fairness Doctrine** to cigarette advertising, giving antismoking groups access to "equal time" on the air to reply to tobacco commercials. The FCC also issued a Notice of Proposed Rulemaking to ban cigarette ads on TV and radio, as Congress debated the issue. Tobacco companies finally agreed to stop advertising cigarettes on the air. In 1970, a congres-

infomercial
....
Also called paid programming, this is a thirty- or sixty-minute television show that seeks to sell a product and that usually involves a celebrity spokesperson and testimony from customers about how good the product is.

fairness doctrine
....
Adopted by the FCC in 1969, it required broadcasters to seek out and present all sides of a controversial issue they were covering. It was discarded by the FCC in 1987.

sional ban on radio and TV cigarette advertising took effect, costing the broadcast business roughly $220 million in advertising.

The hard-liquor industry had a voluntary ban on TV advertising for sixty years, although that ban began breaking down in 2001 when NBC ran a vodka ad on late-night television. The ad drew such a backlash that NBC stopped airing the ad soon afterward. In February 2009, Absolut vodka broke the voluntary ban and ran an ad during the Grammy Awards, which also drew heated reactions from a number of groups. This did not stop Absolut from continuing to advertise, however, or other hard-liquor manufacturers from following with their ads.

Commercialization of the Internet

Although today we are accustomed to a range of advertisements on the Web, with new ones seemingly created almost every month, the fact is the Internet began as a resolutely noncommercial space. It was created, using taxpayers' money, by engineers and computer scientists who were more motivated by learning and the communication potential for the Internet than by profit, and several years went by before commercialism wedged its way in.

The first email marketing message, commonly called **spam**, after the processed meat (though the inspiration for the name came from a Monty Python comedy sketch), was sent on May 3, 1978, by DEC, a now-defunct computer maker. The message, to all of four hundred people on Arpanet, the precursor to the Internet, now seems almost quaint in comparison to the billions of spam messages sent worldwide today. Immigration lawyers Canter and Siegel sent an email message advertising their services to over six thousand Usenet users in 1994. Despite a harsh backlash from the online community, it is widely held to be the start of the commercialization of the Internet.

The same year, the first advertisements on the Web appeared on Hotwired, the online version of *Wired* magazine. Hotwired offered space on the website to fourteen advertisers in the form of the now-familiar **banner ad**. However, because

spam
Unwanted email sent out by advertisers as a mass mailing.

banner ad
An advertisement across the top of a website and the original form of advertising on the Web.

Popular stars and athletes are often used to help sell products, getting lucrative sponsorship deals from companies.

Me 2.0: The Guide to Branding Yourself

Branding is not only important to multinational companies, but it has become important to individuals as well, says personal-branding guru Dan Schawbel, author of *Me 2.0: Build a Powerful Brand to Achieve Career Success.*

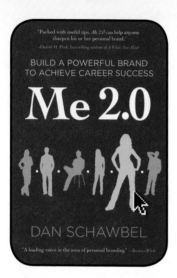

According to Schawbel and dozens of leading technology thinkers he has interviewed, creating a strong personal brand will help define and differentiate the new employee from the competition.

He offers a four-step process for creating a personal brand—discover, create, communicate, and maintain—and includes techniques for using social-media tools to help with the brand.

Schawbel practices what he preaches to the Gen-Y crowd that is his primary audience. His Personal Branding Blog® is ranked as one of the top one hundred marketing blogs and is virtually a case study in itself of how to maximize promotional opportunities by using relevant social-media tools.

It is perhaps no surprise that the age of personal branding has come, given the trends in strategic communications and digital media in recent years. The question that employers may likely face as personally branded potential employees enter the workforce is the same question we typically ask about our corporate brands—how well does image fit reality?

---

online connection speeds were slow in 1994, the ads could not be large graphics and therefore remained fairly small and primarily HTML text.

Today, increased bandwidth has allowed multimedia ads to appear, and advertisers have looked into new types of advertising to further attract consumers' attention. Studies that have tracked consumers online have shown that banner ads have a very low click-through rate, meaning a very low percentage of users—less than 1 percent—actually click on them.

branding
....
The process of creating in the consumer's mind a clear identity for a particular company's product, logo, or trademark.

■ ■ ■ THE RISE OF BRANDING

Developing along with the growing importance of advertising in its various forms, and intertwined with advertising, is the idea of the brand. **Branding** refers to the process of creating in the consumer's mind a clear identity for a particular company's product or trademark. Branding via advertising developed in the 1890s and early 1900s as companies sought to differentiate their products from others in an increasingly cluttered and competitive marketplace. With little differentiation between similar products in terms of what they provided or ingredients they contained, the only way to appear different was to create a memorable brand, or identity, among consumers.

To establish an image of one brand's uniqueness, a catchy slogan and distinctive visual identity are created and then advertised across multiple media, so the desired audience segment or target group gets frequent exposure to the product. Among the first to successfully do this was Campbell's soup, which used the artwork of Grace Weidersein in 1904 depicting "The Campbell's Kids." Campbell's includes Weidersein's artwork in its advertising to this day. Another highly successful advertising campaign was launched in 1970 to promote Coca-Cola. In that year, "Coke" introduced its "I'd Like to Teach the World to Sing" commercial, and the song became an instant hit. Coca-Cola sold a million records featuring a version of the popular advertising jingle.

Some advertising campaigns have been so successful (some would say too successful) that their brand names have become synonymous with the product itself. For example, advertising for Kleenex (introduced in 1924) has branded the product so well that many consumers consider "Kleenex" simply the generic name for facial tissue. This can be both good and bad for the advertiser. On the one hand, this level of branding means that consumers will have extremely high brand-name awareness, but on the other hand, they may go shopping for what they are calling "Kleenex" but actually buy another brand of facial tissue.

Brands are almost always trademarked, and companies can sue individuals or other companies if they believe someone is infringing on their trademark. They can claim that the copycat brand is taking away business from the company by confusing consumers and perhaps hurting the company's reputation in the process if the competitor has inferior products. There are cases of companies zealously protecting their brands, such as Coca-Cola forcing a small café in a remote town in Yunnan Province, China, to change its name from Coca-Cola Café. Yet there are many other cases in which companies have attempted to associate themselves with a more famous brand through visual or written elements.

Protecting a brand is not only about enforcing intellectual property, it is also about the value of a company. Brands have become so important that as much as 70 percent of a company's value may be in its brand rather than in its physical property such as factories or products. Table 12-1 shows the

British Petroleum has successfully rebranded its company with a new logo and a public image as being environmentally friendly.

Brand knockoffs are widespread, especially in Asia.

TABLE 12-1

Some Major Companies and Their Brand Valuations

COMPANY	2002 BRAND VALUE ($ BILLION)	BRAND CONTRIBUTION TO MARKET CAPITALIZATION OF PARENT COMPANY (%)
Coca-Cola	69.6	51
Microsoft	64.1	21
GE	41.3	14
Nokia	30.0	51
Disney	29.3	68
McDonald's	26.4	71

Source: *Business Week*, Interbrand/3P Morgan league table, 2002 estimated brand valuation of some major companies, and the percentage of brand valuation compared to total estimated value. For some company mergers, "buying the brand" may be a major motivating factor in the decision. Brands will become even more important in the digital age, especially in the media industries.

social marketing
....
The practice of using advertising and marketing techniques to persuade people about changing bad or destructive behaviors or adopting good behaviors.

public information campaign
....
Media program funded by the government and designed to achieve some social goal, or what might be called social engineering.

■ ■ ■ SELLING PRODUCTS, SELLING IDEAS

Just as brands can represent a certain image or even lifestyle, the techniques of advertising can be used for more than just selling products or services: they can be used to sell ideas or even political candidates. **Social marketing** applies the lessons learned from years of advertising campaigns and theories of persuasive communications to getting the public to change behaviors for the better through what are called **public information campaigns**.

Social-marketing campaigns often face an uphill battle in changing attitudes, for a number of reasons. First, the behaviors that social marketers are seeking to change, such as underage drinking or smoking, are often considered fun or cool

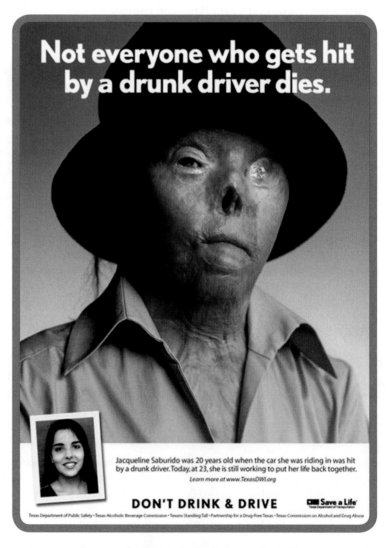

Fear appeals are meant to shock or scare viewers into realizing that they should change their behaviors.

by those engaging in them. Second, determining which advertising channels and types of messages will be most effective for the targeted group can be difficult. Third, ethical questions can sometimes be raised when it comes to which group is deciding what exactly a "prosocial" message is and why other groups may not be targeted. Finally, it can be very hard to determine how effective a social-marketing campaign has been, as its effects will generally not be immediately seen and there may be larger sociocultural forces at work that weaken whatever media messages the target audience sees.

In order to shock the intended audience, some social-marketing campaigns will use **fear appeals** with the hope of changing behavior. Television ads featuring former smokers who have had surgery for throat or mouth cancer, or showing graphic automobile accidents caused by drunk driving, are examples of fear appeals. Fear appeals can be tricky, however. Not only may graphic images offend some viewers, but they may also not be effective for young people who think "that will never happen to me."

One of the more effective social-marketing campaigns in recent years has been the crime-prevention campaign that used the tagline "take a bite out of crime" and featured a cartoon dog, McGruff, dressed as a detective. Using **public service announcements** (PSAs), the series of advertisements covering a range of crime-related issues were widely aired and seen in different media channels. Various surveys have shown a high awareness of the campaign and its anticrime points by adults and children, accompanied by a rise in crime-prevention measures like special locks on doors and windows and security lights.

Social-marketing campaigns play an important role in educating people in developing countries about a range of issues, including safe sex and the risk of AIDS, proper sanitizing techniques to ensure clean water and food and thus prevent disease, and other ways to help the general standard of living. Because of high illiteracy rates and limited access to mass media, such campaigns must use visual symbols in powerful yet easily understandable ways.

■ ■ ■ ADVERTISING CHANNELS

Advertising can of course be seen in a variety of media formats, or channels, and can even include some types that we may not normally consider as mass communications but that are nevertheless important, such as outdoor advertising or direct mail.

Each channel has certain characteristics that have influenced how advertising is done, how it is measured, and what types of advertisements work best. In addition, some channels are more effective at reaching certain types of audiences than others, though of course the type of product or service being advertised also plays a role in determining which audience to target. Here we will look at some of the traditional advertising channels, all of which are still being used, and later we will look at how online advertising is changing some of these.

Print Media

In newspapers and magazines, commercial messages come in either of two forms, **classified advertising** or **display advertising**. Classifieds are short messages appearing together in a special section and posted by individuals and organizations in order to sell specific goods or services.

Classified ads tend to be small and use only text. Because customers pay by the word, or pay a rate up to a certain word limit, messages are usually short and

fear appeals
A type of advertising technique that attempts to scare the audience in order to persuade them, such as anti-smoking ads that show disfigured former smokers.

public service announcement (PSA)
Advertising-like messages for which the media donate time or space to organizations with a worthy purpose that ostensibly benefits the public.

classified advertising
A type of advertising usually found in print media, especially newspapers but also in some magazines, and now increasingly online, that consists of messages posted by individuals and organizations to sell specific goods or services.

display advertising
A type of advertising in print media that usually consists of illustrations or images and text and that can occupy a small section of a page, a full page, or multiple pages. Because of their high costs, display ads are usually bought by large companies or organizations.

Creating persuasive messages can be especially difficult in countries with low literacy rates.

abbreviations are used whenever possible. Despite their small size, the large numbers of classifieds found in most papers have made a significant portion of newspapers' advertising revenue. Online classifieds and auction sites such as Craigslist and eBay have greatly hurt the revenues newspapers get from classified ads.

Display ads are much larger, anywhere from one-eighth of a page to a full page or occasionally foldouts with multiple pages. Display ads often contain images or other graphic elements that help them stand out from other ads.

Costs of running display ads vary by both size and location of the ad on the page and within the publication (back-cover placement is usually the most expensive), as well as whether color is used. If advertisers agree to advertise multiple times, they are able to negotiate rates or receive extra benefits like free color.

A type of display ad that is created to look like an actual article in the publication is called an **advertorial** and usually has tiny print on either the top or the bottom of the page that says "paid advertisement."

Publishing companies create a **rate card**, which lists the various advertising rates based on size and placement of an ad, as well as any discounts available for multiple ads. Usually rate cards are simply used as rough guides, as big advertisers have much leeway to negotiate advertising rates down in the highly competitive print-media world.

Electronic Media

Advertisements on radio or television are called commercials, or "spots," and typically run for thirty seconds. Although the length of time for commercials has gone down and audiences continue to fragment, advertising costs on electronic media are generally high compared to advertising in print media. A primary reason is the larger audience electronic media can command compared to most print outlets. Even large-circulation magazines of over a million readers reach an audience considered relatively small by network-television standards.

Paid programming, or an infomercial, is typically a thirty- or sixty-minute program in which a product is demonstrated or promoted for purchase, oftentimes with endorsement from a celebrity or from highly satisfied consumers, who are typically paid or otherwise compensated. Often actors are used to portray customers.

A concern for a time was something known as **subliminal advertising**. Subliminal advertising supposedly works by flashing messages or images very briefly to produce an unconscious effect on the viewer. Despite early fears, there has been no firm proof that subliminal advertising has any effect at all. Even so, it is illegal.

Another way advertisers get their products noticed is through **product placement**—having products displayed in a show or even used by the characters. This practice also happens in the movies and is increasingly used by advertisers. Product placement has become more important recently as digital video recorders (DVRs) allow viewers to skip commercials.

There is some debate on how effective product placement is in terms of persuading viewers to buy or use a product. Critics argue that most viewers do not notice that product placement is happening and that a product is being advertised, while proponents say that that is exactly what makes it an effective technique.

Perhaps the most famous case of success with product placement occurred with the blockbuster movie *E.T.* The filmmakers approached M&M's to be able to use the famous candy as the snack of choice for E.T., but M&M's refused. So the

Product placement has become a more widely used advertising technique, especially as viewers are better able to skip commercials.

filmmakers used a new candy in the film, Reese's Pieces, and sales of the candy shot up as the film became a global hit.

Outdoor

From billboards to store signs to ads on taxis, buses, and bus stops, advertising messages bombard the public more than most people realize simply because **outdoor advertising** is so ubiquitous. Even wearing brand-name clothing effectively makes the wearer a walking advertisement—and what is good from a company standpoint is that the consumer is paying *it* to advertise its product!

Store signs are some of the oldest forms of public advertising, although their reach is limited to people passing by. Increasingly, municipalities are allowing corporate sponsorship of public vehicles and spaces to help shore up government budgets. Low-power video monitors are allowing advertisements to appear in new public spaces such as above cash registers or in elevators, with news content delivered alongside.

Interactive outdoor advertising is gaining prominence and will continue to grow. Floor-based displays in airports or malls react to activities like footsteps, creating interesting games that people can play and others can watch—all the while engaging with an advertisement.

Direct Mail

Direct mail marketing, commonly called "junk mail" by its recipients, includes ads for everything from lower insurance rates to credit card offers to pleas to donate to various charities or subscribe to magazines. Some companies use tactics to make it appear that the recipient has won a drawing or lottery and needs to send in the material to claim the prize.

outdoor advertising
Billboards and other forms of advertising such as on buses or taxis that are done in public.

Interactive advertising appears increasingly in public spaces.

CONVERGENCE CULTURE

The Super Bowl of Advertising

Advertisements for the Super Bowl have practically become a media event in and of themselves, with advertisers jockeying for the most clever or creative ad that will have people talking days after the game. At times it seems that nearly as much analysis is done of the ads as of the game.

Advertisers pay for the privilege, however. A thirty-second commercial spot was $3 million for Super Bowl XLIII in 2009, up from $2.7 million the year before—compared to costs between $90,000 and $200,000 for a thirty-second spot on a regular Sunday-afternoon football game, depending on the network.

During the dot-com boom in the late 1990s, some Internet start-ups used substantial portions of their marketing funding for Super Bowl ads in order to get as much recognition as possible. Most of these companies shut down soon after the boom ended, although GoDaddy.com still survives and advertises during the Super Bowl.

Most Super Bowl ads in recent years have been from large, well-established companies. They often attempt to use humor or present an edgier advertisement than they normally do, but with mixed success. Sometimes the ads can even create controversy. The Snickers ad in Super Bowl XLI (2007) showing two mechanics accidentally kissing while eating each end of a Snickers bar outraged gay groups, who said that it portrayed men kissing as somehow abnormal or awkward. Snickers decided to stop airing the ad after the complaints, though the company never fully apologized.

Direct mail can be a very effective tool for advertisers, partly because the material is being sent to a very specific audience. Many organizations rent their subscriber lists to potential advertisers on a per-thousand basis, and the more detailed demographic data that is needed, the higher the cost for list rental. Advertisers then use these lists to send very targeted messages. The list owners often seed their lists with some false names to ensure that list renters are only using the list one time. Some savvy citizens are using similar techniques to see who is selling their name: subscribing to a magazine using a pet's name, for example. Subsequent mailings that use the pet's name are an indication that the magazine rented the name to other groups.

Telemarketing involves calling people at home to offer them such things as telephone services or new credit cards. Many people find the calls intrusive and annoying and actively screen calls with an answering machine or with functions like caller ID. Telemarketers use a thoroughly prepared script when giving their sales pitches, complete with prepared responses to a range of expected answers.

The Telephone Consumer Protection Act of 1991 is a federal law that lays out strict guidelines on what times telemarketers may call and that allows people to be removed from companies' call lists. Some states have implemented "Do Not Call" registries that serve the same purpose. An improvement in the act in 2008 keeps

Web Link >>>
National Do Not Call Registry
www.donotcall.gov/

numbers permanently on the registry, so that people do not have to renew their phone numbers every few years anymore.

■ ■ ■ ADVERTISING IN A DIGITAL WORLD

Traditionally, 70 percent or more of commercial-media revenues have come from advertising. Media organizations are now seeing their economic foundation transformed by digital technology. Advertisers have more ability to track consumers and to see what kinds of advertisements work best. They are also finding that many traditional advertising techniques do not work well on the Web. Changes in technology and in user behavior online further complicate the picture.

One of the key aspects of the Web compared to other forms of media is the ability to personalize the user experience, and this is just as important for advertisers as it is for media-content companies. Almost all websites leave **cookies** on users' computers, which are small programs that identify specific users and make it easy for companies to see who is visiting their site and where they are going afterward. Any time a website "remembers" a visitor, as when someone registers for a site and then returns days later, that is because of a cookie. Advertisers also use cookies that are placed in their ads, so are able to track users' behavior on their own.

Through the use of cookies and Web-analytics programs, companies are able to tell what page someone came from before arriving at a page with an ad, how long the person spent on that page, whether the person is a first-time or returning customer, and where he or she went after viewing that page. They can even tell what computer operating system a user has, what type of Web browser, and often roughly where the user lives.

Cookies are just one of the new and unique techniques that are being used by media companies and advertisers in the digital world. Even with the development of many new technologies and social media today, some of the "old" digital media still can be remarkably effective.

Email Marketing

Email is still the most used application on the Internet and as such is an incredibly powerful tool for advertising, despite the rapid growth of spam. Like direct mail, email can provide highly targeted audiences. Even better, consumers have the choice to **opt in** to receive emails, showing their willingness to hear from certain companies.

Email also has the advantage of being cheap to produce and send, especially if the message is only text and does not require any design or graphics. The choice between text or graphics is a difficult one for email marketers. Text-only messages can be seen by anyone but are ugly and can be lost in the clutter of other emails. Emails with images may not appear correctly if the recipient has refused to allow such emails—making any design work for naught.

Advertisements placed within emails by the free online services, such as Yahoo Mail, Hotmail, or Gmail, are also lucrative for these companies. Google uses software that scans each email and, based on the words found in the email, inserts ads that it deems most relevant to the topic.

Banner Ads

In the early days of the Web most online advertising tended to follow the traditional advertising formats—particularly the display-ad model commonly found in print.

cookie

Information that a website puts on a user's local hard drive so that it can recognize when that computer accesses the website again. Cookies are what allow for conveniences like password recognition and personalization.

opt in

The practice of letting consumers choose to receive mailings or marketing material by having them check a box on a web site, usually when registering for the site.

Superstitial ads on websites have become more widespread, partly because they are not as obtrusive as other forms of online advertising.

Called banner advertising, these online ads went across the top of a page like a banner and could typically be clicked on to take the user to the advertiser's website.

Today, there are a variety of shapes and sizes of banner ads, including tower ads that take advantage of the tendency for users to scroll down. Such ads may also contain interactive quizzes, video, or other animation.

Because of the tracking capabilities of the Web, it was learned that banner ads generally had a very low click-through rate. In other words, only a small percentage of visitors to a specific page would actually click on the ads. This caused advertisers to doubt the effectiveness of banner ads and seemed to put the budding online advertising industry in a stall.

Pop-Ups, Interstitials, Superstitials, and Video

It was hoped that pop-up ads would help save advertising online, but they are not without their own weaknesses. There are two main types of pop-up ads. One is the traditional pop-up, which appears in a new window when a website is opened, and can be either an **interstitial ad** or a **superstitial ad**. Interstitial ads have proven unpopular among users because they must close the ad browser window in order to see the website they originally wanted to see. To get around this, some advertisers have their pages open to take up most of a page rather than the whole screen. There are also multiple interstitial ads, in which more than one browser window opens, forcing the user to close multiple windows.

Superstitial ads have become more widespread, partly because they are perceived as less obtrusive, and they allow for ads to be created using a variety of multimedia programs and effects. Ads that show up and crawl across a screen or appear in a corner are examples of superstitial ads.

interstitial ad
An online advertisement that opens in a new window from the one the user was in.

superstitial ad
An online advertisement that covers part of the existing screen or moves over part of it without opening a new window.

Ads in videos are still being experimented with, as the Web has only recently become much more video based. It became clear quite quickly, however, that online users did not want to watch a standard thirty-second commercial before watching a short video, so when there are commercials before a video runs, they tend to be ten or fifteen seconds at most. Some sites have been experimenting with overlays at the bottom of screens, like the ones network television uses to advertise upcoming shows.

Classifieds and Auction Sites

As noted earlier, classifieds online have taken a large chunk of the revenue from newspapers. Online classifieds have several advantages over classifieds in print media. First, since there are no space limitations as with a print paper, there is little need to squeeze text to fit within some predefined word and cost limit. Second, geographic limitations are no longer an issue (at least for some products or services), as long as what is being advertised can be shipped or mailed. This vastly increases the potential audience.

Auction sites have also become popular for many of the same reasons, starting with the rise of eBay. Seller rating and review systems, easy online payment methods, and a large number of users at any one time selling and buying have created a thriving marketplace that has proven to be especially useful for small businesses or those wanting to work from home. The popularity of eBay has of course brought many unusual items for sale, including a British man in 2008 who put his entire life for sale after a bitter divorce. The winning bid was about $380,000, quite a bit short of what he was asking.

Search Engine Ads

Search engine advertising has become one of the most important vehicles for advertisers in recent years and promises to only grow more. It is based largely on people's use of search engines as a primary means of finding content. This has made search engines such as Google, Bing, and Yahoo very important as sites that receive many visitors.

There are two main methods of search engine advertising, search engine optimization (SEO) and search engine marketing (SEM). In broad terms, they could be considered as unpaid and paid forms of advertising, respectively, yet they have the same goal: to show up as the first entry in a search engine search.

SEO uses a variety of techniques that involve website design, keywords, and links to try to raise the rankings of a website in a search. In SEM, the advertiser either pays a search engine company for a sponsored link, which is usually clearly labeled as such (with a colored panel or the words "sponsored links"), or buys keywords that are sold at auction. If an advertiser is the highest bidder for a term like "flowers," it pays the search engine company a set amount every time its site is clicked on when that search term is used.

Viral Marketing

Because the Web is such an excellent distribution medium, some of the most successful advertising online has been without the use of advertising agencies or expensive marketing campaigns. Rather, it has come in the form of **viral marketing**, sometimes called buzz marketing, guerrilla marketing, or word-of-mouth (WOM) marketing.

Viral marketing relies on promoting a product, service, or brand through natural communication channels online, in which people spread a message because

viral marketing
Spreading news and information about media content through word of mouth, usually via online discussion groups, chats, and emails, without utilizing traditional advertising and marketing methods.

they want to, not because they are being paid to. Humorous or strange videos often work best for this, but such videos are not always a good fit for all brands, as many viral videos have an unpolished, amateurish quality to them that is part of their appeal. It is also notoriously difficult to determine what type of content will be viral and what will not.

■ ■ ■ THE ADVERTISING BUSINESS

The advertising industry suffered along with the rest of the economy during the recession that started in late 2007, as companies reduced their advertising budgets at the same time they cut back production and laid off workers. The total ad spend for 2008 in the United States was $136.8 billion, down 2.6 percent from the previous year, with newspapers and business-to-business advertising the big losers, down 10.2 percent and 9.7 percent, respectively. The only areas that gained in 2008 were cable television and Hispanic cable television.

As Table 12-2 shows, cable TV now sits atop the media food chain by ad spend. Until the late 1990s, each analog medium's relative share of total advertising rev-

TABLE 12-2

Ad Spending by Medium, 2008

MEDIUM	AMOUNT SPENT ($ BILLION)	CHANGE FROM 2007 (%)
Cable TV	26.57	7.80
Spot TV Top 100	24.24	−0.30
Network TV	22.05	−3.50
National Magazine	18.82	−7.60
Local Newspaper	11.94	−10.20
Internet	8.56	−6.40
Spot Radio	4.81	−4.00
Business to Business	3.89	−9.70
Outdoor	3.62	−5.00
Hispanic TV	2.93	−.40
Syndication TV	2.59	−0.80
Spot TV, 101–210	1.73	−4.60
National Newspaper	1.57	−9.60
National Sunday Supplement	1.11	−1.90
Network Radio	1.09	−3.30
Local Magazine	0.54	−3.70
FSI Coupon	0.43	−5.20
Hispanic Cable TV	0.24	9.60
Local Sunday Supplement	0.1	−2.60

Source: Media Age, 2008

enue had stayed fairly constant. Network television had received the lion's share, most in the form of national advertising. Newspapers were second in total advertising revenues, most in the form of local retail and classified advertising. Magazines were third, with radio a distant fourth.

Internet advertising now is more than double radio advertising and is fast approaching the amount spent on newspaper advertising, which has been falling rapidly in the past few years. There has been some slowing of growth within some types of Internet advertising, but despite the general decline in 2008 because of the recession, Internet ad spending continues to rise. Although advertisers are of course looking to advertise across mediums or channels, the fact is that an increase in ad spending in one medium, such as the Internet, generally means a decrease elsewhere, such as in newspapers. This has made it especially challenging for the main player in the advertising world today, the advertising agency.

■ ■ ■ ADVERTISING AGENCIES

Advertising agencies are the foundation of much of the advertising business. They perform many important functions in helping create and sell advertising across all media, and they provide a vital link between media and the companies seeking to sell a product or service. There are more than five hundred advertising agencies in the United States that employ more than seventy thousand people.

Advertising agencies have four main areas of operation:

1. Creative, which is the area of the business where advertising content is produced, with copywriters and others working under the direction of creative and art directors

2. Client management, which involves working with the client and is usually handled by account executives

3. Media buying, in which media planners and buyers determine and make the purchase of media time or space; the area that traditionally has produced agency revenues

4. Research, which traditionally involves the collection and analysis of data on consumer characteristics and media and purchase behaviors

Although traditional advertising firms still dominate the advertising landscape and have created interactive divisions, a number of Internet-original firms emerged in the late 1990s. Some have survived as boutique or specialized firms, but many have been bought by the larger agencies that need to add interactive expertise. This followed trends toward consolidation seen with traditional advertising agencies.

Today, most of the world's leading advertising agencies are owned by much larger advertising and media-services companies, and ninety of the top one hundred firms have international operations. Most of these firms also operate both advertising and public relations enterprises,

Advertising campaigns for diamonds have helped make the industry a mainstay of romantic gifts.

making them what are called full-service companies. These types of firms handle all aspects of the communications business, from campaign planning to creative execution, media buying, and public relations. On the opposite end of the spectrum are boutique agencies, or small, specialty advertising agencies.

Table 12-3 presents data on the world's five largest advertising and media-services firms, ranked by their annual worldwide billing in 2008, and their advertising and public relations operations.

■ ■ ■ ETHICAL ISSUES IN ADVERTISING

Mass media are a powerful vehicle to influence the public's opinions, even when they are simply trying to inform or educate. It is no wonder, then, that companies spend billions of dollars on advertising each year, trying to persuade people to buy their products. Yet numerous ethical issues have been raised that often give the discerning consumer a jaundiced eye toward advertising, from snake oil salesmen of the nineteenth century to complaints about billboards in the twentieth century, claims against telemarketers for invasion of privacy, and false and deceptive advertising in the mass media, including actors paid to give "customer testimonials."

Advertising is an important part of how goods and services are marketed in a capitalist economy, and some advertising contains useful product information.

TABLE 12-3

World's Five Largest Advertising and Media-Services Companies

AGENCY	MAJOR SUBSIDIARY GROUPS	HEADQUARTERS	WORLDWIDE REVENUES, 2008 ($ BILLION)
WPP	Young & Rubicam Brands Ogilvy Group JWT Grey Group	London, UK	13.6
Omnicom	BBDO DDB Worldwide Communications Group TBWA Worldwide	New York, U.S.	13.36
Interpublic	McCann World Group Draftfcb Lowe	New York, U.S.	6.96
Publicis	Publicis Leo Burnett Worldwide Saatchi & Saatchi	Paris, France	6.90
Dentsu		Tokyo, Japan	2.93

Source: Advertising Age Agency Family Trees, 2009

Advertising is also the economic engine that drives much of the system of mass communication.

The advertising industry has been less successful at regulating itself than the entertainment industry, and usually the government eventually steps in to create new laws or regulations after receiving consumer complaints—or sometimes after long campaigns regarding certain advertising practices. The Federal Trade Commission (FTC) and the Food and Drug Administration (FDA) are responsible for regulating the advertising industry. Industry self-regulation comes from a variety of trade organizations. One of the main ethical issues, from a mass-communication perspective, is false or deceptive advertising.

Deceptive Advertising

In some cases, advertisers give clearly false or deceptive information, but it is illegal only if it misleads the consumer in some material way. Deception in advertising is not always illegal, because in some cases it does not mislead. For instance, ice cubes photographed in a beverage ad may not be actual ice cubes, as they would melt quickly under the photographer's hot lights, but since the fake cubes do not mislead anyone regarding the taste or look of the beverage, it is fine to use them.

In other cases, however, deceptive claims are made with the intention to mislead the consumer. Offering a "going out of business" sales price is misleading if the store is not actually planning on going out of business, for example. A division of the Federal Trade Commission is assigned responsibility to ferret out deception and can force such advertising from mass media or even levy fines.

The FTC once found a commercial for a toy car misleading even though it was not false. The toy was filmed in extreme close-up next to the track, making it appear to move very rapidly and look like a blur on the screen. The FTC ruled that children would be deceived into believing the car actually moves so fast it is a blur, and the ad had to be canceled or modified.

Web Link >>>
FTC
www.ftc.gov

Puffery

Nevertheless, there is great temptation among those selling goods and services, as well as those sponsoring ads, to exaggerate their claims. This is called **puffery**, and it is an ethical and legal gray area (i.e., sometimes allowed, sometimes not). Puffery usually involves an opinion statement about the product. Examples include these familiar advertising slogans:

puffery
. . . .
A type of advertising language that makes extravagant claims about a product without saying anything concrete.

- "The best in the business" (AT&T)
- "The best part of waking up is Folger's in your cup"
- "World's most refreshing light beer" (Coors Light)

In each case, there is no way to prove the truth or falsehood of the claim. The FTC's position is that audiences do not believe the opinion claims of these commercials because they do not perceive them to be factual. Consequently, the FTC permits most puffery, because it feels people are not deceived.

Public Relations

Just as advertising agencies straddle the advertising and media worlds, public relations firms straddle the worlds of companies wishing to promote themselves and of media organizations who can widely distribute their messages.

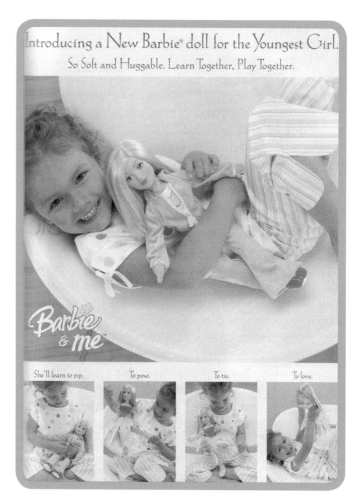

Advertising for children's toys usually portrays the toys as far more fun and exciting than they actually are.

Puffery is a type of advertising that is allowed by the FTC based on the assumption that people do not take it as a statement of fact.

Public relations has been described and defined in many ways. To many journalists, it represents at best a necessary evil. To others, it is far worse: it is the enemy. And to still others, public relations is viewed as a vital part of the three-way relationship among organizations, their publics, and the media. The term "public" refers to the many groups, organizations, and collectives with whom an organization or individual may have some sort of relationship. It will be discussed in more detail in the final chapter on political communication.

Although "the public" is often used to refer to the general population, there are in fact many "publics" with whom an organization might be concerned. For example, a company has many relevant publics, including its employees, consumers, shareholders, activists (who might oppose certain corporate policies), regulators, and of course the media—the primary vehicle by which the general public hears about the company. When a company is in trouble or there is potentially damaging information about it, public relations professionals work to mitigate the negative stories. When there is good news, they seek to promote the news heavily to media outlets.

Edward L. Bernays, the late father of modern public relations, used to say that propaganda was better than impropaganda. The same might be said of public relations. It all depends on how it's done.

Finding the Right Formula for Advertising Regulations

INTERNATIONAL PERSPECTIVES

It may seem like common sense to regulate advertising for harmful products such as tobacco or alcohol, but the reasons for strict regulations of baby formula may not be as apparent.

Unlike the United States, which has very lax advertising regulations for baby formula, most other countries have strict guidelines on what can and cannot be shown on baby-formula packaging and advertising.

One of the biggest restrictions is that no images of a mother feeding her child can be shown. This is not because of religious or cultural restrictions regarding showing a woman's breast, though those exist, but because governments do not want to give the mistaken impression that baby formula is better than breast milk.

The restrictions stem from the 1960s, when Nestle carried out a massive advertising campaign in the developing world to encourage mothers to give their children condensed or evaporated milk (made by Nestle, of course). As a result, countless children became undernourished as mothers stopped breastfeeding or became sick through contaminated water used to mix with the milk.

Corporations have successfully fought such advertising restrictions in the United States but not in Europe and much of Asia. It may seem like a trivial thing, but in countries with low literacy and poor education, especially for women, visual images can have powerful effects.

■ ■ ■ THE HISTORICAL DEVELOPMENT OF PUBLIC RELATIONS

There are some who say public relations is the world's second-oldest profession, but the modern field of public relations has evolved rapidly and in unique ways that connect directly to the rise of mass communications and improvements in communications technologies.

Public relations as a separate, recognized professional field did not develop until the early twentieth century. Prior to that, a number of publishing activities that today we would put into separate categories of journalism or public relations were conducted with little sense of difference between them. Thomas Paine's pro-revolution pamphlets in the 1770s, or the sympathetic writings in newspapers on the Boston Massacre, for example, would be considered public relations or even propaganda, by today's standards, rather than journalism.

During the nineteenth century and early twentieth century, the first stage of public relations emerged. It might best be called the age of **press agentry**. Press agentry

press agentry
....
The practice of getting media attention for a client, often by creating outrageous stunts that would attract journalists.

P. T. Barnum and Tom Thumb.

Web Link >>>
The Museum of Public Relations
www.prmuseum.com/welcome.html

refers to the practice of getting publicity in the press (or other media) for a client. As newspapers developed into a form of mass communications, getting publicity in the press as part of a news story meant that many readers could be exposed to a product or company without the company having to pay for an advertisement.

Press agentry flourished under the practice of Phineas Taylor "P. T." Barnum (1810–1891), the great showman and founder of the famous American circus, which he created in 1870. Barnum used various techniques to communicate with the public and had his greatest success with staged events, or publicity stunts, to attract attention. In the 1830s, Barnum entered the world of promotion, press manipulation, and show business.

Although the term had not yet been coined, it was former journalist Ivy Ledbetter Lee (1877–1934) who was perhaps the first true modern public relations practitioner. Lee was a master of managing the press. He once observed, "Crowds are led by symbols and phrases." He employed a variety of innovative techniques that are staples of modern public relations practice, including press conferences, staged events, and newsreels, which today are known as video news releases (VNRs).

One of Lee's most visible clients was John D. Rockefeller Sr., the founder of the Standard Oil Trust and the world's first billionaire, who managed his companies and employees ruthlessly, even by standards of the day. After Rockefeller had the Colorado state militia put down a miners strike by killing dozens of miners, as well as some women and children, Lee was hired to sway public opinion and manage the likely negative backlash, should the truth come out. Lee produced reports stating that a house fire that had killed women and children was started by an overturned stove, not by the militia, as was actually the case. In response, muckraking journalist Upton Sinclair, author of *The Jungle*, described Lee as "Poison Ivy."

During the years to follow, Lee continued to produce massive amounts of favorable press materials on John D. Rockefeller Sr. Among Lee's successes was his insistence on having photographs and newsreels taken showing Rockefeller handing out dimes to poor children wherever he went. Lee became legendary internationally for his ability to manipulate the media, and in the early 1930s the Nazis in Germany hired Lee to present a more favorable face for the "New Germany" in the United States.[3]

Press agentry features a wide spectrum of PR activities such as special events or stunts. These stunts have ranged from the spectacular to the sublime. In one case, debutantes were invited to march in the 1928 Easter Parade in New York City holding their "torches of freedom"—otherwise known as lit cigarettes—to help get media attention and thereby build public support for women smoking in public, at a time when society frowned upon it. The occasion was sponsored by the American Tobacco Company, manufacturer of Lucky Strike cigarettes, and created by a man many consider the founder of modern public relations, Edward Bernays.

Edward L. Bernays (1891–1995) managed some of the earliest and most famous public relations campaigns of the twentieth century. Trained during World War I as a member of the Foreign Press Bureau of the U.S. Committee on Public Information (CPI), essentially the propaganda arm of the U.S. government, Bernays was a nephew of psychologist Sigmund Freud and often dined with his famous uncle.

Bernays mastered Freud's theories and in fact produced the first Englishlanguage translation of Freud's books. After the war, Bernays applied the principles of both Freudian psychology and social science, a then-budding field, to the strategic influence and shaping of public opinion. He went on to write a classic book titled *The Engineering of Consent*.

Arthur W. Page (1883–1960) was the vice president of public relations for AT&T from 1927 to 1946 and served on many boards of charities and other organizations. He was the first person in a public relations position to serve on the board of a major public corporation. Page helped create ethical guidelines for public relations with his Page Principles, such as "tell the truth," "prove it with action," and "listen to the customer." Today, the Arthur W. Page Society continues his work through a variety of educational programs, networking events, forums for PR executives, and sponsored research initiatives in the field of public relations.

Web Link >>>
Arthur W. Page Society
www.awpagesociety.com/

■ ■ ■ TRENDS IN THE DEVELOPMENT OF PUBLIC RELATIONS

One continuing trend as public relations has developed as a separate profession is the move away from assumptions that the mass audience is passive and mute and toward establishing a dialogue of some kind with the public.

In the earliest forms of PR during much of the nineteenth century, communication was largely asymmetric, going from the public relations agent through the media to the audience. Feedback from the audience was not sought. In the early twentieth century, a limited symmetric model of communications was espoused, with the audience or public brought in to provide feedback to see how effective a campaign may have been in swaying public opinion. Although this had the surface appearance of a dialogue, the organization or PR professional still controlled the flow of communications.

Many of the principles espoused by Page and since adopted by most public relations firms today belong to a **two-way symmetric model** of public relations. This model emphasizes public relations as a system of managing relationships between organizations and individuals and their many publics, internal and external. The media of mass communication are one tool in this system of relationship management. Emphasis is on building mutual understanding and relationships as much as on influencing public opinion.

two-way symmetric model
A model of public relations that emphasizes the profession as a system of managing relationships between organizations and individuals and their many publics.

Research shows that organizational excellence (as defined in terms of accomplishing both short- and long-term organizational objectives) is achieved most effectively when this model of two-way symmetric public relations is practiced. The two-way symmetric model also incorporates the public relations function into the senior management and decision making of the organization, and both formal and informal techniques are used to assess the attitudes, knowledge, behaviors, and intentions of various publics. The symmetric model places a premium on the ethical practice of public relations.

Of course, many practitioners of both public relations and journalism still equate public relations with publicity and media relations, but in the emerging symmetric model this represents merely one activity within the repertoire of tools used in the ethical management of organizational relationships.

One of the best examples of two-way symmetric public relations comes from the story of how Johnson & Johnson handled the well-known Tylenol tampering case in 1982, when seven people died of cyanide poisoning after taking tainted extra-strength Tylenol capsules. After the first reported poisoning in the Chicago, Illinois, area, Johnson & Johnson took immediate steps to prevent further tragedy and established clear and open communication lines with both the media and the public.

Among its efforts, Johnson & Johnson, along with its parent McNeil Consumer Products Company, established a hotline for people to call and offered a $100,000 reward for the arrest and conviction of the person or persons responsible for the deaths. Johnson & Johnson instituted a nationwide recall of all Extra-Strength Tylenol capsules at a cost of some $100 million to remove and destroy all 31 million bottles. The company received thousands of calls requesting information and opened regional poison-control centers to dispense information and assistance.

The capsules were successfully reintroduced into the market in January 1983 with a triple-sealed, tamper-resistant packaging warning. Johnson & Johnson and McNeil Consumer Products Co. were cleared of any legal liability for the deaths and poisonings, and Tylenol sales have recovered. In 1991, Johnson & Johnson and McNeil Consumer Products Co. provided the families of the seven victims with an undisclosed settlement, estimated to be as much as $50 million.

Despite the overwhelmingly negative nature of the event, coverage of the Tylenol tragedy generally portrayed Johnson & Johnson and its parent in a favorable light. Companies during a crisis are often criticized by journalists for hiding information from the press and the public, but many journalists have praised Johnson & Johnson for its openness and the immediacy of its response to the poisonings. John O'Brien, of the *Chicago Tribune*, said, "The public relations people were knowledgeable and available when the media needed to talk to them," he said. "They didn't try to sugar-coat anything."

■ ■ ■ PR AND MEDIA RELATIONS

Although public relations professionals engage in a wide variety of activities, most typically devote a large portion, if not a majority, of their efforts to working with the media, including journalists, producers, and others responsible for the content of those media. By developing and maintaining good working relationships with the media, public relations professionals anticipate that they will be more successful in obtaining fair or positive coverage of their organizations. When a negative story does occur, having maintained a good relationship with the media increases an organization's opportunity to at least communicate clearly and responsibly.

There are several important tools the public relations professional uses in obtaining media coverage, including the pseudo event.

Pseudo Events

One of the most enduring legacies from the early days of modern public relations is the creation of what Daniel Boorstin calls "the pseudo event." Pseudo events are events manufactured by individuals or organizations, typically to capture the attention of the media and thereby the public.

Press conferences, protests, parades, and even awards ceremonies are all examples of pseudo events and are a form of media manipulation. But the media have become dependent on them. In fact, studies show that as much as 75 percent of the news content in even the best of the nation's newspapers, such as the *Washington Post*, was in some way influenced by a pseudo event. Only occasionally is a story generated through pure "enterprise" or original reporting, with no public relations influence.[4]

Distributing News to the Media in the Digital Age

An important development in media relations is the distribution of corporate or other organizational news, information, and data (whether statistical or multimedia, including audio and video), usually through what are called news releases, or press releases. Traditionally done as typed stories sent through the mail, they are today primarily done online and sent via email or posted to the Web.

Journalists prefer digital content because it is easier to look at and evaluate for newsworthiness, since the journalist simply downloads the material to a computer. It's also easier and faster to edit, store, and retrieve than analog content. In an age of information clutter, digital content is also easier to ignore or discard. Now that reaching influential bloggers or others using social media has become perhaps as important as reaching professional journalists, a press release is not even needed. Rather, a well-placed **pitch**, or request to review a client's new product, may be enough to get people writing about it and then to get mainstream media attention.

Similar to the written news release is a video news release. These have caused some controversy in recent years, for example when it was learned that the Bush administration was creating VNRs to promote its health policy. The VNRs were made to look much like a typical story from a reporter in the field, and several television stations around the country ran them without citing the source, making them seem like they had been produced by the news station itself. Many companies produce VNRs, and many are used by television stations, though usually only short clips as part of a larger story—B-roll footage showing pills being sorted, for example.

Press kits give journalists much of the information they need to do a story.

pitch
....
A request to review a client's new product or do a story about the client or the product.

Finding Sources Online

Facilitating the media–public relations relationship has been the growth of various expert-source clearinghouses in the online arena. Although such clearinghouses have functioned in the offline world for many years in a variety of forms (such as media guides published by universities, or *The Yearbook of Experts, Authorities & Spokespersons*), they have thrived online for many of the same reasons that classified advertising works well online: the Web allows highly efficient targeting of communications and searching. *The Yearbook of Experts, Authorities & Spokespersons* is now available online, greatly facilitating the process of finding experts and authorities, especially when on deadline.

Perhaps the biggest of these clearinghouses is ProfNet, an online service that connects more than six thousand news and information officers at colleges and universities, businesses, research centers, medical centers, nonprofits, and public relations agencies with journalists all around the world.

Web Link >>>
PR Newswire
www.prnewswire.com

Web Link >>>
Businesswire
www.businesswire.com

Web Link >>>
MediaLink
www.medialink.com

■ ■ ■ PR FIRMS AND THE PR INDUSTRY

The U.S. public relations industry is tied to the rise and fall in the economy, just as the advertising industry is. When companies are in financial difficulties, they tend to cut back on advertising and public relations services, even though it could be argued that this is exactly when they most need such services. In public relations, revenues are based on a combination of sources.

Web Link >>>
The Yearbook of Experts, Authorities & Spokespersons
www.expertclick.com/

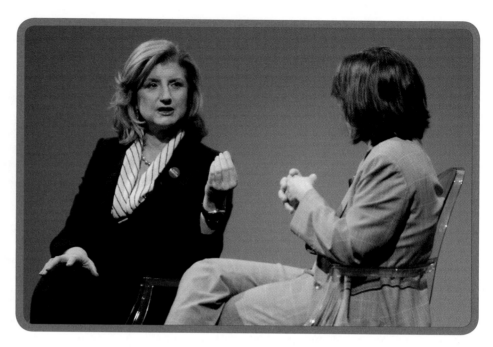

PR professionals help get their clients media attention through interviews as subject experts or writing op-ed columns.

Web Link >>>
ProfNet
profnet.prnewswire.com/

Web Link >>>
Council of Public Relations Firms
www.prfirms.org

These include primarily fees for public relations consulting and services; income from specialized communications services such as research, interactive communications, and employee communications; and markups for production services and other media materials.

The 1990s saw considerable consolidation among public relations firms. But acquisition has slowed considerably in the early years of the twenty-first century, with most consolidation still occurring internationally. Major buyers are European holding companies such as Incepta Group, Havas, Publicis, and Cordiant. Omnicom is the one major U.S. communications firm that acquired several technology firms for Fleishman-Hillard.

Although most organizations maintain their own internal public relations units or offices, many hire public relations firms to help in their efforts, particularly with more specialized services, especially media relations. Media relations can be extremely complex and can require extensive experience with not just local but national media. Oftentimes, public relations firms maintain their own specialists who have the necessary experience to help clients manage their media relations, particularly during campaigns or crises.

PR firms are organized into three main areas:

1. Core practice areas, or the type of relationships the client needs managed, including marketing communications or consumer relations; investor relations; public, nonprofit, and governmental affairs; corporate and employee communications; political communications; and community relations

2. Services, or the type of activity the firm provides to its clients, including media relations, research, interactive or online communications, writing, lobbying, fund-raising, and crisis management

3. Industries, or the business sectors within which the clients operate, including utilities, technology, retail, manufacturing, health care, financial services, and consumer products

Many firms specialize in one or more core practice areas, services, or industries. This enables them to focus resources in one or more areas yet achieve a high enough level of expertise needed to serve clients operating on a national or global scale. Some PR firms also offer integrated communication programs, sometimes called integrated marketing communications. This means the firm provides a comprehensive set of communication management and services to clients, including both public relations and advertising activities. Most of the larger PR firms provide integrated communication programs.

Table 12-4 provides data on the top five U.S. public relations firms according to total worldwide revenues for 2008. Most of the PR firms had revenue losses or lackluster performances in 2008, largely because of the downturn in the economy.

■ ■ ■ ETHICAL ISSUES IN PUBLIC RELATIONS

Public relations people face a unique set of ethical issues compared to journalists, media-entertainment professionals, and advertising people. Like advertising professionals, their loyalties lie with the message their client wants to give, but like journalists, if they present false or misleading information, their credibility and that of their clients can be severely damaged. In addition, although some public relations practitioners like to claim they are the "conscience of the client," the fact is they do not always have access to the corporate channels of power to head off possibly disastrous management decisions. Often they are called in after damage has been done and are asked to minimize or negate it from a public relations standpoint.

Because public relations deals with trying to present an image to the public or trying to improve public opinion about something or someone, a clear-cut line between ethical and unethical behavior is often hard to discern. Guidelines for ethical public relations practices are articulated by professional associations such as the Public Relations Society of America (PRSA) and the International Association of Business Communicators (IABC).

TABLE 12-4

Top Five Independent Public Relations Firms, 2008 Worldwide Revenues

FIRM	HEADQUARTERS	# OF EMPLOYEES	2008 REVENUES
Edelman	Chicago, Illinois	3,000	$449,231,193
Waggener Edstrom	Bellevue, Washington	843	$119,670,000
APCO Worldwide	Washington, D.C.	569	$112,400,000
Ruder Finn Group	New York, New York	545	$96,112,000
Text 100 Int'l	San Francisco, California	540	$63,000,000

Source: O'Dwyer's PR Firms Database

According to the PRSA, unethical behavior for PR practitioners includes lying by omission, as in failing to release financial information from a corporation or giving a misleading impression of a corporation's performance; deceiving the public by employing people to pose as volunteers to speak at public hearings or in "grassroots" campaigns; and giving expensive goods or gifts to journalists or politicians in order to influence their opinion on a product or issue.

On the other hand, their guidelines also state that members must protect the privacy rights of clients and safeguard their confidential information, as well as advise appropriate authorities if they discover that an employee is divulging confidential information. It is easy to see how an ethical conflict could arise for a PR professional if he learns information about the poor financial situation of a company and is asked by the company to encourage positive news reports on its financial health, rather than negative ones.

Similarly, some PR firms have helped create faux grassroots campaigns online, called "astroturf" campaigns, designed to make it appear that there is citizen support for a company or cause. If bringing people to speak at a public meeting is considered unethical, then it is clear that this online equivalent is unethical, too.

Digital media present other new and unique temptations to public relations professionals. Shortly after Infoseek's executive vice president Patrick Naughton was arrested in September 1999 for allegedly planning a sexual encounter with a minor he'd met over the Internet (who turned out to be an undercover policewoman), not only was Naughton fired from Infoseek and his management bio removed from the site, but the public relations department tried to delete all mention of his name in their archived press releases online, to make it seem as if he never worked there. There were protests about this clumsy attempt to rewrite history 1984 style, and within twenty-four hours his name was back in most of the press releases. Infoseek claimed it was "an accident."[5]

In 2006, public relations firm Edelman was publicly lambasted for a blog it concocted for its client, Wal-Mart. The blog was ostensibly written by a couple traveling the country in their RV, blogging about their experiences. What came out later was that they were actually paid to blog on behalf of Wal-Mart, which may explain why they were so eager to park their RV in Wal-Mart parking lots and discuss their friendly encounters with happy Wal-Mart employees.

Ethical lapses in PR can have far-reaching consequences, especially when it comes to politics and war. Hill and Knowlton was widely criticized for its clandestine efforts to influence the U.S. government and the American public during the Gulf War. The firm was hired at a cost of more than half a million dollars by the government of Kuwait to foster support among the American public and the U.S. Congress.

Hill and Knowlton produced and distributed dozens of video news releases (VNRs) to television news operations around the country. Many of the stations aired the VNRs without identifying their source as either Hill and Knowlton or the government of Kuwait. Many aired the propaganda without editing it, presenting it as impartial journalism.

Hill and Knowlton also helped organize the "Congressional Human Rights Caucus," which held hearings on Capitol Hill. In October 1990, a fifteen-year-old Kuwaiti girl, known only as Nayirah, spoke in tears, saying, "I volunteered at the

Web Link >>>
Public Relations Society of America
www.prsa.org/

Web Link >>>
International Association of Business Communicators
www.iabc.com/

al-Addan hospital. While I was there, I saw the Iraqi soldiers come into the hospital with guns, and go into the room where . . . babies were in incubators. They took the babies out of the incubators, took the incubators, and left the babies on the cold floor to die."

For months after her testimony, the Iraqi soldiers' killing of babies was repeated in the media and even by President George H. Bush as a rationale for the U.S. presence in the region. Later it was revealed that Nayirah was a member of the Kuwaiti royal family, that her testimony was a fabrication, and that a Hill and Knowlton vice president had coached Nayirah on what to say during her testimony. After the end of the war, the Canadian Broadcasting Corporation produced an Emmy Award–winning documentary on the Hill and Knowlton campaign, entitled *To Sell a War.*

Changing Trends in Advertising and PR

One thing that has become clear is that the traditional divisions between the two professions of advertising and PR are blurring. It used to be, in the analog media world, that PR professionals dealt primarily with media relations and did not have to be concerned with brand strategy or other aspects of advertising. But today, it is apparent that both PR and advertising professionals have to know what the other is doing in order to maximize the effectiveness of campaigns.

In what is typically called **integrated communications**, strategic-communications professionals are trying to figure out the best ways not only to manage a brand's image across media channels but to learn what the public is saying about the brand through blogs, websites, and other social media—which were traditionally the realm of public relations. Advertising agencies are learning what public relations professionals have long known—a company cannot assume that it can send out a message without the audience talking back.

Similarly, public relations professionals are learning that a company or brand exists within a network of relationships and that thinking on a larger, strategic level can help them better integrate their messages to various publics.

One thing that companies are learning—sometimes the hard way, as in the case with Edelman—is that the online public demands more transparency than in the past. Attempts at deception, through faux-amateur ads or blogs, will likely create a strong negative backlash that will hurt the brand or company. A shift to even more equitable, symmetrical dialogue is happening, as companies learn to talk with their clients, or publics, through forums, blogs, and other means.

integrated communications
The idea that all channels of communication about a company or brand should work together in creating a cohesive message.

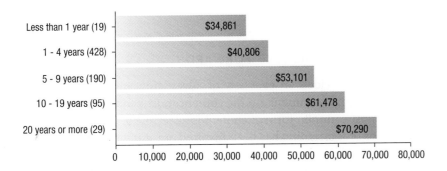

FIGURE 12-1 Salaries and Positions for Advertising Account Managers. Source: Payscale.com

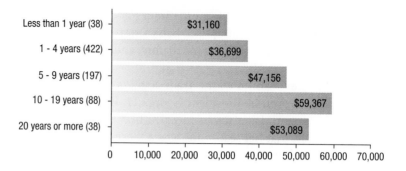

FIGURE 12-2 Salaries and Positions for Public Relations Specialists. Source: Payscale.com

The shift from "controlling the message" to "guiding the conversation" is often seen as threatening by companies who for too long have believed that in order to have an effective brand or to be successful they must control all aspects of communication with the public.

■ ■ ■ CAREERS IN ADVERTISING AND PR

Although very much reliant on larger trends in the economy, a wide variety of interesting jobs exist in both professions, and there is a growing amount of overlap between the two. The trends in media production and consumption tend to favor strategic communications over fields like journalism (which is seeing drastic cuts throughout the industry), and the salaries are generally better.

Young people often find rewarding careers in any of a number of areas within advertising and PR, ranging from the creative side to account management to research. Within the larger firms there is great scope to change career tracks and deal with different clients, so someone who has been working in pharmaceuticals for a few years may switch to telecommunications, in effect starting a different career in learning the details of the new industry.

Social media are creating new job opportunities for people in advertising agencies and PR firms, as well as in large companies that have their own marketing or PR departments. Keeping track of what is being said about a company and reaching influential members of the audience through social media is increasingly vital. More importantly, knowing why a company or client should use (or not use) a particular social-media tool is a skill set that companies are actively seeking.

LOOKING BACK AND MOVING FORWARD

This chapter has provided an overview of advertising and public relations. Although news and entertainment are the content most people go to the media for, in reality the most common form of content is advertising, while much of the editorial content or programming has been inspired or influenced by public relations.

Underlying both advertising and PR, which are forms of strategic communication, is the desire to persuade an audience to change an attitude or belief and take some action. Persuasive communication, historically called rhetoric, has long played a role in human affairs, and today there are more than two dozen theories that attempt to explain how persuasion works.

Advertising has so far failed to be a great success on the Web, for a number of reasons. Technology allows for greater accountability of response rates to advertisements, and the low response-rate numbers have made advertisers feel their money is not well spent online. As a result, advertising agencies have been trying new types of online advertisements, with mixed results and with some Internet-user backlash at larger, more obtrusive ads.

It does raise interesting questions about why advertisers were willing to pay so much for ads in nondigital media, when it was nearly impossible to estimate audience engagement. Even the metrics of circulation numbers for print and viewers for television could be seen as largely fictions, as neither says anything about whether the audience read or watched the ad, let alone remembered it or took some action based on it.

Advertising revenues have provided the means for the majority of content we see today. Advertising helps pay the salaries of journalists and keeps the television studios operating. Few people would be willing to pay the full price for the content they get largely for "free."

However, the content is not of course free. Consumers do pay for the content in the form of higher prices for goods, as the expenses for advertising and marketing have to come from revenues and are considered part of the costs of doing business. Given that such costs are largely hidden from the public, it seems that it will be hard to change to subscription-based or pay-per-use models on the Web.

Social media will continue to greatly affect strategic-communications professionals, who have to learn that transparency and engagement with their audiences will be what gains credibility in the social-media space. Monitoring online conversations about companies—and, more importantly, joining those conversations—will be increasingly imperative for advertising and public relations professionals. Already we are seeing more job titles with the words "social media"—jobs in which the employee is responsible for dealing with social-media components of a company's overall exposure.

One thing is increasingly clear: largely because of the democratization of media and the ability of more people to create and distribute their messages than ever before, it is harder than ever to be heard above the noise. The skills of strategic-communications professionals in knowing how to persuade, how to craft powerful messages, and how to understand audiences will all become even more important in our world than they are today.

- -

DISCUSSION QUESTIONS

1. Choose a brand and keep track of every encounter you have with it throughout the day. Don't forget to include not only the number of radio and television commercials and ads you see in the morning paper, but advertising on websites and on objects like cereal boxes, buses, taxis, and telephone booths and ads outside and inside stores.

2. How effective is persuasive communication? What could make it more effective in today's crowded media environment?

3. Some brands have such successful marketing that the brand name becomes synonymous with the product itself, such as the trademarked name Kleenex. Can you name other trademarked brands that have become commonly used for the generic products?

4. Discuss which advertising format you feel is the most effective and why. Are there some products that are better advertised in a certain format than in others? Why do you think this is?

5. Discuss strengths and weaknesses of the large-advertising-agency model common today. Do you think the trend toward ever-larger agencies is good or bad? Why?

6. Choose a company and see what is being said about it in the social-media space, including blogs, any complaint sites, and what the company itself is doing with social media, if anything. Discuss your findings and suggest any ways the company should do a better job in social media.

FURTHER READING

Ad Land: A Global History of Advertising. Mark Tungate (2007) Kogan Page.

A History of Advertising. Stephane Pincas, Marc Loiseau (2008) Taschen.

The Advertising Concept Book. Pete Barry (2008) Thames & Hudson.

Guerrilla Advertising: Unconventional Brand Communication. Gavin Lucas, Michael Dorrian (2006) Laurence King Publishers.

Ogilvy on Advertising. David Ogilvy (1987) Vintage Books.

PR! A Social History of Spin. Stuart Ewen (1996) Basic Books.

The Father of Spin: Edward L. Bernays and the Birth of Public Relations. Larry Tye (2002) Holt.

Public Relations: The Complete Guide. Joe Marconi (2004) South-Western Educational Publishers.

The New Rules of Marketing and PR: How to Use News Releases, Blogs, Podcasting, Viral Marketing and Online Media to Reach Buyers Directly. David Meerman Scott (2008) Wiley.

The New Influencers: A Marketer's Guide to the New Social Media. Paul Gillin, Geoffrey Moore (2009) Linden Publishing.

MEDIA QUIZ ANSWERS

1. False.

2. False.

3. Putting products in shows in which the actors use them and their logo or brand is displayed.

4. Classified ads generate more revenue for newspapers.

5. Cost per thousand, a unit used for calculating print advertising rates.

6. Search engine marketing and search engine optimization, which are important because searching is how most information is found on the Internet.

7. True.

8. A campaign organized by a corporation to make it look like a grassroots campaign started by the public.

9. The Gulf War.

10. A video is uploaded to a website or blog and sent by users to other people.

Media Theory and Research: From Writing to Text Messaging

● CHAPTER OBJECTIVES

In this chapter we will:

■ Explain the role that theory and research have for media professionals.

■ Examine the differences between quantitative and qualitative research.

■ Describe various types of media research.

■ Critically examine the strengths and weaknesses of various media-research approaches.

■ Examine how digital media and the Internet are being researched both in terms of new media theories being developed and within the framework of old media theories.

13 In today's age of cross-promotional partnerships between nonmedia and media companies the announcement in early 2006 that GM was partnering with the television show *The Apprentice* to promote the new Chevy Tahoe was not unusual. Even the fact that they had created a website for the launch, and provided video clips and other digital production tools on the site to encourage users to create their own commercials, was not entirely groundbreaking.

Several companies had already received lots of publicity for soliciting user-generated content (UGC) and holding contests to determine the best. Doritos was perhaps the most notable example when it encouraged consumers to create commercials, the best of which would be aired during the Super Bowl.

Things did not go as smoothly for GM's UGC video ad campaign, however. Although the vast majority of people used the tools on the website to make positive commercials for the Tahoe, a minority used the tools to create anticorporate messages and to criticize the Tahoe as a gas guzzler and environmentally unfriendly vehicle. These videos were leaked to video-sharing sites such as YouTube and became the dominant story about GM's campaign.

GM executives might have saved themselves some grief if they had considered some of the theorizing

and media research being done about active audiences and how people generate meaning—sometimes oppositional meanings—from what a media producer may have intended. Media theory is not confined to the halls of academia; it can often help inform practical, real-world decisions and strategies being made every day.

Theories about media and communication attempt to explain the underlying processes of media, how we interact with media, and how media affect our cultures, societies, attitudes, and lives. Media research is the systematic and scientific investigation of communication processes and effects that often bases its explorations on theories of media and communication. Some types of media research are more oriented to answering practical questions, such as whether audience members remember a particular advertisement, their impressions of a product or brand, or their media use and consumption habits.

Media-research methodology, or how research is carried out, takes many forms. It can entail social scientific research using quantitative tools such as surveys and experiments, employing statistical analysis of the data, or it can involve critical studies using qualitative methods such as ethnography or focus groups.

The Role of Theory and Research

The significance of research for media professionals may seem clearer than that of media theory. It may not seem important to someone planning to work as a journalist or in advertising to learn about media theories, which seem better suited to the musty halls of universities.

Media theories have had a number of profound effects. They play a foundational role as cognitive constructs, or ways we organize and make sense of the world. They also play a key role in shaping research agendas, which then affect the questions asked during the course of research, the findings or discoveries made, and the funding given to conduct research.

Research findings in turn have been very influential in shaping public policies toward the media and media industries, ranging from ratings systems for movies, music, and video games to decisions on what is regulated or not. This of course has important implications for how media companies are organized and run, touching on everything from job creation to the types of media and media content we have available.

Media research carried out specifically for business purposes helps determine audience numbers for particular shows

Audience-measurement techniques are just one example of how media theories, statistical analysis, and research come together to help media professionals.

Bringing Out Your Inner Researcher

1. Do you believe that there is an objective reality "out there" that we can describe and all agree on or that each of us creates our own reality?
2. (T/F) Concerns about media and their effects on the public originated in the twentieth century.
3. If you worked in a company that was coming out with a new online magazine, what type of research would you do to find out what might be most popular?
4. What words come to mind when you think of the logo of your school mascot?
5. Have you ever tried to copy something you've seen on television, on the Internet, or in the movies? What was it?
6. Did you have a television in your room as you grew up?
7. How much did your parents or guardians supervise your television viewing? Your time on the computer?
8. Do you agree or disagree with the following statement: "Children, especially, need to be protected from media content that is violent or sexual in nature." Why do you feel this way?
9. What does the term "information society" mean to you?
10. (T/F) Some traditional media scholars who died before the Internet became popular have useful theories that help us better understand the current media environment.

or networks (thus determining advertising rates and what kinds of shows are produced in the future). It also helps determine what media campaigns have been effective, what messages are more persuasive to the public, and therefore what areas are of interest to businesses, nonprofit organizations, and politicians.

In short, media theories not only help media professionals better predict or explain various phenomena, they also help us better understand the world we live in and the forces at work in that world.

Media Research: What Type of Science Is It?

It may seem strange asking what "type" of science media research falls under, but the question is an important one because it raises several issues about media studies. At the heart of the question is whether or not the social sciences such as psychology, sociology, and anthropology can (and should) be conducted according to the rules of the natural sciences.

There is no question that for most of their histories as individual disciplines the social sciences have tried to emulate the rules and methods of the natural sciences, but some scholars disagree on whether they can do that properly or not. Is it possible, they ask, to discover the same kind of natural laws for communication and media that we see in the natural sciences, such as a law of gravity? More importantly, in trying to copy scientific models that may not be appropriate to the social sciences, are we missing the point in understanding our social world and asking the wrong questions?

The confusion about where media-studies research sits is also reflected in the range of schools and departments in universities where it can be found. Sometimes media studies may be within a school of journalism; other times it may be within a school of communications or even in an English department.

To further complicate matters, much important research and theorizing on the media has been done by sociologists and psychologists or by scholars trained in those fields or in other areas, such as literary theory, who have focused on media or mass-communication research. The transmission model of communication, as discussed in Chapter 1, was developed by mathematicians to help solve an engineering problem, yet became hugely influential for many years in shaping our understanding of the processes of communication.

Broadly speaking, the debate on the type of science media research should entail can be divided into two main camps regarding how the world is viewed. **Positivism** says that there is an objective reality that can be observed, measured, and explained by a neutral observer. Theories can be hypothesized based on observations, and through rigorous testing and experimentation following the scientific method the hypotheses can be proved or disproved. This leads to a better understanding of the world and an increasing ability to predict behaviors or alter phenomena with predictable results. This has been the dominant **epistemology**, or way to understand the world, for most social scientists, including media researchers, throughout the twentieth century.

There are several other epistemologies that reject positivist claims to varying degrees. These range from **postpositivism**—which largely agrees with most positivist claims but also states that there are areas of knowledge that cannot be under-

positivism
....
The belief, common among scientists in the physical or natural sciences and many in the social sciences, that there is an objective reality that can be discovered and explained through rigorous scientific research.

epistemology
....
A way of or framework for understanding the world.

postpositivism
....
A view that agrees largely with positivism, but acknowledges that there may be some things that we cannot know through scientific inquiry.

Good media researchers use both quantitative and qualitative research techniques to find answers.

stood through scientific means, such as religious faith—to **social constructionism** and **postmodernism**.

Social constructionism says that all meaning and truth are derived from social interactions, including our interactions with symbols and signs, which have relativistic and changeable meanings according to the context. Language is not a transparent medium that describes the world; it creates the world as we know it.

Postmodernism, although it has many variants, largely eschews grand theorizing and what it calls "metanarratives," or overarching narratives that try to explain the world, because any such metanarrative essentially favors one worldview over others, which are then suppressed. It, like social constructionism, questions how knowledge is formed and challenges the assumptions of positivist science that it is a better (or the only) way to find and establish truth.

It is important to note that some of the basic elements of constructionist and postmodern thought are not entirely new or simply a reaction to the dominance of positivist science in the twentieth century. Their histories can be traced back to influential schools of thought in the nineteenth and early twentieth centuries like **pragmatism** and even before that to some important philosophical traditions. In some ways, such thinking is a return to the roots of theorizing about media and the role of communication.

The debate about what type of science media-studies research falls under can also be roughly mapped to the main types of research methodologies carried out today, **quantitative research** and **qualitative research**.

■ ■ ■ QUANTITATIVE RESEARCH

Researchers relying heavily on quantitative techniques tend to have a positivist outlook. They assume that their research will help better predict behavior, find causal effects for certain phenomena, or confirm or deny certain media theories.

Quantitative studies include the familiar methods of experiments, surveys, and statistical analyses. The exact method used depends on several factors, especially on the goals or purposes of the research. If a study is intended to establish causality, such as whether watching violent programming on television causes increased levels of violence among children, then experimental or quasi-experimental methods could be appropriate.

If a study is meant to document how much violence is on television, then a content analysis should be conducted. If an investigation is designed to determine how much televised violence children see, then a survey or direct observation is in order.

In any case, research methods are never perfect indicators, and the design of the study as well as the particular method used can affect results. For example, conducting a laboratory experiment with children on the effect of watching violence on television not only raises important ethical questions, it also creates an unrealistic media environment that will make accurate measurements extremely problematic. The laboratory environment, no matter how much it is changed to look and feel like a home environment, still does not accurately capture the range of environmental factors that may be involved in a normal viewing experience.

Content analysis, such as counting the number of times the word "sex" is used in an issue of a magazine or newspaper, or the number of times images of violence are shown on television, can also be problematic. Although such analysis can provide concrete numbers that can then be analyzed using statistical methods, it often makes big assumptions. For example, what evidence is there that a certain number

social constructionism
A view that says that much if not all of what we know and understand about the world, including scientific knowledge, is constructed through our social interactions and language.

postmodernism
A broad category of viewpoints that claim that there is no absolute truth, that truth is unknowable, and that attempts to create grand narratives that explain the world are faulty.

pragmatism
A school of thought that claims that truth is found in actions that work and that no overarching or purely objective notion of truth can be found.

quantitative research
Research that focuses on numbers and measures and experimentation to describe phenomena. Researchers usually have a hypothesis they are trying to prove or disprove through controlled experimentation.

qualitative research
Research that describes phenomena in words instead of numbers or measures. Ethnographic studies, such as interviews with people to learn about beliefs or trends, are an example of qualitative research, also called critical-cultural studies.

of violent scenes will have an effect on viewers or that seeing the word "sex" fifteen times in a magazine article and not twelve times (or one hundred times) will affect readers?

Analyzing data using statistics raises its own set of problems, including incomplete or missing data that may make analysis difficult, sampling error (taking a sample of the population that does not accurately reflect the entire population), and faulty study design that leads to misleading results. Consider a simple example. Let's say you conduct a ten-question multiple-choice survey among one hundred classmates. You get responses from all one hundred people (itself a rarity in survey research), but you find that only thirty-five people have answered the tenth question. How should it be counted in your results? And why did so few answer it? Because 50 percent of thirty-five is seventeen people, while 50 percent of the other questions would be fifty people, to say "50 percent of the survey respondents believe that..." regarding question ten would not be accurate since only thirty-five answered the question.

These and other methodological difficulties with quantitative research have led to the growth and acceptance of qualitative research methods.

■ ■ ■ QUALITATIVE RESEARCH

Qualitative researchers may reject the assumptions behind quantitative research, or they may simply appreciate the limitations with such research and want other means to explore their areas of interest. They are generally not trying to make predictions, but are focusing on description with the hope of better understanding the world as the participants see it. Qualitative research can include in-depth interviews, focus groups, and ethnography, among other techniques.

Ethnography involves the application of a technique, developed in anthropology, in which the researcher immerses himself in a culture in order to directly observe it. The researcher tries to see the culture in its natural state, disrupting it as little as possible.

An ethnographer might enter into a household, a newsroom, or an advertising agency and spend hours, days, weeks, or even months directly observing the media behaviors of the people or organization involved. The ethnographer might video and audio record the observed activities as a way of documenting the research. A detailed analysis would follow. The results might be used in isolation or in combination with other methods, such as interviews or even quantitative techniques.

A variation of ethnography is **participant-observation**. In this technique, the researcher joins the group he is studying, such as a fan club or an online multiplayer video game. His status as a participant not only helps him better understand the world he is observing, but also helps the participants open up more to the researcher than they otherwise might if they saw him simply as an outsider.

Focus groups are widely used by media researchers. Often the social interaction that takes place among the participants of a focus group, and the way they discuss what is being studied, can provide important insights that the researcher would not get from interviewing people individually or simply conducting a survey.

Qualitative research raises its own ethical concerns and is not without weaknesses. One question is whether or not participants should be informed of the researcher's true role. This is especially important when doing research with groups online, where the researcher's identity may not be obvious. Another ethical issue arises when the researcher sees the participants engaging in risky or dangerous behavior. Does he explain to the participants why they shouldn't do that, thus

ethnography

A variety of qualitative research techniques that involve the researcher interacting with participants, either through observation, participation, interviews, or a combination of methods.

participant-observation

A qualitative research technique in which the researcher participates as a member of the group being studied.

focus groups

A research technique in which small groups of people are gathered together to discuss a topic, with the interactions often recorded and carefully watched to determine what different people think.

changing the results of his research, or does he simply observe?

Qualitative research of course makes no claims to being generalized to the larger population or being reliable in the sense of getting the same results if conducted by another researcher or with another group, even under similar circumstances. It is wrong to try to generate meaningful numbers from a certain set of interviews so the results look like you have talked to a representative sample of the population.

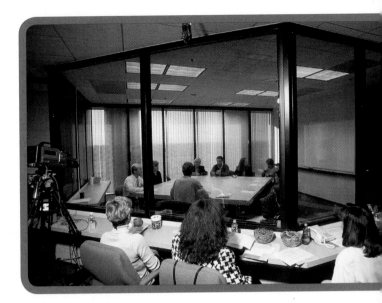

Focus group research can provide rich insights into consumer opinions of products or issues.

■ ■ ■ QUALITATIVE AND QUANTITATIVE RESEARCH WORKING TOGETHER

Each methodology has its place in media research today, and each methodology has strengths and weaknesses. Ignoring one methodology over another because of a philosophical disagreement can create a blind spot for a researcher trying to find answers. They are simply tools to be used; a person can pound a nail with a screwdriver, but a hammer works much better.

Qualitative techniques are often used to provide more depth or texture to quantitative studies. For example, in designing a survey you may not really know what issues are important to your research subjects or perhaps even how they talk about certain things. Conducting qualitative research can help you see various common themes that emerge and help you design a better survey.

Qualitative research, if done properly, helps you see the world from another perspective in a way that quantitative can never do. Simply observing certain behaviors with media can often yield amazing insights on the part of the researcher and will generate even more interesting research questions to ask. Observing who controls the remote control in the living room, and a family's rules around that, may be more telling of television viewing habits than specific preferences for shows.

Quantitative research, with its statistical techniques and its claims of speaking for a much larger population than what was studied, is also extremely powerful. Sometimes simply looking at charts and graphs of numbers can be enough to persuade people that the results must be true.

Now that you have an understanding of some of the current research issues and research methodologies, we will take a look at how media theories and research have developed. Rather than take a purely historical approach, we will explore media theory and research within the framework of what questions people were trying to answer.

The First Media Revolution: The Written Word

Over the last century, public concern has arisen about the possible effects of each new medium of mass communication as it has emerged. Questions have been asked about each medium's impact on culture, political processes, the values and behaviors children learn, and the like. In the 1920s, much of the public became concerned about the depiction of sex, violence, and lawlessness in film. In recent years, concerns have been raised about the Internet and how it may be influencing us.

These concerns are nothing new. In the 1800s, critics warned that newspapers caused juvenile crime. Moralists believed that the flow of sensational news stories about crime and vice would lead people to imitate that immoral behavior. In 1888, *Punch* magazine attributed Jack the Ripper's crimes committed in Whitechapel, a rough inner-city district of London, to "highly coloured pictorial advertisements."

Concern about the effects of media on children has even deeper roots. We know that even in ancient Greece, philosophers Socrates and Plato worried greatly about the influence of literacy on children. Plato was concerned especially about the morally corrupting influence of poetry, particularly allegorical tales such as Homer's *Battles of the Gods*, and sought to ban it.[1] In 360 BCE, Plato offered this reasoning:

> Children cannot distinguish between what is allegory and what isn't, and opinions formed at that age are usually difficult to eradicate or change; it is therefore of the utmost importance that the first stories they hear shall aim at producing the right moral effect.
>
> Plato, *The Republic*

It is hard for us today to see just how profound an effect on society writing had. As Chapter 7 discussed in terms of the storage of information, being able to easily store knowledge in the form of writing changed important aspects of the culture and society.

No longer was a good memory prized the way it was in a nonliterate oral culture, since memorization was not needed to the same extent to store information. The form of storytelling changed with writing, as repetitive phrases were no longer needed as memory prompts for storytellers, and the rhythm and cadences of the written word differed from oral.

Similarly, a storyteller could lose control of his or her words once they were in written form. Someone could take a person's words and twist their meaning, with no chance for an immediate response or perhaps any response at all. In fact, the author of a work had no way of knowing who might read it or when. It is perhaps comical to picture Greek children sneaking off with a scroll of poetry to read in secret, but in a fundamental sense it is no different than kids today sneaking into an R-rated movie in the multiplex or removing the parental controls on the family computer.

Media Representations and Understanding the World

The basic assumption behind concerns about the media is that what we see and hear—the signs, symbols, and words—can somehow affect us in ways that nonmediated communication does not. This assumption has led to a large body of research on media effects, which will be discussed later in this chapter.

Before we can understand the various theories on media effects, however, we should first look at some theories regarding media itself that may affect how we understand the world. We can divide media theories into three broad categories: the role that signs and symbols play in cognition (semiotics), the effect of the type of medium used to convey messages (media ecology), and how media messages bracket or frame our worldviews (framing and agenda-setting).

▪ ▪ ▪ SEMIOTICS

Semiotics, or the study of signs and symbols, goes back in some form to Plato and Aristotle. Today, the field of semiotics has been greatly influenced by Ferdinand de Saussure, the father of linguistics, and his notion of signs as having dual properties. These properties are the signifier, or the form, and the signified, or what the form represents (some semioticians claim a third component, an interpretant, between these two). For example, an image of a rose (see Figure 13-1) is the signifier, and the signified can represent any number of things depending on the context. An image of a rose on a Valentine's Day card may mean one thing, while a rose tattoo with blood-dipped thorns on the arm of a biker may mean something else entirely.

semiotics
....
The study of signs and symbols.

Love
Thoughtfulness
Relationship
Romance
Birthday
Apology

Signifier   Signified

FIGURE 13-1 Semiotic Signifier and Signified. A rose (the signifier) can mean many different things (the signified), depending on the context. Illinois Press.

A main point is that context plays a major role in the audience's understanding of the signified, even when the signified remains the same. The power of signs to affect our thinking should not be underestimated. René Magritte's famous illustration of a pipe that says "This is not a pipe" is an example of how we typically take the sign as reality. Magritte is absolutely correct: his picture of a pipe is not actually a pipe—it is simply a picture of a pipe.

It is also important to remember that in semiotics "sign" does not simply refer to visual images but includes words as well. Words could be considered a more complex form of sign, as we have to learn that certain sounds carry particular meanings (which are entirely arbitrary). There is no logical reason that the color red is pronounced "red" in English, or "rojo" in Spanish, or "aka" in Japanese; all of these are simply linguistic conventions for those particular languages.

If that seems like an obvious point, then another semiotic insight is not always so obvious. Once we learn what certain sounds mean (or what certain visual images mean), we take what we have learned as "natural" and largely accept it without question. This fact makes the creation and use of signs extremely powerful, as it not only influences our thinking but even directs certain behaviors. Think of what you do without question whenever you are driving and come to a stop sign (even if you don't stop entirely—at least you know that you should).

René Magritte's famous "this is not a pipe" picture reminds us how we mistakenly understand the representation of something as the thing itself.

Similarly, an indexical sign is visual but signifies something else that is not actually related to it. Consider the image of a floppy disk in most software programs that has come to represent the "save file" function. Most computers nowadays do not even have floppy disk drives, as portable storage has largely been taken over by USB drives, yet we understand what function the image represents.

Some scholars argue that semiotics is at the heart of communication. Noted semiotician and novelist Umberto Eco, in his book *A Theory of Semiotics*, has claimed: "Every act of communication to or between human beings—or any other intelligent biological or mechanical apparatus—presupposes a signification system as its necessary condition." This means that without a common understanding of what signs mean, whether they are visual or lingual, we would not be able to communicate.

Understanding semiotics is important for a deeper understanding of the processes of communication and how meaning is generated among people and in cultures. It is also important for communications professionals in advertising especially, as they can gain insights into how certain branding and advertising campaigns may be received by target audiences.

■ ■ ■ MEDIA ECOLOGY

media ecology

....

The study of media environments and how those environments may affect people and society.

Media scholar Marshall McLuhan was widely popular even outside of academic circles in the 1960s and 1970s and is noted for coining the phrase "The medium is the message."

Media ecology, as its name suggests, is the study of media environments and how those environments may affect people and society. Just as an ecological system in nature is complex and can be studied from a number of perspectives, or specialties (a chemist studying soil samples will see an ecosystem very differently than a biologist studying bear habitats in the same ecosystem), so it is with media ecology.

Media ecology attempts to examine everything from how our media environment influences our thinking to how specific types of media affect our perceptions because of the medium used (medium theory).

Perhaps the most famous proponent of medium theory was Canadian scholar Marshall McLuhan, with his famous phrase, "The medium is the message." By this, McLuhan claimed that the medium used to transmit messages was far more important to understand than the actual message content or way it was produced.

McLuhan's provocative writings were hugely popular in the 1960s and early 1970s, even outside of academia. His claims that electronic media had transformed the world into a "global village," free of the hierarchical and rigid power relations that were created by the culture of print media, echo what we hear about the role of the Internet, even though he was only speaking about radio and especially television.

His star has fallen dramatically in recent years among scholars. He has been charged with espousing a form of **technological determinism**, or the belief that technology causes certain human behaviors—a charge that some forms of media ecology still must deal with. Some critics also state that by celebrating the technical side of communication he ignored (and thereby left unchallenged) the relations of power and dominance that went into making the media today.

Despite these and other weaknesses in some of his theories, McLuhan did offer important insights into how media have affected our sense of time and space and thus our lives in modern society. Some of his points are even more important when considering digital media. Although technology may not be the most important component to examine when trying to theorize about media, the capability of mass media to reach large audiences almost immediately certainly has far-reaching consequences for how we understand the world.

technological determinism
....
The belief that technology causes certain human behaviors.

■ ■ ■ AGENDA SETTING AND FRAMING

One of the reasons politicians and others seek media coverage is a concept first explained by Paul F. Lazarsfeld and Robert K. Merton in 1948, called **agenda setting**. Lazarsfeld and Merton explained that one of the primary functions of the media is to confer status. The process of singling someone out from the large, heterogeneous masses tends to bestow prestige and authority on those so identified. "The audiences of mass media apparently subscribe to the circular belief that if you matter, you will be at the focus of mass attention and, if you are at the focus of mass attention, then surely you must really matter," wrote Lazarsfeld and Merton.[2]

agenda setting
....
A role the media play in deciding which topics to cover and thus, by virtue of the fact that the media have covered them, which topics the public deems important and discussion-worthy.

As agenda setters, the media can shape our perception of what issues are important, and how important, depending on their prominence in the mass media. Political scientist Bernard Cohen more clearly articulated the agenda-setting model when he wrote, "The press may not be successful much of the time in telling people what to think, but it is stunningly successful in telling its readers what to think about."[3]

Research by communication scholars Max McCombs and Donald Shaw tested and further articulated this phenomenon in the 1970s and demonstrated that in fact the media are especially effective at influencing public views on the importance of various issues. Moreover, McCombs and Shaw's research showed that different media play different roles in the agenda-setting process. In particular, historically newspapers have tended to set the general agenda of public issues. For example, newspapers might determine which issues the public is likely to see as important, such as taxes, education, crime, or health care. Meanwhile, the electronic media of television and radio are especially effective at shaping the public's views on which of those issues are most important.

Television news can not only direct us to what we consider important but also lead us to believe, through heavy coverage of crime, that the world is more dangerous than it actually is.

A major question emerged in the 1990s regarding the role of the Internet and other online media in the agenda-setting process. Although many researchers have followed in the footsteps of pioneers McCombs and Shaw to test and refine the agenda-setting model, little research to date has examined how communication via the Internet and other online media affects public opinion, especially with regard to the perception of importance of different issues.

When the concept of framing is combined with the agenda-setting function of media, it shows how powerful media can be. **Framing** is done in all forms of mass communication, including news. It relies on the notion that we classify, organize, and interpret things into certain schema, or frameworks, in order to simplify our complex lives. We have to do this just to get through the day; if we carefully considered and analyzed every message we received, then we would never be able to leave the house in the morning. Instead, we take mental "shortcuts" with much of what we encounter, letting it go unexamined as we carry on with our lives.

framing
....
The notion that every story is told in a particular way that influences how readers think of the story.

Frames act much like signs and symbols in semiotics in that once they are accepted, they appear natural and largely go unquestioned. They also shape our perceptions of people, places, issues, and events. A simple example of framing can be seen by looking at two words, "rights" versus "benefits." If an Iraq War veteran is fighting the government to have better health care and services for his wounds, there is a different connotation if he is asking for "veterans' rights" rather than "veterans' benefits." The term "benefits" sounds like something he is getting that is extra, something not available to other people and therefore perhaps slightly unequal or unfair. If he is arguing for veterans' rights, on the other hand, then it sounds more fundamental and is something he is being deprived of, rather than something extra he is asking for.

Framing may simply sound like spin, but it is not. We all frame our world, and good communicators know how to frame debates in ways that favor their views and disadvantage their opponents. If a persuasive communicator wins the framing battle, she has largely won that particular persuasive war.

Agenda setting and framing take on such importance in today's world because the media of mass communication are so pervasive. When combined with the echo effect of the Internet and the conversations that can take place (using the frames that were used, or sometimes debating those frames) about what is seen and read in the mass media (agenda setting), it is easy to see how certain types of media coverage can shape our perceptions of the world. Now let us look at how some theories of mass communication developed in the first place.

Mass Society, Mass Communication

The study of mass communication and the theories developed to better understand media have been greatly influenced by a number of larger social, political, cultural, and scientific factors throughout the course of history. We have already discussed how the social sciences and communications research have been influenced by natural science models. Here we will explore some of the historical and sociopolitical forces at work in the development of mass communication and media research.

The dramatic societal and political changes that took place in Europe and the United States during the nineteenth and twentieth centuries, thanks largely to industrialization, provide the backdrop for early theorizing on the role of mass communication. Traditional ways of life that had remained largely unchanged for generations were being replaced by the new demands of factory work and mass migrations of people to the quickly growing cities.

Harsh working and living conditions led to various social and political movements that called for greater democracy and workers' rights and clashes between workers and authorities. Elites tended to see these developments as a threat to their power and found various rationales for why some should lead and most should simply follow.

The notion of "the masses" helped give elites a rationale for why they should continue to rule. The people were seen as largely uneducated, lacking in culture, and not intelligent enough to be able to rule themselves. Others took the opposite side, claiming that more participation, better education, and greater distribution of wealth would help create a more democratic, just society.

During these debates, which we hear echoes of even today, film was starting to be recognized as an important medium of mass communication. Literacy was not needed to understand the stories in silent films, and the moving images were regarded as very powerful influencers, especially for the uneducated, passive "masses" or other supposedly vulnerable groups, such as children. Messages could be created through the medium of film or using other mass communication to educate, persuade, or control the masses; the question then became how it worked and how to best do this.

Media-Effects Research

The obvious way to study how media influenced people was to find effects of media exposure. As noted earlier, the notion that media could harm people was already well established, dating back to at least the ancient Greeks. With new and powerful communication technologies such as film, radio, and television that could reach millions of people at once, it was not hard to imagine the power that mass communication could have over people.

Media-effects research has played a dominant role in the history of media research and continues to be important today. Findings from media-effects studies have influenced the creation of the movie rating system, dictated regulations overseeing the television industry, and determined what types of advertisements we see. Although earlier assumptions of direct and powerful media effects on people have been tempered and scaled back as newer, more subtle theories have been developed, the notion that media directly affect us (usually negatively) is still very prevalent in the public. Tracing the historical development of effects research provides an interesting view of the role that communication technologies have played and the issues and social norms that we deem important.

■ ■ ■ PROPAGANDA AND THE MAGIC BULLET

Some of the earliest media-effects research was conducted in order to better understand how people were persuaded by mass communication. During World War I, both the United States and Germany employed film and other media (including posters) as instruments of propaganda to shape public opinion and generate support for their positions in the war. It was widely believed that such propaganda efforts had a great effect on influencing the public's attitudes.

Propaganda is an attempt to influence an audience through mass communication that usually involves total control of the transmission of information and that is often done without the audience knowing who is actually controlling the message. Although perhaps hard to imagine in today's media environment, particularly with the Internet, many people had extremely limited sources of information—perhaps only a government radio station or single government television station broadcasting a few hours a day.

Political scientist Harold Lasswell coined the term "hypodermic needle," during his analysis of World War I propaganda efforts, to describe the notion that media can act like a drug being injected into a passive audience. The **hypodermic-needle model** is based on the assumption that messages have a profound, direct, and uniform impact on individuals. This model has also been called the "magic bullet" model of communication

Propaganda posters during World War I led researchers to hypothesize how persuasion worked on the public.

and derives largely from learning theory and simple stimulus-response models in behavioral psychology.

As film became more popular and began to share space with radio as a form of mass communication in the 1920s, research was conducted about both mediums that looked beyond specific political or propaganda uses and examined the effect on the general public, especially children, a group seen as particularly vulnerable.

■ ■ ■ PAYNE FUND

The Payne Fund studies were conducted between 1928 and 1933 by some of the most prominent psychologists, sociologists, and educators of the day. Named after the source of funding for the research, they were published in 1933 and included a twelve-volume report on the impact of film viewing on children.[4] The studies provided a detailed examination of the effects of film in wide-ranging areas, including sleep patterns, attitudes about violence, delinquent behavior, and knowledge about foreign cultures.

The Payne Fund studies concluded that the same film would influence children differently depending on those children's varying backgrounds and characteristics, including age, sex, life experience, predispositions, social environment, and parental influence. One study of movies, delinquency, and crime, for instance, concluded that the impact of film on criminal behavior may vary depending on the range of themes presented in the film as well as the social context, attitudes, and interests of the viewer.

Although much of the Payne Fund research started from the assumption that movies would have a variety of negative effects, the research also revealed a variety of positive effects. For example, some research found that children could learn

The Payne Fund studies in the 1920s examined the effects of violence and sex in movies on young people.

positive lessons from film and that information retention was a function of grade in school.[5]

The Payne Fund studies also examined radio. In 1927–1928 they created a "school of the air," which would use radio to educate children on a variety of subjects.[6] This led to the formation of the National Committee on Education by Radio (NCER), as well as the allocation of some $300,000 in the early 1930s to support a reform of U.S. broadcasting, which at that time meant radio.

■ ■ ■ RADIO'S WIDER IMPACT

Radio had other effects in society that reached far beyond the realm of children. Consider the events that unfolded on the night of October 30, 1938, when Orson Welles broadcast a radio program created to sound like a news event, called *War of the Worlds*.

Orson Welles and his *War of the Worlds* radio broadcast had many listeners believing that Martians actually were invading the East Coast.

At 8 p.m. the Columbia Broadcasting System's Mercury Theater of the Air began its radio broadcast from a New York City studio. Regular listeners and others who heard the introduction understood perfectly well what was about to follow. It was simply a radio adaptation of the science fiction writer H. G. Wells's famous 1897 novel, *War of the Worlds*, starring a twenty-one-year-old baritone named Orson Welles.

But many who did not hear the introduction found themselves lulled into a state of calm as the program brought them a supposedly live orchestral performance. When the program was interrupted for a news flash, the calm was shattered by the announcement that Martians had landed at a farm near Grovers Mill, New Jersey. The increasingly frequent and intense news flashes in the broadcast sounded very much like reports by Walter Winchell, whose hurried tenor was familiar to millions and was the radio standard of the day.

As the Martian invasion ensued and it became apparent that the Martians had vastly superior weaponry, numerous people who lived along the eastern seaboard, especially the New York and New Jersey area, panicked. Many listeners gathered their personal belongings and fled their homes or hid in basements. The broadcast made news headlines for weeks because of the widespread panic it caused. A study by a psychologist showed that one in six listeners—1 million people—thought the show was a real broadcast and that Martians were invading (although not all 1 million panicked and fled).

Together, studies of the *War of the Worlds* broadcast and other radio programming demonstrated that media effects could be quite dramatic, but that media did not produce uniform effects across the population. The research indicated that a variety of factors, including different individual personalities, demographics, and psychological variables like good critical thinking ability, could mediate audience members' response to media exposure.

This event focused Americans' attention on the power of mass communication in the form of radio and triggered one of the first major research investigations of a media program on the subject of social panic and mass hysteria, as well as a debate about the government's control over the radio industry. As spectacular and strange as these incidents may be, by far the major reasons researchers have examined media effects have been concerns about depictions of sex and violence. These concerns gained even greater force with the advent of television as a form of mass communication.

■ ■ ■ TELEVISION AND VIOLENCE

Although a lot of television programming is educational and entertaining, much of it is laced with violence, sex, and profanity. Consequently, many adult viewers and policy makers have pondered what effect all this extended television viewing may be having on the minds, bodies, and souls of society's next generation. Is viewing television violence eroding children's morals? Are children learning to be overly aggressive, in imitation of what they see on the television screen? Are they learning more about the Three Stooges than the three branches of government?

Hundreds of studies have been conducted and millions of dollars have been spent to investigate the effects of TV violence on children who viewed it. Among the first was a study that introduced the notion that television had become the new "Pied Piper." In this view, television was providing a model for children to imitate, oftentimes not a very good model.

Yet few early studies could provide conclusive evidence that exposure to TV violence would have negative consequences in the real world. Laboratory research in the 1950s by psychologist Albert Bandura and others had shown that children exposed to TV violence were more likely to repeat the behavior they had witnessed (e.g., beating a "Bobo doll") as well as become more aggressive—while they were still in the lab. Although these studies showed that children learned by watching others, the effects could be documented initially only within a laboratory setting. In the so-called **Bobo Doll studies** the researchers could not confirm that the children continued to be more aggressive once they had left the laboratory and returned to their normal lives.

The 1960s saw a dramatic rise in social unrest and violence in public, much of it politically motivated. In response, President Lyndon B. Johnson in 1968 convened the National Commission on the Causes and Prevention of Violence. He was concerned about a broad range of violence and its social causes, but one major part was the media. Emerging from the commission's media task force in 1969 was a massive three-part report called *Violence and the Media*. It focused on not only the quantity of violence on entertainment television, but also its quality. How did the media portray violence? Who used which weapons to kill whom and what were their motivations and the consequences of their acts? Did the aggressors find reward or punishment? Professor George Gerbner of the Annenberg School for Communication at the University of Pennsylvania was selected as the head of the team to conduct the content analysis. His study defined violence as "the overt expression of force intended to hurt or kill."

Overall, Gerbner and his colleagues found the consequences of television violence were unrealistic. There was rarely pain or much blood. Good guys were often as violent as bad guys but did not suffer the negative consequences of their actions. Bad guys usually got their punishment not from the courts but from the cops. Whites were often the victims, and young black males and other people of color, as well as immigrants, were typically the perpetrators of crime. A follow-up report by Gerbner reached many of the same conclusions.

The 1980s and the 1990s witnessed continued research on TV violence. The American Psychological Association is-

Bobo Doll studies
....
Experiments done in the 1950s that showed that children who watched violent episodes on television in which the violent person was rewarded were more likely to punch a Bobo Doll than children who saw violent episodes in which the violent person was punished. This research seemed to confirm certain assumptions about direct media effects.

Depictions of violence on television continue to be a concern among many groups.

Advertising and Its Potential Negative Effects on Women

Advertising is designed to persuade people in some manner: to buy goods or services or to take some action, such as to vote for a particular candidate. Extensive research is conducted by the industry to measure the effectiveness of particular advertising campaigns. But frequently there are side effects, perhaps unintended. Among the most significant possible side effects are the attitudes and behaviors of young viewers who may be influenced by the characters in television commercials they see depicted in a variety of stereotypical, demeaning or self-destructive behaviors or situations.

One group has been particularly outspoken in its criticism of such advertising, the Advertising Women of New York. On September 28, 1999, the group released a study of 556 young women ages twelve to nineteen. The group had commissioned Smart Girl Internette Inc. in New York to conduct the investigation. In the study, 55 percent of respondents answered "Yes, I see them all the time" to the question "Have you ever seen an ad that made you feel like you needed to go on a diet?" With a high number of teenage girls suffering from eating disorders, the findings are particularly disturbing. "That's frightening," said Ellen Flahive, president of Advertising Women of New York.

Respondents also said many commercials "offend" them by portraying women as if they "only care about their looks," by depicting models as "too skinny," and by skewing camera angles to "focus on sexy body parts." One of the most offending commercials in 1999 was produced by the Frito-Lay unit of PepsiCo, Inc., and BBDO New York of the Omnicom Group. The commercial is for barbecue-flavored Doritos snack chips and shows a library filled with male students studying human anatomy in the form of the model Ali Landry as she saunters by in a clinging dress.[7]

Television and other media make a sizeable portion of their revenues from ads like this one. If you were the president of one of the major commercial television networks, would you consider banning such advertising, knowing it would significantly reduce revenues and might result in the loss of jobs at the network?

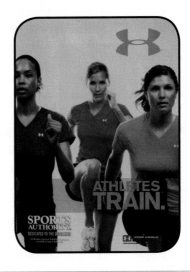

sued in 1992 its TV violence report, *Big World, Small Screen: The Role of Television in American Society*. It argued, "The accumulated research clearly demonstrates a correlation between viewing violence and aggressive behavior. Children and adults who watch a large number of aggressive programs also tend to hold attitudes and values that favor the use of violence." It is important to note that correlation does not equal causation, so although there may be a relationship between television-violence viewing and aggressive behavior, the one does not necessarily cause the other.

One of the most important studies of TV violence in the 1990s was conducted by a team of researchers at UCLA led by Jeffrey Cole. Cole's research shows that U.S. network-television-series programming has gotten somewhat less violent in recent years, but that "shockumentary" reality-based specials have increased dramatically. Funded by the networks themselves, the *UCLA Television Violence Report* showed that overall violence decreased on ABC, CBS, Fox, and NBC during the 1994–1995 season. But the reality-based programs are especially violence filled and are most commonly encountered on Fox. These programs feature real and re-created footage of police shootouts, car chases and crashes, and animals attacking people, in some cases killing them on air.

■ ■ ■ LIMITED EFFECTS

A landmark research investigation of the impact of television on children in North America was conducted by Wilbur Schramm, Jack Lyle, and Edwin Parker in 1960. In their study, *Television in the Lives of Our Children*, Schramm, Lyle, and Parker concluded that some children under some conditions were likely to exhibit some negative consequences of exposure to television violence. But there was no magic bullet of media effects. The results from this and other studies with similar findings developed various kinds of limited-effects models.

In this view, media are seen as a component in a much larger, and more fundamental, system of influences to which all are subject. Institutions such as the family, school, and religion were seen as much more influential on the individual. These institutions were viewed as providing the basic set of forces shaping the individual's tastes, attitudes, and behaviors. Media exposure was seen as contributing to and often reinforcing the individual's worldview, but clearly secondary.

Cultivation Analysis

George Gerbner conducted research on the long-term impact of television watching that led to a theory known as **cultivation analysis**. In this view, television cultivates in audiences a view of reality similar to the world portrayed in television programs. Rather than emphasizing the impact of individual programs on individual viewers, cultivation analysis posits that the cumulative effect of viewing thousands of murders on television is to see the world as a more dangerous place than it actually is. This is known as the "**mean-world syndrome.**" Because television programs are designed as mainstream entertainment and are easy to understand, they provide a means by which people, especially children, are socialized into society.

Research by Gerbner and others has provided evidence that those who watch more television are more likely not only to believe the real world is a more dangerous place, but to be stronger supporters of a more powerful system of law enforcement. Senior citizens who watch more television are more inclined to stay at home because they are more fearful of perceived dangers in the real world. Cultivation effects are not uniform, however.

Spiral of Silence

The **spiral of silence hypothesis** was developed by German communication scholar Elisabeth Noelle-Neumann to explain why people may be unwilling to express publicly their opinions when they believe they are in the minority. Her analysis is based on her own observations of Germans during the Nazi regime in the 1930s and 1940s.

cultivation analysis
....
A theory of media effects that states television cultivates in audiences a view of reality similar to the world portrayed in television programs. For example, it posits that viewing thousands of murders on television is unlikely to increase the chances that one will commit murder but does lead to one's belief that the world is a more dangerous place than it actually is.

mean-world syndrome
....
The notion that the world is a more dangerous place than it actually is, which has come from watching news reports or violent programming.

spiral of silence hypothesis
....
A hypothesis that states people (1) are naturally afraid of isolation, (2) realize that if they are in the minority on an issue they will likely be isolated, and (3) have a kind of sixth sense that helps them gauge when their opinions are contrary to the majority—which makes them refrain from expressing their opinions.

It's a Mean, Mean World—At Least on TV

When looking at data on children's television-violence viewing, it is obvious that most children in the United States are heavy viewers of television, and much of what they see is violent in nature. Evidence accumulated over the past half century indicates that this heavy violence viewing increases aggressiveness, especially among young boys, although the effects are present among girls as well.

- By age twelve, the average American child sees eight thousand murders and one hundred thousand acts of violence on television.[8]
- By age eighteen, that child has seen on TV two hundred thousand acts of violence, including forty thousand acts of murder.[9]
- Longitudinal studies show that eight-year-old boys who viewed the most violent programs were more likely to act aggressively and engage in delinquent behavior by age eighteen and commit criminal behavior by age thirty.[10]
- Fifty-four percent of children have a television set in their own bedroom and often watch with a friend, unsupervised.[11]
- Half (47 percent) of the violent actions include no depiction of pain.[12]
- A national survey of two thousand boys and girls showed that one in ten (9.1 percent) boys and one in fifty (2.2 percent) girls said they were victims of genital assault (being kicked or hit with an object in the genitals) as a result of children imitating movies and television programs such as *The Jungle Book*, *Dumb and Dumber*, and *Three Ninjas*.[13]

The numbers may seem alarming, and most people would likely agree that there is no reason the average American child should see eight thousand murders on television by the time he or she is twelve years old. However, it is also important to remember that cause and effect cannot be attributed to these numbers regarding violence, even the ones showing eight-year-old boys who saw the most violent programs were more likely to engage in criminal behavior.

A common problem with direct-media-effects thinking in trying to pin actions on earlier media use (such as television watching) is that it ignores other potential factors. Perhaps children who watch more television or violent shows tend to live in households in which violence is also more common, or perhaps they are less supervised than their peers. These factors could have more of an effect on subsequent delinquent behavior than simply watching television—which could be merely the symptom of another problem.

The spiral of silence hypothesis has been widely tested and shown to be valid under a variety of circumstances. It is based on three premises:

1. People have a natural fear of isolation.

2. Out of fear of isolation, people are reluctant to express publicly views that they feel are in the minority.

3. People have a "quasi-statistical organ," a sort of sixth sense, that allows them to gauge the prevailing climate of opinion and determine what the majority views are on matters of public importance.

How people gauge the climate of opinion is based on a variety of factors, including their past experiences and interactions with others, but is especially shaped by the media. If a person feels her point of view is in alignment with the prevailing climate of opinion, then she will feel more comfortable publicly expressing that viewpoint. If on the other hand she feels out of step with public opinion, then she will be increasingly less likely to express that opinion, thus leading to a possible spiral of silence. In some instances, it is possible that even a majority opinion, if perceived to be the minority (possibly through biased media reporting), may not be expressed publicly.

Third-Person Effect

Among the most interesting of media effects was first observed outside the United States, although its implications are not limited to the international arena. It is known as the **third-person effect** of communication, and it occurs when a media message does not affect the behavior or beliefs of the intended audience but does affect a different group, which also receives the message and may act in the belief that the message will affect the intended audience.

The third-person effect of communication was first recognized from examining records from World War II in which the Japanese dropped propaganda leaflets to black servicemen stationed in the South Pacific, saying the Japanese were fighting against the white imperialists and had no ill will toward blacks. It encouraged them to surrender and promised them good treatment until after the war was over, by which time they could return home. Although records show this campaign had no effect on the black servicemen it targeted, it did cause the white officers of these black troops to transfer soldiers away from areas where they could be targets of the propaganda in order to avoid any potential loss of morale.

Many researchers have since studied the third-person effect of communication and demonstrated its widespread impact in society and in many different circum-

third-person effect

When a media message does not affect the behavior or beliefs of the intended audience but does affect a different group, which also receives the message and may act in the belief that the message will affect the intended audience.

TV news coverage can affect voter behavior, especially when people see that a race looks like it has already been decided by earlier voters.

stances. In the political-communication arena the third-person effect may play a role in election outcomes if the media publicizes results too early. If the election outcome seems to be decided early by exit polls, many people may decide not to bother voting because it won't seem to make a difference anyway.

■ ■ ■ CRITICISMS OF MEDIA-EFFECTS RESEARCH

Although the direct-effects assumptions and hypodermic-needle model of media power were discredited by subsequent research very quickly, the notion among the general public and policy makers remains strong. When tragedies like the Columbine High shootings in 1999 or the Virginia Tech shootings in 2007 occur, media use by the killers is always discussed. Experts may not blame comic books and radio anymore, but television, the Internet, and video games are all fair game when trying to show blame for violent or antisocial actions.

A basic flaw in much media-effects research is the assumption of the audience as more or less a "passive dupe," or people with no wills of their own and who become easily controlled by media messages. The assumption of a passive dupe is a direct descendant of the belief that the masses are incapable of governing themselves. Although researchers today do not believe that people are simply automatons that can be programmed to act and behave a certain way based on what messages they get, even some of the limited-effects models can lean toward perceiving audiences as passive rather than active.

Even if the media influence us in some way, it is nearly impossible to separate the intertwining social, cultural, psychological, and media factors and find specific links that provide clear cause-and-effect explanations. To say that certain programs, songs, or video games lead to predictable behaviors or attitudes is hardly believable, given all the other influences we potentially have in our daily lives.

Another criticism of media-effects research is that it is examining the wrong end of the communications process. Some scholars claim that in order to actually understand the role that media play in our lives we have to understand the processes and economics of media products. Other scholars choose to focus not on what media may or may not do to us, but what we may or may not do with the media. This is partially what audience-focused research attempts to find out.

Understanding the Audience

To a certain extent mass-communications research has always been about trying to understand the audience. For advertising and public relations, knowing how the audience thinks and the tools to best persuade it can determine success or failure of a campaign or new brand. For political communication the audience, broadly conceived, is essentially the public and public opinion. For media companies, knowing what shows, books, music, and films audiences will like is a vital element for success. In scholarly communications research, the trend in audience studies in recent years has been toward seeing the audience as increasingly active in how it makes sense of the world and uses media.

■ ■ ■ AUDIENCES CREATING MEANING

It may seem odd to think of audiences creating meaning from media content they consume, but remember what was discussed earlier in this chapter about semiotics and how we tend to take a given meaning of a sign or symbol for granted once we know it. Similarly, scholars who use the new audience-studies approaches question the assumption that a media product comes with a predetermined and unchangeable meaning that audiences then ingest like a fast-food hamburger. Rather, they claim that we are always actively participating in creating meaning around the media we encounter, and this happens not only between the media and audience, but between audience members. Some approaches look at psychology, while others focus on the social aspects of creating meaning, while still others examine broader cultural issues and relations of power.

Uses and Gratifications

Uses-and-gratifications research looks at *why* people use particular media. It examines what people do with the media rather than what the media do to people. Uses-and-gratifications research became popular in the 1970s and 1980s. It posits that people have certain needs, especially psychological needs, which they seek to satisfy through media usage. Uses and gratifications makes three basic claims:

1. People actively use the media for their own purposes.
2. People know what those purposes are and can articulate them.
3. Despite individual differences in media use, there are basic common patterns among people.

Uses-and-gratifications research is based on a model of a more active rather than passive audience (i.e., audience members seek to satisfy certain needs through their media use) and may lend itself to future media research on the Internet and interactive media.

Uses-and-gratifications research is not without its critics, however. It has been criticized for being somewhat circular in its reasoning and hard to test empirically. In other words, it's hard to know which came first—the social/psychological need or the media use. Other criticisms include its focus on psychological needs while ignoring the important role that social forces play in media use and the assumption that audiences always do know (and can articulate) why they are using media.

Encoding/Decoding

The **encoding/decoding** model, developed by Stuart Hall in the 1970s as a response to dissatisfaction with media-effects research at the time, takes a broadly cultural approach to audiences and tries to examine them within larger relations of production and social power. It began what is known as the active-audience approach to research.

The model is complex, but in essence it states that media products are encoded with meanings by media producers and those meanings are decoded in various ways by the audience. There is no guarantee that the producer's preferred meaning is the one that will become accepted by the audience, as audience members have three basic options when decoding.

They can choose the dominant, or hegemonic, reading (the one that the media producer likely intended). The dominant reading is one that most people would recognize as "common sense" or would accept as natural. They can choose the oppositional reading, in which they recognize the codes being used but reject them and put their own meanings to the media product. They can also choose a negotiated reading, in which they largely accept the dominant reading but add some variations to it. Audiences will have varied decoding skills and tendencies based on their backgrounds, education, identities, and other social factors.

uses-and-gratifications research
A branch of research on media effects that looks at why people use particular media and examines what people do with the media rather than what the media do to people.

encoding/decoding
A theory that says that messages are encoded with certain meanings by media producers and that audiences then "decode" the messages in various ways, depending on things like their education level, political views, and other factors.

Reception Analysis

Reception analysis was a major break in audience research in a number of respects. First, the starting point for much of the research was the assumption that audience members were active in making meaning with the media they consumed. Second, researchers looked at areas of popular entertainment such as soap operas, women's magazines, and romance novels rather than the traditional areas of news or other "serious" programming that had been studied in earlier years. Third, the areas of study allowed feminist and other scholars to study not only the role of women in media, but women as active audiences.

The findings challenged long-held assumptions about the reasons why women read romance novels, or why they watched a soap opera such as *Dallas*, or how teen girls perceived Madonna. In contrast to some of the notions commonly held, even by feminist scholars, that these forms of popular culture were demeaning to women or taught them to see themselves as sex objects within a patriarchal viewpoint, scholars found that women were active participants in deciding what such content meant to them and freely chose a variety of meanings.

Reception analysis attempts to fill the holes in previous types of theorizing and research by looking at cultural and social patterns of media production and power relations between different groups. However, some critics have argued that it has gone too far in its claims of active audiences, making media almost powerless. Another strand of research on mass communications, cultural studies, attempts to look at media through broad cultural and social frameworks and media production.

Madonna has been a polarizing figure among researchers of pop culture, with some saying she empowers young women and others saying she promotes standard gender stereotypes.

Cultural Studies

The focus on culture and broader societal issues in relation to media, seen in reception-analysis research and the encoding/decoding model of Stuart Hall, falls within a broad category of scholarly research developed in the 1970s called **cultural studies**. Difficult to define concisely because of the wide range of research interests encompassed by the discipline (some even disagree that it can be called a discipline, let alone a scientific discipline), it nevertheless has seen tremendous growth from the 1990s into the early part of the twenty-first century. More and more universities have created cultural-studies departments in recent years.

Cultural-studies approaches to research largely reject the media-effects research tradition and attempt to understand how meaning is produced not only among audiences but among media producers. By looking at popular culture in its many facets and with a critical eye toward dominance and related issues of uses of power and subordination, researchers hope to better understand the role that media plays in perpetuating these social relations.

European versions of cultural studies tend to be Marxist oriented and highly critical of existing politics and culture, while the North American version of cultural studies has tended to be more celebratory than critical of consumer culture and media. Even with these differences, cultural-studies scholars tend to have a normative rather than descriptive bent to their research. In other words, they want to try to make society better rather than claiming they are neutral observers simply describing society.

cultural studies

A framework in studying theories of communication that shuns the scientific approach used by scholars in the empirical school and that tries to examine the symbolic environment created by mass media and the role mass media plays in culture and society.

■ ■ ■ IDEOLOGY AND THE CULTURE INDUSTRY

The normative focus of cultural studies stems from its origins in **critical theory** and the Frankfurt School scholars who created critical theory in the 1930s and 1940s in

Germany at the Institute for Social Research, based in Frankfurt. Theodor Adorno, Max Horkheimer, Herbert Marcuse, and to some degree Walter Benjamin were all German Marxist scholars with a variety of research interests ranging from music theory and philosophy to sociology.

The Frankfurt School coined the term "**culture industry**" to refer to how media businesses created mass-produced "cultural products" that were then consumed by the masses. They distinguished between "high art" (opera, classical music, etc.) and "popular art" (jazz, film, etc.), which they saw as demeaning and crass partly because of its commercial nature.

Although their views may be criticized as artistic snobbery, their larger point was that the culture industry plays an important role in propagating an **ideology** that helps maintain the status quo. In other words, it makes existing power relations and inequality seem natural or inevitable and discourages critical reflection among people—which high art, on the other hand, encourages. In this view, media production is not simply a by-product or reflection of popular tastes and desires; it actively creates those desires and plays a vital role in suppressing freedom.

It is important to note that they are not simply talking about authoritarian governments such as Nazi Germany, although it applies to these kinds of governments as well. They are claiming that even supposedly "free market" systems are actually not free at all, because the media of mass communications promote capitalist ideology as the best way of life while ignoring the fundamental problems of capitalist systems.

Herbert Marcuse was a prominent member of the Frankfurt School and one of the founders of critical theory.

Theories Old, Theories New, Theories Borrowed. . .

INTERNATIONAL PERSPECTIVES

Tracing the intellectual history of currently popular media theories and research can be a fascinating exercise and give us a better sense of how theories may be influencing our thinking.

Most of the theoretical frameworks used in media research have been borrowed in one form or another from European schools of thought in the humanities or social sciences. The sole American-made school of philosophical thought, pragmatism, was largely superseded by European schools of thought after the early part of the twentieth century, although important aspects of pragmatism can be found today in some social theories.

Many ostensibly "new" theories actually have deep roots in combinations of much older theories or are combinations of different schools of thought with unique insights added to create a more relevant theory.

Some of Europe's most interesting thinkers draw from a wide variety of sources as they tackle social issues or the role of the media in society. These include philosophy, literary theory, history, economics, political theory, social theory, and cognitive science.

It is also interesting to note that scholars in some European countries are much more visible than scholars in the United States. For example, in France social theorists Michel Foucault and Pierre Bourdieu were virtually media celebrities in their own right, appearing on television to discuss theoretical issues and writing regularly on political and social topics for popular newspapers.

■■■ POLITICAL ECONOMY

Another area of media research that has been inspired by Marxism and influenced by critical theory is **political economy**. Political-economist media scholars examine the production and ownership of media as main forces that determine the type of media we have and what that means for our social and political systems and our lives.

Scholars such as Robert McChesney study the history and current status of media ownership, regulations and laws applying to media, and especially the conglomeration of media ownership and how that has affected the type of media we have. In other words, political economists would argue that simply looking at how audiences use or are affected by media products misses the point, as it largely ignores the really important question of how we got the media in the first place.

They claim that by examining the forces of media production—by seeing who owns what media companies and studying how their business decisions determine types of media, how they are delivered, to whom, and in what way—we are then better able to understand the underlying forces behind power relations and dominance.

A political-economic viewpoint has an advantage over most forms of audience-studies research in that it enables media scholars to explore areas where an audience does not actually yet exist. For example, an audience-studies researcher would be unable to study Hispanic-language newspaper readership in an area that does not have a Hispanic-language newspaper. But the question "Why isn't there a Hispanic-language newspaper for this audience in this market?" would be a legitimate area of study for a political economist, as would exploring the type of content such a newspaper likely would have if it did exist.

■■■ CRITICISMS OF CULTURAL STUDIES

Cultural studies, despite its rise in popularity in academia, is not without its detractors and faults as a field of study. One common complaint is the often impenetrable, jargon-laden writing style of many cultural-studies researchers, which excludes many people who have not had extensive academic study. This is at odds with the broad goal of helping to bring about positive changes in society by enlightening the public about how it is oppressed and the role that media play in that oppression.

The writing style is also criticized for hiding muddled thinking and masking mundane ideas behind grandiose jargon. In 1996, a physicist at New York University, Alan Sokal, published an article in the postmodern journal *Social Text* entitled "Transgressing the Boundaries: Toward a Transformative Hermeneutics of Quantum Gravity." The title and writing style were typical of many journal articles written from a postmodern perspective, but the article was actually a hoax and purposely written to be nonsensical. Sokal said he perpetrated the hoax to show the danger, in the social sciences, of basing scholarship on fashionable or trendy schools of thought rather than on reason.

In the same vein, other critics of cultural studies say that since it largely rejects scientific tenets such as the importance of rationalism for finding truth, it cannot actually be called a science. Without any basis for measuring the correctness or incorrectness of viewpoints, it is nearly impossible to have any grounds for refuting ideas that are clearly wrong.

As may be expected for a medium that is still relatively new, there are still large gaps in research and theorizing about digital media and the Internet. Early euphoria about the positive transformative effects the Internet would have for society and democracy have given way to more measured, careful statements that also

critical theory
....
An umbrella term for a range of theories, most of which are influenced by Marxism, which attempts to look critically at society and offer ways to make society better.

culture industry
....
A term used by some critical theorists that refers to the mass communication industries and their power in creating culture as a commodity.

ideology
....
A way of belief that goes largely unquestioned by people or that is seen as somehow natural or beyond question.

political economy
....
An area of study inspired by Marxism that examines the relationship between politics and economics with media ownership and the influences they all have on society and perpetuating the status quo.

Robert McChesney is a noted political economist of media and has taken a leading role in the media reform movement, founding Free Press.

Web Link >>>
Alan Sokal's Articles on the "Social Text" Affair
www.physics.nyu.edu/faculty/sokal/#debate_
    linguafrancaDigitalMediaTheoryandResearch

recognize the dangers or weak spots and studies that have sometimes shown surprising effects.

Some scholars have claimed that nothing has fundamentally changed, from the perspective of media theory or social theory, with the rise of the Internet and digital media, and that existing conceptual frameworks are perfectly adequate for researching and explaining new media. This may be true in some cases, but it also leaves large blind spots in the research agenda, such as explaining the changes taking place in the nature of mass communication.

Research and theorizing on digital media and the Internet is further complicated by the fact that rapid technological changes can have drastic effects on usage and perceptions. Studies done two years earlier that involve a certain technology or framework may seem hopelessly outdated by the time a journal article is published, especially if the technology that was studied no longer has the same prominence.

Researchers who focus on digital media tend to draw heavily from research traditions in media studies, sociology, information science, and communication studies, among other disciplines. The broad research frameworks correspond more or less to those applied to traditional media, ranging from the broad-based sociocultural perspectives to Internet use-and-effects research to studying the ways characteristics of the medium itself, such as interactivity, may affect our relation with content.

It is also interesting to note that some pre-Internet scholars could experience a revival of interest in some lines of their work. For example, Marshall McLuhan, with his examination of the way electronic media implode space and time and affect social relations, may have much to offer digital-media scholars studying the Internet. Uses-and-gratifications principles may prove especially fruitful in an interactive medium where users largely control what content they can get and how they get it.

■ ■ ■ INFORMATION SOCIETY

information society

The notion that modern society has transformed from one in which industrial production was dominant to one in which information production has become more important.

The meaning of the **information society**—sometimes also named the "network society," "knowledge society," or "postindustrial society"—is still being debated by social scientists. Information-society theories posit that the prominence of communications and media ushers in a new era that breaks drastically from the industrial society. Networks become hugely important as they bring the world closer together, and economic value lies not so much in the old manufacturing centers, like it once did, but in knowledge centers. Education and training will be the keys to success for workers, who will be valued not for the manual labor they are able to do but for the ideas, knowledge, and creativity they have to make sense of and create information.

There are many critics of the often utopian picture painted by information-society theories. Some scholars, especially those influenced by Marxism or critical theory, claim that the information society is actually making established relations of dominance stronger for transnational media corporations as fewer companies control more media channels, including those on the Internet. They point to the rhetoric used for earlier media types that promised to be emancipatory when they were new, such as radio, and chronicle the relentless control by government and corporations that rendered claims about any new medium bringing freedom or democracy largely hollow.

One criticism with information-society theories is that they take a small slice of the world's population and expand its way of life to almost everyone. One does not have to look far to see that much of the world lives in conditions where clean water is a rarity, let alone ready access to the Internet, or even electricity. This leads to discussions regarding the **digital divide**, one of the most important Internet-audience issues today.

Research has shown that from the early days of public use of the Internet, especially from the first graphical Web browsers, Internet access tended to be much higher among society's economically advantaged—those with higher education and with a legacy of higher overall print-media use. Economically disadvantaged groups, especially minority groups and the rural poor, tended to have less Internet access and lower Internet and overall online usage. Yet, the gap has closed dramatically if not disappeared in some cases. Women, for example, now make up the majority of Internet users in the United States—across economic lines. Problems of equity of access to online media will not disappear soon, however, especially among the economically disadvantaged and those in the developing world.

digital divide

The idea that some groups that do not have access to the Internet become left out of the benefits that online technology can bring.

■ ■ ■ AUDIENCES AS CONSUMERS, USERS, OR PRODUSERS?

In contrasting online media with traditional analog media, perhaps the most basic distinction is that the online audience has to be to some extent interactive in order to access desired media, including reaching other members of the audience. The audience online can be in many ways a full participant in the process of online communication.

Although there are certainly passive media experiences online, they only happen after the user has first engaged them. Although the research to date exploring active audiences online is fairly limited, it is growing rapidly and becoming one of the most important areas of Internet research in the twenty-first century.

The change from viewer to user or producer affects media organizations, the way news and entertainment are presented, and even what types of news or entertainment will likely become popular. Even more importantly, the nature of the relationship between the audience and media producers is changing, affecting a broad swath of social relations and the hierarchical power relations often taken for granted. Even non-media companies have had to start thinking of themselves as content producers, or at least start giving the tools to audiences to produce **user-generated content**.

Giving children access to computers and teaching them media and computer literacy will help them succeed in the twenty-first century.

Because of the newness of the Internet, there is a growing amount of research on the impact of time spent online, on both children and adults. A major study was launched in 1999 to examine the social, cultural, and commercial impact of the Internet. Funded by a consortium of major companies interested in online communication, the study is headed by Jeffrey Cole, director of the UCLA Center for Communication Policy, who had earlier headed the UCLA Television Violence Study. Among the companies sponsoring the twenty-year longitudinal investigation are Microsoft, America Online, Disney, and Sony. Researchers are studying a variety of questions, including how family time, political leanings, and social life are influenced by Internet usage. The study is also designed to examine online banking, shopping and buying habits, comfort with using credit cards online, and other issues related to ecommerce. The initial panel includes two thousand people selected from a national sample, and international representatives will be added later.[14]

Research is being conducted on the effects of video games, including how they may reinforce negative gender or racial stereotypes. How violent video games influence children is not as well known or researched as is the impact of violent television programming. Yet, evidence consistently shows that children have a great

user-generated content

Media content that has been created by consumers or audience members, including videos, music, or other forms of content.

Web Link >>>
The Pew Research Center for the People & the Press
people-press.org/

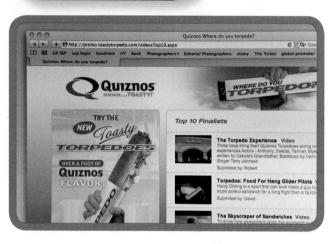

User-generated content (UGC) is an example of the shift in audiences from consumers to produsers.

ability to imitate actions they observe. And young children under five years of age, especially, do not always have the ability to determine whether such violent actions are appropriate or properly motivated or justified. Moreover, the highly repetitive and interactive nature of video games in which the player is often attempting to kill or brutalize a facsimile of a human being would lead one to expect these negative effects to be even greater than with television viewing.

LOOKING BACK AND MOVING FORWARD

This chapter explained the importance of media theory and research to media professionals and to people who simply want to better understand how media works, why we get the type of media content we do, and how it may affect us.

An important divide to remember is the role of quantitative versus qualitative research. Each methodology has strengths and weaknesses, but the two can also be combined to create powerful tools for researchers. At heart, though, they have vastly different philosophies on the nature of the world, knowledge, and what makes up reality.

The fact that most theories of communication and especially of media have originated with scholars outside of media studies may prove to be a strength for the field going forward. First, unlike other social scientific disciplines, which have developed fairly strong traditions of specific lines of inquiry and research considered legitimate, media scholars can borrow from disciplines that are most relevant to them. This kind of interdisciplinary approach to research and theorizing is being seen more and more and can be very effective in asking some interesting questions and in finding answers.

The need for interdisciplinarity is even more important when studying digital media, as technology, media content, media ownership, and social uses of media all readily intertwine. For scholars, having an understanding of a breadth of disciplines, while perhaps specializing in one area, will be necessary to tackle some of the tough theoretical issues involving digital media.

The reams of user information created online through natural usage and tracking provide many opportunities for researchers, but also many challenges. It may be hard to sift through so much data and try to make sense of something like the number of hyperlinks on an average web page or how the frequency of text messages affects our ability to concentrate on complex tasks.

Audience-research questions will likely continue to be largely driven by the same forces as they have been, namely companies that want to better monitor and target audiences. This means researchers will need to be well versed in the rapidly changing technologies in the social-media space and have a solid grounding in principles and theories of human communication and social behavior.

DISCUSSION QUESTIONS

1. Find some recent media or social science studies reported in the news and determine whether they are quantitative of qualitative types of research. What are the strengths and weaknesses of the approaches used in these?

2. Discuss whether you believe there is an objective reality that can be clearly measured and explained or whether there are various realities or truths that defy scientific explanations.

3. Which type of medium do you think may have the strongest influence on people, radio, film, television, or the Internet? Why?

4. Describe some of your own experiences in seeing how television may have affected your behavior or that of your friends in terms of actions, fashion sense, or career goals. Were these changes short- or long-term?

5. Write a list of your television or film heroes from your teens to the present, along with a brief sentence on why you like each one. Compare lists with a classmate of either a different ethnic group, age, or gender and discuss your choices.

6. What implications for media on the Internet could there be as more people from different countries start using the Internet? Do you think these implications are good or bad for an American, English-speaking audience? Why?

7. Discuss ways in which some of the older media theories may be applied usefully to explain social media or practices related to social media.

FURTHER READING

Quantitative Research Methods for Communication: A Hands-On Approach. Jason Wrench, Candice Thomas-Maddox, Virginia Peck Richmond, James McCroskey (2008) Oxford University Press.

Ethnography: A Way of Seeing. Harry F. Wolcott (1999) Rowman & Littlefield.

Understanding Media Theory. Kevin Williams (2003) A Hodder Arnold Publication.

Understanding Media Cultures: Social Theory and Mass Communication. Nicholas Stevenson (2002) Sage.

Anthropology and Mass Communication: Media and Myth in the New Millennium. Mark Allen Peterson (2003) Berghahn Books.

Critical Theories of Mass Media: Then and Now. Paul Taylor, Jan Harris (2007) Open University Press.

More Than Meets the Eye: Watching Television Watching Us. John J. Pungente, Martin O'Malley (1999) McClelland & Stewart.

Communication, Media, and American Society: A Critical Introduction. Daniel W. Rossides (2002) Rowman & Littlefield.

Theories of the Information Society, 2nd ed. Frank Webster (2002) Routledge.

E-Crit: Digital Media, Critical Theory, and the Humanities. Marcel O'Gorman (2007) University of Toronto Press.

Dark Fiber: Tracking Critical Internet Culture. Geert Lovink (2003) MIT Press.

MEDIA QUIZ ANSWERS

2. False.

10. True.

Communication Law and Regulation in the Digital Age

CHAPTER OBJECTIVES

In this chapter we will

■ Outline a legal framework for understanding the nature of freedom of speech and press and how media are regulated in the United States.

■ Describe the key concepts in law protecting and restricting freedom of speech and press, including threats to national security, libel, and censorship.

■ Review the regulation of content in the United States, especially regarding commercial speech and political speech.

■ Discuss the principal legislation that defines communication regulation in the United States, and the principal federal communications regulatory agency, the Federal Communications Commission.

■ Discuss intellectual property issues, especially copyright, and how they are affected in the digital age.

On April 3, 2007, Josh Wolf stepped out of a federal prison in California and into the record books after spending 226 days in jail, the longest any journalist in U.S. history was held for protecting his sources.

There were several ironies with this case, not the least of which was that there were questions about whether Wolf was actually a journalist. A self-described activist, he participated in, videotaped, and blogged about various protests conducted by anarchist or radical-left groups.

In July 2005 he videotaped an anti-G8 demonstration held in San Francisco, posting excerpts of his footage on the local Indymedia site, part of a worldwide network of activists and citizen journalists.

A policeman was injured during the demonstration, and Wolf was subpoenaed by federal authorities to appear before a grand jury and hand over his footage so investigators could determine if any of the protestors could be identified. Wolf refused on First Amendment grounds and was sentenced to jail, then eventually federal prison, as he continued to refuse to surrender his videotapes.

The prosecution claimed that Wolf was not a journalist but an activist who happened to be capturing a public event on tape and thus had no First Amendment protections. Supporters of Wolf claimed that he was acting in a journalistic capacity by his video reporting and blogging and that his imprisonment could have a chilling effect on other journalists who could be threatened by the government.

On the day Wolf was released from prison he posted all his video footage to his blog. After an unsuccessful run for mayor of San Francisco in 2007, in July 2008 he began work as a general-assignment reporter for a local newspaper, the *Palo Alto Daily Post*. The final bits of irony in the case are that he put down his video camera and focused solely on writing for his new job and is doing so for a newspaper that does not even have a website.

Congress shall make no law respecting an establishment of religion, or prohibiting the free exercise thereof; or abridging the freedom of speech, or of the press; or the right of the people peaceably to assemble, and to petition the government for a redress of grievances.

First Amendment to the Constitution of the United States

A lthough the **First Amendment** guarantees that Congress shall make no law restricting freedom of speech or of the press, it has been interpreted by the courts, elected officials, and legal scholars to permit some level of regulatory and legal restriction. Some of these laws deal with libel, obscenity, and other media-content matters. Others deal with technical issues related to broadcast station operation, such as to prevent one station from interfering with another's signals, and others pertain to media ownership, intellectual property rights, and fulfilling the requirements of broadcasting licenses.

And of course it is important to remember that the First Amendment is very much an American invention. Most other countries have no such stipulation in their constitutions, which of course has resulted in sometimes vastly different laws and regulations regarding mass communication and journalism.

First Amendment
....
Guarantees that Congress shall make no law restricting freedom of speech, press, or religion.

The Legal Framework

When printing began in Renaissance Europe, political and religious authorities were quick to recognize the power of publishing to spread not only religious teachings but political edicts as well. However, political and religious dissidents found printing presses equally useful in disseminating their views against authority. The tension between government control of the press and using the press as a means to be free of political or religious control continues to this day.

The reasons underlying the value of freedom from governmental control were perhaps best articulated by U.S. president Thomas Jefferson, who said, "Information is the currency of democracy." When the first U.S. Congress passed the Bill of Rights in 1789, there were fewer than three dozen printing presses in the country. Despite this small number, the importance of the press was recognized by the nation's founders. Jefferson said, "Were it left for me to decide whether we should have a government without newspapers, or newspapers without a government, I should not hesitate a moment to prefer the latter."

The press is a critical watchdog of government as well as other of powerful institutions in society, including business. But it is as an unofficial "fourth branch" of government, or **fourth estate**, that the press must be free from government censorship or control.

Thomas Jefferson's famous quote about his choice between government and newspapers is often cited to show the important role that journalism plays in a democracy.

Legal Limits

Test your legal knowledge as it relates to the First Amendment, media regulations, and copyright. Mark whether the questions are true or false.

1. Libel and slander are simply two different legal terms for the same thing.
2. In the United Kingdom you can be sued for libel even if what you said about the person is true.
3. It is impossible for politicians, but not public figures such as movie stars, to sue for libel.
4. The government can restrict free speech if it feels it will harm national security.
5. Journalists can protect themselves from libel as long as they properly attribute the questionable material.
6. Broadcasting media face more regulations than print because it is felt they have a greater impact on the audience.
7. Only accredited journalists or freelance writers under contract can use the Freedom of Information Act to request public records from the federal government.
8. The FCC enforces its broadcasting regulations by examining station and network programming and flagging material that is objectionable.
9. A hyperlink is not protected by the First Amendment.
10. If I tell my friend my idea for a novel and he then writes a novel based on my idea, I can sue him for copyright infringement.

In societies where government control over the press, or media, is substantial, as in China or other authoritarian countries where journalists must be licensed to operate, the press suffers from an inability to criticize the government, its policies, or its representatives. More often than not, the press becomes a puppet to the government and is used to promote government positions rather than independently evaluate them. In the United States and other democratic societies, the press ideally acts as an independent balance of power to government bodies. However, concentration of ownership, commercialism, and other circumstances can adversely affect the ability of the press to act responsibly or effectively in its role as watchdog of powerful societal institutions. Business interests may sometimes outweigh public interests, for news organizations.

Despite the early constitutional admonitions to protect freedom of speech and press, there have been many attempts by the government at all levels to infringe upon the independence of the press and to censor. In addition, a second problem has plagued the media with regard to acts of general governmental control. This problem is the failure of the government, in each of its three branches, to extend full First Amendment protection to the media in all their forms. Instead, only the print media have received full protection. In *Miami Herald Publishing Co. v. Tornillo* (1974), for instance, the U.S. Supreme Court struck down a Florida statute that

fourth estate

Another term for the press, or journalism, in which it acts as a fourth branch of government: one that watches the other branches (executive, legislative, and judicial).

required newspapers to give space at no cost to political candidates whose personal or professional character the paper had criticized. However, television and radio stations must provide airtime should the station itself editorially endorse or oppose a candidate.

Radio, television, cinema, and today the Internet have received much less protection than print media, and only through extended legal battles have they won a certain degree of freedom. In fact, during the first half of the twentieth century, cinema was not provided any First Amendment protection. Not until the Supreme Court's 1952 *Miracle* decision (*Joseph Burstyn, Inc. v. Wilson*), when the court ruled that the showing of a film could not be prohibited because a censor deemed it sacrilegious, did any constitutional protection extend to motion pictures.

The historical influences and legal and regulatory decisions on print and electronic media are complex, but they are worth exploring briefly in order to better understand the reasons given for restrictions on media content today.

The Foundations of Freedom of Expression

Governments continue to use many means to control print media. One heavy-handed method is to jail journalists and editors, thus not only silencing them but also often having a **chilling effect** on others who may be tempted to write on similar topics.

chilling effect
....
The phenomenon that occurs when journalists or other media producers decide not to publish stories on a topic after a journalist has been punished or jailed for such a story.

However, such tactics can also backfire in that jailed journalists may stoke public anger at the government or damage the government's reputation. More subtle means of control, such as licensing laws for owning a printing press or being a journalist, or special taxes on printing equipment, paper, or ink, have been used in the past. By controlling the materials needed for printing, governments hoped to be able to control the free flow of information. Government censors, or bodies that examine and approve all printed material, have also been used.

Although these measures continue to be used in various countries, it has been harder for governments to control information than in the past. This is partly because vastly more information is available and partly because electronic media, including the Internet, have become important information sources alongside print media.

Though there is still a long way to go, in many countries, to gain freedom of expression, there have been great strides made in many developed countries over the past few hundred years. Today we may look at the strict censorship and licensing laws of seventeenth- and eighteenth-century England and see them as draconian, yet within this period some of England's most noted literary and journalistic voices flourished, such as Jonathan Swift and Samuel Johnson. Nevertheless, it is important to remember that our concept of freedom of expression was not immutable. The notion evolved over time and has largely been influenced by several major court cases that dealt with either national security issues, libel, or censorship.

■ ■ ■ NATIONAL SECURITY

In 1798, only a little over a decade since the creation of the Constitution and Bill of Rights, a series of four acts limiting freedom of speech were passed by the U.S. Congress. The **Alien and Sedition Acts** were passed by the Federalist-controlled U.S. Congress as a response to a threat of war with France and were meant to crush the position of the Jeffersonian Republicans, who were sympathetic to France.

Among other things, the acts prohibited **sedition**, meaning spoken or written criticism of the U.S. government, and imposed penalties of a fine or imprisonment upon conviction. With the end of the threat of war, the Sedition Act expired in 1801, but other sedition acts have resurfaced throughout U.S. history, especially during times of war.[1]

Several important legal concepts have developed with court cases that involved issues of national security, one of the main areas where press freedoms are curtailed.

Clear and Present Danger

The most basic restriction is when the speech in question meets both of the following conditions: (1) it is intended to incite or produce dangerous activity (as with falsely shouting "Fire!" in a crowded theater), and (2) it is likely to succeed in achieving the purported result. This two-part framework is known as the **clear and present danger** test and is subject to the appropriate criminal-law-enforcement authorities and to the judicial system rather than regulatory authorities.

The clear-and-present-danger test emerged from *Schenck v. United States* (1919). In that case, the U.S. Supreme Court unanimously upheld the conviction of Charles T. Schenck for violating the Espionage Act of 1917. Schenck had been distributing handbills urging resistance to U.S. involvement in World War I. He was a Communist but did not commit any violent acts. The Court based its decision on the notion not only that the First Amendment is not absolute, but that in wartime ordinary constitutional rules do not apply.

Alien and Sedition Acts

A series of four acts passed by the U.S. Congress in 1798 that, among other things, prohibited sedition, or spoken or written criticism of the U.S. government, and imposed penalties of a fine or imprisonment upon conviction. Although they expired in 1801, other sedition acts have been passed periodically, especially during times of war.

sedition

Speech or action that encourages overthrow of a government or that subverts a constitution or a nation's laws.

clear and present danger

A restriction on speech when it meets both of the following conditions: (1) it is intended to incite or produce dangerous activity (as with falsely shouting fire in a crowded theater), and (2) it is likely to succeed in achieving the purported result.

During times of war, the courts have often curtailed the public's right to freedom of expression in the interests of national security.

Prior Restraint

An important ruling came in the 1931 Supreme Court case *Near v. Minnesota*. Minnesota courts had stopped the publication of an anti-Semitic weekly on the basis that it was a "malicious, scandalous and defamatory" periodical in violation of the state's nuisance law. The Supreme Court reversed the decision, saying that **prior restraint**, or the government preventing or blocking the publication, broadcasting, showing, or otherwise distributing of media content, whether in print, over the air, or in movie theaters, must only be used in cases of serious or grave threats to national security.

In 1971, the Supreme Court made another important ruling in this regard in the case of *New York Times Co. v. United States*. In this case, the Supreme Court overturned a lower court ruling that had stopped the *Times* from publishing "The Pentagon Papers," a top-secret Pentagon study of U.S. involvement in the Vietnam War. The government failed to prove that national security interest outweighed a heavy presumption against prior restraint.

In 1979, a district court stopped *The Progressive* magazine (*U.S. v. Progressive*) from publishing "The H-Bomb Secret." The magazine had obtained its information from publicly available documents, and six months later the court injunction was lifted after others published similar material.

In sum, the courts have ruled that freedom of speech is not an absolute, especially during time of war. There is, however, a strong presumption against permitting the government any form of prior restraint on publication or distribution of speech, and it is incumbent on the government to clearly show that publication poses a clear and present threat to national security. This framework seems especially relevant in the aftermath of the September 11, 2001, terrorist attack on the World Trade Center and Pentagon.

In his book *Mass Media Law*, Don Pember describes a **preferred-position balancing theory** that has particular utility in this regard. According to this theory, a balance must be struck between speech and other rights, but speech is given a preferred position (especially in print media), and limitations on freedom of speech in print are usually illegal. The burden of proof falls on the government to show that some speech or expression of information is harmful to national security; it is not journalists or media organizations that must prove that it is not harmful.

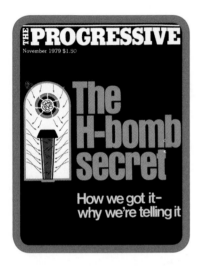

The planned publication by *The Progressive* of how to make a hydrogen bomb was a landmark case regarding the government's right of prior restraint.

■ ■ ■ LIBEL

The foundation for the relationship between freedom of expression and libel in the United States was established in the colonial era. Foremost is the case of John Peter Zenger, a New York printer and journalist who faced a libel suit from the publication of the *New York Weekly Journal*, a political journal opposed to the colonial governor, William Cosby. As publisher of the *Journal*, Zenger was responsible for the articles, which frequently featured scathing attacks on the governor.

In November 1734 Zenger was arrested for libel, and he spent nearly ten months in prison awaiting trial. Zenger's attorney, Andrew Hamilton, requested the jury rule on the veracity of Zenger's printed statements, and in a surprise ruling in August 1735 Zenger was acquitted of libel. This important precedent established the principle of freedom of press in early America and marked a departure from the way much of the world considers libel in the courts, even today. For example, in England someone can successfully be sued for libel even if the statements are true, if the statements damage a person's reputation.

In the United States, libel is a type of defamation, such as a false attack on a person's character, which damages a person's reputation. Libel is different historically from **slander** on the basis that slander involves the spoken word, and libel involves the written word.

With the rise of electronic media in the twentieth century, libel has been extended to broadcasting on television or radio, as well as online communications, even though broadcast media are technically spoken rather than printed.

In the case of *Phipps v. Clark Oil & Ref. Corp.* (1987), the Minnesota court ruled that libel occurs when a publication "tends to injure the plaintiff's reputation and expose the plaintiff to public hatred, contempt, ridicule, or degradation."

The libel case of Peter Zenger in colonial times was a turning point for what defined libel in America.

New York Times v. Sullivan (1964)

Media historians and legal scholars tend to agree that the most important legal decision to establish a free press in the United States was the 1964 Supreme Court ruling in *New York Times Co. v. Sullivan*.

In 1960, the *New York Times* printed a fund-raising advertisement for the civil rights movement, which contained several minor factual errors. L. B. Sullivan, a Montgomery, Alabama, city commissioner in charge of the police, said that some of the false statements in the advertisement regarding Montgomery police actions defamed him, even though he was not mentioned by name. A jury agreed and awarded him a half-million dollars. The *New York Times* appealed the case and it eventually went to the Supreme Court, which overturned the lower court ruling.

The Supreme Court ruled that public figures (defined as publicly prominent) and public officials (defined as public policy makers) may not file suit for libel unless they can prove "actual malice." For nonpublic figures (private citizens), the standard for libel is less stringent, requiring merely that the plaintiff show objectively that a "reasonable person" knew or should have known the defamatory statement was false.

The Court defined "actual malice" in terms of either (1) the intent of the defendant being malicious or (2) the defendant knowing the statement is false but acting with reckless disregard for the truth and publishing it regardless. This is known as the "actual malice" test. The Court ruled that the common law of defamation violated the guarantee of free speech under the First Amendment and that the citizen's right to criticize government officials is too important to be intolerant of speech containing even harmful falsehoods. The result of the ruling has been to maintain a more robust environment for media to publish criticisms of public figures, knowing that they can be found libelous only if they meet the stringent actual-malice test.

Protecting Journalists Against Libel

Most media organizations have libel insurance to protect journalists. Freelance journalists, however, often do not have libel insurance, so the threat of libel can have a serious chilling effect. This is especially true for online journalists and others who operate on a shoestring budget or who are not widely recognized by media organizations as "real" journalists.

slander
....
A type of defamation that is spoken, as opposed to written (libel), that damages a person's reputation or otherwise causes harm.

Moreover, although there is no prior restraint for libel cases, journalists can be imprisoned for contempt in libel cases or others. Most typically this happens when a journalist is protecting sources (i.e., refusing to disclose their identities), but it can also occur for other reasons, such as failing to release one's notes.

There are at least five steps journalists can take to minimize chances of committing an act of libel

1. Engage in thorough research, including investigating the facts and maintaining good records, establishing and adhering to written criteria in making decisions about when and what to publish, and using reliable sources.

2. Confirm the identity of the target of your report.

3. Use quotations whenever possible and attribute statements to sources.

4. Report facts only and avoid language that draws conclusions.

5. Avoid bias in reports and strive for balance (i.e., give the different sides in a debate fair play).

Shield Laws

Shield laws are laws intended to protect journalists from legal challenges to their freedom to report the news. Journalists have received neither blanket protection from the Supreme Court nor a federal shield law. Yet thirty-four states have enacted laws to protect journalists from being required to answer every subpoena.[2] In these states, journalists are not required to testify or produce materials obtained from sources in confidence. Most of the other states and territories provide some court protection for journalists, although they have no shield laws.

Without these shield laws, unrestrained legal action might exert a chilling effect on journalists, some suggest, including Reed Hundt, former chairman of the FCC.[3] "Newsgatherers might be less aggressive and cease to pursue confidential sources or information. Whistle-blowers and other sources could be left without any legal protection from discovery," Hundt said.

Evidence suggests that shield laws have limited effectiveness, based on studies done on the number of subpoenas served to journalists in states with shield laws compared to the number in those without. Opponents of shield laws argue that journalists should not be given special protections from answering subpoenas, given how difficult it is to define what a journalist is. Others worry that trying to explicitly state what defines a journalist could be a first step toward official licensing for journalists, which most news organizations strongly oppose as a curtailment of their First Amendment rights.

Web Link >>>
The Reporters Committee for Freedom of the Press
www.rcfp.org

■ ■ ■ CENSORSHIP

Censorship is the third major dimension of government control over media. It refers to the act of prohibiting certain expression or content. In a sense, it is a form of prior restraint, only rather than prohibiting an entire publication, it targets specific content within that publication, broadcast, film, or website. Censorship is not generally permitted in the United States, although it is routine in some countries, especially ones with authoritarian regimes that prohibit criticism of the government or rulers. In the United States, censorship is most common in two circumstances: (1) during wartime, when content, especially that being reported from the battlefield, is subject to censorship under the principle of national security, and (2) with pornographic or obscene content, which can sometimes include graphic violence or detailed accounts of criminal behavior.

An important censorship case is *Hazelwood School District v. Kuhlmeier* (1988). This case established that not all citizens have the same First Amendment rights. In particular, people still in school, typically but not necessarily those under eighteen, are not afforded full First Amendment protection. In this case, a school principal was permitted to censor school newspaper articles dealing with pregnancy and divorce. The court found that school-sponsored publications are not a public forum and thus may be subject to censorship to protect the young from harm.

Indecent Content

Although not prohibited, **indecent speech** is also subject to federal regulation. Broadcasters may not air indecent speech when children are likely to be in the audience or between 6 a.m. and 10 p.m. This has been called a safe harbor period, and concerned groups sometimes request portrayals of violence or sex to be barred from the time period as well.

Federal law defines indecent speech as "language or material that, in context, depicts or describes, in terms patently offensive as measured by contemporary community standards for the broadcast medium, sexual or excretory organs or activities." Exempted from this definition is profanity that is neither indecent nor obscene. "Damn" is an example of a permitted word. Indecent speech was put to the test in a landmark First Amendment case involving comedian George Carlin.

Carlin recorded before a live California audience a twelve-minute monolog titled "Filthy Words." He opened his routine by contemplating "the words you couldn't say on the public airwaves, the ones you definitely wouldn't say, ever." He then listed those words and repeated them in a variety of contexts. The Supreme Court decision in *Federal Communications Commission v. Pacifica Foundation* (1978) was the basis for subsequent regulations on indecent speech for broadcasters.

Other entertainers have tested and the pushed the limits of freedom of speech in the electronic media as well, including radio "shock jock" Howard Stern, whose frequently crude and vulgar on-air commentary before he moved to satellite radio drew criticism not only from citizen groups but from government regulators. In 1995, Infinity Broadcasting Corp. (owned by CBS), the producer and broadcaster of Stern's radio show, agreed to pay $1.7 million without admitting guilt to settle a variety of indecency charges that had been leveled by the FCC since 1989 against Stern, whose comments are frequently sexually graphic.

As part of the **Telecommunications Act of 1996**, the first sweeping federal legislation to rewrite the foundation of communications regulation in the United States since 1934, legislators had sought to curb "indecent" speech online, but the Communications Decency Act (CDA) passed as part of the act was ultimately struck down by the U.S. Supreme Court in *ACLU v. Janet Reno* (1998). The CDA made it illegal to "depict or describe" on the Internet anything considered indecent and made no distinctions between scientific or literary works and pornography. The ACLU filed a lawsuit against the government the same day the Telecommunications Act was passed,

The courts have ruled that high-school students do not have full First Amendment rights with student publications.

indecent speech
....
Language or material that, in context, depicts or describes, in terms patently offensive as measured by contemporary community standards for the broadcast medium, sexual or excretory organs or activities.

Telecommunications Act of 1996
....
The first major regulatory overhaul of telecommunications since 1934, designed to open the industry to greater competition by deregulating many aspects of it.

George Carlin's comedy routine "Filthy Words" turned into a landmark case regarding indecent content.

Web Link >>>
"Filthy Words" by George Carlin transcript
www.law.umkc.edu/faculty/projects/ftrials/
conlaw/filthywords.html

and a lower court ruled the CDA unconstitutional, which the Supreme Court affirmed.

In late 2008 and early 2009 Facebook found itself the object of "lactivists" who protested its policy of removing photos of breastfeeding mothers from member pages. Threatened with banishment from Facebook for violating its policy on showing exposed breasts, women created the group "Hey Facebook, breastfeeding is not obscene!" and staged online and offline protests, which quickly grew to the tens of thousands.

The protestors pointed out the hypocrisy of Facebook's policies, which accept pictures of women in thongs striking sexy poses and couples making out. Despite getting soundly ridiculed in the press and blogosphere, Facebook refused to change its policy.

Obscenity

obscenity
....
One of the forms of speech not protected by the First Amendment, and thus subject to censorship. Although an exact definition of the term has been difficult to achieve in various court cases, generally a three-part standard is applied for media content: it must appeal to prurient interests as defined by community standards, it must show sexual conduct in an offensive manner, and it must on the whole lack serious artistic, literary, political, or scientific value.

Pornography, or **obscenity**, is one of the major forms of speech deemed unprotected by the First Amendment, and is subject to censorship by the government. A landmark case in this regard was *Miller v. California* (1973), in which Miller had been convicted in California of mailing unsolicited pornographic brochures. He appealed his conviction on the grounds that it inhibited his right to free speech, but the Court disagreed and outlined three criteria for determining whether content is obscene

1. An average individual applying contemporary community standards must believe the content, taken as a whole, appeals to prurient interest.

2. The content must show or describe in an offensive manner sexual conduct.

3. The content on the whole must lack serious literary, artistic, political, or scientific value.

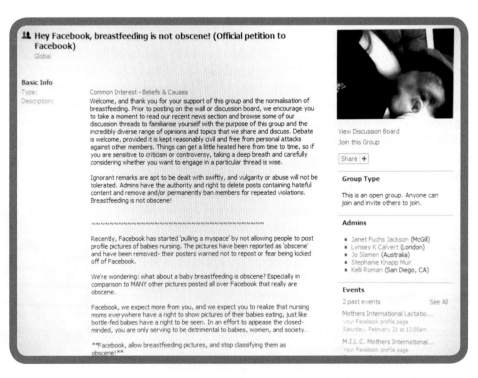

"Lactivists" have protested in vain Facebook's policy of removing photos of women breastfeeding.

Defining obscenity, however, is difficult, and some would say simply that "I know it when I see it (or hear it)."

The digital age has produced unique issues for obscenity cases. One is the ease with which pornography can be distributed across national boundaries. Another is computer-generated pornography in which increasingly realistic images can be created. In April 2002, the Supreme Court reaffirmed that free-speech principles applied online when it struck down provisions in the Child Pornography Prevention Act of 1996, which made it a crime to create, distribute, or possess "virtual" child pornography, or computer-generated images of children in sexual acts (as opposed to images of actual children). Justice Anthony M. Kennedy wrote for the majority, saying the act "prohibits speech that records no crime and creates no victims by its production." Although some justices voted in favor of keeping penalties for computer-generated images, and the government argued that real children could be harmed and exploited if a market for virtual child pornography were sustained, Justice Kennedy said, "The mere tendency of speech to encourage unlawful acts is not a sufficient reason for banning it."[4]

Criticism, Ridicule, or Humor

As objectionable as they may be, stereotypes and other offensive material are protected by the U.S. Constitution. Criticism, ridicule, and jokes about individuals (including government officials), groups, or institutions based on race, religion, gender, national background, or other factors are protected speech, whether in print or electronic media, and may not be regulated by the FCC. In the case of licensed broadcasters, it is incumbent upon station owners and operators to act responsibly in offering programming that meets the needs of the communities they serve.

The following discussion of the origins and evolution of electronic-communications regulations will highlight how the FCC came about, its role, how regulations differ from those of print media, and how they have influenced the programming and communication networks we have today.

The Evolution of Regulating Electronic Media

The origins of U.S. electronic-communications regulations lie in the development of broadcasting in the early part of the twentieth century, starting with radio and later including television. The approach has evolved considerably over the years as a result of changing technical and economic factors surrounding and underpinning those media.

■ ■ ■ EARLY DAYS AND THE RADIO ACT OF 1912 (1911–1926)

The regulation of broadcasting in the United States has moved through a series of four stages. Prior to 1911, there was no regulatory authority for broadcasting, which at the time meant specifically radio transmissions. The technology of radio was in its infancy, and so little was known about the new medium or its potential that there was little to regulate. Because radio emerged as a vital medium for ships at sea, especially for making distress calls, the Commerce Department's Bureau of Navigation was put in control of radio and made it a legal requirement in the **Radio Act of 1912** that all large ships maintain radio contact with ships or shore stations. Responsibility for radio regulation rested with the Commerce Department until 1927.

Radio Act of 1912
....
The act assigned frequencies and three- and four-letter codes to radio stations and limited broadcasting to the 360-meter wavelength.

In its earliest days, radio was primarily seen as a ship-to-shore communications tool and was regulated by the Commerce Department's Bureau of Navigation.

During this period, radio broadcasting was done largely by amateur technology enthusiasts. The process of obtaining a frequency on which to broadcast was very informal. As broadcast historian Mark Goodman points out, "By mailing a postcard to Secretary of Commerce Herbert Hoover, anyone with a radio transmitter, ranging from college students experimenting in science classes, to amateur inventors who ordered kits, to newspaper-operated stations, could broadcast on the frequency chosen by Hoover."[5]

By 1926 there were 15,111 amateur radio stations and 536 broadcasting stations in the United States. Despite geographic separation of radio transmitters and various power restrictions on those transmitters, there was a great amount of interference between the different stations' signals. Radio became what historian Erik Barnouw calls "A Tower of Babel," and the need for regulation grew. In the 1920s much public attention became focused on the new medium of radio and how the government was attempting to regulate it.[6]

▪▪▪ INCREASING REGULATION AND THE FEDERAL RADIO COMMISSION (1927–1933)

"The airwaves by 1927 were an open forum for anyone with the expertise and equipment to reach a forum with 25 million listeners," explains Mark Goodman.[7] But the rapid and largely uncontrolled growth of the new medium required a new regulatory structure. The **Radio Act of 1927** was signed into law in February and borrowed from railroad regulations. It said that anyone who owned a radio frequency and radio should operate for the "public convenience, interest, or necessity"—even though it didn't define those terms.[8]

The Federal Radio Commission (FRC) was established by the act. The FRC comprised five politically appointed commissioners and a limited staff whose mandate was to sort out the mess in radio. They revoked the vast majority of radio licenses and instituted a new system that favored fewer, high-powered stations over many, low-powered stations.[9] This change effectively favored radio for big companies over educational institutions or other groups that had small radio stations at the time.

Radio Act of 1927
....
The act replaced the Radio Act of 1912 and created the Federal Radio Commission, the precursor to the FCC, and gave the government greater regulatory and enforcement powers over radio, as well as establishing the premise that the airwaves were a public good and limited.

▪▪▪ THE COMMUNICATIONS ACT AND SPECTRUM SCARCITY (1934–1995)

In 1934, Congress enacted the Communications Act, which became the foundation of communications law for the next sixty-two years. The act was based on the premise established in the Radio Act of 1927 that the airwaves were a public good, a limited natural resource that belonged to the people. Broadcasters were granted licenses to use those airwaves at no cost, but were public trustees and bore a responsibility to use the airwaves in "the public interest, convenience, or necessity." Because of the limited nature of the airwaves, the act established regulations based on the notion of "spectrum scarcity," or limited channel capacity. It was under this model that news, whether profitable or not, came to meet the public service requirements for radio and television broadcasters.

CONVERGENCE CULTURE

(Low) Power to the People

Although the FCC's policies have encouraged large commercial broadcasters over the past several decades, and it is believed that the concentration of media ownership among radio stations in the United States has been spurred in part by the Telecommunications Act of 1996, one throwback from an earlier era in radio has also come from the act.

In 2000, after several years of efforts on the part of radio activists, Congress passed the Radio Broadcasting Preservation Act to encourage local radio diversity by encouraging the development of low-power FM (LPFM) stations.

LPFM stations must be operated on an educational and noncommercial basis and are licensed by the FCC. Operating at 100 watts or less, they can broadcast only a few miles. Although opponents of LPFM claimed that their signals would interfere with full-power stations, an FCC-commissioned study in 2003 known as the Mitre Report showed that they do not, which promises to open even more spectrum to LPFM stations if new legislation is passed to ease current restrictions.

Today there are over three thousand LPFM stations throughout the United States. Many are religious stations, while others focus on matters of community interest or education. The stations help foster a sense of community identity and also can be good training grounds for budding journalists or radio producers.

The Prometheus Radio Project is a group that encourages the creation of LPFM stations through educational resources, ideas for fund-raising activities, and barnstorming events in which activists from throughout the country gather for a weekend to work together and build an LPFM station.

Web Link >>>
Prometheus Radio Project
prometheusradio.org

The Communications Act of 1934 established the Federal Communications Commission (FCC), with five political appointees, including one chair, and a series of bureaus, each assigned responsibility for an area of the growing radio industry. The FCC would eventually assume regulatory responsibility for the emerging medium of television as well.

■ ■ ■ THE TELECOMMUNICATIONS ACT AND ITS EFFECTS (1996–PRESENT)

The technological transformation of the communication system in the United States and throughout the world, of which the Internet was an important part, was the impetus for Congress enacting the Telecommunications Act of 1996, the first major overhaul of the Communications Act of 1934. The convergence of telecommunications, computing, and traditional media in a digital, networked environment created the need for a basic reconstruction of the regulatory framework for the media of mass communication.

The act introduced that new framework. Although it preserved the requirement to serve in the "public interest, convenience, and necessity," the act's new mandate was to foster competition in the communications marketplace. The preamble of the act states it is intended "[t]o promote competition and reduce regulation in order to secure lower prices and higher quality services for American telecommunications consumers and encourage the rapid deployment of new telecommunications technologies." The motivation for this new mandate was the digital revolution that made the premise of channel scarcity virtually obsolete. The public no longer only had three or four network channels to watch—it now had broadcasting choices ranging from cable or satellite television to, increasingly, Internet-based programming.

More than one hundred pages in length, the complex Telecommunications Act of 1996 raises a variety of issues that affect not just the structure of the communications industry and how it is regulated, but the nature of programming and production. The act promotes direct competition among all telecommunications providers, including terrestrial broadcasters, direct broadcast satellite providers, mobile communication services, cable providers, and the regional Bell telephone companies. Further, the act specifically targets two forms of programming: violent or sexual programming and interactive services.

Since passage of the act, there has been dramatic growth in the concentration of media ownership. Whether this trend will have the stated desired effect of fostering competition or whether it will simply create powerful media cartels has been a subject of some debate. Another trend has been an increase in alternate media-service providers: cable companies are allowed to provide telephone service, for example, and telephone companies could provide, in theory, programming content.

The act puts no limit on the number of television stations a single person or organization may own in the United States, as long as the combined reach is no more than 35 percent of U.S. households. This also will spur greater concentration of ownership, which has already occurred in the radio industry. As a result of these regulatory, economic, and technological trends, Eli Noam and Robert Freeman point out that the media offer unprecedented programming diversity at the national level and ever-dwindling diversity at the local level.[10]

Because the act eliminates the legal barriers preventing telephone and television companies from competing in the areas of telephone and video services, consumers have seen an increased array of alternative service providers. Similarly, consumers have seen an increase in the range of both phone and video services, such as video-on-demand, voicemail, and call waiting. There have been several attempts in recent years to pass further sweeping legislation that deals with issues such as Net neutrality, voice-over IP (VOIP), and other new technologies that either did not exist or were just emerging in 1996.

■ ■ ■ ELECTRONIC MEDIA REGULATION INTERNATIONALLY

Electronic media of course developed differently in various countries throughout the world, and it is impossible to thoroughly cover the historical development within each country or even each region here. However, several general trends and patterns can be explored.

In many countries, the development of radio as mass communication was an extension of the already existing telegraph services, which were generally run by the government. Unlike the United States, where commercial forces tended to dominate, in Europe and European colonies a public service ethos for electronic media was most prevalent. What this meant for the public was a limited number of radio or television networks that were licensed or directly run by the government. Because of the principle of public service, programming content tended to emphasize news, education, and cultural shows rather than pure entertainment.

In the European Union in the last twenty years there has been a steady trend toward privatization and less regulation of the radio and television industries. As a result, more U.S. programming has been licensed by European broadcasters, making shows like *Baywatch* or *The Simpsons* highly popular throughout the world. This trend, although perhaps good from the audience's perspective, as it can now see more types of programming, also raises charges of cultural imperialism. Local broadcasters may too easily choose to simply buy U.S. programming rather than supporting home-grown productions.

Nevertheless, the EU is moving toward more liberalization and privatization, so it is likely that the EU, like the United States, will also see growth in the

The Rise and Fall of Russian Media

INTERNATIONAL PERSPECTIVES

After the demise of the Soviet Union in 1991 there was great hope for the rise of a democratic Russia and the role that a free press would play in rebuilding the country. There has been tremendous growth in the numbers of newspapers, magazines, and books available to Russians, as well as growth in radio and television stations and the type of programming they offer.

However, since 2000 there have been many disturbing trends in Russia that have raised alarm among journalists and media scholars. One is the concentration of media ownership and the expectations that owners have regarding uncritical coverage of themselves and their interests. Although it is not as clear-cut as Soviet-era media control, the private owners of many media companies nevertheless exert undue influence over editorial content and programming.

Of even greater concern is how dangerous Russia has become for journalists critical of the government. Since Vladimir Putin became president in 2000, Russia has become the third most dangerous country for journalists, trailing only Iraq and Algeria, according to the Committee to Protect Journalists. Fourteen Russian journalists have been killed since 2000, and none of the murders has been solved.

More recently, the term "extremism" has had its definition expanded to include any criticism of the government, which means journalists who criticize the government or government policies face jail time and the publications they work for can be shut down.

concentration of media ownership. Asian countries each have their own regulations and laws, but with the exception of Japan, India, the Philippines, and South Korea, most Asian countries have stronger degrees of government control over electronic media than the EU or the United States. For example, it is illegal to own a satellite dish in Malaysia, and countries like Singapore and Indonesia have strict regulations on content, especially criticism of the government.

The Federal Communications Commission (FCC)

The Federal Communications Commission (FCC)
....
The principal communications regulatory body, established in 1934, at the federal level in the United States.

The **FCC** is the principal communications regulatory body at the federal level in the United States. Some would say the FCC is also a lightning rod for criticism because of its prominent position on the communications regulatory landscape. Oftentimes, regardless how the commission rules, some group is left unhappy and frequently is quite vocal in expressing its displeasure.

The principal mandate of the FCC is "regulating interstate and foreign commerce in communication by wire and radio so as to make available, so far as possible, to all the people of the United States a rapid, efficient, nation-wide, and world-wide wire and radio communications service. . . ." In this sense, the term "radio" is interpreted to include television. The commission is authorized to "make such regulations not inconsistent with law as it may deem necessary to prevent interference between stations and to carry out the provisions of [the] Act." The FCC mandate was reaffirmed under the Telecommunications Act of 1996, which supplanted the 1934 act. The new act added an emphasis on fostering competition in the newly converged digital landscape, in the hopes of both supporting and expanding the communications industry and bringing a greater range of communications services, at an affordable price, to the American public.

The FCC consists of five commissioners appointed by the president, each of whom must be confirmed by the Senate. The commission must include at least two representatives of each of the major parties to help ensure its nonpartisan nature.

Web Link >>>
FCC website
www.fcc.gov

■ ■ ■ REGULATING RADIO AND TELEVISION

Among its principal duties, the FCC allocates new broadcast radio and television stations and renews the licenses of existing stations, ensuring that each licensee is complying with the laws mandated by Congress. The FCC does not license TV or radio networks, such as CBS, NBC, ABC, Fox, UPN, WB, or PBS, except when they are owners of stations.

The commission considers two basic sets of factors regarding the allocation of new stations. First, it evaluates the relative needs of communities for additional broadcast outlets. This depends on a variety of considerations, including a community's population and its heterogeneity. Second, the commission considers various engineering standards that eliminate interference between stations.

In fulfilling its duties, the FCC invites public comment on its proposed rules, publishes those rules, and implements them through a set of seven bureaus and eleven offices. The bureaus include the Mass Media Bureau, which regulates radio and television stations (and absorbed the Cable Services Bureau, which had regulated cable television), and the Common Carrier Bureau, which regulates wireline and wireless telephony.

Cable and satellite television are not under the same FCC rules as broadcast stations or those transmitted via terrestrial frequencies. Cable TV and satellite channels are available only to subscribers and have fewer rules to abide by than network broadcasters. Among the most important rules administered by the Cable Services Bureau are the following:

1. Basic service, which is the lowest level of cable service a subscriber can buy. It includes, at a minimum, all over-the-air television broadcast signals carried pursuant to the must-carry requirements of the Communications Act and any public, educational, or government access channels required by the system's franchise agreement.

2. "Must carry," in which every broadcast TV station, whether commercial or noncommercial, is entitled to have its programming carried on any local cable TV system. The station receives no compensation, but its programming is carried via the cable system. A broadcaster may opt instead to grant permission to the cable system to carry the station and receive compensation for the programming. This is called retransmission consent and is available only to commercial TV stations.

■ ■ ■ UNIVERSAL SERVICE

An important item for the FCC is the definition of universal service, a long-cherished notion central to the 1934 act. The act does not go so far as to provide a definition of universal service, however. It states, "Universal service is an evolving level of telecommunications services that the commission shall establish periodically under this section." It identifies six principles central to this evolving notion of universal service:

1. Quality services at reasonable and affordable rates
2. Access to advanced telecommunications and information services throughout the United States
3. Access in rural and high-cost areas
4. Equitable and nondiscriminatory contributions to the preservation and advancement of universal service
5. Specific, predictable, and sufficient federal and state mechanisms to preserve and advance universal service
6. Access to advanced telecommunications services in elementary and secondary schools and classrooms, health care providers, and libraries

The outcome of this evolving notion is a new model of universal service. One scenario would include fully interoperable high-bandwidth, two-way communication service—the twenty-first-century equivalent of "plain old telephone service" (POTS) mandated in the 1934 act. This would create a powerful network engine to drive a new information infrastructure linking wired and wireless technologies and empower the development of fully interactive, multimedia communications. An alternative paradigm, however, would simply mandate that all homes have access to at least two communication-service providers capable of delivering both traditional and new media services (including the Internet).

■ ■ ■ SPECTRUM AUCTION

Since 1994, the FCC has held auctions for available electromagnetic spectrum. The auctions are open to any individual or company that makes an upfront payment and that the FCC deems a qualified bidder. Many countries auction spectrum, and the auctions can generate large revenues for the governments. Some critics claim that the spectrum tends to be leased too cheaply, resulting in essentially corporate give-aways, considering the money that the winning bidders make from the spectrum.

The auction in the United States in 2008 drew special attention thanks in part to disagreements and lawsuits among several major telecommunications companies and Google, all bidders for the spectrum. Google requested that the auctioned spectrum be open, meaning that the winning bidder would have to keep the spectrum available to anyone to develop applications and communication tools that could be used by anyone else, along the lines of open-source business models. Google claimed that this would give consumers more choices and spur greater innovation in mobile communication devices.

Open communications like this directly threaten the established business models of telecommunication companies, and Verizon filed a lawsuit against the FCC to stop the open requirement. In the end, Google got two of its four requests, creating a partially open system, and the auction generated close to $20 billion for the government.

■ ■ ■ THE FCC, STATION ID, AND LICENSE RENEWAL

Each station must air station-identification announcements as it signs on and off each day, and it must air announcements hourly, at what the commission calls a natural programming break. The requirements for station identification foster a certain level of uniformity in programming style in the broadcast media, but they do not mandate that programmers insert station IDs at the top of the hour and at other well-defined intervals.

The FCC licenses stations to operate either as commercial or noncommercial-educational (public) broadcasters for up to eight years, after which the station must renew its license. This is the case for both radio and television broadcasters licensed to transmit their signals via terrestrial frequencies.

At the time of license renewal, a station must meet five basic requirements, primarily that it has served in the public interest and met all legal requirements. A station must also accept and respond to viewer or listener complaints. Audience members, journalists, or anyone else may also review what is called the station's "public inspection file," which contains a variety of information about the station.

■ ■ ■ FCC LIMITS ON STATIONS

There are a variety of station activities that are either regulated or prohibited by federal law. Among the regulated activities are station-conducted contests, television games and quiz shows, and the broadcast of telephone calls. When a station hosts a contest, it must fully disclose all terms and rules of the contest, including in any advertising promoting the contest. Stations are required to inform any parties to a phone call before recording it for broadcast, or broadcasting it live, although there are certain exceptions, such as call-in shows, when callers can reasonably be expected to understand their calls may be broadcast.

If a licensee violates the rules, the FCC is authorized to levy a fine or even to revoke a station's license. Among the programming concerns for which the FCC may levy fines or revoke licenses are the airing of obscene or indecent language when children are likely to be viewing, and nudity. The FCC does not advise stations regarding artistic standards, format, or grammar. Stations must rely on their

Today the FCC regulates broadcast stations, allocating spectrum, renewing licenses, and levying fines for violations.

own judgment. Generally, only the stations themselves are responsible for selecting the material they air, including coverage of local issues, news, public affairs, religion, sports events, and other subjects.

Among the prohibited activities for stations are knowingly broadcasting a hoax, including false information regarding a crime or catastrophe (defined as a disaster), especially when a broadcast might cause public harm. This rule came about largely as a result of the 1938 *War of the Worlds* radio broadcast.

Regulating Content

In addition to the ways content is regulated in electronic media by the FCC and the federal controls over libel, obscenity, and speech that threatens national security, there are at least eight other types of content restrictions in the United States. These are largely, but not entirely, unique to the broadcast media and may involve other agencies besides the FCC. The restrictions are primarily aimed at protecting children, controlling political communication, and limiting commercial speech.

In the cases of libel, copyright, clear and present danger, and obscenity and pornography, the judicial system has authority over broadcast or publication. In the case of false or deceptive advertising, the Federal Trade Commission has primary responsibility, although the Food and Drug Administration (FDA) has authority when food or drugs are involved. Most of the remaining content restrictions are subject to the jurisdiction of the FCC.

■ ■ ■ COMMERCIAL SPEECH

Commercial speech, including advertising, has generally been afforded less First Amendment protection than other forms of speech, especially political speech or the news. In a landmark decision, the U.S. Supreme Court ruled in 1942 in *Valentine v. Chrestensen* that "purely commercial advertising" was unprotected by the First Amendment. Chrestensen was a businessman who was displaying a World War I–era submarine at a pier in New York City and dispersed leaflets advertising tours of the submarine. The leaflets were becoming litter, and the police commissioner in New York forbade him from distributing them. Even though Chrestensen attempted to subvert the ruling by adding political messages on the opposite side, the city still barred him from distributing his advertising leaflets, and the Supreme Court agreed, giving commercial speech no protection under the First Amendment.

In the 1970s the broad powers granted to government regarding commercial speech were restricted somewhat by cases that allowed some First Amendment protection, although not on par with other forms of speech. In 1976, the Court ruled in *Virginia State Board of Pharmacy v. Virginia Citizens Consumer Council, Inc.*, that speech that does "no more than propose a commercial transaction" is entitled to at least some First Amendment protection. This was in response to a case brought by some citizens' groups in Virginia that wanted to see pharmacies advertise prices of drugs, which the state legislature had prohibited.

In some cases, however, commercial speech has been afforded more protection than one might expect. An interesting example comes from a case involving former New York City mayor Rudolph Giuliani. Giuliani was lampooned in an advertising campaign by *New York* magazine in 1997 on the city buses of New York, which said that the magazine was "possibly the only good thing in New York that

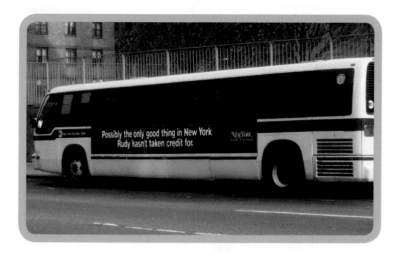

Former New York mayor Rudolph Giuliani tried unsuccessfully to get bus advertisements that poked fun of him removed.

Rudy hasn't taken credit for." Giuliani, who had often taken credit for everything from drops in the crime rate to a booming economy, found the ads to be offensive and ordered them removed from the buses. In this case, commercial speech won. Consider the conclusion of United States District Judge Shira Scheindlin, who said, "Who would have dreamed that the mayor would object to more publicity?" She ruled that Giuliani's administration violated the First Amendment when it ordered city buses to remove paid ads.

Tobacco and Alcohol Advertising

Most products can be legally advertised on electronic media under the jurisdiction of the FCC. However, one type of product generally may not be legally advertised by broadcasters: tobacco. Advertising cigarettes, small cigars, smokeless tobacco, or chewing tobacco is prohibited on radio, television, and any other electronic medium regulated by the FCC, such as telephony. It is permissible to advertise smoking accessories, cigars, pipes, pipe tobacco, or cigarette-making machines. There are no federal laws or FCC regulations prohibiting the advertising of alcoholic beverages, such as beer, wine, or liquor, on television and radio.

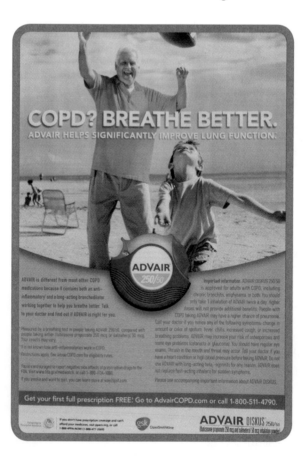

Drug companies must follow many regulations in advertising their products, including listing possible side effects.

False Advertising

One other area of commercial speech that is subject to federal regulation is false or deceptive advertising. However, this form of commercial speech is regulated by the Federal Trade Commission (FTC), not the FCC. In the case of food or drug products, the Food and Drug Administration is also involved. It has strict regulations on what can be said on the air in prescription drug commercials, which is why such commercials usually include long lists of possible side effects. Areas of commercial speech that are not regulated or prohibited by any federal law or agency include loud commercials (which the FCC has shown through research are only perceived as louder than programs but actually are not), offensive advertising, and subliminal programming.

In the latter case, the FCC states that use of subliminal messages, which are meant to be perceived only on a subconscious level, is "inconsistent with a station's obligation to serve the public interest." However, it does not officially prohibit subliminal programming. Research does not provide conclusive evidence that subliminal messages are even understood or have an influence on behavior.

■ ■ ■ POLITICAL SPEECH

Historically, the heart of freedom of expression is in political speech, or speech that deals with the political process, government, elected officials, or elections. Some go so far as to contend that the only speech the founders intended when they wrote the First Amendment was political speech. Political speech is also one area where federal regulations have been most extensive.

Equal-Time Rule

Stations are required to adhere to an **equal-time rule**, outlined in the 1934 Communications Act, which says that broadcasters must give "equal air time" to candidates running in elections. Under this provision, if a station permits a qualified candidate for public office to use its facilities, including commentaries or paid commercials, the station is required to "afford equal opportunities to all other such candidates for that office." Two circumstances are exempted from the equal-time provision: when the candidate appears in a newscast, interview, or documentary and when the candidate appears during on-the-scene coverage of a news event.

Candidate debates have been ruled as "on-the-spot" news coverage and thus are exempt from equal-time-rule provisions. Early in the 2008 election season there was some question whether the town hall forums conducted by McCain and Obama, even before they declared their candidacies, would be considered the same way by the FCC.

The U.S. Supreme Court ruled in 1981 in support of the equal-time rule, saying that it is the right of viewers and listeners, not of broadcasters, that should be considered paramount. It went on to say, "As defined by the FCC and applied here, [it] does not violate the First Amendment rights of broadcasters by unduly circumscribing their editorial discretion, but instead properly balances the First Amendment rights of federal candidates, the public, and broadcasters."

The equal-time rule says that TV stations must allow equal opportunities for all political candidates to air paid commercials.

equal-time rule

The requirement that broadcasters make available equal airtime, in terms of commentaries and commercials, to opposing candidates running for election. It does not apply to candidates appearing in newscasts, documentaries, or news-event coverage.

Fairness Doctrine

The equal-time rule is not the same thing as the **Fairness Doctrine**, though it is often confused with it. The equal-time rule deals only with giving political candidates equal time compared to other candidates, with the exceptions noted above. The Fairness Doctrine was much broader in scope, requiring broadcasters to seek out and present all sides of an issue when covering a controversy, allowing people who were personally attacked on-air a chance to respond, and giving candidates airtime to respond to a station's endorsement of another candidate. The Fairness Doctrine, which the FCC had adopted in 1949, was largely discarded in 1987.

In 1969, in *Red Lion Broadcasting Co. v. FCC*, which required Red Lion Broadcasting to provide equal airtime for a politician's response to an attack on him, the Court held that, because of the scarcity of broadcasting frequencies, the government might require a broadcast licensee to share the frequency with others who might not otherwise have a chance to broadcast their views. The Court thus gave the public a right of access "to social, political, esthetic, moral, and other ideas and experiences."

Even after the overturning of the Fairness Doctrine in 1986, two parts of it in particular remained in effect until October 2000, when they too were discarded by the FCC and the decision of a federal court. These were political editorials and personal attacks.

The FCC defined a political editorial as "when a station endorses or opposes a legally qualified candidate(s) during a broadcast of *its own* opinion." It distinguished the opinions of third parties broadcast by the station as "comments" or

Fairness Doctrine

Adopted by the FCC in 1949, it required broadcasters to seek out and present all sides of a controversial issue they were covering. It was discarded by the FCC in 1987.

The prevalence of conservative talk shows such as *Rush Limbaugh* has given rise to attempts by liberals to reinstate the Fairness Doctrine.

"commentaries" and thus exempt from these rules. A station had a week to provide other qualified candidates for the same office, or the candidates that were opposed in the editorial, with these three things: (1) notice of the date and time of the editorial, (2) a tape or script of the editorial, and (3) free and comparable airtime in which to respond.

The FCC defined a personal attack as "during the presentation of views on a controversial issue of public importance, someone attacks the honesty, character, integrity, or like personal qualities of an identified person or group." After such an occurrence, the station had one week to provide the attacked party with the same three things provided candidates opposed in political editorials. Stations were not required to maintain copies of the material they broadcast, with two exceptions: personal attacks and political editorials.

In early October 2000, the FCC suspended these last vestiges of the Fairness Doctrine and a federal court overturned the provision entirely, ruling that the FCC had not demonstrated the value to the public of the doctrine, given the limitation it places on broadcasters' First Amendment rights.

Despite a number of attempts in 2005 and 2008 to resuscitate the Fairness Doctrine with new legislation, mostly by liberals and Democratic politicians who claim the imbalance in conservative versus liberal talk shows on radio and TV skews public debate and perceptions on important issues, such moves are strongly resisted by libertarians and conservatives. The FCC has refrained on the basis that the doctrine never really produced more diversity in programming and that with channel proliferation there is more diversity than could have been hoped for when television was dominated by three major commercial networks.

Children's Programming Protections

Parents, elected officials, and others have long sought to protect children from unwanted or offensive speech and to create a media system that actively nurtures and nourishes children. As such, there has been considerable regulation designed to both protect and promote children's welfare in the context of the media, especially the electronic media. Among the most important pieces of regulation in this regard is the **Children's Television Act**.

Children's Television Act
....
Created in 1990, it places limits on the amount of commercial content that programming can carry, forces stations to carry certain amounts of educational programming for children sixteen and under, and includes other provisions to help protect children.

■ ■ ■ THE CHILDREN'S TELEVISION ACT

The Children's Television Act (CTA) took effect in 1990. It places limits on the amount of commercial content permitted in children's TV programming (including broadcast, satellite, and cable). The act also mandates that each television station provide programming specifically designed to meet the educational and informational needs of children age sixteen and younger. The FCC determination of whether programming meets this criterion is based on four standards

1. The programming is primarily designed to meet children's educational and informational needs (i.e., it can't be primarily entertainment, such as a cartoon, and have as a by-product some educational value).

2. It is broadcast between 6 a.m. and 10 p.m., hours when children are likely to be viewing.

3. It is scheduled to run regularly each week.

4. It is at least a one-half-hour program.

In addition, commercial stations are required to identify their educational programs for children at the beginning of those programs; they must identify these programs to publishers of program guides as well. Moreover, all programs aimed at children twelve and younger may not contain more than 10.5 minutes of advertising per hour on weekends and 12 minutes on weekdays. The FCC also established that stations that air at least three hours of "core" children's programming a week would be in fulfillment of their obligations under the CTA, "core" being defined primarily in terms of item number one above.

■ ■ ■ VIOLENT AND SEXUAL PROGRAMMING: THE V-CHIP

Violent and sexual programming receives special attention from the FCC because of concern about the implications of such material for young viewers. With the passage of the Telecommunications Act of 1996, the federal government began regulating televised violent content in addition to sexual content, which it already regulated. The act seeks to give parents greater control over their children's viewing of violent and sexual programming. The act begins by summarizing research findings that demonstrate the negative impact of television-violence viewing on children. It notes, "Parents express grave concern over violent and sexual video programming and strongly support technology that would give them greater control to block video programming in the home that they consider harmful to their children."

In order to give parents control over what kind of programming their children are able to watch, the government mandated that from January 2000 all television sets thirteen inches or larger come equipped with what is called a **V-chip**, or "violence chip." The V-chip is a computer device that enables parents or any other viewer to program a TV set to block access to programs containing violent and sexual content, based on the program rating.

The rating system developed for the V-chip is also called the "TV Parental Guidelines." At the request of the government, the television industry created its own voluntary ratings system and agreed to broadcast signals that contain programming ratings that can be detected by the V-chip. The ratings are shown on the TV screen for the first fifteen seconds of rated programming and permit viewers to use the V-chip to block those programs from their sets. On the basis of the First Amendment, all news programming is exempted from the V-chip.

In the digital age, the V-chip is no longer the only tool at parents' disposal to restrict television viewing among their children. All digital media systems, including digital cable and satellite television, contain software controls that can block individual programs, entire channels, or classes of programs based on their ratings.

The V-chip lets parents block certain types of programming unsuitable for children.

V-chip
....
A computer device that enables parents or any other viewer to program a TV set to block access to programs containing violent and sexual content, based on the program rating.

■ ■ ■ TV PARENTAL GUIDELINES

The new television rating system identifies six categories of programming. The first two refer to programming designed solely for children, and the final one is programming aimed solely at adults. The middle three ratings refer to programming that has not been designed for children, but that may be suitable for some children, and it is up to parents to decide. The rating system is similar to the system developed for motion pictures. Following are the categories and their official definitions.

Programs designed specifically for children

TV-Y (All Children. This program is designed to be appropriate for all children.) Whether this program is animated or live-action, the themes and elements in it are specifically designed for a very young audience, including children from ages two to six. This program is not expected to frighten younger children.

TV-Y7 (Directed to Older Children. This program is designed for children ages seven and above.) It may be more appropriate for children who have acquired the developmental skills needed to distinguish between make-believe and reality. Themes and elements in this program may include mild fantasy or comedic violence or may frighten children under the age of seven. Programs where fantasy violence may be more intense or more combative than other programs in this category will be designated TV-Y7-FV.

Programs not designed for children, but possibly suitable for audiences including at least older children

TV-G (General Audience. Most parents would find this program suitable for all ages.) Although this rating does not signify a program designed specifically for children, most parents may let younger children watch this program unattended. It contains little or no violence, no strong language, and little or no sexual dialogue or situations.

TV-PG (Parental Guidance Suggested. This program contains material that parents may find unsuitable for younger children.) Many parents may want to watch it with their younger children. The theme itself may call for parental guidance and/or the program contains one or more of the following: moderate violence (V), some sexual situations (S), infrequent coarse language (L), or some suggestive dialogue (D).

TV-14 (Parents Strongly Cautioned. This program contains some material that many parents would find unsuitable for children under fourteen years of age.) Parents are strongly urged to exercise greater care in monitoring this program and are cautioned against letting children under the age of fourteen watch unattended. This program contains one or more of the following: intense violence (V); intense sexual situations (S); strong, coarse language (L); or intensely suggestive dialogue (D).

Programs designed only for adult audiences

TV-MA (Mature Audience Only. This program is specifically designed to be viewed by adults and therefore may be unsuitable for children under seventeen.) This program contains one or more of the following: graphic violence (V); explicit sexual activity (S); or crude, indecent language (L).

Intellectual Property Rights

intellectual property
....
Ideas that have commercial
value, such as literary or
artistic works, patents,
business methods, and
industrial processes.

Of significant and growing concern to those in mass communication is protecting their **intellectual property** (IP). IP refers to ideas that have commercial value, such as literary or artistic works, patents, software programs, business methods, and industrial processes, particularly in the form of copyright protection. Copyright law ("copy-right" refers to the legal right to make a copy of a work) is one form of intellectual property rights protection that deals with protecting specific expressions of ideas. The other two main areas of intellectual property law are patents and trademarks.

Patents are intended to protect a specific form of intellectual property known as "inventions." Once granted, a patent prohibits anyone from copying the invention, pattern, or design. Anyone can apply for a patent, as long as the idea is new. **Trademarks** refer to images, designs, logos, or even words or phrases. For example, in March 2004 Donald Trump, host of *The Apprentice* reality TV show, attempted to trademark his phrase "You're Fired!" so it could be sold on clothing and other items. However, the U.S. Patent and Trademark Office turned down his request because it was too similar to another phrase, "You're Hired!", an educational board game that had that phrase trademarked in 1997.

Donald Trump tried to trademark his famous phrase "You're Fired," from the reality show *The Apprentice*.

A copyright exists from the moment a work is created in its fixed form, such as being written down or recorded, so simply claiming an idea does not give you a copyright to it. Inserting a © symbol (although in the case of a musical recording the symbol is a P in a circle, but that symbol may be hard to find on your keyboard), along with a date and the name of the copyright owner, also helps show that you are copyrighting a work, but it is not necessary. In the case of a work for hire, the employer generally owns the copyright. A copyright is in effect for the lifetime of the author, plus 70 years, although it may be up to 125 years in the case of a work for hire. The rationale of a copyright is to protect not only the intellectual product but the author/owner's financial interests. In 1989, the United States joined the Berne Convention for the Protection of Literary and Artistic Works, extending copyright protection globally.

Copyright law protects a wide range of expression, primarily the creations of authors or artists. A book or an article is protected by a copyright, not a patent. Included are literary works (including newspapers, books, magazines), musical works, dramatic works, pantomimes and choreographic works, pictorial, graphic, and sculpture works, motion pictures and other audiovisual works, sound recordings, and architectural works. Under the **Digital Millennium Copyright Act**, it extends to digital works as well, including those on the Internet or other online media, because if something exists on hard drive it is considered a fixed form.

■ ■ ■ FAIR USE

Holding a copyright to a work provides the owner an exclusive right to reproduce, distribute (over any media), perform, display, or license that work. There are limited exceptions to the rights under copyright law, including primarily for **fair use** of an expression, such as in a movie or book review where the reviewer might include an excerpt, or in criticism or commentary. In general, there are four factors considered in deciding whether the use of another's copyrighted work is legal under the "fair use" provision of the act:

1. The purpose and nature of the use (i.e., is it purely commercial, educational, or for the news, the latter two of which are generally more likely to qualify)

2. The character of the copyrighted work (some works are inherently more protected; this is a subjective matter determined by the courts)

copyright
....
The exclusive right to use, publish, and distribute a work such as a piece of writing, music, film, or video.

patent law
....
Protects the right to produce and sell an invention, rather than a literary or artistic work, which is covered by copyright law.

trademark
....
A type of intellectual property that refers to signs, logos, or names.

Digital Millennium Copyright Act (DMCA)
....
An act of Congress in 1998 that reformed copyright law comprehensively in trying to update it for the digital age. Key provisions addressed the circumvention of copyright protection systems, fair use in a digital environment, and Internet service providers' (ISP) liability for content sent through their lines.

fair use
....
Allowable use of someone else's copyrighted work that does not require payment of royalties, with a number of factors used to determine if something falls under fair use or is a violation of copyright.

Web Link >>>
U.S. Copyright Office
lcweb.loc.gov/copyright/

Web Link >>>
The Copyright Website
www.benedict.com/

3. The amount and extent of the excerpt used, in proportion to the copyrighted work in its entirety (this is more qualitatively than quantitatively determined, however, and there are no exact rules on the permissible number of words one may borrow from a text or the amount of video, audio, or image one may excerpt, since even a small clip may represent the most significant creative aspect of the work)

4. The effect of the use on the copyrighted work's market potential (i.e., in dollar terms), especially when the copyrighted work is used as the basis for a derivative work (i.e., a movie based on a book)

The issue of fair use has become a flash point for digital media, especially in relation to content aggregators such as Google News or video search engines. There have been several court cases in the past ten years in which copyright holders have sued content aggregators, claiming copyright infringement. However, if the content aggregator has been able to show that it has sufficiently transformed the content—for example, by making low-resolution thumbnails of images or video clips—and to show that it is not profiting directly from doing so, it has generally won the case. Other aggregators have arrived at licensing agreements with media companies in order to continue to display or aggregate their content. An example is a deal Google struck with Associated Press to aggregate its news stories and keep them on Google News for a limited time.

Legal Issues in the Digital World

The courts and legal system have not been able to keep up with the many changes to mass communication that the Internet and digital media have brought. As a result, cases decided by the courts from the mid-1990s through today can have dramatic effects because they can establish precedent, meaning they become the basis for subsequent court decisions and legislation.

One example of just how far the legal system has had to come occurred in a 2000 ruling against Eric Corley (Emmanuel Goldstein), publisher of *2600: The Hacker Quarterly*. He included links in the online version of the magazine to a site that contained the code to DeCSS, a computer program that opened encrypted DVDs and allowed them to be freely copied. Corley argued that being forced to remove the hyperlinks was an infringement of his First Amendment rights. The court disagreed, saying that a hyperlink was not an example of free speech because it acted as a kind of "mechanism" that allowed users to go to the site. However, posting the URL of a site without it being hyperlinked would still be considered free speech. An appellate court agreed with this decision in May 2001, and Corley decided not to take the case to the Supreme Court.

Because digital media have certain characteristics unlike analog media, there have been a host of new issues raised that our legal system has been ill-equipped to deal with. In some cases the courts are able to rely on existing laws and apply them to digital media, but in other cases the fit has been awkward, at best.

■ ■ ■ DIGITAL RIGHTS MANAGEMENT

File-sharing and royalty issues related to music, and increasingly video, have been discussed in earlier chapters, and this continues to be one of the main areas of contention in the digital space. Record labels have tried various measures to deter free file sharing, including suing customers and having universities hold seminars for incoming students on the matter, but with little success.

Broadly speaking, **digital rights management**, or DRM, is about finding ways using technology to rein in copyright infringement of digital content. Encryption has had some success, although, as the DeCSS example demonstrates, it is not foolproof. **Digital watermarks** are a very important part of DRM. Watermarks are computer code (usually invisible, but sometimes visible) inserted into any digital content—images, graphics, audio, video, or even text documents—that authenticates the source of that content. Copyright owners value watermarks because they can protect media assets, or intellectual property, from theft—or at least make them easier to track when they are used illegally.

For example, if a media company sends digital video over the Internet and someone else tries to copy the video and distribute it without obtaining permission, the original copyright holder, an end user, or even an intelligent software agent can examine the content for an embedded digital watermark. If the watermark is present and is that of the original copyright holder, then it can be easily demonstrated that the redistributor is in violation of copyright law. In essence, the digital watermark is analogous to a brand placed on cattle by a rancher in order to deter or catch cattle rustlers.

DRM has faced resistance from some groups, such as the Electronic Frontier Foundation, who claim that media companies are trying to limit the capabilities of new technologies simply to increase their revenues and force media to behave like their analog counterparts. In some cases, new DRM technologies have severely limited use of content, not allowing someone who has purchased a CD to copy songs more than once, for example, or not allowing transfer between different devices. These restrictions have angered consumers and raised serious questions about what exactly a person is "buying" when purchasing a CD and what rights the purchaser has to that content.

digital rights management (DRM)
Technologies that let copyright owners control the level of access or use allowed for a copyrighted work, such as limiting the number of times a song can be copied.

digital watermark
Computer code (usually invisible, but sometimes visible) inserted into any digital content—images, graphics, audio, video, or even text documents—that authenticates the source of that content.

TV commentator Bill O'Reilly won a decision by WIPO to get ownership of the domain name billorielly.com, even though the name was spelled differently and it was the name of the prior owner.

Creative Commons License

Creative Commons is a nonprofit organization founded in 2001 that is "dedicated to making it easier for people to share and build upon the work of others, consistent with the rules of copyright."

The rationale behind Creative Commons is that the more material that is available in the public domain for others to borrow and create from, the more it will enhance the creative pool for everyone. Creative Commons argues that copyright law as it is practiced today has become too restrictive in the interests of copyright holders (specifically large media companies) at the expense of the public interest.

The organization allows creators to license their works the way they want to license them and offers a range of options that encourage mixing, reuse, and commercial sales. For example, a creator can stipulate the "attribution" type of Creative Commons license, which means that others can freely use, copy, distribute, and perform the copyrighted work, and derivatives of that work, but only if the creator is given credit as specifically requested.

The most restrictive of the six main types of licenses Creative Commons offers is sometimes called the "free advertising" license, as it allows free distribution of a work but no changes to the work, credit must be given as stipulated, and a link back to the original work must exist.

By 2008, there were 130 million CC-licensed works, and the band Nine Inch Nails released their album *Ghosts I-IV* that year under a CC license.

Nine Inch Nails released their 2008 album
Ghosts I-IV under a Creative Commons license.

Although not DRM per se, companies have also had to learn to manage their online presence through company websites and domain names. Some who did not see the value of the Internet in its early years discovered later that others had already leased their company name as a domain name, usually with the intent to sell it at a higher price, in a practice called **cybersquatting**. The World Intellectual Property Organization (WIPO) handles complaints from parties who claim others are unfairly using their names for personal gain.

WIPO decides on each case and generally applies standards of fair use, although there is no hard-and-fast rule. For example, Fox news personality Bill O'Reilly brought a case to WIPO to acquire www.billorielly.com. The person who had the site was actually named Bill O'Rielly (note the "i" and "e" are reversed in the spelling of his name), yet WIPO ruled in favor of O'Reilly and he got that domain name as well.

Keywords have also come before the courts as contested intellectual property. This has become especially important, as search engines dominate how people

cybersquatting

The practice of getting a domain name, usually of someone famous or a well-known company, with the intention of reselling the domain name at a high price.

find information on the Web. Although keywords have become less important in terms of how search engines find and rank websites, they still play a role and can mislead users.

The courts have generally ruled that as long as a keyword fairly represents the content of a website, it can be used. However, a company cannot put a competitor's name in its keyword list in the hope of drawing people who were searching for the competitor.

■ ■ ■ PRIVACY

Privacy issues have become increasingly important on a number of levels with the Internet and digital media. Not only can websites track users in ways that are impossible with analog media, but they can insert code, called a cookie, onto users' computers and track them even after they have left that particular website. Not all cookies track users so relentlessly, however, and in fact cookies are needed to make the Web a more user-friendly environment.

Still, the overuse of cookies can be a problem. Just as a website will add a cookie to your computer, so will advertisers on a website. These **third-party cookies** also track your Web usage and send information directly to the advertisers, who can determine how long you've stayed on a page and where you went afterward.

third-party cookies

Cookies put on a computer by those other than the website being visited, such as advertisers inserting their own cookies on a web page.

■ ■ ■ CONTENT RIGHTS AND RESPONSIBILITIES

Another new area that media companies have had to deal with is the status of user-generated content (UGC). It is virtually impossible for a company to police all the content that is uploaded to the Internet, and the question of who is responsible for the content on a site arises when someone is defamed in a user comment as opposed to something the company itself wrote.

In general, the courts have made a "safe haven" provision for content providers, protecting them to some extent from libel lawsuits as long as they promptly removed the offending content and showed good efforts in preventing such content. Similarly, Internet service providers (ISPs) have been considered largely immune from responsibility for what is sent over their networks, although the threat of a lawsuit can sometimes be enough to get them to remove offending content.

LOOKING BACK AND MOVING FORWARD

The Internet has raised a host of legal and regulatory issues regarding media, and the legal system lags generally far behind in dealing with them. The apparently simple question of whether a hyperlink is protected by the First Amendment can generate some complex discussions about the nature of digital media and the online environment. Similarly, the question "Where does publishing occur?" brings up complex legal debate.

The global nature of the Internet also raises questions on which laws should be followed if content that is offensive or illegal in one country can be viewed online.

With analog media, the answer was obvious—publishing occurred in the country where the printing press was located. A book might be legally printed in one country but banned in another; thus if a copy was smuggled into the country where it was banned, the person caught with the book would be penalized, not the printer.

But on the Internet the question of where something is published is not at all clear. A person may create some banned content in his country for his website, which is hosted by a company in another country, where the content is not banned. Someone else may come across the content in a third country, where the material is considered harmful, sacrilegious, or defamatory. Several issues are raised in this scenario, including what country's laws will be used if a lawsuit is brought, and what constitutes libel, since it differs from country to country.

A pertinent highly controversial case was settled in December 2002. *Dow Jones and Co. Inc. v. Gutnick* involved an article in *Barron's* (published by Dow Jones) in October 2000 that mentioned Melbourne businessman Joseph Gutnick several times. He sued for libel and claimed that the case should be heard in Australia, where he was defamed.

Although the number of print copies of *Barron's* sent to Australia was minuscule, the online readership of the magazine was over half a million, and Gutnick claimed that many more people would see the article in Australia than just those who subscribed to the print version. Dow Jones argued that the article was actually published in the United States, where Dow Jones's web servers were located, and thus the case should be heard in the United States (where libel charges are harder to win than in Australia). The Australian High Court agreed with Gutnick, however, and Dow Jones eventually settled with him in 2004.

The case was of serious concern to Internet watchers and media companies because of its potential implications for publishers on the Web. If this case becomes a precedent, then anyone could sue a media company or website according to his or her own country's laws, which may be stricter regarding types of acceptable content than where the material was published. On the other hand, it can be argued that it is not fair to impose another country's views of acceptable free speech simply because it is on the Internet. The question remains open and will likely come up again in the future.

. . . .

DISCUSSION QUESTIONS

1. In light of the terrorist attacks on the World Trade Center and Pentagon on September 11, 2001, do you think the government should have more or less power to exercise prior restraint and block publication or broadcast of material it feels might hurt national security interests? What would some of the effects be, both positive and negative, if the government adopted your opinion?

2. Tobacco and tobacco products cannot be advertised on electronic media such as TV and radio, yet alcohol can. Should similar restrictions be placed on these products on the Internet, or should there be even stronger restrictions?

3. Can traditional standards of what makes a "community" be applied when dealing with Internet obscenity or pornography? If so, what would those criteria be? If not, what standards could be applied?

4. Given the harm that ridicule or stereotyping can cause for the groups being ridiculed, do you think there should be greater legal restrictions on ridicule or offensive stereotypes in the media? Why or why not?

5. Do you think television and movie rating systems are effective in protecting children? Why or why not? Could there be a better system than ratings to protect children from objectionable content?

6. What dangers are there in a media industry that regulates itself or self-censors? Why could self-censorship be a good thing?

7. Put yourself in the role of a young novelist or struggling musician who is trying to make a living writing stories or making music. Would you oppose or support greater government or corporate control on copyright if the technology promised that unauthorized copies of your work could not be circulated?

· ·

FURTHER READING

Mass Communication Law: In a Nutshell, 6th ed. Juliet Lushbough Dee, Harvey Zuckman (2006) Thomson West.

Freedom for the Thought That We Hate: A Biography of the First Amendment. Anthony Lewis (2008) Basic Books.

The Associated Press Style Book and Briefing on Media Law. Norm Goldstein (2007) Basic Books.

The Journalist's Guide to Media Law: Dealing with Legal and Ethical Issues, 2nd ed. Mark Pearson (2004) Allen & Unwin Academic.

We're All Journalists Now: The Transformation of the Press and Reshaping of the Law in the Internet Age. Scott Gant (2007) Free Press.

Insult to Injury: Libel, Slander and Invasions of Privacy. William Jones (2003) University of Colorado Press.

Rethinking Global Security: Media, Popular Culture, and "The War on Terror." Andrew Martin, Patrice Petro, eds. (2006) Rutgers University Press.

Intellectual Property Law and Interactive Media: Free for a Fee. Edward Lee Lamoureux, Steven Baron, Claire Stewart (2009) Peter Lang.

The Future of Ideas: The Fate of the Commons in a Connected World. Lawrence Lessig (2001) Random House.

Remix: Making Art and Commerce Thrive in the Hybrid Economy. Lawrence Lessig (2008) Penguin Press.

· ·

MEDIA QUIZ ANSWERS

1. False.

2. True.

3. False.

4. True.

5. False.

6. True.

7. False.

8. False.

9. True.

10. False.

Mass Communication and Politics in the Digital Age

CHAPTER OBJECTIVES

In this chapter we will:

■ Describe the role of mass communication in democratic and nondemocratic countries.

■ Highlight the role of the public and public opinion in political communication.

■ Present what research tells us about the evolving role of the media in political elections, especially the nature of sound bites, election coverage, and opinion polls in campaigns.

■ Discuss the increasing presence of political advertising in campaigns and what research tells us about its impact.

■ Outline the emergence of talk shows and the Internet in political campaigns.

■ Identify the most significant theories that explain, describe, and predict the impact of mediated political communications.

■ Examine the increasing role of new media in political campaigns.

15

It was a historic night for *The Tonight Show*. It was the first time a sitting president appeared on the show, and the president to do so was America's first African American president, Barack Obama.

President Obama had earlier appeared on an ESPN show and discussed his picks for the upcoming NCAA March Madness basketball tournament, and now he was talking about a variety of things to host Jay Leno. Obama's appearance was part of a larger campaign to persuade the American public about his proposed economic plan to help America recover from a recession, and he showed his characteristic wit and charm during the interview.

When asked by Leno when President Obama's daughters would get the dog they long wanted, Obama quipped, "This is Washington. That was just a campaign promise."

However, another offhand joke got the most media attention. After President Obama said that his poor bowling score was "like Special Olympics or something," for days, stories covered the remark and the public's reactions to it, and the subsequent apology from the president.

The story seemed to get more coverage than another video from President Obama aired the same day—a videotaped message to Iran that extended an olive branch and an offer to repair relations between the two countries, reversing thirty years of U.S. government policy toward Iran.

Although political candidates had long been going on late-night talk shows, some commentators worried that President Obama's appearance on *The Tonight Show* may have demeaned the office of the presidency. Others worried that politicians might lose more than they gain if, in their effort to become closer to the American people, they should commit a gaffe like President Obama did.

A s the brief story about President Obama demonstrates, there have been dramatic changes in recent years regarding media and politics. Journalism has long considered itself the main conduit through which politicians inform the public, thereby playing a key role in democratic processes. Journalism is the mechanism through which the public obtains unbiased, impartial information about candidates for office, sitting elected officials, and the agencies they represent and operate.

Although this is the goal, media critics contend the media are anything but unbiased. Consider the words of Joseph Pulitzer, the former publisher of the *New York World* and the founder of the Pulitzer Prize, the highest award for journalistic excellence. In support of his proposal for the founding of a school of journalism, Pulitzer summarized his credo: "Our Republic and its press will rise or fall together. An able, disinterested, public-spirited press, with trained intelligence to

Comedy sketches in shows like SNL have sometimes received
as much media attention as statements from actual candidates.

Playing Politics

Test your political and media knowledge.

1. (T/F) Bill Clinton was the first presidential candidate to appear on a late-night talk show.
2. Who was the politician whose campaign for reelection was ruined when a video of him calling a campaign worker "macaca" was widely distributed?
3. Name a country that follows the authoritarian theory of communication.
4. What form of mass communication would be most useful in a developing country, print media or radio?
5. What is the digital divide?
6. Describe an example of horse-race coverage in an election.
7. (T/F) Expenditures on political advertising make up by far the largest part of a campaign budget.
8. What social-media site has been credited with radically changing the nature of elections in 2008?
9. (T/F) So far, the changes to politics from social media and online communications have only taken place in industrialized countries.
10. (T/F) You can find online how much your neighbor donated to a politician.

know the right and courage to do it, can preserve that public virtue without which popular government is a sham and a mockery. A cynical, mercenary, demagogic press will produce in time a people as base as itself. The power to mould the future of the Republic will be in the hands of the journalists of future generations."[1]

However, it is more than journalism that drives the engine of media and politics. In fact, especially in times of presidential election campaigns, it is advertising that drives this machine. Political advertising, especially on television, is how most candidates, particularly presidential candidates, reach most voters most often. Negative political advertising is one of the mainstays of the political world in the United States, and it has been extensively researched. Political advertising also provides substantial income for media organizations and has made it necessary for political candidates to raise large sums of money from donations.

Entertainment has played an increasingly important role in helping political candidates create a more down-to-earth image, with appearances on late-night talk shows and even comedy shows like *Saturday Night Live* now becoming the norm. "Fake news" shows such as *The Daily Show* are often a main source of political news for young people.

Furthermore, the Internet and other types of online communication have not only become important information sources for the public but played key roles in helping candidates organize and raise funds. Similarly, political and activist groups have been able to generate money or support for their causes using online communication tools. Candidates have had their political careers ruined thanks in part to the ease of distribution of video and documents. A case in point was Virginia senator George Allen, who on a campaign stop during the 2006 election publicly called an opponent's campaign worker of Indian descent "macaca," a racial slur for

George Allen's political campaign was badly hurt by the video that showed him calling a campaign worker of Indian descent "macaca" during a rally.

African immigrants used in Europe. The video of Allen saying this at the rally was widely spread on the Internet, leaving an indelible impression of Allen's character that no amount of official press release apologies could successfully whitewash or counter.

But mass communication is not only important at election time; the media are directly connected to government and the public in many complex ways. The following section examines what research tells us about the process and effects of journalism and mass communication in the sphere of political communications in the United States and abroad.

Four Theories of International Mass Communication

Four theories of international mass communication were presented in 1956 by Fred S. Siebert, Wilbur Schramm, and Theodore Peterson.[2] These three social scientists were looking for ways to explain how the press operates in different political, historical, and cultural environments around the world. Although they referred specifically to "the press," we can extend their theories to embrace all the media of mass communication, including television, radio, and online.

Siebert, Schramm, and Peterson's four theories of the press are these:

1. The authoritarian theory
2. The libertarian theory
3. The social responsibility theory
4. The Soviet theory

■ ■ ■ THE AUTHORITARIAN THEORY

authoritarian theory
of the press
. . . .
A theory of international
mass communication in which
authoritarian governments exert
direct control over the media.

The **authoritarian theory** describes the oldest system of mass communication, which has its roots in sixteenth- and seventeenth-century England. This system exists in authoritarian states in which government exerts direct control over the mass media. Countries where government consists of a limited and small ruling class are especially likely to have an authoritarian media system.

Media in authoritarian systems are not permitted to print, broadcast, or webcast anything the government feels might undermine its authority. Content that

Searching for Truth:
Self-Censorship in China

INTERNATIONAL PERSPECTIVES

As growing numbers of Chinese go online, the Chinese media market becomes increasingly tempting to Western media. However, China's restrictions on the press and tight control over Internet access often run afoul of Western notions of a free press.

For example, China blocks access to a wide range of websites, from pornographic sites to those that mention the 1989 protests and deaths in Tiananmen Square or the banned group Falun Gong, to sites that are critical of the Chinese government.

Google was criticized in the press in 2006 when the company chose to censor itself in order to enter the Chinese search engine market. Many observers noted the irony in Google's "Don't Be Evil" mantra regarding its business philosophy and wondered how the search engine giant could rationalize its decision to not include full access to sites on the Internet.

Google representatives said that it was better that Google provide some access, with the hope that it helps China open its media system more, than to not offer anything at all. Despite its compromise to gain entry to the Internet in China, Google still remains less popular there than home-grown search engine company Baidu.

Competitor Yahoo faced heavy criticism from the press a year earlier, when the company provided user information, requested by the Chinese government, that helped put a Chinese journalist in jail for ten years.

As long as the Communist government in China maintains its strict controls over media access and the types of content allowed, Western media companies will have some difficult ethical choices to make if they do business in China.

threatens or challenges the existing political system and its values is strictly prohibited. Anyone who violates the rules is subject to harsh punishment, including imprisonment, expulsion, or even death.

Government uses the media not only to inform the public of important events but also to shape public opinion in support of its policies. Although ownership of media can be private or public, media professionals are not permitted to have editorial independence within their organizations. Foreign media are subordinate to governmental authority. Countries where the authoritarian theory best describes current systems of mass communication include China, Cuba, and Myanmar.

■ ■ ■ THE LIBERTARIAN THEORY

Libertarian theory is often also called the free press theory. Libertarian theory rests on the notion that the individual should be free to publish whatever he or she likes. Its roots lie in the work of seventeenth-century philosopher and writer John Milton, whose *Areopagitica* (1644) argued, "And though all the winds of doctrine were let loose to play upon the earth, so Truth be in the field, we do injuriously by licensing and prohibiting to misdoubt her strength. Let her and Falsehood grapple; who ever knew Truth put to the worse, in a free and open encounter?"

In the libertarian theory, criticism of the government and its policies are accepted and even encouraged. There are no restrictions on the import or export of media messages across the national borders. Media professionals have full autonomy within their media organization.

In some ways, however, the libertarian theory is an ideal type, and not one that realistically applies in full anywhere. There are few if any countries where the libertarian theory perfectly describes the system of mass communication. Yet, there are many countries where elements of the theory clearly play a role in the media system.

■ ■ ■ THE SOCIAL RESPONSIBILITY THEORY

Social responsibility theory best describes the systems of mass communication in most democratic societies. The theory rests on the notion that the media play a vital role in informing citizens in a democratic society and, as such, should be free from most governmental constraints in order to provide the best, most reliable and impartial information to the public.

To operate effectively in this environment, the media must exercise self-restraint and act responsibly. The Commission on Freedom of the Press (known as the Hutchins Commission) in 1947 articulated the media's obligations to society. These included truth, accuracy, objectivity, balance, diversity, and being informative. The commission argued that a responsible media system must do more than simply report the facts. It must place them in context. This means the media must provide analysis, explanation, and interpretation.

Although the social responsibility theory may best describe the system of mass communication in democracies such as the United States, Canada, France, and the United Kingdom, the growth of global corporate media organizations challenges media to place the public good over profits and to do so internationally as well as domestically. Siebert, Peterson, and Schramm cautioned, "The power and near monopoly position of the media impose on them an obligation to be socially responsible, to see that all sides are fairly presented and that the public has enough information to decide; and that if the media do not take on themselves such responsibility it may be necessary for some other agency of the public to enforce it."

John Milton was a proponent of the libertarian theory of the press.

libertarian theory

A theory of international mass communication that is rooted in the idea of the individual's right to publish whatever he or she wants, even material that is critical of the government or of government officials.

social responsibility theory

A theory of international mass communication that perhaps best describes the media's role in democratic societies. It rests on the notion that the media are vital to informing citizens in a democratic society and, as such, should be free from most governmental constraints in order to provide the best, most reliable and impartial information to the public.

They add, "Freedom of expression under the social responsibility theory is not an absolute right, as under pure libertarian theory. . . . One's right to free expression must be balanced against the private rights of others and against vital social interests." For example, a socially responsible news organization would exercise extreme care in preparing reports about terrorist activities, especially ones that might detail how bioterrorism is conducted or provide information on a city's disaster plans, because such information could be used by terrorists to help plan attacks.

■ ■ ■ THE SOVIET THEORY

The **Soviet theory** of the press is based on a specific ideology: the communist system of government practiced in the former Soviet Union. Siebert traced the roots of this theory to the 1917 Russian Revolution and the views of Karl Marx and Friedrich Engels. According to the Soviet theory, media should serve the interests of the working class and should be publicly owned, not privately owned.

The Soviet Union's main newspaper was *Pravda*, meaning "truth."

Although there are some similarities between the Soviet and authoritarian systems, such as the media being subordinate to government, there are also important differences. In particular, the Soviet theory posits that the media should recognize their responsibility to the people and self-regulate their content. Government censorship is not to be the norm. With the demise of the Soviet Union in the 1980s, this theory is most useful as an historical reference point. However, one can see elements of its philosophy in the growing number of citizen-journalism and alternative-media organizations that are challenging mainstream journalism for the public's attention.

The Public, the Public Sphere, and Public Opinion

The notions of "the public" and "public opinion" are surprisingly complex, and their definitions are still being debated by scholars today. In some ways, the public can be considered as an audience for governments or politicians, but this viewpoint fails to take into account how exactly the public today differs from the public in the Middle Ages, for example.

Most scholars agree that the idea of "the public" did not come about until the late sixteenth or early seventeenth century, when Europe was beginning to enter the modern era and governments were changing from monarchies to more representative forms. A new class arose, the **bourgeoisie**, which began to recognize the differing economic and political interests among business, government, and citizens. More importantly, the bourgeoisie recognized themselves as a separate group, apart but also a part of government and economics. Through tools of communication at the time, primarily newspapers, pamphlets, journals, and other periodicals, the bourgeoisie were able to communicate with each other about common interests and challenge government policies that did not match them.

The forums in which the bourgeoisie debated matters of public interest included the popular coffeehouses, where conversations were spurred by the material in the print publications that were disseminated, and where a sense of

soviet theory
....
A theory of international mass communication that states the media should be publicly owned and used to further the needs of the working class.

bourgeoisie
....
A class of society that translates approximately to "middle class," which distinguishes the class from the aristocracy above them and the proletariat (or workers) below them.

"conventional wisdom" developed through debate and discussion among peers. The notion of the **public sphere**, as first discussed by German social theorist and philosopher Jürgen Habermas, captures this atmosphere in ideal terms, where the most rational argument won the day and where rank or privilege took a back seat to the quest for knowledge and truth.

This ideal was never realized, of course, but the notion of the public sphere remains a powerful one in media and mass-communication research today. Some scholars see a kind of "fall from grace," in that commercial media have taken over the public forum and imposed new forms of (often hidden) control over what is discussed and how it is discussed. Other scholars claim that the public sphere of the seventeenth-century European coffeehouses never actually included the public, as women and the majority of people were excluded from the conversations.

Coffeehouses in the eighteenth century were important locations for development of the public sphere.

Today there is debate on whether the Internet can actually rejuvenate the notion of the public sphere in which citizens can discuss freely and openly without interference from government or commercial interests. However, with so many different types of people online and so many different types of interests, getting any sense of a coherent public sphere in which participants all abide by certain rules of rational argument and civic-mindedness has proven elusive.

The public sphere ostensibly plays a role in the formation of **public opinion**, itself a contested concept, which can nevertheless be broadly defined as "what the public thinks." The notion of public opinion goes back directly to trying to define who exactly "the public" is and how a commonly shared opinion is formed and spread. Is public opinion simply the aggregate of individual beliefs, writ large, or does it become something greater than the sum of its parts? If so, how does it change and what effects are there of such changes?

Whatever the disagreements over the definition, public opinion plays an important role in democratic countries today, and the media play an integral part in creating, shaping, and spreading ideas that become commonly accepted. Few major policy decisions are made without first testing the waters among the public to see what the reaction is.

This is not to say that government is controlled by mob rule, however, as the notion of "the public" is more complex than simply thinking of a mass of people. Public opinion can and often is manipulated to suit the ends of various groups, and an entire media industry—public relations—exists for the primary purpose of swaying public opinion in favor of clients or policies.

But PR professionals are not the only ones who can influence the public today. Just as the bourgeoisie in seventeenth-century coffeehouses found themselves with new tools of mass communication that gave them power to communicate that they previously did not have, citizens today have a wide range of powerful communication tools at their disposal. They can start online petitions, create complaint sites about companies or parody sites of politicians, post news scoops on blogs about embarrassing moments in the lives of politicians, and act as citizen reporters to inform the world of injustices when media are silent (either by their own decision or by decision of a government).

An example of the latter happened in 2007 in Myanmar, a country in Southeast Asia that is run by a military junta. Antigovernment protests that were started by Buddhist monks were forcefully repressed by the military, and the only images released of the violence were from citizens taking pictures with mobile phones, as the international media were not allowed in the country and the state-run media did not report accurately on what was happening.

With so many communication tools accessible, media have become even more intertwined with various political issues, both in the United States and internationally.

Political Issues with Media

Radio and television are often used to reach persons in remote agricultural regions in developing countries to provide information on agricultural techniques and government policies. Broadcast stations are often among the first places taken in a coup, as those in power—or those wishing to gain power—realize the importance of controlling the means of distributing information. Print media are often used to foster the business development of a region, although their effectiveness is limited in countries with low literacy rates or where many different languages are spoken.

Foreign governments tend to control the content of their mass-communication organizations, especially television and radio, far more than is seen in the United States. In some cases, broadcasting stations are entirely government owned or government run, while in other cases licensing restrictions for television sets or media devices such as satellite dishes limit the ability of the public to have complete access to the media.

■ ■ ■ MEDIA IN DEVELOPING COUNTRIES

The media and accompanying communication technologies are instruments for economic development throughout the world and can have exceptional potential to improve the economy in developing nations. Western companies looking to

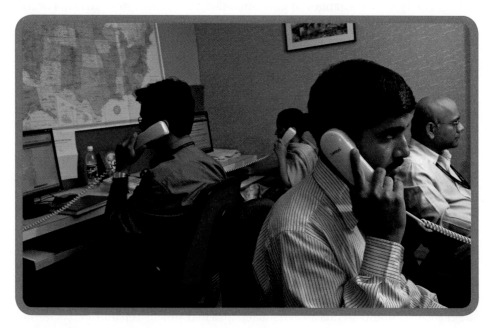

Outsourcing IT services to developing countries has provided
new job opportunities for workers in those countries.

establish factories overseas to take advantage of cheap labor costs look for developed infrastructure, such as passable transportation routes and communication networks, as part of what makes a good place to locate. Of course, such things as stable governments and corporate-friendly government policies (like low taxes) are also sought.

Countries such as India have become sources for relatively cheap software developers and computer-programming workers, as well as database centers and information-processing centers. India is positioned nicely because it has a generally well-educated workforce that speaks English, letting the country take advantage of "low-end" information-economy needs, such as scanning documents, transcribing documents, and providing technical support for computer makers and software companies.

Some countries in Africa have been making moves toward similarly fulfilling information-processing needs of industrial countries. A data-processing company in Ghana, for example, inputs into a database minor violations that occur in New York City, ranging from parking tickets to jaywalking. For Ghanian workers the pay is better than other jobs and the working conditions are better than in many other industries, although hours are long and breaks are short by Western standards.

Although some critics charge that moving information-processing work overseas is no different than sending factories overseas to obtain cheaper labor and avoid dealing with pollution problems and employee-benefits costs, others have supported this trend. They claim that the information technology (IT) industry is not like industrial-era factories: it is generally nonpolluting, it can be created using existing buildings, and the type of work raises workers' level of education, better positioning them for other jobs within information societies. In short, it is hoped that developing countries can skip the worst effects of the industrial age and move directly into the information age, although whether this is the case or not remains to be seen.

Some factors keep IT from growing as fast as it could in developing countries. Excessive government regulation often hampers development of a good telecommunication infrastructure that could better reach all citizens within a country. Political instability, drastic changes in government policies, corruption among government officials, a lack of other infrastructure, such as regular electrical power—all these can hurt development of telecommunication technologies in a country.

Southeast Asian nations such as Singapore and Malaysia have been promoting themselves as high-speed Internet ecommerce zones that will provide the most technologically advanced support for online business operations in the hope of attracting Western businesses. However, important concerns arise regarding the free flow of information, from a cultural or political, rather than a technical, perspective. Singapore strictly controls access to most forms of media, even banning some Western newspapers that have criticized the government, and it attempts to tightly control citizens' access to the Internet. Western companies, especially media companies, may balk at these restrictions on access to information.

■ ■ ■ THE DIGITAL DIVIDE

digital divide

The idea that some groups that do not have access to the Internet become left out of the benefits that online technology can bring.

As developed countries see a growing number of their citizens get online, often with percentages between 60 and 70 percent, the problem of the **digital divide** rears its head. The digital divide is not caused by the Internet. Rather, it reflects larger socioeconomic trends and characteristics that already separate citizens—but some worry that, if ignored, it could have serious negative implications for society.

In the United States, the early users of the Internet tended to be wealthier and more educated than later users. Given the importance of the information economy, people who are online have a distinct advantage over those who are not in terms of getting important information, making decisions, and engaging in a host of other activities that could accelerate their upward motion on the social and economic ladder.

Meanwhile, it is feared that people who are less educated, or without the income to afford typically more than one hundred dollars a month for complete telecommunications service, including Internet access, could fall behind. These people tend to be members of groups that already have faced various forms of discrimination in society or have other socioeconomic or educational disadvantages compared to dominant groups.

Being able to simply have access to the Internet is one component, but having access to high-quality information is also a matter of some concern. If all that is available for free or low cost

Providing low-cost or free Internet access is an important part of closing the digital divide.

is lowbrow entertainment that does little to inform or educate the public, then simply having access will have no effect on bridging the digital divide. What is important is to provide the kind of education and critical-thinking skills that allow people to discern the quality of information they get and to use it for helpful purposes.

Thus, there are two major components to the digital-divide issue. One is technological: providing access to the communications technologies needed to access the Internet, such as computers, cheap or free software, and other tools. Cost plays a key role in this as well. Two hundred dollars a month for communications may not seem like much to someone making eighty thousand dollars a year, but it is a much larger percentage of the income of someone making minimum wage or working part-time. The other main component is education: teaching people how to use the online communication tools available to them. Entertainment will always be a part of online communication, but it should not be the sole consumption for the less privileged, just as it is not for the affluent.

Political issues like the digital divide and the role that the Internet plays in our society are complex and will require long-term commitments and widespread discussions among everyone involved. Media will play a role in guiding (or hampering) these discussions, though that role may not always be readily apparent. Given media's chronically poor job of covering themselves in the news, business interests may win out over public interests if companies see their profitability at stake when it comes to discussions on the digital divide. However, one area of politics in which the media are far more visible, and where they have often changed some fundamental aspects of politics, is in elections.

The Role of Media in Political Elections

Since the earliest days of the Republic, the media have been intimately involved in our political process. The colonial newspapers were a "partisan" press, typically aligned with a particular political party or trying to persuade the public of a certain viewpoint. In some countries, there is still a partisan press. Media also played a role in helping the Revolutionary cause. Journalism in the nineteenth century evolved into an impartial press, but it still considers its core mission to provide the

Editorial cartoons in the nineteenth century often used caricature and could often have biting commentary.

information citizens need to make sound decisions—in other words, journalism sees itself as an engine of democracy.

Since the first use of radio in political campaigning, in 1924, the electronic media have played an increasingly important part in political elections. In both 1936 and 1940, while the majority of newspapers throughout the United States openly endorsed Republican candidates for office, radio had become the more heavily used medium by Democrats. President Roosevelt was masterful in his use of radio to reach the masses, providing his regular "Fireside Chats" during both the 1930s and 1940s. Radio had emerged as the politically potent medium of mass communication during this time, with even greater impact than newspapers and magazines, and radio itself was soon to be replaced by television as the dominant medium in the 1950s. It began an era in which the personal qualities of candidates, rather than their political-policy stances, would take center stage in the campaign process.

■ ■ ■ SOUND BITES AND HORSE RACES

With the rise of electronic media, especially television in the past half century, the process of political communication and debate in the media has been transformed from one of generally some substance into one increasingly characterized by superficial examination of the issues.

More often than not, the horse-race aspect of the campaign, or chronicling who's ahead, who's behind, and what the latest campaign tactic might be to move ahead in the polls, becomes the whole story at the expense of coverage of issues.

In 1968, Kiku Adatto of Harvard University did a study on political **sound bites**—specifically, how long a source in a television news story was allowed to speak without being edited by the reporter. In 1968 the average sound bite was 42.3 seconds. Nearly a quarter of all political sound bites were at least a minute in length, providing considerable room for context. Twenty years later, in 1988, the average TV sound bite of a political candidate had shrunk by some 80 percent to just 9.8 seconds, and virtually none were a minute or longer—in fact, entire stories were often not a minute in length.

sound bite
....
The length of time a news subject is allowed to speak without being edited by a reporter. It also has come to refer to short utterances that are catchy and designed to capture the media's attention.

■ ■ ■ THE CHANGING TONE OF TELEVISION POLITICAL COVERAGE

The tone of television political coverage has also changed. Consider the research findings of Syracuse University political scientist Thomas Patterson, author of *Out of Order*. He found that in the 1960 presidential election, three-quarters (75 percent) of the news reports about leading candidates John F. Kennedy and Richard M. Nixon were positive in tone; only a quarter (25 percent) were negative. Thirty years later, in the 1992 presidential election, news reports had become predominantly negative in tone: more than half (60 percent) of the reports about then candidate Bill Clinton and then president George H. Bush were negative, and less than half (40 percent) were positive. Patterson's research also shows that the length of candidate statements in election stories on the front page of the *New York Times* had similarly shrunk. In 1960, the average quote was fourteen lines. In 1992, the average quote was less than seven lines.

CONVERGENCE **CONTEXT**

Sound Bite Shakespeare

University of San Diego professor Daniel C. Hallin puts the shrinking sound bite into context.[3] In 1968, if a commercial network television reporter had included a sound bite from William Shakespeare's *Julius Caesar* (Act III, Scene II, at the Forum), he would have had time to include the following statement from Antony:

> Friends, Romans, countrymen, lend me your ears;
> I come to bury Caesar, not to praise him.
> The evil that men do lives after them;
> The good is oft interred with their bones;
> So let it be with Caesar. The noble Brutus
> Hath told you Caesar was ambitious:
> If it were so, it was a grievous fault,
> And grievously hath Caesar answer'd it.
> Here, under leave of Brutus and the rest—
> For Brutus is an honourable man;
> So are they all, all honourable men—
> Come I to speak in Caesar's funeral.
> He was my friend, faithful and just to me:
> But Brutus says he was ambitious;
> And Brutus is an honourable man.

Here's what we'd hear from Antony in 1988 on the commercial network television evening news:

> Friends, Romans, countrymen, lend me your ears; I come to bury Caesar, not to praise him.

Some hold out hope that the sound-bite culture of commercial television news may change thanks to competition from YouTube and online video sites that let users watch video clips as long as they want without commercial breaks. There is some early evidence that large numbers of viewers have turned to YouTube to watch speeches, or at least longer excerpts of speeches, than what the mainstream news has traditionally presented. If mainstream news wants to remain relevant for viewers, it will likely have to likewise offer longer clips than in the past.

Has this situation changed with the rise of online news? Not by much. Although there is scant research evidence yet to point to, the fact is that much of the online political coverage is no different than the political coverage in other media, since much of that coverage is lifted and repurposed from other media, including television, radio, newspapers, and magazines. The sound bites are the same, and the quotes are the same.

Many of the better online news operations, such as CBS News online, typically add further reporting to stories that are adapted from on-air coverage, turning the text of a sixty-second video report (what might be less than two hundred words) into a five-hundred-word or longer report with more depth and possibly additional quotes. Repeated quotes are sometimes the same length but occasionally longer than in the broadcast text. Much of the additional reporting is drawn from wire service copy (e.g., Reuters, the Associated Press) pulled off the Internet or sometimes from original reporting conducted via telephone or email interviews. Increasingly, graphics such as maps are used as well.

■■■ OPINION POLLS

Campaign coverage has also become heavily driven by **opinion polls**. Patterson's research shows that the news about a candidate becomes more favorable when his or her support in the polls increases markedly or if he or she leads by a wide margin. Conversely, media coverage becomes more negative if there is a drop in the candidate's standing in the polls or if he or she trails significantly.

Media organizations usually use one of several professional polling organizations, such as Gallup, to conduct polls. These polling organizations try to take random samples of the public in order to assess what the population as a whole is likely feeling about a candidate or issue. However, lower telephone response rates in recent years, as people screen calls to avoid telemarketers, have made conducting telephone polls more expensive.

Opinion polls or surveys show up increasingly on news websites, although they are not considered scientifically valid, since the answers only represent users who have visited the website and chosen to answer the poll. Online polls are being used by some polling organizations, such as Harris Interactive, although these are largely derided by other organizations and the American Association for Public Opinion Research (AAPOR) for being nonscientific. Internet users still do not fairly represent a broad sampling of the general populace since they tend to be more affluent than average, white, and male. They also have voluntarily signed up to participate in online polls, usually with the promise of a chance at winning prizes, and are therefore a self-selected group that is also not considered to be representative of even the online population. Despite the poor image of online polls among some polling professionals, they continue to be used more and more and are gaining more respectability. Some of the issues regarding accurately representing the population are also rapidly becoming less relevant as more and more people go online.

Sometimes telephone "polls," called **push polls**, are actually political advertising. Push polls try to sway voters by giving them false or misleading information about opposing candidates under the guise of conducting a poll or try to make a candidate look good by asking leading questions. Push polls ask deliberately misleading questions, such as, "Would you support the policies of a candidate who will curtail some of our freedoms and raise taxes?" Few would answer "yes" to such a question, but the respondent may not realize that the pollster was referring to a certain candidate when asking it. Yet the results would be publicized as showing that "90 percent of the people polled say they do not support Candidate Y."

■■■ POLITICAL ADVERTISING

Partly as a result of the shrinking sound bite, the poll-driven horse-race media coverage of campaigns, and the political candidates' and parties' interest in controlling their own messages to the voter, candidates have turned increasingly to paid advertising. Of course, candidates have historically used a wide variety of techniques to directly reach as many people as possible, from whistle-stop speeches to political rallies. However, campaigning has become increasingly expensive in the

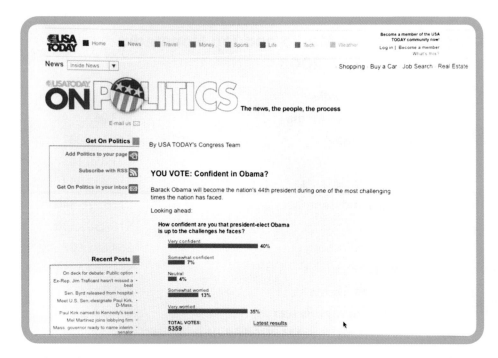

Online polls are increasingly used, although they are still not considered as accurate as traditional polls.

United States as campaigns and technology become more complex and candidates attempt to reach people through the media.[4]

The 2008 presidential elections were the first in which the candidates raised more than $1 billion combined. By far the largest single expenditure, over $478 million, was on advertising in broadcast media, as **Table 15-1** shows. Other media expenditures, including advertising on the Internet, which in 2008 was more than double that spent on print advertising, make up over 50 percent of campaigns' total expenditures. In 1952, only 5 percent of campaign expenditures went for broadcast media. When you count direct mail and telemarketing expenditures, the amount spent on political advertising is even bigger.

The Impact of Negative Advertising

Some people say that political advertising is no different than other product advertising, except that in a political campaign there is a one-day sale. It is this mentality that drives the industry. As a result, many candidates gravitate toward negative advertising. Based on an examination of more than 1,100 political commercials, political-communications scholar Larry Sabato concluded:

> Even when television is used to communicate political truth (at least from one candidate's perspective), the truth can be negatively packaged—attacking the opponent's character and record rather than supporting one's own. If there is a single trend obvious to most American consultants, it is the increasing proportion of negative political advertising. . . . At least a third of all spot commercials in recent campaigns have been negative, and in a minority of campaigns half or more of the spots are negative in tone or substance.[5]

Although some of the paid political spots on television are intended to simply provide information about the candidate and his or her position on the issues, the

TABLE 15-1

Political Campaign Expenditures on Media and Top Nonmedia Expenditures, Presidential Campaign 2008

Media Expenditures	**Broadcast Media**	$419,170,183
	Miscellaneous Media	$73,067,264
	Internet Media	$43,551,881
	Print Media	$21,850,143
	Media Consultants	$11,477,888
Nonmedia Expenditures	**Salaries and Benefits**	$176,276,340
	Travel	$167,302,536
	Postage/Shipping	$64,685,987
	Rent/Utilities	$57,063,635
	Campaign Events	$71,248,680
	Polling/Surveys/Research	$44,947,223
	Fund-raising Direct Mail/Telemarketing	$66,420,094

Source: OpenSecrets.org, May 2009

ads that have captured the most criticism and research have been the negative ads that are intended to attack the opposing candidate rather than shed light on the issues. The rise of political advertising has also led news media to increasingly focus their coverage of the candidates on the candidates' advertising.

Much of the negative political advertising has been problematic for a number of reasons. One of the biggest problems, Kathleen Hall Jamieson points out, is that many of the ads contain falsehoods or lead the audience to make false inferences.[6] Republican presidential candidate John McCain was criticized for running negative political ads about Barack Obama at one point in his campaign, despite his promises that he would not run negative ads. Obama's advisers suggested Obama fight back with his own ads rather than ignore McCain's negative advertising, because they worried that he would look weak if he did not respond strongly.

Negative Advertising Effectiveness

Researchers Richard Lau and Lee Sigelman tested three hypotheses regarding negative political advertisements: (1) that they work (i.e., they get voters to endorse the candidate doing the attacking), (2) that voters dislike negative ads, and (3) that negative ads tend to have an unintended side effect of disenfranchising the electorate.

Regarding the first hypothesis, Lau and Sigelman found in a study of voters in 1997 that negative ads do not work; they actually decreased the favorability of voters' attitudes toward the candidate whose campaign ran the negative ad. Conversely, the favorability of voters' attitudes toward the "target" of the ads increased. A study of the 1992 campaign similarly revealed that candidates who initiated negative ads lost eighteen out of twenty-five elections. They also found there was no strong preponderance of evidence indicating that negative political ads were more memorable than positive ads.

Regarding the second hypothesis, that voters dislike negative ads, the results are clear again. "Six of the nine studies found negative political ads being rated

Negative political advertising is controversial, with some claiming that it turns off voters and actually hurts the politician making the negative ad.

less ethical, less fair, and otherwise less liked than positive political ads, while two studies came to the opposite conclusions and one uncovered no significant differences," Lau and Sigelman report.

Third, whether negative ads contribute to voter apathy or disenfranchisement, the results are somewhat mixed. Although there is some evidence to support this hypothesis, it is not clear. "Of the 20 relevant findings, ten report no significant differences and two associate positive outcomes with negative political ads (e.g., higher turnout), but eight report significant negative consequences," Lau and Sigelman explain.

Some research indicates that one of the most important effects of negative political advertising is to alienate young viewers from the political process. Negative political advertising increases the level of cynicism among young viewers and decreases their interest in becoming politically active and involved.

■ ■ ■ POLITICAL DEBATES

One of the most important areas of political communication is the debate. Ever since the great debates between Abraham Lincoln and Stephen A. Douglas during the U.S. Senate race of 1858, debates have been a proving ground for candidates to test their mettle against an opponent and for the voting public to better understand both the character and the content of each candidate.

Notably, these early debates were in many ways quite different than the televised debates the public has come to know since the first televised debate in 1960. For example, a debate between Lincoln and Douglas might last more than five hours, with each candidate offering detailed commentary of an hour or more on a single issue, such as abolition—which was the topic of the first debate, held on August 21, 1858. Further, since television or radio did not yet exist, these debates were not heard by anyone other than those present for the live event, although the public could read about them in newspapers.

The Kennedy-Nixon presidential debate in 1960 showed how powerful television could be for political candidates in influencing public perceptions.

Arguably the most important debate between U.S. presidential candidates in the twentieth century occurred in 1960, when for the first time presidential candidates debated live on broadcast television and radio. The debate pitted John F. Kennedy and Richard M. Nixon against each other. Research conducted at the time showed that among those who watched the debate on television, Kennedy, who was handsome and well groomed, was rated clearly superior. Nixon, whose dark stubble and "shifty" eyes gave him a more sinister look (the debate was scheduled for the evening and Nixon had not shaved since the morning), was deemed to have lost.

Meanwhile, on radio, with listeners only able to hear the candidates' voices, the clear winner was deemed to be Nixon because it seemed he had the more convincing arguments. Kennedy ultimately won the presidential contest in an extremely close election, and it is not clear whether the debate was the deciding factor. But it has been the touchstone for televised campaigning ever since. Today it is a given that one's television persona is an essential quality in winning an election.

The Internet and Political Campaigns

One phenomenon that emerged as a strong force in political elections is the direct-access medium of the Internet. Never before have candidates and the public had such great ability to directly communicate with each other. Voters can simply go online and visit a candidate's website to obtain information about where the candidate stands on an issue, make a campaign contribution, or volunteer to help the candidate's party. Conversely, the voter can also create a website voicing approval or disapproval of a candidate or support for or opposition to an issue. Some have even bought website domain names to create websites that make fun of candidates. Voters use the Internet to supplement their knowledge of the candidates and to compare what the candidates have to say with what the news media report.

Although having a website may have been considered groundbreaking for a candidate in 1998, by 2008 it was fully expected and not nearly enough if that was all a candidate had. All candidates had websites, and all sites had areas in which the candidates outlined their beliefs and viewpoints on issues. All also had online donation capabilities and sold items to help with fund-raising. But the most successful candidates went far beyond a simple website and utilized the growing array of social-media tools to further engage the public with the candidate and with each other.

Building on some of the techniques pioneered by Howard Dean's failed presidential bid in 2004, in which he tapped into an informal network of grassroots support and small donations to raise large sums of money, Obama's campaign team—some of whom were veterans of the Dean campaign—further refined the techniques. Obama's campaign was so successful at getting small donations from

CONVERGENCE **CULTURE**

Image Is Everything

Although the obsession with a politician's image did not begin with television, it certainly took on much greater importance than it ever had in the age of print. Even so, politicians then were hardly groundbreakers in fashion. A look at presidential portraits shows that after a spate of presidents with facial hair in the latter 1800s, the last president with a beard or mustache was William Howard Taft (1909–1913). Today, except perhaps for Sinn Fein president and Irish MP Gerry Adams, almost no Western politicians have facial hair. Of course there is no correla-

tion between one's ability to govern and having facial hair, yet it has been considered a political taboo for at least eighty years.

Television has only added to the importance of how politicians look, and it is said that several presidents would have never been elected if television had existed when they were running, because of their looks or disabilities. These include Abraham Lincoln, with his gawky, awkward appearance; William Howard Taft, weighing in at three hundred pounds; and wheelchair-bound Franklin Delano Roosevelt, stricken by polio. FDR would never be able to get the press today to agree, as the press did then, to not publish images of him getting in and out of his wheelchair.

Today, image consultants help political candidates look the part, with advice on everything from what color shirt and tie to wear to what hairstyle they should have. Republican vice-presidential candidate Sarah Palin got a thorough makeover and wardrobe change—a sticking point for some in the Republican Party when it was revealed that the Republican National Committee paid $150,000 for her clothes when she was trying to cultivate an image of a middle-class soccer mom.

many people that he was the first presidential candidate to refuse taxpayer funding (and, not coincidentally, the spending restrictions that went with that).

Some have even claimed that President Obama, often called the first "Black-Berry President" because of his obsession with his BlackBerry, owes his election win to the Internet. Joe Trippi, Dean's campaign manager in 2004, said that the extent and kind of organizing that Obama was able to do through the Internet would have required "an army of volunteers and paid organizers on the ground."[7]

■ ■ ■ THE ROLE OF YOUTUBE

YouTube played a major role in helping Obama, according to Arianna Huffington, founder of the influential blog the Huffington Post. By being able to post videos that the public could watch when it wanted to, without commercials, candidates could speak at greater length than in the sound-bite culture that dominates the mainstream news. YouTube also allowed people to watch repeatedly and to forward videos to friends.

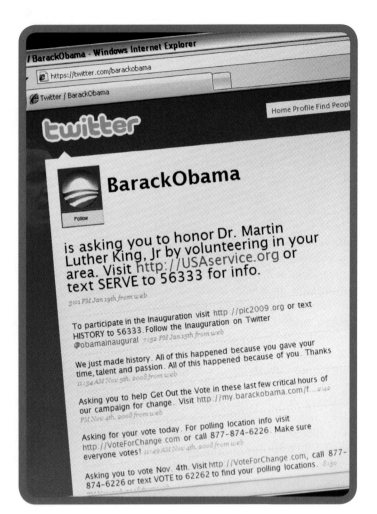

The ability of the public to repeatedly watch and forward short videos was of course a double-edged sword for politicians. On the one hand, they could communicate directly with the public without depending on news organizations to disseminate their speeches and messages. On the other hand, gaffes or other mistakes that were videotaped could be spread just as easily as prepared speeches.

YouTube purposely positioned itself to play a potentially important role in the elections by launching the YouTube You Choose '08 campaign, which gave presidential candidates their own YouTube channels. YouTube also encouraged people to videotape their questions to candidates during a series of debates, called the CNN/YouTube debates, and worked with Video the Vote, an organization that has people videotape difficulties with voting.

The success of these efforts likely surprised even YouTube itself, and some commentators have called 2008 the YouTube election. The implications for future campaigns are only starting to be analyzed by scholars and political consultants, but the changes brought by YouTube are even more remarkable given that YouTube did not even exist during the presidential election of 2004, and it is owned by Google, itself barely ten years old.

■ ■ ■ CHANGING RULES FOR POLITICIANS

President Obama's campaign created a website specifically to dispel the myriad false rumors circulating about him during the campaign.

The changes brought to political campaigns by YouTube, Facebook, and other Web 2.0 social-media technologies are still not fully understood and will likely change as technologies continue to evolve. However, there are some fundamental shifts that are already apparent from the 2008 presidential campaign.

As candidates from both parties learned, to their dismay, there is no such thing anymore as an "off the record" event. It used to be that journalists attending fundraisers or other events that were off the record respected that whatever was said there by a candidate could not be reported on. But now, with a variety of citizen journalists and bloggers attending such events, there is no guarantee that these rules will be respected.

One of the biggest scoops of the campaign came during the Democratic primary, when Obama commented about people in small towns in Pennsylvania "clinging to guns and religion." The comment was made to a group of wealthy Californians at an event that was closed to the media, but citizen journalist Mayhill Fowler blogged about the comment as part of her "Off the Bus" campaign coverage, and it was picked up by the mainstream media.

Fowler also broke the story of former president Clinton's tirade, about a writer of a scathing article about him, in which he called the writer "a scumbag." She captured all this after asking him a question in a handshake line of supporters and posted the audio recording of it.

Web Link >>>
Video the Vote
www.videothevote.org/

Another change seen in the 2008 election is that candidates are less able to repeat untruths about opposing candidates, thanks to online communication tools. Obama created a site specifically to address the falsehoods spread about him, including his religious beliefs, as the Republicans encouraged the falsehood that he was Muslim. McCain's campaign initially said that his vice-presidential running mate, Sarah Palin, had opposed the wasteful "bridge to nowhere" project in Alaska, where she was governor. However, people online continued to hammer at this false statement and showed that she did not oppose it until it became unpopular, and eventually McCain's camp stopped making that claim. The mix of blogs, online videos, citizen journalism, and political-information sites has also helped the public get a wider range of information than it could from only traditional media sources.

YouTube and CNN partnered to have video debates hosted on the site, one reason the 2008 presidential election became known as the "YouTube election."

Candidates have learned that a great number of small donations can have more of an effect in mobilizing the public than smaller numbers of large donations. They also have had to find a balance between encouraging online communication between supporters and offering ways for supporters to meet and interact offline as well. Al Gore's 2000 campaign for president, although prior to most of the social-media tools available today, was faulted for concentrating only on online participation and forgetting the real need of people to interact face-to-face.

One other change seen with the rise of the Internet in political campaigns is the ability to attract young people and get them involved in the political process. Not only do many young people today have a better sense of how to best utilize social media and networks than older generations, they have proved a powerful force in helping organize and volunteer. This bucks a trend, going back at least thirty years, of steadily declining youth participation in elections.

Online Media and Political Communications

Online databases and sites that provide direct information about political donations, voting records, and other political activities have become especially useful tools for journalists and citizens. Visitors to such sites can customize information on demand about any community in the United States or any person who may have contributed to a candidate, using data from the Federal Election Commission. The user simply enters a zip code and immediately obtains a list of everyone in that geographic area who has contributed to federal campaign committees. Alternatively, the user can enter the first three or more letters of a person's last name and obtain a detailed inventory of her or his contributions during any election cycle dating back to 1990.

The database is maintained by OpenSecrets.org, which also offers a wide range of other useful online political information, such as details on the activities of political action committees (PACs), the spending of lobbyists (which can be extremely

Citizen journalist Mayhill Fowler broke two of the bigger stories of candidate gaffes during the 2008 presidential campaign.

smart mob
....
A term coined by author Howard
Rheingold to define a group
of people communicating with
each other via text messaging
or wireless networks in order
to coordinate their activities
even though they are in
different places.

revealing in how organizations or industries are trying to shape the nation's political agenda), and which political races have raised and spent the most. Not everyone thinks making public records such as these widely available on the Internet is a good idea, however.

Political activists have found the Web to be an effective place to organize people as well as to distribute their messages. The website e.thePeople encourages citizens to email their politicians, create and sign online petitions, and discuss various political topics with others online.

Email initially seemed to promise a faster, more efficient way for constituents to communicate directly with their members of Congress, but a report released in 2001 by George Washington University and the Congress Management Foundation as part of the Congress Online Project said that the reality of email communications did not bear out that promise. There was growing frustration on the part of constituents who felt that their politicians were not responding to their communications and likewise a frustration on the part of politicians who felt that the public did not adequately understand how Congress worked and had unrealistic expectations of how quickly they could receive responses. Some House offices were receiving eight thousand emails a month and some Senate offices were getting fifty-five thousand emails a month, far more than their staff could read or answer in addition to doing their various regular duties. The report also said that there was a general perception among politicians that emails were a more casual form of communication than a telephone call or written letter and were thus given lower priority than those other forms of contact.

Some political activists are also using digital media to not only organize online but physically gather as well. Dubbed **smart mobs** by author Howard Rheingold,

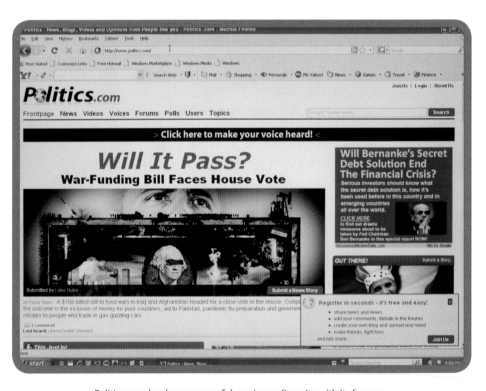

Politico.com has been successful as a journalism site with its focus on providing the most up-to-date, insider news on Washington politics.

these groups use cellular phones and wireless networks to communicate rapidly with each other and organize. Smart mobs contributed to the overthrow of President Suharto in Indonesia in 1998 and to the overthrow in 2001 of Philippine President Joseph Estrada as organizers orchestrated demonstrations against him via forwarded cell phone text messages. Protestors at the World Trade Organization meeting in Seattle in 1999 were able to check the electronic network to see which way the tear gas was blowing. Through the use of wireless technology, mass demonstrations in various parts of a city can be roughly coordinated in real time, giving protestors almost as good a communication network as police or military might have in such a situation.

Handheld video- and audio-recording equipment has also helped activists, in some cases. Hundreds of activists were arrested during the Republican National Convention in New York City in 2004 and in some of the subsequent trials activists were able to show video that directly contradicted police testimony regarding their actions and why they were arrested.

Filipinos used text messages to quickly organize crowds to protest President Joseph Estrada as he was being investigated for corruption charges.

LOOKING BACK AND MOVING FORWARD

As we have seen, the government has become more active in recent years in writing bills that attempt to counter some of the trends online media bring, such as the general breakdown in the ability of media companies to protect copyrighted material. These and issues regarding online privacy, encryption, and online pornography are likely to continue to be hot topics that involve politicians and the court system for some time.

It will be important for citizens to be knowledgeable about these issues and willing to sacrifice convenience to preserve fundamental rights of privacy. The role of mass communication in democracies will likely be even more important in the future than it has been, even as the focus may shift from the notion of simply informing the public to that of engaging in a dialog with the public. In this regard, social media will also play an important role, in facilitating conversations between members of the public and between the public and its elected officials.

The move toward more dialog may be one of the biggest shifts in the role media play in the political process and in elections. If participation and discussion are encouraged, far more people may become engaged in the political process than has been the case in recent history. Even something as simple as blogging about what took place at a local school board meeting on a microblog site or for a local news organization could affect the way leaders govern.

Just as maintaining our rights to privacy will be an ever more important struggle in the future, keeping governance as transparent as possible will likewise be an ongoing effort. It is the shift toward more transparency that social media in part represent and that many government leaders may find the most threatening to standard ways of conducting political business.

Web Link >>>
The Center for Voting and Democracy
www.fairvote.org/

Web Link >>>
e.thePeople
www.e-thepeople.org/

Transparency will also be hugely important in the international arena, in which a growing number of transnational organizations make policy decisions that can affect entire nations and the global economy. Most of the leaders of these organizations are not elected officials and thus have little if any incentive to make their policy decision-making processes transparent. While leaders within democratic nations may have increased pressure to be more transparent, the leaders of these transnational groups, who arguably have more power to affect national policies, will not be beholden to any specific public.

There has been a growing awareness among some activist groups and social movements that the increased powers of some organizations, such as the World Trade Organization (WTO), must be monitored. Regular, sometimes violent protests accompany WTO meetings, trying to raise publicity about the policy decisions the WTO is making for global business and trade. Using organizing and protest tactics similar to those used with antinuclear and environmental protests in the 1970s and 1980s, these new social movements also use powerful social-media communication tools to talk with each other and to get media attention for their causes.

DISCUSSION QUESTIONS

1. Do you agree with Joseph Pulitzer's statement on the importance of the press in preserving American democracy? Why or why not? What trends and events both historical and current support your views?

2. Discuss some of the important trends in media coverage of elections, such as sound bites and horse-race coverage, and what can be done to change these trends if you feel they are detrimental to good journalism and the political process.

3. Considering that most media organizations rely heavily on advertising for revenue, is it fair to deny them the revenues that come from political advertising? Are there any potential conflicts of interest that could come from a media organization's coverage of fund-raising or election issues because of the current arrangement? How might this situation be changed so that media companies can still earn money, politicians can effectively reach the public, and the audience can be thoroughly informed on issues?

4. Compare and contrast the coverage of a current political issue in a liberal publication or blog and a conservative one. How do they frame and talk about the issue? How do they discuss certain facts about it? Which do you find more credible, and why?

5. If you go to a nonnews website to get information on candidates, what do you look for that makes you trust the information it provides? Do you visit more than one site to read about a particular candidate, or do you stay with one site?

6. Discuss what role you played, if any, in the 2008 presidential election, whether through volunteering, voting, or simply going to candidates' websites to learn more about their policies and stands on issues.

7. What are your perceptions of social movements that protest things like WTO meetings or policies created by international organizations? What influenced these perceptions?

FURTHER READING

Mosh the Polls: Youth Voters, Popular Culture and Democratic Engagement. Tony Kelso, Brian Cogan (eds.) (2008) Lexington Books.

Into the Buzzsaw: Leading Journalists Expose the Myth of a Free Press. Kristina Borjesson (ed.) (2002) Prometheus Books.

Breaking the News: How the Media Undermine American Democracy. James Fallows (1997) Vintage.

Media Spectacle and the Crisis of Democracy: Terrorism, War, and Election Battles. Douglas Kellner (2005) Paradigm Publishers.

Media Politics: A Citizen's Guide. Shanto Iyengar, Jennifer McGrady (2006) W. W. Norton.

Tuned Out: Why Americans Under 40 Don't Follow the News. David Mindich (2005) Oxford University Press.

The Press Effect: Politicians, Journalists, and the Stories That Shape the World. Kathleen Hall Jamieson (2003) Oxford University Press.

The Nightly News Nightmare: Network Television's Coverage of U.S. Presidential Elections, 1988–2000. Stephen J. Farnsworth, S. Robert Lichter (2002) Rowman & Littlefield.

Mass Media and American Politics, 8th ed. Doris A. Graber (2009) CQ Press.

(Un)Civil War of Words: Media and Politics in the Arab World. Mamoun Fandy (2007) Praeger.

Cyberprotest: New Media, Citizens, and Social Movements. W. Van De Donk (ed.) (2004) Routledge.

MEDIA QUIZ ANSWERS

1. False. John F. Kennedy appeared on *The Tonight Show* in 1960.

2. George Allen, Virginia.

3. China, Myanmar, Cuba.

4. Radio, as low literacy rates make print media reach smaller audiences.

7. True.

8. YouTube.

9. False.

10. True.

Further Reading

Glossary

actualities: Edited audio clips from people interviewed.

ad-agency commission: A percentage amount of the cost of an advertisement that is taken by the advertising agency that helped create and sell the ad.

advertising: An ancient form of human communication generally designed to inform or persuade members of the public with regard to some product or service.

advertorial: A type of display advertisement that is created to look like an article within the publication, although most publications have the words "advertisement" or "paid advertisement" in tiny print somewhere nearby.

agenda setting: A role the media play in deciding which topics to cover and thus, by virtue of the fact that the media has covered them, which topics the public deems important and discussion-worthy.

Alien and Sedition Acts: A series of four acts passed by the U.S. Congress in 1798 that, among other things, prohibited sedition, or spoken or written criticism of the U.S. government, and imposed penalties of a fine or imprisonment upon conviction. Although they expired in 1801, other sedition acts have been passed periodically, especially during times of war.

analog media: Term originally used in audio recording for media analogous to the sound being re-created. It now refers to all nondigitized media, such as print media, audio and video recordings, photography, and film.

Armstrong, Edwin Howard: Inventor of FM radio transmission; Columbia University engineering professor.

aspect ratio: The ratio of a screen's height to its width. Incompatible aspect ratios of films and television mean that either films have to be cropped to fit within a television screen, or, in order to keep the original aspect ratio, black borders must appear on the top and bottom of the screen.

Associated Press: Founded as a not-for-profit members' cooperative in 1848 by a group of six New York newspaper publishers in order to share the costs of gathering news by telegraph. Today 1,700 newspapers and 5,000 television and radio stations are members of this news-gathering organization.

Astroturf/Astroturfing: The practice of creating a movement or campaign so that it looks like it was created by concerned citizens as a grassroots movement, but was actually created or controlled by a large organization or group.

asynchronous media: Media that do not require the audience to assemble at a given time. Examples of asynchronous media are printed materials and recorded audio or video.

auteur: French for "author," it is usually applied to directors who stamp their vision on the films they make, as opposed to directors who have but one role among many other professionals in the making of a film.

authoritarian theory of the press: A theory of international mass communication in which authoritarian governments exert direct control over the media.

Baird, John Logie: Scottish inventor who created the first mechanically scanned television device, in 1923. His thirty-line TV had better resolution than the first attempts at electronic televisions.

balance: In news coverage, the concept of presenting sides equally or of reporting on a broad range of news events.

banner ad: An advertisement across the top of a website and the original form of advertising on the Web.

beat: A reporter's specialized area of coverage based on geography or subject. Common beats in large or medium-sized newspapers include education, crime, and state politics.

Bennett, James Gordon: Founder of the *New York Herald* in 1835. He started many features found in modern newspapers, including a financial page, editorial commentary, and public-affairs reporting.

blog: Short for "weblog," a type of website in which a person posts regular journal or diary entries with the posts arranged chronologically.

Bobo Doll studies: Experiments done in the 1950s that showed that children who watched violent episodes on television in which the violent person was rewarded were more likely to punch a Bobo Doll than children who saw violent episodes in which the violent person was punished. This research seemed to confirm certain assumptions about direct media effects.

bourgeoisie: A class of society that translates approximately to "middle class," which distinguishes the class from the aristocracy above them and the proletariat (or workers) below them.

Brady Mathew B.: A famous photographer of the nineteenth century who took portraits of many well-known people of his day as well as Civil War battlefield photographs.

branding: The process of creating in the consumer's mind a clear identity for a particular company's product, logo, or trademark.

broadcast: The original usage was agricultural, referring to casting seeds widely in a field rather than depositing them one at a time. The notion was transferred to the fledgling electronic medium of radio and later television.

byte: The most common base unit used to measure computer storage and information, it consists of eight bits, in a combination of 0's and 1's, to form letters, numbers, and all modes of computer information that are displayed.

camera obscura: A dark box or room with a small hole in it that allowed an inverted image of an outside scene to be shown on the opposite inner wall.

Carey, James: Communications scholar and historian who has shaped a cultural-studies approach to communication theory.

Cary, Mary Shadd: The first African American woman to edit a weekly newspaper. She founded and edited the *Provincial Freeman* in Canada after leaving the United States so she would not be captured and put into slavery because of the Fugitive Slave Act.

cathode-ray tube (CRT): A device, still used in most television screens and computer monitors, in which electrons are transmitted to a screen for viewing.

censorship: The act of prohibiting certain expression or content. Censors usually do not target the whole publication, program, or website, but seek to prohibit some part of the content.

Children's Television Act: Created in 1990, it places limits on the amount of commercial content that programming can carry, forces stations to carry certain amounts of educational programming for children six-teen and under, and includes other provisions to help protect children.

chilling effect: The phenomenon that occurs when journalists or other media producers decide not to publish stories on a topic after a journalist has been punished or jailed for such a story.

circuit switching: The original system used for telephony, in which circuits connected two people communicating. Once the circuit was connected, or "on," the people on either end of the circuit used the whole circuit exclusively, even if they didn't speak. When they hung up, the circuit was disconnected by an operator and available for others to use.

classified advertising: A type of advertising usually found in print media, especially newspapers but also in some magazines, and now increasingly online, that consists of messages posted by individuals and organizations to sell specific goods or services.

clear and present danger: A restriction on speech when it meets both of the following conditions: (1) it is intended to incite or produce dangerous activity (as with falsely shouting fire in a crowded theater), and (2) it is likely to succeed in achieving the purported result.

click-through rate: Rate in which people click on the ad.

client/server: A network model, predominant in the Internet today, that relies on a centralized computer, or server, that stores content that the audience, or clients, access.

coaxial cable: An insulated and conducting wire that is typically used for most cable television connections.

codex: A manuscript book of individually bound pages.

Community Antenna Television (CATV): Also known as cable television, it was developed in 1948 so communities in hilly or remote terrain could still access television broadcasts.

consolidation: The process of large companies merging with each other or absorbing other companies, forming even bigger companies.

convergence: The coming together of computing, telecommunications, and media in a digital environment.

cookie: Information that a website puts on a user's local hard drive so that it can recognize when that computer accesses the website again. Cookies are what allow for conveniences like password recognition and personalization.

copyright: The exclusive right to use, publish, and distribute a work such as a piece of writing, music, film, or video.

correlation: The ways in which media interpret events and issues and ascribe meanings that help individuals understand their roles within the larger society and culture.

cost per thousand (CPM): The standard unit for measuring advertising rates for publications, based on circulation.

critical theory: An umbrella term for a range of theories, most of which are influenced by Marxism, which attempts to look critically at society and offer ways to make society better.

crowd sourcing: Utilizing raw data that the public has gathered, in addition to reports from citizen journalists, to help create a news report.

cultivation analysis: A theory of media effects that states television cultivates in audiences a view of reality similar to the world portrayed in television programs. For example, it posits that viewing thousands of murders on television is unlikely to increase the chances that one will commit murder but does lead to one's belief that the world is a more dangerous place than it actually is.

cultural studies: A framework in studying theories of culture and communication that shuns the positivist scientific approach used by scholars in the empirical school and that tries to examine the symbolic environment created by mass media.

cultural transmission: The transference of the dominant culture, as well as its subcultures, from one generation to the next or to immigrants, which helps people learn how to fit into society.

culture industry: A term used by some critical theorists that refers to the mass communication industries and their power in creating culture as a commodity.

cybersquatting: The practice of getting a domain name, usually of someone famous or a well-known company, with the intention of reselling the domain name at a high price.

Daguerre, Louis: A French scene painter and inventor of the daguerreotype, an early type of photography.

Day, Benjamin: Publisher of the *New York Sun*, he ushered in the era of the penny press when, on September 3, 1833, he began offering his paper on the streets for a penny.

daypart: A segment of time used by radio and television program planners to decide who the primary audience is during that time of day or night.

de Forest, Lee: Considered the "father" of radio broadcasting technology because of his invention that permitted reliable voice transmissions for both point-to-point communication and broadcasting.

deep linking: Creating a hypertext link to another website's inside page or pages rather than to its homepage.

Digg: A popular website in which users submit material (called "digging") to be voted on by other users, with the most popular material appearing on the homepage.

digital divide: The idea that some groups that do not have access to the Internet become left out of the benefits that online technology can bring.

Digital Millennium Copyright Act (DMCA): An act of Congress in 1998 that reformed copyright law comprehensively in trying to update it for the digital age. Key provisions addressed the circumvention of copyright protection systems, fair use in a digital environment, and Internet service providers' (ISP) liability for content sent through their lines.

digital rights management (DRM): Technologies that let copyright owners control the level of access or use allowed for a copyrighted work, such as limiting the number of times a song can be copied.

digital watermark: Computer code (usually invisible, but sometimes visible) inserted into any digital content—images, graphics, audio, video, or even text documents—that authenticates the source of that content.

digitization: The process in which media is made into computer-readable form.

dime novel: The first paperback book form, which cost ten cents. This made it accessible even to the poor.

direct effects model: A model of mass communication that says that media has direct and measurable effects upon audiences, such as encouraging them to buy products or become violent.

Disney, Walter Elias: Creator of animated cartoon characters such as Mickey Mouse, Goofy, and Donald Duck and classic cartoons such as *Bambi*, *Snow White and the Seven Dwarfs*, and *Fantasia*. Founded the Disney media empire.

display advertising: A type of advertising in print media that usually consists of illustrations or images and text and that can occupy a small section of a page, a full page, or multiple pages. Because of their high costs, display ads are usually bought by large companies or organizations.

distributed computing: Individual, autonomous computers that work together toward a common goal, typically a large, complex project that requires more computing power than any individual computer could have.

Edison, Thomas Alva: Inventor whose inventions include the electric light, the phonograph, and the Kinetoscope. Edison's lab in Menlo Park, New Jersey, had over sixty scientists and produced as many as four hundred patent applications a year.

electronic news-gathering (ENG) equipment: Tools such as video cameras and satellite dishes that allow journalists to gather and broadcast news much more quickly than in the past.

electronic program guides (EPG): Guides available on television that provide program listings and some simple interactivity, such as ordering pay-per-view programs or buying CDs or DVDs of listed music or shows.

embargo: The practice of sending news releases to news organizations with the stipulation that the information cannot be broadcast or print until after a specific day or time.

encoding/decoding: A theory that says that messages are encoded with certain meanings by media producers and that audiences then "decode" the messages in various ways, depending on things like their education level, political views, and other factors.

entertainment: A function of mass communication that is performed in part by all three of the other four main functions (surveillance, correlation, cultural transmission) but also involves the generation of content designed exclusively to entertain.

epistemology: A way of or framework for understanding the world.

equal-time rule: The requirement that broadcasters make available equal airtime, in terms of commentaries and commercials, to opposing candidates running for election. It does not apply to candidates appearing in newscasts, documentaries, or news-event coverage.

ethnography: A variety of qualitative research techniques that involve the researcher interacting with participants, either through observation, participation, interviews, or a combination of methods.

fair use: An exception to copyright law that allows someone to use an excerpt of a work without paying for its use. Reviews of works or their use in commentary or criticism are examples of fair use.

fairness: In news coverage, the concept of covering all relevant sides of an issue and allowing spokespeople representing those various sides a chance to be covered in the same way.

Fairness Doctrine: Adopted by the FCC in 1949, it required broadcasters to seek out and present all sides of a controversial issue they were covering. It was discarded by the FCC in 1987.

fear appeals: A type of advertising technique that attempts to scare the audience in order to persuade them, such as anti-smoking ads that show disfigured former smokers.

Federal Communication Commission (FCC): The principal communications regulatory body at the federal level in the United States, established in 1934.

Federal Radio Commission (FRC): Formed by the Radio Act of 1927, the commission was the precursor to the FCC and created a policy that favored fewer, high-powered radio broadcasting stations rather than more numerous, low-power stations.

First Amendment: Guarantees that Congress shall make no law restricting freedom of speech, press, or religion.

focus groups: A research technique in which small groups of people are gathered together to discuss a topic, with the interactions often recorded and carefully watched to determine what different people think.

folksonomies: A collection of tags created by users that provide meta-data, or data about data, regarding information.

fourth estate: Another term for the press, or journalism, in which it acts as a fourth branch of government: one that watches the other branches (executive, legislative, and judicial).

frame: The notion that every story is told in a particular way that influences how readers think of the story.

genre: A type of story that has recognizable and defined elements, that distinguish it from other types of stories or nonfiction.

gramophone: Developed by inventor Emile Berliner, it used a flat disc to record sound rather than the cylinder that was used up to that time.

graphophone: An improvement on Thomas Edison's phonograph in recording audio, it used beeswax to record sound rather than tinfoil. Developed by Alexander Graham Bell and inventor Charles Tainter.

graphical user interface (GUI): A computer interface that shows graphical representations of files structures, files, and applications, in the form of folders, icons, and windows.

Gutenberg Bible: One of a handful of surviving Bibles printed by Johannes Gutenberg; considered the first mechanically printed works in Europe.

Gutenberg, Johannes: German printer credited with creating the first mechanical printing press in Europe in 1455.

Hays Code: A code established in 1930 by the movie industry to censor itself regarding showing nudity or glorifying antisocial acts in movies. Officials for the Hays Office had to approve each film that was distributed to a mass audience.

hub: A node that has many connections to other nodes in a social network.

human-computer interaction: The general term for any interaction between humans and computers, either through devices such as keyboards, mice, touch screens, or voice recognition.

hyperlink: A clickable pointer to other online content.

hypertext: Text online that is linked to another web page, website, or different part of the same web page by HTML coding.

hypodermic-needle model: A model of media effects, also called the "magic bullet" model, largely derived from learning theory and simple stimulus-response models in behavioral psychology, that states media messages have a profound, direct, and uniform impact on the public.

ideology: A way of belief that goes largely unquestioned by people or that is seen as somehow natural or beyond question.

indecent speech: Language or material that, in context, depicts or describes, in terms patently offensive as measured by contemporary community standards for the broadcast medium, sexual or excretory organs or activities.

independent films: Films made by production companies outside the main Hollywood studios.

independent labels: Any small record-production and distribution companies that are not part of the four major-label companies. They include companies producing only one or two albums a year, as well as larger independents such as Disney. The independent labels produce 66 percent of the albums each year but only 20 percent of the sales.

influencer: A person who can influence others in their social network to perform an action or change an attitude.

infomercial: Also called paid programming, this is a thirty- or sixty-minute television show that seeks to sell a product and that usually involves a celebrity spokesperson and testimony from customers about how good the product is.

information overload: The difficulties associated with dealing with the vast amounts of information available to us and making sense of it.

information society: The notion that modern society has transformed from one in which industrial production was dominant to one in which information production has become more important.

instant messaging: Often abbreviated to IM, it is a form of real-time communication through typed text over a computer network.

integrated communications: The idea that all channels of communication about a company or brand should work together in creating a cohesive message.

intellectual property: Ideas that have commercial value, such as literary or artistic works, patents, business methods, and industrial processes.

interactivity: Although an exact definition is still being debated, for digital-media purposes interactivity can be defined as having three main elements: (1) a dialog that occurs between a human and a computer program, (2) a dialog that occurs simultaneously or nearly so, and (3) the audience has some measure of control over what media content it sees and in what order.

interpersonal communication: Communication between two or more individuals, usually in a small group, although it can involve communication between a live speaker and an audience.

interpretive reporting: A type of reporting that tries to put the facts of a story into a broader context by relying on knowledge and experience the reporter has about the subject.

interstitial ad: An online advertisement that opens in a new window from the one the user was in.

joint operating arrangements (JOAs): Legal agreements that permit newspapers in the same market or city to merge their business operations for reasons of economics yet maintain independent editorial operations.

keyword auction: One method in search engine marketing in which companies bid for words and pay the search engine a certain amount every time the word is searched and their listing is clicked on.

laugh track: A device used in television sitcoms that generates prerecorded laughter, timed to coincide with punch lines of jokes.

libel: A type of defamation that is written and published, such as a false attack on a person's character, which damages a person's reputation.

libertarian theory: A theory of international mass communication that is rooted in the idea of the individual's right to publish whatever he or she wants, even material that is critical of the government or of government officials.

listservs: Also known as listserves, they are automated mailing-list administrators that allow for easy subscription, subscription cancellation, and sending of emails to subscribers on the list.

localization: The ability of media-content producers to provide content based on a user's locale, either done automatically based on an ISP or after the user has provided information such as a city name or zip code.

long tail: The notion that selling a few of many types of items can be as profitable or even more profitable than selling many copies of a few items. The concept works especially well for online sellers such as Amazon or Netflix.

lurker: A person on an online discussion board who does not contribute to discussions by posting messages but who simply reads what others write.

major labels: The four biggest recording-arts companies that control much of the music industry partly through their powerful distribution channels and ability to market music to mass audiences. They are Universal Music Group, Sony Music, EMI, and the Warner Music Group.

Marconi, Guglielmo: Italian inventor and creator of radio telegraphy, or wireless transmission, in 1899.

mash-up: Combining textual information over geographic, map-based information so users can access multiple layers of data.

mass communication: Communication to a large group or groups of people that remain largely unknown to the sender of the message.

massively multiplayer online role-playing games (MMORPGs): Online games played by a number of people at the same time in which they develop characters or roles and interact with each other while completing quests or adventures.

McLuhan, Marshall: A communication scholar who wrote *Understanding Media* and *The Gutenberg Galaxy*, among other books. He is perhaps most famous for creating the "global village" metaphor regarding electronic media and his often-misunderstood phrase "the medium is the message."

mean-world syndrome: The notion that the world is a more dangerous place than it actually is, which has come from watching news reports or violent programming.

media ecology: The study of media environments and how those environments may affect people and society.

media literacy: The process of interacting with media content and critically analyzing it by considering its particular presentation, its underlying political or social messages, and ownership and regulation issues that may affect what is presented and in what form.

media oligopoly: A marketplace in which media ownership and diversity is severely limited and the actions of any single media group substantially affect its competitors, including determining the content and price of media products for both consumers and advertisers.

media spotlight effect: The phenomenon that occurs when the media has intense coverage of a certain event or person for a short time, but then moves on to other issues soon after.

mediated communication: Communication that takes place through a medium, such as writing or recording, as opposed to unmediated communication, such as face-to-face discussions.

medium: A communication channel, such as talking on the telephone, instant messaging, or writing back and forth in a chat room.

Méliès, Georges: An early French filmmaker who pioneered the use of special effects in film in order to show imaginative stories.

metasearch engines: A search engine that searches search engines for information, compiling the results for users.

Metcalfe's Law: The value of a network rises in proportion to the square of the number of people on that network. In other words, the more people who are connected to a network in which they can communicate with each other, such as the Internet, the more valuable that network becomes.

modem: Derived from the terms **mod**ulate-**dem**odulate; a device that converts digital signals from a computer to analog signals for transmission over a phone line, as well as converting transmitted analog signals to digital signals.

mods: Short for "modification," it refers to the practice of changing parts of the code in some games to alter how they are played or how they look..

MPEG: Moving Picture Experts Group, established in 1988 and responsible for creating the standards for digital and audio compression. The abbreviation is also used to denote the types of compression, such as MPEG-1, MPEG-4, and so on.

muckrakers: A group of journalists in the latter nineteenth and early twentieth centuries who investigated business and political corruption. Their activities were likened to raking up mud, or muck, by Theodore Roosevelt, who meant it as a term of derision.

multicast: Simultaneously transmitting multiple channels of compressed digital content over the television airwaves.

multimedia: A combination of different types of media in one package; thus, film or video with sound is a type of multimedia, because it combines visual and audio elements. Web pages that combine text, video, animation, audio, or graphics are another type of multimedia.

multipoint multichannel distribution system (MMDS): A type of terrestrial wireless service that can transmit as many as thirty-three analog TV channels over the air via microwave transmission and up to ninety-nine compressed digital channels.

Murrow, Edward R.: A radio and, later, television journalist and announcer who set the standard for journalistic excellence on television during television's golden age.

nanotechnology: A cutting-edge field of technology research that involves items that are nanometers (10^{-9}. meters) in length and that promises to revolutionize many fields, ranging from electronics, information storage, and even medicine.

narrowband: A network connection that does not provide very much bandwidth, thus receiving and sending information more slowly than broadband connections. Dial-up modems and some of the early wireless connections with speeds of 56 kHz or under are considered narrowband.

Net neutrality: A principle that states that broadband networks should be free of restrictions on content, platforms, or equipment and that certain types of content, platforms, or equipment should not get preferential treatment on the network.

news hole: A term typically used with newspapers, it refers to the amount of total space available after advertisement space has been blocked out.

newsgroups: Categories for discussion groups within Usenet.

Newspaper Preservation Act: Created in 1970, it is intended to preserve a diversity of editorial opinion in communities where only two competing, or independently owned, daily newspapers exist.

objectivity: A journalistic principle that says journalists should be impartial and free of bias in their reporting. This principle has come under attack in recent years, because of the impossibility of people being completely objective, and has largely been replaced by the concepts of fairness and balance.

obscenity: One of the forms of speech not protected by the First Amendment and thus subject to censorship. Although an exact definition of the term has been difficult to achieve in various court cases, generally a three-part standard is applied for media content: it must appeal to prurient interests as defined by community standards, it must show sexual conduct in an offensive manner, and it must on the whole lack serious artistic, literary, political, or scientific value.

OLED: Organic light-emitting diode screen, a type of thin, flexible screen that will change how and where we are able to view content on screens.

oligopoly: An economic structure in which a few, very large, very powerful and very rich owners control an industry or collection of related industries.

open source: Any program whose source code the programmer allows others to see. This lets others modify and improve it. Most proprietary software programs do not allow the public to see their source code.

opinion poll: A poll that is usually conducted by a professional polling organization asking members of the public their opinions on issues or political candidates.

opt in: The practice of letting consumers choose to receive mailings or marketing material by having them check a box on a web site, usually when registering for the site.

optical fiber: A transparent filament, usually made of glass or plastic, that uses light to carry information. This makes transmission of information much faster and with much greater capacity than twisted-pair copper wires or coaxial cable.

optical storage: Uses light in the form of lasers to store and read data of all types, whether text, audio, or video. Using light is highly efficient: it permits storage devices to record vastly greater amounts of data in small spaces and enables faster retrieval of the stored data than from magnetic storage devices.

outdoor advertising: Billboards and other forms of advertising such as on buses or taxis that are done in public.

packet switching: A type of switching within a network, in which information is divided up into pieces, or packets, and transported as separate packets using the least congested routes. At the end of the route the packets are reassembled in their proper order and delivered over the telephone line or Internet.

participant-observation: A qualitative research technique in which the researcher participates as a member of the group being studied.

patent law: Protects the right to produce and sell an invention, rather than a literary or artistic work, which is covered by copyright law.

payola: Cash or gifts given to radio disc jockeys by record labels in exchange for greater airplay given to the label's artists or most recent songs. The practice is now illegal after several scandals involving payola in the 1950s.

peer-to-peer network (P2P): A network in which all computers on the network are considered equal (peers) and can send and receive information equally well. This is the basis of file-sharing services.

penny press: Newspapers that sold for a penny, making them accessible to everyone. They differed from older newspaper forms in that they tried to attract as large an audience as possible and were supported by advertising rather than subscriptions.

performance-based advertising: Any form of online ad buying in which an advertiser pays for results rather than paying for the size of the publisher's audience, or CPM.

personalization: The ability of media-content producers to provide content that is of interest to a specific user based either on criteria the user has selected, such as a zip code, or on automated tracking of their Web-viewing habits.

phonograph: First patented by Thomas Edison in 1877 as a "talking machine," it used a tinfoil cylinder to record voices from telephone conversations. Successive technological improvements in electronics and the type of material the sounds were recorded on made sound quality better.

pitch: A request to review a client's new product or do a story about the client or the product.

political economy: An area of study inspired by Marxism that examines the relationship between politics and economics with media ownership and the influences

they all have on society and perpetuating the status quo.

positivism: The belief, common among scientists in the physical or natural sciences and many in the social sciences, that there is an objective reality that can be discovered and explained through rigorous scientific research.

Postmodernism: A broad category of viewpoints that claim that there is no absolute truth, that truth is unknowable, and that attempts to create grand narratives that explain the world are faulty.

Postpositivism: A view that agrees largely with positivism, but acknowledges that there may be some things that we cannot know through scientific inquiry.

Pragmatism: A school of thought that claims that truth is found in actions that work and that no overarching or purely objective notion of truth can be found.

preferred-position balancing theory: A legal theory that says that a balance must be struck between speech and other rights, although speech has a preferred position compared to other rights.

press agentry: The practice of getting media attention for a client, often by creating outrageous stunts that would attract journalists.

prior restraint: When the government prevents or blocks the publication, broadcasting, showing, or distribution of media content, whether in print, over the air, in movie theaters, or online.

product placement: The practice of advertisers paying for actual products to be used and shown prominently in television shows and movies.

produsers: The notion that audiences cannot simply be considered consumers anymore but also often take an active role in producing content or information.

propaganda: The regular dissemination of a belief, a doctrine, a cause, or information, with the intent to mold public opinion.

pseudo events: An event that is created specifically to attract the attention of the media, particularly the news.

public information campaign: Media program funded by the government and designed to achieve some social goal, or what might be called social engineering.

public opinion: The notion that the public, as a group, can form shared views or ideas about topics and that these ideas guide the public's actions.

public service announcement (PSA): Advertising-like messages for which the media donate time or space to organizations with a worthy purpose that ostensibly benefits the public.

public sphere: An idealized conversational "space" in which people discuss and debate their interests separate from the interests of the state and civil society.

puffery: A type of advertising language that makes extravagant claims about a product without saying anything concrete.

push poll: A type of political advertising that appears to be a telephone poll but is actually a telemarketing campaign to sway voters by giving them false or misleading information about opposing candidates or to make a candidate look good.

qualitative research: Research that describes phenomena in words instead of numbers or measures. Ethnographic studies, such as interviews with people to learn about beliefs or trends, are an example of qualitative research.

quantitative research: Research that focuses on numbers and measures and experimentation to describe phenomena. Researchers usually have a hypothesis they are trying to prove or disprove through controlled experimentation.

Radio Act of 1912: The act assigned frequencies and three- and four-letter codes to radio stations and limited broadcasting to the 360-meter wavelength.

Radio Act of 1927: The act replaced the Radio Act of 1912 and created the Federal Radio Commission, the precursor to the FCC, and gave the government greater regulatory and enforcement powers over radio, as well as establishing the premise that the airwaves were a public good and limited.

random-access memory (RAM): Usually used for a type of computer memory and abbreviated to RAM, in storage-technology terms it is a type of medium that allows for a reader or viewer to randomly obtain specific pieces of content by doing searches, using an index, or taking some other action.

rate card: A listing of advertising rates by size, placement, and other characteristics, such as whether ads are black and white or full color. Frequency discounts are also usually offered, and the listed rates are usually negotiable, especially for large advertisers.

rating: Used in broadcast media to explain the number of households that watched a particular show.

Reed's Law: The utility or value of an interactive communication network with n members increases exponentially, or 2 to the nth power.

rhetoric: One of the ancient arts of discourse, it involves using language to persuade others.

RSS feed: Short for really simple syndication, it lets users easily subscribe to feeds from a blog or website.

Sarnoff, David: Head of RCA. He helped push the development of television as a mass medium yet blocked the development of FM radio for years because its adoption would hurt AM listenership and reduce demand for AM radio receivers, which RCA produced and sold.

Sarnoff's Law: Created by RCA executive David Sarnoff, it states that the value of a network increases linearly with the number of people on it.

scrolling: The practice of simply repeating the same message in a chat room, which quickly draws the ire of other participants.

search engine marketing (SEM): Paying a search engine such as Google to have a listing appear prominently when searched.

search engine optimization (SEO): A strategy that utilizes website design, careful choice of keywords, links, and other techniques to show prominently in online searches.

sedition: Speech or action that encourages overthrow of a government or that subverts a constitution or a nation's laws.

semiotics: The study of signs and symbols.

sensational journalism: News that exaggerates or features lurid details and depictions of events in order to get a larger audience.

sequential-access memory: A type of medium in which a reader, viewer, or user must go through the medium in the order received in order to find specific information.

serious gaming: A growing area of gaming that creates video games that have educational value or purpose to them.

shield law: A law intended to protect journalists from legal challenges to their freedom to report the news.

simplified communications model: Developed by Wilbur Schramm in 1954 and based on the mathematical theory of communication. It includes a source, who encodes a message, or signal, which is transmitted (via the media or directly via interpersonal communication) to a destination, where the receiver decodes it.

six degrees of separation: The idea that everyone in the world is separated from each other by at most six other nodes in a social network.

slander: A type of defamation that is spoken, as opposed to written (libel), that damages a person's reputation or otherwise causes harm.

Slashdot effect: The occurrence of a website's servers crashing because of a large increase in visits to the site after its being mentioned on the popular website Slashdot.org.

small world: A tight-knit social network with many strong ties.

smart mob: A term coined by author Howard Rheingold to define a group of people communicating with each other via text messaging or wireless networks in order to coordinate their activities even though they are in different places.

soap opera: A type of programming that began on radio and successfully moved to television but that is now threatened by the increased variety of media types, as well as changes in lifestyles. Soap operas are dramatic story series that involve numerous characters and are aimed at a daytime audience of homemakers.

social constructionism: A view that says that much if not all of what we know and understand about the world, including scientific knowledge, is constructed through our social interactions and language.

social marketing: The practice of using advertising and marketing techniques to persuade people about changing bad or destructive behaviors or adopting good behaviors.

social responsibility theory: A theory of international mass communication that perhaps best describes the media's role in democratic societies. It rests on the notion that the media are vital to informing citizens in a democratic society and, as such, should be free from most governmental constraints in order to provide the best, most reliable and impartial information to the public.

soft news day: A day in which not much of importance happens, so that editors are more likely to add features with less real news value, such as human-interest stories.

sound bite: The length of time a news subject is allowed to speak without being edited by a reporter. It also has come to refer to short utterances that are catchy and designed to capture the media's attention.

soviet theory: A theory of international mass communication that states the media should be publicly owned and used to further the needs of the working class.

spam: Unwanted email sent out by advertisers as a mass mailing.

spiral of silence hypothesis: A hypothesis that states people (1) are naturally afraid of isolation, (2) realize that if they are in the minority on an issue they will likely be isolated, and (3) have a kind of sixth sense that helps them gauge when their opinions are contrary to the majority—which makes them refrain from expressing their opinions.

storage technology: Any type of device or medium in which information can be maintained for later retrieval.

strong ties: In social network analysis, the tight bonds between people in a "small world" of close connections.

subliminal advertising: Persuasive messages that supposedly happen below the level of consciousness, such as quickly flashing an image or word on a screen. Despite concerns about subliminal advertising, there has been no firm proof that they work.

subtext: The message beneath the message—the underlying, or implicit, message that is being conveyed by media content.

superstation: A local TV station that reaches a national audience by beaming its programming nationwide via satellite to local cable systems, which then transmit the program to local subscribers.

superstitial ad: An online advertisement that covers part of the existing screen or moves over part of it without opening a new window.

surveillance: Primarily the journalism function of mass communication, which provides information about the processes, issues, events, and other developments in society.

swarming: The process used by some P2P systems in which multiple downloaders of the same file are temporarily coordinated in order to speed up the downloading process.

synchronous media: Media that take place in real time, such as live television or radio, that require the audience to be present during the broadcast or performance.

tagging: Defining a piece of information, file, image, or other type of digital media in a non-hierarchical system that helps describe what the information is.

technological determinism: The belief that technology causes certain human behaviors.

Telecommunications Act of 1996: The first major regulatory overhaul of telecommunications since 1934, designed to open the industry to greater competition by deregulating many aspects of it.

theory of cognitive dissonance: A theory of persuasion that states we act first and then rationalize our behavior afterward in order to fit our actions into self-perceived notions of who we are.

third-party cookies: Cookies put on a computer by those other than the website being visited, such as advertisers inserting their own cookies on a web page.

third-person effect: When a media message does not affect the behavior or beliefs of the intended audience but does affect a different group, which also receives the message and may act in the belief that the message will affect the intended audience.

time shift: Recording an audio or video event for viewing later rather than when the event was originally broadcast. Setting a VCR to record a favorite program while one is out is an example of time shifting.

time-space compression: The idea that electronic communication has essentially reduced distances between people because of nearly instantaneous communication, which has also "sped up" our notions of time.

trademark: A type of intellectual property that refers to signs, logos, or names.

transmission control protocol: A part of the main protocol for the Internet that allows for computers to easily communicate with each other over a network.

troll: A person who purposely vandalizes Wikipedia entries by inserting false or nonsensical information.

two-way symmetric model: A model of public relations that emphasizes the profession as a system of managing relationships between organizations and individuals and their many publics.

user-generated content (UGC): Media content that has been created by consumers or audience members, including videos, music, or other forms of content.

uses-and-gratifications research: A branch of research on media effects that looks at why people use particular media and examines what people do with the media rather than what the media do to people.

V-chip: A computer device that enables parents or any other viewer to program a TV set to block access to programs containing violent and sexual content, based on the program rating.

vertical search engines: A specialized search engine that searches within a highly specific field, thus giving users more relevant results within that field than more general search engines.

viral marketing: Spreading news and information about media content through word of mouth, usually via online discussion groups, chats, and emails, without utilizing traditional advertising and marketing methods.

voice-over: An unseen announcer or narrator talking while other activity takes place, either on radio or during a television scene.

watermark: A symbol or mark embedded in a photograph that identifies who owns the copyright for that photograph. With digital media, any piece of content can be watermarked, and the watermark, itself digital, can be completely invisible.

weak ties: In social network analysis, the connections between people in different "small worlds," which tend not to be as tight or as close as strong ties but that are nevertheless extremely important in social networks.

weblog (blog): A type of website in which a person posts regular journal or diary entries with the posts arranged chronologically.

Wells, Ida B.: A female African American journalist in the latter nineteenth century who wrote and fought against racism and black lynching.

widget: A portable chunk of code that can be embedded in HTML pages and that often gives users extra functionality to their pages.

wiki: A website that lets anyone add, edit, or delete pages and content.

Woods, Granville T.: Inventor of railway telegraphy in 1887, a type of wireless communication that allowed moving trains to communicate with each other and with stations, greatly reducing the number of railway collisions.

word-of-mouth marketing: Marketing that takes place among customers through discussions with each other.

yellow journalism: A style of journalism practiced especially by publishers Joseph Pulitzer and William Randolph Hearst during the late 1890s in which stories were sensationalized and often partly or wholly made up in order to be more dramatic.

Zworykin, Vladimir: Inventor of an improved cathode-ray tube he called the "iconoscope" that is the basis for the CRTs still used today in television sets and many computer monitors. He is considered one of the fathers of electronic television.

Notes

CHAPTER 1

1. Thomas L. Friedman, "Global Village Idiocy," *New York Times*, May 12, 2002. Retrieved May 30, 2002, from http://www.nytimes.com.

2. Gary Gumpert and Robert Cathcart, eds., *Inter/Media: Interpersonal Communication in a Media World*, 3rd ed. (Oxford: Oxford University Press, 1986).

3. Irving Fang, *A History of Mass Communication: Six Information Revolutions* (Boston: Focal Press, 1997).

4. Harold D. Lasswell, "The Structure and Function of Communication in Society," in *The Communication of Ideas*, ed. Lyman Bryson (New York: Institute for Religious and Social Studies, Jewish Theological Seminary of America, 1948), 37.

5. Claude F. Shannon and Warren Weaver, *The Mathematical Theory of Communication* (Urbana, IL: The University of Illinois Press, 1964), 7.

6. Wilbur Schramm, "How Communication Works," in *The Process and Effects of Mass Communication*, ed. Wilbur Schramm (Urbana, IL: The University of Illinois Press, 1961), 5–6. Retrieved January 25, 2002, from http://muextension.missouri.edu/xplor/comm/cm0109.htm.

7. J. W. Carey, "A Cultural Approach to Communications," *Communication* 2 (1975): 1–22.

8. Werner J. Severin and James W. Tankard Jr., "Introduction to Mass Communication Theory," in *Communication Theories: Origins, Methods, and Uses in the Mass Media*, 5th ed. (New York: Addison Wesley Longman, 2001), 16.

CHAPTER 2

1. "Dow Does the Right Thing," The Yes Men website, http://www.theyesmen.org/hijinks/bbcbhopal. Retrieved October 10, 2008.

2. W. James Potter, *Media Literacy*, 2nd ed. (Thousand Oaks: Sage Publications, 2001): 4–7.

3. Sherwood Schwartz, "Send Help Before It's Too Late," *Parents' Choice* (Winter 1984): 2.

4. Jim Giles, "Internet Encyclopaedias Go Head to Head," *Nature* 438 (December 15, 2005): 900-901.

5. "About Hallmark Channel," Hallmark Channel website, http://www.hallmarkchannel.com/tv/about/index.asp. Retrieved October 12, 2008.

6. "Who Pays for Public Broadcasting?" Corporation for Public Broadcasting website, http://www.cpb.org/aboutpb/faq/pays.html. Retrieved July 31, 2009.

7. Clifford G. Christians, Mark Fackler, Peggy Kreshel, and Kathy Brittain McKee, *Media Ethics: Cases and Moral Reasoning*, 8th ed. (Boston: Allyn & Bacon, 2008), 51–53.

8. Ibid., 41–43.

CHAPTER 3

1. "Interactivity," Whatis.com, http://whatis.techtarget.com/definition/0,,sid9_gci212361,00.html. Retrieved May 15, 2002.

2. Sheizaf Rafaeli, <"Networked Interactivity," Journal of Computer-Mediated Communication>, http://jcmc.indiana.edu/vol2/issue4/rafaeli.sudweeks.html#Interactivity. Retrieved August 3, 2009.

3. Jon Krakauer, "Into Thin Air," *Outside* (September 1996): http://outside.away.com/outside/destinations/199609/199609_into_thin_air_1.html. Retrieved August 3, 2009.

4. Elizabeth Dinovella, "U.S. Slipping in Internet Access," *The Progressive* (June 25, 2008). Retrieved October 15, 2008, from http://www.progressive.org/mag_wxld062508.

5. Judith Newman "Ray Tomlinson: Inventor of E-Mail, a New Discourse" Intelligent Systems (July 2002), Volume IX, No. 2. http://www.chenaultsystems.com/articles/Intell33.htm.Retrieved August 3, 2009.

6. Robert Hobbes' Zakon, "Hobbes' Internet Timeline," version 5.6, Zakon.org, http://www.zakon.org/robert/internet/timeline/. Retrieved June 20, 2002.

7. George T. Hawley, "DSL: Broadband by Phone," *Scientific American* (October 1999): 102–105.

8. P. William Bane and Stephen P. Bradley, "The Light at the End of the Pipe," *Scientific American* (October 1999): 110–115.

9. David D. Clark, "High-Speed Data Races Home," *Scientific American* (October 1999): 95–96.

10. John Carey, "Winky Dink To Stargazer: Five Decades Of Interactive Television" (Dobbs Ferry, NY: Greystone Communication, 1998). http://www.columbia.edu/cu/business/courses/download/B9201-XX/carey/history_of_interactive_tv.pdf. Retrieved August 3, 2009.

CHAPTER 4

All book sales data, etc. comes from: Book Industry Trends 2008, published by Book Industry Study Group 2008, New York, NY.

1. National Endowment for the Arts, "Reading at Risk: A Survey of Literary Reading in America" (June 2004). Research Division Report #46, http://www.nea.gov/pub/ReadingAtRisk.pdf.
2. Heinrich Wilhelm Wallau, The Gutenberg Society (Mainz, 1902). Translated by Bryan R. Johnson for the Catholic Encyclopedia (New York: Encyclopedia Press, Inc., 1913).
3. *Book Industry Trends 2008* (New York: Book Industry Study Group Press, 2008).
4. *Editor & Publisher International Year Book,* 88th ed. (New York: Editor & Publisher, 2008).
5. Steve Mariotti, Debra DeSalvo, and Tony Towle, *The Young Entrepreneur's Guide to Starting and Running a Business* (New York: Three Rivers Press, 2000).

CHAPTER 5

1. "Biography of Alan Freed," Alan Freed website, http://www.alanfreed.com. Retrieved August 18, 2002.
2. "Granville Woods," Black Inventor Online Museum, (n.d.). http://www.blackinventor.com/pages/granville woods.html. Retrieved August 3, 2009.
3. Bob Lochte, "The Life and Legend of Nathan B. Stubblefield: A Chronology." Retrieved May 17, 2002, from http://campus.murraystate.edu/academic/faculty/bob.lochte/NBSDates.htm.
4. Thomas White, "'Battle of the Century': The WJY Story," United States Early Radio website, http://earlyradiohistory.us/WJY.htm (January 1, 2000). Retrieved August 18, 2002.
5. Albert N. Greco, "The Structure of the Radio Industry," in *The Media and Entertainment Industries,* ed. Albert N. Greco (Boston: Allyn & Bacon, 2000).
6. National Public Radio website, http://www.npr.org. Retrieved May 18, 2002.
7. Public Radio International website, http://www.pri.org. Retrieved May 18, 2002.

CHAPTER 6

1. Robert Leggat, "The Beginnings of Photography," A History of Photography website, http://www.rleggat.com/photohistory/. Retrieved May 15, 2002.
2. Ibid.
3. Elizabeth Valk Long, "The Life and Death of Kevin Carter," *Time,* September 12, 1994. Retrieved June 2, 2002, from http://home-4.tiscali.nl/~t892660/msp/time.htm.
4. John V. Pavlik, *New Media Technology* (Boston: Allyn & Bacon, 1999).

5. "Sprocket Holes: The Lumière Brothers," presscard.com/www.presscard.com/sprocketholes2.html, retrieved June 3, 2002; "The Biography of Thomas Alva Edison," ThomasEdison.com, http://www.thomasedison.com/biography.htmlretrieved August 3, 2009.
6. Erik Barnouw, *Documentary: A History of the Non-Fiction Film,* 2nd rev. ed. (New York: Oxford University Press, 1993).
7. Barry R. Litman, *The Motion Picture Mega-Industry* (Boston: Allyn & Bacon, 1998), 74–88.
8. "Curtains Rise Halfway on Digital Cinema," *Business 2.0* (May 29, 2001): 32–33.
9. "Television Bureau of Advertising Online: Television Facts," Television Bureau of Advertising, http://www.tvb.org/tvfacts/index.html. Retrieved May 20, 2002.
10. Nielsen Media Research, 1999; *Cable TV Facts* (New York: Cable Television Advertising Bureau, 1996), 5.

CHAPTER 7

1. "Google Flu Trends," Google website, http://www.google.org/flutrends/. Retrieved November 1, 2008.
2. Steve Lohr, "Is Information Overload a $650 Billion Drag on the Economy?" *New York Times,* December 20, 2007. Retrieved October 21, 2008, from http://bits.blogs.nytimes.com/2007/12/20/is-information-overload-a-650-billion-drag-on-the-economy/.
3. Lisa Napoli, "A Gadget That Taught a Nation to Surf: The TV Remote Control," *New York Times,* February 11, 1999. Retrieved January 10, 2002, from http://www.nytimes.com/library/tech/99/02/circuits/articles/11howw.html.
4. John Carey, *Winky Dink to Stargazer: Five Decades of Interactive Television* (Dobbs Ferry, NY: Greystone Communication, 1998).
5. "Internet World Users by Language," Internet World Stats, 2008. Retrieved November 13, 2008, from http://www.internetworldstats.com/stats7.htm.
6. "Control Data Corporation Historical Timeline," Charles Babbage Institute Collections website. Retrieved August 3, 2009, from http://www.cbi.umn.edu/collections/cdc/histtimeline.html .
7. "Panel: Interactivity Ethics" (Jan. 25, 2006), washingtonpost.com. Retrieved October 20, 2008, from http://www.washingtonpost.com/wp-dyn/content/discussion/2006/01/24/DI2006012400817.html.

CHAPTER 8

1. David F. Gallagher, "Star of 'I Kiss You' Site Moves from Farce to Folklore," *New York Times,* July 4, 2002. Retrieved July 10, 2002, from http://www.nytimes.com.
2. Susan Taylor Martin, "Scrappy Al-Jazeera Stands Up," *St. Petersburg Times,* September 22, 2002.

CHAPTER 9

1. John Jantsch, "The Definition of Social Media," Duct Tape Marketing blog, September 25, 2008. Retrieved February 20, 2009, from http://www.ducttape marketing.com/blog/2008/09/25/the-definition-of-social-media/.

2. Brian Solis, "The Definition of Social Media," Web-Pro News, June 29, 2007. Retrieved February 20, 2009, from http://www.webpronews.com/blogtalk/2007/06/29/the-definition-of-social-media.

3. Anvil Media, "Resources: SEM Glossary of Terms," n.d. Retrieved February 20, 2009, from http://www.anvilmediainc.com/search-engine-marketing-glossary.html.

4. Jessica Clark and Patricia Aufderheide, "Public Media 2.0: Dynamic, Engaged Publics," February 2009. Retrieved March 17, 2009, from http://www.centerfor socialmedia.org/documents/whitepaper.pdf.

5. Erin Kutz, "Just a Few on Twitter Do All the Tweeting: Study," Reuters, June 5, 2009. Retrieved June 5, 2009, from http://tech.yahoo.com/news/nm/20090605/wr_nm/us_twitter_study_3.

6. Danah M. Boyd and Nicole B. Ellison, "Social Network Sites: Definition, History, and Scholarship," *Journal of Computer-Mediated Communication* 13, no. 1 (2007): article 11. Retrieved April 4, 2009, from http://jcmc.indiana.edu/vol13/issue1/boyd.ellison.html.

7. Axel Bruns, *Blogs, Wikipedia, Second Life, and Beyond: From Production to Produsage* (New York: Peter Lang, 2008).

CHAPTER 10

1. The Write Site, "Tracing the Story of Journalism in the United States." Retrieved July 5, 2002, from http://www.writesite.org/html/tracing.html.

2. Joseph Pulitzer, "The College of Journalism," *North American Review* (May 1904).

3. Michael G. Robinson, American Culture Studies, "1890s" course, spring 1996. http://ernie.bgsu.edu/~wgrant/1890s/yellowkid/introduction.html.

4. George Seldes, "Farewell: Lord of San Simeon," in *Lords of the Press* (New York: Julian Messner, 1938).

CHAPTER 11

1. Dolf Zillman, "The Coming of Entertainment," in *Media Entertainment: The Psychology of its Appeal*, Peter Voderer, ed. Dolf Zillman (Mahwah, NJ: Lawrence Erlbaum Associates, 2000), 17.

2. Dolf Zillman, "The Coming of Entertainment," in *Media Entertainment: The Psychology of its Appeal*, Peter Voderer, ed. Dolf Zillman (Mahwah, NJ: Lawrence Erlbaum Associates, 2000), 9.

3. *Les Brown's Encyclopedia of Television*, 3rd ed. (Detroit, MI: Gale Research, 1992).

4. David Becker, "When Games Stop Being Fun," CNET News.com, April 12, 2002. Retrieved August 22, 2002, from http://news.com.com/2100-1040-881673.html.

5. Christine Hanson, Ranald D. Hansen, "Music and Music Videos," in *Media Entertainment: The Psychology of Its Appeal*, Peter Voderer, ed. Dolf Zillman (Mahwah, NJ: Lawrence Erlbaum Associates, 2000), 179–181.

6. For example, *A Fool There Was*, Fox, 1915; Eve Golden, *Vamp: The Rise and Fall of Theda Bara*. (West Vestal: Emprise Publishing, 1996).

CHAPTER 12

1. A project of the Digital Scriptorium, Rare Book, Manuscript, and Special Collections Library, Duke University. Copyright 2000 Duke University. Retrieved October 31, 2002, from http://scriptorium.lib.duke.edu/eaa/timeline.html.

2. Kathleen Hall Jamieson, *Dirty Politics* (New York: Oxford University Press, 1992), 54–55.

3. Stephen Millies, "The Ludlow Massacre and the Birth of Company Unions," *Workers World*, January 26, 1995. Retrieved October 31, 2002, from http://www.hartford-hwp.com/archives/45b/030.html.

4. Daniel J. Boorstin, "From News-Gathering to News-Making: A Flood of Pseudo Events," in *The Modern World: The Image* (New York: Vintage, 1961).

5. Andrew Marlatt, "Patrick Doesn't Work Here Anymore," *Wired* (December 1999): 114.

CHAPTER 13

1. Tom Gormley, "'Ruination Once Again': Cases in the Study of Media Effects," theory.org.uk, 1998. Retrieved November 4, 2002, from http://www.theory.org.uk/effec-tg.htm.

2. Paul F. Lazarsfeld and Robert K. Merton, "Mass Communication, Popular Taste and Organized Social Action," in *The Communication of Ideas*, ed. Lyman Bryson (New York: Institute for Religious and Social Studies, 1948), 95–118.

3. Bernard Cohen, *The Press and Foreign Policy* (Princeton, NJ: Princeton University Press, 1963), 13.

4. Garth S. Jowett, Ian C. Jarvie, and Kathryn H. Fuller, eds., *Children and the Movies: Media Influence and the Payne Fund Controversy* (Cambridge: Cambridge University Press, 1996).

5. P. W. Holaday and G. D. Stoddard, *Getting Ideas from the Movies* (New York: Macmillan, 1933).

6. Garth Jowett et al., "Payne Fund Radio Broadcasting Research, 1928–1935," in *Children and the Movies: Media Influence and the Payne Fund Controversy* (Cambridge: Cambridge University Press, 1996).

7. Stuart Elliott, "Women's Group to Present Good, Bad and Ugly Awards," *New York Times*, September 28, 1999.

8. R. S. Lichter and D. Amundson, *A Day of Television Violence* (Washington, D.C.: Center for Media and Public Affairs, 1992).

9. Rolf Wigand Lichter, "Communication and Violent Behavior," *ICA Newsletter* (July 1999): 5.

10. Leonard Eron, University of Illinois at Chicago, testimony before the Senate Committee on Commerce, Science and Transportation, Subcommittee on Communications, June 12, 1995.

11. Statistics compiled by TV-Free America, Washington, D.C., 1996.

12. National Television Violence Study, issued by Mediascope, February 1996.

13. The UCLA Television Violence Monitoring Report, issued by the UCLA Center for Communications Policy, September 1995.

14. Jeffrey Cole, "Surveying the Digital Future: A Longitudinal International Study of the Individual and Social Effects of PC/Internet Technology." Retrieved November 5, 2002, from http://www.webuse.umd.edu/abstracts2001/abstract_2001_cole.htm.

CHAPTER 14

1. Dwight L. Teeter Jr. and Don R. Le Duc, *Law of Mass Communications* (Westbury, NY: The Foundation Press, 1992).

2. "How Effective Are Shield Laws?", *Agents of Discovery: A Report on the Incidence of Subpoenas Served on the News Media in 1997*, Reporters Committee for Freedom of the Press website, http://www.rcfp.org. Retrieved November 8, 2002, from http://www.rcfp.org/agents/shieldlaws.html.

3. Reed E. Hundt, FCC Chairman, transcript of speech given at the Museum of Television and Radio, New York, New York, June 3, 1997. Retrieved November 8, 2002, from http://www.fcc.gov/Speeches/Hundt/spreh729.txt.

4. Linda Greenhouse, "'Virtual' Child Pornography Ban Overturned," *New York Times*, April 17, 2002. Retrieved April 17, 2002, from http://www.nytimes.com.

5. Mark Goodman, "The Radio Act of 1927 as a Product of Progressivism," vol. 2, no. 2. Media History Monographs. Retrieved November 8, 2002, from http://www.scripps.ohiou.edu/mediahistory/mhmjour2-2.htm.

6. Erik Barnouw, *A Tower of Babel: A History of Broadcasting in the United States*, vol. 1 (New York: Oxford University Press, 1966).

7. Mark Goodman, "The Radio Act of 1927 as a Product of Progressivism," vol. 2, no. 2. Media History Monographs. Retrieved November 8, 2002, from http://www.scripps.ohiou.edu/mediahistory/mhmjour2-2.htm.

8. M. S. Mander, "The Public Debate About Broadcasting in the Twenties: An Interpretive History," *Journal of Broadcasting* 28 (1984): 167–185.

9. Alan B. Albarran and Gregory G. Pitts, *The Radio Broadcasting Industry* (Boston: Allyn & Bacon, 2001), 27–29.

10. Eli Noam and Robert Freeman, "Global Competition," *Television Quarterly* (1998) Vol. 29, number 1, 18-23.

CHAPTER 15

1. Joseph Pulitzer, "The College of Journalism," *North American Review*, May 1904.

2. Fred S. Siebert, Wilbur Schramm, and Theodore Peterson, *Four Theories of the Press: The Authoritarian, Libertarian, Social Responsibility, and Soviet Communist Concepts of What the Press Should Be and Do* (Champaign, Illinois: University of Illinois Press, 1956).

3. Daniel C. Hallin, "Sound Bite News: Television Coverage of Elections 1968-1988," Journal of Communication, Vol. 42, 1992.

4. Herbert E. Alexander, "Financing Presidential Election Campaigns," *Issues of Democracy*, USIA Electronic Journals 1, no. 13 (September 1996). Retrieved November 7, 2002, from http://usinfo.state.gov/journals/itdhr/0996/ijde/alex.htm.

5. Larry Sabato, *The Rise of Political Consultants: New Way of Winning Elections* (NY: Basic Books, 1981), 165–166.

6. Kathleen Hall Jamieson, *Dirty Politics* (New York: Oxford University Press, 1992), 19–20.

7. Claire Cain Miller, "How Obama's Internet Campaign Changed Politics," *New York Times*, November 7, 2008.

Credits

Corbis; page 229, REUTERS/Mohammed Dubbous/Landov; page 230 (top), Sheila Terry/Science Photo Library; page 230 (bottom), TEK Image/Science Photo Library; page 235, Michael Newman/PhotoEdit; page 237, Jeff Kravitz/FilmMagic/Getty Images; page 238, Mark Richards/PhotoEdit; page 240, Justin Sullivan/Newsmakers/Getty Images; page 243, Courtesy of BitTorrent Inc.; page 244, WARNER BROS/SOUTHSIDE AMUSEMENT CO/THE KOBAL COLLECTION/DUHAMEL, FRANCOIS; page 247, Sven Torfinn/Panos Pictures

CHAPTER 9

page 251, WISSAM NASSAR/Maxppp/Landov; page 254, FOX-TV/THE KOBAL COLLECTION; page 258, Xinhua/Landov; page 259, Andy Sheppard/Redferns/Getty Images; page 260, David Young-Wolff/PhotoEdit; page 261, Susan Van Etten/PhotoEdit; page 264, TIM SHAFFER/Reuters/Landov; page 265, David Young-Wolff/PhotoEdit; page 271, Michael Tran/Getty Images for Time

CHAPTER 10

page 281, © CNN ImageSource; page 284, Jim DeLillo, Photographer; page 285, Bettmann/Corbis; page 286, The Granger Collection, New York; page 287, Bettmann/Corbis; page 288, Hulton Archive/Getty Images; page 289 (top), Hulton Archive/Getty Images; page 289 (bottom), Mike Margol/PhotoEdit; page 291, Courtesy of APCOR—Portuguese Cork Association; page 293, Jeff Greenberg/PhotoEdit; page 294, Brendan Smialowski/Getty Images for Meet the Press; page 295, MUSA AL-SHAER/AFP/Getty Images; page 296, Spencer Grant/PhotoEdit; page 297, Richard Levine/Alamy; page 299, Laura Dwight/PhotoEdit; page 301, Spencer Grant/PhotoEdit; page 303, David Young-Wolff/PhotoEdit; page 305, Mike Margol/PhotoEdit; page 306, claude thibault/Alamy; page 309, Richard Lord/PhotoEdit; page 312, Courtesy of Condace Pressley/Photo by Ian Irving; page 313, Kevork Djansezian/Getty Images

CHAPTER 11

page 319, Boston Globe/Pat Greenhouse/Landov; page 320, Rudi Von Briel/PhotoEdit; page 322, Mary Evans Picture Library; page 324, CBS/Landov; page 326, Frank Micelotta/Getty Images for Zomba Label Group; page 327, Imagestate Media Partners Limited—Impact Photos/Alamy; page 329, Courtesy of Truth or Consequences/Sierra County Chamber of Commerce; page 330, Kelsey McNeal/TM and Copyright © 20th Century Fox Film Corp. All rights reserved, Courtesy: Everett Collection; page 331, PETER KNEFFEL/dpa/Landov; page 332, Jeff Greenberg/PhotoEdit; page 334, Bettmann/Corbis; page 336, Sunset Boulevard/Corbis; page 337, UNIVERSAL/THE KOBAL COLLECTION; page 338, CONSTANTIN FILM/DAVIS-FILMS/THE KOBAL COLLECTION; page 339, © 1997–2009 Netflix, Inc. All rights reserved.; page 340, Mike Margol/PhotoEdit; page 342 (top), Bettmann/Corbis; page 342 (bottom), KMazur/WireImage/Getty Images; page 343, Dave Hogan/Getty Images; page 344, John Shearer/WireImage/Getty Images; page 345, Ted Streshinsky/Corbis; page 346, WARNER BROS/THE KOBAL COLLECTION; page 347, Matt Sullivan/Getty Images; page 348, MICHAEL DE LUCA PRODUCTIONS/THE KOBAL COLLECTION

CHAPTER 12

page 353, Courtesy of EepyBird, www.eepybird.com; page 354, Win McNamee/Getty Images; page 358, Michael Newman/PhotoEdit; page 359, CHRIS RADBURN/PA Photos/Landov; page 360, The Granger Collection, New York; page 361, The Granger Collection, New York; page 362, Photo by Jeanne Strongin, courtesy of www.tonyschwartz.com; page 363, Mike Margol/PhotoEdit; page 364,

Book cover design by Carly Schnur, reproduced courtesy of Kaplan Kaplan Test Prep and Admissions and Dan Schawbel; page 365 (top), © 1999–2009 BP p.l.c; page 365 (bottom), Kevin Foy/Alamy; page 367, Courtesy of Texas Department of Transportation; page 368, Borderlands/Alamy; page 369, WAYANS BROS. ENTERTAINMENT/THE KOBAL COLLECTION; page 370, Mike Margol/PhotoEdit; page 371, Catchyoo by LM3LABS; page 373, Neno Images/PhotoEdit; page 376, © Harry Winston, 2007; page 378 (top), © 2005 Mattel, Inc.; page 378 (bottom), Bill Aron/PhotoEdit; page 379, Jock Fistick/Bloomberg News/Landov; page 380, Bettmann/Corbis; page 383, Derek Capitaine Photography; page 384, Franco Origlia/Getty Images

CHAPTER 13

page 393, Mike Margol/PhotoEdit; page 394, © The Nielsen Company. All Rights Reserved.; page 396, Canadian Press/Phototake; page 399, Spencer Grant/PhotoEdit; page 401, Banque d'Images, ADAGP/Art Resource, NY; page 402, Bettmann/Corbis; page 403, Tom Carter/PhotoEdit; page 405, The Granger Collection, New York; page 406, FIRST NATIONAL/WARNER BROTHERS/THE KOBAL COLLECTION; page 407, CBS/THE KOBAL COLLECTION; page 408, NBC/UNIVERSAL TV/THE KOBAL COLLECTION; page 409, Derek Capitaine Photography; page 411, UNIVERSAL TV/THE KOBAL COLLECTION; page 412, DON EMMERT/AFP/Getty Images; page 415, Neal Preston/CORBIS; page 416, Bettmann/Corbis; page 417, Courtesy of University of Illinois at Urbana-Champaign, Department of Communication; page 419, A. Ramey/PhotoEdit; page 420, Mark Herron Photography/PhotoEdit

CHAPTER 14

page 423, David Paul Morris/Getty Images; page 424, Bettmann/Corbis; page 427, Bettmann/Corbis; page 428, © 2009, The Progressive Magazine; page 429, The Granger Collection, New York; page 431 (top), James Shaffer/PhotoEdit; page 431 (bottom), BILL GREENBLATT/UPI/Landov; page 432, Mike Margol/PhotoEdit; page 424, © Corbis; page 435, Courtesy of Prometheus Radio Project; page 437, ANATOLI ZHDANOV/UPI/Landov; page 440, Corbis Premium RF/Alamy; page 442 (top), Jonathan Elderfield/Liaison/Getty Images; page 442 (bottom), Derek Capitaine Photography; page 443, Michael Newman/PhotoEdit; page 444, ALEXIS C. GLENN/UPI/Landov; page 447, TRUMP PROD./MARK BURNETT PROD./THE KOBAL COLLECTION; page 449, Robin Nelson/PhotoEdit; page 450, LUCAS JACKSON/Reuters/Landov

CHAPTER 15

page 455, LARRY DOWNING/Reuters/Landov; page 456, NBC-TV/THE KOBAL COLLECTION/EDELSON, DANA; page 458 (right), Alex Wong/Getty Images; page 459, Robin Nelson/PhotoEdit; page 460, Bettmann/Corbis; page 461, STF/AFP/Getty Images; page 462, Mary Evans Picture Library; page 463, Atul Loke/Panos Pictures; page 465, Mark Richards/PhotoEdit; page 466, The Granger Collection, New York; page 467, David Young-Wolff/PhotoEdit; page 469, Michael Newman/PhotoEdit; page 471, Neno Images/PhotoEdit; page 472, The Granger Collection, New York; page 473, Chris Hondros/Getty Images; page 474, ICP-UK/Alamy; page 475 (top), CARLOS BARRIA/Reuters/Landov; page 475 (bottom), Courtesy of Mayhill Fowler, photo by Lisa Keating Photography; page 476, Spencer Grant/PhotoEdit; page 477, CHERYL RAVELO/Reuters/Landov

Image in insert at the back of the book: Dmitry Krasny/Deka Design, © 2007, Foundation for National Progress

Index

social media
  careers in advertising and PR, 389
  definitions of, 253
  differences between traditional media, 254–256
  ethical issues, 274–276
  implications for politicians, 474–475
  legal issues, 275–276
  types of, 260–268
social networking sites, 266–268
social networks
  explanation of, 268–272
social responsibility theory, 460–461
Social Text, 417–418
Society of Professional Journalists Code of Ethics, 310
soft news day, 283
Sony Music, 139–141
Sony Reader, 85–86
sound bite, 466, 467
soviet theory, 461
spam, 234, 261, 364
spectrum auction, 439–440
spiral of silence hypothesis, 410–412
sports programming, 330–331
Sputnik I, 228
Star TV, 48
stereotypes, 347
Stern, Howard, 157
storage technology. *See also* information storage
  capacity sizes, 198
  characteristics of, 190–193
  definition of, 190
  historical development of, 198–199
strategic communications, 356–357
strong ties, 269
Stubblefield, Nathan, 148
subliminal advertising, 369
subscriptions
  as revenue model for digital media, 96
subtext, 37
Sunstein, Cass, 14
superstation, 184
superstitial ad, 372
surveillance, 20, 111, 282
swarming, 243
synchronous media, 19

T

tagging, 257
technological determinism, 76, 403
Telecommunications Act of 1996, 184, 185, 431, 435–436
telecommunications companies
  conflicts between cable and phone, 82–83
telecommunications networks
  characteristics of, 235–237
  government vs. private industry, 224–225
  historical development of, 222–230
  nature of, 230–231
telegraphy, 225–226
telephony
  as example of convergence, 4–8
  historical development of, 5–7, 226–227
  mobile. *See* mobile telephony
  texting. *See* text messaging
television
  broadcast. *See* broadcast TV

cable. *See* cable TV
  development of programming types, 324–328
  digital. *See* digital television
  distribution of, 181
  functions of, 179
  historical development of, 179–181
  influence of flat-panel displays, 180–181
  parental guidelines for, 445–446
  satellite. *See* satellite TV
  time spent watching of, 178
  types of programming, 328–332
television violence, 408–410
  children viewing of, 411
text messaging, 36
theory of cognitive dissonance, 358
third-party cookies, 451
third-person effect, 412–413
Thomson Reuters, 110
3-D movies, 172
time-shifting, 19, 178
time-space compression, 223
tobacco and alcohol advertising, 442
touch-sensitive screens, 209
trademark, 447
transmission control protocol, 78
transparency, 74, 275–276, 478
trolling, 215, 266
trust, 74–75, 273–274
TV/PC convergence, 89–92
two-way symmetric model, 382
Tylenol, 382

U

UGC. *See* user-generated content
Understanding Media, 195
Universal City Studios v. Reimerdes, 77
Universal Music Group, 139–141
universal service, 439
URL, 80
USA Today, 112
user-generated content, 10, 73, 350, 393, 419
user interface. *See also* desktop metaphor; graphical user interface
  development of natural input methods, 209–210
  future of, 216–218
  historical development of, 204–212
  implications of in mass communication, 202–203
  problems of, 203–204
  role of keyboards in, 206–207
uses and gratifications research, 414
utilitarianism, 54–55

V

V-chip, 445
veil of ignorance, 55
Verizon, 83
vertical search engines, 201
Viacom, 52
video games
  addiction of, 340
  as entertainment, 339–341
  role in converging TV and computers, 91
video news release, 383
Video Volunteers, 59
viral marketing, 14, 248, 374

visual media,
    media grammar of, 40–41
voice over, 40

W

Wall Street Journal, 43–44, 112, 122, 273
War of the Worlds, 407
Warner Brothers, 333
Warner Music Group, 139–141
Watergate, 196–197
watermark, 245
weak ties, 269
Weaver, Warren, 22
Web. *See also* Internet; World Wide Web
Web 2.0, 252. *See also* social media
weblog. *See* blog
Webster, Noah, 106–107
WELL, The, 263
Wells, Ida B., 286
widget, 258
wiki, 45, 73
    as social media, 264–265
Wikipedia, 38, 44, 45, 265–266

wireless networks, 235–236
wireless telecommunications, 227–228
wireless telegraphy, 147–148
Wolf, Josh, 423
Woods, Granville T., 147–148
word-of-mouth marketing, 274
World Wide Web
    creation of graphical browsers, 80–81
    historical development of, 78–81

Y

Yahoo, 52, 201
yellow journalism, 287
The Yes Men, 29, 43
Yomiuri Shimbun, 112
YouTube, 20, 48, 89, 186
    role in political elections, 473–474

Z

Zenger, John Peter, 428–429
Zworykin, Vladimir, 179–180